Principles and Applications of Economic Geography

Principles and Applications of Economic Geography

Economy, Policy, Environment

DEAN M. HANINK
University of Connecticut

John Wiley & Sons, Inc.

•   •   •   •   •

ACQUISITIONS EDITOR	Nanette Kauffman
MARKETING MANAGER	Catherine Faduska
PRODUCTION EDITOR	Sandra Russell
COVER & TEXT DESIGNER	Nancy Field
MANUFACTURING MANAGER	Dorothy Sinclair
PHOTO EDITOR	Lisa Passmore
PHOTO RESEARCHER	Elaine Paoloni
ILLUSTRATION EDITOR	Edward Starr
ILLUSTRATION ASSISTANT	Sandra Rigby
COVER PHOTO	Arnulf Husmo/Tony Stone Worldwide

This book was set in 10/12 New Baskerville by Bi-Comp, Incorporated and printed and bound by R.R. Donnelley & Sons Company, Crawfordsville. The cover was printed by Phoenix Color Corporation.

Recognizing the importance of preserving what has been written, it is a policy of John Wiley & Sons, Inc. to have books of enduring value published in the United States printed on acid-free paper, and we exert our best efforts to that end.

The paper in this book was manufactured by a mill whose forest management programs include sustained yield harvesting of its timberlands. Sustained yield harvesting principles ensure that the numbers of trees cut each year does not exceed the amount of new growth.

To order books or for customer service please, call 1(800)-CALL-WILEY (225-5945).

Library of Congress Cataloging in Publication Data
Hanink, Dean M.
    Principles and Applications of Economic Geography: economy,
  policy, environment/Dean M. Hanink.
        p.   cm.
    Includes bibliographical references and index.
    ISBN 0-471-10933-9 (cloth: alk. paper)
    1. Economic geography.   I. Title.
HF1025.H2943   1996
330.9—dc20   96-34962
                                                                CIP

Printed in the United States of America

10 9 8 7 6 5 4 3

Preface

The purpose of this text is to introduce basic principles of economic geography concerning location and spatial interaction to undergraduate college students. In addition, the book is designed to bridge the gaps between theory, models, and concepts and their applications to real-world situations. This intention requires a broad interpretation of economic geography that emphasizes not only "pure" spatial-economic considerations, but also the political, historical, and especially the environmental contexts in which locational decisions are made and which underlie a number of issues of regional change. It also requires the presentation of a sufficient number of brief cases to illustrate the applicability of economic geography in making decisions about both public and private location and in promoting an understanding of issues of general public concern.

The book's contents are ordered in a conventional way. The first chapter introduces the student to some basic principles of economic geography that are used in the following chapters, and attempts to start the student thinking about the evaluation of costs and benefits in making geographical decisions. Chapter 2 serves as a foundation for the next two chapters; it concerns land use, a fundamental geographical issue across all economic sectors. Chapter 3 concerns variations in the geography of agriculture around the world, whereas Chapter 4 considers the usually more localized problems of land-use conflicts. The issue of land as a resource, and the way the resource is used, is raised in Chapter 4. That discussion flows into Chapter 5, with its coverage of the use of other natural resources and the link between resources, population, and technology. The next chapter focuses on transportation, both with respect to supply and demand for transport services at places and the connections among places that are revealed in patterns of spatial interaction. Chapter 7 considers the location of manufacturing, and Chapter 8 centers on the location of services: both those services used by households and those used by businesses. Chapter 9 focuses on fairly technical ways of considering urban and regional economic growth. The geographical scale of the text shifts in Chapter 10 to a more international one. It contains material on international trade that links well to Chapter 11, which covers national and international issues of economic development. The final chapter concerns the future as much as the present in its material on sustaining economic growth and development from a geographical perspective.

Although specific chapters focus on environmental topics and international topics such as trade, these issues, along with those of government policy and political economy, are integrated within the remainder of the text as well. Nature-human systems and political-economic systems are quite well integrated. Although it is sometimes useful to consider things independently, often relying on the phrase "other things being equal," it is often useful to consider the effects of their integration in trying to understand how things work.

In closing this preface I would like to thank a number of people, not least of whom are the students in economic geography at the University of Connecticut. I have also had interesting discussions on economic geography with other faculty members of the UConn Geography Department, including Bill Berentsen and especially R. G. "Bobby C." Cromley. I also would like to thank the good folks at John Wiley and Sons, Inc. and all the publishers who granted their permission for the use of copyrighted material in this book. Finally, I really appreciate the support of my family during the writing of this book, including Barbara and Don, Emily, Mary, Sarah, Hanne, and the love of my life, Maureen. This book is dedicated to the memory of my father, John D. Hanink.

Contents

Chapter 3
Global Patterns of Agricultural Land Use   64

Chapter 4
Land-Use Transition, Conflict, and Control   105

Chapter 5
Resource Use: Population, Technology, and Accessibility   141

Chapter 6
Transportation and Spatial Interaction   193

Chapter 7
The Location of Manufacturing   228

Chapter 8
The Location of Services   272

Chapter 9
Urban and Regional Economic Growth   310

Chapter 10
International Trade: Patterns and Management   340

Chapter 11
Economic Growth and Development: National Patterns and Processes

Chapter 12
Geographic Perspectives on Sustainable
Economic Growth and Development   442

Chapter 1

Introduction to the Study of Economic Geography

This chapter

- provides an overview of the field of economic geography, emphasizing spatial interaction among places of production and consumption.
- indicates the breadth of factors of importance to locations of production and consumption: markets, politics, history, and environment.
- illustrates basic principles of market demand and its effects on economic flows between places.

- describes the importance of politics and public policy, history, and environmental factors to economic flows between places.
- outlines cost-benefit analysis as a tool for locational decision making.

Courtesy of United Nations

This chapter introduces basic principles of location and spatial interaction as the foundation for understanding economic geography. The chapter also gives the flavor of what is to come: an effort toward bridging the gap between principles, theories, and concepts of economic geography and real-world situations. Theory is not reality, of course, so its application requires a contextual interpretation of economic geography that emphasizes not only "pure" spatial-economic considerations, but also the political, historical, and environmental contexts in which locational decisions are made and which underlie a number of issues of regional change.

LOCATION, LOCATION, LOCATION

Geography is about location; accordingly, *economic geography* is about location in the economy. Production and consumption, two fundamental economic activities, occur at particular locations. Because the locations of production and consumption are seldom identical, a third fundamental economic activity is the distribution of goods and services from their points of origin to the destinations where they are consumed. Realistically, understanding an economy requires that the *fundamental economic activities*—production, consumption, and distribution—be treated as integrated parts of a system. Obviously, production of a good doesn't last very long if it can't reach consumers, and consumers cannot consume what isn't reaching the marketplace. As a field of study, economic geography focuses on the flows in the economy: the activities of distribution. Yet this does not mean that it ignores the activities of production and consumption; rather, it concentrates on their locational characteristics and requirements. If we understand the location of production and the location of consumption, then we can understand their geographical links in the economic flows between them. The economic flows of interest in economic geography are not confined to goods and other materials, however, because flows of people, services, and information also are necessary in an economy.

Our interest in flows requires a focus on location. As we go along in the book, it may seem that economic geography stresses location too much. If you've studied introductory economics, you may recall complete texts on microeconomics and on macroeconomics that never even mention location. Economists are interested in the locational characteristics of the economy but often consider production and consumption in the aggregate, such as national totals, so that the costs of transporting and distributing goods and services are ignored. For example, economists can forecast gasoline consumption during the next year or sales of automobiles based on their knowledge of prices and incomes and so on. For specific sellers, however, the general expectations of sales based on aggregates is only a helpful background. Their particular success rests on a number of specific factors, with their location often being a very important one.

Table 1.1   Considerations in Valuing Small Business

Business	Considerations
Apparel stores	LOCATION, competition, reputation, specialization
Car dealerships	LOCATION, reputation, boutique image
Employment agencies	Reputation, specialization, client relations
Fast food outlets	LOCATION, competition, neatness of premises, lease terms
Gas stations	Sales volume, lease terms, LOCATION, competition, other services
Grocery stores	LOCATION, lease terms, presence of liquor, condition of facilities
Insurance agencies	Client demographics and transferability, carrier characteristics
Manufacturers	Distributor relations, market position for products, condition of plant
Newspapers	LOCATION, demographics, economic conditions, competition, lease terms
Real estate agencies	Tenure of salespeople, franchised office, reputation
Restaurants	Competition, LOCATION, reputation
Retail businesses	LOCATION, competition, reputation, specialization, lease terms
Travel agencies	Revenue mix, LOCATION, reputation, lease terms
Video shops	LOCATION, competition, inventory

SOURCE: "Valuing Small Business: A Guide to What They're Worth." *Willimantic Chronicle,* May 11, 1991, p. 15. Emphases added.

Of the 14 types of business listed in Table 1.1, 10 cite location as a prime consideration in their valuation. Will an individual gas station thrive? Yes, but only if it has high individual sales volume and a reasonably inexpensive lease, does not have too much competition, provides other services, and boasts a good LOCATION. Actually, the existence of a strong aggregate demand for gasoline has only a minor bearing on the success or failure of an individual gas station, even though it is very important for the industry in general. As an analogy, we may point out that people eat all the time, but not all grocery stores are successful. Again, the cost of the store's lease is an important consideration, as is the condition of the facility. Apparently, the ability to sell liquor, which like food has steady demand, is also beneficial, but the first cited factor is LOCATION. This point is illustrated in Case 1.1, which describes the problems encountered by a Builders Square store in a suburb of Hartford, Connecticut. A better located competitor, Home Depot, was doing a thriving business at the same time Builders Square was going out of business. The pivotal difference lay in location. Home Depot was on the "good" side of the interstate highway, whereas Builders Square was on the "bad" side—out of sight and out of mind of the local home improvement market.

According to Table 1.1, some types of business don't place a high priority on their locations. That may be true but only at the local scale of analysis.

Certainly, being on one side of a street as compared to the other can have an impact on the sales of a retail outlet, but it is unlikely to affect the sales of a manufacturer or a real estate brokerage, two types of businesses that do not list locational considerations. At a different scale, however, locational considerations are very important. Real estate brokers, for example, specialize in particular geographical regions that are fairly small. Real estate booms and busts vary from one region to another, and the profits and losses of most brokerages vary strongly with local real estate market conditions. Manufacturers, of course, also pay attention to location. Some manufacturers are tied to particular sources of raw materials, must be in close proximity to particular consumers, or require a location where cheap labor is available.

Retail stores may sink or swim depending on which side of the street they are located; real estate brokerages may find the side of a city to be the important locational consideration, and factories may be placed to take advantage of conditions in a particular country. In this sense, location is always important, but its importance is a function of geographical scale. As we go along in the book, different scales of analysis, from local to international, will be used to illustrate different principles of economic geography. Changes in scale often mean changes in level of generalization. For example, rather than be concerned with the flows of goods and services between a single place of production and a single place of consumption, we might be concerned in a more general way with regional flows within a country or flows between blocs of countries in the international economy. Although the flows in the economy often appear different at one scale than at another, you may be surprised at how often they tend to follow basic principles of economic geography.

◪ CASE 1.1
Builders Square

MANCHESTER—The booming Buckland Hill's retail market has suffered its first major casualty with the announcement that the Builders Square home improvement store will shut its doors Nov. 1.

Builders Square also is shutting its store in Orange and four stores in other states. The company earlier this summer closed its Farmington store.

A company spokeswoman said Builders Square, a Kmart subsidiary, is cutting back its existing operations to refocus its efforts on a new chain of larger home stores it calls Builders Square II.

But the Buckland Hills shutdown concedes the lucrative east-of-the-river home improvement market to Builders Square's arch-rival, Home Depot.

It has been evident for some months that Home Depot was getting the lion's share of the business. Its parking lot and store aisles are often jammed with customers, particularly on weekends, compared with the quieter Builders Square.

Frank DiBesceglie, manager of the Builders Square in town, blamed the store's location—on the south side of I-84, opposite the Pavilions at Buckland Hills mall—for the store's inability to compete.

"This particular situation was directly attributable to the location," DiBescegli said. "In this industry, location is everything. The [Buckland] area is good, but you really can't be invisible and hard to get to."

About 80 employees at the town store will lose their jobs when it closes, but the company said it would try to place them with other employers.

It was not immediately known what would become of the Builders Square Building. Jeanne Janes, a spokeswoman for the company, said it is trying to lease it.

The Farmington store was turned over to another Kmart subsidiary, Sports Authority, a large sporting goods store. But that is unlikely to occur in town, where a Sports Authority store is already under construction—not far from Home Depot.

The Builders Square store opened in town last year as part of a retail boom that was triggered by construction of the Buckland mall. The store shares a 29-acre parcel with the Pace membership warehouse club, another Kmart subsidiary.

In all, Builders Square expects to consolidate about 180 stores nationwide into the new Builders Square II format. The company hopes to complete the consolidation by 1996.

Founded in 1983, Builders Square is a $2.4 billion-a-year company based in San Antonio.

SOURCE: "Builders Square Closes Six Stores," by John M. Moran. *Hartford Courant*, August 31, 1993, pp. D1–D2. By permission of the *Hartford Courant*.   ◪

FOR DISCUSSION

Does the closing of the Builders Square store suggest that interstate highways can be a barrier to spatial interaction even though they are intended to facilitate travel?

PRICE, DEMAND, SPATIAL INTERACTION, AND AGGLOMERATION

Location is indeed a vital component of much of the economy, but why? What is the difference between a good location and a bad one? Location can be considered in two ways. *Absolute location* is a geometric construct. If you have two directional coordinates—latitude and longitude are used frequently—you can pinpoint an absolute location. Absolute location, however, has no more than a coincidental bearing on the economic value of a site. The important economic characteristic of a site's position is its *relative location:* its location in relationship to other relevant places. A good location for a gasoline station is at the intersection of two busy roads. It is more accessible to higher traffic volume, and, therefore, more potential customers, at an intersection than in the center of a block with access to only one street of traffic. The important factor lending economic value to its site is not the address of the gas station, or its absolute location, but rather its easy access to the busy roads or its location relative to its potential customers.

So a location is good if it is in proximity to other relevant locations. A retail store has a good location if it's close to a large number of potential customers. A factory may have a good location if it's close to its suppliers, or to its customers, or to a source of particular labor skills, and so on. The point here is that locations can't be treated independently because no company and no household is economically independent. Economic flows must occur between places—these are termed *spatial interactions*—and the more efficiently these flows can take place, the better off an economy is in general. Good locations enhance the potential for relevant spatial interaction, and poor locations diminish the potential for relevant spatial interaction. It's as easy as that.

The principle that a good location enhances spatial interaction is straightforward, and so are the economics that underlie it. To begin with, consider a basic demand curve (also called a demand schedule) as suggested by the left-hand diagram in Figure 1.1. Demand for a product typically decreases as the price increases. You and I would rather pay less for an item than more. After all, the more money we spend on cheese, let's say, the less we have to spend on crackers. Sellers understand the basic demand curve: if they want to increase sales of an item, they cut its price. As the figure indicates, high prices yield smaller sales volumes, and lower prices yield higher sales volumes. This indicates a condition called *price elastic demand* (see Insights 1.1). The diagram defines an aggregate relationship; that is, it describes the demand–price relationship over a large population. It is a generalization of a large number of individual purchase

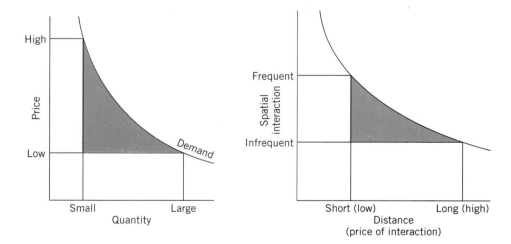

Figure 1.1   The left-hand diagram describes a basic demand schedule, with demand decreasing as price increases. The right-hand diagram describes the basic principle of distance decay; the demand for spatial interaction decreases as distance, or the price of spatial interaction, increases.

decisions and shows that while more of the product will be sold at low prices, some of it will be sold at the higher price. Finally, note that the price–demand relationship is represented by a curve and not a straight line. The curve indicates that the price elasticity of demand changes with price level. At higher price levels, price cuts must be large in order for consumption to increase much, whereas at lower price levels consumption can increase quite a bit even if price cuts are fairly small. Think about it this way: if I cut the price of a good by $1 from $100 to $99, I can't expect the same increase in sales volume as I would if I cut the price from $2 to $1; the increment is the same, but the proportion is quite different.

The demand for spatial interaction is similar to the demand for a good, or better yet, service, in that it too, is likely to decline with price. The right-hand diagram in Figure 1.1 is very close in its construction and meaning to the left-hand diagram of the demand schedule. Here, however, the price of interaction, or simply distance in this example, is on the horizontal axis, and quantity, or level of spatial interaction, is on the vertical axis. The cost of spatial interaction over long distances is high, in terms of both time and out-of-pocket expenses for gasoline or air fare or other direct costs; thus, levels of spatial interaction over long distances are relatively low. Short distances mean relatively lower costs, so spatial interaction levels over shorter distances are relatively high. Generally, spatial interaction in the economy conforms to the basic relationship called downward-sloping demand (also see Insights 1.1). In economic geography, downward-sloping demand is most often in the form of *distance decay*, or the decline in interaction that occurs with distance. For example, people are more likely to buy their groceries at a nearby supermarket than at one farther away, and friends who live near each other get together more often than friends who live far apart. Spatial interaction is necessary for a real economy to exist because not every individual is self-sufficient. Each person, each firm, each corporation, interacts with other entities in the economy in carrying out their patterns of production and consumption. Because spatial interaction is costly, there is a tendency toward geographical concentrations of people and industries called *agglomerations*.

Agglomerations develop because people (and companies) are better off if they are able to pay less for a good or service than they are willing to pay. It makes you happy if the price of a movie is $3.50 when you would be willing to pay $5.00 to see it. In the aggregate, the difference between what people would be willing to pay for a product and what they do pay for it is called *consumer surplus*. The left-hand diagram in Figure 1.2 describes the consumer surplus for the product in question as the area of the triangle *ABC*. (Note that the demand "curves" in Figure 1.2 are actually straight lines, making the graphs simpler to present and allowing us to avoid integral calculus in describing areas under the curve.) The market price is *C*, which intersects the demand schedule at *B*, which denotes the market demand for the good. Quantities in demand decrease as one moves up the schedule from *B* to *A*, but they are not zero because there is still some demand even at much higher prices. Wealthy people, for example, may be willing to pay high prices, but their volume of demand is limited. In addition, some people have preferences that would make them willing to pay

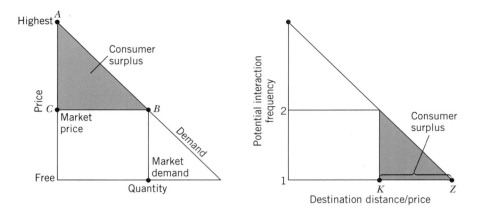

Figure 1.2 The left-hand diagram indicates consumer surplus as the shaded triangle *ABC*, the value of consumption that would occur at higher than the market price. The right-hand diagram indicates that geographical consumer surplus increases with proximity to a destination. For example, a person at *K* can visit the destination for one-half the price paid by a person at *Z*, or the person at *K* can visit the destination twice for the same price of one visit by the person at *Z*.

very high prices for a particular good, even if it creates hardship in other areas. Both the wealthy person and the one with particular preferences (especially the latter) are better off in that they are able to pay a lower price.

The need for spatial interaction in the economy means that people and companies are frequently made better off by being located within an agglomeration. The proximities that come with agglomeration yield consumer surplus with respect to necessary spatial interactions within the economy. An individual at *K* in the right-hand diagram in Figure 1.2, for example, has consumer surplus with respect to spatial interaction when compared to the individual at *Z*. Given a common destination that must be reached, the geographical consumer surplus can be measured for individuals simply as the difference in their required distances to be traveled. In this case, the surplus for the individual at *K* as compared to the individual at *Z* is distance *KZ*, or its associated cost. In the situation described in the diagram, a person at *K* could travel to the destination twice for what a person at *Z* pays for one trip. More concretely, think of the money and time you could save during a year if you lived 1 kilometer closer to work, or 1 kilometer closer to a shopping center. The savings from a closer location to work or shopping would be your consumer surplus gained from a shift in your location. When consumer surplus is placed in this geographical context, it's not surprising that people and companies tend to cluster together in agglomerations that reduce the costs of spatial interaction.

Agglomerations vary in size. Cities, for example, which are one type of agglomeration in the economy, don't all have the same populations or population densities. Shopping malls don't have the same areas, and manufacturing agglomerations don't have the same number of factories. An explanation for the variation in size of different agglomerations can begin with considering the importance of transaction costs in the workings of the economy. As we know, prices of goods and services have a direct impact on their volumes of sale, but so do other indirect costs. Sales taxes, for example, usually charged as a percentage of a product's price, or the value-added taxes used in Europe, increase the effective price of a product, so that lower quantities are purchased than if the taxes are not imposed. Other indirect charges are in effect as well. A trip to the shopping mall takes time, and we all know that time is money, and there is the price of bus fare or gasoline as well. If the trip to the mall is for the purpose of buying goods and services, and not simply a recreational end in itself, then the trip's costs can be added to the total price paid for the goods purchased as a form of *transaction cost*, or cost incurred in making the purchase. As long as people do not have unlimited budgets of time and money, as any transaction costs (not just those involving transportation) increase so do total prices, and demand for goods and services decreases. Because transportation is not free, spatial interaction between places tends to decrease as the distance between places increases. For example, if you need a loaf of bread, would you be more inclined to buy it at a store within a half-mile of your apartment or at a store five miles away? The time and trouble of traveling the five miles probably would not seem worth it for a loaf of bread; that much travel incurs too high a transaction cost, especially if you can purchase the bread at a much nearer store. Proximity increases geographical consumer surplus by decreasing transaction costs of spatial interaction.

The economist Richard Coase has suggested that firms are formed as a type of small-scale agglomeration of people with similar business objectives. These people concentrate their interests in order to minimize the transaction costs of communicating and of working with each other that would be incurred if they acted as independent operators. Savings result from sharing the costs of transmitting and using information. These kinds of savings are typical of those referred to as *economies of scale*, which are technically defined as a decrease in the average cost curve with an increase in production, as described in the left half of Figure 1.3. Economies of scale occur for a number of reasons, in addition to the reduction of transaction costs. Experence increases with production, so that the cost of making the billionth hamburger is lower than the cost of making the first. Larger companies have more market power because they buy so much. Even individuals can experience this type of scale economy; notice the average price of a can of soda pop when it is purchased in a case as compared to buying it singly. In addition, fixed costs of production, such as some machinery, property taxes, or sponsoring bowling teams, can be spread more widely over large production runs, again lowering the average cost per unit of output.

As long as economies of scale are being achieved, total cost increases at a decreasing rate. A volume of production may be reached, however, where the average cost curve and, therefore, the total cost curve begin to swing up. Bottlenecks may develop on overloaded production lines, requiring expansion of plants and purchases of new equipment. Also, large-scale production runs limit the flexibility of reaction to market changes that may arise, so that large volumes of

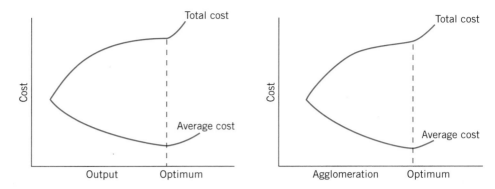

Figure 1.3   The left-hand diagram describes internal economies and diseconomies of scale with respect to output. The right-hand diagram describes external economies and diseconomies of scale with respect to agglomeration.

output have to be sold at deep discounts. An increase in the average cost curve with an increase in production is indicative of *diseconomies of scale.*

Just as average costs frequently decrease with an increase in production, they can also decrease with an increase in agglomeration as described in the right-hand diagram of Figure 1.3. So-called *agglomeration economies* can arise from a number of sources, but in general average costs decrease in an agglomeration because of the lower costs of spatial interaction that is required if it can take place within a geographical concentration. As indicated in Insights 1.2, which discusses the potential location of biotech companies in Connecticut, agglomerations can offer local supplies of specialized labor, financing, and other special business services that would be much more costly if obtained from multiple sources over long distances. In general, when producers and consumers cluster together, the geographical costs of their transactions are lowered. Just as in the case of the single company, however, agglomerations may reach a size that causes the onset of agglomeration diseconomies, so that large centers become high-cost rather than low-cost locations. As population density increases, for example, congestion may actually cause spatial interaction to become more costly over fairly short distances, thereby raising geographical transaction costs.

Congestion alone is a good reason why agglomeration is not so complete that everybody lives in one huge city, or even in a handful of very large cities. It's easy enough to see that settlements around the world vary in size from village to metropolis and that while many companies are found in big cities, many others are found in smaller ones and are even located at fairly inaccessible sites. The importance of spatial interaction and its costs is not uniform across people or across companies. Certain companies, for example, may find it necessary to locate away from agglomerations in order to minimize certain direct production costs. Companies that require large amounts of land in their production processes, or proximity to natural resource sites, may incur unneeded additional costs if they locate within agglomerations in order to cut the costs of other types of spatial interaction. Land may be more expensive, for example, in an agglomeration than in a more rural place. These types of producers, as well as others, can actually impose extra costs on themselves by limiting relatively minor costs by locating in an agglomeration but raising other major costs of production. These *opportunity* costs result from taking one action, or picking one location, when another action or location would be less costly in total.

Agglomerations themselves vary in size because the relative importance of the transaction costs of spatial interaction vary from company to company and even from person to person. If the volume of necessary spatial interactions is light for a producer, then that producer can take advantage of other locational requirements that may be available only in smaller centers. Over time, technological advances have led to a *space–time convergence* in which distance has become less costly because it can be covered more quickly. A simple conversation between a person in Japan and a person in Canada would have required significant travel 100 years ago; now the distance is meaningless because they can speak over a telephone. As distance becomes shorter in terms of time and expense, the need for agglomeration decreases because transaction costs dissipate. The use of fax machines, computer links such as the Internet, and so on allow people and companies to be farther apart than in the past and still maintain necessary levels of spatial interaction without incurring prohibitive transaction costs. Case 1.2 illustrates the impact of improved communications technology on the need for agglomeration in many industries, right down to the level of the firm. Agglomerations grew with the Industrial Revolution because the need for spatial interaction in the economy increased as production became more specialized. Now, even though spatial interaction requirements remain strong for most industries, its declining role as a transaction cost may bring about a deconcentration in the economy's geography.

➤ INSIGHTS 1.1
Elastic Demand and Distance Decay

The diagrams in Figure 1.1 can be expressed as basic mathematical functions. For example, a downward-sloping demand curve is a map of a mathematical function that takes the general form

$$-Q = (P) \tag{1.1}$$

which indicates that quantity of demand, Q, decreases as price, P, increases. Another way to indicate this demand–price relationship is

$$Q = P^{-k} = \frac{1}{P^k} \tag{1.2}$$

so that demand is shown to respond reciprocally to price that is weighted by some coefficient, k, of elasticity.

In the same way, the demand for spatial interaction in the economy can be generalized as

$$-I = (D) \qquad (1.3)$$

so that interaction, *I*, decreases as distance, *D*, increases. This in turn implies the general distance decay function:

$$I = \frac{1}{D^k} \qquad (1.4)$$

with interaction responding reciprocally to some weighted measure of distance.

➤ Insights 1.2
Agglomeration Economies in the Biotech Industry

Biotech companies would consider locating in Connecticut over other states, biotechnology analyst Kenneth J. Pounds said, primarily for access to Yale University and the University of Connecticut. Yale's medical school, for example, was among the top recipients of grants from the National Institutes of Health last year.

For research—which includes biotechnology—it received 455 awards totaling more than $125 million. During the same time, the UConn Health Center received 87 awards for $20.3 million.

There are already a number of biotechnology companies located near Yale, another reason why start-ups may want to locate here.

"Those that spawn out of universities like to stay close for the professional relationships, shared resources and collaborative opportunities in which services—and research—are bought and brokered," said Debra K. Pasquale, president of Connecticut United for Research Excellence, a biotechnology advocacy organization.

Along with highly educated graduates from the universities, the state has a highly skilled work force to draw from, experts say. It also has the fourth-largest concentration of privately managed venture capitalists in the country, according to the Department of Economic Development.

In addition, Connecticut features several major pharmaceutical companies—which are increasingly looking at forming alliances with small biotechnology companies as a way of speeding new-drug discovery and development.

In return, the pharmaceutical companies provide capital and assistance with the U.S. Food and Drug Administration's regulatory process, as well as support with marketing and manufacturing.

Source: "Beckoning to Biotech Businesses," by Dee Siegel in the *Hartford Courant Business Weekly*, July 4, 1994, p. 8. By permission of the the *Hartford Courant*.

■ CASE *1.2*
Electronics Revolution Affects Jobs

In the late 1700s, steam power drove the first Industrial Revolution right over a world of farmers and cottage workers. It rearranged the global workforce, drawing people in from the countryside to live near new factories in the city.

In the early 1990s, silicon chips and electronic superhighways have begun a second industrial revolution, reversing the trends of the first.

Driven by newly affordable—and powerful—small computers, it threatens once again to restructure the marketplace and the workforce.

Plugged into new electronic networks, those computers will let individuals work at home with access to data bases worldwide while harnessing a power reserved for their company's mainframe just a decade ago.

"Ultimately, the essence of work will be totally revolutionized," said William Davidow, author of "The Virtual Corporation." "Companies that grasp this opportunity are going to ride the wave into the future."

Those that don't may be headed for the corporate graveyard to find a resting place alongside other dinosaurs that couldn't adapt to a changing environment.

"The first industrial revolution was characterized by machines that extended, multiplied and leveraged our physical capabilities," said Raymond Kurzweil, head of a Massachusetts software-design company and author of "The Age of Intelligent Machines."

"The second industrial revolution . . . is based on machines that extend, multiply and leverage not our physical capabilities, but our mental abilities," he said.

Desktop computers, for example, now allow one person to take the place of a whole printing plant, as well as an army of distributors.

Today, chips that process 1 million instructions a second—or MIPS—cost about $100. That's the equivalent of a 1980 mainframe computer costing $100,000.

And personal computers are keeping pace; for $1,500, you can buy a system with 20 MIPS. For about twice that price you can get 100 MIPS.

It means vast changes for many industries, from real estate and finance to defense and publishing.

Creating documents electronically and sending them over a data highway such as Time Warner, Inc.'s Full Service Network will likely produce a new segment of "cottage" publishers, consultants and entrepreneurs.

Already 7 million people "telecommute" to work with computers at home. That number is expected to grow to 10 million by the year 2000 and has spawned a new buzzword, SOHOs—small-office, home office workers.

But for workers, the changes also mean unemployment or retraining.

Increasing automation could put 5 million to 25 million American jobs at risk by the year 2000, according to the Gortner Group, a market research and analysis firm.

Nearly two-thirds of all U.S. workers are now considered information or knowledge workers, according to federal reports. But the transformation has just started to hit home in several key industries.

Workers who adapt may find themselves empowered by at-home computing that will give them the freedom to live wherever they want—as small-business people or independent contractors.

Although letting employees work at home might seem awkward at first, its benefits multiply rapidly.

Telecommuters translate into smaller offices, less upkeep and lower overhead.

An employee who trips and falls while working at home is clumsy. An employee who falls at work is a mountain of paperwork—worker's compensation claims, witness reports, safety inspections and perhaps even a drug test.

Fewer employees at the workplace mean fewer managers as well.

Some corporations may evolve into a small circle of managers who assemble groups of freelance information workers from throughout the country.

They will post want ads on networks, receive resumes and references online and even interview candidates with two-way video conference calls, said Thomas W. Malone, professor of information systems at the Massachusetts Institute of Technology.

Department meetings can be held the same way. If there are actually any departments.

Once a team's specific task is completed, the group could be disbanded, allowing the company to redesign its departments "every month, every week and, sometimes, every day," Malone said.

Unlimited flexibility will mean a company can try out new directions and respond quickly to new consumer trends.

With that, the second industrial revolution will begin to reverse another centuries old convention—mass production.

It will be mass customization, not mass production, say the analysts, that keeps companies alive in the new revolution.

SOURCE: "Electronics Revolution Gathers Force" by Jay Hamburg of the *Orlando Sentinel*, May 31, 1994. By permission of the *Orlando Sentinel*.

FOR DISCUSSION

This case suggests some fairly sweeping changes in the economy as a result of the "second industrial revolution." Can you think of some reasons why the predictions made in the case may not come to pass?

MORE THAN MARKETS

The supply and demand for a good or service is a *market.* . So far, our discussion of location has been completely in the context of current markets for spatial interaction. Simply stated, *current costs of spatial interaction between economic interests determine the quality of a location.* If that were completely true, then this book wouldn't be so thick, nor would locational problems be hard to analyze and solve. In addition to markets for spatial interaction among economic enterprises, two other types of interaction are important in affecting the quality of a location: interaction between economic enterprises and governments, and interaction between economic enterprises and the physical environment. In addition, the quality of a location can change over time as a type of historical process. Markets, government policy, and technology all change over time so that the best location at one time can become a poor location at another and yesterday's bad location becomes very attractive under current conditions.

Government policy can affect the economic characteristics of a place or region, or it can directly modify patterns of spatial interaction. Over the last three decades, international trade has taken on such importance that we now frequently think of ourselves as operating within a global economy. Certainly, flows of trade in the global economy between different countries have a basis in supply and demand for the goods being traded. A large porportion of trade, however, is guided by government policy. Many national governments subsidize certain industries in their countries, paying some of their costs so that those industries will be in a better position to export in the global economy. Trade flows, as forms of spatial interaction, are directly affected by governments in their policies on currency exchange rates and tariffs. High tariffs, for example, make imports relatively expensive and so limit the demand for them relative to that for domestically produced goods. Government at other levels can also affect locational quality through policy and regulation. In the United States, for example, state governments can either encourage or discourage particular types of economic activities through tax laws, labor legislation, and a variety of business regulations. Local governments can also use taxes to affect locational decisions and also may regulate land use in order to limit economic activity in one part of their jurisdiction and direct it toward another.

Given government's power to affect economic activity, certain groups expend a considerable amount of effort to influence the government's policy in their favor. In general, the subject matter of the field of economics is the allocation of scarce resources. The term *political economy* is used to describe the process of groups using the government to effect a favorable allocation. Tariffs on foreign imports, for example, usually result from the pursuasive pleas of domestic producers of similar goods rather than from careful analysis of the country's best interests in general. Recent efforts by some states in the United States to maintain flow control of trash provide a good illustration of political economy at a more local level (Insights 1.3). Over the last 10 years, most municipal and other local landfills have been closing in the United States, for they have been filled to capacity. Transfer stations, as centralized collection facilities, and incinerators are being built to handle trash disposal but their cost is not low. Usually, their construction is financed by public bonds—money borrowed by local governments.

In order to ensure that the incinerators built on borrowed money would earn enough revenue to pay off the loans, many local governments enacted flow-control regulations determining that trash generated within their jurisdiction would be brought to the disposal sites that had been financed by their borrowing. Flow control meant that spatial interaction between points of trash "production" and least cost points of trash "demand" (cheaper disposal facilities), either locally or across the country, was blocked by local governments in the interests of their bondholders. Large amounts of trash lower the average operating costs of the facilities, and the lower average costs ensure sufficient revenues to pay interest and principal on the bonds. Unfortunately for the local governments and bondholders, this type of flow control was found to be unconstitutional in the United States because only the federal government is allowed to make regulations and laws concerning interstate commerce.

The flow-control issue also illustrates one facet of the importance of the interaction between economic enterprise and the physical environment in affecting locational quality. Waste disposal is an increasingly important environmental consideration in making location decisions, especially in goods-producing businesses such as manufacturing. It was not so long ago that the only concern for the environment in making locational decisions was in its context as a provider of raw materials. Certain soil and climate characteristics guided the location of particular agricultural crops, for example, while an abundance of local mineral supplies led to the development of certain metallurgical industries. Two hundred years ago, manufacturing plants were built on rivers for two reasons: running water provided a direct source of cheap power in an age before the use of electricity, and running water also offered a free waste-disposal system. Unfortunately, the view of water as a free disposal system outlasted its direct power-generating benefits, and industrial water pollution remains a significant environmental problem in many parts of the world.

Technological change, a type of historical process, has altered the quality of past locations in the same way that it alters locational quality today (see Case 1.2). Southern New England has enough abandoned mill sites on its streams to keep an army of industrial archeologists busy for years. The mills were abandoned when their locational advantage declined following the manufacturers' ability to generate and transmit electricity at low prices. Other once-thriving industrial regions have lost much of their advantage, too. The Monongahela Valley of Pennsylvania has the hulks of old steel works, and southeastern Michigan has empty auto plants. Locational change does not affect just manufacturing; downtown retail sites in the United States are also diminishing, and once prime farmland has decreased in acreage. At the same time, of course, economic development is occurring in other locations. Markets for textiles, steel, and autos remain strong, whereas suburban sites of retail shopping centers are expanding on former farmland, and agricultural production is increasing on formerly fallow land. With changes in the geography of production costs and the geography of consumers over time, locational quality changes as well.

Case 1.3 illustrates changing locational quality as an historical process. Production technology and plant logistics have changed in the firearms business, and markets have changed, too. As a result of these changes, production has moved from an original to a suburban location, bringing the end of an era. In addition, the case of Colt's Manufacturing Company shows that personal factors may play a role in establishing locational patterns. Colt's success was due in no small part to its regional location. At the time of its establishment, many of the world's most highly skilled craftspeople lived in Connecticut. Firearms production, especially at Colt's, was a cutting-edge industry that required a level of worker expertise that was not easily found elsewhere. There were other specific locations, however, that would have served just as well: New Haven, also in Connecticut, Springfield and Worcester, in Massachusetts, or Providence, in Rhode Island, seem to have had the requisite labor and other factors, and so did the larger centers in the region of Boston and New York. Hartford, however, had Sam Colt, the critical factor not only in the location of his own plant but also the establishment of a regional firearms industry that still exists today. Colt's impact in Hartford was about the same as Henry Ford's around Detroit in the automobile industry. Both men served as catalysts for establishing significant industrial agglomerations.

Markets, public policy, environmental factors, and historical context all come together in Case 1.4, which describes the closing of an electricity-generating plant in Fort Fairfield, Maine. Aroostook County in northern Maine, where Fort Fairfield is located, is the end of the line in the eastern United States. The county is poorly placed for spatial interaction with the rest of the Unites States' economy, and the area around Fort Fairfield may be better integrated with the Canadian Province of New Brunswick than it is with southern Maine. The region probably had its best days during the 1920s when local starch factories were a ready source of demand for the huge potato crop grown in the eastern part of the county. While potato farming remains at a reduced scale, all of the county has been under economic duress for some time and the closing of the U.S. Air Force (Loring AFB) eliminated the region's single largest employer.

The electricity-generating plant at Fort Fairfield was established as a result of public policy that anticipated a market that never came to pass. During the period of rapidly increasing oil prices engineered by the Organization of Petroleum Exporting Countries in the early 1970s' and later with the revolution in Iran, government policy in the United States encouraged the generation of electricity at nonpower company sources by mandating the purchase of this energy by electrical utilities. This policy was designed to provide a variety of sources of electricity outside of the existing power companies, but to use the power companies to distribute the electricity to consumers. The government mandates usually required the power companies to purchase the electricity at high prices in order to encourage alternative producers such as the one at Fort Fairfield. Also, at the time, the mandated prices were assumed to be in line with anticipated increases in consumer demand for electricity and rising energy costs in general. To make a long story short, the oil price bubble burst, and energy prices decreased rather than increased at the same time that power consumption efficiency increased. Power companies in many places, not just in Maine, have urged the elimination of requirements of purchasing so-called co-generated electricity, especially at old high prices.

The plant at Fort Fairfield was established not in response to an actual market for electricity produced there, but to a market contrived by government policy. The location was a good one, however, after the fact, because it provided a ready supply of wood as fuel for the plant. Aroostook County is as much a center of the wood products industry, primarily pulp and paper, as it is a center of potato farming. Furthermore, local agricultural production benefited from the plant's establishment because it could use the ash byproduct as cheap fertilizer, and a system of localized spatial interaction was developed. Unfortunately, times changed and so did public policy. Without the policy, there is little demand for the electricity generated, and the other factors making Fort Fairfield a good location for electricity production make no difference to the plant's survival.

All the cases in this chapter ultimately concern the quality of certain locations for certain businesses. In each case, the locational decisions described were ultimately based on weighing the enterprise's worth at the particular location in question. Ultimately, the decision to open, maintain, or close a plant is a decision concerning capital investment in a project (Insights 1.4). Each capital investment made by a company must have a location, and locational quality plays an important role in investment decisions. Over time, however, the original characteristics of a location that made it a good one for investment may change, or the needs of a business for a place's particular characteristics may change. In either case, we have the basis for a dynamic pattern of locations in the economy.

➤ INSIGHTS 1.3
Flow Control

SUPREME COURT OF THE UNITED STATES
Syllabus
C & A CARBONE, INC v. TOWN OF
CLARKSTOWN, NEW YORK
CERTIORARI TO THE APPELATE DIVISION, SUPREME COURT
OF NEW YORK, SECOND JUDICIAL DEPARTMENT
No. 92-1402. Argued December 7, 1993—Decided May 16, 1994

Respondent town agreed to allow a private contractor to construct within town limits a solid waste transfer station to separate recyclable from nonrecyclable items and to operate the facility for five years, at which time the town would buy it for one dollar. To finance the transfer station's cost, the town guaranteed a minimum waste flow to the facility, for which the contractor could charge the hauler a tipping fee which exceeded the disposal cost of unsorted solid waste on the private market. In order to meet the waste flow guarantee, the town adopted a flow control ordinance, requiring all nonhazardous solid waste within the town to be deposited at the transfer station. While recyclers like petitioners (collectively Carbone) may receive solid waste at their own sorting facilities, the ordinance requires them to bring nonrecyclable residue to the transfer station, thus forbidding them to ship such waste themselves and requiring them to pay the tipping fee on trash that has already been sorted. After discovering that

Carbone was shipping nonrecyclable waste to out-of-state destinations, the town filed suit in state court, seeking an injunction requiring that this residue be shipped to the transfer station. The court granted summary judgment to the town, finding the ordinance constitutional, and the Appellate Division affirmed. *Held:* The flow control ordinance violates the Commerce Clause.

(a) The ordinance regulates interstate commerce. While its immediate effect is to direct local transport of solid waste to a designated site within the local jurisdiction, its economic effects are interstate in reach.

➤ INSIGHTS 1.4
Making Locational Decisions by Discounting Costs and Benefits

From a purely economic perspective, any project is feasible if it has a net present value of costs and benefits that is positive. The *net present value* of a project is the value in today's money that is obtained by adding the actual current and forecasted future net costs and benefits of the project over its anticipated useful life, so that

$$NPV_P = \frac{(B_0 - C_0)}{(1 + r)^0} + \cdots + \frac{(B_t - C_t)}{(1 + r)^t} \tag{1.5}$$

where NPV_P is the net present value of the project, B_0 and C_0 are the benefits and costs, respectively, incurred at the outset of the project, or at time zero, $1 + r$ is the discounting factor with discount rate r, and B_t and C_t are the benefits and costs, respectively, incurred in the last time period, t, of the project's existence. It is convenient to use summation notation for this type of series, so that Equation 1.5 is more often portrayed as

$$NPV_P = \sum_{t=0}^{t} \frac{(B - C_t)}{(1 + r)^t} \tag{1.6}$$

Benefits and costs should be considered in a comprehensive way. Equally important, however, is the selection of the *discount rate, r,* because its value is the weighting factor of the net costs and benefits that are earned in the future. Future values are discounted because money has a time value of its own. People and the enterprises they operate tend to prefer having money now rather than later. We would, for example, rather have $5 now than the assurance of having $5 next year, much less than $5 ten years from now. When loans are made, lenders forgo the current use of their money until the loan is paid back. Interest charges are a form of payment that offsets the time preference of money. Even loans to the U.S. government, which are usually considered to be risk free, carry interest rates of a sufficient magnitude to make lenders prefer to have their money later rather than now. Otherwise, government bonds would not be loans; they would be gifts.

The higher the value of r, the greater the discount of future net benefits and costs. To illustrate the effects of variation in discount rates, let's begin with a hypothetical project that costs $50,000 to start and then earns $17,000 per year for five years of useful life at operating costs of $2,000 per year, yielding a net nominal benefit of $15,000 in years 1 through 5. If the discount rate is zero—that is, the future values are not discounted at all—then the net present value is calculated to be $25,000, as

$$NPV_P = \frac{-\$50,000}{(1+0)^0} + \frac{\$15,000}{(1+0)^1} + \frac{\$15,000}{(1+0)^2} + \frac{\$15,000}{(1+0)^3} + \frac{\$15,000}{(1+0)^4} + \frac{\$15,000}{(1+0)^5}$$

If the discount rate is 5%, or 0.05, then the NPV is lowered to $14,950:

$$NPV_P = \frac{-\$50,000}{(1+0.05)^0} + \frac{\$15,000}{(1+0.05)^1} + \frac{\$15,000}{(1+0.05)^2} + \frac{\$15,000}{(1+0.05)^3}$$
$$+ \frac{\$15,000}{(1+0.05)^4} + \frac{\$15,000}{(1+0.05)^5}.$$

While at a 10% discount rate,

$$NPV_P = \sum_{t=0}^{t} \frac{(B-C_t)}{(1+0.10)^t} = \$6,870$$

So the discount rate is pivotal in calculating the net present value of a project. Higher rates yield lower net present values, while lower rates make them higher, other things being equal. How are discount rates selected? It depends on who is planning a project. In the private sector, a targeted rate of return is frequently used. For example, a company may require that its projects earn a 10% internal rate of return on investments, so that would be the discount value it employs in cost-benefit analysis. Again if the net present value is greater than zero, then the project is economically feasible. Feasibility, however, is no guarantee that investment in a project will take place. Investment in a project should only take place if it is optimal, meaning the project has the highest net present value of any comparable feasible projects that the enterprise is considering. Investment in feasible but nonoptimal projects create opportunity costs.   ◄

■ *CASE 1.3*
Colt's Relocation Closes Chapter in City's History

The annoying buzz of flickering fluorescent light resounds through the near-empty Colt Armory in Hartford.

It is one of the few sounds here, save the silent echos of the men and women who, over the past 140 years, changed the way Americans worked and fought and thought about themselves.

It is an eerie emptiness. This is where Connecticut, arguably even America, abandoned its agrarian past and began the sometimes glorious, sometimes painful evolution into an industrial power.

Sam Colt was the man who designed the famous single-action revolver that won the West. And it was on the clattering machines that carve chunks of raw metal into weapons that Colt workers churned out 10,000 M-16 rifles a week during the Vietnam War. In the late 1980s, just outside the factory gates, angry workers staged a bitter four-year strike.

But the quiet these days is real, for an era is drawing to a close. Colt's Manufacturing Co., the modern version of the company Sam Colt founded, is leaving the Colt complex. By mid-May, operations are scheduled to shut down and move to a more modern facility.

The company's president, Ron Whitaker, keeps a collection of classic Colt guns behind glass in his office. He has respect for the past, but his mission is to save the ailing gunmaker, which has been languishing in Chapter 11 bankruptcy for more than two years.

The sprawling complex along the Connecticut River with its trademark blue dome on the top no longer suits the modern gunmaking processes Whitaker has put into place. The huge pillars that support the hulking edifice get in the way of his revamped assembly lines.

Besides, Whitaker said, Colt's has not owned the property for about 40 years, and consolidating operations in the West Hartford plant Colt's has used since the early 1960s will save the cash-strapped company about $3 million a year.

"That's so sad," said Frances Williams, one of the handful of employees still working at the Hartford plant. "We've been in here a long time. It's history."

In a now-vacant wing where firearms executives once made decisions about bullet widths and barrel lengths, a smattering of desks and chairs sprawl in a haphazard clutter. Much of the plant's machinery is outdated and will soon be scrapped.

Sam Colt would no doubt be shocked to learn that within a couple of weeks, guns bearing the distinctive Colt trademark of a rearing horse gripping a broken spear in its mouth will no longer be made under the famous blue dome.

And, of all reasons, because the cutting edge factory Colt built is now an industrial relic, no longer well-suited to the craft of making quality guns.

"I think it's sad we are leaving this plant with so much historical significance, not only for Colt's but for the city of Hartford," Whitaker said. "But there's no way for us to compete in today's competitive environment, with a broken-up factory like this."

Colt was a dynamic man, whose dreams captured the imagination of a changing nation. In 1851, he started buying up swampy land in Hartford's South Meadows and embarked on a project that at first sparked skepticism among city leaders.

But four years later, Colt succeeded in building a factory that would bring sweeping changes not only to Hartford, but to the nation. He capped his accomplishment with an onion-shaped dome that still catches the attention of travelers speeding down I-91.

The factory became an industrial magnet. Young men eager to learn the latest in manufacturing and engineering flocked to Colt's palace on the river and later went on to start their own companies, helping establish Hartford as one of the leading hubs of the industrial era.

Immigrants hungry for work swarmed into the city, carving out neighborhoods that changed Hartford forever. Many lived in company homes and danced in the huge Charter Oak Hall Colt built near his plant. When the building burned down in 1864, two years after Colt's death, his widow rebuilt the complex.

Year after year, guns were made in Hartford. And, as the company grew, so did the complex. More than 20 buildings now sprawl over six square blocks, with Colt's now taking up only about a third of the space. The rest is occupied by 180 different tenants ranging from artists to manufacturers.

The company itself went through many changes—different owners, stepped up competition, the paralyzing strike of the 1980s. A host of troubles came to a head in 1992, when Colt's took the drastic step of filing for protection from its creditors in U.S. Bankruptcy Court.

In 1993, scrambling to keep the company alive, Colt executives decided they were spending too much money keeping both of the company's major gun-making facilities open. They considered moving everything to Hartford, but the aging facility just didn't lend itself to making guns the way they wanted to.

They decided the company's future was not under the blue dome, but in a nondescript industrial space on New Park Avenue marked by little more than a company sign, relatively small and easy to miss.

The departure is certainly an end, although much of what this particular move speaks of is already history.

The demise of urban manufacturing in the Northeast is a decades-old story, one easily measured in blighted abandoned factories. Nor is the flight of jobs and money from the city a new notion. The poverty and despair that have damaged so many neighborhoods is a painful testament to the trend.

Source: "Colt's Move Signals End of an Era," by Andrew Julien. *Hartford Courant*, May 1, 1994, pp. A1–A2. By permission of the *Hartford Courant* and Andrew Julien.

FOR DISCUSSION

Make a quick list of the apparent costs and benefits of operating the Colt's plant. Should the costs and benefits listed be extended to those incurred outside the plant in the community affected? If so, do you think the decision to close the plant would be changed?

◪ *CASE 1.4*
Wood to Energy in Northern Maine

FORT FAIRFIELD—Safety posters at the Fairfield Energy Venture power plant remind workers to protect their eyes and heads, but there's no warning telling them how to save their jobs. What they need is a flashing neon sign: "Caution, watch for shifting public policy."

State policy in the 1980s replaced foreign oil with 100 small power plants that run on wood, water and trash. Electric rates soared, but the policy brought energy independence and thousands of jobs, a good tradeoff at the time.

Times change. Now state loans may help close some of the same plants and throw people out of work.

This potato farming town of 4,000 people is set to suffer the first hit. Up here, the shifting outline of public policy is about to take on a human face.

Just eight years ago an out-of-state partnership came here to the Canadian border and sank $60 million into a giant wood-chip and mill-waste burner. It cranks out enough electricity for Central Maine Power Company [CMP] to run 9,000 homes downstate. Back then, clean-burning, home-fueled power was patriotic and the plants were heroes.

But many of the plants got bad names when demand fell and bills soared to pay for all the new, unneeded power. With customers in revolt, CMP went to its highest-cost plants and asked for new deals. Most refused.

So last spring CMP went to the Legislature. Down in Augusta, CMP blamed the power plants for rate hikes and sought a controversial tax. As a compromise, lawmakers approved $100 million in state-backed funds to help refinance costly contracts, or buy them out.

Folks here knew their plant was costly, almost double today's going rate. They figured CMP would use the money to negotiate a lower contract. So they were shocked three weeks ago to learn that CMP wanted $78 million of the bond money to buy the plant, and shut it down.

The deal will save CMP customers $35 million over the next eight years. Put another way, the average homeowner will pay 50 cents less on a monthly bill.

But for a customer in Portland to save $6 a year, people in Aroostook farm country will bear a high cost.

The plant contributes one-third of Fort Fairfield's taxes. It employs 37 workers who earn an average of $12.50 an hour, good money in the county. Loggers, truckers and sawmills send 355,000 tons of biomass a year in the front end. Farmers get leftover ash out the back door to fertilize their soil. Almost everyone has a meal in town or tops up a gas tank.

In eight years, Fairfield Energy Venture has become more than just a good corporate neighbor. It's a white-hot light in a darkening local economy. Residents have struggled the past two years with a potato blight that has ravaged the crop. They watched millions of dollars fly out of the county when the last bomber took off from Loring Air Force Base. They're still cleaning up from the April flood, when the fickle Aroostook River reared up and spread icy havoc along Main Street.

Now this.

BITTER OVER POLICY CHANGE

Two weeks ago, a group of plant operators sat nervously in the control room and talked about the gathering doom. These are young men with families, mortgages and car payments, bitter about a policy change they couldn't see coming and don't understand. . . . They can't believe they're being sold out, with state backing, so southern Mainers can save $6 a year.

CMP says there's another side to the story.

Its 500,000 customers are the real victims, the company says. They've been subsidizing unneeded or overpriced plants for years. Why should electric customers support what amounts to a jobs program?

Paying too much for power also costs jobs in southern and central Maine, CMP says. An economist estimates the financial impact of excess power payments for independent energy at about $200 million, the equivalent of roughly 4,000 potential jobs.

Now the debate over the future of this isolated power plant in Aroostook County is expanding into a high-stakes battle with statewide implications.

CMP fears that if opposition derails the deal, it will set a precedent that will deter other private power plants from renegotiating. That would handcuff CMP's attempts to stabilize rates.

The buyout must be approved by the Maine Public Utilities Commission. The PUC will decide over the next several weeks on the rate-saving merits of the deal. The town, northern Maine lawmakers and other intervenors will argue against approval.

If the deal makes it through the PUC, state loans must then be approved by the Finance Authority of Maine. If both agencies sign off, CMP plans to close the plant at the end of September.

VENTURE BENEFITS FARMERS

Frustration has blanketed Fort Fairfield like a late-spring snow.

In the countryside, John Durepo works in his barn on the family farm. He just put 200 acres of potatoes in the ground and the green vines have begun to emerge. Alfalfa, barley and oats alternate on the rest of the land.

For farmers, the power plant is a perfect fit. It's a new source of income from their woodlots. It's free fertilizer, a renewable resource that can save $190 a ton on potash. And since farmers are the biggest landowners in town, they know just how much the plant has kept their taxes down.

Farmers here expect to cope with changing weather and markets. They didn't expect to lose their power plant, and they are angry.

"We were just beginning to get things in place and find some solutions," Durepo says. "This is a complete waste. Our state isn't thinking long-term. They're doing everything on emotion, politics and the dollar."

At Earlan Turner's Exxon station, where a handful of plant-bound chip trucks stop each day for fuel, a sign reads: "If you can't see the bright side—polish the dull side."

A short distance away, Lenny Willette hasn't given up. He had 69 inches of water in Lenny's Family Restaurant, but he's back at the grill for the lunch crowd. He thinks the power plant closing will be a bigger blow.

"It's going to affect everybody, not just the low-lying areas on Main Street," he says. "The flood is a one-shot deal. You crawl out and pick up the pieces. This is long-range. It's going to hurt for years."

Willette sees the familiar faces of plant workers at his tables. Night-shift workers order pizza. Truck drivers grab a meal on their way to the mill.

"I need the business climate we presently have, if not more, to keep this thing going," he says.

Scott Seabury can take the pulse of Main Street from his second-floor window at Town Hall. The town's manager, he was already swamped with trying to speed federal relief to help offset the $100 million worth of damage caused by the flood. Now he's also trying to build a legal and political defense machine to fight against CMP and state policy makers.

Seabury is plenty frustrated. He was quoted in the Bangor Daily News saying the new policy is to "satisfy the desires of our yuppie friends to the south." Now he says the reporter must have misunderstood him about "yuppie." What he really said involved profanity.

Seabury depends on the plant's $60 million valuation to help run the town. CMP now says that, minus the power contract, the 7-year-old facility is worth only $2 million, the value of the machinery. That could mean cutting the town staff, laying off half the five-person police force, closing the library and ending the recreation program.

Local residents got a chance late last week to tell the PUC how much the closing would hurt their town. More than 400 people came to a public hearing, including northern lawmakers who said the governor should call a special legislative session to change the law.

Seabury and other locals say they thought the state financing would help CMP focus on renegotiating rates, or buying out unbuilt facilities—not shutting down existing plants.

"We knew the game was going to change with the legislation," Seabury says. "But we never expected this."

BIG PLANTS EXEMPT

Down in Augusta, officials say the new law is doing what it was supposed to do.

The new law exempts plants with a capacity above 50 megawatts. Lawmakers feared that closing a large cogeneration plant in a papermill, for example, could affect thousands of manufacturing jobs. The language they finally drafted favors buy-downs for other plants, but it doesn't forbid buyouts, like the one proposed in Fort Fairfield.

Unless you close some big, expensive plants, policy makers say, the law won't have much impact on rates. And when you do close a big plant, some people lose their jobs.

Fairfield is 33 megawatts and has a contract price of 13 cents a kilowatt hour. The buyout will cost $78 million, but avoid future operating costs of $113 million. The tradeoff is 37 jobs, and an economic blow to a small town.

The power company has contracts with 86 private plants. Roughly 25 with above-market rates are targeted for renegotiation or buyouts. Almost all are in CMP's service area.

"Politically, there's going to be fallout in northern Maine on this," says Mark Ishkanian, a CMP spokesman. "But our customers are 80 percent of the state's population, and for years they've paid higher-than-market rates for that power. Any benefits that come to them are long overdue."

ALTERNATIVE SOUGHT

CMP says it will continue looking this summer for ways to keep the plant operating. Another utility could buy it. Perhaps it can be mothballed for a time when the region's power appetite returns. Maybe it can be run as a wholesale generator by some future subsidiary of CMP, to sell power out of state.

But the most likely outlook now is also the most bleak: This modern, reliable source of renewable energy and economic vitality may be dismantled and sold for salvage.

Fort Fairfield will survive without its power plant. But for residents who have watched the unit rise against the rural landscape, and have quickly come to depend on it, the closing is part of a grim continuum that is pulling the vitality from that community. It's not a pile of steel that's at risk, not even a bunch of jobs, really. It's a way of life.

SOURCE: "Shifting Public Policy Takes on a Human Face in Northern Maine," by Tux Turkel. *Maine Sunday Telegram*, July 3, 1994, pp. 1A, 14A. By permission of the *Maine Sunday Telegram*.

FOR DISCUSSION

Is there any evidence of agglomeration economies benefiting the local economy of Fort Fairfield?

POINTS IN SUMMARY

1. Economic geography is about location in the economy. It is concerned with production, distribution, and consumption as fundamental economic activities. Its emphasis, however, is on the

flows in the economy which constitute spatial interaction.

2. Relative location is important because it tells us something of a location's accessibility to relevant places in the economy, and accessibility is vital to spatial interaction.

3. Distance decay is the geographical manifestation of downward-sloping demand. Distance between places tends to raise their costs of spatial interaction and so decreases their level of spatial interaction.

4. Costs of spatial interaction can be considered directly, as in the case of transport costs, or indirectly as transaction costs that raise prices of goods and services. Either way, we would rather have lower costs of spatial interaction than higher ones.

5. Costs of spatial interaction have led to the formation of agglomerations, or geographical concentrations, of industries and people. Agglomerations generate geographical consumer surpluses.

6. Technological advances can lower the costs of spatial interaction in a process called space-time convergence. Depending on relative needs for spatial interaction, space–time convergence can lead to the dissipation of agglomerations.

7. Locational quality depends on more than markets, or current price–demand relationships of spatial interaction. Public policy, characteristics of the physical environment, and historical conditions have important impacts on locational patterns.

8. Location decisions may be treated as investment decisions that consider the present value of the costs and benefits of a project.

TERMS TO REMEMBER

absolute location	diseconomies of scale	market	space–time convergence
agglomeration	distance decay	net present value	spatial interaction
agglomeration economies	economic geography	opportunity costs	transaction cost
consumer surplus	economies of scale	political economy	
discount rate	fundamental economic activities	price elastic demand	
		relative location	

SUGGESTED READING

Erickson, Rodney A. 1989: "The Influence of Economics on Geographic Inquiry." *Progress in Human Geography*, Vol. 13, pp. 223–250.

Erickson presents a review of the use of economic thought by economic geographers, in terms of both concepts and methods. His article covers a series of topics such as international trade, economic development, and production and consumption, in a brief but thorough way. It also contains a comprehensive list of bibliographic references.

Hugill, Peter J. 1993: *World Trade Since 1431: Geography, Technology, and Capitalism*. Baltimore, Md.: Johns Hopkins University Press.

This book, like the one by Neil Smith noted later in these references, covers economic geography without using economics or spatial analysis. It is noted here for two reasons: its historical perspective ties together technological developments and changes in economic flows in a very effective way, and it is simply a very interesting book.

Meyer, William B. 1994: "When Dismal Swamps Became Priceless Wetlands." *American Heritage*, Vol. 45, No. 3, pp. 108–116.

This well-written article uses changing attitudes toward wetlands in the United States as an example of changing attitudes toward the physical environment in general. The "before" and "after" photographs of a marsh in Wisconsin are especially interesting.

Millward, Hugh. 1994: "Process and Pattern in the Agricultural Settlement of the Maritimes." *NESTVAL Proceedings*, Vol. 23, pp. 21–31.

This brief article is not easily accessible because of its publication in a limited circulation serial. It's worth the effort of acquisition, however, because of the way it ties together environmental, historical, and economic factors in the early settlement of Atlantic Canada.

O'Sullivan, Patrick. 1981: *Geographical Economics*. New York: John Wiley & Sons.

This thin volume bridges the gap between economic geography and spatial economics nicely. If you only read one more book on economic geography during the rest of your life, this should be it.

Smith, Neill. 1984: *Uneven Development: Nature, Capital and the Production of Space*. New York: Basil Blackwell.

This is not a long book, but it contains lots of ideas centered on an important theme: the subjectivity of nature and of the economy's geography. Most spatial analysis implies that scale and factors of production and so on are objective items, but they are, in fact, cultural constructions with historical and political contexts. Smith describes the geographical effects of these constructions from a Marxist perspective.

Stern, Paul C., Oran R. Young, and Daniel Druckerman, eds. 1992: *Global Environmental Change: Understanding the Human Dimensions*. Washington, D.C.: National Academy Press.

This is an outline of suggested research initiatives on the interaction of people and nature at the global scale as well as a review of some of the research pertinent to this topic that had already been conducted. Much of the work cited in this landmark volume was done by geographers, and geographers contributed to the design of the initiatives presented.

Stone, Kirk H. 1972: "A Geographer's Strength: The Multiple-Scale Approach." *Journal of Geography*, Vol. 71, pp. 354–362.

The title of this article aptly summarizes its contents. Using examples, Stone describes variations in geographical analysis that occur with changes in scale and appropriate methods of presenting multiscale research findings.

Taaffe, Edward J. 1974: "The Spatial View in Context." *Annals of the Association of American Geographers*, Vol. 64, pp. 1–16.

This well-known piece provides a review of the development of spatial analysis in the discipline of geography. Its value is in its tracing of the spatial perspective's evolution and in its outline of geography's links to other disciplines, especially economics.

Academic Journals

Several academic journals frequently publish articles of interest to students of economic geography. The leading periodical in this regard is *Economic Geography* published by Clark University in Worcester, Massachusetts. The Association of American Geographers publishes two journals: the *Annals* and *The Professional Geographer* which carry relevant articles with some frequency, as do the *Transactions* of the Institute of British Geographers and its companion publication, *Area*. The Canadian Association of Geographers publishes two journals that frequently carry articles on topics in economic geography: *The Canadian Geographer* and *The Operational Geographer*. Both are bilingual (French and English). Other journals that are of particular interest to economic geographers are *Progress in Human Geography*, published in England by Edward Arnold Ltd. It provides an ongoing series of literature reviews on such topics as industrial geography as well as articles describing original research. Important work of a more quantitative and theoretical nature is published frequently in the Ohio State University Press's *Geographical Analysis*. Some of this work in economic geography is similar to that found in regional science journals, such as *Papers in Regional Science*, published by the Regional Science Association International.

Chapter 2

Location Principles and Land Use

This chapter

- develops the concept of economic rent in the context of the relationship between market price and supply.
- connects the concept of economic rent to the concept of location rent as the market basis for the relative location of agricultural land uses.
- extends the market-based model of agricultural land use to land use in cities.
- outlines cost-benefit analysis as a tool for making land-use decisions.

Courtesy of The Warmington Company

In Chapter 1, we took up some basic principles of location and spatial interaction and used them to develop a simple pattern of economic geography. The basis of cities in markets was drawn out from some basic relationships between price levels and demand. We considered cities as a series of agglomerations that have developed so that consumers and producers can minimize the transaction costs arising from their need for spatial interaction. Chapter 1 focused on the demand side of the market as the basis of locational quality, and now this chapter turns to the supply side of the market to consider locational quality in the context of land use. It begins with a review of the simple supply and demand schedule and then draws out a framework for maximizing profits by matching the appropriate economic activity with the appropriate location.

While the general theoretical market foundations of land-use patterns are established here in Chapter 2, Chapters 3 and 4 concentrate more on environmental, historical, and public policy factors. Always keep in mind that in real life all these factors are constantly intertwined in determining locational quality.

SUPPLY, PRICE, AND ECONOMIC RENT

As indicated in Chapter 1, the basic definition of consumer surplus is the difference between the maximum price at which something could be sold and the actual price at which it is sold. It's not just consumers, however, that can enjoy surpluses. Consumer surplus has a type of mirror image in *producer surplus*, which is calculated from the difference between the actual price at which something is sold and the minimum price at which it could be sold. The term "producer surplus" can apply to any seller of a good or service, including retailers, colleges, baseball players, and so on. Consumer surplus is an amount of money that consumers gain by buying at prices lower than they are willing to pay, and producer surplus is money that producers gain by selling at prices higher than the minimum they would be willing to charge.

Producer surplus, as you might expect, is something that producers would rather have than not, and so it plays a strong role in their behavior. Let's begin our thinking about that role by looking at Figure 2.1. The left diagram describes a conventional supply and demand schedule. There are two demand curves, D_1 and D_2; both are downward sloping, indicating price elastic demand. The demand curve D_2, however, indicates a demand shift that can come about because of a general increase in incomes, for example, or perhaps because the product in question is much more popular than at an earlier time represented in D_1. As an example of the shift stemming from popularity, think of hotel rooms in resort areas. Demand for their use increases, as does their price, during common

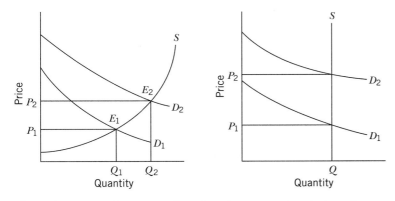

Figure 2.1 The left diagram describes the conventional case where supply is price elastic; it reacts to price changes. A demand shift from D_1 to D_2 raises the market-clearing, or equilibrium, price from P_1 to P_2, generating an increase in economic rent for earlier producers and bringing new producers to the market. The right-hand diagram concerns the case of inelastic supply, which characterizes the land market. An increase in demand from D_1 to D_2 raises prices from P_1 to P_2, a pure rent for the resource owner.

vacation periods such as midsummer. Because it is higher on the diagram, D_2 indicates a higher price being paid for a particular quantity than when demand is described by D_1.

The supply schedule on the diagram also indicates price elasticity, but the supply curve S is upward sloping rather than downward sloping like the demand curves. In general, the upward slope indicates that more product is for sale at higher prices than at lower prices; supply increases as prices increase, just as demand decreases as prices increase. Supply increases in reaction to price increases have two sources: existing producers bring more goods to market as prices increase, and more producers enter the market as prices increase. Think of home construction, for example. When housing prices are high, existing contractors tend to build more houses and more firms enter the house-building business.

Both sources of increased supply can be traced to the never-ending search for producer surplus in market economies. Point E_1 on the left diagram in Figure 2.1 is the intersection of the supply curve S and the lower demand curve D_1. It defines the *market equilibrium*—the point at which demand and supply just match each other—at quantity Q_1. The price at which demand just equals supply is called the *market-clearing price*, P_1 in this case, because it's the price that "clears the market" of surplus production—more of the product will not be produced than is in demand at that price. It also "clears the market" of unmet demand—demand for the product is no more than is produced at that price. It turns out that the equilibrium price is the price at which both consumer and producer surpluses disappear. As long as the demand curve is above P_1, then there are consumer surpluses, and as long as the supply curve is below P_1, there are producer surpluses. Any product on the market to the left of Q_1 earns producer surplus because the supply curve indicates that it would have been brought to the market at a lower price. The quantity Q_1 includes one unit of production that has a producer surplus of zero. This *marginal product*, or last unit produced, is brought to market because it sells for just enough to provide satisfactory revenue to its seller. One more unit of product brought to market, $Q_1 + 1$, could not be sold at the existing level of demand D_1 because its satisfactory revenue requires a price higher than P_1.

In effect, an upward-sloping supply curve is indicative of different levels of efficiency among the producers in an industry. Those producers that are most efficient would be able to sell their products for a much lower price than is actually being paid by the market and so earn large producer surpluses. Less efficient producers must earn more revenue to stay in business because their inefficiency means they have higher costs of production. The supply curve is an inverted measure of producer efficiency. Those producers represented by the lower levels of the supply curve are the most efficient, while the higher levels of the supply curve represent the less efficient producers.

The same relationship holds true even if the source of increased supply is expansion of output by existing producers. We assume that their asking prices are based on their costs when producing at their most efficient levels of production. If that production expands, their selling prices must rise so that increasing *marginal cost*, or the cost of producing an additional unit of output, can be covered. If this were not the case, then the whole supply curve would shift to the right, but we won't let it do that in this example. Unless the market price goes up, producer surplus first shrinks and then dissipates with the expansion of production. (Some of this effect is due to the law of diminishing returns, which is described in Chapter 3.)

Producer surplus has a synonym in *economic rent*. Economic rent, *ER*, associated with the sale of a good or service, *i*, is the difference between the price paid for a good or service, p_i minus the cost, c_i, of providing the good or service. In short, we have an economic rent identity:

$$ER_i = p_i - c_i \qquad (2.1)$$

Of course, you can see that economic rent is not the same sort of rent you pay to live in an apartment or to use a car. That payment is referred to as contract rent, which is related to economic rent in a way that will be described later in this chapter. Businesses are well served if they can operate in such a way as to maximize their economic rent, and this maximizing behavior has an impact on production and its location.

Let's go back to the left diagram in Figure 2.1. If demand increases from D_1 to D_2, economic rents, or producer surpluses, increase all along the supply curve up to the quantity Q_2 that is associated with the new market-clearing price of P_2. Established producers can continue doing what they had done before but now enjoy significant increases in economic rent. In addition, new producers can enter the market even though their inefficiency remains as before. The new higher equilibrium price now allows the formerly marginal producer of Q_1 to earn large amounts of economic rent which are earned right up to the new marginal product at Q_2. Higher prices, by generating higher rents, lead to an increase in production. Note that a decrease in production costs, perhaps because of improvements in production technology, could lead to the same result: more economic rent and more producers.

The left diagram in Figure 2.1 describes a market for a product that exhibits price elastic supply. The right-hand diagram concerns a good or service marked by its price inelastic supply, *S*, which is parallel to the price axis. Local markets for natural resources, especially land, have inelastic supply. No one is replenishing the coal taken out of a mine or refilling an existing oil well. So-called *made land* exists in many places in the form of drained wetlands and filled waterfronts, but its proportion of total land is negligible. (A real estate sales agent once told me, "Buy your land now, they're not making any more of it.") In this case, a shift in the demand schedule from D_1 to D_2 does not generate an increase in the supply of land, which remains steady at Q. It does, however, raise the price for the available quantity from P_1 to P_2. The difference is a windfall for the seller, and it is sometimes called a *pure economic rent*. Pure economic rent is different from the economic rent described earlier because it can be taxed without causing any change in the economy's behavior. If the tax, as a transaction cost, is equal to the price difference between P_1 and P_2, the same quantity of resource stays on the market. The result holds whether the seller or buyer, or both, pay the tax. In the upper diagram, such a tax would cause a decrease in production from Q_2 back to Q_1 because it would affect the price paid by consumers or the costs paid by producers. In either case, the less efficient producers would be the hardest hit.

ECONOMIC RENT AND THE LOCATION OF AGRICULTURAL PRODUCTION

The economic rent identity shown in Equation 2.1 is sometimes referred to as *Ricardian rent* after David Ricardo, a very influential British economist of the late eighteenth and early nineteenth centuries. He was concerned with the relationship between land use, its price, and the price paid for the land's output. At the time, many people thought that food was expensive because the land it was grown on had high prices. Ricardo demonstrated that the price of food usually determined the price of land, and not the other way around. As food became more expensive, the demand for land on which food could be grown increased. So the rising price of food led to an increase in its ultimate source, the land where it was grown. A rising tide raises all ships, but as increasing food prices drive up the price of land, not all landholders benefit equally. The difference in the benefits is the difference in the economic rents that are earned by different parcels of land. The difference in *land rent* from parcel to parcel is due, according to Ricardo, to differences in the costs of agricultural production on some land parcels relative to others.

In effect, Ricardo put Figure 2.1 on the ground. At any market price for a good that provides sufficient demand for its production to take place, lower cost producers have higher profits, or earn more rent, than do higher cost producers. The equilibrium price limits the number of producers in the marketplace because it defines the maximum production costs for goods on the market. The segment of the supply curve above the equilibrium price represents producers with costs that are too high for the market at current levels of demand. Raise the good's market price, and more producers can operate profitably; lower the price, and producers must leave the market unless their costs can come under the lower revenues.

In agriculture, variability in production costs from one plot of land to another can occur for a number of reasons. Even if all farmers have exactly the same abilities, the soil they farm can vary in fertility, moisture, and other environmental characteristics that all have a bearing on the cost of crop production. If soil fertility is insufficient, then fertilizer can be added. If the soil is too dry, then it can be irrigated. Land with poor environmental characteristics can be brought up to speed, but only by paying costs that do not have to be paid by farmers who enjoy land with superior environmental characteristics. Even if the land is worked in a less fertile condition, the crops not produced represent an opportunity cost to the farmer that should approximate the costs of increasing the land's crop output. For any price paid for a crop at the market, the following relationships obtain: The higher the environmental quality of the land on which the crop is grown, the lower the cost of producing the crop, the greater the economic rent earned by the land, and the greater the value of the land. Conversely, the lower the environmental quality of the land on which the crop is grown, the higher the cost of producing it, and the lower the economic rent and value of the land.

An example of the dependence of land rent on production cost is presented in Figure 2.2. The top of that figure contains a grid of 25 cells, each labeled with a hypothetical production cost per ton of crop produced. The numbers are laid out on the grid randomly and are meant to represent the differences in production costs that we might associate with fairly local differences in soil quality and so on. The lowest cost of production is in cell B2, at $114 per ton, and the highest cost of production is in cell A1, at $193/ton. We'll assume that output levels are the same across all the cells so that the example only has to concern average costs and prices and not their totals. Part B of the figure shows the rent per ton of crop produced at each of the parcels if the price paid at the market is $140 per ton. At this price, only six parcels yield positive rents: A2, A4, B2, B4, C2, and C5. All the other parcels have negative rents that arise because their production costs are higher than the price paid for the crop. At the price of $140 per ton, only the six parcels paying positive rents would be in production, and their value would be in the order of the rents they earn. Again, the value of the land is usually derived from the value of its output (and not the other way around).

A. Production Cost Per Unit of Land

	1	2	3	4	5
A	$193	$117	$149	$139	$172
B	$171	$114	$184	$136	$143
C	$162	$132	$171	$184	$123
D	$181	$160	$141	$188	$180
E	$185	$164	$144	$172	$177

B. Economic Rent

	1	2	3	4	5
A	−$53	+$23	−$9	+$1	−$32
B	−$31	+$26	−$44	+$4	−$3
C	−22	+$8	−$31	−$44	+$17
D	−$41	−$20	−$1	−$48	−$40
E	−$44	−$24	−$4	−$32	−$37

C. Sequence of Production

	1	2	3	4	5
A	25	2	10	6	16 tie
B	14	1	21 tie	5	8
C	12	4	15	21 tie	3
D	20	11	7	24	19
E	23	13	9	16 tie	18

Figure 2.2 Part A at the top contains a 5 × 5 grid of agricultural plots, with each cell indicating its hypothetical production costs per ton of output. Part B shows the same 5 × 5 grid, but now the cells are labeled with the rents they would earn at the production costs described in Part A and a market price of $140. When a cell bears a negative rent, it would not normally be used to produce the product. Part C shows the same grid, with the numbers in the cells indicating the order they would be put into production as their product's price rises at the market. Ties occur where cells have equal production costs.

The last part of Figure 2.2 describes the sequence of land entering production as a response to prices paid for its output. Ricardo noted that the best land was used first and poorer land later on as long as food prices were rising. In the hypothetical landscape described here, parcel B2 would be the first in production, as soon as the market price reached $114 per ton of output. It would be followed by parcel A2, which would enter into production when the price reached $117 and by parcel C5 when the price hit $123. The last parcel to be used to grow the crop would be A1, which would only be worth farming if the price at the market reached $193 per ton. As prices rise, higher cost land—land with lower environmental quality—becomes economically viable and is put to use in the same way that the rise in the equilibrium price represented in Figure 2.1 induced an increase in supply.

A point of contention over Ricardo's analysis of land use was raised in the historical examination of some agricultural settlement patterns in early America. It was found that agrarian settlers often used land of relatively poor quality first and higher quality land later on, after the local economy had been established. There are two explanations for the deviation between experience and theory (assuming that Ricardo was right in general—a fairly safe bet). One is that the settlers wrongly perceived the land that they used first to be more productive than the land used later—a misperception that would be unlikely to last long. The other is that access is an important factor of the cost of production that needs to be added to the costs incurred owing to the environmental characteristics of a piece of land. The pattern of settlements followed river valleys in many cases; the land was accessible, even though it flooded frequently. In other cases, new farms were established along the ridge lines because the higher land was more sparsely wooded than the bottoms: easier to clear and easier to get around. Accessibility was not nearly as important in terms of the farmer getting to the land, however, as of getting the land's production to the market. Any crop grown above a subsistence supply was worthless unless it could be sold to consumers at the marketplace.

LOCATION RENT

A German economist, Johann Heinrich von Thünen, working about the same time as Ricardo, focused on market access as the key to the location of agriculture in the same way that Ricardo focused on variations in environmental quality. In effect, von Thünen extended the basic identity of economic rent ($ER_i = p_i - c_i$) to *location rent*: producer surplus that is earned because of the location of production. The location rent identity is

$$LR_{ij} = Q_i(p_i - c_i) - Q_i f_i k_j \qquad (2.2)$$

where LR_{ij} is the location rent of growing crop i at place j, Q_i is the volume of production (tons and bushels are examples), p_i and c_i are again the respective price and cost of a unit of the crop, f_i, is a transport charge per unit of distance for the crop (so much per kilometer, for example), and k_j is the distance between the place of the crop's production, j, and its place of consumption, or the "market." (A numerical example is presented in Insights 2.1.) The location rent identity in Equation 2.2 is the economic rent identity in Equation 2.1 extended to include the cost of spatial interaction between place of production and place of consumption. Even if land is of particularly high quality, its economic rent will decline as transport costs increase. The rent can decline in two ways. One is that transport costs reduce economic rent because they are a special, particularly important, cost of production that varies with distance from the market. The other is that transport costs reduce demand and, therefore, quantity sold. They are transaction costs, and as we saw in Chapter 1, higher transaction costs reduce demand. Note that in the location rent identity, if Q_i decreases, location rent does too.

A simple geography of agriculture based on location variations in location rent is illustrated in Figure 2.3. Let's say two crops, wheat and maize, are in

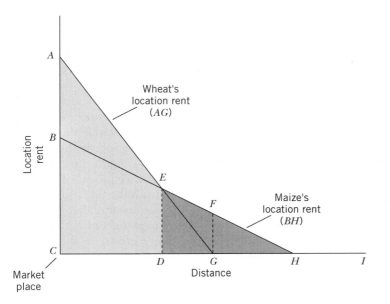

Figure 2.3 The relationship between location rent and distance is described, hypothetically, for wheat and maize. Wheat's location rent is higher than is maize's at the market. Its rent gradient is steeper than maize's as well, so wheat production gives way to maize production at distance *CD* from the market. Commercial crop production ends at distance *CH* because beyond that point the price paid by consumers would be less than the cost of producing and delivering either crop to the market.

demand at a central market. We will assume that variations in soil quality or other environmental characteristics are not important in this instance. As represented, wheat's location rent is higher than maize's location rent at the market, but it decreases more rapidly with distance. This results in a pattern of wheat being grown in and around the central marketplace, up to distance CD in Figure 2.3, and then maize being grown from D to H. The point D marks the place of crop transition from wheat to corn because it corresponds to the intersection point, E, of wheat's location rent line, AG, with maize's location rent line, BH. At D, therefore, maize offers a return superior to wheat's. Wheat could be grown profitably at any point between C and G, and maize could be grown profitably at any point between C and H. However, the location of a crop is determined by rent maximization. Although it would be profitable to grow maize from point C to point D, to do so would generate an opportunity cost in terms of the loss in economic rent that could be earned by growing wheat. This is represented as triangle ABE in Figure 2.3, or the area encompassed by the differences between the higher rents for wheat production and the lower rents for maize production.

There is also an opportunity cost of growing wheat rather than maize from points D to G; this is represented by triangle EFG in the figure. Opportunity cost aside, it simply would be unprofitable to grow wheat at any distance from the market beyond point G, and maize ceases to be grown profitably beyond point H. Beyond distance CH, commercial agriculture would cease in our example because places beyond that distance are too far from the market. Points from H to I would be either uncultivated or employed in subsistence agriculture as long as only wheat and maize are grown.

The picture given in Figure 2.3 is a half cross-section of the idealized land-use pattern of maize and wheat production. Assuming that transport costs are uniform around the market center, the crop patterns would encircle the market center as portrayed in Figure 2.4, with the marketplace serving as the center of a circle of land in wheat surrounded by a doughnut-shaped area of land in maize. Any market-based zonation of agricultural land requires, of course, wheat production inside a doughnut of maize. Viewed from the air, agricultural landscapes, under idealized conditions, would appear as circular patterns around commercial centers. In order for such a regular pattern of agricultural land use to develop, it's necessary that the crops being grown in the region have different location rents at the market and that their location rents decrease with distance in such a way that they intersect at some distance from the central market. Because of varying levels of demand that lead to variations in prices from one crop to another, and because of varying crop characteristics such as perishability and weight to volume ratios, location rents can vary in the way described by theory. It is unlikely, however, that theoretical location patterns will ever be closely matched by reality. First of all, environmental quality does vary locally, so that the location rent gradients would be more bumpy than smooth as costs of production vary for reasons other than distance from any single point of consumption. Second, except in limited cir-

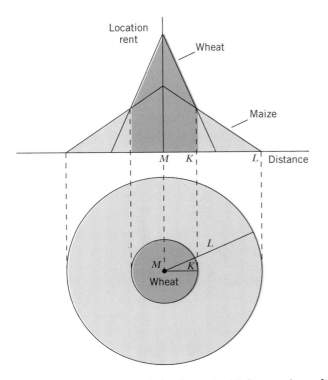

Figure 2.4 Concentric circles form the bird's-eye-view of the crop patterns that would arise from the simple decay of location rents with distance from a central marketplace.

cumstances, locally produced products have the potential to be consumed in many markets, not just one, and some of those markets may be very far away, indeed.

So we have spent a lot of time developing a location theory that doesn't replicate reality all that well. Why? Although reality isn't replicated fully, important parts of it are accounted for by the principles of land use that theory draws out. Is access to markets important in agriculture in the way that theory tells us? The account given in the first half of Insights 2.2, concerning agriculture in Utah in the early part of the twentieth century, indicates that it is. As long as the farms remained isolated, no clear value of agricultural production could be determined because of the literal case of "no market" for the product. The second half of Insights 2.2, concerning the failure of pioneer farming in Alaska, also emphasizes the importance of location in farming, but in a more complicated way than in the story about Utah. In Alaska, the low costs of production initially offset the high costs of transport. When the local production costs were no longer low relative to the cost of production elsewhere, the costs of transport began to outweigh the revenues of pioneer agriculture, and frontier farming in Alaska collapsed.

> INSIGHTS 2.1

A Numerical Example of Location Rent and Distance from a Central Market

The location rent identity given as Equation 2.2 is a definition and not a true predictive equation. We should not, therefore, get too carried away in its extension, but it can be used to demonstrate the development of the theoretical patterns described in Figures 2.3 and 2.4. To plug in some numbers, let's use the values that follow (each is made up):

	Wheat	**Maize**
Bushels per acre (Q)	100	60
Price paid per bushel (p)	$1.50	$0.50
Production cost per bushel (c)	$0.90	$0.10
Transport cost/bushel/mile (f)	$0.20	$0.05

At the market, the location rent of wheat is

$$100 \times (\$1.5 - \$0.9) - 100 \times \$0.5 \times 0 = \$60$$

Note that k_j, distance to the market in the location rent identity, is zero in this case because the crop is grown at the market. Wheat's location rent of $60 at the market is its Ricardian rent. At the market, the location rent of maize is

$$60 \times (\$0.5 - \$0.1) - 60 \times \$0.05 \times 0 = \$24$$

Now at one mile from the market, distance does have an effect on location rent. Wheat's location rent one mile from the market is

$$100 \times (\$1.5 - \$0.9) - 100 \times \$0.5 \times 1 = \$10$$

whereas the location rent of maize is

$$60 \times (\$0.5 - \$0.1) - 60 \times \$0.05 \times 1 = \$21$$

So maize is grown one mile from the market instead of wheat. In the case of wheat, the distance decay in its location rent is $50 per mile, or 100 times × $0.5. In the case of maize, it's $3 per mile. Potential commercial wheat cultivation can take place where the location rent is zero or more. Given our numbers, that's 1.2 miles from the market, found by dividing the $60 location rent at the market by its decay rate of $50 per mile. Maize has a much slower rate of decay and can be grown to 8 miles from the market ($24/$3). The actual transition from wheat to maize takes place where their location rents are equal, found by solving for k in

$$60 - 50 \times k = 24 - 3 \times k$$

or, by manipulation, $36/k = 47$. So the point of change from land in wheat to land in maize is 0.766 mile from the market, where both maize and wheat earn location rents of about $21.70.

➤ INSIGHTS 2.2
Location Constraints and Farming the American Frontier

To place 95,000 acres of semidesert land under cultivation entails a vast amount of physical labor. It necessitates also the utilization of tremendous quantities of equipment. These allotments were as nature fashioned them—wide expanses of sagebrush, juniper, and cedar—no roads, no fences, no buildings, no supply of domestic water. In addition, there was no market for farm produce. There being no means by which it could be shipped to the outside world, the local market was the only market. Such farming as was done by the Mormons was almost wholly of the subsistence type. Every family owned a farm and endeavored to raise enough foodstuffs to meet its own requirements and little more. Should one bushel of wheat or one ton of hay be produced in excess of local demands, it possessed no value. . . . We could have all the eggs we needed if we would but visit the farmer and gather them ourselves. Poultry was likewise a glut on the market. Noting a flock of turkeys, I asked the farmer what one was worth. "Really, I don't know," he replied, "I never sold one. If you want one you can have it for fifty cents or, if that is too much, name your own price."

SOURCE: *Indian Agent*, by Albert H. Kneale (Caldwell, Id: Caxton Printers), 1950, pp. 294–295.

Two major reasons for the decline of pioneering can be seen by examining the traditional economic rationale of the frontier farm. Cheap land and a fertile, virgin soil were important assets, and in theory, these outweighed the handicaps of long distance to markets and an absence of many of the amenities of established society. . . . Rich soil, with the growing use of fertilizers, insecticides, and better soil conservation practices, became no longer the sole property of the the virgin lands. . . . With new wheat varieties and the development of greater skill in utilizing the subhumid lands of the Great Plains, there was no longer any need for the crop to be grown on the Alaskan frontier, thousands of miles from markets of the East.

SOURCE: "The Collapse of Frontier Farming in Alaska," by James R. Shortridge, *Annals of the Association of American Geographers*, Vol. 66, 1976, p. 595.

LOCATION EQUILIBRIUM

The diagrams in Figures 2.3 and 2.4 represent a *location equilibrium*. Just as a market equilibrium represents a balance between supply and demand for goods, a location equilibrium represents a balance in the supply and demand for locations. In order for a location equilibrium to be achieved, individual users of locations must be as well off as they can be at a particular place. This means that their net incomes must be maximized. Location equilibrium is not achieved, for example, when maize is grown at a place where wheat can earn a higher location rent. It also means that as long as location rents are not negative, any individual is indifferent with respect to their location. How can this be? We have seen that location rents, which are measures of profit, decrease with distance from the market center. Wouldn't everyone prefer, therefore, a close-in farm rather than a more distant one? No, not if the land market is perfectly competitive. A *perfectly competitive market* (like the one represented on the left half of Figure 2.1) is one that has many buyers and sellers, so that neither group can ordinarily fix the price of a good, or in this case, land. Let's take a closer look at such a market.

If there are many buyers in the land market, the price of land near the market center will be high because bidders will be interested in the more profitable land. Land at some distance from the market will be less valued because its location rent is lower. Theoretically, bidding contests for various parcels of land will lead to land prices that perfectly reflect variations in location rent. Sometimes the location rent lines shown in Figures 2.3 and 2.4 are called *bid-rent curves* for that very reason; they represent the maximum bid anyone should make for using a location. (The precise relation between location rent and bid rent is described later in this chapter.) Location rent is an inverse linear function of transport costs; when transport costs are low, rent is high, and when transport costs are high, rent is low. The bidding process eventually leads to locational prices that are perfect tradeoffs with transportation cost. At the market center, the location rent is the highest, but transport costs are zero. Where location rent is zero, transport costs are at their highest for any product that can actually be sold at the central market. Between those two points the tradeoff is constant; as rent decreases, transport costs increase to just balance a decrease in the price of land. Because transport charges and land prices sum to a constant value in this way, land users are indifferent with respect to their location as long as location rent is not negative. The same relationship can be extended to economic rent in general. In the broader theoretical context, all costs, not just those associated with transport, are just offset by lower land prices if the land market is perfectly competitive. As in the locational case, the inverse relationship between costs and land prices can lead to a location equilibrium.

LOCATIONAL SHIFTS

Any location equilibrium is likely to hold only for a static set of conditions. Any change in prices or costs will upset the balance fairly quickly. These shifts happen all the time, but locational shifts take place fairly slowly because the transaction costs of locational changes are high. In the agricultural sector, for example, it's usually cheaper to change a selection of crops to match changing market conditions than to sell one farm and buy a different one. In this way, crop locations can change even if the producers don't change theirs.

Some simple conclusions about the relationship between changes in location rent and changes in land use are illustrated in Figure 2.5. Let's say that some crop, any crop, has a starting locational equilibrium defined by the location rent line LR_1 so that it is grown from the market out to distance K_1. One way in which an equilibrium can be unbalanced is by a shift in transport costs. If we could hold everything else constant (yield per hectare, price, and production cost) but lower transportation costs, the resulting location rent line could be represented by LR_2. The location of crop production would be extended to K_2 as the decrease in the crop's location rent with distance from the market becomes

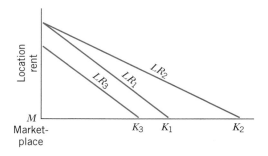

Figure 2.5 This diagram represents some simplified changes in land use that would result as location rents change. In some initial location equilibrium for a hypothetical crop described by LR_1, the crop would be grown from the market to distance K_1. The crop's location rent can be altered by decreasing transport costs, which could result in a new location rent line represented by LR_2, or by an increase in other costs, which could result in location rent LR_3. Either type of change requires a shift in the amount of land used to grow the crop.

less severe. The general result of a decrease in transport costs is that the area of cropland increases, all other things held equal.

Alternatively, let's hold yield and transport costs constant but allow either costs or price (but not both) to vary. The location rent line LR_3 in Figure 2.5 represents a parallel but downward shift in location rent as compared to LR_1. It could result from a decrease in price offered at the market for the crop or an increase in its cost of production. In either case, the amount of land devoted to producing the crop shrinks from a boundary at K_1 to the inner boundary of K_3. The slope of the location rent curve does not change because transport costs have not changed, but a decrease in the product's rent at the market causes it to decrease everywhere else on a perfectly proportional basis, regardless of distance. Thus, either a change in rent at the market or a change in transport costs can lead to a change in land use that results in a change in quantity produced. It makes sense that a decrease in price at the market would shrink the area of a crop's production because the price decrease signals a decrease in demand. Would changes in cost of production or cost of transportation also lead to a reduction in land use (if they increase) or an expansion of land use (if they decrease)? Not necessarily.

The demand for food is price elastic, but not considerably so. If its price decreases, demand for it does not increase that much unless a very poor population is considered. As long as people are living at or above a true subsistence level, a decrease in food prices would not generate much in the way of additional food production. Therefore, a decrease in the cost of producing food, or its transport to market, is more likely to result in different areas being used for food production, or shifts in the location of food production, rather than an expansion of the area under cultivation. This is the point illustrated by the failure of frontier farming in Alaska; a general decrease in the cost of food production left Alaska at a locational disadvantage as its relative production cost advantage dissipated.

By way of analysis, we'll start with a conventional supply and demand diagram similar to the one we used before, but this time we'll add a supply shift (and straighten out the supply and demand curves for easier explanation). The left half of Figure 2.6 has two supply curves, S_1 and S_2. Let's say that S_1 represents the original supply curve and its intersection with the demand curve occurred at the market-clearing price of PE_1, and that the quantity produced and consumed was QE_1, the equilibrium quantity of our hypothetical product. The new supply curve is represented by S_2, indicating a supply shift to the right on the quantity axis. Such a supply shift could take place, for example, if the costs of production were generally reduced by a broadly adopted technological improvement. The line S_2 results from lower costs of production, which mean that for any price that exists more of the product can now be brought to market. If the old equilibrium price of PE_1 was maintained after the supply shift occurred, then Q^* would be brought to market. The new market equilibrium, however, is at QE_2 because that is the equilibrium quantity associated with the new market-clearing price of PE_2. There is more of the product on the market, but the market price is much lower than before. Any producer using the old technology (and therefore inefficient given current practices) is likely to go out of business

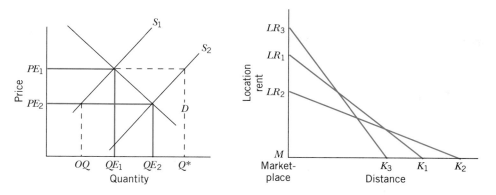

Figure 2.6 The left diagram represents the implications for the prices and quantities of a supply shift associated with a general decline in production costs of a product. The right-hand diagram shows implications for the location of agriculture of similiar supply shifts. Note that this more comprehensive approach leads to a more complicated set of locational shifts than those described in the more simplified context of Figure 2.5.

rapidly because there is very little demand, *OQ*, for that output at the new prices. After the supply shift, more is consumed and more is produced, but the producers are not necessarily the original ones.

The locational shifts associated with changing location rents are more complicated than represented in Figure 2.5 when the relationships between price, cost, and demand are considered in a more integrated way than in the cases with "all else held constant." The right half of Figure 2.6 illustrates the same changes as described in Figure 2.5, but this time related changes in prices and demand are taken into account in assessing changes in land use. As before, let LR_1 define a location rent gradient—a change in location rent over distance—for some hypothetical crop at an initial equilibrium, and as before let's say that transport rates decrease for some reason. With cheaper transportation, a new locational equilibrium may be defined by the rent gradient LR_2 that indicates that cultivation can take place profitably much farther from the center than before. Is there more output, as in the case above? Not necessarily. Any significant decrease in transport costs could be expected to lead to a supply shift of the type described in the left half of Figure 2.6. Increases in location rents on the outskirts of the region would be counterbalanced by rent decreases in the interior as more land was opened to agriculture. Any large increase in supply of the product in question, such as might be associated with the new agricultural potential at greater distances from the market, would lead to a decrease in the price paid at the market. Rent increases on the outskirts of the region would be counterbalanced by rent decreases in the interior as more land was opened to agriculture. The same process would limit rents at some distance from the market as well, so that farmland would not extend as far as might be determined by the decrease in transport prices alone. If transport costs decrease at a faster rate than prices, however, agricultural production will take place farther from the market than before, but much of the new production will replace, and not expand, former production.

Historically, the geographical extension of agricultural potential owing to declining transport costs has led to the decline of agricultural production in the most accessible locations, such as those near the market in the right half of Figure 2.6. A decline in location rent near the market from LR_1 to LR_2, for example, would likely lead to a loss of farmland because other land uses—urban ones—would be more profitable in and around the market center now that crop production has become less profitable. Even though LR_2 remains higher near the center than farther away, more distant sites are used for agriculture because they do not have the opportunity costs associated with that type of production that affect more central locations where there are uses more profitable than agriculture. It's the competition for land that makes agricultural (and other) land prices functions of location more than anything else. In 1990, the highest prices per acre of farmland in the United States, excluding Alaska and Hawaii, were in the Northeast. In descending order, Rhode Island, New Jersey, Connecticut, and Maryland had the highest prices. The association between average price per acre of agricultural land and population density is very high because location rents are highest near large markets. Farm income per acre is also strongly associated with population density, but farming in these centers is not a big business. In the states listed here, agriculture accounts for a fairly small proportion of state income and uses a small proportion of land. Income is high because only the highest earning land remains in agriculture, a sector that does not compete well with other commercial uses, such as retailing, which can generate more profits per unit of land than can most types of farming.

So land leaves agriculture, or any other use, when a more profitable use of the land becomes available. The other side of the coin is that land is entered into agricultural production, or any other use, once that becomes a more profitable use of the land than the way it is currently employed. Let's say there is a general decrease in agricultural production costs that leads to a change in the locational equilibrium defined by LR_1 in the right half of Figure 2.6 to a new equilibrium defined by LR_3. Again, we have a different result in Figure 2.6 than the one described in Figure 2.5. The geographical extent of agriculture can actually decrease under declining production costs as more farmers start production nearer the market in response to rising location rents. Essentially, the process is the reverse of the one described earlier. In that case, rents declined and land left agriculture; in this case, rents increase and more land is entered into crop production. Distant farmers lose out as basic production costs decrease because transport costs become more important even if they themselves do not change. The shift from LR_1 to LR_3 in the diagram describes wht happened to the Alaskan frontier farmers. Decreased costs nearer the market increased output there, but a supply shift followed that made Alaskan crops, with their high transport costs, uncompetitive in the market.

As you can see, changes in price, production costs, and transport costs can lead to changes in land use at particular locations that create both winners and losers. An extended example is provided in Case 2.1, which describes the now-ended Canadian rail transport rate called the "Crow." The case involves an anticipated shift from a location equilibrium based on very cheap transportation to a new location equilibrium that accounts for more realistic transport costs. Under the Crow, the market in Quebec generated positive location rents in the Canadian Prairies of the type described by line LRQ_1 in Figure 2.7. Local rents to the Prairie producers under the Crow are low, say at LRP_1, because significant local consumption in the form of a livestock industry and grain processing facilities never developed inasmuch as it was so profitable to send the grain out of the region. Notice that under the Crow, Quebec's grain farmers could have shipped west as well, but the rental rate of LRP_1 is much less than LRQ_1, so that flow was nonexistent. If the transport rate is raised, what happens? Distance decay in demand rears its ugly head as transport rates rise, and a shift from LRQ_1 rents to LRQ_2 rents could result. At LRQ_2, the Prairie growers are beyond the range of the market in Quebec and would be confined (ignoring the Asian market) to a more local market that is perhaps defined by LRP_2. The local rents would be higher than before as some livestock production and processing would develop, but the new rate of LRP_2 would not be as great as the old LRQ_1. If it were, then nobody would complain. As you can see from the case of the Crow, politics enters mightily into location problems involving land use. The political economy of the location of land use will be taken up in much more detail in Chapters 3 and 4.

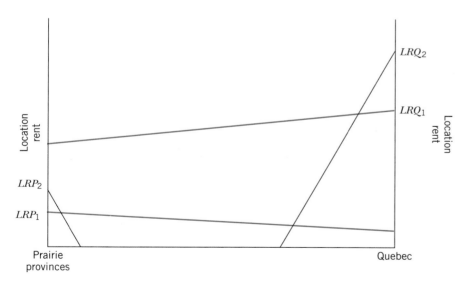

Figure 2.7 This diagram stylizes the location rents to Prairie grain production both with and without the Crow transport rate. With the Crow rate, Prairie grain producers have positive location rents with respect to the large eastern market of Quebec, as represented by LRQ_1, which are higher than their rents from the local market, LRP_1. Without the Crow rate, Prairie producers will be cut off from Quebec, as rents associated with LRQ_2 develop, and must rely on their local market's lower rents, LRP_2, to define the extent of their production.

◤ CASE *2.1*
The Sacred Crow

For years the first lesson a freshman politician in Canada's prairie provinces learned could be summed up in four words: "Don't touch the Crow." That is the nickname for what may well be the longest-lived piece of special-interest legislation in North America, and over the years it has taken on the aura of an economic and social birthright for Canada's western grain producers. But now the sacred Crow is being "touched," and the reaction is thunderous.

It all began in 1897. In return for a subsidy to build a branch line through the Crow's Nest Pass in Alberta, the Canadian Pacific Ry. (now CP Rail) agreed to transport all major grains grown anywhere in Western Canada at 0.5¢ per ton mile—in perpetuity. By 1960 the rate covered only 60% of the real cost of moving grains. After the inflationary 1970s, the proportion was down to a mere 20%. Last year, CP and the state-owned Canadian National Rys. lost an estimated $480 million in revenues because of the Crow's Nest freight rate.

It has also distorted Canada's agricultural economy. Says Lloyd Axworthy, Canada's Transport Minister: "It has certainly been seen by an increasing number of agricultural and business people as being a serious retardation to growth there." Because the rate encourages long-distance shipment of grain, it has stifled grain processing and livestock raising in the west and perpetuated an outdated system of inefficiently placed grain elevators served by inappropritaly laid railroad branch lines.

Now the two railroads think they have the ammunition to shoot down the Crow. When the Crow's Nest Pass rate was instituted, virtually all export grain was being shipped to Europe. Today, huge amounts cross the Rockies destined for the Orient. The two railroads, whose tracks through the Rockies were built with 19th century technology, will soon have to ration westbound freight unless they can upgrade their mountain track. To do this, they have promised to spend up to $13 billion over the next 10 years—if the Crow rate is repealed. Ottawa legislators are expected to adopt a bill wiping out the Crow rate and ultimately moving grain freight to realistic levels. That could fundamentally alter Canada's export trading ability—particularly vis-a-vis the U.S. But the possibility that the Crow might die has set off a roiling political clash. Some fear it could spark economic battles among Canada's provinces and erode Ottawa's control over the country's agricultural economy.

Changing the Crow could be crucial to sustaining the growth of Canada's export grain business. Helped by artificially low rail transportation rates, Canada's grain exports have shot up almost 50% since 1979, to an annual rate of about 30 million tons, worth $4.8 billion.

But the railroads say that if they do not have the money to improve their tracks over the mountains, grain will be the victim in the freight rationing that will follow, because it is such a money-loser.

The Liberal government of Prime Minister Pierre Elliot Trudeau last year agreed to provide a $520 million annual fixed subsidy to wean farmers away from the Crow and clear the way for the railroads to finance their modernization. A federal study panel advised the government to divide the subsidy between the railroads and the farmers. eventually paying nearly all of the subsidy to the farmers.

But large prairie wheat pools with their investments in existing grain-handling systems, combined with Quebec livestock growers, who also benefit from low Crow rates, to pressure the Liberals into shifting the subsidy to the railroads. That would provide funds for the rails' expansion but would preserve most of the economic distortions in the western economy. "We were whiplashed between the western pools and the Quebec farmers," concedes Transport Minister Axworthy.

With a clear majority in Parliament, Trudeau's Liberals should prevail in passing the Crow bill. However, opposition critics are predicting increased farm failures on Canada's prairies when sharp increases in freight rates begin in approximately two years. "Nothing has really changed," says Donald Mazankowski, transportation critic for the Conservative Party. "The economic distortions are still in place, but producers are going to be paying dramatically higher prices."

The worst fallout from changes to the Crow may soon be seen. Subsidies to western grain producers would have prompted them to sell locally—a boon for the western livestock industry but a blow to livestock raisers in Quebec, who have benefited from the low rail rate on grain. But now that the subsidies are scheduled to go to the railroads, livestock owners are vowing to lobby for provincial subsidies to wipe out the advantage of their Quebec competitors, whom they blame for killing the original Crow reform bill.

SOURCE: "Canada's New Uproar over an Old Rail Rate," Reprinted from October 24, 1983 issue of *Business Week* by special permission, copyright (c) 1983 by McGraw-Hill, Inc.

FOR DISCUSSION

This case on the former Canadian rail rate called the Crow describes some of the locational implications for agriculture from a change in transport prices. Would a change in production prices have the same sort of effects? What would be the implications for grain production in Quebec, for example, if costs of grain production in the Prairie provinces increased significantly even if the Crow had remained in place?

ECONOMIC RENT AND LAND USE IN CITIES

Up to this point we have focused on agricultural land use, but the same logic of location can be extended to urban land uses, too. In this section we consider some extensions to the land-use model we have developed so far. Just as the basics of that model can be used to analyze both agricultural and urban land uses, the extensions that follow concerning asking prices, the impact of nonlocal markets, barriers to interaction, channels of interaction, and multicentered local markets are also applicable to both types of land use.

So far we have assumed that the land use with the highest location rent at a particular site will occupy it. This glosses over the likelihood that a transaction between buyer and seller or renter and landlord is going to be required before any occupation takes place. Essentially, a transaction in the land market will occur only if there is an agreement between what the seller thinks the land is worth and what the buyer thinks the land is worth. If there is an agreement, then a location transaction will take place, as illustrated in Figure 2.8. Two land users are described by their different bids for land with respect to distance from the region's center of accessibility. This center of accessibility serves the same role as the marketplace in the agricultural context; by definition, it's the place where costs of local spatial interaction are minimized, so that location rents are maximized. (The relationship between location rent and purchase and rent bids is discussed in the next section of this chapter.) The difference in the two location bids is based on the different premium each bidder's business places

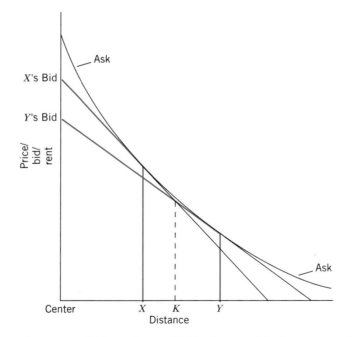

Figure 2.8 Asking prices and bid prices must be in agreement before a location can be occupied. The bid by use *X* for a location in this stylized land market corresponds to a seller's asking price at point *X*. Point *Y* is occupied by a use with different location preferences than has *X*, as indicated by the different bid-rent lines.

on accessibility. Access carries a higher premium for *X* than for *Y*, as evidenced by *X*'s higher bid for the location at the market and its steeper rate of decline with distance as well. Many retail businesses, for example, need to be easily accessible to a large number of customers. They are willing to pay relatively high prices to occupy sites with high levels of access because such sites improve their general business prospects. The location bids of *X* and *Y* intersect at distance *K* from the center of the market: from the center to that point, *X*'s bid is higher, and beyond *K* the location bid of *Y* is higher. The derivation of a business's bid for a particular location in a city is described in Insights 2.3 in some detail. Ultimately, it involves the weighing of the costs and benefits of a particular location against the costs and benefits of all other locations.

Earlier, we would have indicated that *X* would occupy locations from the center to *K* and *Y* would occupy the locations beyond, but now we are more specific because we are concerned with particular users rather than with more general classes of land use such as crop types. Furthermore, we now consider that the location selected is the place where a market equilibrium exists: the point where the seller of the land is asking the same price as the buyer is willing to pay. Just as the buying price for the land is a function of the buyer's anticipated location rent, the seller's asking price is a function of the seller's attempt to gain from that location rent. The "ask" curve in the diagram is a true curve because it consists, theoretically, of a very large number of straight segments describing location rents for a very large number of potential land users. (If you've taken an introductory calculus course, you will understand how all the little straight lines become a curve; otherwise, just take it on faith.) Note that the ask curve intercepts the vertical rent axis, indicating that there is some definable maximum or ceiling price of land in the region. It does not, however, intercept the distance axis because that would mean that at some distance from the center land becomes free. It's cheaper at a distance, but it certainly isn't free.

Even though we are now looking at individual enterprises rather than aggregate crop types, we can still expect the type of circular zonation in land-use patterns in the city that we found in the country. Although each location bid line of individual businesses is at least slightly different from that of any other business, companies in the same sector of the economy, retail for example, or perhaps automobile repair, are quite similar in their general costs and ways of doing business. They will share the same kind of locational tradeoffs alluded to in Insights 2.3, and their bid-rent lines will be quite similar. A simplified version of the result is shown in Figure 2.9, which shows the location pattern that might arise in an economy with three types of sectors, defined largely, in this case, with respect to the location of their markets: local high frequency, local low frequency, and external.

Any business that requires a high frequency of interaction with a local market will place a premium on locations near the region's center of accessibility. If high frequencies of interaction are required, then they will lead to a large expense that can be reduced only at more accessible locations. Such companies are willing to pay more for a location at the center because it lowers their cost of doing business significantly. (Examples of such businesses are listed in Table 1.1.) As

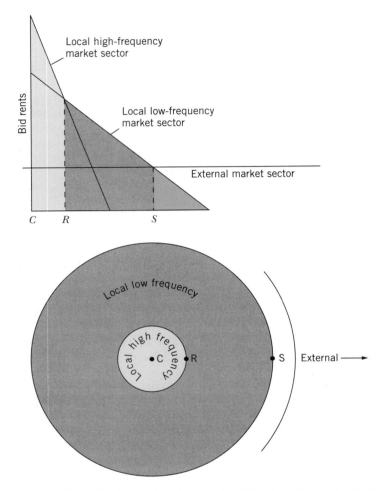

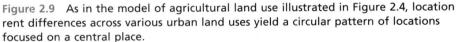

Figure 2.9   As in the model of agricultural land use illustrated in Figure 2.4, location rent differences across various urban land uses yield a circular pattern of locations focused on a central place.

costs decrease, producer surplus, in this case in the form of location rent, increases so that central locations carry high values for companies that require a high frequency of local transactions. Any business with a local market would prefer, other things being equal, a central location rather than a location on the outskirts of town.

If a business requires fairly low frequencies of interaction with its market, however, its valuation of a central location would not be as great as that of a company that requires high frequencies of market interaction. A comparison that might apply here is a wholesaler to a retailer. The retailer requires a high frequency of market interaction to turn a decent profit; few stores can survive with only a handful of customers each day. The wholesaler, however, may serve each of its retailer customers only once a day or even less frequently. The bid-rent line of the local low-frequency market sector indicates a lower valuation of more centralized locations than held by the high-frequency sector. The local low-frequency market sector is more likely to be found away from the center than nearby because its costs of interaction are relatively low and it can afford to operate in locations that are less accessible.

Whether they have requirements for a high frequency of interaction or a low frequency of interaction, businesses with local markets should exhibit decreasing location bids with respect to decreasing proximity to centers of accessibility. The vital element here is "local markets." If a business has an international market, or even one that is simply external to the local economy, then its location bid would not be associated in any way with local access. Its location bid, as indicated for the external market sector in Figure 2.9, would not vary with distance from the center. There is no location rent gradient here because the center is no more important than any other point in the local area with respect to its market. To go back to the discussion on agricultural rents, any sector with an external market would have its rent defined on Ricardian terms—that is, price of product, or service, minus cost of production. Local market sectors, however, have their rents defined as in the von Thünen approach; they earn location rents because distance counts. You know, of course, that external markets also exist for agricultural products, so the same principle applies out in the country as well. (External markets for agricultural products are considered in more detail in the next chapter.)

Businesses with external markets may have apparent positive location rents throughout an urban region, but their location bids won't be successful until they exceed the location bids of companies with local markets. This is most likely to occur at the edge of the region, so that the map of our hypothetical city is represented in the lower diagram of Figure 2.9, with the center surrounded by the local high-frequency market sector, which is itself surrounded by the local low-frequency market sector, followed by the external market sector. You might ask, where do the people live in the region? Good question. There are location rent models for households, too. Part of William Alonso's general urban location rent model is devoted to a household sector that has certain assumed locational preferences. That part of the model is not given in Insights 2.3 because it is more complex than our current analysis requires. Moreover, in talking about market-based competition for land in a region, individual households are not often a significant factor.

Housing is a *residual land use,* so-called because it occupies land that is left over after commercial interests are satisfied. None of the land-use zones outlined in Figure 2.9 is likely to be used up completely by the relevant sector, especially the exterior zone of the external market sector which appears to go on forever. Where an empty location occurs, it can be occupied by housing. Although the circular zonation system doesn't explicitly apply to housing in this context, it does have an apparent effect. Because land prices tend to decrease with distance from the region's center of accessibility, housing densities will be highest near the center and lowest at the region's exterior. High-rise apartments, for example, are more likely to be found near the center than far away because they spread the high cost of central locations over a large number of households. Apartment buildings are more rare on the outskirts because land is cheaper there and individual households can more easily afford it.

Housing is not the only large sector of residual land use today. Agriculture also appears to be a residual land use in many circumstances, even though it is a commercial sector. (The problems of housing and agriculture in competing in land markets are discussed more thoroughly in Chapter 4.)

The location principles we have put forth have led to logical but unrealistic patterns of land use. After all, we don't often see nice circular patterns of urban and rural land uses. Why not, if the economic logic is there? One reason is that in real life spatial interaction does not cost the same in every direction as if we lived on some featureless plain (or geometric plane). In real life there are discontinuities in the costs of interaction caused, for example, by barriers. The left half of Figure 2.10 illustrates the location rent effect of a barrier to spatial interaction, at *D*, on the spatial extent of a city in one direction. The barrier causes a discontinuity in location rent, which declines precipitously as the cost of spatial interaction increases in the same way. The segment *BC* is longer than the segment *CB'*, because positive location rents occur at greater distances from the center of accessibility toward the left of the diagram than toward the right. The region is stunted in its spatial extent where spatial interaction costs are higher.

The Hartford (Connecticut) metropolitan region provides an example. The city of Hartford is separated from its eastern suburbs by the Connecticut River. Recently, rental rates for office space in Hartford's western suburbs ran about 70% of those in downtown Hartford. The rates in the eastern suburbs were only

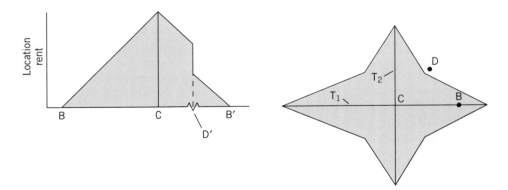

Figure 2.10 The left diagram describes the discontinuity in location rent that can occur due to a barrier, at *D*, to spatial interaction in a region. The right-hand diagram illustrates the mapped pattern, or bird's-eye-view of an area around some center C, which is crossed by two channels of spatial interaction, T_1 and T_2. The channels provide low-access costs away from the center and so elongate the area of positive location rents along their axes.

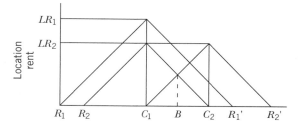

Figure 2.11 An initial center of accessibility, C_1, has maximum location rent LR_1 that declines with distance to R_1 and $R_{1'}$, which define the spatial extent of the region. A second center of accessibility, C_2, is developed, which causes the maximum location rent of C_1 to decline to LR_2 and displaces the spatial extent of the region by defining new boundaries at R_2 and $R_{2'}$.

about 56% of those in downtown. The river is a barrier to spatial interaction that has limited the accessibility and growth of towns to the east of the region's center in Hartford as compared to the suburbs to its west.

Just as barriers to spatial interaction limit the spatial extent of a region, special channels for spatial interaction that reduce its cost can extend a region's area and distort it with respect to a circular form. The right half of Figure 2.10 presents a bird's-eye view of the star-shaped area of a region's positive location rents that would result from two roads, T_1 and T_2, crossing at C. Land more distant from C, at B, for example, can have a positive location rent as long as it is close to one of the channels, while a site nearer C, D for example, does not have a positive rent because it is not near one of the channels.

The extension and improvement of metropolitan highway systems, especially in the United States, but in other countries as well, has led to the development of urban regions with multiple points of high regional accessibility. Downtowns have declined as suburban shopping centers have grown in response to changing levels of accessibility. For example, let's say that place C_1 in Figure 2.11 is a region's center of accessibility at some time when C_2 did not exist. The maximum location rent of LR_1 grades to zero at R_1 and $R_{1'}$, thereby defining the region's spatial extent. If a new center forms at C_2, peak location rent could decline to LR_2, but occur at each of the two points. The region would have two centers, with an intersection of their location rent gradients at B, and the region's spatial extent would be displaced from R_1–$R_{1'}$ to R_2–$R_{2'}$. As the region grows from $R_{1'}$ to $R_{2'}$, locations from R_1 to R_2 are abandoned due to a loss in *relative* accessibility and declining location rents.

➤ INSIGHTS 2.3
William Alonso's Model of Urban Land Use

The model of urban land use written by William Alonso serves as the foundation for most urban land-use modeling in the neoclassical school of economics.

Neoclassical economics is, as the name implies, an updated version of the work of the classical economists such as David Ricardo, Adam Smith, and John Stuart Mill. It focuses on equilibrium points in the economy which are points of balance in supply and demand in markets. Land market models of this type, including the Alonso model, lay out these points of balance in mathematical terms, most often in equations using differential calculus. Fortunately, the Alonso model is straightforward enough that its logic and the location behavior that results can be readily understood even if the equations appear at first glance to make the model too difficult.

The model begins by establishing identities that describe the pertinent characteristics of the urban land market:

$$G = V - C - R \tag{2.3}$$

where G is profit, V is sales, C is nonland cost, and R is land cost. Simply put, sales minus costs equals profit. In this model, sales are assumed to be a function of a business's location and its size, as indicated in the function

$$V = (t, q) \tag{2.4}$$

where t is the business's distance from the region's center of accessibility and q is the size of the business's site of operation. Nonland costs, such as labor and advertising, are also assumed to be functions of location and size of site, and sales volume as well:

$$C = (V, t, q) \tag{2.5}$$

Finally, land cost is taken as a combination of location and size characteristics:

$$R = P(t)q \tag{2.6}$$

with $P(t)$ defining the price of land at t.

Given these definitions, an equilibium location for a business is defined by

$$0 = \frac{dV}{dt} - \frac{dC}{dV} \times \frac{dV}{dt} - q\frac{dP}{dt} \tag{2.7}$$

It's useful to break down the location equation into its individual entries. First of all, the location equation is set equal to zero to indicate a locational equilibrium. A locational balance is achieved when movement cannot yield a gain or loss. In this case, if all the changes in costs and sales and so on that occur with a change in location are neither positive or negative, then the business's best location has been found. (The symbol d indicates derivatives are being taken, in this case changes in one variable that correspond to changes in another.) The term

$$\frac{dV}{dt} \tag{2.8}$$

concerns the marginal revenue lost with a shift in location away from the region's center of accessibility. In turn:

$$\frac{dC}{dV} \times \frac{dV}{dt} \qquad (2.9)$$

covers the change in marginal operating cost caused by a change in volume of business caused by relocation, which is distinguished from

$$\frac{dC}{dt} \qquad (2.10)$$

the marginal increase in operating cost directly attributable to moving, and

$$q\frac{dP}{dt} \qquad (2.11)$$

is a decrease in land cost associated with the land's decrease in value with distance from the center. The model describes a balancing act: sales decrease with relocation away from the region's center of accessibility and operating costs follow the same pattern. Land costs, however, become lower with distance from the center. On the opposite track, land costs are higher in more accessible places, but they may be offset as other costs are lower and sales volume increases.

Remember, however, that sales is a function not only of location, but also of size of site (or establishment), so another equilibrium equation is required in the model:

$$0 = \frac{dV}{dq} - \frac{dC}{dV} \times \frac{dV}{dq} - \frac{dP}{dq} \qquad (2.12)$$

This equation defines the equilibrium point of site size, as

$$\frac{dV}{dq} \qquad (2.13)$$

describes the change in sales volume with a change in site size:

$$\frac{dC}{dV} \times \frac{dV}{dq} \qquad (2.14)$$

covers the change in marginal operating cost caused by a change in volume of business caused by changing the size of the establishment, and

$$\frac{dP}{dq} \qquad (2.15)$$

is the change in land price with a change in the size of the site. The location equation and the site equation have to be solved simultaneously in order to find the locational equilibrium of a business.

SOURCE: *Location and Land Use*, by William Alonso (Cambridge, Mass.: Harvard University Press, 1964).

LAND PRICES, RENT, AND HIGHEST AND BEST USE

All the discussion of land use in this chapter has been couched in terms of economic rent and location rent. Although rent in this usage is abstract, it can be translated into property prices and therefore a direct valuation of land. The *market capitalization* of any asset, including land, is its fair price as determined by its earnings in perpetuity. Remember the discussion of net present value at the end of Chapter 1. Present value is calculated as the sum of future benefits discounted by an appropriate rate so that earnings in the future don't count as much as earnings right now. It can be shown that the present value (*PV*) of a consistent stream of earnings, so many dollars per year for example, can be calculated as

$$PV = \frac{\$A}{i} \tag{2.16}$$

where $\$A$ is the consistent annual stream of earnings and i is the discount rate (as a decimal).

The present value of all future earnings associated with a piece of land is the price that should be paid for the land now because that is what the land is worth. Let's use the data from Insights 2.1 to calculate land prices based on location rents. There, the location rent per acre of wheat at the market is listed as $60, whereas maize's location rent at that location is listed as $24. At one mile from the market, wheat's location rent is $10 and maize's is $21. The location rents are earnings streams for a single period. If we can assume that the rents will be stable forever (a very strong assumption to make), then we can plug them into the market capitalization formula (Equation 2.16) and calculate the value of land under the different circumstances. At the market center, land in wheat is worth $60/.05, or $1,200 per acre, assuming 5% is the appropriate discount rate. Land in maize would be worth $24/.05, or $480 per acre. At one mile from the market, an acre of land in maize is worth $21/.05, or $420, whereas wheat is only worth $10/.05, or $200 per acre. The value of the land is a simple function of the present value of its earnings stream. That land use with the highest earnings stream is considered the *highest and best use* of the land, and the value of the land in its highest and best use is the market value of the land. In other words, just because someone wants to grow maize near the market center doesn't mean she can buy the land for a lower price. In this example, wheat production is the highest and best use, so the price of land is determined as land being used for growing wheat.

The use of land can be obtained over shorter terms than is implied by the market capitalization formula. The *contract rent* on an asset is the price paid for its use over a limited period. If you live in an apartment, you probably pay contract rent to your landlord on a monthly basis. Farmers frequently farm land that is owned by others and so must pay contract rent. The contract rent can be calculated in the same way that you calculate a purchase price, except that the earnings streams are discounted over a finite number of periods. The present value of the earnings stream is divided appropriately to calculate the contract rent payments: by 12 in the case of a monthly payment schedule.

Of course, the calculation of prices according to simple formulas is one thing in a textbook and another thing in reality. Actual real estate prices are implicitly calculated in the way described, but two people would rarely come up with the same price for a given piece of land even if they are competent professional appraisers. First of all, who can tell the future with certainty? Our price of wheat land, for example, was calculated under the assumption that wheat prices and the costs of wheat production are never going to change. Different people will have different expectations concerning future trends in prices and costs, and this will lead to different capitalized values. In addition, the discount rate for such calculations is not engraved in stone. Different purchasers and sellers often have different discount rates because of differences in their past experiences, what they anticipate will happen in the future, or for a number of other reasons. Differences in discount rates also lead to differences in capitalized values.

Case 2.2, which discusses Pratt and Whitney's land in East Hartford, Connecticut, illustrates the discrepancies that can arise in land valuation. The gap in this case is huge, with one estimate of $40,000 per acre and another of $500,000. The discrepancy, however, is not the main point of the case. The main point is that the highest and best use of the land has changed over time with the fortunes of Pratt and Whitney's production process and market for jet engines. As production is shifted to other plants, the economic rent of the production site decreases with respect to jet engines, while the location's high accessibility within a large metropolitan region suggests high location rents for housing developments or other commercial users. Maintaining the land in factory production is irrational when other uses could earn more income. Although, the president of Pratt and Whitney, Mr. Krapek's appraisal may be questionable, his plan for the land appears to be very rational.

◪ *CASE 2.2*

Pratt and Whitney and the Highest and Best Use of a Location

Pratt and Whitney's president has confirmed to employees what had long been speculated: The company's likely course—maybe a decade down the road—is to sell its sprawling 1,200-acre complex in East Hartford and move its headquarters to its Middletown site.

"Probably by the year 2005, this (East Hartford) facility will have all moved to Middletown," Krapek said in the phone exchange.

East Hartford Mayor Robert M. Decrescenzo said the comment was further evidence his town was in transition. "I'm going to make it my duty to find out how much of that is an official statement and how much of it is off-the-cuff theorizing," he promised.

"It's very gratifying to know a corporate friend is going to remain here and expand here," Middletown mayor Thomas J. Serra said.

In his remarks, Krapek called the East Hartford site, tucked between two interstate highways, "the best piece of land left in America."

The site, which Pratt has occupied since 1929, contains two dozen buildings and hangars as well as Rentschler Airfield, long the private airport for Pratt's parent company, Hartford-based United Technologies Corp.

"If we sell at the right time, which isn't now . . . we'll get $500,000 an acre, which is $600 million," Krapek said. "Therefore the facts are that we'll probably end up vacating it."

Krapek, however, said Pratt isn't in a position to move its headquarters and other East Hartford operations to Middletown immediately.

"If I could wave a magic wand today and could afford it, and we weren't laying people off," Pratt's president said, "I'd build a headquarters building in Middletown and I'd take customers there. Because that's where you can best show off Pratt. You can show the product, the assembly, the test (operations). . . . So probably by the end of the year 2005, this facility will have all moved to Middletown.

The likelihood of Pratt's eventually moving its headquarters to Middletown, a scenario often rumored by Pratt's workers but denied by its management, was first broached by Krapek in a private meeting with some Pratt engineers last month.

"Middletown is where the action is," an employee at that meeting wrote in a computer message sent to *The Courant.* "Karl will be moving down there sometime because that's where the engines are built and the selling will be done. We plan on selling the East Hartford site because it's simply too valuable to do anything else with it."

However, a Waterford firm that assessed Pratt's land last year, Flanegan Associates, said it was worth $40,000 an acre—far less than the $500,000 an acre Krapek said it might be worth in the future. The discrepancy could not be explained Wednesday night.

Pratt has been moving work out of its once-bustling East Hartford complex for several years.

Last year, it completed the transfer of its military-engine production line to Middletown. Its military-engine testing operation will be moved to Middletown by midsummer. Pratt has torn down some older office and maintenance buildings on the East Hartford site, while parent UTC has announced plans to move its corporate flight operation to Bradley International Airport.

East Hartford remains Pratt's largest site, however. The company continues to keep its headquarters and administrative, engineering, marketing, experimental test, some overhaul and repair and some machining operations there. The complex in East Hartford employs just under 9,000 workers, down from 13,900 at the end of 1991.

Pratt's complex in Middletown, which assembles civilian as well as military engines, employs 2,600 workers. That is down from 2,856 at the end of 1991. But the company is planning to shift to Middletown most of the workers from its Southington parts plant, which is being phased out by the end of this year. Pratt will be closing half of another parts plant in North Haven.

Joseph Cohen, a spokesman for the state Department of Economic Development, said Krapek's comments should be put in perspective.

"If Pratt is going to move jobs a few miles, that's not nearly the significant problem of Pratt moving out of Connecticut," Cohen said. "With all the Pratt bashing that's going on, all parties should keep in mind that this company can go anywhere at any time, and it's been a tremendous asset to Connecticut."

A move to consolidate Pratt's headquarters, engineering and marketing with its production and testing would be consistent with the trend in U.S. industry, said Luis A. Chong, and Avon-based manufacturing productivity consultant.

"You want designers and engineers close to production," Chong said. "At the same time, having too many people at one location can make things difficult to manage. Companies have to look into what's the most efficient thing to do."

SOURCE: "Middletown to Become Pratt Base, Leader says," by Robert Weisman in the *Hartford Courant*, March 31, 1994, pp. A1 and A12. By permission of the *Hartford Courant* and Robert Weisman.

FOR DISCUSSION

This case concerns the likely transition from manufacturing to other land uses. Pratt and Whitney's president claims that the plant occupies the "best piece of land left in America." Why isn't it the best for manufacturing jet engines?

POINTS IN SUMMARY

1. Producer surplus, or economic rent, is the difference between the price actually paid for a good or service and the price required by the seller to stay in business.

2. The market equilibrium price is defined by the intersection of the demand curve for a good or service and its supply curve.

3. For any crop price paid at the market, the higher the environmental quality of the land on which it is grown, the lower the cost of the crop's production, and the higher the economic rent due to the land.

4. The value of the land is usually derived from the value of its output (and not the other way around).

5. Access to markets is a necessary foundation of commercial agriculture.

6. Location rent incorporates accessibility costs into the calculation of economic rent.

7. Location rent is inversely related to transport costs. When transport costs are low, location rent is high, and when transport costs are high, location rent is low (other things being equal).

8. The demand for food is only weakly price elastic. Its demand does not increase that much unless a very poor population is considered.

9. Price changes, changes in production costs, and changes in transport costs can lead to changes in land-use locations.

10. Location rent models of land use can be applied in both rural and urban location analyses.

11. Location decisions ultimately involve the weighing of the costs and benefits of a particular location against the costs and benefits of all other potential locations.

12. If a business requires fairly low frequencies of interaction with its market, its valuation of a central location is not as great as that of a company that requires high frequencies of market interaction.

TERMS TO REMEMBER

bid-rent curve	location equilibrium	market capitalization	producer surplus
contract rent	location rent	market-clearing price	pure economic rent
economic rent	made land	market equilibrium	residual land use
highest and best use	marginal cost	perfectly competitive market	Ricardian rent
land rent	marginal product		

SUGGESTED READING

Alonso, William. 1964: *Location and Land Use.* Cambridge, Mass.: Harvard University Press.

Alonso pioneered the extension of the type of land-use model first used by von Thünen to the analysis of urban land patterns. This is the best book-length work to use as a starting point for understanding contemporary urban land-use modeling. The book by Papageorgiou cited later in these references will bring you up-to-date.

Anas, Alex. 1984: "Land Market Theory and Methodology in Wildland Management," pp. 89–114 in *Valuation of Wildland Resource Benefits,* edited by George L. Peterson and Alan Randall. Boulder, Colo.: Westview Press.

This paper spells out in detail the cost-benefit rationale for a land-use transition—in this case from wild land to developed.

Chisholm, Michael. 1967: *Rural Settlement and Land-Use.* New York: John Wiley & Sons.

Chisolm describes not only the market basis of land use in differential rents, but also history, policy, and technological change in their impacts on rural patterns in the landscape.

Cromley, Robert, and Dean M. Hanink, 1989: "A Financial-Economic von Thünen Model." *Environment and Planning A,* Volume 21, pp. 951–960.

This paper links agricultural land-use patterns with investment strategies that minimize financial risk. One of the resulting diagrams looks, by coincidence, like a cornucopia.

Dunn, Edgar S., Jr. 1954: *The Equilibrium of Land-Use in Agriculture.* Gainsville: University of Florida Press.

Dunn, like Alonso, was a pioneer in the development of neoclassical land-use models. This book is a reworking and extension of von Thunen's work on agricultural land use.

Norman, George. 1993: "Of Shoes and Ships and Shredded Wheat, of Cabbages and Cars: The Contemporary Relevance of Location Theory," pp. 38–68, in *Does Economic Space Matter? Essays in Honour of Melvin L. Greenhut*, edited by H. Ohta and J.-F. Thisse. New York: St. Martin's Press.

At the beginning of this essay, Norman links Ricardo and von Thünen and then extends von Thünen to the urban arena under changing needs for accessibility. Other location models are also considered.

OECD Group on Urban Affairs. 1992: *Urban Land Markets: Policies for the 1990s*. Paris: OECD.

This short volume describes efforts by governments in the world's richer countries to develop and implement policies that reinforce the operation of land markets in the allocation of urban land uses.

Papageorgiou, Yorgos Y. 1990: *The Isolated City State: An Economic Geography of Urban Spatial Structure*. New York: Routledge.

This highly mathematical work builds on the tradition established by Alonso. It is much more comprehensive, however, in its treatment of behavioral issues and externalities, for example.

Wilson, A. G., and M. Birkin. 1987: "Dynamic Models of Agricultural Location in a Spatial Interaction Framework." *Geographical Analysis*, Vol. 19, pp. 31–56.

As the title states, Wilson and Birkin recast the von Thünen model in an explicit framework of spatial interaction. By altering parameters, the land-use patterns developed initially are made dynamic.

Chapter 3

Global Patterns of Agricultural Land Use

This chapter

- describes basic differences in agricultural production around the world.
- introduces the use of production functions in assessing types of economic activity.
- considers the environmental differences underlying regional agricultural patterns.
- takes up the role of technological differences in forming regional agricultural patterns.
- describes the impact of national government policies on agricultural land-use patterns.
- examines the role of global markets in affecting local agricultural land-use patterns.

Courtesy of USDA

Chapter 2 described land use in largely abstract terms. The development of land-use patterns was viewed as the result of differences in producer surpluses, or economic rents, that are available to different users of land. Rent variations were given simple causes: some parcels have higher rent than others because they are more productive, and some parcels have higher rent than others because they have a better location with respect to local markets for the land user's product. This chapter considers land use in more specific ways. First, it concerns only one use of the land: agriculture. Second, it explores some of the real-world causes of variations in land's economic rent for agriculture. Agricultural land is not a homogeneous factor of production around the world. Environmental differences, of course, affect the pattern of agriculture in a basic way. In addition, agriculture as an economic endeavor occurs within a variety of cultural patterns. Neither technology that links the economy of agriculture to its environmental base nor the political and legal institutions that affect agricultural production are consistent from place to place. Finally, most agricultural production is increasingly being embedded within the global economy, so that the spatial interaction of agricultural production and consumption is increasing in complexity.

AGRICULTURAL SYSTEMS

Agriculture can be simply defined as the practice of producing crops and raising livestock. Most agricultural output is used for food by people and animals, but a large proportion is used for industrial purposes. In many parts of the world, the hides of cattle and other animals are used to produce articles of clothing, while the fibers of plants such as hemp, jute, and cotton are put to a variety of uses. By considering the end use of agricultural production then, we can immediately think of a simple way to classify agriculture: as food or as input to another production process. Actually, although agriculture may be defined simply as we have done here, it really is complex when you try to understand its implications for land-use patterns.

The market for agricultural output is important for the the way land is used. Chapter 2 contains an extensive discussion of the location of the market and agricultural land use; here we back up a step and observe that the type of output is important, not just where it is sold. If the type of output is important, then the physical environment must play a critical role in agricultural land use. Weather and climate, soils, degree of slope, and other elements of the physical environment have a bearing on what types of crops can be grown with a reasonable chance of success. We also need to add technology, the link between the market and the physical environment, as an important factor in agricultural land use. The institutional ground on which agriculture takes place is sometimes just as important as the physical ground, so we also must pay attention to government policy and legal practices when we think about agricultural land use.

The location of markets, types of products, the physical environment, technology, and institutional factors are therefore necessary elements to consider in studying agricultural land use, and this list is not exhaustive. Obviously, agriculture is a complex sector of the economy, but useful generalizations concerning agricultural land use around the world can be drawn from thinking about *agricultural systems*. Agricultural systems include not only crop types, but also the environmental, social, economic, and technological contexts in which the crops are grown. B. L. Turner II and Stephen Brush, in *Comparative Farming Systems*, have classified the world's agricultural systems into three groups based on similarities in technology and market. One group, "paleotechnic and consumption-oriented systems," contains farming systems that use basic technology in growing products for subsistence and otherwise local consumption. An example is dry rice cultivation in northern Thailand. A second group, the "neotechnic and commodity-oriented systems," includes, for example, wheat farming in northeastern Colorado. This group uses advanced technology in producing agricultural products for commercial markets that are likely to be national in scope or even international. In between lies a mixed group, "mixed technic and production systems," which consists of production systems with diverse technological levels and end-markets. This group contains producers such as those engaged in irrigated cereal production in Punjab (India) who use an intermediate amount of inanimate energy in agricultural production compared to the low levels of the first group and the high level of energy used by the second group.

Let's take a simple approach to classifying world agriculture by focusing on productivity. Usually, *productivity* is measured as output per unit of productive input. The output may be measured in terms of quantity (e.g., bushels harvested per hectare of cultivated land) or in terms of value of output. The value of output per worker is a common measure of *labor productivity*, not only in agriculture but also in other industries. A related measure is the value of agricultural output per person in a country, which is an indicator of the strength of the country's agricultural sector. This measure of productivity can vary from country to country for a number of reasons. We would not expect, for example, Singapore to have large values of agricultural output per person because the amount of land available for agriculture in that small country is very limited. Conversely, the value of agricultural output in a country might be higher than otherwise expected simply because it produces crops that have much higher than average values. In general, however, the value of output in agriculture per person varies systematically with a country's per capita national income; richer countries have relatively stronger, more productive agricultural sectors, and poor countries have weaker, less productive agricultural sectors.

The relative differences in average agricultural output around the world in the early 1990s are indicated in Figure 3.1. The World Bank, a leading international financial institution that is weakly affiliated with the United Nations, classifies the world's countries by their per capita *gross national product* (*GNP*). This

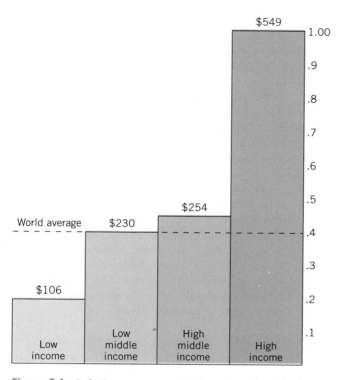

Figure 3.1 Relative average agricultural productivity by World Bank income group in 1992.

measure of national income sums the value of goods and services produced and provided in a country during a year. Agricultural output is one component of GNP that appears to be representative of a country's entire economy on a per capita (per person) basis. High-income countries have more than twice as much agricultural output per person than the two groups of middle-income countries and over five times the output per person, on average, than the low-income countries. (The use of per capita GNP and similar measures in describing levels of national wealth is described in more detail in Chapter 11. In 1992, low-income countries such as Bangladesh and Honduras had per capita GNPs of U.S. $675 or less, whereas high-income countries, including the United States and Japan, among others, had per capita GNPs of over $8,355.)

Classifying agricultural systems by their productivity gives us a geography—high productivity in rich countries and low productivity in poor countries—but this is an insufficient basis for talking about systems. The array of characteristics that lead to agricultural productivity problems in the world's poor countries are revealed, however, in Insights 3.1, which concerns the problems of agricultural development in the world's poorest countries. Items (a), (b), and (h) point to problems in markets, both national and international, for agriculture in those countries and a lack of financial support systems. Point (c) concerns problems of distribution stemming from a lack of roadways and rail lines that are necessary for the distribution of agricultural products within a country. Point (d) also concerns distribution problems and other factors limiting access to world markets for agricultural products. Points (e) and (g) concern technological problems in the agricultural sector of poor countries, with respect both to production and to problems of environmental degradation. Point (f) concerns problems of land-tenure systems in poorer countries. Land tenure is the way land is owned and operated in a legal context (see Chapter 4 for a more detailed discussion).

Insights 3.1 summarizes the main disadvantages of agriculture in poor countries: those having to do with markets, technology, environment, legal factors, and government policy. In rich countries, these same items often constitute advantages by comparison. For example, inadequate access to agricultural technology may limit agricultural productivity in poor countries, while, by comparison, ready access to agricultural technology in richer countries is one reason for that group's higher level of per capita agricultural output. A major difference in the agricultural sectors of rich countries and poor countries not alluded to in Insights 3.1 is in their *production functions*—the relationship between the quantity of inputs to the production process and the quantity of output. Because this is an important difference, let's explore it in more detail.

Agriculture has a long list of productive inputs. Soil, water, and seed, for example, may be supplied by nature, labor is supplied by people working the land, and machinery and pesticides are used as capital inputs. This short list is not meant to be comprehensive. Even a complete list of productive inputs, often called *factors of production,* for one type of crop would be at least a little different for another crop. Production functions are often simplified to two factors of production: labor and capital. Labor refers to the number of people working to produce a good or service, or the value of their contribution measured by their wages and salaries. Capital refers to just about everything else that is used in production, including buildings, land, and machinery. In agricultural production, items such as tractors and hoes are capital inputs, and so are water wells, fertilizers, pesticides, and so on.

A typical production function is illustrated in Figure 3.2. Larger amounts of the two factors, capital and labor, used in production are indicated by K_1, K_2, K_3, and L_1, L_2, L_3, respectively. In addition, increasing quantities of output are indicated by curved lines on the graph marked with Q_1, Q_2, and Q_3. These curved lines are called *isoquants,* because they define equal quantities of output. An important characteristic of production in agriculture, and in other sectors of the economy as well, illustrated by the left graph in Figure 3.2 is that the factors of production work together in yielding output. Labor cannot produce much without capital, and capital cannot produce much without labor. A hectare of land, for example, won't produce wheat on its own except in strange circumstances because labor is required to operate the land in a productive manner. In turn, just wishing for wheat isn't at all effective because the farmer needs capital inputs of some sort to cultivate the crop. Production, however, doesn't usually require equal volumes or values of the inputs of capital and labor. De-

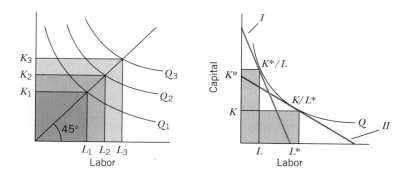

Figure 3.2 The diagram at the left illustrates the general production function with output, Q, increasing from Q_1 to Q_2 to Q_3 in proportion to combined increases of the capital inputs, C, and labor inputs, L. The right-hand diagram illustrates that different factor intensities may be employed to produce the same quantity of output. There is a higher ratio of capital-to-labor in K^*/L than in the combination represented by K/L^*, but the quantity of output, Q, is the same.

pending on the good or service that is being produced, factor intensities, or relative amounts of factors used in production, can be expected to vary. *Labor-intensive production* uses relatively more labor than capital; *capital-intensive production* uses relatively more capital than land.

Sometimes the same product can be produced by either capital-intensive or labor-intensive methods. Textiles, for example, are produced by capital-intensive mechanized methods in many of the world's richer countries, but by labor-intensive methods in many poorer countries where labor costs are relatively low. Construction projects are another example; many people with picks and shovels are used to dig building foundations in many poorer countries, but bulldozers and other machines are used for the job in richer countries.

The tradeoff between capital and labor in production is illustrated in the right half of Figure 3.2. Isoquant Q can be achieved by either the capital-intensive factor ratio K^*/L or the labor-intensive factor ratio K/L^*. If both production factor ratios can produce the same amount of output, why would one be used in practice rather than the other? The relative costs of the factors usually determine the factor ratios. If labor is scarce, it is probably expensive and as much capital as possible will be used instead. On the other hand, if labor is inexpensive compared to capital, then as much labor as possible will be used in production. Line I on the right-hand diagram of Figure 3.2 traces the tradeoff between capital costs and labor costs. Line I is called an *isocost line* because it shows the factor combinations that could be used in production for a particular constant cost. A different set of tradeoffs is indicated by isocost line II. Capital costs are relatively low in the case of line I, and this is represented by the higher point of intercept of line I on the vertical capital axis as compared to the intercept of line II. Labor costs are relatively low in the case of line II, and this is represented by the higher point of intercept of line II on the horizontal labor axis as compared to the intercept of line I. The exact factor ratios are determined by the point of tangency between an isocost line and the isoquant. Because isocost lines I and II represent different relative factor costs, they have different slopes on the graph and different points of tangency with the isoquant.

Again, a basic difference between agriculture in rich countries and agriculture in poorer countries is in their production functions. The poorer countries, in general, have labor-intensive production functions in agriculture (as well as in their other economic sectors), whereas agriculture in rich countries is generally capital intensive by comparison (Figure 3.3). In 1980, nearly three-quarters of the labor force in the average low-income country was employed in agriculture, while only 7% of the average high-income country's labor force was employed in that sector. (The percentages have declined since 1980, the last year for which comprehensive data were published by the World Bank, but the relative proportions are probably about the same.) Is the difference in factor intensities between rich-country agriculture and poor-country agriculture the source of the differences in their average levels of agricultural productivity? Yes, although not because of any inherent inferiority of labor-intensive production compared to capital-intensive production, but simply because of a barrier to output in poor

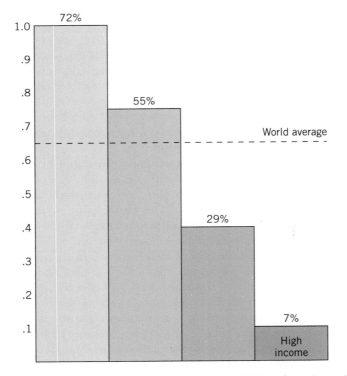

Figure 3.3 Relative average proportion of labor force in agriculture by World Bank income group in 1980.

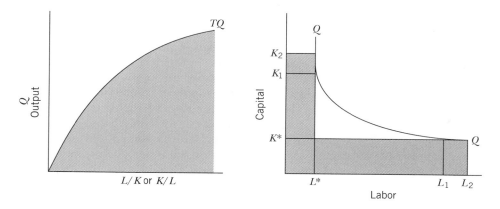

Figure 3.4 In the left diagram, total output, *TQ*, increases at an increasing rate and then a diminishing rate on the margin as either the labor-to-capital ratio, *L/K*, or the capital-to-labor ratio, *K/L*, increases. Early on, labor or capital additions to existing stocks of capital or labor allow rapid increases in production because factor shortfalls are eliminated. On the other hand, continuing rapid increases of one factor while the other remains fixed in supply simply leads to bottlenecks in production. The right-hand diagram represents the law of diminishing returns with respect to the marginal substitutability of one factor for another. As long as capital is fixed in supply at *K*, then increasing labor from amount L_1 to L_2 does not increase production. As long as labor is fixed in supply at *L**, then increasing capital from amount K_1 to K_2 does not increase production.

countries raised by the *law of diminishing returns.* This law states that if one factor of production is held constant, it's difficult to increase output even if another factor is used in much greater amounts.

This law is illustrated at the left of Figure 3.4, where total output, *TQ*, increases rapidly at first and then at a diminishing rate as either the labor-to-capital ratio or capital-to-labor ratio increases. When one of these ratios is low, there is an imbalance in the factors of production that limits output. If, for example, you have 100 hectares of land and only one person to work it (low *L/K*), your production will be limited by the shortage of labor. By increasing the labor factor by just one person, production should increase significantly; add another and output will continue to grow. Eventually, however, a limit will be reached where marginal productivity of labor begins to decline; the 15th additional worker, for example, will not be adding what the second did, and the 101st additional worker probably will not add anything at all but only get in the way. The same sort of limits affect capital, and sometimes quickly. You can cut a lot more grass with a lawn mower than without one, but two lawn mowers can't be used at the same time by one person. This last point is generalized in the right half of Figure 3.4, where the limits to substitutability of one factor for another are illustrated. You can't keep adding capital to a fixed labor supply and increase output forever, and, conversely, you can't keep adding labor to a fixed supply of capital and expect output to maintain a steady rate of growth.

Many of the points raised in Insights 3.1 concern methods of increasing the capital-to-labor ratio of agriculture, and therefore reducing its labor intensity, in the hope of improving agricultural productivity in poor countries. The establishment and maintenance of *physical infrastructure*, which consists of capital that serves the economy in general, such as transport and other communications systems, is an important part of enlarging the supply of capital in an economy. The last paragraph of the box also addresses the issue of changing the capital-to-labor ratio in poor-country agriculture in its call for equal gender access to technology and agricultural support services. Neither women nor any other group can be fully productive if their access to capital is denied, any more than labor in general can be fully productive if it faces a capital shortfall. This type of discrimination is not only inequitable but also inefficient.

➤ INSIGHTS 3.1
The Agricultural Sector in the Least Developed Countries

The development of the agricultural sector will continue to rank high among the transformational objectives of the least developed countries in the 1990s. Around 80 per cent of the population of the least developed countries live in rural areas, and agriculture is the dominant sector of production. Rural development thus constitutes an indispensable element of any agricultural development strategy. Moreover, expansion of food production and food security continue to be a priority objective of the least developed countries. Towards this end, least developed countries should, with adequate international support, at the minimum strive to increase agricultural and food production at an annual growth rate significantly ahead of population growth if poverty alleviation and eradication, nutritional improvement as well as food security goals are not to be at risk.

The development of the agricultural sector will require the formulation, by the LDCs with the support of the competent international organizations and donor countries, of an "agricultural development strategy." This strategy for development of the agricultural sector requires, among other things:

a. Adoption of appropriate agricultural price and credit policies, taking into account market signals, as well as the need to ensure adequate incentives for agricultural development; support for farmers' initiatives; LDCs will study the impact on their agricultural production of cereals which are sold at low prices on world markets;

b. Improving income distribution patterns and broadening income earnings opportunities at the national level so as to strengthen the purchasing power of the low-income strata of the population, and thereby expand the national demand for agricultural goods;

c. Effective participation by the public sector, in particular with regard to the improvement of the physical and institutional infrastructure on which agricultural production depends directly in order, at any time, to help supply the zones affected by shortages from surplus regions, as well as the formulation and implementation of cooperation arrangements at regional and subregional levels aimed at fostering agricultural development;

d. The diversification of the agricultural base through the integration of crop and livestock farming and by the promotion of fisheries, livestock, horticulture and forestry, and the improvement of productivity and competitiveness through more effective processing, distribution and marketing from production to consumption or export, especially for products intended for the world market;

e. The development and application of agricultural research and improvement of the technical skills and know-how of farmers, groups of farmers or agricultural workers through flexible and decentralized agricultural extension systems;

f. Reform of farming and land-tenure systems, where appropriate, aimed at encouraging investment in land;

g. Adoption of agricultural techniques and farming practices keeping in mind the preservation and protection of the environment, including stepped-up efforts for afforestation and the prevention of soil erosion arising from land misuse and over-use;

h. The establishment of agricultural support services—in particular agricultural credit systems, including mutual groupings—storage facilities and other relevant measures to minimize pre-harvest and post-harvest losses.

Within their agricultural development programmes, the least developed countries should provide appropriate incentive structures to small-holders, who are the major producers of food crops and who thus have a crucial role to play in the attainment of national food security, as well as gainful employment to landless workers, who represent the large majority of agricultural producers in the least developed countries. Their success, or failure, has a direct impact upon the well-being of the mass of the rural population. Women's role in food production should be similarly strengthened through the recognition of the need for laws and regulations ensuring equal access to more efficient food-processing technologies, credit, land tenure and agricultural training and support services.

SOURCE: *Paris Declaration and Programme of Action for the Least Developed Countries for the 1990s*, by United Nations Conference on Trade and Development, UNCTAD/RDP/LDC/58 (New York: United Nations), 1992, pp. 47–49.

CAPITAL INTENSIVE AGRICULTURE

In comparison to agriculture in poor countries, agriculture in rich countries is capital intensive indeed. The high degree of capital intensity, however, is relatively new. In the United States, for example, even though paid labor has been relatively expensive by international standards for hundreds of years, capital-intensive agriculture only became typical in the years following World War II. Between 1950 and 1990, the number of people employed in agriculture declined by well over two-thirds, from nearly 10 million to just over 3 million, and the number of people living on farms dropped from over 14% of the country's population to under 2%. The decline in labor was not accompanied by a decline in agricultural output in the United States. Production per hectare more than doubled on American farms between 1950 and 1990, and total output nearly doubled during the period. The increase in output as labor declined is the measure of increased labor efficiency in production brought about by replacing people with machinery, chemicals, and other forms of capital.

The increase in output per worker and per hectare underline the importance of economies of scale (see Chapter 1) in bringing about higher rates of agricultural output per person in richer countries such as the United States. In this context, the important factor ratio seems to be capital-to-land rather than capital-to-labor because farms that are larger in area lend themselves more readily to applications of capital. For example, machinery often is used more easily on larger farms—tractors are less appropriate on 2-hectare farms than on 200-hectare farms. Fertilizers and pesticides are more cheaply purchased in large quantities, and large quantities are only useful on large plots of land.

The number of farms has decreased significantly in the United States over the last 40 years but not the area of land in agricultural production. Smaller farms are being consolidated into larger ones so that capital can be more cheaply deployed on an average cost basis. The relationship between economies of scale and the increasing use of capital factors in contemporary agriculture is discussed with specific reference to the American pork industry in Case 3.1, but the conditions described are typical of capital-intensive agriculture around the world.

Capital-intensive agriculture is also intensive in its use of commercial energy (purchased inanimate energy). Commercial energy use per hectare of land in agriculture and per worker in agriculture are at their highest levels in North America, Western Europe, and Australia and New Zealand (Table 3.1). These are the richer regions of the world and have capital-intensive production throughout their economies. They rely on favorable energy prices, however, to maintain their style of production. By one measure of efficiency, based on output quantities, a lot of the energy is wasted.

It seems ironic that in places where a lot of energy is used, levels of output per energy input are low. At the same time, in regions such as Africa and East Asia where energy use is very low, energy is most productive on a per hectare and per worker basis. These differences are evidence of market forces, and the market's measure of efficiency is financial. The relative cost of energy, as a form

Table 3.1   World Regions Ranked by Commercial Energy Use and Efficiency in Agriculture[a]

Energy Use per Hectare	Energy Efficiency per Hectare
Western Europe	Africa
North America	East Asia
Oceania	Middle East
Eastern Europe	Latin America
Latin America	East Europe
Middle East	North America
East Asia	West Europe
Africa	Oceania

Energy Use per Worker	Energy Efficiency per Worker
North America	Africa
Oceania	East Asia
Western Europe	Middle East
Eastern Europe	Latin America
Latin America	East Europe
Middle East	North America
East Asia	Oceania
Africa	West Europe

[a] Energy is measured in joules ($\times 10^9$). Efficiency is defined with reference to output in metric tons and should not be mistaken for cost efficiency.

of capital, is often lower in the richer countries than in the poorer countries. As long as the marginal revenue of crops is greater than the marginal cost of commercial energy to grow them, and the marginal cost of commercial energy is less than the marginal cost of other factors, agriculture will be relatively energy intensive. If those conditions don't hold, as in many poorer countries, then commercial energy won't be a major factor of production.

◪ *CASE 3.1*
Economies of Scale in Pork Production

Two key economic factors will drive the U.S. pork industry toward more consolidation and integration in the years ahead (1) a drive to cut costs by capturing economies of scale, and (2) efforts to control the industry's increasing risks. Cutting production costs by shifting production to more efficient, larger farms will fuel further consolidation in the industry.

A steady stream of new production technologies will lead to further economies of scale in hog farming, spurring the current trend toward fewer, larger farms. Many industry observers believe the widening cost disadvantage of small farms points to a swift decline in the number of hog farms, from 250,000 today to only 100,000 by the year 2000. The erosion in hog farms will be fastest among small farms, which are at the greatest cost disadvantage. As small farms leave the industry, hog production will concentrate further on bigger farms

Technology will drive the shift to fewer, larger hog farms. New production technologies are pushing down production costs on the nation's hog farms. But the industry's cost savings are achieved primarily by capturing economies of scale. For example, average production costs on farms producing 10,000 hogs annually, the largest size tracked by the U.S. Department of Agriculture, are nearly 30 percent lower than costs on small farms producing only 140 hogs a year. The steady, downward slope of the cost curve in the chart suggests that even larger production units—like the new mammoth farms producing half a million or more hogs a year—have an even bigger cost advantage over smaller farms.

The newest technologies coming on stream are likely to push down production costs even more, especially on large farms. Some of the new technologies—like pST (a growth hormone)—are said to be "size neutral," indicating they could lower production costs on both small and large farms. But these technologies are likely to be used more effectively on large farms where sophisticated production and management systems are already in place.

The economies of scale that are driving the industry's consolidation should improve pork's competitiveness with other meats—especially budget-priced poultry. The sharp drop in the price of poultry relative to beef and pork in the last two decades boosts its appeal to budget-conscious consumers. To remain

Average hog production costs in the United States

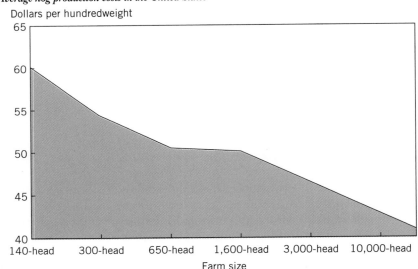

competitive at the supermarket, the pork industry must hold down its costs—while simultaneously satisfying more discriminating tastes. Thus, further consolidation in the pork industry will be driven by the consumer's demand for convenient and nutritious pork products in a highly competitive food market.

The industry's further consolidation on bigger hog farms is making hog production a much riskier business than before. The highly specialized equipment used on big hog farms has little value in uses other than hog production. These modern pig factories have less flexibility than small farms to cut back production or liquidate assets altogether if hog prices fall or if a market cannot be found for market-ready hogs. Thus, uncertain marketing arrangements expose investors in modern hog farms to large losses. A relatively high capital-labor ratio points to the critical role of large investments in specialized technology on big hog farms. Average production expenses on the 10,000-head farms shown in the chart are lower than on the 140-head farms in every expense category. But the biggest difference is in the labor expense, which is nearly two-thirds less on the big farms than on the small farms. As a result, the capital-labor ratio on the larger farms averages more than half again as large as on the small farms.

SOURCE: "The Changing U.S. Pork Industry: A Dilemma for Public Policy," by Alan Barkema and Michael L. Cook, *Economic Review*, Federal Reserve Bank of Kansas City, Vol. 78, No. 2, 1993, pp. 56–58.

◪

FOR DISCUSSION

Does this case indicate that agriculture can become too specialized if it relies on capital-intensive production methods?

AGRICULTURE AND THE ENVIRONMENT

The cultivation of crops and the raising of livestock can be viewed as taking place within an *agro-ecosystem* that consists of close interrelationships between the natural environment and the human pursuit of raising crops and livestock. Agro-ecosystems are like natural ecosystems because they consist of a necessary interdependence among a host of physical factors such as soil and moisture. Unlike natural ecosystems, however, agro-ecosystems would not exist without interaction with people as well, and so they exist in social contexts that include economic, political, and historical concerns.

Case 3.2, which describes canola cultivation in the Canadian Prairie provinces, illustrates the interdependence of social and physical factors in agricultural decision making. Wheat cultivation had been the mainstay of the region, but declining subsidies from the Canadian government meant reduced land rents on that crop. A new variety of rapeseed, canola, was developed as a source of cooking oil that appeals to the increasing number of people looking for low fat substitutes in their diets (it can also be used in gasahol). Because of a growing market for its derivatives, canola cultivation raises land rents, but only where the physical environment is appropriate, as in the Prairie provinces.

The supply of land that can be used for agriculture, or *arable land*, is limited by environmental conditions. Basic limitations arise from the needs of various crops, and even types of livestock, for certain soil nutrients available, certain levels of moisture, particular growing seasons, and so on. Sometimes, environmental constraints can affect farmers so that cultivation is limited. Problems of malaria, for example, or sleeping sickness, limit the ability of people to live and farm in certain parts of the world, although these environmental constraints do not affect cropping directly.

Perhaps the most important single physical factor in agricultural production is climate, or average conditions of air temperature, solar radiation, and moisture availability, and their seasonality. Some climatic limits on agriculture are obvious; extremely high latitudes have impossibly short growing seasons, for example. Other climatic effects are less obvious. An important factor in crop production such as soil pH is directly affected by fairly subtle climatic differences in the yearly amount and seasonal pattern of precipitation. Extremes of temperature and seasonal variations in temperature and solar radiation may also affect agricultural production by narrowing the range of crops that may be grown in an area.

◪ *CASE 3.2*
Canada Counts on Canola

PENNANT, SASKATCHEWAN—It's been a long time since Canadian farmers were caught smiling, but these days it's nearly impossible to wipe the grins from their faces. A "wonder" plant is sweeping prairie agriculture.

The new game in town is a fragile-looking little oilseed called canola, a genetically altered version of a plant with the unfortunate name of rapeseed. With the lowest saturated fat content of any oil, about 6 percent, canola has become the darling of health food enthusiasts, and industrial uses are growing.

The Agriculture Department expects that when farm receipts are toted up for 1994, canola will have overtaken wheat as Canada's biggest agricultural earner.

"The crushing industry in Canada and exporters have asked us for eight million tons," said a gleeful Doug Sword, a canola farmer and president of the Canadian Canola Growers Association. "We can't supply it."

Perhaps even better news: Canola likes cool weather. That is something Canada has plenty of. Though some canola is grown in the north-central United States and the Pacific Northwest, warmer weather generally makes it an unsuitable crop for farmers south of the border.

Don Dowdeswell farms 3,500 acres around Pennant, a village in southwestern Saskatchewan. Growing canola in his area is very new, even scary for beginners used to more traditional crops such as durum and barley.

Canola is more difficult to grow than wheat. It is more fragile, vulnerable to more diseases and pests, harder to seed, and difficult to harvest. The recommendation is to plant canola in a rotation of one year in four.

Dowdeswell jumped into canola in 1992, driven to it by low wheat prices in recent years. He now has 400 acres of the yellow-flowered oilseed.

"We have been limited in the crops we thought we could grow," Dowdeswell said over a cup of coffee on a frosty autumn morning in the office of his small seed company. "Wheat prices drop, and we all wring our hands."

"I see canola being able to offset some of the big ups and downs in wheat. A good part of the world is getting on the health wagon, and industrial uses of canola are increasing, which will make it a bit of a stabilizer for a farm operation. It's about as exciting as grain farming can get," he said.

Rapeseed has been around for a long time, grown in more northerly reaches of Saskatchewan, Manitoba, and Alberta. Its oil was first used as a marine lubricant during World War II.

Then, about 20 years ago, Canadian researchers came up with a new rapeseed variety that could be processed into a cooking oil. They dubbed it canola—coined from the words Canadian and oil—to give it a more marketable name than rapeseed.

Canola produces seeds in a pod, similar in shape to a pea pod, but about five times smaller. The seeds, like small buckshot, are crushed to obtain oil, about 40 percent. The remainder of the seed is processed into meal for livestock.

With 6 percent saturated fat, canola is comfortably ahead of corn oil at 13 percent, soybean oil at 15 percent and peanut oil at 18 percent.

Apart from edible oils, canola is now also used as an ingredient in cosmetics, lubricants, pharmaceuticals, inks, plasticizers and fertilizer, as well as a fuel additive.

Canola production is exploding in Canada. In 1994, 14.4 million acres were planted, shattering the 1993 record by 40 percent. The 7.39 million tons expected to be produced in 1994 is 75 percent more than the previous high.

SOURCE: "Canola Bids to Be King of Canadian Agriculture," by Jeffrey Ulbrich, Associated Press Writer, January 2, 1995. By permission of the Associated Press.

FOR DISCUSSION

This case illustrates that changing preferences for food can play an important role in the geography of agricultural production. Can you describe other examples of the relationship between consumer preferences and the location of certain types of food or livestock production?

ENVIRONMENTAL MODIFICATION AND DEGRADATION

Agriculture interacts directly with the physical environment on a two-way street. The environment affects what types of agriculture can occur at a place, and agriculture also affects the environment. Agriculture can lead to environmental modification, if not outright degradation. Land for cultivation is expanded by burning or cutting existing cover, such as forests. Land is drained if it's too wet for farming or irrigated if it's too dry. Livestock grazing has led to change in plant cover since animals were first domesticated. Land expanded for agriculture frequently reduces wildlife habitat, and wild animals that interfere with agriculture practices are often exterminated.

Agriculture's impact on the environment can be considered at three different geographical scales: on-site or local, off-site or regional, and interregional or global. One of the most important on-site problems is soil degradation. This degradation can take place in a number of ways, including erosion and chemical change. Soil degradation by agricultural practices is an example of negative feedback in an agro-ecosystem. Productive agriculture can only be assured in the long run if soil quality is maintained, but many efforts to increase crop productivity in the short run lead to soil degradation. For example, certain types of cropping patterns can lead to increased rates of soil erosion by wind and by action of sheet runoff. Annual rates of soil erosion in the United States are estimated at about 3 billion tons of soil, and nearly one-third of its cropland is eroding at a rate that leads to real declines in agricultural productivity.

Salinization is a common form of chemical soil degradation that occurs naturally owing to the evaporation of rainfall. It becomes a severe problem, however, more often as a result of crop irrigation practices. The additional water on the fields brought by irrigation also means additional salts and other minerals left in the soil as evaporation takes place. Severe declines in crop productivity occur on about 10% of all irrigated land owing to excessive salinization, while about one-quarter of all irrigated land experiences at least some decline in soil quality.

On-site environmental degradation by agriculture frequently spills over to create off-site regional problems. Soil erosion, for example, which often can be traced to practices on individual farms, may lead to sedimentation of local drainages that can pollute many downstream waters. Water pollution over entire watersheds can result from several agricultural practices, including the use of chemical pesticides and fertilizers. Water contamination by agricultural chemicals and by sedimentation from eroding fields is referred to as *nonpoint source pollution* because it doesn't enter water from a single source like a drainage pipe from a factory (a *point source*). Instead, it enters water in sheet runoff along whole water courses. Capital-intensive agriculture, in particular, generates nonpoint source pollutants in the carcinogenic and otherwise toxic chemicals it uses as herbicides, insecticides, fungicides, and rodenticides. Each chemical used has a positive effect on farm output, but negative environmental costs often lead to their removal from use. The pesticide DDT is probably the best known case of an agricultural chemical with positive impacts on farm output but larger negative impacts on the health of people and animals. Its dangers were first brought to popular attention by Rachel Carson in her book *Silent Spring* (Greenwich, Conn.: Fawcett). The book was published in 1962, but DDT was not banned for use in the United States until 10 years later. The length of time the chemical stayed in use after its dangers became well-known is a testament to its success in agricultural applications.

Sugar cultivation and other agriculture in south-central Florida provides a strong example of the effect of farming practices in causing regional environmental problems. The regional watershed affected by agricultural practices extends from near Orlando to Florida Bay (Figure 3.5). The key flow is the Kissimmee

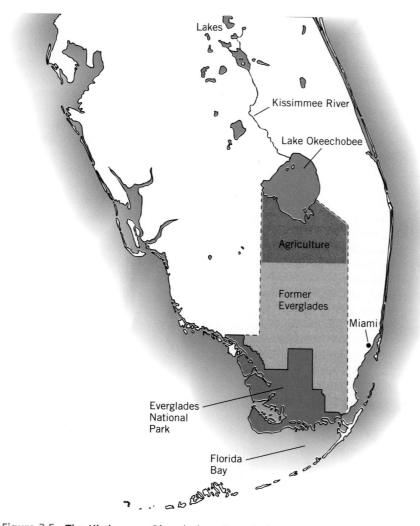

Figure 3.5 The Kissimmee, Okeechobee, Everglades ecosystem.

River to Lake Okeechobee (the home lake of Roland Martin) into the Everglades, which in turn border Florida Bay on the south. Before Florida was densely settled in the way it is today, say about 75 years ago, the Kissimmee gradually wound its way to Okeechobee, and Okeechobee graded slowly into wetlands that formed the northern edge of the Everglades. Today the map is different; the Kissimmee was straightened to control its hydrology and put it to productive use, much of the wetlands south of Okeechobee were drained and put into agriculture, and a significant amount of the fresh water in the Everglades was diverted to the Miami metropolitan area. About one-half million acres of the upper Everglades is now in sugar. Diversion of water and reduction of wetlands has led to a shrinking of the Everglades to about one-half of their original size. In addition, the water in Florida Bay has become saltier owing to the diversion.

Florida's sugar cultivation is a capital-intensive system that uses large amounts of phosphorus as fertilizer. Each year about 200 tons of the fertilizer enters the remaining Everglades as nonpoint source pollution. The phosphorus does a good job of fertilizing wherever it goes, and the Everglades are no exception. Plant growth, especially cattails, has choked out other vegetation that has been an important part of the habitat for a variety of species. Plant growth is accelerated as the water is drained, and the Everglades became in danger of disappearing. In short, a regional ecological system has been damaged by agriculture and other human actions. The cost of this type of damage is not frequently considered until after the fact, because it is external to the individual producers (see the discussion of externalities in Chapter 4). Current estimates of the cost of reclamation range as high as $2 billion over a 20-year period required to complete the work.

An example of the interaction between agriculture and the environment at the interregional or global scale is the greenhouse effect described in Insights 3.2. Again the focus is on capital-intensive agriculture because fossil fuel consumption by farm machinery is a major source of carbon dioxide forced into the atmosphere by farming practices. Although even primitive farming practices such as slash and burn agriculture can contribute to global climate change, the large-scale capital-intensive farming practices that take place in fairly limited areas have the strongest global effect. Environmental degradation and agricultural productivity seem to be joint outcomes of capital-intensive agricultural practices.

➤ INSIGHTS 3.2
Agriculture and the Atmospheric Greenhouse Effect

The greenhouse effect, although widely discussed, is still widely misunderstood. Part of the confusion is that the greenhouse effect is both natural and induced. The *natural greenhouse effect* results from gases like carbon dioxide and water vapor forming an atmospheric thermal blanket around the earth, trapping the warmth of sunlight and making the earth habitable. It has been estimated that without the natural blanket of greenhouse gases, sunlight would simply be re-flected back into space and the earth's temperature would be colder by 33 degrees Celsius (C), or 59 degrees Fahrenheit (F). The *induced greenhouse effect,* or what scientists call climate forcing, is the result of additional greenhouse gases put into the atmosphere through human activities, such as the release of carbon dioxide when fossil fuels are burned. The induced greenhouse effect is well understood, and the rise in greenhouse gases from human activity is well docu-mented. What remains unclear is how and when the increase will affect the earth's climate.

Agriculture has three vital links to the greenhouse effect. First, agriculture is made possible only through the natural greenhouse effect, and any changes to the current climate will change agriculture itself. Second, agriculture contri-butes to the induced greenhouse effect; burning fossil fuel to power tractors, for example, releases carbon dioxide. Finally, agriculture can reduce the amount of greenhouse gases in the atmosphere because trees and plants absorb carbon dioxide from the atmosphere and store carbon in wood or soil.

THE GREENHOUSE EFFECT AND GLOBAL WARMING

Without doubt, the atmosphere contains more of the major greenhouse gases than it did a century or two ago. There are four main greenhouse gases: carbon dioxide, methane, nitrous oxide, and chlorofluorocarbons (CFCs). Carbon diox-ide is the biggest culprit in climate forcing, or the induced greenhouse effect. From 1980 to 1990, carbon dioxide accounted for an estimated 55 percent of climate forcing. To stabilize the concentration of carbon dioxide at current levels,

Sources of Global Climate Forcing Based on 1990 Emissions

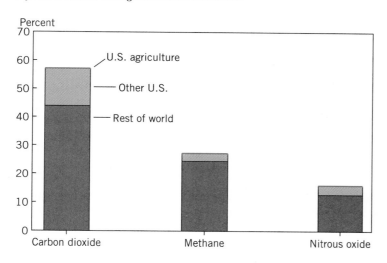

emissions from human activities—largely the burning of fossil fuels—would have to drop more than 60 percent, a highly unlikely prospect.

The more important issue is how these rising concentrations of greenhouse gases will change tomorrow's climate. To answer that question, climatologists and physicists have constructed ambitious computer models called General Circulation Models (GCMs). GCMs quantify the complex processes of the global climate system and are so massive that they can be solved only by running the biggest supercomputers for weeks or months on end. Once constructed, model parameters can be changed to examine the effects of rising concentrations of greenhouse gases. Nearly all projections are based on carbon dioxide concentrations doubling from pre-industrial revolution levels, an outcome that might happen by 2050 if the current rate of greenhouse gas emissions continues.

The United Nations Intergovernmental Panel on Climate Change (IPCC) is widely regarded as issuing the benchmark prediction of future change. Drawing on GCM projections, the panel's 1990 report predicted that a doubling of carbon dioxide would ultimately raise the earth's mean temperature 1.5° to 4.5° C (2.7° to 8.1° F), with 2.5° (4.5° F) the best guess. They also estimate that the earth will warm 1° (1.8°F) by 2030. Along with a rise in temperature, global precipitation would increase 3 to 15 percent.

All of the IPCC projections must be tempered, however, by the many shortcomings of the GCMs that lie behind the projections. The models divide the world into segments roughly the size of Colorado—a scale too big to capture important regional effects. And for agriculture, the regional effects are far more important than global averages. The models do not capture the dynamic interaction between temperature, evaporation, and cloud cover. That is, the models cannot predict whether global warming means more or fewer clouds, a key point in deciding how much sunlight is reflected and how much is trapped. Most important of all, the models do not effectively couple the atmosphere and the oceans, a crucial link in the earth's climate system.

The future climate cannot be predicted with a lot of certainty, but if the IPCC scenario proved true, the change in climate would have a major impact on U.S. agriculture. Higher temperatures might cut crop yields, especially if temperatures were significantly higher during critical periods such as corn pollination. Shifting temperature and precipitation patterns might force regional shifts in production—a northward drift of the corn belt, for example. Increased rates of evaporation would make irrigation more costly and perhaps impractical in many parts of the country, including the Great Plains. But these negative impacts would be counterbalanced by the positive impact of more carbon dioxide available for photosynthesis and new technologies and production practices enabling plants and animals to adapt to the new climate.

The Council for Agricultural Science and Technology (CAST) panel (commissioned by the U.S. Department of Agriculture in 1991) began its work with the premise that the steady enrichment of the atmosphere by greenhouse gases makes warming likely. Whether the global climate will change inconsequentially, change differently among regions, or warm even more in the future, only time will tell. But the responsible course today is to examine how agriculture might adapt to a degree or two of warming.

U.S. AGRICULTURE'S CONTRIBUTION TO THE GREENHOUSE EFFECT

The emission of greenhouse gases is a by-product of agricultural production: carbon dioxide is released when fossil fuel is used to power tractors. Methane is released by rice paddies and by cattle and other ruminants—animals that have more than one stomach enabling them to digest grass. And nitrous oxide is released when fertilizer decomposes in the soil. Contrary to perception, agriculture's emissions of greenhouse gases are small. The CAST panel found that emissions of carbon dioxide, methane, and nitrous oxide from U.S. agriculture comprise only 0.8 percent of global climate forcing by these three greenhouse gases. While cattle and other ruminants are often viewed as major contributors to global warming, in fact, emissions from U.S. ruminants are a very small portion of total climate forcing from methane. Thus, it is clear that strategies aimed at reducing emissions from U.S. agriculture will have a very minor impact on total global warming.

AGRICULTURE'S POTENTIAL CONTRIBUTION IN REDUCING GREENHOUSE GASES

Although ways could be found to cut the industry's emissions of greenhouse gases, the greater opportunity for U.S. agriculture to help mitigate climate change lies in "stashing" carbon in soil and trees and displacing fossil fuel. Stashing is a term for any process that stores or sequesters carbon out of the atmosphere and keeps it out. Agriculture is a unique industry in that it not only emits greenhouse gases, it also stashes carbon. Through photosynthesis, plants and trees use carbon dioxide and in the process store carbon in plants and trees. The consumption or decay of crops and trees returns some carbon to the air as carbon dioxide, but much is stored in timber or as organic matter in soil. (A molecule of carbon stored in a tree that becomes a piece of furniture can be kept out of the atmosphere for a very long time.)

Agriculture can also produce biofuels, fossil fuel substitutes made from renewable crops, such as trees or corn. Ethanol, for example, can be produced from either wood or corn. The advantage of biofuels is that the carbon in them comes from the atmosphere. That is, photosynthesis uses carbon dioxide to produce the corn or trees that yield the biofuel. The carbon in fossil fuels, on the other hand, has been stored in the earth for millennia. When biofuels are burned, therefore, they simply recycle the carbon already in the atmosphere, unlike fossil fuels which release new amounts of carbon into the atmosphere.

The biofuels approach to reducing atmospheric carbon dioxide, however, is not economical today. Under some circumstances, biofuels are economically competitive, but displacing more fossil fuels will require more incentives than current markets provide. To become more feasible, either the price of fossil fuels must rise or the public must be willing to tax their use.

SOURCE: "Agriculture's Portfolio for an Uncertain Future: Preparing for Global Warming," by Mark Drabenstott. *Economic Review*, Federal Reserve Bank of Kansas City, Vol. 77, No. 1, pp. 6–10.

AGRICULTURAL TECHNOLOGY AND DIFFUSION

It is difficult to define *technology*. Sometimes it is considered simply as applied science, implying that procedures developed in laboratories constitute technology when they are used in the more practical situations of the outside world. Sometimes the word is used as a synonym for a set of techniques. Terms such as "primitive technology" and "modern technology" imply ways of doing things in an historical context, "computer technology" implies the general use of computers as a set of tools, and "automotive technology" indicates the set of techniques that are used in building motor cars and trucks. The term "agricultural technology," too, implies a whole series of techniques and processes that are linked by their application to a particular type of production. In general, agricultural technology consists of a series of tools and techniques that effectively enhance the two major factors of agricultural production, land and labor, or even provide substitutes for them, in ways that cause agricultural productivity to increase.

The level of technology in agriculture has grown dramatically over the last 200 years, a very short period by historical standards. American farmers, for example, at the beginning of the nineteenth century had only basic tools: axes and fire for clearing land, rough plows pulled by animals and sometimes people, hoes for tilling, and basic cutting tools like scythes for harvesting. Most of the energy used to operate the day's agricultural equipment was animate. Technological progress, however, was very rapid during the early 1800s. The cotton gin was invented by Eli Whitney at the end of the eighteenth century but came into widespread use in the U.S. South in the early nineteenth century. John Deere first built iron plows with steel blades in 1837, and the McCormick harvester had been adopted by many grain farmers by the 1850s. By the end of the century, gasoline-powered tractors had replaced the steam-driven ones developed earlier, and farm mechanization began in earnest in the United States.

Not all technological advances in agriculture are embodied in machines. Advances in irrigation and drainage practices, for example, are improvements in agricultural technology. And while mechanization was in fact the primary area of technological change in agriculture from about 1800 to 1930, since that time scientific changes seem to have been more important than engineering changes. The development of chemical fertilizers and pesticides, for example, is the result of increased knowledge of biochemistry. Currently, *biotechnology*, or genetic engineering that merges both biology and engineering skills, is being used to improve agricultural productivity in a number of ways. Bacteria have been designed, for example, that can protect strawberry and potato plants from mild frosts; other dead bacteria are being used as pesticides in almost the same way as dead bacteria are used as vaccines in people and animals; and yet other bacteria have been engineered to help legumes such as alfalfa and peas fix soil nitrogen more rapidly in order to increase yields.

Technology is the loophole in the law of diminishing returns. Diminishing returns occur because of an imbalance in factor inputs. If one factor, say land, is fixed in supply, then at some point further additions of labor are not productive. If we can add land, then additional labor will be productive. But the Earth is finite, and the supply of agricultural land is therefore limited—except for the effects of technology. Irrigation and drainage increase the amount of land available for productive agriculture. Pesticides and fertilizer effectively increase land supply by increasing its productivity, and biotechnology does the same. Technology also works on the labor factor. Machinery can be used to increase the productivity of labor or even as a substitute for labor itself. Mechanized agriculture, as a suite of technologies, was largely developed in the United States and Canada where labor was the limiting factor in agricultural production. Both countries have huge land areas, but their populations were relatively small, so machines were developed as substitutes for labor.

All technology has some geographical source, or sources, from which it spreads to other places in a form of spatial interaction called *spatial diffusion*. Agriculture, as a general set of technologies affecting food and fiber production, did not begin all over the world at the same time, but it diffused from its original early starting points over a very long period. Most Western agriculture, for example, can probably be traced to the area around the Tigris and Euphrates rivers in the Middle East as its source region. Modifications have been adopted from other parts of the world, again over long periods of time.

Diffusion is actually a temporal process as well as a spatial one. The rate of adoption of a new technology, or technological innovation, is often characterized as a logistic one (Figure 3.6). Adoption of a new technololgy begins slowly as information concerning its benefits and drawbacks first becomes known in a region. In a second stage, adoption rates increase as information becomes more widely disseminated. Adoption slows down in the third stage as saturation sets in; there is some upper limit to the number of people who can and will adopt the new technology.

Spatially, *contagious diffusion* is marked by distance decay (Figure 3.7). Contagious diffusion is a complex mixture of temporal and spatial changes. In its primary stage, a source of diffusion is established as a technological innovation first develops. An actual diffusion stage then takes place during which the innovation is adopted fairly rapidly at places near the innovation's source. The condens-

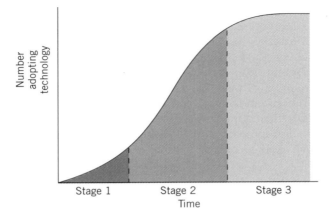

Figure 3.6 The diffusion of a new technology over time is often represented as a logistic curve.

ing stage of the contagious diffusion process then occurs as the rate of acceptance of the innovation in more distant places from the source becomes rapid, but declines nearer the source. This happens because the more distant places are operating at the more rapid growth segment of the logistic curve than the more nearby places where growth is flattening out. The final stage of contagious diffusion is the saturation stage, when all places within reach of the source are at the upper limit of their rate of adoption of the technological innovation.

Physical distance is a barrier to diffusion simply because it frequently corresponds to time. This was more true in the past than today, because modern telecommunications systems allow the virtually instantaneous spread of informa-

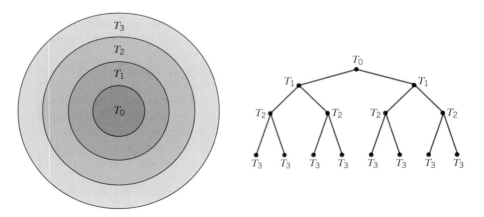

Figure 3.7 Spatial diffusion can be represented as a contagious process as in the left-hand diagram or as a hierarchical process as in the right-hand diagram. In both diagrams, the place marked with T_0 is the origin of a technological innovation, while places that adopt the innovation at later times are marked T_1, T_2, and T_3.

tion around the world. Actual implementation of an innovation takes more time, but knowledge of the innovation is a necessary first step in its diffusion. Distance is less of a barrier to the spread of information in *hierarchical diffusion* (Figure 3.7). As long as communication links are established or as long as other channels of spatial interaction are in frequent use, information can spread rapidly regardless of physical distance. Often, the probability of information spreading along hierarchical lines is a function of the frequency of other contacts between places. Links between Tokyo and New York are well established despite the distance between them, so the diffusion of any new information between the centers can be expected to occur quickly. Links between Tokyo and New Paltz (a small town not far from New York) are thinner, so we might expect New Paltz to receive the new information from Tokyo via a secondary source in New York. A type of hierarchical diffusion strategy is often used to spread the word on better agricultural practices in poorer economies. A general approach is to have an agricultural extension specialist relay information to a limited number of extension agents, who then inform local farm leaders, who in turn inform a number of local farmers in their vicinity. If 1 extension specialist informs 10 agents, 10 agents inform 10 farm leaders each, and each of the farm leaders informs 10 local farmers, the original information will have diffused to 1,000 farmers on a hierarchical path.

TECHNOLOGY AND PRODUCTIVITY

Once they become known, technological advances in agriculture and in other sectors should be adopted in order to increase economic rent. In the case of agriculture, land rent is raised when productivity is increased per unit of land. Fertilizers, irrigation, and the other land-enhancing technologies must lower the average cost of production, like economies of scale, therefore raising rent, or they would not be used. It seems to be a pretty easy decision rule: use a technology if it increases income more than costs; if not, don't. This rule is too simplistic when we consider the adoption of technology in the real world. We have seen that agricultural productivity varies around the world, with the general trend of richer countries having higher levels of productivity than poorer ones. The productivity trend simply reflects the regional incidence of capital-intensive agriculture, which is also intensive in applications of technology. The difference in technological intensity between rich and poor countries indicates that cost is a primary barrier to the widespread diffusion of a number of agricultural technologies. Poorer farmers in poorer countries cannot afford to adopt many technologies, simply because they cost too much up front.

Costs other than financial ones are also incurred when new technologies are adopted, creating significant barriers to the diffusion of new technologies. Applications of new technologies often have spillover effects with environmental and social consequences that are not often completely understood. An often-cited example of the full effects of adopting new technology in agriculture is the *green revolution*—the development of certain high-yielding varieties of cereals by hybridization. This advance began in the 1940s in the richer countries, but it was not diffused widely in the poorer countries until the late 1960s. By the mid-1980s, the effects of the green revolution were fairly widespread on a global basis. Undoubtedly, the most important effect of this technological advance has been the increase in cereal yields it generated. The green revolution's success with respect to productivity gains may have meant the difference between chronic food shortages and surplus cereal production in the world over the last 25 years.

In addition to yield increases, the green revolution has brought about other changes in those countries where capital-intensive production is the norm. The higher yields in agriculture associated with the green revolution require not only the right strains of cereals but also large amounts of fertilizer and often irrigation. In short, green revolution agriculture favors relatively capital-intensive production. It also favors taking advantage of economies of scale that are important in lowering capital costs on a per unit basis. However, because of the traditional labor intensity of production in poor-country agriculture, many farms are small and unable to take advantage of economies of scale. The favorable effects of the green revolution on the production side tend to give the larger landholders the edge over the smaller ones. Many small farmers in poorer countries have been forced to leave agriculture because of their inability to compete with the larger landholders and their new technology. In addition, many farm laborers who did not own land lost their employment as mechanization replaced them on many of the larger parcels that were formed when single smaller farms were consolidated. Environmental problems have also been caused by the green revolution's emphasis on irrigation and fertilizer use in increasing productivity. These practices have caused water pollution and increased use of commercial energy in agriculture.

The social and environmental costs of the green revolution have led to a more serious and comprehensive assessment of new technologies and their effects. *Appropriate technology* improves productivity in a narrow sense of economic efficiency by lowering a producer's financial cost and keeps the social and environmental costs in its application at a stable level.

THE IMPACT OF NATIONAL POLICY

Because of the high costs of agricultural practices associated with the green revolution, many governments in poorer countries have had to subsidize them. By bearing some of the costs of fertilizers and irrigation, for example, governments are investing in their country's agricultural sector by raising its output in particular and the national standards of living in general. Government involvement in agriculture is hardly unique to this particular circumstance. Government policy is an important element of agriculture in almost every country of the world and might even be considered a separate factor of agriculture production. Policy plays a strong role in determining what crops will be planted, how much will be grown, where crops will be produced, and where agricultural production will be consumed.

National farm policy in the United States has traditionally focused on improving farmer incomes. This general policy can be implemented in two ways, which are not always used exclusively. One is to subsidize the costs of farm production; if market prices hold constant, then the lower costs should increase the farmer's income. The other way is to boost prices; if costs hold constant, then the higher prices should increase the farmer's income. Until the New Deal policies of Franklin Roosevelt, federal policy largely concentrated on subsidizing costs. The Homestead Act, for example, provided land to farmers and developed the land grant college system, and the Department of Agriculture subsidized the development and spread of agricultural innovations at very low cost to farmers.

With the New Deal, direct cost subsidies rather than indirect cost subsidies were expanded considerably through the development of farm credit systems that revitalized the financial base of American agriculture. The Farm Security Administration (later called the Farmers Home Administration), for example, provided credit for the acquisition of farmland and related purchases. In addition to cost-subsidizing efforts, agricultural policy was also expanded to affect prices during the New Deal. Voluntary marketing agreements were developed among producers to fix allotments of land for growing particular crops. The allotments, used in tobacco production, for example, were developed to control the volume of production so that prices could be controlled as well. Floor prices were established for certain grains so that producers could count on receiving a preset price for their crops. While specific programs come and go, cost subsidies and price supports have been the backbone of American agricultural policy. (Farm policy in the United States is undergoing revision as this book is being written. New farm legislation, for example, is likely to end the system of subsidies over a period of years.)

The kind of farm policy recently practiced by the U.S. government is fairly typical of the policies practiced by national governments in almost all of the world's rich countries. The incomes of Scandinavian farmers, for example, are made up mostly of subsidies from their governments, and Japanese farm income is about two-thirds subsidy. Canadian farmers receive, on average, about 45% of their income from government subsidies, whereas the average in the United States has been just under one-third. Some countries with highly productive agricultural sectors run counter to the trend. Australia's farmers have incomes that consist of only about 15% government subsidies, and New Zealand's subsidies to its farmers average less than 4% of their incomes. On average, over 50% of farm incomes in the European Union are in the form of government subsidies. The countries in the European Union have a *Common Agricultural Policy* (*CAP*), which consists of a set of subsidies, price supports, and restraints to international trade in agricultural products.

Although cost subsidies and support prices are common features of agricultural policies in the richer countries, they are not common in the poorer ones. Until the 1980s, agriculture was anything but subsidized in most poor countries. Rather than subsidize costs, farm costs were raised artificially by overtaxation and the support of artificially high prices for agricultural tools and other inputs. Rather than support prices, a common policy in poorer countries was to suppress agricultural prices. Governments would establish official prices for agricultural commodities or control prices by acting as the single legal purchaser of output on the farm. These policies were used in the poorer countries to subsidize the consumers of food rather than to subsidize the producers of food as in the richer economies. This subsidy to consumption was also a primary goal of the agricultural policy in most communist countries where agricultural production and distribution were almost completely controlled by the government. During the 1980s, many agricultural policies that suppressed food prices or meant excessive taxation of farmers were repealed, in Sub-Saharan Africa as well as in Eastern Europe, because of their negative effects on farm productivity.

It is ironic that rich countries with high agricultural productivity should support artificially high crop prices and that poor countries with low rates of agricultural productivity should suppress crop prices. The higher support prices tend to encourage excess production, and the suppressed prices tend to lead to deficits in output. The price–supply relationship is illustrated in Figure 3.8. Market equilibrium occurs at the price *PM* and yields quantity *QM*. If the government holds prices higher, at *PT*, then production increases from *QM* to *QT*. If the government suppresses prices to *PS*, it can expect production to shrink from *QM* to *QS*. Remember that a supply curve is also a producer cost curve. As prices rise, more producers can operate profitably, and as prices drop, fewer producers can stay in business.

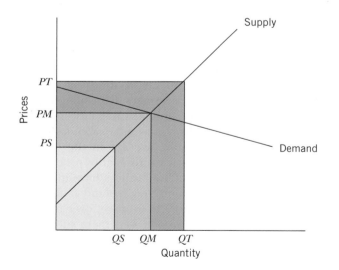

Figure 3.8. *PM* is the equilibrium, or market, price of a good that is determined by the intersection of the supply and demand curves. At that price, quantity *QM* is supplied. If the government supports prices at a higher level such as *PT*, then quantity *QT* is supplied. The difference between *QT* and *QM* is excess supply with respect to the market. On the other hand, the difference between *QM* and *QS* is the shortage that would occur if the government suppressed the price to *PS* from its market level.

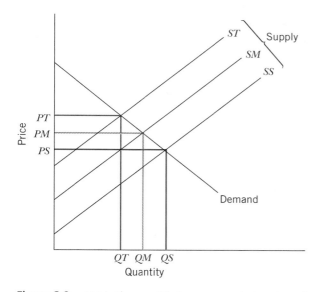

Figure 3.9. *PM* is the equilibrium, or market, price of a good that is determined by the intersection of the supply curve labeled *SM* and the demand curve. At that price, quantity *QM* is supplied. If the government policy is to subsidize costs, a supply shift to the right might take place as represented by *SS*. The new market price is *PS*, as determined by the intersection of *SS* and the demand curve. At this price, quantity produced and consumed rises from *QM* to *QS*. Conversely, if the government taxes agriculture excessively, the supply curve might shift to the left as represented by *ST*. The new price would be *PT* as the quantity produced shrinks from *QM* to *QT*.

This price–output relationship is fairly strong in most types of agricultural production (see Case 3.3, which describes the use of price supports in the American dairy industry). The price supports were instituted in an effort to maintain a balance, or parity, between milk prices and the cost of milk production throughout the year. Often, however, the milk support price program had the unintended effect of encouraging surplus milk production because it guaranteed prices that were higher than average cash expenses of milk production. Sometimes so much milk was produced under the price support program that it created storage problems. Dried milk and cheese were sometimes given to people with low incomes as much to lower storage expenses as to supplement their diets.

There is also irony in the existence of cost subsidies to agricultural producers in rich countries and excessive taxation of farmers in poor countries. As illustrated in Figure 3.9, cost subsidies can lead to increased output at lower direct prices to consumers. A shift in the supply curve from *SM* to *SS* brought about by government subsidies can lead to a drop in prices from *PM* to *PS* and an increase in quantities from *QM* to *QS*. A shift in the supply curve from *SM* to *ST* induced by excessive taxation leads, however, to a very bad thing: a decrease in supply at higher consumer prices.

Government policies toward costs and prices have implications for the amount of land used for agriculture in a country. Some subsidies, for example, are directly used for land purchases, but the effects are mainly indirect. Subsidies and price supports encourage increased production under most circumstances. The increase in production can come about in two ways: more intensive use of existing land and more extensive use of land. Subsidies can generate positive economic rent on land that would not normally be used for agriculture because some production costs are borne by the government and not the farmer. Price supports have the same effect because high-cost land can earn economic rent as long as prices paid for its output are higher still. Excessive taxation and price suppression lead to the opposite outcome. Less land would be used for agriculture under these policy regimes because land rent is reduced. Less intensive use of existing land would not be a reasonable response to these policies, so land abandonment is encouraged.

Shortfalls in food production were never intended as policy goals for agriculture in poor countries. The shortfalls were unintended effects of policy that had other purposes. Food prices were suppressed so that consumers could be subsidized. Farms paid high taxes so that higher rates of investment could be directed toward other industries. Unfortunately, good intentions could go awry in agricultural policy as well as in other areas. Subsidies to irrigation, for example, hurt the competitive capability of farmers who didn't irrigate their land at all. Recall from Chapter 2 that the economic rent of a parcel of land is a function not only of its own productivity but also of its productivity relative to other parcels. If government subsidies are not fully uniform, then their unevenness will affect the economic rent of the farmers in an uneven way.

Agricultural policy also has implications that go beyond the farm sector. One of its unintended effects in most countries has been environmental degradation. Policies that encourage surplus production, in particular, have been found harmful to land and water. Many agricultural policies are now being recast with direct consideration for environmental impact. The European CAP, for example, was reformed in a number of ways in 1992, but some of the most important changes include new emphasis on forest planting on agricultural land and encouragement of less capital-intensive farming practices. Poorer countries are benefiting to some degree from the experience of the richer countries, and the environmental effects of increasing capital intensity in their agricultural sectors are considered as policies are developed.

◪ CASE 3.3
Milk Price Supports in the United States

Throughout most of the history of government milk programs prices have been pushed upward by the rising support price level, and lower dairy incomes in response to price reductions could result in pressure on Congress to raise dairy support levels. Since the mid-1930s, federal, state, and municipal programs have evolved to adjust milk supplies and support prices. The rationale for these controls rests in the seasonality of milk production, which prior to regulatory efforts, caused great volatility in the supply of milk over the course of the year.

In the fall and winter months, both the quality and quantity of feed for dairy cows dwindled; milk production fell sharply below the levels of spring and summer, when high-quality green forage crops are usually more abundant. Thus prices tended to fluctuate with the changes in the volume of milk available: during the spring and summer, farmers typically had surplus milk that was difficult to sell at any price, while prices were high but producers had less to sell in the fall and winter. This volatility led to strong demand for government programs that would cover costs.

Beginning with the Agricultural Adjustment Act of 1935, supplies have typically been regulated through marketing orders that specify the amount of fluid milk producers are entitled to sell during given periods of the year. Since fluid milk deteriorates in storage, surplus production has been relegated to nonfluid uses such as butter, cheese, and nonfat dry milk. These applications usually command lower prices than milk allocated to fluid uses.

To support milk prices the federal government buys milk powder, butter, and cheese in sufficient quantities to keep manufacturing milk at a designated price level. In an effort to maintain a parity relationship between the average milk price and the cost of items dairy farmers purchase to produce milk, the designated price has tended to be set at levels that encourage surplus production.

Until the early 1980s law required the Federal Price Support Program to maintain milk's price between 75 and 90 percent of parity. The parity pricing formula did not take into account the productivity improvements many farmers have been able to achieve over time to cut the relative cost of per-unit milk production. Given greater efficiencies, even support prices set at 75 percent or less parity can return increasing profits to producers.

From 1978 to 1983 support prices exceeded not only cash expenses but total costs as well, greatly increasing the profit incentive to expand output. During this period, government-owned stocks of manufactured milk commodities became burdensomely large. In 1983 inventories of cheese and nonfat dry milk rose to inordinately high levels, and stocks of milk-equivalent dairy products reached 17.4 billion pounds—about 12.5 percent of annual milk production.

Not until the mid-eighties were support prices permitted to decline rather than ratchet upward each year. Though inventories in 1984 and 1985 fell well below 1983 peaks, they were still high enough to warrant the Dairy Termination Program. By early 1988, the support price had fallen to $10.60 (40 percent of parity) from a peak of 13.49 per hundredweight.

SOURCE: ''F.Y.I.—What's Behind Milk Price Movements?'', by Gene D. Sullivan, *Economic Review*, Federal Reserve Bank of Atlanta, January–February 1990, pp. 36–37.

FOR DISCUSSION

The United States had a dairy termination program in the 1980s that reduced milk cow numbers by killing them. Describe the effect of such a program using basic supply and demand curves.

THE ROLE OF EXTERNAL MARKETS

Did you have a cup of coffee or tea this morning or a chocolate bar for an afternoon snack? If so, you were likely participating in the global agricultural economy by consuming an agricultural product that was produced very far away. In Chapter 2, the use and value of land was said to be a function of its proximity to a local market for whatever the land could produce. On general principles, the relationship between land value and market proximity holds, but not all markets are local ones. In a sense, crops face two markets and two sets of prices: local markets and prices and world markets and prices.

Local prices represent the interplay between demand and costs of production in local markets, whereas world prices represent general conditions outside the local economy. In theory, whether an agricultural product will be exported or imported depends on the relationship between local prices and world prices. If the world price is higher than the local price, then the product will be exported, and if the world price is lower than the local price, then the product will be imported. If flows of agricultural products could be as simple as basic theory tells us, then the notion of a "local" market as opposed to a "global" market wouldn't be very meaningful because they would be one and the same thing. (See Chapter 10 for more about flows in international trade.)

The difference between local markets and world markets is real, however, and exists for two basic reasons: transport costs and political-economy. The cost of transportation between places is a primary barrier to any sort of spatial interaction, including trade in agricultural commodities. If a local price is higher than the world price, imports won't take place if the cost of transportation is more than the difference in prices. If consumers pay a local price of $3.50 per bushel of corn and the world price is $3.00 per bushel, they will prefer to import corn from outside the local region. This preference will only be exercised, however, as long as their cost of transporting the corn is less than 50¢. From another perspective, if local farmers are happy to sell corn for $3.00 per bushel while the world price is $3.50, they will only be able to participate in the global agricultural market if they can get their corn to the outside world for under 51¢ per bushel.

The market for agricultural products has become increasingly global because of improvements in transportation. One hundred years ago, for example, the price of an orange in Cleveland, Ohio, was prohibitive for most consumers because of the care required in shipping perishable fruit long distances. Today, oranges can be purchased in Cleveland at fairly low prices because the technology for shipping and otherwise handling them has improved so much that transport charges are no longer meaningful additions to the price of the fruit. The same goes for bananas, coffee beans, coca beans, and just about any other agricultural product. Cotton is grown in one country, spun into cloth in another, and the cloth is sewn into shirts in a third for export back to the country where the cotton was initially grown. Again, the cost of transporting the raw cotton is negligible as a proportion of the cost of the shirt.

While transportation improvements have become a less important barrier to trade in agricultural products, a second barrier to this type of spatial interaction has become more dominant. The integration of agricultural markets that has been facilitated by the lowering of transport costs and such integration leads to lower consumer prices. On the producer side, however, there are losers as well as winners, and this is where the political economy comes into play as the basis of agricultural policy. Earlier we saw that governments affect agricultural patterns greatly through the use of subsidy or taxes and price supports or price suppression. Many of these policies are formed at the urging of special interest groups in a country and not because they are in the best interest of the general population. Agricultural policies are also used to develop barriers to trade that are intended to benefit domestic agricultural producers.

If a country's wheat growers, for example, are high-cost producers, they will prefer that their government limit the importation of wheat so that they won't have to compete with foreign sources of production that operate at lower costs. At worst, such competition could drive them from business altogether; at best it would mean a reduction in their land rent, if it brings about any reduction in prices on the local market. Even if the domestic producers are operating at globally competitive costs, they will prefer a limit on wheat imports simply to maximize their land rents. Recall that if producer rents are high, then consumer surplus must be low; thus, any policy that benefits the limited number of producers will tend to harm the larger number of consumers. The harm to consumers is large in the aggregate but small on an individual basis. Consumers, therefore, tend to be less vocal on agricultural trade protection than the growers who have much to gain or lose on an individual basis.

The sugar industry in the United States provides a good example. American sugar producers are protected by a quota on sugar imports. The quota is a physical limitation on the amount of sugar that may be brought into the United States. The sugar that can enter the country is subject to an import tax called a tariff. The combined quota and tariff barriers recently led to the price of sugar in the United States averaging 21.8¢ per pound while the world price was 15¢ per pound. Sugar producer rents were estimated to be $616 million higher than expected owing to their protection from foreign imports—a pretty sweet deal for the growers.

Not all trade policies benefit domestic producers over foreign ones. Though not directly targeted on agricultural products, some governments keep their currency's international exchange value artificially high. If a currency is overvalued in this way, then that country's products will have higher prices outside the country than inside and exports are discouraged. At the same time, foreign producers would find that their goods are worth more in the country with the overvalued currency than in their own domestic market, leading to more exports to that country. Overvalued exchange rates are like taxes for a country's own producers and subsidies for foreign producers; since they affect prices, they impact the international flow of agricultural products. Undervalued exchange rates, which are difficult to maintain, work the opposite way. Other policies that are used to encourage exports include special forms of financing and extending cheap credit to foreign buyers as well as direct provision of special subsidies to exporters as provided under the European CAP.

Agricultural trade protection in one form or another increased dramatically around the world in the early 1980s. Given that trade in agriculture was about the most protected sort of trade around the world to begin with, the impacts of the increase in protection were significant. The world's poorer countries were the hardest hit by the strengthened trade barriers, and they lost out on markets worth hundreds of billions of dollars. In the 1990s, the trend has been toward reducing barriers to agricultural trade, and this trend has been institutionalized in the recent revision of the General Agreement on Tariffs and Trade referred to as the Uruguay Round. Real free trade in agriculture would require the removal not only of quotas and tariffs, but also of all production subsidies and price supports. Case 3.4 on the regional impacts of free trade in the United States suggests some of the political problems that would occur if these changes took place. The current GATT revision calls only for phasing out export subsidies and replacing quotas on agricultural imports by tariffs. The move toward real free trade in agricultural products around the world remains far in the future, so the distinction between the local market and the world market remains in force.

◪ CASE 3.4
State-by-State Effects of Agricultural Trade Liberalization

According to a USDA study, full multilateral trade liberalization would only slightly reduce overall U.S. agricultural output, but the composition of production would change significantly. Like countries, states are not equally well-suited to produce all agricultural commodities. The profitability of agricultural production depends on natural factors such as soil and climate and on the proximity to large metropolitan centers or transportation.

Current agricultural subsidies and trade protection generally do not affect each state's inherent efficiency characteristics. Rather, these programs merely alter the costs of operation. In most cases, costs have been reduced, permitting some marginally less productive farms to remain in business. In the case of livestock, where trade protection has suppressed demand, marginally efficient ranches may have been pushed out of operation.

According to the USDA study, current subsidies and trade barriers encourage U.S. farmers to overproduce many grains and underproduce pork, beef, lamb, and oilseeds. Multilateral trade liberalization would reduce income from most crops and increase income from most livestock. Because each state specializes in the production of a different mix of crops, changes in income and output would affect each state differently.

Some states already specialize in producing commodities for which multilateral trade liberalization would increase income, but in most states overall farm income would decline. The greatest declines in agricultural income would be in states that produce large quantities of sugar, rice, or other subsidized crops but not much livestock.

In general, the farm economies of most states would realize little or no net effect from trade liberalization if 60 percent or more of the state's agricultural income comes from the production of livestock. Livestock production is important because the greatest increases resulting from free trade would be in producer prices, output, and income from the production of livestock. The reason is because beef producers are among those least affected by the U.S. market distortions currently imposed by farm subsidies and would therefore benefit from the elimination of trade protection. Beef producers also would benefit from a multilateral elimination of protection because it could allow them to sell to more foreign markets.

THE MOST NEGATIVELY AFFECTED STATES

With free trade, fourteen states would reduce agricultural income by 7 percent or more. These states produce large volumes of subsidized or protected crops and low volumes of livestock. Increases in livestock production in these fourteen states would likely not be sufficient to compensate for the reduced production of subsidized commodities.

Hawaii, Louisiana, and North Dakota would have the largest reductions in agricultural income, with declines greater than 20 percent (see Figure). Currently, more than 35 percent of agricultural income in each of these states comes from the production of grains, cotton, sugar, and rice. Producers of these crops receive large subsidies and trade protection that artificially raise income and producer prices. Elimination of farm support and protection would reduce producer prices, output, and income from these crops.

Because sugar production is heavily subsidized and protected, free trade would hurt sugar-producing states, such as Hawaii, Louisiana, Florida, and Idaho. According to USDA estimates, income from sugar production would fall more than 80 percent with free trade, while output would decline more than 40 percent.

Cotton and rice production are also subsidized heavily, and income from these crops would fall 43 percent and 63 percent, respectively, with free trade. Cotton and rice prices would fall significantly because of the loss of support and protection. Producer prices for cotton would fall more than 35 percent, while rice prices would fall nearly 60 percent. Production of rice and cotton would fall about 10 percent. Louisiana would lose income from both of these crops. Reduced cotton income would also affect Mississippi and Arizona, while loss of rice income would affect Arkansas.

The states most negatively affected by free trade also would sustain income losses because of reduced output and producer prices for wheat, corn, and other coarse grains. With free trade, income from wheat production is expected to fall nearly 50 percent. Although wheat output would fall only 5 percent, the loss of government subsidy and protection would reduce producer incentive prices by 45 percent. Corn output would drop only slightly with free trade, but a nearly one-third reduction in producer prices would lower income from the production of corn 34 percent. Loss of corn income would be significant in Illinois, Indiana, and Ohio. Similarly, income from the production of other coarse grains, such as sorghum, oats, and barley, would fall more than 40 percent. Montana and North Dakota would be hurt by the loss of income from wheat and other coarse grains.

Illinois, Indiana, and Ohio also would experience a nearly 10 percent loss in soybean income. A slight increase in the production of soybean output would not compensate for a 12 percent reduction in producer incentive prices.

Not all the large losers fit this pattern, however. North Dakota and Montana would both significantly reduce agricultural income with free trade, despite reasonably large livestock sectors. Livestock production contributes 25 percent of agricultural income in North Dakota and 55 percent of agricultural income in Montana. Free trade would increase livestock production 11 percent, not enough to compensate for the loss of income from heavily subsidized crops such as wheat and other coarse grains. More than 30 percent of agricultural income in North Dakota and 25 percent in Montana comes from the production of wheat. Income losses in Montana would be less severe than those in North Dakota because of Montana's relatively larger livestock sector.

WHICH STATES BENEFIT FROM FREE TRADE?

Free trade would increase gross agricultural income in six states: Colorado, Nevada, New Mexico, Utah, West Virginia, and Wyoming (see Figure). Overall, agricultural producers in these states are currently being hurt by world trade protection and subsidies. Nevada, Utah, and West Virginia produce little or no heavily subsidized crops such as cotton, sugar, wheat, and other coarse grains. Colorado, New Mexico, and Wyoming receive a small amount of agricultural income from subsidized crops. All these states already have large livestock sectors that contribute more than 40 percent of agricultural income. With free trade, these already large sectors would expand and benefit. Currently, beef, pork, and lamb production receive virtually no subsidy, and trade barriers limit U.S. producers' access to foreign markets. Increased foreign demand for beef, pork, and lamb would bolster livestock prices. These increases would more than compensate for rising feed grain prices.

Income from the production of sheep and lamb would increase nearly 25 percent with free trade. Production would increase 9 percent, while producer

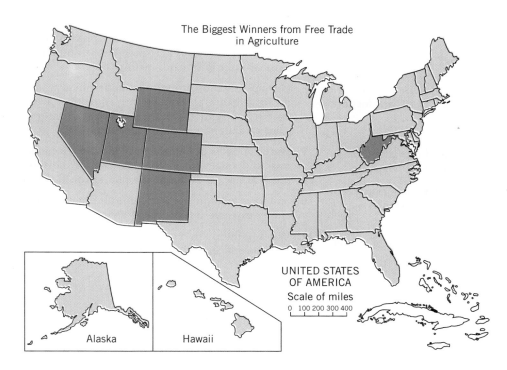

The Biggest Winners from Free Trade in Agriculture

UNITED STATES OF AMERICA
Scale of miles
0 100 200 300 400

Alaska   Hawaii

prices would increase 14 percent. Wyoming and Utah, the largest U.S. producers of mutton and lamb, would benefit. Income from the production of beef would increase 11 percent, and income from the production of pork would rise 8 percent. Both would benefit from moderate increases in price and output. Iowa, Indiana, and Illinois would benefit from increased income from the production of hogs, while Wyoming, Kansas, Oklahoma, Colorado, New Mexico, Texas, Nevada, Nebraska, and Montana would increase income from the production of cattle and calves.

SOURCE: "Regional Effects of Liberalized Agricultural Trade," by Fiona D. Sigalla, *Economic Review*, Federal Reserve Bank of Dallas, Second Quarter, 1992, pp. pp. 47–52.

FOR DISCUSSION

Describe the impacts on land use that can be expected in a country that decreases its farmers' protection from foreign imports.

POINTS IN SUMMARY

1. Agricultural systems include crop types and the environmental, social, economic, and technological contexts in which the crops are grown.

2. Production functions define the relationship between the quantity of inputs to the production process and the quantity of output. They are often simplified to two factors of production: labor and capital.

3. Because of the law of diminishing returns, labor cannot produce much without capital and capital cannot produce much without labor.

4. In general, poorer countries have labor-intensive production functions, and richer countries have capital-intensive production functions.

5. Between 1950 and 1990, the number of people employed in American agriculture declined from nearly 10 million to just over 3 million, but production per hectare more than doubled and total output nearly doubled during the period.

6. Capital-intensive agriculture is also intensive in its use of commercial energy, and it also benefits from economies of scale.

7. Agro-ecosystems are like natural ecosystems in that they consist of a necessary interdependence among a host of physical factors. Unlike natural ecosystems, however, agro-ecosystems would not exist without interaction with people, too.

8. Perhaps the most important single physical factor in agricultural production is climate, or average and extreme conditions of air temperature, solar radiation, and moisture availability.

9. Water budgets use combined measures of moisture and solar energy that encompass the biophysical energy available for plant growth.

10. Soil degradation by agricultural practices includes erosion and chemical change.

11. Water pollution over entire watersheds can result from several agricultural practices, including the use of chemical pesticides and fertilizers.

12. Technological advance is the loophole in the law of diminishing returns.

13. Mechanized agriculture was largely developed in the United States and Canada because labor was a limiting factor in agricultural production.

14. Diffusion is a spatial and temporal process.

15. Fertilizers, irrigation, and other land-enhancing technologies must lower the average cost of production, therefore raising rent, or they would not be used.

16. Government policy plays a strong role in determining what crops will be planted, how much will be grown, where crops will be produced, and where agricultural production will be consumed.

17. Subsidies generate positive rent on land that would not normally be used for agriculture. Price supports have the same effect because even high-

cost land can earn rent if prices paid for its output are higher still.

18. One unintended effect of agricultural policy in most countries has been environmental degradation.

19. Theoretically, whether an agricultural product will be exported or imported depends on the relationship between local and world prices.

20. Recent trends have been toward the reduction of barriers to the international trade of agricultural products.

TERMS TO REMEMBER

agricultural systems
agro-ecosystem
appropriate technology
arable land
biotechnology
capital-intensive
  production
Common Agricultural
  Policy (CAP)

contagious diffusion
factors of production
green revolution
gross national product
  (GNP)
hierarchical diffusion
induced greenhouse
  effect
isocost line

isoquant
labor-intensive
  production
labor productivity
law of diminishing
  returns
natural greenhouse
  effect

nonpoint source
  pollution
physical infrastructure
point source pollution
production function
productivity
spatial diffusion
technology

SUGGESTED READING

Bowler, I. R., C. R. Bryant, and M. D. Nellis, eds. 1992: *Contemporary Rural Systems in Transition, Volume 1. Agriculture and Environment.* Wallingford Oxon, U.K.: C A B International.

This is part of a two-volume publication that arose from a conference on rural geography. This volume contains 18 chapters divided over five general topics, including the changing relationship between agriculture and the environment and the development of agricultural policies.

Crosson, Pierre R. 1991: "Cropland and Soils: Past Performance and Policy Challenges," pp. 169–203 in *America's Renewable Resources: Historical Trends and Current Challenges,* edited by Kenneth D. Frederick

and Roger A. Sedjo. Washington, D.C.: Resources for the Future.

This work addresses succinctly the interplay of natural environment, government policy, and technological change in shaping the agricultural landscape of the United States. It provides an historical perspective on American agricultural productivity that illustrates the impact of post–World War II mechanization on farm output.

Food and Agriculture Organization of the United Nations. 1951–: *The State of Food and Agriculture.* Rome: FAO.

This annual provides an overview of major developments in the world's agriculture over the preceding year. Most issues contain regional reports, discussions of a particular topic such as energy, and coverage of international trends.

Goudie, Andrew. 1995: *The Human Impact on the Natural Environment.* Oxford: Basil Blackwell.

This is the latest edition of an important work that traces the impact of people on their natural environment. Much of this volume concerns the impact of agriculture on natural environments as viewed from an historical perspective.

Gould, Peter R. 1969: *Spatial Diffusion.* Resource Paper No. 4. Washington, D.C.: Association of American Geographers, Commission on College Geography.

An oldie but a goodie, this is the basic primer on spatial diffusion.

Pierce, John T. 1990: *The Food Resource.* New York: Longman.

This work presents a comprehensive examination of agricultural systems around the world. The coverage includes consideration of economic, demographic, and other social concerns of food production as well as agriculture's place in the physical environment. This volume provides an excellent starting point for a thorough examination of contemporary agriculture.

Reitsma, H. A., and J. M. G. Kleinpenning. 1985: *The Third World in Perspective.* Totowa, N.J.: Rowman & Allanheld.

The second part of this book, "The Rural-Agricultural Scene," contains six chapters on agricultural systems in poorer countries and includes a number of case studies.

Shaw, Anthony B. 1985: "Constraints on Agricultural Innovation Adoption." *Economic Geography*, Vol. 61, pp. 25–45.

The article contains a case study of the barriers to the diffusion of green revolution rice varieties in Guyana. Structural and institutional factors are found to be more important than personal ones in affecting the diffusion patterns.

Siddle, David, and Kenneth Swindell. 1990: *Rural Change in Tropical Africa: From Colonies to Nation-States*, No. 23 of the Institute of British Geographers Special Publication Series. Oxford, U.K.: Basil Blackwell.

A survey of Africa's changing agricultural politics, legal institutions, and production systems is placed within the context of economic development theory.

Simmons, I. G. 1989: *Changing the Face of the Earth: Culture, Environment, History* New York: Basil Blackwell.

The fourth chapter of this book is especially pertinent as it provides a discussion of agriculture from the perspective of cultural evolution. It also examines a variety of current agricultural systems in the context of their use of energy.

Turner, B. L., II, and S. B. Brush, eds., 1987: *Comparative Farming Systems.* New York: Guilford Press.

This collection of 14 papers covers the world's farming systems from an integrated perspective of market, environment, and technology.

Visser, Sent. 1982: "On Agricultural Location Theory." *Geographical Analysis*, Vol. 14, pp. 167–176.

This is a technical paper that integrates the Cobb–Douglas production function and the von Thünen land-use model.

Chapter 4

Land-Use Transition, Conflict, and Control

This chapter

- considers the conflicts that arise because of most land potential for multiple uses.
- describes various forms of land tenure and types of property rights.
- develops the implications of externalities for land use markets.

- examines the role of national governments in controlling the way land is used.
- examines the role of regional and local governments in regulating the location of various land uses.

Mimi Forsyth/Monkmeyer Press Photo

In the previous chapter we discussed the role of government policy, particularly at the national level, in guiding agricultural production. Subsidy payments and other types of government policies directly affect agricultural production, and in doing so indirectly affect the way agricultural land is used. One point raised in the discussion of agricultural policies was their tendency to have unintended effects. Other unintended effects of certain actions were also described, such as the rural unemployment in poorer countries that has resulted from the adoption of agricultural practices associated with the green revolution. These actions have such unintended effects, or spillovers, because of the interconnectedness of social and economic pursuits and their context in the physical environment. This chapter concerns the problems of spillovers in most types of land use that can lead to conflicts among potential land users. Many of these land-use conflicts arise because of different views of rights to own and use land. Governments play active roles in setting rules for using land so that land-use conflicts can be minimized. Therefore, political economy is often more important than highest and best use in determining land-use patterns.

COMPETITION FOR LAND

You should recall from Chapter 2 the idea of "highest and best use" of the land. It's any use of the land that has the highest discounted present value. If we think of the land market in an abstract economic fashion, then land-use patterns are generated as patterns of highest and best use in the same way that auctions are settled by the prices people bid. In the model described in Chapter 2, one crop rather than another was grown at some distance from the market because it had the highest location rent. In an urban context, one type of commercial activity, retailing, for example, would occupy a particular location rather than another, perhaps manufacturing, because retailing's superior location rent indicated it was the highest and best use of that particular piece of land. Uses compete for parcels of land and for particular locations through land-location markets, with the highest bidder winning the prize. In the narrow sense of highest and best use, the competition for land is a simple and straightforward process.

Based on the criterion of highest and best use, the way a particular piece of land is used can be characterized as the placing of an investment. Land-use possibilites can be evaluated in the context of potential income streams from possible projects. The project, or land use, with the highest net present value is the best project in which to invest. More often than not, the land-use investment decision will involve a transition from one type of use to another, so the cost of the transition must be reckoned with as a transaction cost. A transition from one type of land use to another may require tearing down buildings, for example, and even so-called vacant land may require significant preparation before entering commercial use. Because of the cost of transition from the current land use to the alternative one, the net present value of the alternative land use must be substantially higher than the net present value of the current one before a land-use change will take place. Transaction costs tend to reinforce current patterns of investment in general because they make change expensive, and transition costs tend to reinforce current patterns of land use.

In addition to transaction costs, other factors affect a change from one type of land use to another. In addition to variations in a property's value based on variations in its possible use, its price also can be affected over time by general conditions in the local real estate market. While the use of a single parcel of land can be viewed in the narrow sense of its highest and best use, real-world competition for land and locations often has broader implications than what type of land use will occupy a particular piece of real estate. The characteristics of a residential neighborhood, for example, or the vitality of a downtown shopping district, can often be traced to certain transactions in the land market. Land-use transitions that result from competition in land markets often have spillover effects and are often affected by local connections with more distant places, as described in Insights 2.2 in Chapter 2.

The shrinkage of agricultural land is a common and controversial land-use transition in many urban regions. The spread of the builtup area of metropolitan regions, called *urban sprawl*, has led to concerns over the decline of local agriculture and other more open uses of land. Urban sprawl is illustrated in Figure 4.1. At the left of that figure, an initial distribution of land between urban and agricultural uses is defined by the intersection of the two bid-rent curves, Urban 1 and Agricultural 1, which dictate a land-use boundary at B_1. If a city's population grows, then the location rent for urban uses can be expected to increase to Urban 2, which would lead to urban encroachment on agricultural land. Now the encroachment by urban land can have two effects on agricultural land use.

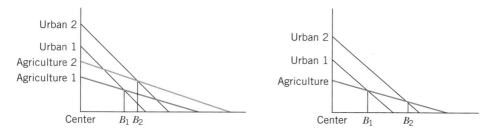

Figure 4.1   The left diagram describes the competition for land between growing urban uses and local agriculture that does not compete with imports from outside the region. An increase in location rents for urban uses leads to an expansion of both urban and agricultural land because demand for food expands the land under cultivation at the edge of the region. The right-hand diagram illustrates the more common result; if local agricultural production competes with imports, then an increase in location rent to urban uses can lead to shrinkage of a region's land in agriculture.

The first is illustrated on the left side of Figure 4.1. There, agricultural land expands because the location rent for agricultural land increases to Agriculture 2. Agriculture's location rent increases because of the need for an increase in food production to serve the growing local population. Even though agriculture's location rent increases, it can't compete with urban uses for land near the region's center, so it expands on the region's periphery. The peripheral expansion can more than compensate for the land lost to urban uses closer to the region's center. The expansion of agricultural land illustrated here, however, would occur only if the region could not import any food.

If food can be imported, then local agriculture has to compete with sources of food outside the region, and its location rent may not be able to adjust upward in response to an increase in the local population. Remember, location rent depends on the price of the product sold at the market; food imports can force the price to remain stable even as local demand grows. This takes us to the second potential effect of urban sprawl on agricultural land. It can shrink, as described on the right side of Figure 4.1. As location rent for urban land grows from Urban 1 to Urban 2, the location rent for agriculture remains unchanged and the built-up area of the region extends from B_1 to B_2 without any compensating extension of agricultural land. Local agricultural land is lost as the city sprawls. In this case, local land-use patterns are not fully "local" in their formation, but hinge on connections with the outside world.

The loss of local agricultural land in the face of urban sprawl can be considered a land-use transition that follows the investment rules described earlier. Wherever agriculture's location rent is lower than the location rent of an urban use, then agriculture's net present value must be lower than the net present value of the urban use. That is why urban uses can encroach on agricultural uses and why any commercial use can encroach on any noncommercial use. Wilderness, for example, is a noncommercial use that doesn't generate any location rent in the conventional sense. Wilderness is a residual land use if highest and best use is the determining factor in land allocation, and it is often best preserved outside of market processes.

As shown in Figure 4.2, the boundary of wild land is usually determined in a market system by the value of commercial land use. Initially, the population of the region may yield a generalized location rent labeled Commercial 1. Wild land begins at that distance from the region's center where Commercial 1 drops to zero. If the region's population grows, or there is any other reason for local demand for commercial products to increase, then commercial location rents may increase to Commercial 2. The increase in commercial location rents leads to an expansion of commercial land use and a decrease in wilderness from Wild Land 1 to Wild Land 2.

Based on the doctrine of highest and best use, it seems that loss of agricultural land and loss of wilderness are actually beneficial since incomes are being maximized because of the land-use transition. The land market appears to allocate land uses to various locations in a rational way. Why, then, should people be concerned about losses of farmland and losses of wilderness? The concern is expressed in many ways but can be boiled down to a fear of failure in the land market. *Market failure* occurs when exchange is based on incomplete information,

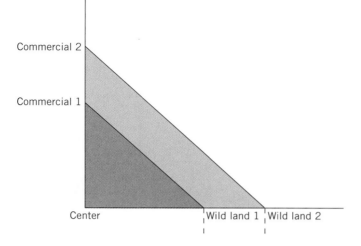

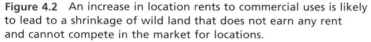

Figure 4.2 An increase in location rents to commercial uses is likely to lead to a shrinkage of wild land that does not earn any rent and cannot compete in the market for locations.

so that costs and prices are inadequately determined. You would think it odd, for example, if Leonardo's *Mona Lisa* were valued in terms of the costs of the paints it contains. Its value, and therefore price, is simply not determined in that way. The loss of agricultural and wild land to urban land uses may be the result of market failure because the net present values of these lands are not calculated correctly. In the case of agricultural lands, their net present values may be underestimated if other sources of food become unreliable in the future. Wilderness may have a net present value that is quite high if many of its individual characteristics are fully considered. You would probably pay for a beautiful view, but because it's free the market tells us its worthless. Land-use transition is often associated with market failure. Comprehensive land valuations are hard to come by simply because land has so many possible uses and not all the uses are mutually exclusive. Any land's potential for multiple uses generates a potential for multiple perspectives on its true value.

LAND TENURE

Land ownership and property rights have critical implications for the way land is used. The models we have looked at so far are based on the implicit assumption that land is privately owned and that the owner holds full rights to the property's use. *Land-tenure systems* are much more variable, however, than is implied by the model. The variety of land-tenure systems is listed in Table 4.1, ranging from

Table 4.1   Types of Land Tenure

Land Tenure
Open access
State tenure—state operated
State tenure—state controlled
Collective tenure
Common property tenure—by custom
Common property tenure—by law
Private tenure—regulated and distributive
Private tenure—regulated and aggregative
Private tenure—regulated in use
Private tenure—unregulated

SOURCE: M. D. Young and O. T. Solbrig, eds., 1993: *The World's Savannas: Economic Driving Forces, Ecological Constraints and Policy Options for Sustainable Land Use*, Man and the Biosphere Series, Vol. 12 (Paris: UNESCO), p. 68.

open access as the least restrictive, or most public, form of land tenure to its most restrictive and least public form: private and unregulated holdings. Both the first and last forms are idealistic. Any open access land is at least nominally owned by a government at one level or another. Furthermore, government always has at least a managerial interest in the use of any land within its jurisdiction, so that any private land is bound to be regulated in some way even if the restrictions on its use are quite minimal. Public safety regulations, for example, that require buildings to be set back a particular distance from a road are a common government-imposed restriction on land use.

The forms of state tenure exist in almost all countries. In the United States, for example, the national parks are in the category of state-owned and state-operated land (state meaning government entity, and not individual states in the nation). National forests fit the category of state-controlled land because private interests can use and even own parcels of land within their boundaries. Farming in the former Soviet Union and most of the other countries controlled by communist parties took place on land that either was owned by the state or held collectively by a group, as in the brigade, or commune, system used in the People's Republic of China until the mid-1980s. Common property tenure differs from collective tenure in that on common land farmers practice as individuals, whereas in collective systems the land's output belongs to the entire membership on an equal basis.

Private tenure systems hold that rights of ownership and use are held by individuals, but that governments have jurisdiction over land use, so that private property rights are effectively limited by the state. Distributive land policies, which call for land ownership across a country's population, primarily in the agricultural sector, favor smallholders over larger ones. Land reform has been a critical issue in the Latin American countries, where an estate system of agriculture called *latifundia* was transplanted from its source in the Mediterranean countries. The breakup of the large estates owned by a few very wealthy people and worked by a large number of fairly poor tenants has been a basic land reform policy of all but the most right-wing governments in the countries where that form of land tenure is common. The resulting smallholdings, called *minifundia*, are usually more productive as private holdings than they were when they were aggregated and worked by sharecroppers or tenants. The same kind of land reform, from estate to smallhold farm, was instituted in Japan during its occupation by the Allies after World War II.

Aggregative policies encourage smallholdings to grow in areal extent, so that economies of scale, for example, can be realized in the interest of improving agricultural productivity. As you should recall, one outcome of the green revolution in many places has been the growth in the size of individual landholdings and a decrease in the number of farmers as a result of government-sponsored changes in agricultural technology. The average size of landholdings is related to dominant forms of land tenure, and, in turn, applications of agricultural technology are often dependent on farm size. British agriculture, for example is more capital intensive than would otherwise be expected because many of its large landholdings were maintained intact by the policy of primogeniture, in which the oldest son has exclusive rights of inheritance. Other offspring had to make their own way under this system, while the family lands were held together under the single ownership of the oldest son.

Because land-tenure systems are part of legal traditions, they exhibit a geographical pattern that is strongly associated with cultural patterns. As mentioned earlier, the latifundia system was transplanted with other Iberian-Mediterranean cultural practices from the Old to the New World. Indigenous land-tenure systems in most of Africa south of the Sahara are collective systems, based on kinship, or common property systems, based on the village. The private tenure system that is typical of the United States and other English-speaking countries is part of the British legal tradition. With the settlement of English-speaking people across the globe, it spread to other areas, such as southern Africa and North America. As described in Insights 4.1, private property is a truly foreign concept in some cultures.

> INSIGHTS 4.1
Extreme Cultural Differences in Systems of Land Tenure

By provisions of the General Allotment Act, the land comprising a reservation, or a portion of such land, could be apportioned among the Indians, each individual receiving a proportionate share. Each share was termed an allotment. Title to this allotment was to remain in the United States Government "in trust." An instrument, termed a "Trust Patent," was to issue, granting to the individual, whose name appeared on the face of the patent the exclusive right to use and occupy the tract described therein. The patent was to provide further that, at the expiration of a twenty-year trust period, the government, if it deemed it was wise so to do, could recall the trust patent and cause a patent in fee simple to issue in its stead. On the other hand, if, for any reason, the government should deem it unwise to permit this second patent to issue, the trust period could be extended. The same idea might have been expressed something like this: Here is a piece of ground which you may make believe is your own; after enjoying this pretense for a period of twenty years perhaps you will come into possession and perhaps you will not.

Like many a plan, devised with excellent intent solely for the benefit of the Indian, this act did not produce the expected results. It was conceived in an erroneous idea of the value that an Indian placed on ownership of land. Few of the Indians of that period had any interest whatever in the ownership of a small portion of the earth's surface. They did not think of land as something to be possessed by an individual. They considered land much as the white man considers the high seas. The white man insists that he has the right to traverse the seas to his heart's content and to remove from its waters any of its denizens. But he would have little interest in some small area of the ocean that had been set aside as his individual allotment. No more did the Indian prize individual ownership of a small portion of the earth's surface.

Several years subsequent to the enactment of this statute, being in charge of the Uinta and Ouray jurisdiction in Utah, I was endeavoring to interest Red Cap, an old war chief of the White River band of the Ute tribe, in his allotment. The old man became very angry, "You say this little piece of land is mine!" he said. "You do not know what you are talking about." Then, sweeping his arm in a circle entirely around his head, he added, "Everything is mine. This whole land is mine. You look down and see everywhere the tracks of white men, but under these tracks are the tracks of my people. It is all mine. You lie, when you say that only this little piece is mine."

SOURCE: *Indian Agent*, by Albert H. Kneale (Caldwell, Id.: Caxton Printers, 1950), pp. 107–108.

RIGHTS OF STAKEHOLDERS

Land-tenure variations are not important only in rural situations. Homelessness, which now seems endemic in American cities, can be considered a function of the predominant disposition toward residential private property in the United States. Public shelters are always viewed as temporary, and the use of government-owned public housing is diminishing in favor of rent or purchase subsidies that can be employed in private property markets. In many poorer countries, most cities have large populations of squatters that live in semipermanent housing on public land. The system is effectively one of common property for residential rather than agricultural purposes. In industrial countries, too, squatting seems to be evolving as a form of land tenure. Almost any vacant building in any city now seems to be viewed as a potential residence by many groups, and government often accords this residential use some rights that compete with the rights of the actual owner of the property.

The idea that users of a piece of property can have rights to its use that are distinct from the owner's rights was not developed by urban squatters. Part of this distinction comes from the separation of the land as property from what passes over it. In northern lands, for example, the general population's free access to large tracts of private land is a common tradition. Open access to wild, but private, land in the North Woods of Maine and in Scandinavia is widely held as a right. The tradition seems to be tied to hunting; the deer and other game that travel across the land are viewed as public property that cannot be constrained in any way by private land interests. In another northern country, Scotland, trespass is not even considered a criminal act, but rather a matter for the civil courts.

In addition to rights of access, other rights have been recognized that are effectively property rights that don't require actual ownership of land. People have a right to earn a decent livelihood, for example, and that right may require that land be used in a particular way. People also have a right to a clean environment as part of their right to good physical health. Because water and air pollution that occur at particular sites can easily affect other locations that are some distance away, landowners cannot pollute their own properties with impunity. People also have an increasingly recognized right to a visually pleasing landscape. Again, this right affects the way land is used by its owner, so private property rights are subordinated to public rights of land use if restrictions are imposed.

Because rights to use of the land go beyond conventional property rights, there may be many stakeholders in a piece of land in addition to its owner. Case 4.1 illustrates the variety of stakeholders in a large, fairly remote, piece of land around the Owyhee Canyon. The land in question is used as rangeland for grazing, as recreational land, and even as a corridor for the transmission of electricity. The land's stakeholders are local people, people passing through, and people who live away from the land and may never see it (those who use the electricity). Some uses of the land are seasonal, and some are ongoing through the year. There are likely as many views of the appropriate way to value the land as there are land uses and maybe even land users. Although the government owns and manages most of the land considered in the case, there are also multiple stakeholders in private lands.

As access to land increases, so do the number of stakeholders in its use. The Interstate Highway System was expanded into the North Woods of New York, Vermont, New Hampshire, and Maine at about the same time that the woods products industry in the region developed its own system of roadways. The industry's roads restored access to its own forest lands that had been cut off by new laws against logging drives on waterways, and opened new access to other woodlands. Recreational demand increased dramatically as the huge urban population of the U.S. Northeast took advantage of the new convenience of the semiwild woods for vacations and second homes. At the same time that highway technology changed the landscape's accessibility, changes in financial appraisal of the forest resources of the region as productive assets also took place, and state and federal governments undertook a wholesale reassessment of land use in the North Woods as a resource.

The North Woods region is now viewed as a comprehensive set of land uses that goes beyond easy single-use definitions. In addition to standard land uses associated with the wood products industry, the current land-use inventory of the region includes historical sites and places of particular importance to recreation. Public policy decisions are now supported by a *geographic information system* (*GIS*) that has been designed to store a series of spatial databases in digital form, integrate their information as appropriate, and provide analysis as well as display of geographical relationships of all the land uses in the North Woods. As land-use issues broaden, GIS has become a vital technology for land management in a large variety of contexts (Insights 4.2).

> ➤ INSIGHTS 4.2
The North Woods Inventory

The Northern Forest Resource Inventory (NFRI) is a state-based program designed to assist states in the gathering of natural and economic resource information, largely from existing data sources. The purposes of the inventory are to: (1) assist state land conservation work; (2) establish an information baseline; and (3) provide a clear picture of the forest resource and the economy that relies upon it. The information gathered provides a factual basis for discussion and analysis of land conservation issues and policies in the Northern Forest. It will provide the framework for private sector and government applications beyond the life of the NFLC (Northern Forest Lands Council).

The inventory is Geographic Information Sytem-based. A Geographic Information System is a computer system capable of storing and using data describing places on the earth's surface. A GIS is more than a tool to make maps. It is a tool that allows the user to perform complex spatial analyses that integrate databases containing information about locations on the earth's surface. For example, emergency service providers can use GIS to identify the shortest routes to an incident. Shortened response times can save lives and reduce property damage.

OPERATIONAL PROCESS

Each state is responsible for carrying out the inventory in a manner consistent with the ''Operating Procedures, Standards, and Guidelines'' report. The four state coordinators, working in concert with a state technical working group, developed the approach for each state's inventory. An outside contractor worked with the coordinators, state Geographic Information Systems administrators, and other technical personnel to develop the technical standards for the inventory. State coordinators are responsible for technical and financial oversight of the NFRI project.

The inventory project began in late summer of 1991. During the first year the states concentrated on automating base map features. The finalization of the "Operating Procedures, Standards and Guidelines" report allowed work to continue in an orderly fashion. By the end of 1994, all states will have finished, or be very close to finishing, the highest priority data layers: base maps, public and private conservation ownerships, land habitat, cover and use, population densities, and elevations. New Hampshire and Vermont will likely complete their full inventories by the end of 1994. Due to funding and staff constraints, Maine and New York are less likely to complete the inventory by that time, although all funds have been committed to ongoing or scheduled projects.

USES OF THE DATA

Geographic Information Systems provide an efficient framework to store, manage, and exchange information about locations on the Earth's surface. The information automated as part of the NFRI will enable the private sector and all levels of government to make more informed decisions about land use, facility siting, service delivery, and other matters.

The base map information automated as part of the NFRI is of particular importance. The accuracy of analyses using all other databases depends upon an accurate link between information and a particular spot on the Earth's surface, using latitude and longitude, or some other coordinate system. The base map data layer is, and will continue to be for the forseeable future, of universal utility.

States will be responsible for the management, updating, and future uses of NFRI data. States are already using the automated data in a number of ways. For example, Maine's Land Use Regulation Commission is using elevation, land use guidance, and other data to evaluate the impact of a large-scale windpower project. Graphic displays of the information can assist the public in evaluating the potential impact of policy changes affecting forest lands. Such displays may also help to indicate the level of protection accorded the region's natural resource base.

SOURCE: Northern Forest Lands Council, 1994: *Finding Common Ground: Conserving the Northern Forest* (Concord, NH: Northern Forest Lands Council), pp. A11–A14, A57–A58, and A60.

◪ CASE 4.1
Multiple Use in the Owyhee Canyonlands

DESCRIPTION

This environmental impact statement (EIS) assesses the environmental consequences of managing all or portions of eight wilderness areas (WSAs) totalling 446,067 acres and 4,205 acres of adjoining non-WSA lands as wilderness or nonwilderness. The WSA are clustered along the high sagebrush desert plateau

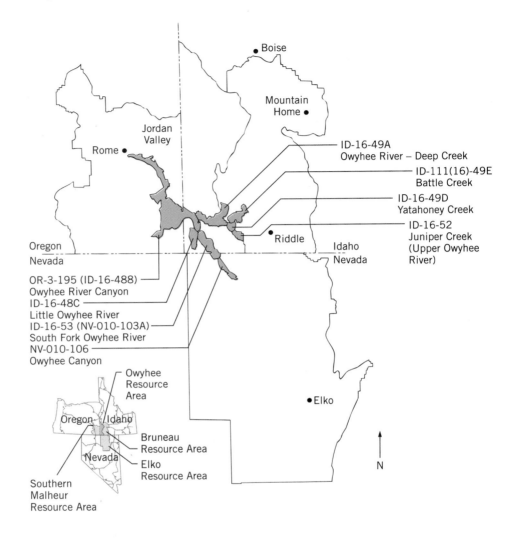

and canyonlands of the Owyhee River system where the three states of Oregon, Idaho and Nevada join (see map). The WSAs contain 124 miles of the Owyhee River from Highway 95 in Oregon to the Duck Valley Indian Reservation in Idaho and 45 miles of the South Fork Owyhee River in Idaho and Nevada.

PURPOSE AND NEED

The purpose of the Proposed Action is to manage and preserve wilderness characteristics on 377,560 acres (including 2,275 acres of non-WSA lands) as part of the National Wilderness Preservation System and to manage for uses other than wilderness on the remaining 70,782 acres of WSA lands and 1,930 acres of non-WSA lands. There are few designated wilderness areas in the Intermountain Basin of the western United States and they are generally in the mountainous areas adjacent to the desert and semi-desert regions. The Proposed Action would provide a relatively large desert area with opportunities for wilderness experiences not yet available in the National Wilderness Preservation System in this region.

SCOPING AND ENVIRONMENTAL ISSUE IDENTIFICATION

In December 1982, over 1,800 individuals, organizations, and agencies were contacted to determine their concerns with the Owyhee Canyonlands Wilderness Study. As a result, 211 comments were received prior to the preparation of the draft EIS. A total of 517 written and oral comments were received during the review period on the draft EIS in 1984. Additional comments were submitted by agencies in 1985. The scoping process identified the environmental issues listed below that were selected for detailed analysis in this final EIS.

ENVIRONMENTAL ISSUES SELECTED FOR ANALYSIS

Impacts to Wilderness Values

The wilderness values of naturalness, opportunities for solitude, opportunities for primitive recreation, and special features (bighorn sheep and cultural resources) within the WSAs could benefit from wilderness designation. The same values may be adversely affected by uses and actions that would occur should the WSAs not be designated wilderness. The significance of beneficial or adverse impacts on wilderness values is an issue for analysis.

Impacts to the Condition and Amount of Native Vegetation

The Owyhee Canyonlands WSAs support a sagebrush-bunchgrass ecosystem where species composition and ecological condition was historically dependent on natural fires prior to livestock use. Livestock grazing practices and limited natural fire occurrence have resulted in a change in the amount and ecological condition of native vegetation. Wilderness designation or nondesignation could affect the type and amount of vegetative treatment undertaken to change the species composition of plant communities primarily for the benefit of livestock grazing. The significance of beneficial or adverse impacts to the condition and amount of native vegetation is an issue for analysis.

Impacts to the Level of Selected Wildlife Populations

The Owyhee Canyonlands WSAs support a diversity of wildlife species which are dependent upon the relatively undisturbed habitats found there. Wilderness designation or nondesignation could affect the amount of habitat modifications which could occur. The degree of habitat modifications could affect species populations and distribution. The wildlife species of primary importance in the area and those that are selected for detailed analysis are mule deer, pronghorn antelope, sage grouse, and redband trout. The significance of beneficial or adverse impacts to these wildlife populations is an issue for analysis. California bighorn sheep are also found in the area and are addressed as a special feature of wilderness value.

Impacts to the Level of Semi-Primitive Motorized Recreation

The Owyhee Canyonlands WSAs are used for semi-primitive motorized recreation activities. Recreation use is primarily associated with hunting activities and to a lesser extent sightseeing and rock (gemstone) collecting. Wilderness designation would affect the continuation of motorized recreation access into the WSAs and could result in changes in the amount and type of recreation activities in the area. The significance of impacts to semi-primitive motorized recreation is an issue for analysis.

Impacts to the Level of Livestock Use

Grazing use is managed through grazing systems and rangeland developments including reservoirs, springs, fences, seedings and vegetative manipulation. Wilderness designation could impact livestock levels by precluding potential range developments designed to increase livestock use or improve range condition and by restricting the level of livestock use allowed. The significance of impacts to the level of livestock grazing use is an issue for analysis.

Impacts to the Level of Soil Erosion

Wilderness designation or nondesignation could affect the level of soil erosion by changing the level of livestock use and the extent of vegetation treatment projects. Soil erosion could also be affected by mineral and energy related activities. The significance of impacts to the level of soil erosion is an issue for analysis.

Impacts to Water Quality

Wilderness designation or nondesignation could affect water quality by changing livestock use levels and the extent of vegetation treatment projects. Water quality could also be affected by mineral and energy related activities. The significance of impacts to water quality is an issue for analysis.

Impacts to Local Income and Jobs

The Owyhee Canyonlands WSAs provide income and jobs to the local communities of Oregon, Idaho, and Nevada through livestock grazing use and recreation use. Wilderness designation could impact jobs and revenues generated by different types and amounts of recreation use. The significance of impacts to local income and jobs from changes in livestock and recreation use is an issue for analysis.

Impacts to Overhead Transmission Line Development in Nevada

The Elko Resource Management Plan identifies five-mile wide planning corridors (for future use) to the south and to the east of NV-010-106. These planning corridors, which run east-west and north-south beyond the boundaries of the WSA, allow for construction of overhead high-voltage electric transmission lines to accommodate future energy needs. For analytical purposes it is projected that without wilderness designation, the east-west five-mile wide planning corridor would traverse and occupy the southern one-third of WSA NV-010-106 and would allow for overhead transmission line construction through this WSA. No other powerline construction is projected in this vicinity in the forseeable future. The projected transmission lines would be constructed through WSA NV 010-106 in all alternatives except for the all wilderness alternative. In the All Wilderness Alternative, the transmission lines would be routed around the WSA in order to accommodate possible future energy transmission needs. The impact that routing these transmission lines around WSA NV-010-106 in Nevada would have on the utility industry is an issue selected for analysis. This issue is only analyzed in detail in the All Wilderness Alternative since the transmission lines would be routed through the WSA in all other alternatives with no impact on the industry.

SOURCE: *Owyhee Canyonlands Wilderness Final Environmental Impact Statement*, 1989 (Boise District Office, Bureau of Land Management, U.S. Department of Interior), pp. I1–I4.

FOR DISCUSSION

Should stakeholder priorities with respect to land use be established? For example, should uses that generate employment take priority over recreational uses?

EXTERNALITIES

In addition to accessibility, the number of stakeholders in a piece of property also depends on the geographical extent of the positive and negative spillovers that develop because of the way the land is used. These spillovers can be defined as either costs or revenues that are generated by a particular land use but affect people beyond the land's boundaries. Such spillovers fall under the heading of externalities. *Positive externalities* yield income to people for actions taken by others, whereas *negative externalities* impose costs on people because of actions taken by others. In the case of land use, one parcel's use can impose costs on the users of neighboring parcels, or it can add to the income generated by other parcels. Household real estate markets provide an example. If your neighbor's house is run down and the yard littered with trash, it will decrease the selling price of your house. The difference between the price you would normally expect and the lower price you receive because of the condition of your neighbor's property is a cost imposed as a negative externality. On the other hand, if your neighborhood is especially well-kept owing to a high density of compulsive residents, then the sales price of your house would be higher than normally expected, with the difference in revenue due to a positive externality. The boundary problems of national parks can easily be characterized in the context of externality because land use outside the parks affects the quality of the land inside them.

The geographical extent of externalities is most often marked by distance decay, as illustrated in Figure 4.3. The left diagram shows the distance decay in the negative externalities imposed by a hypothetical landfill. The closer you are to the landfill, the greater is the concern over water pollution from leakage, odor problems, noise of operation, and so on. These things have a decreasing effect with distance, so that any negative effects of the landfill on property prices disappear at the distance indicated. The right-hand diagram shows the same sort of distance decay in the positive externalities generated by a public park. Recreational opportunities and views of open land decline with distance from the park, and their positive impact on property prices also disappears at some distance.

A single parcel can generate both positive and negative externalities. A public park, for example, can provide benefits during the day but impose costs at night

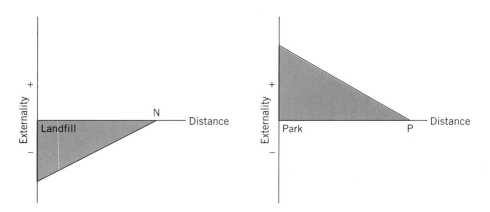

Figure 4.3 The incidence of a spatial externality is often marked by distance decay. The left diagram illustrates a decrease in the negative spatial externality that might be associated with a landfill. The effect of the externality is strongest near its source and declines toward zero at distance *N*. The right-hand diagram indicates that the positive externality of a park undergoes distance decay to distance *P*.

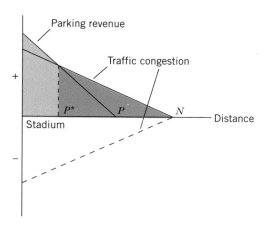

Figure 4.4 A single source may yield both positive and negative spatial externalities. Here, a stadium generates both negative and positive externalities on households in the neighborhood. Negative externalities such as traffic congestion decrease with distance from the stadium to point *N*, and the positive externality of parking revenue decreases to point *P*. The difference between the negative and positive externality gradients is the net externality effect. Positive net externalities dominate to distance *P** in the diagram, and net negative externalities dominate from *P** to *N*.

as nasty people are attracted to its unlit areas. A single parcel of land even can generate positive and negative externalities at the same time, as illustrated in Figure 4.4. Say you live very close to the University of Michigan's football stadium in Ann Arbor. Every Saturday that the Wolverines play a home game in the fall, you can expect a serious onset of traffic congestion as more than 100,000 fans descend on the stadium. The traffic congestion imposes costs on you, especially if you are not interested in the game, because your mobility is limited. On the other hand, because of your house's proximity to the stadium, you are able to earn over $100 in fees charged for parking on your lawn. This income is a positive externality of the game because nobody would pay to park on your lawn on any other day. The difference between the two externality gradients is the net externality. In this case, there is a positive net externality from the stadium to distance *P**, net negative externality from distance *P* to *N*, and no externality effect beyond distance *N* from the stadium.

   If the University of Michigan paid a fee to people surrounding the stadium to compensate them for their loss of mobility caused by the football game, then there would be no definable negative externality. It would be paying the cost it imposes on others by its use of the stadium. In turn, if homeowners turned over their parking revenues to the school, then a positive externality would no longer exist. The University of Michigan would be receiving all the revenues that are generated by the use of the stadium, even those earned beyond the stadium's boundary. Payments, therefore, provide the linkage between externalities and property rights.

A famous proposition in economics that concerns this linkage is the Coase theorem. It states that the initial distribution of property rights has no bearing on the use of the property because its use will ultimately be acquired by the person who values it the most. As stated by R. H. Coase in *The Firm, the Market, and the Law* (1988, p. 157), ''Whether a newly discovered cave belongs to the man who discovered it, the man on whose land the entrance to the cave is located, or the man who owns the surface under which the cave is situated is no doubt dependent on the law of property. But the law merely determines the person with whom it is necessary to make a contract to obtain the use of the cave.'' Coase's theorem may be applied in a number of land-use contexts. If the costs imposed by a negative externality become extreme, a market will be established so that the externality, as an unpaid cost or unpriced benefit, will be eliminated. For example, if water pollution becomes too severe, the polluter will be paid not to pollute. In effect, the right to pollute will be purchased from the polluter. The type of land trusts established by a number of conservation organizations around the world are examples of Coase's theorem at work. In order to maintain the environmental benefits of certain land parcels, the property source of the benefits—land—is simply purchased outright.

Libertarians have suggested that governments, in light of Coase's theorem, overstate problems of externalities as an excuse to unnecessarily intervene in markets. Externalities of land use, for example, are frequently cited as the basis for zoning and other forms of land-use restriction (see the following section). Under Coase's theorem, however, negative externalities will be bought off, and the benefits associated with positive externalities will be purchased outright. Land-use zoning is unnecessary because, theoretically, private property markets will provide any compensation required for costs to one property owner raised by the actions of another property owner. The only drag on the process is transaction cost. If transaction costs are high, externalities remain because the total purchase price of an externality's source can exceed the social cost or benefit of the externality. If transaction costs are high, government intervention may indeed be necessary, even under Coase's theorem, to prevent a loss to one property owner from the actions of another. It would be difficult, for example, for a few households that are injured by water pollution to buy a whole factory that is dumping waste in the stream that runs through their properties.

GOVERNMENT MANAGEMENT OF LAND USE

In order to limit the impact of negative externalities, most governments believe that the public interest is served if they try to control their impacts. In controlling these impacts, the conflicts that arise owing to the imposition of externalities can be mitigated in an orderly way. In short, externalities arise because of market failure, and governments offer alternative mechanisms to markets in the effort to reduce their negative effects. This generalization holds for externalities associated with land use, and governments at every level around the world—national, regional, and local—have developed land-use management policies of one type or another. Even international land-use management programs have been developed, such as the international network of biosphere reserves coordinated by the United Nations.

National land-use policies in the United States can be divided into two broad classes. The first class concerns land that is owned outright by the federal government, and the second concerns land owned by other levels of government and by private interests. Most of the land owned by the federal government is managed by one of two cabinet departments. The Department of Interior manages most of the federal lands in the United States through three separate agencies: the Bureau of Land Management, the National Park Service, and the Fish and Wildlife Service. The Department of Agriculture, through the U.S. Forest Service, also manages a significant amount of the federal lands. Most federally owned land is in the western part of the United States.

Although the management of federal lands has always been a matter for debate, it has become more contentious over the last 20 years as environmental concerns have become more widespread. The guiding concept of federal land managment, as directed by the U.S. Congress, is *multiple use.* Given that the market cannot determine highest and best use of the public lands, the multiple-use concept states that the government should not play favorites but should instead allow competing uses to share stakes in the land. Mining, grazing, and recreational uses, for example, have been allowed to share the public lands, except for those officially designated as wilderness (see Case 4.1).

When environmental concerns were more limited, multiple-use principles could be maintained fairly easily because the uses were not in direct conflict with each other. Recreational use of national forest lands was displaced by logging, for example, but it was not eliminated. Moreover, logging, grazing, mining, and even recreational use can seriously degrade certain habitats, even to the point of elimination. Species preservation does come into direct conflict with other uses, and this and other environmental considerations have led to a call for rethinking the multiple-use concept.

Some people have suggested that environmental degradation would be reduced if the federal government did not subsidize commercial use of the public lands. They point to the low fees paid for grazing rights and mining rights on public lands and the subsidy provided to the forest products industry in the form of roads built on national forest lands. If costs were raised to market levels, then the subsidized overuse of the federal lands would be eliminated and environmental preservation would be more easily accomplished. Because the government has replaced the market on these lands, however, their allocation to various uses is not determined by economics. Instead, their use is based in political economy, and the commercial users form powerful interest groups for maintaining the status quo. They argue that environmental preservation is not worth the loss in employment that would occur if their subsidies were eliminated, but their primary interest is in maintaining the healthy producer surpluses generated because their costs of production are reduced under the current system.

Over the last 25 years, most of the federal policies affecting the use of land not owned by the U.S. government have been directed toward environmental preservation. Some of the policies have been directly targeted at land use, such as regulations concerning surface mine reclamation and coastal zone management. The Food, Agriculture, Conservation, and Trade Act of 1990 authorized the Department of Agriculture to withhold benefits from farmers who converted wetlands to croplands after November 1990. It also contained provisions for two major land-use programs: the Conservation Reserve Program, designed to facilitate wildlife habitat restoration on farmland, and the Wetlands Reserve Program. In addition to those policies aimed directly at land use, other environmental policies, such as those affecting endangered species and water and air quality, have effects on the way land can be used.

The United States is not, of course, the only country with environmental land-use policies. According to data compiled by the World Bank, countries

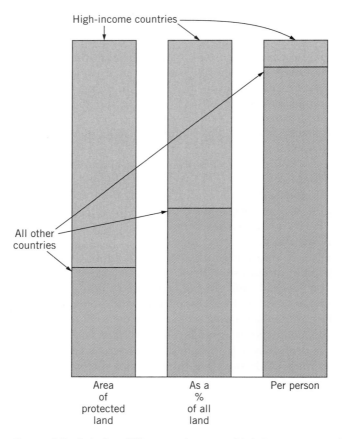

Figure 4.5 Relative differences between high-income countries and the rest of the world in amount of protected lands.

around the world have placed an average of 52 square kilometers of their land under protection for ecological reasons. Environmental protection is often viewed as a luxury that can only be afforded in richer countries, and the average area enjoying protection is much larger in the high-income countries than in the rest of the world (Figure 4.5). The gap diminishes, however, when the area protected is considered in proportion to a country's total area, and it almost disappears when protected areas are considered on a per person basis.

Increasingly, concerns about the environment are being treated as basic components of land-use policies that are integrated with economic and social factors. Part of this comprehensive approach to national land-use management that is now being taken up around the world was described at the UN Conference on Environment and Development, held in Rio de Janeiro in 1992 (Insights 4.3).

Below the national level of government, regional governments often exercise land-use controls. Regional governments often have goals for their land-use policies that are similar in scope to those of national governments, but also often have additional policies that are developed for their specific circumstances. Rhode Island, for example, has general policies on land use that are probably consistent with the policies of most American states (Insights 4.4). In addition, it has specific concerns for coastal zone management, and perhaps urban sprawl, that are due to its particular geography. California may have the most comprehensive array of environmental and land-use regulations of any state in the nation, including its own specific regulations on surface mine reclamation and special air quality standards. The rigor of the state's policies may be the result of its experience of rapid population growth in and near areas of special environmental concern.

➤ Insights 4.3
An Integrated Approach to the Planning and Management of Land Resources

BASIS FOR ACTION

Land resources are used for a variety of purposes which interact and may compete with one another; therefore, it is desirable to plan and manage all uses in an integrated manner. Integration should take place at two levels, considering, on the one hand, all environmental, social, and economic factors (including, for example, impacts of the various economic and social sectors on the environment and natural resources) and, on the other, all environmental and resource components together (i.e., air, water, biota, land and geological and natural resources). Integrated consideration facilitates appropriate choices and trade-offs, thus maximizing sustainable productivity and use. Opportunities to allocate land to different uses arise in the course of a major settlement or development projects or in a sequential fashion as lands become available on the market. This in turn provides opportunities to support traditional patterns of sustainable land management or to assign protected status for conservation of biological diversity or critical ecological services.

ACTIVITIES

Governments at the appropriate level, with the support of regional and international organizations, should ensure that policies and policy instruments support the best possible land use and sustainable management of land resources. Particular attention should be given to the role of agricultural land. To do this, they should:

a. Develop integrated goal-setting and policy formulation at the national, regional and local levels that takes into account environmental, social, demographic and economic issues;

b. Develop policies that encourage sustainable land use and management of land resources and take the land resource base, demographic issues and the interests of the local population into account;

c. Review the regulatory framework, including laws, regulations and enforcement procedures, in order to identify improvements needed to support sustainable land use and management of land resources and restrict the transfer of productive arable land to other uses;

d. Apply economic instruments and develop institutional mechanisms and incentives to encourage the best possible land use and sustainable management of land resources;

e. Encourage the principle of delegating policy-making to the lowest level of public authority consistent with effective action and a locally driven approach.

Governments at the appropriate level, with the support of regional and international organizations, should review and, if appropriate, revise planning and management systems to facilitate an integrated approach. To do this, they should:

a. Adopt planning and management systems that facilitate the integration of environmental components such as air, water, land and natural resources, using landscape ecological planning or other approaches that focus on, for example, an ecosystem or a watershed;

b. Adopt strategic frameworks that allow the integration of both developmental and environmental goals; examples of these frameworks include sustainable livelihood systems, rural development, the World Conservation Strategy/Caring for Earth, primary environmental care and others;

c. Establish a general framework for land-use and physical planning within which specialized and more detailed sectoral plans (e.g., for protected areas, agriculture, forests, human settlements, rural development) can be developed; establish intersectoral consultative bodies to streamline project planning and implementation;

d. Strengthen management systems for land and natural resources by including appropriate traditional and indigenous methods; examples of these practices include pastoralism, Hema reserves (traditional Islamic land reserves) and terraced agriculture;

e. Examine and, if necessary, establish innovative and flexible approaches to program funding;

f. Compile detailed land capability inventories to guide sustainable land resources allocation, management and use at the national and local levels.

SOURCE: United Nations Conference on Environment and Development, 1992: *Agenda 21*: *Programme of Action for Sustainable Development. Rio Declaration on Environment and Development, Statement of Forest Principles* (New York: United Nations), pp. 84–86. ◄

> ➤ **INSIGHTS 4.4**

Rhode Island's Policies for General Land Development

Policies are numbered for ease of reference and do not reflect priorities.

1. Conserve natural resources and areas.

2. Preserve and enhance the distinctiveness of urban, suburban, village, and rural communities and landscapes.

3. Control urban sprawl and scatteration.

4. Develop residential, commercial and mixed-use areas which are compactly grouped, attractive, and compatible with the ability of land and water resources to support the development.

5. Use open space to control and shape urban growth.

6. Relate the use of land to its natural characteristics and varying suitability for development.

7. Relate the use of land to the level of public facilities and services available or planned to be available.

8. Promote the establishment of higher residential densities and smaller lot frontages in urban and suburban areas, and town centers, where public water and sewer service is present or planned.

9. Promote low overall densities where public services are unavailable and are not planned. Promote the clustering of development in these areas.

10. Protect and enhance those values of the coastal region, including scenic values, which contribute to the quality of life of the people of the state. Examine proposals for changes in the coastal region in terms of their importance to the state-as-a-whole.

11. Prevent filling of coastal and inland waters and wetlands except when necessary to the health or welfare of the people of the state and there is no other alternative.

12. Limit the use of land along the coastline and shores of inland waters to water dependent uses, or to mixed-use development in which a water dependent use is combined with other uses. Clarify land uses as "water dependent" and "non-water dependent" according to their characteristics and need for adjoining a water body in order to perform their basic functions.

13. Guide development in a manner that will prevent encroachment on floodways, dunes, barrier beaches, coastal and freshwater wetlands, and other natural features that provide protection from storms, flooding, and sea-level rise.

14. Preserve historic buildings, districts and archeological sites.

15. Encourage development patterns that promote energy efficiency and help attain state air quality objectives.

16. Encourage development patterns that protect water resources.

17. Identify and seek to protect and expand greenways of state, municipal, and privately-owned protected land.

18. Achieve a livable, coherent, and visually pleasing environment.

SOURCE: Division of Planning, 1989: *Land Use 2010: State Land Use Policies and Plan*, State of Rhode Island and Providence Plantations, State Guide Plan Element 121 (Providence: Rhode Island Department of Administration), p. 3.2.

AGRICULTURAL LAND-USE PRESERVATION POLICIES

States in the United States have been particularly active in developing and implementing policies targeted at maintaining land in agriculture and other rural and open space uses. Problems arise in rural land-use preservation for reasons described in Chapter 3. Most urban land uses, including housing developments, have higher present values on land near population centers than do agricultural uses or other rural ones (Figure 4.1). The crunch comes in two ways. First, anyone holding land in agriculture (or any other use) that could earn higher returns if used in a different way is incurring opportunity costs. They are effectively losing money even if their farming operations are profitable. Second, property taxes are *ad valorem taxes*—that is, they are based on the value of the land. The market value of the land is derived from its highest and best use. In many rural situations, the highest and best use and the current use of the land are not always the same. Because the highest and best use is more valuable than the current use, property taxes can be significantly higher than the current land use can bear.

Let's consider a hypothetical situation in which there are two plots of land next to each other, both consisting of 160 acres. Let's say that the price of land in agriculture is $1,000 an acre and that price holds for both plots at some starting point. If the property tax rate is 1% per year, then each farmer pays 1% of $160,000, or $1,600 per year in property taxes. Let's say Farmer Brown sells out to a developer who puts a shopping center and some apartment buildings on that plot of 160 acres. The market value of the developed land could be 20 times its value as farmland. Based on principles of highest and best use, the value of the land remaining in agriculture is pushed up by the growth in value of the neighboring parcel that is developed. An assessor might easily argue that if the fully developed land is worth $20,000 per acre, exclusive of buildings, then the neighboring agricultural land is worth $15,000 per acre. By *ad valorem* taxation, the property tax on the land remaining in agriculture would increase from $1,600 per year to $24,000 per year. In a purely economic sense, the higher tax is just because the market value of the land has increased. It's very difficult, however, for Farmer Jones to keep the land in agriculture and pay the tax.

Farming often faces a liquidity crunch, or lack of cash on hand, because funds are tied up in land. Even a rich farmer, in terms of total assets, may be strapped for the kind of cash that is due at tax time. In order to pay taxes, the farmer has to sell land. (This is also a problem when estate taxes are due. Land bequests often have to be liquidated in order to pay federal and state inheritance taxes.) The land isn't sold to other farmers in these circumstances because they would face the same problem. The land is sold to developers who can pay the taxes because they convert the land from its current use to its highest and best use. If the government wants to maintain land in its current rural use, then it must implement policies that alleviate the opportunity cost of withholding land from its highest and best use and that alleviate the tax differential between current uses and highest and best use. Several policies have been developed that facilitate the maintenance of open and agricultural lands. Most of the programs require cooperation between state and local governments.

One method is *agricultural zoning* which designates certain areas of land as being limited to agricultural production alone. If agriculture is the only use allowed, it becomes the highest and best use possible so that property taxes are reduced to a current-use basis. This type of single-use zoning also eliminates any opportunity cost imposed by the current use because no other uses of the land are allowed. The down side of all this is that it also does away with any chance of earning significant capital gains on the land should the owner eventually wish to do so. The farmer can never sell to a developer at a high price because the land can't be developed.

Another method of preserving particular land uses is the imposition of *use-based taxation* on targeted land rather than *ad valorem* taxation. These programs usually are limited in time, so that a farmer may pay taxes on current use over five- or seven-year periods. During that time, the farmer has a contract with the state, or a more local jurisdiction, not to develop the land in any way. The contract is enforced through a lien on the property covering the value of the foregone taxes during the period. There are often additional penalties for early withdrawal from such programs. These programs are most effective when states reimburse local governments for taxes lost to the program, but most local governments also find that farmland pays for itself even at lower tax levels because its low density of use requires little in the way of local services.

Tax abatement programs like those just described are only temporary measures for preserving rural land uses because landowners can convert their land to other uses when the period of the agreement ends. These programs are popular with landowners because they don't eliminate the potential for capital gains the way that agricultural zoning and other single-use zoning policies do. A policy that provides both tax reduction and the effective realization of capital gains at the same time that rural land uses are preserved is the *purchase of development rights*, as illustrated in Case 4.2. Based on the hypothetical prices given earlier, if land in agriculture is worth $1,000 per acre and is worth $15,000 developed, then the development rights are worth $14,000 (at least on paper). If a farmer sells the farm's development rights to the state, the land can no longer be developed, but the farmer has gained in the same way as if the land were sold to a developer. In addition, once the development rights have been sold, the land's highest and best use is in agriculture or other current use, so the property taxes are lowered as well. Such programs are costly but effective because they offer permanent solutions to land preservation problems that do not penalize the current landowner in the long run. In addition to state and local programs in the United States, the federal government has recently started a program to purchase development rights to privately owned forest land. Called the Forest Legacy Program, its purpose is to maintain geographically integrated tracts of forested land in places threatened by urban growth.

Preservation of forest land is also the intention of agroecological zoning in the Brazilian state of Rondonia. Unlike the situation in the United States, the Brazilians are concerned about the encroachment of agriculture on the rain forest. Zoning plans take into consideration the physical potential for agricultural productivity, as well as the land's special ecological or social characteristics. About 20% of the state's land has been set aside for its indigenous people. Additional policies concerning land tenure, agricultural subsidies, and regional transportation improvements have been designed to support the zoning policy. Outreach programs have also been established to educate recent migrants to the area about the importance of preserving the rain forest.

◪ *CASE 4.2*
Agricultural Land Preservation in Lebanon, Connecticut

LEBANON—"If I stopped to talk with everyone who comes to look at this place, I'd never get anything done," the 74-year-old farmer said.

Still Kalmon Kurcinik is clearly proud that his land is so eye-catching that people stop to take photographs or just gaze at the vista.

"You don't see places like mine much anymore, with ponds like that. I take good care of it. I keep it clean," he said. "When people come here, they generally come back again."

In fact, over the last three years, representatives from the state Department of Agriculture's Farmland Preservation Program have made a number of visits to the 170-acre farm on Bog Lane, off Kick Hill Road.

Those visits resulted in an offer to buy the development rights to Kurcinik's land in order to ensure the farm will always be used for agriculture.

On Dec. 10, Kurcinik's farm was one of three properties approved by the governor and the State Bond Commission for purchase of development rights.

Kurcinik will be paid $480,000—$3,200 an acre for 150 acres of the farm's total of 170 acres.

In return, a covenant will be placed on the property and filed with the land records, preventing it from ever being subdivided or used for anything other than agriculture, according to Joseph Dippel, director of the Farmland Preservation Program.

The farm is full of memories for Kurcinik, including wintertimes when he'd plow the ice on the man-made ponds so family, friends and neighbors could skate. "I'd make a nice wood fire and put out hay bales so they'd have a place to sit and warm themselves," he recalled.

He also remembers Saturday nights at the Echo Grange in Mansfield where he'd go for square dances, "after dark, when the work was all done." Although he had plenty of dancing partners, Kurcinik remained a bachelor.

"I built the house I live in. It's not a big house, but it's plenty big enough for me, and it will probably stand for a long time," he said proudly.

"I must have been a year-and-a-half when my parents moved here. Over the years we made a living. . . . We kept working, working, working and got the damned place going. But then I was left alone," Kurcinik said.

The family raised dairy cows but now the land is primarily farmed for hay for other farmers.

Kurcinik said he has mixed feelings about his agreement with the state. "It took me a long time to make up my mind. Does it feel good? I don't know. In a way, I feel like I don't own the place anymore," he said.

At the same time, he's seen a lot of farms disappear, replaced by housing subdivisions, including land directly across the road, he said.

"Used to be a lot of milk produced here in Lebanon, but not anymore," he said. "A lot of them have given it up. They've sold their land for building lots, that's pretty good money. Farmers, when they get a little bit older, they say the heck with it."

Although Kurcinik is still allowed to sell the land, or bequeath it to someone else after his death, the restrictions will also apply to the new owner, Dippel said.

"The object of the program is to preserve the state's land resource base so land is available forever for farming," Dippel explained.

The state approached Kurcinik about his farm partly because it neighbors another farm already preserved by the program, Dippel said.

"Kurcinik's farm abuts what was Oliver Manning's farm. It's a 280-acre dairy farm. It's been sold to Robin Chesmer, who has a productive dairy herd on it, and he rents a piece of property for hay from Kurcinik," Dippel said.

"We try to work where there's still a strong farming community and where there are support services, like feed and tractor dealers, and where there are good farm soils. We try to cluster farms together in that respect. In eastern Connecticut, we still have a strong dairy community," Dippel said.

"The price paid for development rights to a property is calculated by deducting its value as agricultural land from the fair market value, the price the land would sell for without restrictions," Dippel said.

"The next step is to survey the property, then the attorney draws up documents and holds the closing—we'll probably close in five of six months—then (Kurcinik) is paid," Dippel said.

"Throughout Connecticut, 154 farms—totaling 23,535 acres—are part of the program," Dippel said. The program celebrated its 15th anniversary this year and the goal is to preserve 140,000 acres.

SOURCE: "Popular Panorama Preserved for Posterity," by Brenda Sullivan, *Chronicle* Staff Writer, *The Chronicle*, December 29, 1993, pp. 1, 11. By permission of *The Chronicle* and Brenda Sullivan.   ◪

FOR DISCUSSION

What unintended effects might agricultural land preservation policy such as the one described in this case have on land markets for residential and other commercial uses?

OTHER LAND-USE POLICIES

In the United States, local governments seem to be more involved with managing land use than is any other level of government. The single most commonly used method of management is land-use zoning. Land-use zoning is a power granted to local governments in every state in the nation, although not every local government uses it. Land-use zoning can be classified in two basic ways. In the first, *single-use zoning* can be contrasted to *multiple-use zoning*. An example of single-use zoning is the agricultural zoning described earlier, where no other uses than conventional farming are allowed. Multiple-use zoning, on the other hand, allows alternative land uses as long as they are compatible. A local jurisdiction, for example, may have multiple zoning for agricultural and low-density residential uses. The other classification is *cumulative zoning* versus *noncumulative zoning*. Cumulative zoning is hierarchical: single-family residential zones preclude all other uses, multiple-family residential zones include single family zones, and so on. At the bottom of the heap, land zoned to allow heavy industrial use could also be used for any other purpose. In contrast, noncumulative zoning is exclusive. Either a single-use or multiple-use classification precludes any other use of the land.

The difference between cumulative and noncumulative zoning may be traced to different explanations for using zoning in the practice of managing land use and land markets. One rationale is the reduction of the impacts of negative externalities. Cumulative zoning is based on this rationale; heavy industry does not suffer from negative externalities imposed by other uses of nearby land, so any other use in its zone is permitted. Single-residential use, however, can be negatively affected by any other use, so no other uses are permitted in single-residence zones. The other rationale for zoning is that the land market is inefficient owing to the inability of some uses to compete for certain locations. The uncompetitive uses are the residual ones, most often housing and agriculture, that would only occupy areas not wanted for more competitive land uses. Zoning in this context is a way to preserve selected parcels for targeted uses. Making the zones noncumulative preserves the zone from competition with other uses, regardless of potential externality effects, so that land is more affordable. The agricultural zoning described above accomplishes this goal for farming, and its application to housing is illustrated in Figure 4.6. The bid rent of excluded uses in any zone is effectively zero, so the targeted land use is automatically the highest and best.

In some places, Houston, for example, land-use covenants take the place of zoning regulations. Covenants are restrictions on land use that are written into titles and deeds, as described in Case 4.2. They are also used as additions to zoning regulations in some places because they are applied to individual properties. Other methods adopted by local governments in managing land include subsidies that promote certain uses. Tax abatements or construction cost sharing are common forms of subsidies to land uses found desirable by the government but not provided by the market in sufficient amounts. As illustrated on the right-hand of Figure 4.6, subsidies provide boosts to otherwise uncompetitive bid rents that allow a targeted land use to compete in the land market.

Some land-use management programs involve governments in the taking of *exactments* from certain land users. One type of exactment, designed to preserve open space in housing developments, is described in Insights 4.5. Exactments

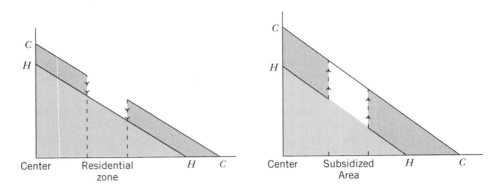

Figure 4.6 The effect of zoning on the land market is illustrated in the left diagram. The bid-rent line *CC*, representing commercial interests, has a gap in it where it corresponds to the area zoned for housing. In the zone, housing, represented by bid-rent line *HH*, is the highest and best use of the land because competition is prohibited. An alternative to zoning would be to subsidize housing or any other targeted land use. As illustrated in the right-hand diagram, the effect of a subsidy is to raise a bid rent up to competitive levels.

usually involve the establishment or preservation of an uncompetitive land use as a requirement for permission to proceed with a land development project. Sometimes, however, they affect the design or operation of the project itself so that it yields some perceived public benefit. For example, permission for an office building to be erected may be contingent upon its developer setting some land aside on the property for a small public park. In concept, the use of exactments requires that a development yield some positive externality.

Insights 4.5 describes an unintended effect of state and local land-use policy. Neither the town of Mansfield nor the state of Connecticut intended to limit the financing of land development projects by exacting open space set-asides or affordable housing units as requirements for developing housing subdivisions. Such unintended effects, however, are common results of land-use management programs. Consider the two primary intended effects of zoning: the reduction of negative externalities and the provision of affordable land for selected and otherwise uncompetitive uses. Zoning programs that severely limit the location of fairly undesirable uses tend to cause those uses to become concentrated in limited areas. Because of their concentration, their externality effect is much greater than if they were dispersed in many locations around a metropolitan area. A concentration of undesirable uses can serve as the core of a large area that is perceived as undesirable. The intention of reducing negative externalities may therefore have the unintended effect of shifting and concentrating them in particular places. Zoning programs that are designed to intervene in property markets and lower land costs for particular uses are very effective in their intended result. They are also fairly effective in the unintended result of raising land prices for every other use. For example, every program that zones or otherwise devotes an acre of land to agriculture reduces a region's available stock of real estate for every other use by the same amount. Because agricultural land is threatened most often by conversion to use for housing, agricultural preservation programs often have the unintended effect of driving up local housing costs.

Critics of government land-use policies often cite their unintended effects as reason enough for less policy and more reliance on the market for allocating land use. They believe that the land-use market is more efficient than government policymakers would have the public believe. They also believe, like Coase, that the impact of negative externalities is highly overstated and is more an excuse than a true reason for government intervention in the land market. In addition, critics of government land-use policy in the United States often cite constitutional reasons for severely limiting any intervention by the public sector in the land market. An extreme position on this issue is that of the *county supremacy movement* in parts of the western United States. Proponents of this view argue that the U.S. Constitution does not expressly describe the role of the federal government in owning land or even its management. The Constitution does, however, state explicitly that any powers not held by the federal government automatically belong to the states or people (Tenth Amendment). Accordingly, federal lands in the United States are held unconstitutionally, and any land-use policy that affects them or any other land is unconstitutional as well.

A more commonly used appeal to the U.S. Constitution as the basis for limiting government land-use policy, at all levels of government, is the final phrase in the Fifth Amendment, "nor shall private property be taken for public use, without just compensation." The important terms here are "public use" and "just compensation." When highways are built, for example, land is appropriated for public use, or "condemned," by eminent domain (the ultimate right of government to control land), and a fair market price is paid to the land's owner. Zoning and other land-use regulations are different, however, because the land in question is not purchased outright by a government body. Although the value of the land is often altered by the restrictions on its use, the owner is not compensated for any decrease in property value. This lack of compensation is referred to as a *taking* by many people who feel that such restrictions are unconstitutional. The value of a taking can be determined simply by comparing the present value of a property's highest and best use and the present value of the use to which it is restricted. Case 4.3 describes a probable case of taking by the federal government, one that would likely have been found unjust in a federal court. Most court actions involving so-called takings are not as clear cut, however, because the government's interest in restricting a property's use is most often a legitimate one intended to enhance the general welfare. Again, because land often has many stakeholders, property "rights" tend to be very complex.

> INSIGHTS 4.5

Conflicting Policies and Unintended Effects

MANSFIELD—A state law that was supposed to encourage towns to build affordable housing hasn't worked very well in this town.

The two-year-old law gives developers a break from land use laws that require giving a town a certain percentage of land—to be preserved as open space—if they offer to set aside 20 percent of their subdivision's units as affordable housing.

The law is supposed to promote building more affordable housing. The reasoning is that having to give the land to the town raises the cost of developing the remaining lots.

However, banks have proved unwilling to offer mortgages for homes that can only be sold to those who meet state guidelines for affordable housing. And so, the houses don't sell, say the developers.

Last week, Mansfield's planning and zoning commission approved a motion to "reluctantly" release the developers of The Crossing at Eaglebrook on North Eagleville Road from such an agreement.

After months of discussion, the developers' lawyer, Sam Schrager, convinced the PZC and town council that local banks won't finance the three lots designated for affordable houses. The town council agreed to accept about an acre of land, pending the PZC's agreement to remove the affordable housing restriction.

PZC members criticize that state law as "poorly drafted legislation," because it pits two desirable elements of a community against each other, affordable housing and open lands.

Schrager says the problem is compounded in Mansfield where the PZC adds a restriction requiring these homes to remain affordable, by state guidelines, permanently.

The restriction is meant as insurance, to keep developers from slipping out of the deal at some point in the future. "Otherwise, the town permanently loses the open space as well as the affordable housing," PZC member Steve Lofman said.

SOURCE: "Affordable Housing Effort Backfires," by Brenda Sullivan, *Chronicle* Staff Writer, *The Chronicle*, August 12, 1994, p. 3. By permission of *The Chronicle* and Brenda Sullivan.   ◄

◪ CASE 4.3
I'm from the Government, and I'm Here to Help You

WASHINGTON—Gaston Roberge's quiet $338,000 Christmas-season real estate settlement with Uncle Sam should spread cheer—and hope—to thousands of property owners involved in regulatory disputes with government agencies across the country.

Blind in one eye, 81 and a victim of several heart attacks, Roberge stood his ground and in mid-December got the Justice Department to do what legal experts say has never been done before: agree to pay big bucks for a "temporary regulatory taking" of a citizen's free use of his real estate. Here's his story— something akin to Kafka does Christmas. Back in 1964, Roberge and his wife, Monique, bought 2.8 acres in the coastal town of Old Orchard Beach, Maine.

The idea, he said, was to hold onto the property—just 300 feet from the sea—"as an investment for our retirement years, when we wouldn't be earning anything."

In 1975 and 1976, the town installed a new sewage system and with the Roberge's permission, dumped some excess fill from the job on a low-lying section of the Roberge's land.

Fast forward to 1986. New England's economy was in full boom, and a home builder approached the Roberges with a tantalizing proposition: He'd give them $440,000 for their 2.8 acres. The Roberges said yes.

Then their nightmare began. The Army Corps of Engineers informed the builder that the lot was a "wetland" under its legal jurisdiction and that the land had been illegally filled. The Corps ordered that all the fill from the mid-1970s had to be cleaned out—a procedure that would cost between $50,000 and $100,000.

The builder said no thanks and backed out of the $400,000 contract. The Roberges, meanwhile, were stunned.

"No one here had even heard of the Corps of Engineers having anything to do with land in this town," he recalls. "And we certainly never thought of our property as a 'wetland.' "

In fact, the Corps received regulatory jurisdiction over property like the Roberge's lot in July 1977—well after the fill had been brought in by the town.

Gaston Roberge was now determined to do whatever was necessary to make the land salable, so he spent $50,000 on soil experts, lawyers and other consultants to make a formal application for what the Corps calls an "after-the-fact" permit.

In 1991—three years after Roberge first applied for the permit—the Corps rejected his request. It told Roberge, now in his late 70s and short of cash, that before anyone could use the land, he'd have to remove the 28,000 square feet of fill the town left there back in 1975 and 1976.

Roberge could have simply thrown in the towel at that point. But he said "I was really angry. I knew that this was completely unjust." He decided to keep fighting.

This time he contacted Peggy Reigle, head of a national grass-roots organization called the Fairness to Landowners Committee, based in Cambridge, Md. She in turn brought in a prominent Washington environmental lawyer, Stanley W. Legro, a former top enforcement administrator for the Environmental Protection Agency, and Bernard N. Goode, an engineer based in Burke, Va. who formerly headed the Corps of Engineers' regulatory office.

In the face of all this technical and legal expertise, the Corps backed down. By October 1992, it admitted that it had no legal jurisdiction over the Roberges' lot in the first place. The Corps' letter offered no explanation, no apology, no compensation for its actions during the prior six years. But the Corps said the property was now "free" of the earlier entaglements—it could be sold without removing the fill.

Great. The only problem was that from 1986 to 1992, New England's—and especially Maine's real estate market had gone into free fall. Not only was there no builder around who'd pay $440,000 for the lot, there was "nobody who wanted to buy anything," says Roberge.

So with the help of his legal and technical team, Roberge filed suit in 1992 in the U.S. Court of Federal Claims. He charged that the U.S. government, acting through the Corps, had unjustly taken away much of the economic value of his property. The case went to trial this October and was heading for a decision.

But for reasons the Justice Department declined to discuss, it decided not to wait for the results. In the spirit of the season—and perhaps to avoid a far more generous cash award to the long-suffering Roberges—the Feds offered $338,000.

The Roberges said yes.

SOURCE: "Taking on Uncle Sam—and Winning," by Kenneth Harney, *The Hartford Courant*, January 29, 1995, pp. J1, J2. By permission of the *Hartford Courant*.

FOR DISCUSSION

This is a case of obvious abuse of government power to intervene in land markets. What methods, ranging from nonintervention to outright purchase, would you consider as appropriate for government to use in controlling land markets?

POINTS IN SUMMARY

1. The highest and best use of the land is that use with the highest present value.

2. There is an opportunity cost if the current land use is not the highest and best use.

3. Because of transaction costs, the net present value of an alternative land use must be substantially higher than the net present value of the current one before a land-use change will take place.

4. Wherever one land use's location rent is lower than the location rent of another use, its net present value must also be lower.

5. Market failure occurs when exchange is based on incomplete information so that costs and prices are inadequately determined.

6. Comprehensive land valuations are hard to make because land has many possible uses, and not all the uses are mutually exclusive.

7. Conventional land-use models are based on the implicit assumption that land is privately owned and that the rights to the property's use are held fully by the owner.

8. Systems of private tenure hold that rights of ownership and use are held by individuals, but that governments have jurisdiction over land use so that private property rights are effectively limited by the state.

9. The average size of landholdings is related to dominant forms of land tenure in a region.

10. Users of a piece of property may have rights to its use that are distinct from the owner's rights.

11. The number of stakeholders in a piece of property depends to some degree on the geographical extent of the positive and negative externalities that develop because of the way the land is used.

12. The Coase theorem states that the initial distribution of property rights has no bearing on the use of property because its use will ultimately be acquired by the interest that values it the most.

13. If transaction costs are high, externalities persist because the total purchase price of an externality's source can exceed the social cost of the externality.

14. Externalities arise because of market failure, so governments offer alternative mechanisms to markets in the effort to reduce their negative effects.

15. Most federal lands in the United States are managed for multiple use.

16. Some people have suggested that environmental degradation of federal lands would be reduced if the government did not subsidize their commercial use.

17. If the government wants to maintain land in its current rural use, then it must implement policies that alleviate the opportunity cost of keeping land from its highest and best use and that alleviate the tax differential between current uses and highest and best use.

18. The government's purchase of the landowner's development rights provides the landowner both tax reduction and the effective realization of capital gains at the same time that rural land uses are preserved.

19. There are two primary intended effects of zoning: the reduction of negative externalities and the provision of affordable land for selected and otherwise uncompetitive uses.

20. Although the value of the land is often altered by government-imposed restrictions on its use, the owner is not often compensated for any decrease in property value.

TERMS TO REMEMBER

ad valorem tax	geographic information system (GIS)	multiple use	purchase of development rights
agricultural zoning	land-tenure system	multiple-use zoning	single-use zoning
county supremacy movement	latifundia	negative externalities	taking
cumulative zoning	market failure	noncumulative zoning	urban sprawl
exactment	minifundia	positive externalities	use-based taxation

SUGGESTED READING

Bowler, I. R., C. R. Bryant, and M. D. Nellis, eds. 1992: *Contemporary Rural Systems in Transition, Volume 2. Economy and Society.* Wallingford Oxon, U.K.: C A B International.

This is part of a two-volume publication that arose from a conference on rural geography. This volume contains 20 chapters divided over five general topics, including social change in rural areas and the development of recreation and tourism in the countryside.

Coase, R. H., 1988: *The Firm, the Market, and the Law.* Chicago: University of Chicago Press.

This book summarizes much of Coase's work that led to the award of his Nobel Prize in economic science. The conservative nature of this work is typical of the Chicago School of economics.

Graf, William L. 1990: *Wilderness Preservation and the Sagebrush Rebellions.* Savage, Md.: Rowman & Littlefield.

The key word in the title is the plural one. Graff is a physical geographer who has written as fine a cultural history as any human geographer, or anyone else, could. His focus is the politics of land use in the American West that led to "rebellions" against the irrigation, forest, grazing land, and wilderness policies of the federal government.

Healy, Robert G. 1985: *Competition for Land in the American South: Agriculture, Human Settlement, and the Environment.* Washington, D.C.: The Conservation Foundation.

This volume describes the competition and the competitors for land in the southern United States. It considers the way land is used by competing interests in agriculture, forestry, and settlement.

Kneale, Albert H. 1950: *Indian Agent.* Caldwell, Id.: Claxton Printers.

Kneale worked for the U.S. Bureau of Indian Affairs (BIA) for more than 30 years and played a leading role in the development of commercial agriculture on Native American reservations in the West. In addition to the details of irrigation projects, Kneale provides a very critical appraisal of the BIA's management and its politics.

Mason, Robert J. 1992: *Contested Lands: Conflict and Compromise in New Jersey's Pine Barrens.* Philadelphia: Temple University Press.

Mason begins by describing the development and current state of regional planning in the United States and then details the tensions affecting regional and environmental planning in maintaining the integrity of the pine barrens.

Northern Forest Lands Council. 1994: *Finding Common Ground: Conserving the Northern Forest.* Concord, NH: Northern Forest Lands Council.

This volume contains a list of the problems affecting the northern forest in Vermont, New Hampshire, New York, and Maine, and summarizes their solutions. Unfortunately, the work leaves the impression that it was commissioned by the region's paper and lumber interests.

Platt, Rutherford H. 1991: *Land Use Control: Geography, Law, and Public Policy.* Englewood Cliffs, N.J.: Prentice Hall.

The author is a lawyer as well as a geographer and so is equipped to bring special insight to the general problems of land use and its control by governments.

Wallach, Bret. 1991: *At Odds with Progress: Americans and Conservation.* Tucson: University of Arizona Press.

This may be the most interesting book concerning land use ever written. The author understands much about the relationship between land and people, and he also knows about Maine's Route 11.

Wright, John B. 1993: "Cultural Geography and Land Trusts in Colorado and Utah." *Geographical Review,* Vol. 83, pp. 269–279.

This paper argues that cultural predispositions toward land preservation explain the geographical patterns of land trusts in the United States.

Young, M. D., and O. T. Solbrig, eds. 1993: *The World's Savannas: Economic Driving Forces, Ecological Constraints and Policy Options for Sustainable Land Use.* Man and the Biosphere Series, Vol. 12. Paris: UNESCO.

This volume provides a comprehensive comparison of developing understanding and evolving principles of public policy toward use of savanna lands around the world.

Chapter 5

Resource Use: Population, Technology, and Accessibility

This chapter

- extends concepts of property rights to natural resources other than land.
- contrasts the Malthusian model of population growth with the model of the demographic transition.
- applies the economic principle of rent maximization to the exploitation of natural resources.

- describes the role of technological advance in extending supplies of natural resources.
- outlines the importance of accessibility in evaluating three different sets of resources: energy, fisheries, and forests.

Courtesy of Kennecott Copper Corporation, Photo by Don Green

The general topic of the three previous chapters is land, and we have examined it with respect to its use in general, its use for agriculture in particular, and the types of conflicts raised by land's potential for multiple uses. Land, of course, is a natural resource, and this chapter applies many of the same principles and concepts developed in the discussion of land use to the use of the wider variety of natural resources.

The economic geography of natural resources has two major components: natural resource production and natural resource consumption. As described in Chapter 1, however, the location of production and the location of consumption are inextricably linked. A coal seam is endowed by nature in the Earth's crust for a number of reasons best described by a geologist, but a coal mine's operation depends on the ties between costs at the mine, prices at the market, and the transportation costs in between. Interests in coal mining, or in the production of any other natural resource, are at least twofold, with producers on one side and consumers on the other, and conflicts over natural resource rights are just as common as conflicts over the use of land. The valuation of resources is often biased by perspective—producer versus consumer—and can change rapidly as technology is employed to widen the base of natural resources available for use in the economy.

THE TRAGEDY OF THE COMMONS

The great classical economist, Adam Smith, described an ''invisible hand'' that guided the market in determining the proper allocation of production and consumption of goods and services in an economy. In addition, he said that the common good was increased by individuals acting with their own best interests in mind. Proponents of the free market as the proper foundation of an economy often base their arguments against government intervention in the economy on the guidance of the invisible hand. Outside guidance of the market is unnecessary, they argue, and what's best for individuals is best for the group.

Garret Hardin, in ''The Tragedy of the Commons,'' provides a parable that calls into question the universal application of these free market principles. Think of a village economy based on herding cattle. Let's assume that its land-tenure system is one of common property, in this case a commons in the center of the village. (American readers from New England should recognize the ''commons'' which still exists in most of the region's towns, although they are no longer open to the grazing of livestock.) Each family's wealth is reckoned by the size of its herd, so each family is bent on increasing its holding of livestock. The use of the commons is free, with open access guaranteed because it is common property. Given these conditions, the *tragedy of the commons* is twofold: One part of the tragedy is that the village economy is doomed; the second part is that the decline of the local economy cannot be forestalled under its current system. The village economy is doomed because if each family maximizes its cattle holdings, thereby acting in its individual best interest, the commons will be ruined by overgrazing. And this situation cannot be forestalled. No individual family has an incentive to stabilize, much less reduce, its holdings because the grass it doesn't use will simply be used by others. There is no point in personally conserving something if it's only going to be consumed by someone else, acting in *their* own best interest.

Proponents of the free market argue that the tragedy of the commons occurs because there is no market in the village, not because the market has failed. Recall that basic relationships between supply and demand can be defined by price. If there is a shortage of a good on the market, prices can be expected to rise so that consumption becomes limited. (If prices rise high enough, then we can expect additional supply to come on the market, but not in the case of land in the commons, which is fixed in extent.) High prices are symptomatic of scarcity, and as any commodity becomes more scarce, the market makes its price rise and its consumption decrease. If the land in the commons was not commonly held with open access to all, but instead was subject to market forces, then individual farmers would use the land more judiciously. If, for example, the land was divided into pieces of private property, with each family allocated a particular share, then the families would have an interest in conserving their land so that its use could be prolonged into the future. Another market solution would be to charge contract rents on the use of the land that are paid into a village kitty. Use of the commons would decrease if there was a cost, and the cost could be raised or lowered depending on conditions in the commons during any particular season. Ultimately, free market proponents see the tragedy of the commons as a problem of externality in which free use by one person imposes costs on others. A land-use market would provide the mechanism by which the externality could be priced, along with the tragedy, out of existence.

Hardin lists remedies to the tragedy of the commons that call for one kind of rationing or another. Pricing is an obvious form of rationing, but other systems could be based on a lottery, or "first come, first served" up to some predetermined capacity, or there might be some system based on generally perceived individual merit of potential users of the commons. Each of these systems could be used, but each system has its drawbacks in terms of the fairness of the allocation of rights to use the commons. What is the most effective and fairest way to allocate natural resources to people who require them for sustenance? It's a tough question when raised hypothetically and even tougher when raised in practical circumstances. Hardin suggests that the question won't have to be answered if population growth can be controlled.

If population is limited, the tragedy of the commons goes away. The problem in the commons is with adding cattle; if cattle are not added, then overgrazing will not occur. The tragedy of the commons is forestalled not by changing the way it is used, but by changing the number of its users. As noted by Hardin, the problem in the commons is one of density of use and not type of use, and the same sort of problem occurs in the use of a variety of natural resources. The intensity of the externality, or costs imposed on others by an individual's consumption, is directly related to the density of the population with respect to the quantity of the resource. The "tragedy of the commons" raises an issue that has been raised often: the impact of population growth on natural resource consumption. The analysis of this issue was first brought to widespread attention by Thomas Malthus in his *Essay on the Principle of Population*, first published in 1798.

MALTHUSIAN POPULATION THEORY

Malthus's basic argument was that population tends to grow at a geometric rate, such as 1, 2, 4, 8, 16, 32, 64, and so on. Unfortunately, food and every other product based in natural resource use increases at a much slower rate because of the law of diminishing returns (recall from Chapter 3). Malthus suggested that the effect of doubling the Earth's population would be no different than that of halving the Earth's area. Under the best of conditions, population growth would lead inevitably to declining standards of living as per capita incomes would be forced downward over time. More labor would be added with population growth, but the Earth's finiteness would limit output and fewer natural resources would be available to provide sustenance for each new person. The relationship between Mathus's view of the interplay between population growth and natural resource consumption and the "tragedy of the commons" should be clear.

If declining per capita incomes would be the best result, what would be the worst result? A worse result would be entry into what has been called the *Malthusian trap*, as illustrated in the left diagram of Figure 5.1. When population growth exceeds the level of output, it exceeds the carrying capacity of the land. This condition can't last very long, and population crashes to a much lower level. The crash is traumatic. It could be caused by famine, disease, or warfare resulting from an unevenness in the distribution of output across countries in a particular region of the world. Unfortunately, population growth then returns to its tendency toward geometric growth, and the Malthusian trap is entered again. Under the *Malthusian model*, the future of the planet is dismal.

So far, the Malthusian model has not proved accurate. Supporters of the model argue that its basic propositions are irrefutable, but that certain developments have delayed the inevitable population crash. The effect of the *Industrial Revolution*, the replacement of animate energy by inanimate energy in production processes that began in the mid-1700s, is often cited as a primary reason for the delay. Malthus's model is based to a large extent on the limits to production that he observed, and while the Industrial Revolution began during his lifetime he could not see its full impact. Many observers believe that the Industrial Revolution is now running out of steam and that its effect in raising output levels has been fully realized. It has merely delayed the inevitable, since its addition to output will eventually be outpaced by inexorable and rapid population growth (Figure 5.1). According to this view, the law of diminishing returns has been bent but not broken. Recent extensions to the Malthusian model include the

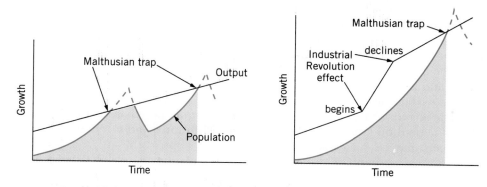

Figure 5.1 The left diagram outlines the Malthusian model of population growth exceeding the economy's ability to support it. The Malthusian trap is entered when population, growing at a geometric rate, exceeds its carrying capacity as defined by the level of output. Even after the population crashes, it will return to its rapid growth rate and again enter the Malthusian trap. The right-hand diagram illustrates the delaying effect of the Industrial Revolution in the Malthusian model. The Industrial Revolution caused output to increase dramatically and delayed the inevitable entry to the Malthusian trap. Eventually, however, the dramatic increases in output made possible by the Industrial Revolution will be insufficient to carry the rapidly increasing population.

degrading impacts of population growth on the environment as well as the continued depletion of natural resources (see Insights 5.1).

Given that some extensions to the resource base can take place owing to technological advance, as illustrated by the large-scale impacts of the Industrial Revolution, the Malthusian model rests on its argument that human population has a tendency toward geometric growth. It's the same problem that the commons has: not the nature of the use itself but the fact that there are too many users. If population growth occurred at a geometric rate in the United States, the population in 1990 would have been about 400 million. This estimate is based on an initial population in 1790 of about 4 million people and 30-year generations, and does not include the effects of any immigration. In 1990, the U.S. population was about 250 million. This and similar evidence generally contradicts the Malthusian proposition that there is a tendency toward extremely rapid growth in the world's human population.

➤ INSIGHTS 5.1
The Population Debate

Nafis Sadik, Executive Director of the UN Population Fund

When Thomas Malthus observed at the close of the 18th century that population growth might threaten food supply, our current world population of 5.3 billion people would have been literally unimaginable to him. Even 150 years later, it was hard for Paul Ehrlich and the other prophets of the "Population Bomb" to swallow; they thought that civilization would come to an end first.

Yet here we are in 1990, ticking along at an extra 92 million a year and rising; expecting 6.25 billion people by the end of the century, 8.5 billion by 2025, and a total of maybe 10 or 11 billion by the time growth finally stops. Should we be worried?

The answer is: Yes, we should. The momentum of population growth is like that of a giant oil tanker, slow to develop, hard to turn, and very hard to stop. The reefs may be far ahead, but if you haven't stopped the engines, you are going to run aground. The momentum of population is indeed slowing, but quite gradually. Birth rates are down in most parts of the world, but simple arithmetic means that annual additions will continue to rise until the end of the century, and only then start to decline. Population growth, according to the United Nations' most likely projection, will not halt altogether until about 2085.

Nearly all population growth, about 96% of it, is in developing countries, and the largest additions are in the poorest countries. Potentially, these new arrivals are all contributors to the solution; but they need at least a 15-year supply of food, clothing, health care, and education before they can begin to fulfill their potential.

Although we may be able—theoretically—to supply everyone's needs from the resources known to be available, the Earth is not merely a collection of resources, but a vast and complex life-support system. It has enormous built-in flexibility and capacity to absorb punishment, but it is showing signs of overload. Damage to the ozone layer, buildup of greenhouse gases and toxic wastes, and increasing acidification are all symptoms. Most of the burden of responsibility falls on the "rich billion" people in industrialized countries, but developing countries, the other 80 percent of the population, are doing their best to catch up.

Consider also the "bottom billion," the fifth of the world's population who live in deepest poverty. Their need is so desperate that they are forced into a ferocious assault on their environment simply to survive. The damage done by each individual is small, but the cumulative effects are enormous. Look at the equatorial rain forests, the eroding river basins, the filth and squalor of urban shanty towns: Can the Earth survive such a combination of poverty and destruction?

This concerns all of us. Clearly, development must continue—if only because poverty as well as wealth is wrecking the ecological balance. Equally, development cannot proceed on the basis of "business-as-usual." There has to be an all-out attack on the roots of poverty. There has to be a determined effort to find technologies which permit development without despoiling the environment. There also has to be an attack on rapid population growth.

Ben J. Wattenberg, Senior Fellow at the American Enterprise Institute

Due to recent demographic trends in less developed countries, much of the argument about the "population explosion" has become moot. While fertility rates were climbing, or while those rates were essentially at a high plateau, explosionists could cry disaster. Opponents, on the other hand, could maintain that whatever problems existed in those countries, be they economic or environmental, they were not primarily demographic in in origin. Culture counts, we anti-explosionists said: It's what people do, not how many there are or how fast they reproduce, that makes an economy sound or sick, an environment healthy or polluted.

But new fertility rates now coming in show that we're off the demographic plateau. Total fertility rates have either fallen dramatically, or are now falling, typically fairly rapidly, just about everywhere.

It's been about two decades since any major industrialized nation, including the United States, has had a total fertility rate at or above replacement-level.

Although from much higher levels, Asian and Latin American total fertility rates have also been dropping for several decades. During the period 1960–65 to 1985–90, South Korea went from 5.4 to 2.0; Indonesia from 5.4 to 3.3; India from 5.8 to 4.3; China, assisted by coercive government policy, from 5.4 to 2.0; Brazil from 6.1 to 3.5; and Mexico from 6.8 to 3.6.

Down, down, down. And fertility rates are clearly going to come down much, much further as modernization runs its course.

However, the built-in demographic momentum of earlier high-fertility rates will produce an increase in the total population, probably doubling it by the middle of next century. Can this decline be speeded up? Perhaps. Let's do what can be done, but in a non-coercive way.

If population growth is not a key cause of environmental degradation, which is what I suspect and is the clear conclusion of a 1986 blue-ribbon National Academy of Science report, we will still want to do the best we can to let people control their fertility.

We will be helped by continuing economic modernization, hopefully accelerated due to the sweeping global victory of market economics. The economic boost provided by free-market philosophy may prove to be as important to lowering fertility as family planning, and perhaps more so. Are environmentalists prepared to support market incentives with the same vigor that supply-siders support contraceptive programs?

Herman E. Daly, Senior Economist in the World Bank's Environment Department

Human impact on the environment is not simply the product of the impact of one person times the total number of people. All people and their impacts are not equal. Rich people use more matter and energy per capita than do poor, and thus one rich person is equivalent to many poor people in terms of load on the environment.

Apparently affluence, not poverty, is the big environmental problem. Yet we hear a lot about the close connection between poverty and environmental degradation, and with reason. Poverty hurts the environment mainly because there are so many more poor people that their per-capita consumption adds up.

In addition, the poor often are forced to live on—and overexploit—marginal land for immediate survival at the expense of the land's long-run productivity.

Fertility among the poor is also significantly higher than for the rich. Unless direct efforts are made to reduce population growth, there will be further degradation of the environment, increases in absolute poverty, and a widening gap in the distribution of income. And the theory of demographic transition, relied upon by many to provide the "automatic" solution to population growth, is a false hope.

Even if it were true that the fertility of the poor would fall to the lower level of the rich as the poor began to consume more, there is still the question of the environmental impact of that much extra consumption. If the consumption of the average Indian has to rise to that of the average Swede for the Indian fertility level to fall to the Swedish level, then there is not much hope for saving the environment from total ruin. Transition enthusiasts forget that affluence is harder on the environment than poverty, other things being equal. Population control is essential—but we must practice birth control for cars, airplanes, buildings, etc., as well as for people.

We must recognize that 10 billion lives are better than five billion lives—as long as they are not all lived simultaneously! We should strive to maximize the cumulative number of lives ever to be lived over time at a per-capita standard of resource consumption sufficient for a good life. But if we have too many people and too much consumption at any one time, we will erode the Earth's long-run carrying capacity and therefore reduce the cumulative total of lives ever to be lived at a decent level of consumption.

James T. McHugh, Bishop of the Roman Catholic Diocese of Camden, New Jersey

The doubling of world population in the next 40 years is a projection that is tenuous at best because most demographers refrain from projecting beyond 10 to 20 years. Nor is the doubling alone the critical issue. One has to consider a nation's natural resources, financial structure, workforce, and productivity in assessing the impact of population growth rates.

Looking at the global picture, one sees a variety of population situations. Most developed nations face the problem of seriously declining growth rates and aging populations. With the exception of Ireland, every nation in Western Europe has a birthrate below the replacement level. Europe's population is growing older as its workforce continually declines. The U.S. birthrate is also below replacement level and many sectors of the workforce rely on immigrant labor—legal or illegal.

In the developing nations, population growth rates have begun to decline and the problem of *rapid* population growth now exists in a small number of countries, mostly in sub-Saharan Africa and Western Asia. The increase in world growth rates from 1950 to 1970 was due primarily to a decrease in mortality, not to an explosion of births.

Concern about environmental problems was expressed at both the 1974 and 1984 United Nations World Population conferences. There is general agreement among population specialists and ecologists that environmental issues should always be considered in the context of socio-economic development. The solution to environmental problems requires more careful monitoring and control of economic and production strategies by the industrialized countries, since air and water pollution—such as acid rain and global warming—cross geographic boundaries. Industrialized countries also influence developing nations through their trade activities and importation of natural resources. Demographers and economists increasingly recognize that patterns of production, consumption, and economic activity, particularly in the least populated industrialized countries, have more to do with present ecological problems than population growth.

Two fundamental ethical principles should inform our strategies and guide our efforts: the integrity of all creation and respect for human life and human dignity. We must come to understand that the goods of the Earth are part of the heritage of the entire human family.

It is not simply a matter of counting heads and proclaiming there are too many people. Rather it is a matter of adjusting our lifestyles and global strategies to protect, enhance, and sustain human life as well as the global environment.

SOURCE: "A Forum: How Big Is the Population Factor?" in *EPA Journal,* Vol. 16, No. 4, 1990, pp. 29–33.

TRENDS IN WORLD POPULATION GROWTH

Over the last few years, population growth rates have been declining around the world (Table 5.1). On average, the world population growth rate averaged 2.2% from 1970 to 1980, which would lead to a doubling of the world's population in just under 33 years using the *rule of 72.* This rule states that the doubling time of any growing population is 72 divided by its rate of growth. If a growth rate is 6% per year, for example, the population will double in size in $72/6 = 12$ years. (The rule also works for compound interest and growth of principle; put away $1,000 at 5% per year, and you'll have $2,000 in 14.4 years.) Based on the average for 1980–92, the doubling time increased to over 42 years, and given the estimated current average growth rate the doubling time is now 48 years.

Population growth rates are declining in each of the World Bank's income groups, on average; nevertheless, poorer countries still have much faster rates of population growth than do richer countries. *Total fertility rates,* which basically describe the average number of children each adult woman will bear over her lifetime, have decreased around the world from nearly 5 in 1970 to just over 3

Table 5.1   Selected Demographic Statistics:
The World and World Bank Income Groups

Income Group	Average Annual Growth (%)		
	1970–80	**1980–92**	**1992–2000**
Low	2.2	2.0	1.7
Lower-middle	3.5	1.8	1.4
Upper-middle	2.5	1.8	1.5
High	0.8	0.7	0.5
World	2.2	1.7	1.5

Income Group	Total Fertility Rate		
	1970	**1992**	**2000**
Low	6.0	3.4	3.1
Lower-middle	4.5	3.1	2.9
Upper-middle	4.8	2.9	2.5
High	2.4	1.7	1.8
World	4.9	3.1	2.9

Income Group	Population (millions)			
	1992	**2000**	**2025**	**Stationary**
Low	3,191	3,654	5,062	7,600
Lower-middle	941	1,055	1,422	2,011
Upper-middle	478	540	717	965
High	828	865	922	903
World	5,438	6,133	8,122	11,479

SOURCE: World Bank, 1994: *World Development Report, 1994* (New York: Oxford University Press).

in 1992 and are expected to be under 3 in 2000. Total fertility rates in the world's richest countries are currently below the population's replacement level (2.1 children per couple, a rate that allows for some infant mortality), indicating that those countries will experience population declines in the future unless immigration can make up the shortfalls. Again, although total fertility rates have been declining in general, they are not at uniform levels across all income groups. While a majority of the world's population already lives in a country belonging to the lowest income group, by the year 2025 that number is expected to increase by almost 2 billion. During the same span, the world's richest inhabitants will increase by only about 100 million.

The different rates of growth from region to region around the world are leading to a drastic redistribution of the world's population (Figure 5.2). In 1950, China had the single largest population, and although it still held that

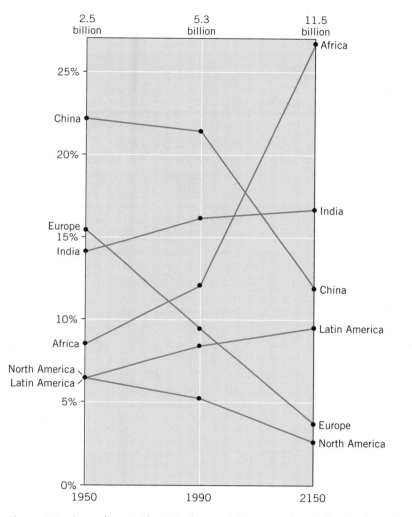

Figure 5.2 According to the UN, the world's proportional distribution of population changed significantly from 1950 to 1990 and will change even more dramatically in the future.

status in 1990, current forecasts indicate that India will hold first place by 2150. Whereas Europe held over 15% of the world's population in 1950, it is expected to hold only about 4% in 2150. North America's share is expected to decline from about 6.5% in 1950 to about 2.5% in 2150, whereas Latin America, which had the same proportion as North America in 1950, is expected to see its share rise to about 9.5% by that year. The most dramatic increase in population has occurred in Africa. It held about 8.5% of the world's population in 1950 and 12% in 1990, but by 2150 it is expected to hold more than one-quarter of the global population. That means more people will live in Africa in 2150, based on projections, than lived everywhere in 1950.

THE DEMOGRAPHIC TRANSITION

Obviously, these forecasts of future population shares assume that population growth rates will continue to vary well into the future, but all populations are expected to be stabilized by 2150. Such stability requires that population growth be uniform by that time at zero. This expectation is based on a model called the *demographic transition*, which describes a population's transition from a condition in which birth and death rates are at high levels to a condition in which birth and death rates are low (Figure 5.3). The model can be divided into several stages. In the first stage, both birth rates and death rates are at high levels. The dynamic balance of the two, with short-term fluctuations forming a longer term equilibrium, means that natural increases in population cannot occur. (Natural increases are those that take place within the population solely as a result of births and deaths. Migration has no effect in this context and is ignored in the model.) According to the UN, populations in all countries have passed this stage, and today it only serves as a theoretical baseline for the transition model.

Natural increases in population take place during the second and third stages of the demographic transition. During the second stage, death rates de-

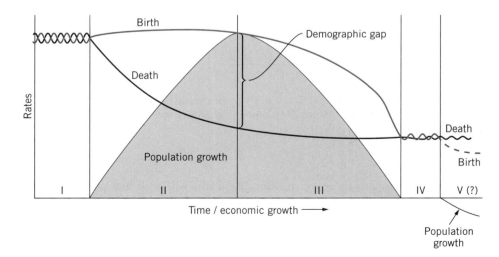

Figure 5.3 The demographic transition model describes a population's shift from a balance of high birth rates and death rates to a balance of low birth rates and death rates. Because death rates decrease at a slower rate than birth rates, a demographic gap occurs that yields rapid increases in population until the gap is closed.

crease rapidly but birth rates remain high. The difference between birth and death rates is the *demographic gap*. When the demographic gap is large and positive, that, is birth rates are much higher than death rates, then natural increase in population takes place; the wider the gap, the faster the population grows. Population continues to grow during the third stage of the demographic transition as well, but at a slower rate than during the second stage. Population increases more slowly during the third stage because the demographic gap begins to narrow as birth rates begin to decline.

Population growth stops, and the population stabilizes, at the fourth stage of the demographic transition. In fact, the transition has taken place by the fourth stage as birth rates and death rates are again in short-term equilibrium, but at a much lower level than in the first stage of the model. The demographic gap is closed at this point, but it may reopen in a fifth stage of the model in which birth rates sink below death rates. This yields a negative demographic gap that, in turn, leads to a natural decrease in population. So far, the existence of a well-defined fifth stage is debatable, but some European countries appear to have entered such a demographic situation. Furthermore, the stable population forecast for the world's richest countries is smaller than the population they are expected to have as a group in 2025 (Table 5.1). Thus, a population decrease in that group of countries as a whole appears to be expected.

It is not fully clear why the transition from high rates of births and deaths to low rates of births and deaths takes place. From the viewpoint of economics, the demographic transition takes place because of the sectoral shifts that usually occur in a country's economy as it grows. *Sectoral shifts* are movements of labor and income from the primary sector (activities directly associated with natural resources, such as farming and mining) to the secondary sector (mainly manufacturing), and then to the tertiary sector, which includes services, government, and everything else not included in the primary and secondary sectors. (The tertiary sector is often subdivided, as described in Chapter 8.)

From the standpoint of the demographic transition, the important sectoral shift is the one from the primary to the secondary sector. This shift implies some broad technological advances that not only have economic implications but also provide health benefits that cause the death rate to decline dramatically. Clean drinking water can be made available because of technology, for example, and medicines may also be considered a result of technological advances. As the death rate declines and birth rates remain high, population growth takes off. The sectoral shift works more slowly on birth rates, but eventually it causes them to decline, too. Birth rates are higher in rural, primary-sector economies because children are productive family assets. They can be put to work in the fields, for example, at fairly young ages. Also, when death rates are high, birth rates must also be high in order to maintain the family's economic output. Once the secondary sector becomes dominant, it is more difficult for children to contribute to the household's wealth. In economic terms, they become more of a liability than an asset, especially after child labor laws are passed. Furthermore, the lower death rates mean that lower birth rates can support any particular size of family that is deemed desirable. Fewer births are necessary to provide ''replacements'' for children who have died.

As an economy becomes more urbanized and shifts its major source of income from the secondary to the tertiary sector, population growth continues to slow down until population stabilizes, as in the fourth stage of the model. From an economic standpoint, it is not clear why population should decrease as predicted for the model's fifth stage. There are a host of sociological, cultural, psychological, and physical factors that affect population growth and decline that are not included in the economic explanation.

Malthus lived in England during the early second stage of the demographic transition, and he couldn't have been expected to anticipate how population growth would play itself out. In any case, his prediction regarding the extent

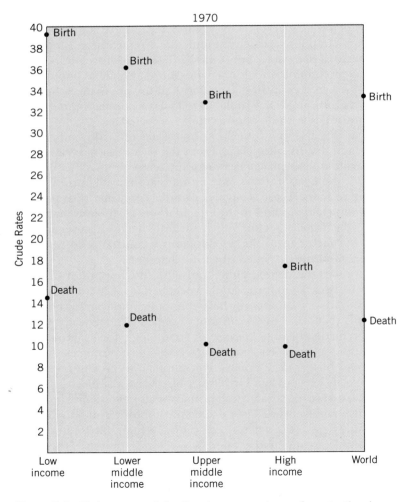

Figure 5.4 Birth rates and death rates appear to conform to the demographic transition model geographically as well as temporally.

of population growth was wrong, and today there is little argument that the demographic transition is a good descriptive model of population growth in countries around the world (Insights 5.1). It has to be fairly accurate because it is a generalization of the actual experiences of a number of countries over time.

Although the demographic transition is supposed to describe a temporal process, additional evidence for its association with economic growth can also be found in a cross-sectional geographical context. In 1970, for example, the World Bank's low income group of countries had the greatest demographic gap, while the high income group had the smallest demographic gap (Figure 5.4A). Both birth rates and death rates decreased as incomes increased. The same pattern is evident in the data for 1992 (Figure 5.4B). The demographic gaps

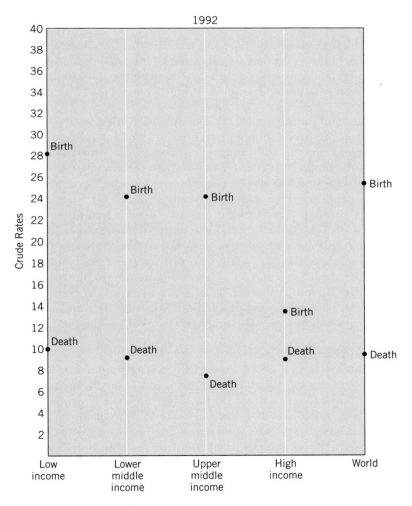

Figure 5.4   Continued.

for all countries have decreased over time as predicted by the demographic transition model.

RESOURCE USE AND LOCATION

Although Malthus was wrong, there is no question that the current world population of nearly 6 billion people and the future stable population of 11.5 billion people cannot consume natural resources without restraint; if they do, the tragedy of the commons will be applicable on a global scale. The primary constraint on resource consumption around the world is the price placed on resources by the market. Although some resources are held as common property, most are rationed by the market through the mechanism of price. The market effectively allocates a natural resource to its "highest and best use" in the same way that land is allocated to its highest and best use. Because of international trade, the size of a country's population may not even be relevant to the consumption of some of its local natural resources because the resources are actually consumed in other countries.

The production of aluminum provides an example of the different locations that can be involved in the production and consumption of any particular raw material. To simplify, producing aluminum is a three-stage process: (1) mine the basic raw material, bauxite; (2) refine bauxite to an intermediate material, alumina; and (3) refine alumina to the final product, aluminum. An alternative third stage involves the recycling of used aluminum products.

Bauxite develops through a soil-forming process called laterization, which requires large amounts of precipitation and very warm temperatures. Bauxite, therefore, is found mostly in semitropical and tropical regions. Oceania (places in and around the Central and South Pacific) and Africa are the most important sources of bauxite (Figure 5.5). Although a significant amount of alumina production takes place in Oceania, not much takes place in Africa. Instead, when it comes to the use of bauxite in alumina production, North America and Europe have proportionately high shares, even though their shares of bauxite production are quite small.

North America and Europe account for more than half of the world's production of aluminum, but less than 20% of the world's bauxite production. Africa, on the other hand accounts for about 18% of the world's bauxite production but only about 3% of the production of aluminum. The difference in proportions exists because of trade, with bauxite-producing countries exporting much of their ore.

The story is more distinct when individual countries are considered. Within North America, Jamaica provides about 10% of the world's bauxite, whereas the United States has less than one-half of 1% of the world's supply. The United States, however, produces about 23% of the world's aluminum, while Jamaica does not produce any (although it does produce alumina). As you

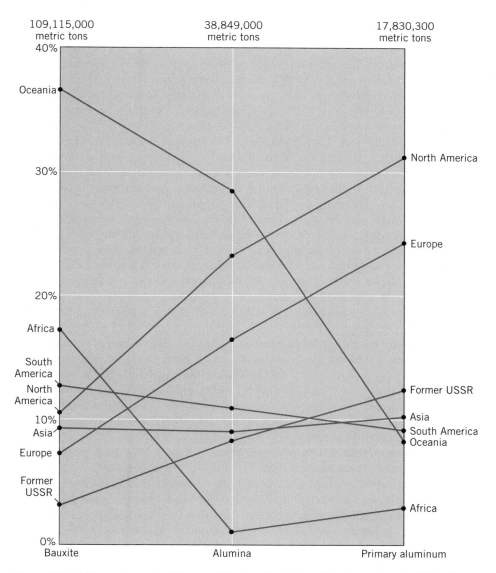

Figure 5.5 Although most of the world's bauxite is found in Oceania and Africa, its refinement into alumina and then aluminum is more commonly found in North America and Europe, where little bauxite is found. SOURCE: United Nations, 1991: *Industrial Statistics Yearbook* (New York: Statistical Office of the UN).

can see, the consumption of bauxite as a natural resource has nothing to do with the populations of Africa or Jamaica, where it is produced, but everything to do with the populations of Europe and the United States, where it is consumed.

CLASSIFICATION OF RESOURCES

What is a resource? We often think of resources as objects found in nature that can be used as factors of production, such as coal or iron ore. For the most part, that is the way resources are defined in this chapter. In the discussion of the Malthusian model, the press of growing population is a problem because it places too much of a demand on limited resources that cannot sustain the necessary increases in production. The definition of resource as an item found in nature that is a factor of production is too limited, however, to be a general one. Wilderness, for example, is often discussed as a natural resource. While wilderness is found in nature, it is not in its full sense ever employed as a factor of production. There are human resources, too. The labor people provide is a factor of production, but although people are "natural," they are not the type of item found in nature that we usually think of when we are defining resources.

Ultimately, a resource is a means to an end. Coal is a resource in producing electricity, for example, and wilderness is a resource in maintaining species diversity. In this sense, the end defines the means, and as the natural resource economist, E. W. Zimmerman, has said, "Resources are not, they become" (*Introduction to World Resources*, New York: Harper & Row, 1964). Something (or someone) is a resource if useful in accomplishing a goal, and whether or not something is useful depends on related economic and technological circumstances. Uranium deposits in the western United States have been there a long time. Native people that occupied the region for thousands of years did not recognize the uranium as any kind of resource because they had no use for it. By the mid-twentieth century, however, the uranium was recognized as a resource that had military and civilian applications. It had "become" as a function of a change in its cultural context.

Generally recognized natural resources are often classified into two groups: exhaustible and renewable. *Exhaustible resources* are those that can be consumed in their entire useful amount without any hope of replenishing their geological supply. Examples include coal and zinc ore. *Renewable resources,* such as soil, wood, and fish, can be replenished at the same time that they are being consumed, as long as their consumption does not proceed at too fast a rate. Solar energy, including wind, and geothermal energy sources are called perpetual resources. They are not exhaustible resources because they cannot be used up, and they are not subject to managed replenishment in the way renewable resources are.

Another method of classifying resources concerns their availability in terms of quantity. The *resource pyramid* can be used to illustrate the relative quantities of a particular mineral resource (Figure 5.6). The entire amount of a mineral resource available in the Earth's crust, even if only at the molecular level, is called the *resource base*. A significant constituent part of the resource base is the *mineral endowment*, which consists of the resource in the Earth's crust that occurs in mineral ore. Not all of the mineral endowment is considered a resource in this classification system.

Resources have technological and economic contexts. Resources are defined with reference to prices that imply more favorable economic conditions for

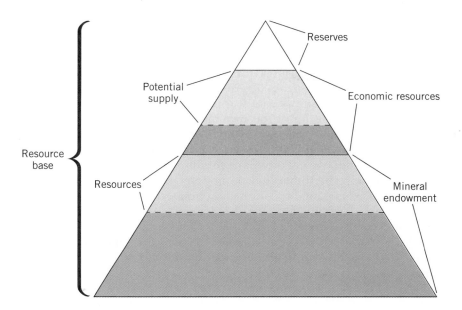

Figure 5.6 The resource pyramid illustrates the relative quantities of a mineral that make up the entire resource base. The resource base is the complete supply of the mineral on Earth. It is larger than the Earth's mineral endowment, which, in turn, is larger than that part of the mineral stock that can be used as an economic resource. The potential supply of the mineral is that part of the economic resource that can be brought to market under current prices and exploration technology. Reserves, the smallest component of the resource base, are deposits of the mineral that are undergoing current exploitation.

exploitation than current ones. *Economic resources* are those that could be employed at current prices, with a smaller subset of *potential supply* consisting of that part of the resource base that can also be used given current exploration efforts. The smallest part of the resource base consists of *reserves*, which are particular deposits of the mineral. Reserves define specific inventories of a mineral, but these inventories are often modified to fit market and technological circumstances so that words such as "proven," "probable," and "possible" are often used as qualifiers on estimates of available reserves.

The resource pyramid in Figure 5.6 describes the relative quantities of a mineral in terms of its difficulty and cost of mining. Economic resources, in particular, are defined in the context of price because minerals are not such resources unless they can pay a nonnegative economic rent (recall that a rent of zero is acceptable because normal profits are still being earned, even though there isn't any surplus). In this sense, the question of which minerals will be mined is the same question as which crops should be grown. Just as those crops yielding the highest rent are the crops that should be grown, those minerals that yield the highest rent are the minerals that should be mined.

The relationship between resource use and rent is not limited to minerals, but can be extended to the broadest definition of resources. The upper part of the resource pyramid, consisting of economic resources and reserves, forms a smaller pyramid that illustrates the general distribution of any type of natural resource by quality, where the term *quality* denotes ease of consumption of the resource. The highest quality supplies of a resource are those that are the purest grades of ore, for example, or the easiest to extract, and so make up current reserves. These make up the tip of the pyramid, while the middle and larger part consists of those minerals of lower quality. The largest part of this pyramid, at the bottom, consists of those parts of the economic resources that are not expected to be used under current economic conditions at all. Their poor quality raises their cost of use so high that they do not enjoy any current demand. As prices rise, or costs of exploitation shrink, economic rents increase at lower qualities and resource use moves down the pyramid. Again, resource use in general is no different than the use of land in this respect, and it follows Ricardo's model. The best resources, like the best lands, are used first, and lower quality resources, like lower quality lands, are not used until they can return rents.

The relative proportions of a resource held in reserve as compared to the amount consumed is a function of its price at the market, as long as production costs are held constant (Figure 5.7). Consumption slows in the face of high resource prices and increases if resource prices decrease. The rate at which an exhaustible resource will be depleted follows the *Hotelling Rule*, named for the

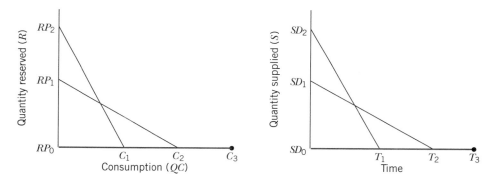

Figure 5.7 The left diagram illustrates the relationship between the amount of a natural resource held in reserves and the amount consumed as a function of price. High market prices, P_2, leave more of the resource in reserve because consumption is low at C_1. If the price is lowered to P_1, then consumption increases to C_2. Nothing is left in reserve if the resource is free, because consumption increases to C_3 at price P_0. The right-hand diagram illustrates the relationship between the amount of a natural resource supplied to the market and and its rate of consumption as a function of discount rates. High discount rates, D_2, lead to more of the resource being placed on the market as consumption occurs rapidly. Exhaustion at time T_1 occurs earlier than if the discount rate is lower, with discount rate D_1 leading to exhaustion at T_2. If the resource's value is not discounted into the future at all, as represented by D_0, then the resource would be supplied over the longest period.

economist who found that the value of a mine's output is related to the rate at which future earnings are discounted (see Chapter 1). If the discount rate is high, the resource will be more rapidly depleted because its future value is expected to be low (Figure 5.7). On the other hand, low discount rates preserve the value of the resource in the future, and its current rate of use decreases. The rule works on the side of demand as well as the supply side. If discount rates are high, consumers are unlikely to practice conservative habits of consumption, and resources will be depleted more rapidly owing to heavy demand. If the future is held more important, as would be true if discount rates are low or zero, then conservation is more likely because future consumption becomes more attractive.

LOCATION RENT AND RESOURCE EXPLOITATION

Location rent, as a form of economic rent, also applies to cases of resource exploitation. Resource use is like land use in that the relative location of resource sites with respect to markets is a very important determinant of the resource's ability to return rent. Transportation charges due to distance, rough terrain, or some other form of inaccessibility can limit the use of otherwise high-quality resources, as described in Case 5.1. For example, oil from Alaska's North Slope fields was exploited only after petroleum prices underwent an extraordinary increase in the early 1970s. Despite its relatively high quality, its inaccessibility kept it from potential supply during the earlier era of lower prices. Even after the field was developed, it would have made more economic sense to sell it on the Japanese market, because of low shipping costs, than to bring it to market in all but the West Coast of the United States. However, given the well-publicized costs of exploiting Alaskan oil, most Americans wanted it directed only to domestic consumption. Following the location rent model, holding other qualities constant, natural resources that are closer to markets will be used before natural resources that are more distant. If qualities are not uniform, then transport charges and other costs of accessibility are weighed against the costs of using less than best quality resources in deciding the best natural resource location to exploit.

Location rent can vary in two ways in the land-use model: costs of production can change and market prices can change. When applied to exhaustible natural resources, however, a third change can affect location rent; the reserves at a particular site can be fully depleted, even beyond the point of potential supply. Think of all the old western movies that revolved around ghost towns, towns that at one time were booming because of their proximity to gold, or silver, or some other type of mine. When the ore was depleted, the town's location rent also was depleted until there were no remaining means of earning a livelihood. The process continues. Uranium City, in Saskatchewan, is rapidly becoming a ghost town. In the early 1960s, it had over 5,000 people, but the uranium mines were played out, the mining companies shut down, and the town's population began to disperse in 1981. By 1994, the population was down to 200 and shrinking even from that low level. The Lake Athabasca region, where Uranium City is located, is hard pressed to provide alternative occupations. The same thing can occur if renewable resources are overexploited. There are ghost towns in the western United States, Maine, and Michigan that once were thriving lumber towns, but their potential supply of lumber was eliminated by clear-cutting and other high-discount harvesting practices.

Despite many cases of ghost towns and related depletion of natural resources at a local level, larger scale depletion of resources is uncommon. With the exception of species extinction induced by human action, have any natural resources ever been exhausted on a global scale or even a continental one? No, but not because of any altruistic efforts at preservation. The market responds to increasing scarcity of a resource by raising its price. Extraction costs increase, for example, as better reserves are used up. As these costs rise, economic rents are reduced, and so production is either curtailed or prices are forced up so that rents are raised as well. Such price increases, induced by increases in extraction costs, signal *Ricardian scarcities*. Ricardian scarcities are qualitative; they occur as better supplies of a resource diminish and poorer quality resources are exploited. Absolute quantitative scarcities are referred to as *Malthusian scarcities*. Such scarcities occur only on a localized basis, as in ghost towns, but they often signal Ricardian scarcities at a larger geographic scale as lower quality resource sites are exploited to make up for shortfalls in production that arise when better quality sites are used up.

◪ CASE 5.1
Moving Down the Resource Pyramid in Alaska

The recent opening of Alaska's Red Dog Mine provides an example of how a native for-profit corporation and a responsible, major international private minerals company, working closely with the local population, the environmental community and state agencies, can successfully achieve the agreements necessary to open a remote mine in Alaska.

The Red Dog Creel Zinc Deposit, 80 kilometers from the Arctic northwest coast of Alaska, was first explored by mining companies in 1978. Its zinc reserves are the second largest in the world. Red Dog's proven reserves contain about two-thirds of all U.S zinc reserves. In seeking to develop this deposit, however, the native corporation owning the minerals and its partner minerals company faced many of the obstacles that have made mining more difficult in Alaska than is popularly supposed. The deposits are just outside the boundaries of a national park unit. The 80-kilometer overland route to a port site on the coast lay through the Cape Krusenstern National Monument. The Northwest Alaska Native Association (NANA) Regional Corporation, one of the 13 Alaska Native regional corporations, negotiated with the federal government to allow an access route through the monument.

In 1979, NANA shareholders approved mineral development of the region, subject to three stipulations: protection of maximum employment for the shareholders; adherence to strict environmental controls, including the right to shut down any or all parts of the operation that threatened subsistence habitats; and a guarantee of an adequate cash return to NANA.

In 1980, NANA's selection rights were ratified by Congress, and NANA began considering joint-venture opportunites with companies that had been exploring the region. The winner was Cominco, a company based in Vancouver, Canada, the largest zinc and lead producer in western North America, which had substantial Arctic mining experience, and had a proven policy of hiring local Native residents as workers in its Canadian mining operations.

Under the joint-venture agreement negotiated with NANA, Cominco is to have an all-Alaska Native work force by the 12th year of operation. Annual production will be capped at a rate that guarantees at least 50 years of production. Development and production will abide by environmental protection decisions made by a committee of Inupiat elders (representatives of the Alaska Native residents of the area). A royalty package was worked out that gives some upfront roylaties but reserves the major portion of the royalties for later years.

The alliance with NANA was a major factor in meeting some other environmental concerns. NANA elders worked out a 83-kilometer corridor through the Cape Krusenstern National Monument that carefully avoided environmentally sensitive sites or mitigated impacts. This route received the endorsement of some environmental groups, and in 1985 Congress approved an easement for the corridor, giving it to NANA in exchange for other NANA lands coming to the federal government. Meanwhile, Cominco, with NANA's support, successfully persuaded the Alaska state government to invest in the transportation infrastructure necessary for operation of the mine by promising payment of 50 years of guaranteed toll fees for the use of the road. The fees serve as a guarantee of payment of development bonds sold by the state of Alaska.

With the major hurdles cleared, the mine that many industry experts had once considered an impossibility was finally constructed in the late 1980s. In 1990, the mine went into partial production; in 1991 it reached full production. More importantly, the Red Dog development may have shown others a way to undertake environmentally compatible development of Alaska's mineral resources.

SOURCE: Council on Environmental Quality, 1992: *United States of America National Report, United Nations Conference on Environment and Development* (Washington, D.C.: Council on Environmental Quality), p. 288.

FOR DISCUSSION

Do you think that environmental and cultural considerations such as those that affected the opening of the Red Dog Mine can be addressed in cost-benefit analysis? In other words, do environment and culture have economic meaning?

TECHNOLOGY AND RESOURCE SUBSTITUTION

The use of lower quality resource sites to make up for the decline in quantity at higher quality resource sites is only one form of substitution that takes place in resource production and consumption. Table 5.2 lists nine overlapping mechanisms for resource substitution, beginning with the innovation that makes something a resource, a means to an end, in the first place. Another form of substitution is the development of new materials; plastics replace metals, and synthetics are used instead of natural fibers. Extraction processes can be improved so that even Malthusian scarcities can be turned around. For example, a steam injection process reopened closed oil wells in Texas during the late 1970s, so that the new process created reserves where they had once been depleted.

In addition to improving extraction processes, technological advances can lead to more efficient use of resources, as described in Case 5.2 which discusses improvements in consumption efficiency in California. That case describes some of the results of statewide negotiations among major utilities, environmental and consumer groups, and the state government. Such conservation programs often lead to win–win situations. Both the utilities, as producers, and the consumers are rewarded by lower costs of power; environmental costs are lowered, too.

Over time, technological change has been induced by increasing resource prices. High prices are signals both of scarcity and of high rewards to those who can develop new sources of potential supply. Other technological advances, in refining, for example, or in shipping, have made lower quality resources more useful. The increase in size of oil tankers and ore carriers has greatly increased the market accessibility of oil fields and mines. Another application of technology, recycling, is an indirect type of resource substitution. Aluminum is more often recycled in order to reduce energy costs rather than bauxite requirements. Higher prices, in general, allow lower quality resources to be substituted for higher ones simply because of the increases in economic rent that occur as prices

---

Table 5.2   Nine Mechanisms of Resource Substitution

1. Innovation that enables a given resource to be used for a particular purpose.
2. The development of new materials.
3. Improvement of extraction processes.
4. Technological advance that makes exploration cheaper.
5. Technological advance that makes resource use more efficent.
6. Technological advance that makes lower quality resources economic to use.
7. Developments in recycling processes.
8. Price changes that make lower quality resources economic to exploit.
9. The substitution of manufactured capital for resources.

SOURCE: Partha Dasgupta, ''Natural Resources in an Age of Substitutability,'' Chapter 23, pp. 1111–1130, in *Handbook of Natural Resource and Energy Economics*, Vol. 3, edited by Allen V. Kneese and James L. Sweeney (Amsterdam: North-Holland, 1993). The items in the table are from pp. 1114–1115.

rise. Finally, some manufactured capital can be substituted for natural resources in the same way that some manufactured capital can be substituted for labor. For example, nylon fibers are used in rope instead of hemp.

As Table 5.2 indicates, technological advance is a major mechanism for resource substitution and expansion of the set of resources available for use in production. The Industrial Revolution, as a broad-scale development of a wide variety of technologies, was able to bend the law of diminishing returns to such a degree that rapid population growth could take place. In effect, industrialization expanded resources in the aggregate in a way that Malthus could not have anticipated. As resources expanded, the population-carrying capacity of an economy also expanded, and population grew rapidly. Initially, this growth took place in Europe, but it soon spread to other places around the world as a byproduct of the spatial diffusion of industrialization. Eventually, however, the process of the demographic transition began to limit population growth. This occurred in about the same geographical sequence as that followed by the rapid increases in population: The first countries to industrialize were the first countries to experience rapid growth, in general, and they were the first countries around the world to approach population stability. The industrializing countries have experienced population booms more recently, and their populations are not expected to stabilize until well into the future.

Resource substitution also plays an important role in international trade. Many poorer countries export primary products, especially raw materials (also see Chapter 10). However, the ability to substitute one resource for another through technological mechanisms has served over time to suppress the prices of most raw material exports in world markets. As illustrated in the discussion of bauxite and aluminum production, richer industrial countries form the major markets for the raw material exports of the poorer countries. If raw material prices increase, the industrial countries will most likely have the technological capabilities either to develop synthetic substitutes or to open alternative reserves of raw materials. In effect, technological advance not only provides a substitute for raw materials, but it also can provide a substitute for their international trade by expanding alternative domestic resources when import prices are too high. Inevitably, resource booms in international markets are followed by resource busts.

■ *CASE 5.2*

Reducing Resource Consumption in California by Increasing Consumption Efficiency

Numerous studies have shown that the least expensive and most environmentally beneficial source of additional electric energy in the United States is energy efficiency—using the energy we now have more efficiently. Increasing the efficiency of existing uses of electric power reduces the need for expensive additional generating plants, avoids their associated environmental impacts, and allows utilities to meet additional energy needs with their existing generating capacity.

Pacific Gas and Electric Company (PG&E), a privately-owned utility serving northern and central California, conducted an assessment of the technical and market potential for Customer Energy Efficiency (CEE) in its service territory. The initial results suggested that a savings potential existed for as much as one-third of their current generation.

PG&E plan includes several new supply sources, including upgrades at existing fossil and hydroelectric facilities, and substantial renewable energy sources to be used beyond the year 2000. However, most customer energy efficiency programs are expected to provide electricity from savings more cheaply than electricity can be produced from these new sources. On the average, efficiency savings cost the company $0.05 per kilowatt-hour (kwh), while the lowest-cost supply alternative broadly available costs $0.08 per kwh. The company has committed itself to provide 2500 megawatts from CEE sources by the year 2000 out of a total projected increase of 3300 megawatts in customer demand.

PROGRAM DESCRIPTIONS

PG&E now offers efficiency services to all of its 4.2 million electricity customers and 3.5 million gas customers. Spending in 1991 for CEE is expected to be at least $180 million, of which about one-third is in the form of direct cash incentives to customers. The plan for the years 1990 to 2000 calls for more than $2 billion in total CEE program spending; programs offered include the following:

- Commercial, Industrial and Agricultural Rebates: PG&E provides cash rebates to cutomers in these classes who make improvements to their lighting systems, refrigeration units, motors and other machinery.

- New Construction Programs: The company offers rebates to builders of new residential or commercial buildings if they exceed minimum California construction standards for energy efficiency by at least 10 percent. Most rebates are for advanced lighting and cooling systems.

- Residential Appliance Programs: PG&E provides cash rebates to residential customers who purchase refrigerators, air-conditioners, light bulbs and other home appliances that are more efficient than federal or state standards require.

- Low-Income Service Programs: PG&E offers weatherization services and certain home appliances at no charge to qualified low-income customers. More than 500,000 homes have been weatherized through these programs. Weatherization of low-income homes involved the following procedures: application of weather stripping for both doors and windows, incorporation or increase of attic insulation, use of water heater blankets, use of low-flow shower heads, insulated wrapping of air conditioning and heating ducts, and insulated wrapping of hot water pipes.

- Advanced Demonstrations: The company is subsidizing the construction of a super-efficient home in each of its 25 operating divisions as a demonstration to builders and home-buyers. Also, a $7 million energy center is being built in downtown San Francisco as a site for demonstrating commercially available CEE technologies to the public and for training professionals in their application.

SOURCE: Council on Environmental Quality, 1992: *United States of America National Report, United Nations Conference on Environment and Development* (Washington, D.C.: Council on Environmental Quality), p. 138.

FOR DISCUSSION

This case describes various conservation strategies that can be employed in order to increase the efficiency of energy use. Do you think that simply raising energy prices would be a better way to achieve the same goal?

PRIVATE VERSUS PUBLIC GOODS

We saw at the beginning of the chapter that market pricing can be considered as one solution to the tragedy of the commons; that is, pricing can be used as a means of allocating resources. However, market allocation via pricing works most efficiently on resources that are *private goods*. Pure private goods are exclusive in their use, meaning that their owner can effectively prevent others from using them, and they are rival, meaning that consumption by one user reduces the amount that may be consumed by another. Coal in a mine has the characteristics of a pure private good; the mine's owner can keep others from using the coal, and when one ton of the mine's reserves is consumed by one user, there is one less ton that could be consumed by others.

Goods that are nonexclusive and nonrival are pure *public goods*. The classic example of a pure public good is the national defense. Every resident of a country is protected by the national defense, and the protection of one does not reduce the protection of another. At sufficiently low populations, the commons is a pure public good; access to the commons is open to the community and grazing by one family's herd should not reduce the grazing by another family's herd. The nonrival characteristic of the commons, however, has a population context: that's what drives the tragedy. If the population of the community gets too large, the commons takes on the characteristic of a *congestible good*, one that is nonrival at lower levels of aggregate demand but rival at higher levels. As the population grows, the commons becomes less of a public good and more of a private good, but it is never either purely public or purely private. As long as access is open, it is a nonexclusive resource and the market is not a player in allocating grazing rights. If access is priced by the market, the commons is no longer a "commons" but has been turned into a private good.

Because they have some characteristics of public goods, congestible resources are often allocated completely by governments, or else governments intervene actively in the market's allocation process. Water use in the United States provides an example of government intervention in the market for a congestible resource. There are two basic systems of water right allocations in the United States: *riparian rights* and *appropriative rights*. Riparian rights to water use are granted to those who occupy the riparian zone (shore, river bank, etc.), and allow reasonable use of the water supply. Riparian rights are allocated in the East, where water is in such sufficient supply that it almost constitutes a nonrival good. In most states, no one owns larger bodies of water and streams, so that while riparian rights give the occupant priority in the water's use, they do not limit anyone else's access to the water and its normal use. In short, the basic principle is that there's plenty of water to go around.

The West is very much drier, and the water in that region is treated as a congestible resource that has rival characteristics under most circumstances. Its system of appropriative rights considers rights to water as rights of consumption based on demonstrated need and historical precedent of "first come, first served." Except in Colorado, water rights are for beneficial uses and exclude rights to wasting water. The definitions of "beneficial" and "waste" vary from state to state, but agriculture and other industrial uses are invariably viewed as beneficial, as are most domestic uses. These rights can be lost if use is not maintained, and the rights are tied to present needs for use rather than future needs. If the year is a wet one, then all rights of consumption should be met. If the year is a dry one, unmet needs for water will occur among those users who came late to the water supply because earlier users have the right to fully satisfy their needs first. This system of water rights has come under fire in recent years because environmental preservation seems to be precluded under its method of allocation. Concern for the environment is fairly recent, however, and competing interests often view preservation as more of a waste than as a beneficial use.

ENERGY RESOURCES

Energy consumption is marked by two patterns of substitution: the substitution of particular resources for others as sources of energy and the increasing efficiency of energy consumption over time. For example, in the United States coal is increasingly becoming a source of energy while natural gas is slowly declining. At the same time, electricity generated by hydro sources is now secondary to electricity generated by controlled nuclear fission (Figure 5.8). Between 1972 and 1990, technological changes made fuel consumption by automobiles in the

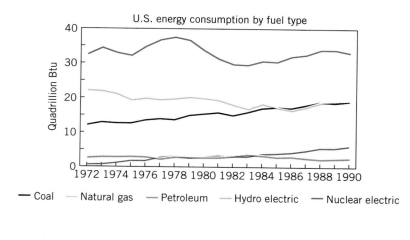

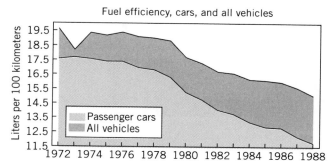

Figure 5.8 The upper graph shows the changing levels of consumption of various fuels, whereas the lower one illustrates the remarkable growth of automotive fuel efficiency in the United States between 1972 and 1988.

United States more efficient. Mileage per gallon improved as engines were made more powerful per liter of gasoline consumed, and automobiles were redesigned to be lighter and therefore require less fuel. Not only were cars generally reduced in size, but also lighter materials were substituted for heavier ones—plastic for steel—in order to further lighten their load (Figure 5.8). The overall improvement in energy consumption in the United States was about 30% (Figure 5.9). Technological improvements, rather than conservation, formed the primary foundation of the growth of American energy efficiency. Per capita energy consumption over the period basically matched the country's business cycle. It had a brief decline during the national recession of the mid-1970s and bottomed out during the recession of the early 1980s, a recession induced by very high petroleum prices.

The same kinds of substitutions taking place in the United States have been occurring around the world (Figure 5.10). In 1950, the world's consumption of commercial energy equaled about 27 billion barrels of oil. The single largest

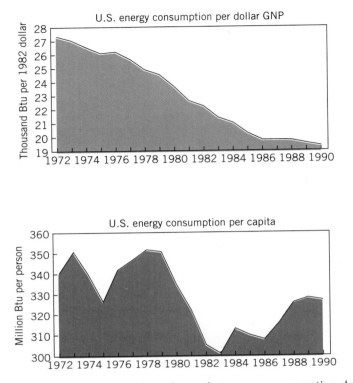

Figure 5.9 The upper chart shows that energy consumption decreased at a fairly constant rate in the United States between 1972 and 1990. As the lower chart shows, however, per capita consumption during the period was a function of general economic conditions.

source of commercial energy was coal, followed by oil. Third came renewable sources of energy, including biomass, geothermal, and later nuclear sources (after 1956). Natural gas and hydro sources rounded out the list. By 1990, the world consumed the equivalent of 64.5 billion barrels of oil. Oil had supplanted coal as the world's leading source of energy, and natural gas had passed renewable sources. Hydro sources were in last place on the energy list. By 2020, the forecast is for coal again to be the leading source of the world's energy requirements, which are expected to equal about 126 billion barrels of oil. Natural gas is expected to increase proportionately, again followed by renewable sources of energy and then hydro sources. Note that if hydro sources were considered as part of the set of renewable resources on the chart, their combined use would be about equal in proportion to natural gas as an energy source by 2020, and would have been greater in 1990 and 1950.

    Although world energy consumption is expected to increase over time, consumption efficiency should increase as well. Between 1971 and 1992, the efficiency of energy consumption increased on average in all the world's countries. As illustrated in Figure 5.11, the greatest increase in average energy efficiency

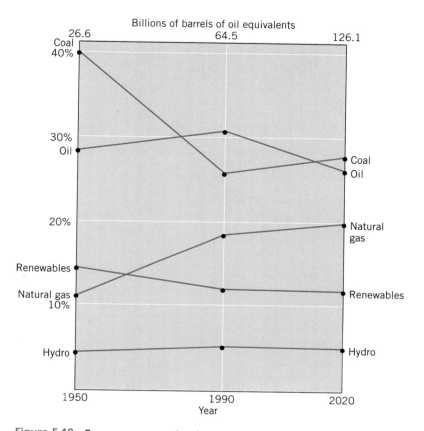

Figure 5.10   Energy consumption increases steadily over time, but sources of energy differ in their relative consumption.   Source: "A Survey of Energy," by Edward Carr, in *The Economist*, June 8, 1994, supplement p. 4).

over the period was in high-income countries. Both low- and middle-income countries improved at lower rates, with the middle-income countries, on average, having the lowest rate of energy efficiency. The world's average increase in energy efficiency of about 200% during the period is heavily weighted by the success of the high-income countries, which have a disproportionately high level of per capita energy use.

The role of technological advance in improving energy efficiency is implicit in Figure 5.11. Look at the relative levels of productivity in 1971. At that time, the high-income countries were the least efficient users of energy (recall their inefficient use of energy in agriculture, as described in Chapter 3). That year marked the near-end of the era of cheap energy in the industrial countries, when it was inexpensive to substitute energy for other factors of production. Even at low prices, however, its cost was more meaningful in poorer countries, so they used energy more efficiently. By 1992, energy efficiency in the high-income countries was well advanced beyond levels in the poorer countries as

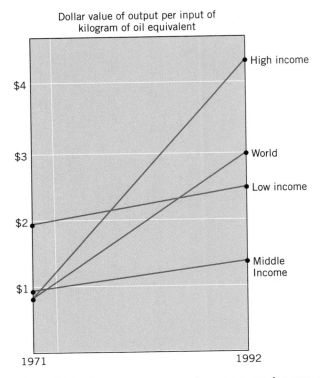

Figure 5.11 On average, energy became a much more efficient factor of production around the world between 1971 and 1992. Increases in its efficiency, however, were much higher in the world's high-income countries than in the medium- and low-income countries. SOURCE: World Bank, 1994: *World Development Report 1994* (New York: Oxford University Press).

increases in energy prices in the 1970s and 1980s led to technological advances that provided substitutes for energy consumption. Much of this technology is expensive in its own right and requires considerable capital investment that is not widely available in poorer countries. Because energy-conserving technology has not fully diffused from rich countries to poorer ones, energy consumption in poor countries lags the rich countries in average efficiency.

The improvements in energy efficiency and substitutions over time among energy sources are symptomatic of Ricardian scarcity. So far, however, Malthusian scarcities have not appeared except at local scales. The world's natural gas reserves tripled between 1970 and 1995, and reserves of oil doubled during the period. Consumption has increased over the period, but reserves have expanded at a much greater rate. Between 1971 and 1980, a period when Malthusian concerns were heightened, the world's average annual rate of energy consumption was greater than its average annual rate of production. This gap, of course, would be unsustainable over too many years, and by 1980 it had begun to close. Averaged

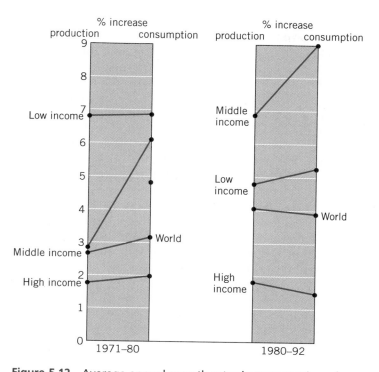

Figure 5.12   Average annual growth rates in consumption of energy were higher around the world than average annual growth rates in production between 1971 and 1980. Such a divergence is unsustainable, and by the period 1980–92, rates of increase in production were higher than average annual rates of increase in consumption. The world's average, however, was heavily weighted by the high-income countries. Rates of increase in consumption in the low-income countries and the medium-income countries remained greater than their rates of energy production.   SOURCE: World Bank, 1994: *World Development Report 1994* (New York: Oxford University Press).

over the period 1980 to 1992, annual growth in world consumption of energy had fallen below the annual rate of growth in energy production (Figure 5.12). However, consumption continued to outpace production, on average, in all but the world's richest countries. Because the rich countries, despite their efficiency, remain the arena of highest energy consumption, the world average is driven by their trend.

POLITICAL ECONOMY AND ENERGY PRODUCTION

Energy consumption, increases in energy efficiency, and substitution of one type of energy for another are all driven by price in a way that can be expected.

Energy prices, however, are not often determined solely by markets. Over the last quarter-century, petroleum prices in particular have been as much functions of political economy as they have been of fundamental relationships between supply and demand. In 1973, a war between Israel and its Arab neighbors was used as the starting point for many oil-producing nations, primarily the *Organization of Petroleum Exporting Countries (OPEC)*, to wrest control of the international oil market from multinational oil corporations. In effect, those countries that produced a large proportion of the world's oil began to take control of the market away from those countries that consumed the largest proportions of the world's oil. OPEC raised petroleum prices unilaterally. In 1972, the price of a barrel of Arabian oil was $2.48; in 1973, it was $5.04; and in 1974, it was priced at $11.25 per barrel.

The price increases had three effects. The price increases (1) sent most of the world's countries, excluding its oil producers, into recession by 1975; (2) raised the economic rents of alternative sources of petroleum and also the rents of substitute fuels; and (3) induced increased efficiency in energy usage, by means of technological advances and by government mandates. It was during this period, for example, that the federal government began to require increased fuel efficiency for cars built in the United States. The increase in fuel efficiency illustrated in Figure 5.8 is as much a result of government-imposed standards as of changes in market demand for fuel efficiency. All three results caused prices to stabilize and even decline after inflation was taken into account.

Worldwide recession caused the demand for petroleum to weaken and undercut the gross revenues earned by OPEC members and other oil producers, too. The decline in revenues led to cheating by some OPEC members as well as to a slowing of the rate price increases, so that economic growth would restore the demand for petroleum to its longer term trend of rapid increase. By 1978, Arabian oil was priced at $12.70 a barrel, having been raised only $1.45 in four years. The overall price increase, however, of well over 400% between 1972 and 1978 caused significant efforts to explore and recover petroleum in a number of places that could not have yielded positive rents to their petroleum deposits just a few years before. Thus, Canada, Mexico, and the United Kingdom all became significant oil producers because of the price hikes, with oil coming to market from Alaska at the same time. None of these producers is a member of OPEC, and as production of oil outside OPEC increased, OPEC's ability to control prices was diluted.

By 1978, the effect of high oil prices on the world's economy appeared to have been played out. In 1978, however, the Iranian revolution cut off supply from that country and oil prices skyrocketed. In 1979, Arabian oil was priced at $24; by 1980, the price had gone up to $32; and by 1981, it was at $34 per barrel. It held at that price until 1984, when it began to slide as OPEC lost the discipline of its members and non-OPEC supplies again increased. By 1987, the price had decreased to $17.50 a barrel, and the oil crisis had ended. One country that experienced a production increase in the early 1980s was the United States. Despite high international prices in the 1970s, oil production in the United

States, with the exception of Alaska, was stable with a tendency toward decline. The lack of production effort was mainly due to a complex system of price controls, first enacted by President Richard Nixon as part of an ill-fated effort to subdue inflation in the late 1960s. The system was modified to include different prices for "new oil" and "old oil," but it generally left most American oil fields with 1960s prices and 1970s costs that yielded negative economic rents. When President Ronald Reagan took office, he lifted the price controls on petroleum, and the American oil industry experienced a significant boom for about six years. The increase in production, though relatively short-lived, went a long way toward putting international prices on more of a market basis than they had been under OPEC's control.

Most governments have two points of interest in energy resources. Energy can be considered a *strategic resource* that is necessary not just for the well-being but for the very survival of a country's economy. As a strategic resource, government has an obligation to ensure its supply and manage its use. A stated goal of American energy policy is to provide energy independence by developing a sufficient array of stockpiles and domestic sources of renewable and exhaustible energy sources, so that the country is immune from any significant foreign intervention in its domestic production. Governments are also interested in energy markets because international energy sales can have a significant impact on a country's balance of trade. Exporting countries, as in OPEC, have tried to increase oil prices so that they can earn foreign exchange that can be used in their own economic growth and development. Importing countries try to keep energy prices lower and to reduce their domestic consumption, thereby ensuring that their balance of trade does not go into deficit simply because of energy consumption.

Currently, much of the impetus for substituting one energy source for another has arisen from a broadened definition of the cost of natural resource use. Until recently, most cost-benefit analyses of resource use have been narrow, or naive, in assessing direct costs. The costs of environmental degradation are now being addressed in determining the relative efficiency of comparable sources of energy. Nuclear power was regarded as the savior of the world's economy at the end of World War II. Albert Einstein even thought that nuclear power would provide electricity so cheaply that nobody would have to work. Electricity would completely substitute for labor in production. Unfortunately, Einstein was wrong and even less hopeful predictions of the spread of nuclear power for peaceful purposes have been scaled back because the environmental costs are often deemed too high. The costs of disposing nuclear waste are high, but the costs of nuclear accidents such as the one that occurred at Chernobyl in Ukraine in 1986 are prohibitive. Even energy sources that at one time were considered environmentally benign have been found problematic because of their broader environmental impacts. Hydro power, for example, is generally considered a clean source of electricity, especially compared to nuclear generation or the burning of carbon fuels such as coal and oil. Unfortunately, hydroelectric systems usually have significant negative effects on the waterways required for their installation. As environmental costs become better recognized, the substitution of one energy resource for another is more likely going to take the form of better conservation rather than material development.

MODELS OF NONEXCLUSIVE RESOURCE USE

The most commonly used energy resources are exhaustible ones that seem to respond more to market prices than to geological factors. These resources are usually in the form of private goods so that their use can effectively be rationed by markets through pricing, and price increases lead to efforts to bring more of these resources to the market. However, a large number of renewable resources are nonexclusive in their use. For example, nondomesticated animals that are used for commercial purposes and for sport fit easily into the category of impure public goods and often face the same sort of tragedy faced by the commons. Economists have analyzed the problem of nonexclusive consumption of renewable resources through fishery models, but the word "fishery" simply indicates the models' most common application. The same models can be used to consider the exploitation of other wild animal species as well. In addition, although the models were developed to address commercial problems, they can be applied to recreational and sporting uses of such resources as well.

The nonexclusive nature of a fishery usually makes it difficult to maximize the economic rent of its resources. In other words, most fisheries are not being exploited at their highest and best use. The sustainable yield of the renewable fishery resource is traced as a half-moon with respect to fishing effort (Figure 5.13). The fishery's yield and revenue are zero when no fishing effort is expended and with fishing effort they increase until a peak is reached. Beyond that peak, increased fishing effort causes both yield and revenue to decrease because of overexploitation. Too much effort causes the resource's rate of renewal to decline as overfishing raises the mortality rate of the fishery to a level that causes the fish population to shrink. If the rate of fishing, or take, is higher than the fishery's rate of reproduction, the fishery will decline. If the rate of take becomes high enough, it can lead to exhaustion of the resource and Malthusian scarcity in the fishery. Overfishing can wreck the fishery in the same way that overgrazing can wreck the commons.

The rent-maximizing level of fishing effort, E_O is less than actual fishing effort, E_A. Because fisheries are nonexclusive, their economic rent is dissipated by competition. Additional fishers enter the water as long as their rent is nonnegative. Fishing continues beyond the maximum sustainable yield, E_{MSY}, because the fishery's economic rent remains positive beyond that point. As fishing technology improves—sonars become more developed, global positioning sytems more widely used, and economies of scale more widely available in the form of factory ships—costs can be expected to drop. As the marginal costs of fishing effort decrease, more rent is generated and then dissipated. And as fishing effort

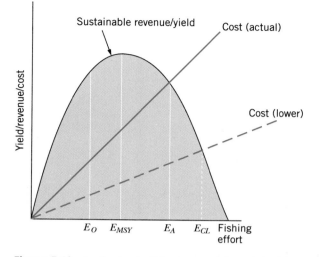

Figure 5.13 In the basic fisheries model, sustainable revenue from a fishery initially increases with fishing effort but soon peaks and then declines even as effort increases. The point on the diagram marked E_O corresponds to the maximum difference between higher revenue and lower cost. It is the optimum level of effort with respect to maximizing resource rents. The point marked E_{MSY} corresponds to the maximum sustainable revenue of the fishery. The actual effort in the fishery, E_A, corresponds to that point where cost and revenues intersect. At lower costs, fishing effort is expanded to E_{CL}, the point that corresponds to the intersection of the revenue curve and the lower cost line.

expands, the resource is diminished. As described in Case 5.3, part of the continued success of Maine's lobster fleet is attributed to its use of obsolete technology. Figure 5.13 illustrates why less technology and higher costs can be beneficial in this circumstance.

As with exhaustible resources, the fishery resource has a location rent (Figure 5.14). Fish close to the fleet's home port are the first to be harvested. Fish caught in proximity to their consumer market are less costly to take. They have lower costs of storage, they do not require as much processing, the market can be supplied more quickly, and so on. Low costs lead to maximum rents on the resource, but the rents can be dissipated not only by competition but also by depletion of the local resource supply. Local depletion can raise prices at the market for the resource, as illustrated in Figure 5.14, and the rise in price can lead to a rise in the fishery's location rent in the same way that an increase in the price of wheat can affect the location rent of that crop. The extent of the fishery increases owing to the increase in rent, but no rent is available near the port because the resource has been exhausted. The increase in price doesn't mean an increase in the fishing fleet's economic rent because its costs increase as fishing effort occurs at greater and greater distances from the home port. In Figure 15.14, even though potential rents are much greater near port as marked

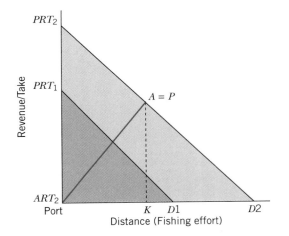

Figure 5.14 The take and revenue of a fishery are functions of distance from the home port. At lower rents to the resource, associated with potential revenue and take point *PRT₁*, rent on the fishery decays to zero by distance *D₁*, where fishing effort ceases. At the higher rent associated with *PRT₂*, rent decays to zero at distance *D₂*. Actual fishing effort, *ART₂*, may be displaced away from the port at the higher rent because of earlier overharvesting. The actual take and revenue from the fishery does not equal its potential until distance *K* from the port is reached.

by PRT_2 than by PRT_1 (Potential Rent at Time), actual maximum rents are no different except in their location. Under the higher prices associated with PRT_2, the same rent available in port under conditions PRT_1 is not available until distance K and only with a much greater expenditure of fishing effort.

The hunting of whales to near extinction has always followed the process of rent maximization. Right whales, for example, acquired that name because they are the "right" sort of whale for commercial purposes. One of their most important characteristics is that they float when they are dead, thereby minimizing carcass losses in the water. About a thousand years ago, the Basques began taking right whales in large numbers in the Bay of Biscay, where the whales swam in shallow water and would often beach themselves. Although the potential location rent of the whales in the Bay of Biscay was high, the actual location rent earned diminished rapidly as local whale stocks were used up. The Basques are skilled at fishing and whaling, however, and they soon developed the technology to take whales in deeper water and farther away. By the mid-sixteenth century, the Basques were whaling off Newfoundland, and other Europeans were copying their methods because of the high prices that whale oil and baleen products were able to command.

The Dutch advanced the technology by developing factory ships so that whole carcasses no longer had to be brought to shore for processing. This practice lowered the rate of distance decay in whaling's location rent, and the industry soon became a global one. Additional improvements included the development of double hulls for traveling in ice packs. Better and faster whale-killing methods, including the exploding harpoon fired from a gun, meant that right whales such as bowheads no longer had to be targeted alone; sperm whales, for example, could always be hunted and were especially targeted by whalers operating from New England's ports. By the beginning of the twentieth century, the whaling industry had collapsed as whales approached extinction. Right whales had become almost impossible to find, and commercial whaling had extended even to small belugas. As extinction approached, substitutes for whale products were developed. Steel was substituted for baleen in corsets, and "land oil," petroleum, was increasingly used as a low-cost, widely available substitute for whale oil. The whaling industry recovered to some degree in the late 1940s under regulation by the International Whaling Commission. By that time, whaling's principal commercial product was whale meat for food, which was especially in demand in Japan and the Scandinavian countries. By the 1970s, whale stocks again came very close to mass extinction, even under regulation, and since 1986 almost all commercial whaling has been prohibited.

Most patterns of animal exploitation for commercial purposes follow paths that would be expected from rent-seeking behavior. Initial takes are confined to larger animals, or only those members of a species with particular characteristics. In all cases, animals closest to the location of markets are taken first. As local and higher quality reserves are depleted, areas of exploitation become wider, and poorer and poorer quality animals are taken. This same process was described in the case of mineral resources that exhibit Ricardian scarcity. In the case of fish, birds, and mammals, however, the tragedy of the commons is relevant because they tend to be nonexclusive in their use. Their rate of exploitation is often far higher than the rate that would sustain a maximum yield, and shortages often develop.

In some circumstances, private developers establish commercial reserves of animal resources. Ranch mink, for example, is a privately held substitute source for wild mink. Private fish hatcheries and fish farms for catfish and salmon are often successful exclusive substitutes for nonexclusive reserves. More often, however, government manages the supply and exploitation of such resources because of the market's failure to do so in a way that serves the general interest. Limits are placed on the number or weight of fish a commercial interest can take from the sea. Licenses are required in an effort to limit participants in commercial fishing, and regulations are established concerning methods used in fishing and the length of the season during which a particular species may be taken. Because fish and whales don't observe political boundaries, most fishery regulations are ineffective unless there is strong international cooperation in their establishment and enforcement. The International Whaling Commission has had its share of detractors over the years, but any regulation enforced under its umbrella is far more effective than any single country's regulation of whaling could ever be.

The same sorts of regulations applied to fisheries are also used to manage the taking of land species. In the United States, for example, some species are protected at the federal level by the Endangered Species Act, and other species are managed at the state level through various licensing, season, and other hunting and trapping regulations. Until the 1890s most game animals were subject to commercial exploitation. Birds, especially ducks and geese, were open to wholesale hunting so that their meat could be sold at butcher shops and in restaurants. Deer and moose, and any other animal that was popular as food, were also taken for commercial purposes. Around the turn of the century, most of these birds and animals were listed as *game species* by states and so were prohibited to commercial exploitation. Although recreational consumption of these species still puts pressure on their numbers, it is not as threatening to a species' survival, and recreational hunting seems easier to control than commercial hunting.

The same policies have been extended to many inland fish species. Black bass (smallmouth and largemouth), for example, used to be taken for commercial purposes, but they are now listed as gamefish only. In the future it would not be surprising if ocean species were declared game fish, with the fish that people eat being raised on farms. Even fishing for sport, however, can rapidly deplete a fishery unless takes are minimized by regulation or by cooperation. The cooperative approach is becoming a more widespread method of fishery preservation. Most recreational fishing associations now promote the practice of *catch and release fishing*, in which fish are not kept for eating or as trophies but are simply released with as little harm as possible.

Conservation practices help maintain any fishery, but they cannot ensure its sustainability unless water pollution is sufficiently controlled to maintain fish habitat. Overharvesting of animal species is one side of a two-sided problem of maintaining living resource stocks. The other side is habitat degradation. In the case of fisheries, spawning grounds have been destroyed by thermal pollution and sediment inflows, water oxygen depletion has resulted from phosphate pollution, bacterial infestations are caused by dumping untreated sewage, and the list goes on. If water quality cannot be maintained at sufficient levels, a fishery can be exhausted despite the strictest fishing regulations.

◪ CASE 5.3
Maine Lobster

YORK, MAINE—Waves rain down on the pilot house as Pat White steers his 33-foot lobster boat through 6-foot swells en route to his favorite fishing spot on a crisp New England morning. Aboard the tossing boat, the stench of fish bait, diesel fumes and bleach are enough to turn the stomach of a newcomer who tries to avoid falling flat on the wet deck littered with fish debris.

But White is cheerful.

Good luck and stable prices have given lobstermen such as White plenty to smile about this summer.

As some New England fisheries struggle, Maine's lobster catch has topped 30 million pounds twice during the last three years, and the state's 4,000-strong lobster boat fleet is expected to have another exceptional season.

Prices have remained relatively stable with consumers willing to pay premium prices such as $10 a pound at a Los Angeles supermarket, or $40 to $74 for a dinner at the Manhattan Ocean Club. At Maine seafood markets, the crustaceans are available for less than $4 a pound and some restaurants in the state sell two-lobster dinners for as low as $10.

Fishermen and scientists wonder how long such good fortune can continue.

With more than 2 million traps crowding the ocean floor, lobster is already overfished, the federal government says.

And lobstermen fear that their livelihoods could be further threatened if fishermen who used to target dwindling fisheries such as cod and haddock are pressured to begin exploiting lobster to make a living.

"It's like squeezing a balloon," said Robert Morrill of the National marine Fisheries Service in Portland. "You squeeze the balloon, it will bulge somewhere else."

For now, the fishing is good.

Most lobstermen in the York area fish between 600 and 1,000 traps, hauling in enough lobster to earn a decent living, said White, the executive director of the Maine Lobstermen's Association.

At the lobstermen's association, White has been trying to bring fishermen together to reach a consensus on conservation rules, such as minimum and maximum size for lobsters that can be caught.

Fishermen cannot harvest egg-bearing female lobsters, which can carry 5,000 to 50,000 eggs. Small lobsters that don't measure up on a metal rule—they must be at least 3.25 inches from their eye sockets to the start of their tails—are tossed back into the ocean as well.

A "good trap" might contain eight or 10 lobsters. At least half are usually thrown back.

As sea gulls flutter overhead, White cuts a notch into the tails of the mature females to declare them off-limits and flips "snappers" that don't measure up back into the cold water.

Such conservation measures, along with the inefficiency of the old-fashioned traps used by generations of lobsterman, have helped the lobster population thrive even though it's generally thought to have peaked, he said.

White said Maine lobstermen want to reach a consensus on stricter voluntary regulations—possibly a moratorium on new licenses—to avoid having the federal government step in to regulate the industry.

One worry lobstermen don't have is whether there's demand for their catch. Back on shore, dealers are busy shipping the lobsters to supermarkets, processors and restaurants coast to coast.

"There's no problem selling them," said Tom Philbrick, manager of the Atwood Bros. lobster pound at Tenants Harbor. "They're wanting more of them than we have to sell."

SOURCE: "Lobster Hauls Fill the Boat in Maine," by David Sharp, Associated Press Writer, September 8, 1994. By permission of the Associated Press.

FOR DISCUSSION

The U.S. government has recently instituted a policy of buying out fishing boat owners in order to reduce commercial fishing pressure off the New England Coast. Can you explain the rationale for this policy in the context of the fisheries model?

RENEWABLE RESOURCES WITH MULTIPLE USES

In recent years, concern for depletion of the world's forest resources has strengthened to the point that forest preservation and other forms of comprehensive management are now considered of vital importance to the world's future. Forests, like fisheries, are renewable resources. Unlike fisheries, however, forest resources have multiple uses whose characteristics range from pure public goods to pure private goods. For example, forests have public good characteristics in their recreational use, even though congestion may cause a decline in the quality of this use. On the other hand, lumber and paper products are examples of private goods taken from forest resources.

Ultimately, the chief problem of the forest resource is its potential application in so many uses and the need to balance its consumption among the wide number of competing interests. The extent of the forest's use and of the related problems of forest management is indicated in Insights 5.2, which contains statements on the ecological, economic, and social importance of forest resources. Although the principles summarized there target all the world's countries, their development was prompted by the recent large-scale reduction of forest in the developing countries.

On average, the world's poorest countries are losing forest most rapidly among the World Bank's income groups (Table 5.3). The low-middle and high-middle-income countries are experiencing somewhat less rapid declines in forest

Table 5.3 Changes in Forest Area
by World Bank Income Group

Income Group	Current Median Rate of Forest Reduction	
	%/Year	Halving Time
Low	0.80	90 years
Lower-middle	0.60	120 years
Upper-middle	0.55	131 years
High	+0.20	360 years (doubling time)
World	0.60	120 years

SOURCE: World Bank, 1994: *World Development Report, 1994* (New York: Oxford University Press).

area, on average, but the high-income countries are actually experiencing an increase in forest cover. Even in the low-income countries, the rate of forest loss does not seem very high, but over long periods it means that half of their current forest cover will be gone in only 90 years. Worldwide, the current average rate of loss would lead to a halving of the globe's forest resources in 120 years, and the annual deforestation of an everage of 500 square kilometers per country.

The trend toward *reforestation* in the richer countries, in contrast to *deforestation* in the poorer countries, suggests the same sort of wealth differential in forest use that is found in the demographic transition with respect to human population growth. The difference occurs for a number of reasons. One is that wood substitutes, especially fuels, are more commonly available in richer countries than in poorer ones. Wood charcoal is a major fuel for cooking and wood a major fuel for heating in many countries, but they are less important in wealthy countries. Another reason why forests are consumed at slower, more sustainable rates in richer countries is that those countries' era of agricultural expansion is past. In Brazil, for example, agricultural expansion rather than the harvest of wood for use as fuel or any other purpose is the single largest cause of deforestation. The same sort of agricultural deforestation took place in the past in North America and Europe, but the decline of many agricultural regions in rich countries has led to a recovery of forest land. New England now has more forest cover than it did 150 years ago, when the extent of cultivation was still expanding. Around the world, the expansion of agricultural land is the most important cause of deforestation, and the reduction of land in agriculture is the most important cause of reforestation.

A third reason for the different rates of forest resource use in rich and poor countries is their pattern of trade. In general, richer countries have diversified export sectors that may include wood products, but consist more of manufactured products and specialized services that tend to earn more in international markets. While many rich countries such as Canada, the United States, and Scandinavia have large wood-product export sectors (see Case 5.4), as a group they tend to be net importers of wood. Many poorer countries, on the other hand, have export sectors that are dominated by primary products. The largest shares of their exports consist of agricultural products and natural resources, including wood, because their manufacturing sectors are not efficient enough to compete internationally with those of the richer countries. Because of the pattern of trade, richer countries can maintain or even increase their wood consumption at the same time that their forests increase in size. That relationship can only be supported, of course, by their pressure on the wood resources of other countries. The implications of the international trade of wood products for North American exports are described in Case 5.4. (The economic geography of international trade is taken up in Chapter 10.)

The economics of forestry are complicated by a number of factors, as illustrated in Case 5.4. Factors affecting aggregate supply include prices, the results of past management practices, current management objectives, and government policy. As a renewable resource industry, forestry is subject to many of the same economic principles that affect fisheries. Achieving a balance between current yield objectives and sustainability over time is a common problem of forest management. Because forests are land-bound, however, rationing of the forest resource is easier. On public lands, cutting can be controlled by the government; the Hotelling Rule can be modified to accommodate sustainability on private forest lands.

Sustainable forest practices are not always the rule, however, even on private land. The practice of *clear-cutting*, for example, which is one of simply leveling every tree over a wood holding, is often employed. Although clear-cut land can regenerate forest cover, it takes dozens of years or longer in most environments for the full renewal of the forest resource. On the other hand, selective harvesting can lead to sustainable forestry in the true sense of the term, with wood lots being thinned on an annual basis over many consecutive years.

As you should expect by now, the geography of forestry follows the principles of rent maximization. The forest industry in the United States, for example, spread from the Northeast to the Midwest, the Midwest to the Southeast, and the Southeast to the Northwest and back again as resources were depleted on a regional basis over time. For example, in the early 1800s, as the supply of merchantable white pine disappeared in Maine, much of the industry moved to Michigan, where the supply was depleted by the middle of the nineteenth century. Unless forest practices are sustainable, the location rent of a lumber operation is dissipated over time as local forest resources are consumed.

The center of a hypothetical lumber operation is designated as the sawmill in Figure 5.15. The current price of lumber yields a location rent gradient that decreases from the site of the mill to a level of zero at distance D_1. The distance

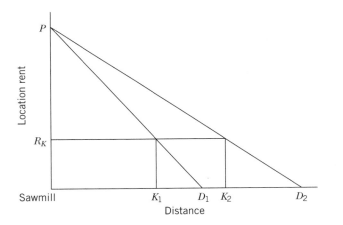

Figure 5.15 Location rent determines the extent of a sawmill's use of the forest resource. At a price for lumber marked *P* and an initial technology, the sawmill will consume wood out to distance D_1. If technology is improved in some way, positive location rent may be earned out to point D_2, indicating the extension of the sawmill's supply area even if market prices for lumber remain stable. A particular level of rent, R_K, can be earned at distance K_1 under the initial technology but at more distant K_2 under the better technology.

decay in the location rent of the sawmill occurs because of the increasing cost of hauling timber from greater distances for processing at the mill. Given the rent gradient marked P to D_1, a location rent of R_K can be earned on lumber felled at location K_1. The same location rent can be earned at location K_2, but only if costs are decreased enough so that a new location rent gradient can be defined that extends the area of potential lumber supply from a boundary at D_1 to one at D_2. The pattern of cutting for the sawmill would be one of expansion from the sawmill, where location rent is highest, toward the periphery of its supply area, where location rent declines toward zero. Unless practices designed to achieve sustainability are followed, such as selective harvesting, any sawmill would eventually consume all its economic supply.

A decrease in costs, as illustrated here, or an increase in the market price for wood products would extend the supply area of the sawmill and keep it in operation. Technology that induces productivity gains could accomplish this extension, or it could come about because of a decrease in transport costs as new roads are built. For example, recent extensions of lumbering in the Northwest of the United States have come about because of road building in the region's national forests, and deforestation in the Amazon basin has simply followed the pattern of road expansion there.

➤ INSIGHTS 5.2
The Importance of Forests

NON-LEGALLY BINDING AUTHORITATIVE STATEMENT OF PRINCIPLES FOR A GLOBAL CONSENSUS ON THE MANAGEMENT, CONSERVATION AND SUSTAINABLE DEVELOPMENT OF ALL TYPES OF FORESTS

Preamble

a. The subject of forests is related to the entire range of environmental and developmental issues and opportunities, including the right to socio-economic development on a sustainable basis.

b. The guiding objective of these principles is to contribute to the management, conservation and sustainable development of forests and to provide for their multiple and complementary functions and uses.

c. Forestry issues and opportunities should be examined in a holistic and balanced manner within the overall context of environment and development, taking into consideration the multiple functions and uses of forests, including traditional uses, and the likely economic and social stress when these uses are constrained or restricted, as well as the potential for development that sustainable forest management can offer.

d. These principles reflect a first global consensus on forests. In committing themselves to the prompt implementation of these principles, countries also decide to keep them under assessment for their adequacy with regard to further international cooperation on forest issues.

e. These principles should apply to all types of forests, both natural and planted, in all geographical regions and climatic zones, including austral, boreal, subtemperate, temperate, subtropical and tropical.

f. All types of forests embody complex and unique ecological processes which are the basis for their present and potential capacity to provide resources to satisfy human needs as well as environmental values, and as such their sound management and conservation is of concern to the Governments of the countries to which they belong and are of value to local communities and to the environment as a whole.

g. Forests are essential to economic development and the maintenance all forms of life.

h. Recognizing that the responsibility for forest management, conservation and sustainable development is in many States allocated among federal/ national, state/provincial and local levels of government, each State, in accordance with its constitutional and/or national legislation, should pursue these principles at the appropriate level of government.

Source: *Report of the United Nations Conference on Environment and Development, 1992* (New York: United Nations), p. 480.

■ CASE 5.4

Wood as an Economic Resource

MAJOR FACTORS AFFECTING U.S. SUPPLIES

The current growth removal balances for timber show that the hardwood forests and eastern softwood forests can support additional harvests. However, these are only an indicator of the future harvest potential. The actual harvest over the next twenty years will depend upon ownership objectives, past investments in forest management, stumpage prices (prices paid for forest land) and institutional constraints.

For private lands, market forces will be a predominant factor; stumpage prices in the United States have shown wide fluctuations in the past several decades but have generally followed an upward trend. Demand rather than supply shifts have been the predominant factor in these movements. Demand increases which cause further upward movement in stumpage prices will influence ownership behavior and facilitate further increases in timber supply where inventories are sufficient.

Timber sale offerings on public lands are generally determined by institutional constraints rather than the market. As a general rule, these institutional constraints are aimed at a sustained volume of timber output. On this basis, harvests from National Forest lands may generally increase over time. However, there is a degree of uncertainty in this forecast. In both the West and South, these lands provide habitat for a number of animal species considered threatened or endangered. Timber management activities must be altered to account for these species' habitats. The number of species listed as threatened or endangered may increase in the future and have the effect of reducing timber sale offerings.

Also, some of the timber supply comes from non-growing stock sources such as tops and limbs, fence rows and forested land other than timberland. In recent years, timber output from non-growing stock sources has been increasing, mainly because of increased demand for fuelwood. In 1986, this represented 9.3% of total softwood output and fully 38% of total hardwood output. While this is not expected to be a major factor with respect to the industrial roundwood market, it could be extremely important in meeting fuelwood demand.

FUTURE PROSPECTS FOR UNITED STATES TIMBER SUPPLIES

Given the constraints on supplies from public lands, increased harvests to the year 2005 must almost entirely originate on private lands. In the East, the timber inventories on private ownerships have been building for decades, and there is volume to respond to demand increases. In the West, the old growth inventories on private ownerships are being rapidly depleted, and by the year 2000 will be largely gone.

During the decade beyond 2000, there may be an unprecedented age class situation for softwood inventories in the United States. The United States since European settlement has had large reserves of virgin softwood timber as exploitation moved from the Northeast to the Southeast and then to the West. By 2000 or thereabouts, large diameter softwood timber will have been harvested on private lands and the harvest on public lands will be constrained by non-market forces. The effects of this situation on timber availability will depend to a large degree on the size and timing of forest product demand growth over the next twenty years. There is the potential for fluctuations in roundwood prices if demand cycles as in the past.

FACTORS INFLUENCING DOMESTIC AND EXPORT DEMAND

Various factors are more or less important for markets for individual products. In general, however, demands for forest products are tied to population and the economy. Markets for some products are relatively stable while others are cyclic. The construction industry—new construction and repair and remodeling of existing structures—is the primary market for solid wood products and cycles according to changes in interest rates necessary to finance mortgages. The demographics of the population also influence housing demand. For example, the "baby boom" generation in the United States had a major influence on U.S. housing demand in the 1980s.

Demands for paper and paperboard are also cyclic in the domestic North American economy. For example, demands for newsprint depend in part on advertising in newspapers which cycles with the economy and the demand for paperboard depends in part on the level of general manufacturing activity with its consequent demand for packaging materials.

Despite cycles in consumption, the overall trend in North American consumption has been upward because of growth in population and economic activity. Projections of population and economic activity underlie projected North American consumption of forest products.

Demands in the export market depend on demand conditions in the importing countries, exchange rates, competing sources of supply, the demand-supply situation in North America, and tariff and non-tariff factors. Export markets for North America have traditionally been the industrialized countries and this is expected to continue. Thus, Japan and Europe are the major sources of offshore demand. Other developing markets include the Republic of Korea, Taiwan and the Peoples Republic of China. Market development activities are in place in other countries, but low per capita incomes and/or lack of tradition of use of the various forest products are formidable obstacles to overcome.

Exchange rates have been free floating since the early 1970s and have major influences on North American shipments to offshore markets. Trends in exchange rates are very difficult to project in the current world economic environment and thus any projections of trade flows are uncertain to the extent that exchange rates may change.

Japan—The main competition for North American softwood exporters in the Japanese market consists of domestic Japanese sources and coniferous logs from the Soviet Union, and secondarily coniferous logs from New Zealand and Chile. The Japanese market for temperate hardwoods has generally been limited, in part because of lack of market familiarity with them and in part because of the availability of tropical hardwoods. Market development activities are having some effect on the market, but it is expected to remain relatively small. Controversy over harvest of the tropical rain forest is stimulating interest in temperate hardwoods.

There is every reason to be optimistic about exports of pulp, paper, and paperboard to Japan. Per-capita consumption of paper and paperboard is expected to increase. The domestic pulp industry has been relatively stable in terms of production and environmental concerns limit the outlook for new mills. As mills are modernized, there will be some increases in domestic capacity, however.

Unlike the situation for softwoods where North America is one of the few sources for world markets, the world market for pulp and paper has many current and potential sources of supply. Japan is also a major importer of waste paper for recycling. Brazil, South Africa, and various Pacific Rim countries are all potential sources of fiber-based products. The outlook for Japan thus is upbeat, but the expectation is that it will be a very competitive market.

Europe—In general, the market can be characterized as mature with growth paralleling increases in population. In a mature market, growth in market share for any one supplier must come at the expense of another supplier. Projections of North American exports to Europe are based largely on judgments about the future course of trends of the past 25 years.

North America supplies to Europe mainly coniferous and temperate hardwood lumber, wood pulp, newsprint, and linerboard. Coniferous plywood and temperate hardwood logs and veneer are also important. Currency valuations affect the competitive position of North America with respect to newsprint and other paper producers in Scandinavia.

SOURCE: United Nations Economic Commission for Europe and Food and Agriculture Organization, 1990: *Timber Trends and Prospects for North America* (New York: United Nations, ECE/TIM/53), pp. 25–27 and 38–40.

FOR DISCUSSION

What impact does international trade have on the supply of forest resources in any individual country? Are their arguments for forest preservation in a single country if wood and other forest products can be imported?

POINTS IN SUMMARY

1. High prices are a symptom of scarcity, and as any commodity becomes scarce, the market makes its price rise and its consumption decrease.

2. The tragedy of the commons arises as a growing population is faced by a fixed set of resources.

3. Malthus's basic argument was that population tends to grow at a geometric rate, but that food supplies increase at a much slower rate because of the law of diminishing returns.

4. Supporters of the Malthusian model argue that its basic propositions are irrefutable, but that certain developments have occurred that have delayed the inevitable tragedy.

5. Poorer countries have much more rapid rates of population growth than do richer countries.

6. The different rates of growth from region to region around the world are leading to a drastic redistribution of the world's population.

7. The demographic transition model describes a population's shift from a high-level equilibrium of birth rates and death rates to a low-level equilibrium of birth rates and death rates.

8. When the demographic gap is large and positive (birth rate minus death rate), then natural increase in population occurs; the wider the gap, the faster a population grows.

9. Sectoral shifts are proportional movements of labor and income from the primary sector's activities to the secondary sector to the tertiary sector. The overall shift with economic growth is from a natural resource economy to a service economy.

10. Although some resources are held as common property, most are effectively rationed by the market through the mechanism of price, and the market effectively allocates a natural resource to its "highest and best use" in the same way that land is allocated by the market.

11. Because of international trade, the size of a country's population may not be relevant to the consumption of some of its domestic natural resources because they are actually consumed in other countries.

12. Something is a resource if it is useful in accomplishing a goal, and whether or not something is useful depends on related economic and technological circumstances.

13. Natural resources are often classified into two groups: exhaustible and renewable.

14. Resource use follows Ricardo's model. The best resources, like the best lands, are used first, and lower quality resources, like lower quality lands, are not used until they can return rents.

15. The relative proportion of a resource held in reserve as compared to the amount consumed is a function of its price at the market, as long as production costs are held constant.

16. Malthusian, or quantitative, scarcities occur only on a localized basis, but they often signal Ricardian, or qualitative, scarcities at a larger geographic scale.

17. Technological advance is a major mechanism of resource substitution and expansion of the set of resources available for use in production. The ability to substitute one resource for another by technological mechanisms has served over time to suppress the prices of most raw material exports in world markets.

18. Because they have some characteristics of a public good, either congestible resources are often allocated completely by governments or governments intervene actively in their market allocation.

19. Energy consumption is marked by two patterns of substitution: the substitution of individual resources for others as sources of energy and the increasing efficiency of energy consumption over time.

20. Because energy-conserving technology has not fully diffused from rich countries to poorer ones, energy consumption in poor countries lags the rich countries in average efficiency.

21. Energy can be considered a strategic resource that is necessary for the very survival of a country's economy.

22. Costs of environmental degradation have only recently come under consideration in determining the relative efficiency of comparable sources of energy.

23. The hunting of whales to their near extinction has always followed the process of rent maximization. Most patterns of animal exploitation for commercial purposes follow from rent-seeking behavior.

24. Conservation practices help maintain any fishery, but they cannot ensure its sustainability unless water pollution is sufficiently controlled to maintain fish habitat.

25. The main problem of the forest resource is its potential application in so many uses and balancing its consumption among the wide number of competing interests.

26. Agricultural deforestation took place in North America and Europe, but the decline of many of their agricultural regions has led to a recovery of their forest land.

27. Unless forestry is practiced on a sustainable basis, the location rent of a lumber operation is dissipated over time as local forest resources are consumed.

TERMS TO REMEMBER

appropriative water rights	catch and release fishing	clear-cutting congestible good	deforestation demographic gap

demographic transition

economic resources

exhaustible resources

game species

Hotelling Rule

Industrial Revolution

Malthusian model

Malthusian scarcities

Malthusian trap

mineral endowment

Organization of
  Petroleum Exporting
  Countries (OPEC)

potential (resource)
  supply

private goods

public goods

reforestation

renewable resources

reserves

resource base

resource pyramid

Ricardian scarcities

riparian water rights

rule of 72

sectoral shifts

strategic resource

total fertility rate

tragedy of the
  commons

SUGGESTED READING

Hardin, G., 1968: "The Tragedy of the Commons." *Science*, Vol. 162, pp. 1243–1248.

This is arguably the most influential paper ever written on the relationship between population growth and natural resource consumption. Hardin's work is steeped in lifeboat ethics, and this piece is similar to his others. He simply finds the world too crowded.

Kneese, Allen V., and James L. Sweeney, eds. 1985–93: *Handbook of Natural Resource and Energy Economics*, Vols. 1–3. Amsterdam: North-Holland.

These are three thick volumes on natural resource, energy, and environmental economics. The contributions are unequal as to length, specificity, mathematical presentation, and so on, but the area of study is so broad that the imbalance in the selections seems impossible to avoid. Chapter 23, in Vol. 3, pp. 1111–1130, "Natural Resources in an Age of Substitutability," by Partha Dasgupta, was a particularly important resource in writing the chapter you just read.

Mowatt, Farley. 1984: *Sea of Slaughter*. Boston: Atlantic Monthly Press.

Mowatt is a noted Canadian author of fiction but turns his hand here to natural history. The book describes the decimation and downright extirpation of a number of species along the coast of Atlantic Canada and New England. The problem for most species he describes was one of increasing accessibility to the European settlers of the region.

Odum, Howard T., and Elisabeth C. Odum. 1976. *Energy Basis for Man and Nature*. New York: McGraw-Hill.

Written in the wake of the first energy crisis of the 1970s, this book possesses a sense of urgency that may seem misplaced today. It does, however, provide an alternative, ecological, framework for evaluating projects that many observers consider to be more appropriate now than ever.

Rees, Judith. 1989: "Natural Resources, Economy and Society." Chapter 6 in *Horizons in Human Geography*, edited by Derek Gregory and Rex Walford. Totawa, N.J.: Barnes & Noble.

Rees provides a thorough, but brief, summary of natural resource economics and geography. In addition, she presents an interesting discussion of the political economy of resource scarcity on the international scale.

Roberts, Rebecca S., and Jacque Emel. 1992: "Uneven Development and the Tragedy of the Commons: Competing Images for Nature-Society Analysis." *Economic Geography* Vol. 68, pp. 249–271.

The authors redefine the tragedy from the socioeconomic perspective of "combined and uneven development." In doing so, they attempt to show that the tragedy is not objective but defined by a social context.

Williams, Michael. 1989: "Deforestation: Past and Present." *Progress in Human Geography*, Vol. 13, pp. 176–208.

This paper contains a thorough review of the changing extent of forest land around the world. It contains a lengthy list of references that cover the literature well.

The *Limits* Trilogy

Meadows, Donella, H., Dennis L. Meadows, J. Randers, and William H. Behrens III. 1972: *The Limits to Growth*: *A Report for the Club of Rome's Project on the Predicament of Mankind*. New York: Universe Books.

Cole, H. S. D, ed. 1973: *Models of Doom*. New York: Universe Books.

Meadows, Donella, H., Dennis L. Meadows, and J. Randers. 1992: *Beyond the Limits*: *Confronting Global Collapse, Envisioning a Sustainable Future*. Post Mills, Vt.: Chelsea Green.

Is the sky falling or not? The first volume listed has been the source of much debate concerning not only the future of human society but also economic forecasting and the use of computer simulation. Its decidedly Malthusian tone is denounced in the second volume, which uses its title to disparage the first volume. The Malthusians return in the third volume to tell us that many of the predictions made in *Limits to Growth* have come true, only we haven't noticed, but it's not too late to prevent further calamity.

Chapter 6

Transportation and Spatial Interaction

This chapter

- considers the supply and demand for transportation services in the context of local infrastructure requirements.
- introduces gravity models and other models of spatial interaction to describe the demand for transportation services between places.
- outlines the basic costs and pricing of different modes of transportation.

- explores the impacts of regulation and deregulation of transport services in the United States.
- introduces the effects of spatial pricing policies on the market areas of producers and wholesalers.

Courtesy of Missouri Pacific Railroad Co.

So far, spatial interaction has been emphasized as the foundation for the geography of the economy, but only in a general way. Rural land-use patterns, for example, have been shown to develop in response to the varying requirements of accessibility between producers and consumers of agricultural products. Urban land-use patterns often are determined by the relative needs of sellers and buyers for spatial interaction in a local economy. As spatial interaction becomes less costly, land-use conflicts arise as more users compete for more accessible land. But while increasing accessibility can sometimes lead to conflict, it more often leads to gains in economic efficiency. Recall that the costs of spatial interaction are like any other transaction cost; they put a drag on the exchange of goods and services in an economy. The establishment and improvement of transportation systems are expensive, but the costs are an investment in an economy's future. As part of economic infrastructure, transport systems lower costs of spatial interaction in general and raise the productivity of the economy. By lowering the costs of exchange between places, transport systems lead to the geographical integration of markets. Market areas of producers get larger, consumers have more choices of products and services to consume, and economies become more efficient.

TRANSPORT SERVICES: SUPPLY AND DEMAND

Considering the supply and demand of transport services is not much different from considering whether the chicken or the egg came first. Transport services provide physical links between places, and allow the supply and demand for goods and services to be met over distance. If wheat is in demand in one place, for example, and it is in supply in another, a transport route between the two places allows the wheat market to function. In this case, the demand for a transportation route occurs in response to the needs of producers and consumers for spatial interaction—flows between places. On the other hand, the development of a transport route for one purpose may be the reason why spatial interaction can occur for other reasons. For example, the trade in wheat that might cause a route to be established might also result from the establishment of the route for other purposes. Historically, for example, transport links that have been developed for military purposes are easily and beneficially used for economic purposes by civilians.

Transport routes are one component of *economic infrastructure*. Infrastructure is the basic physical framework of the economy. It consists of transport lines, communications systems, water, and other utilities that benefit the economic activity of a place and better allow that place to interact with others. The benefits of infrastructure are usually intended not for one company or even one general sector of the economy, but for the economy as a whole. Because of its general benefit, infrastructure is often owned outright and operated by governments. Almost every highway system, for example, is owned and operated by a government body. Where government does not own infrastructure, it often regulates its operation in the interests of the public at large, often by controlling prices and service quality. The so-called public utilities in the United States—the electric companies, telephone companies, and so on—are regulated by either the federal, state, or local governments in most instances, even though they are owned and otherwise operated most often as corporations or corporate subsidiaries.

Currently, there is a trend toward the privatization and deregulation of infrastructure in many countries, but some government regulation is always likely to be maintained so that the general benefits of infrastructure can be ensured at relatively low prices (see Insights 6.1). In many circumstances, transport infrastructure must be subsidized by governments because it provides benefits in the form of externalities. Such benefits are not accounted for in most conventional cost-benefit analyses (as outlined in Chapter 1), and private companies cannot afford to provide services that are not profitable in the conventional sense (Insights 6.2). For example, although a mass transit system can provide general benefits to a region by decreasing road congestion and atmospheric pollution, a private company would be unable to collect revenues from providing such services. Its revenue base would be limited to its ridership, a much smaller population that cannot be expected to pay for the general benefits received by others. Government operation or subsidy of transport systems is necessary because of the market's failure to value the complete set of benefits such a system may provide.

The chicken and egg analogy can be applied to transport infrastructure as well as to transport services. Transport systems raise levels of productivity and therefore lead to increases in wealth. As wealth is increased by developing transport systems, part of it can be reinvested in new transport systems or in the rehabilitation of old ones. Such additional investment again leads to higher productivity, more wealth, and so on. Transport infrastructure can produce an increase in wealth, but wealth is required to develop transport infrastructure. There is an old saying, "It takes money to make money," and the development of transport systems works in about the same way.

The relationship between transport systems and wealth is illustrated in Figure 6.1, which shows the relative average road densities of the World Bank's income groups of countries. In high-income countries, there is almost one and one-quarter kilometer of paved roadway for every square kilometer of territory. The next highest income group has less than 0.2 kilometer of paved road for every square kilometer of territory, and the world's poorest countries average about 3/100 of a kilometer of paved road for every square kilometer, or about 1/40th of the density of roads found in the average rich country. Certainly, much of the higher density of roads found in the rich countries can be attributed to their

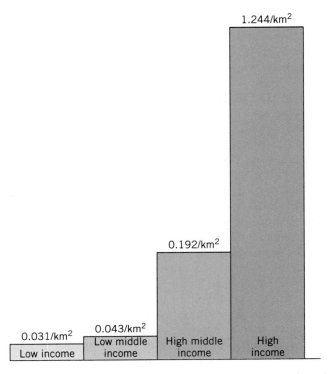

Figure 6.1 The relative density of paved roads (km of road/area in square km) is related to average income. Source: World Bank, 1994, *World Development Report, 1994* (New York: Oxford University Press).

very high rate of ownership of automobiles. Highways, however, have multiple uses ranging from private transport for recreation to freight movement. Their higher density in the richer countries underscores the point that rich countries have more transport services than do poor countries; the disparity in transport services helps maintain the disparity in incomes.

Supply and demand for transport services is largely a function of income at the international scale, with richer countries having a higher density of transport infrastructure than the poorer countries. Within a country or region, however, as long as incomes are fairly equal, the density of transportation services is a function of two variables: population and economic specialization. Centers with large populations usually have a variety of transport services available. In the United States, for example, a big city such as Chicago is an intersection of interstate highways, has frequent rail service for freight and passengers (both long distance and commuter), has two major commercial airports within its metropolitan area, and because of its location on Lake Michigan, boasts active port facilities. Chicago's size ensures sufficient demand for a wide variety of transport services. Smaller places have less general demand for transport, and so the general supply of transport tends to decline accordingly.

> **INSIGHTS 6.1**

General Transport Policies in Rhode Island

1. Develop and maintain a balanced, integrated, safe, and cost-efficient transportation system, giving full recognition to long-term land use and environmental impacts associated with transportation facilities.

2. Locate residential, industrial, commercial and institutional development in a way that will minimize the need for transportation.

3. Develop transportation systems that will help to shape and serve development in accordance with state land use policies, rather than simply to accommodate growth.

4. Provide a variety of transportation modes designed to meet the differing needs of different people, activities, and purposes of travel, and the needs of industry and commerce, within the framework of current and planned land development patterns.

5. Relate the design and location of transportation facilities positively to the natural and cultural landscape. Avoid intrusion of noise or other traffic impacts on recreation and open space resources. Provide a high aesthetic quality in the transportation system.

6. Consider likely future transportation needs in current land development projects. Provide adequate capacity to accommodate planned future growth.

7. Establish and enforce transportation safety measures, and design and maintain the transportation network to avoid or minimize transportation related negative impacts on the environment, including adverse effects of noise, air emissions, road salting, stormwater runoff, and hazards to vehicles, travelers, pedestrians and wildlife.

8. Consider regional transportation requirements and coordinate with neighboring states in the earliest stages of system and project planning to assure compatible planning and execution of transportation projects.

SOURCE: Division of Planning, 1989: *Land Use 2010: State Land Use Policies and Plan.* State of Rhode Island and Providence Plantations, State Guide Plan Element 121 (Providence: Rhode Island Department of Administration), p. 3.5.

> **INSIGHTS 6.2**

Net Present Value versus Cost-Effectiveness Analysis as a Basis for Transit Investment Decisions

Many transit authorities, as well as the federal government, use cost-effectiveness tests to help guide investment decisions. Tests such as cost per new-rider do help in the search for investments that maximize the number of travellers attracted to transit for each dollar spent on facilities and services. Such tests do not, however, indicate which alternatives offer the highest net economic returns nor whether the economic benefits of transit projects, such as time savings and environmental gains, outweigh their costs and thus contribute to productivity and economic growth.

Tests confirm that cost-effectiveness and net present value tests can yield very different economic signals to decision makers. The Table below indicates that, for the city in question, the cost-effectiveness test favors a light rail option whereas the net present value criterion indicates that an express bus approach is likely to yield a higher net economic benefit.

The Table also indicates a risk that none of the options considered are likely to yield benefits in excess of costs (all net present values being negative). This information would be unavailable with only cost-effectiveness information.

Like any forecast, however, net present values should be viewed in the context of sensitivity and risk analysis. Express Bus Option Two, for example, produces an NPV near zero, indicating a broadly satisfactory rate of return. As well, a longer assumed life for each of the options shows that the Light Rail Two alternative is likely to yield a positive Net Present Value. The Express Bus Option Two, however, remains the most economically attractive from an economic perspective.

Economic Benefits of Alternative Transit Improvements in a Selected Urban Area, by Alternative Decision Criteria

Alternative	Cost-Effectiveness (Cost Per New Rider)	Net Present Value (Millions)
Transportation System Management	$3.71	−$5.60
Express Bus Option One	$18.18	−$16.40
Express Bus Option Two	$3.12	−$0.30
Light Rail Option One	$5.86	−$46.90
Light Rail Option Two	$2.87	−$8.60

Source: Lewis, David, 1991: *Primer on Transportation, Productivity and Economic Development* (Washington, D.C.: Transportation Research Board, National Research Council), p. xii.

TRANSPORT, SPECIALIZATION, AND LOCATIONAL INERTIA

Specific transport systems are not always tied to the general demand raised by large populations but often are supplied because of the demand created by an area's particular economic specialization. Places with economies based on natural resource extraction or refining often have fairly small populations, for example, but high densities of rail transport services. The products produced in these places are bulky and expensive to ship in small quantities. Such bulk cargo is most efficiently moved by railroad or by ship or barge where water access is available. The river-canal-coastal waterways in the eastern United States, for example, have been vital in the agricultural and industrial development of the region (Figure 6.2). The relationship is part of another chicken-and-egg situation; economic specialization generates demand for high densities of certain types of transportation services, and a supply of transportation services allows certain types of economic specializations to develop.

Unfortunately, as described in Case 6.1, if a transport service is withdrawn from a region, any economic specialization that depends on the service can be threatened with rapid decline. The abandonment of a portion of Canadian Pacific Rail's track undermines the local economy of Saint John, which depends on the rail line for shipment of wood products. Although improvements in accessibility can lead to improved productivity owing to decreased costs of spatial interaction, loss of accessibility raises those costs and lowers the region's ability to compete with alternative producers. The same thing occurs at smaller scales.

Figure 6.2 The river-canal-coastal waterways of the United States have been vital in the development of heavy industry and agriculture in the East and Midwest.

Patterns of land use and transport services form around each other. When transport systems change, so does accessibility, and when accessibility changes, so does the pattern of land use. For example, local retail centers have grown around the stations on Atlanta's relatively new rapid transit system because they are centers of accessibility in that metropolitan area. An increase in accessibility usually raises the value of a location, and a decrease in accessibility usually lowers a location's value.

Transportation services available at a place and the place's economic functions exist in a type of symbiosis; each reinforces the other to cause *locational inertia*, or a stable geographical pattern of production and consumption. Over time, transport technology changes, but the density of transport services and the geographical pattern of routes has a tendency to remain the same. Early transport routes and related patterns of settlement were often determined by the physical environment. River systems and coastlines had the highest density of settlement because water transport was easy compared to overland movement of people or goods. Once established, locational inertia in the pattern of settlement took hold. Although advances in transport technology have lessened the importance of waterway transport over time, most of the world's population still lives in close proximity to navigable water.

Because of locational inertia, contemporary surface routes often follow routeways that were established for other modes of transportation in earlier times. In New York, for example, most of the current interstate highway routes follow the waterway system. Initially, the Native Americans in the region used the waterways and connecting paths for their trade and seasonal shifts in settlement because lengthy overland travel was much more difficult. Later, European and other settlers used the waterways for their own commerce and linked them better by developing a set of canals, most notably the Erie Canal, in the early 1800s. Rail lines followed the canal and river systems by the mid-1800s, and modern highways now follow the same routes (Figure 6.3). Additional routes have been added over time; I-81 runs north-south in central New York, for example. Rather than replace the old pathways, they serve as extensions.

Although routes often remain the same over time, as in the case of New York, the transport systems they support are often replaced through the process of competition. The canal system that was put in place in the early 1800s established large-scale commercial transport service in New York, but the canal system was soon replaced by the railroads, which could offer faster service over longer distances and at lower prices. Furthermore, rail added flexibility to transportation because its routes were not limited to existing waterway locations. By the early 1920s, rail transport in the region (and elsewhere in the United States) was giving way to automotive transport. Highway transport has even more locational flexibility than rail transport, and although it has not replaced rails in the same way that rails replaced canals, automotive transport is now the dominant surface mode wherever it is available. In sum, whereas the demand for transport services is driven by population and economic specialization, the supply of transport services responds to an additional factor: competition.

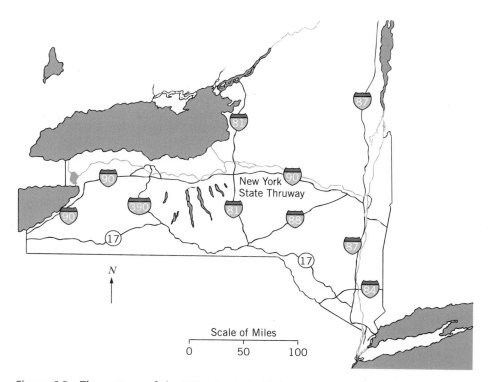

Figure 6.3 The pattern of the U.S. Interstate Highway System in New York mainly follows the earlier transport arterials formed by waterways. The waterways induced an economic geography in the region that provided the demand for the current highway network.

☑ CASE 6.1
The Implications of Losing a Line of Accessibility

BAILEYVILLE—The National Transportation Agency of Canada has given Canadian Pacific Rail permission to abandon portions of its track between Sherbrooke, Quebec, and Saint John, New Brunswick.

The decision was unwelcome news for officials of Georgia-Pacific Corp. The company relies on rail transportation over CP lines at its manufacturing complex in Woodland.

Company officials have said that 11,000 more tractor-trailers would have to travel Route 9 each year to make up for the loss in rail service.

In the decision released late Monday, CP was permitted to close its Canadian Atlantic Railway subsidiary between Sherbrooke and the Maine border at Jackman. The railroad can also close the line between the Maine border at Vanceboro and Saint John.

If allowed to go through, the abandonment would be a blow to the economy of Saint John.

"We have had better days," Mayor Elsie Wayne said in a press release. "We want a moratorium put on this until there is a national policy review. At that time, you look at the needs and the services that are required for the people in the region. It isn't over for us."

Canadian Pacific will continue to operate the track for one more year because another line, Via Rail, uses it for passenger trains between Montreal, St. John and Halifax, Nova Scotia. After the track is abandoned, Via Rail can still provide passenger service to Halifax, but not to St. John, over a longer route operated by the Canadian National Railways.

A related CP application to abandon its 202 miles of track in Maine is still pending before the U.S Interstate Commerce Commission, which has scheduled public hearings for October.

According to Dames & Moore, a Maryland consulting firm hired by the ICC, about 30,000 freight cars travelled along the Maine portion of the line during 1992. More than half of the cars carried logs, lumber or paper products.

According to Dames & Moore, CP is trying to sell some or all of its line in Maine. If a buyer is found, G-P might still be able to ship its products out of Woodland by rail.

CP has said the line loses too much money. The National Transportation Agency agreed, noting that the line has lost more than $30 million Canadian between 1990 and 1992.

"The agency also examined the nature of the operation of these lines and determined that further operating efficiencies could not be achieved," the agency said Monday in a statement.

"After reviewing all of the evidence, the agency concluded that there would be insufficient revenues generated to offset the significant losses being incurred."

Source: "CP Gets Nod to Abandon Rail Service," in *Bangor Daily News*, August 25, 1993, p. 21. By permission of the Bangor Publishing Company.   ◢

FOR DISCUSSION

Case 6.1 describes the potential loss of rail service in a region and the related impact on truck traffic. Use this case in describing some of the limits to competition in the transport sector.

MODELS OF SPATIAL INTERACTION

Although the density of transport infrastructure at a place tells us something about its demand for transport services in general, the geographical pattern of transport links among places identifies the demand for spatial interaction in the economy. The geographical pattern, or *spatial structure*, of supply and demand in an economy is revealed by transport links that have been established for specific purposes (Insights 6.3), or to satisfy more general demand for interaction among particular places. How is the demand for spatial interaction established? E. L. Ullman, an economic geographer, listed three elements that form the foundation for spatial interaction: complementarity, transferability, and intervening opportunity.

In general, *complementarity* exists between places if they have a supply and demand relationship. For example, if oranges are in supply in Southern California and demand for oranges exists in New Jersey, then Southern California and New Jersey have a complementary relationship (at least in this respect). All other things held equal, the spatial interaction between the two regions would consist of a flow of oranges from Southern California to New Jersey, and a flow of money in payment from New Jersey to Southern California.

As in most cases, however, other things are not necessarily equal, and that's why transferability and intervening opportunity are also important considerations in the demand for spatial interaction between places. In general, the characteristic of *transferability* has to do with transportation costs. If, for example, an orange's transport cost between California and New Jersey were a penny per mile, spatial interaction involving oranges between the two would be unlikely. The high cost of transport would give the oranges a very low level of transferability, and even though Southern California and New Jersey would still be complementary with respect to oranges, spatial interaction would not take place. Transferability, and therefore spatial interaction, are dependent on transport technology, and as advances in transport technology take place, the volume of spatial interaction increases.

Although spatial interaction between places is positively affected by complementarity and by transferability, the flows between any two particular places are negatively affected by the existence of an *intervening opportunity*. For example, the opportunity for people in New Jersey to purchase oranges from growers in Southern Arizona rather than Southern California could mean that spatial interaction between New Jersey and California would be replaced by spatial interaction between Arizona's orange growers and New Jersey's orange consumers. Of course, other opportunities to meet supply or demand don't have to be intervening in a literal way. The existence of any alternative opportunity for spatial interaction, as long as complementarity and transferability requirements are met, is likely to offer competition to any other similar opportunity for spatial interaction. Oranges from Florida compete with oranges from Arizona and California (as well as oranges from Brazil) in the New Jersey market.

The supply and demand for spatial interaction is often assessed by the use of a *gravity model*. Gravity models of spatial interaction are taken, as the name indicates, from Isaac Newton's equation for measuring gravitational force:

$$F_{ij} = G \frac{M_i M_j}{D_{ij}^2} \tag{6.1}$$

where F_{ij} is the gravitational force exerted between two objects i and j, M is the mass of an object, D is the distance between the two objects, and G is the gravitational constant. (For the appropriately curious, $G = 6.67 \times 10^{-11}\ nt - m^2/kg^2$.) The gravitational force. therefore, between the Earth and the Sun is positive in the product of their masses but declines in the reciprocal of the squared distance between them. (Not all spatial interaction models are derived from Newton's equation. See Insights 6.4.)

So, the attraction between two bodies increases with their mass but decreases with the square of their distance. The rule for describing the demand for spatial interaction is very similar; the attraction between two places increases with their populations but decreases with their distance. The populations of the places define their complementarity in a general way. The larger a center is, the more likely it will attract people and economic flows from other places. Conversely, larger centers should, in general, be able to generate more flows as well. Smaller centers are less attractive as destinations and less likely to be the sources of large volumes of outward flows in an economy. Longer distances, like low transferability, are assumed to make spatial interaction more costly. Spatial interaction, therefore, is subject to distance decay. It's interesting that basic physical principles of gravity can be applied effectively in socioeconomic contexts. There really is no theoretical reason why gravity models of spatial interaction should work well in describing economic flows, but they do. In a sense they are like automatic transmissions. Everybody knows what they do, but nobody knows how they do it.

The basic gravity model of spatial interaction is

$$I_{ij} = K\frac{P_i P_j}{D_{ij}^{\ X}} \tag{6.2}$$

where I_{ij} is the interaction between two places i and j, and D is their intervening distance. In the spatial interaction model, K is not a constant like G in Newton's equation but is used instead as a scaling measure; that is, it takes on a different value depending on what type of flow is being analyzed. The volume of telephone calls between two cities, for example, would be much larger than the volume of recreational trips between them, but the difference would not be captured if a value like K was not used to scale the expected volume of interaction. For example, K might be equal to 0.1 if the spatial interaction of a good with low transferability is being considered, but it might be equal to 10 in the case of something with very high transferability. In addition, unlike the constancy of gravitational force, the effect of distance on spatial interaction varies from one context to another. That is why the distance is raised to the Xth power in the spatial interaction model rather than assuming that the square of distance is always the appropriate measure of distance decay. For example, there seems to be less distance decay in air transport for business travel between cities than business travel by automobile. The appropriate value of X might be 1.0 when air travel for business is considered as compared to a value of, say, 2.5 for auto transport.

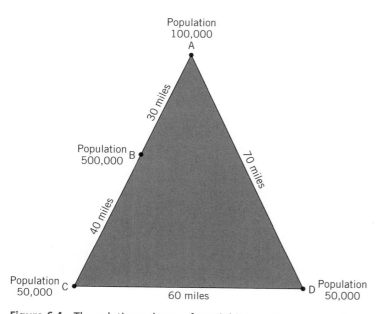

Figure 6.4   The relative volume of spatial interaction among the towns on this map can be calculated from a gravity model of spatial interaction.

Let's run through a quick application of the gravity model using the data in Figure 6.4. Let's say that the square of distance is the appropriate measure of distance decay in this instance and that $K = 1$, so that we can drop it from our calculation. The measure of interaction between cities C and D is calculated as $(50,000 \times 50,000) / (60 \times 60) = 694,444$. The measure of interaction between cities C and A is calculated as $(50,000 \times 100,000) / (70 \times 70) = 1,020,408$. Interaction between cities D and A is expected to be the same as between cities C and A because C has the same population as D, and they are the same distance from city A. Now the actual numbers calculated for the interaction values are not of interest, but their relative magnitudes are. Given the size and spacing of the cities on the map (Figure 6.4), the volume of spatial interaction between C and A (or D and A) is expected to be about one and one-half times the volume of spatial interaction between cities C and D.

The results in the example depend on some assumptions concerning the basic gravity model of spatial interaction that are not always easy to make. First, the entire population of a place may not be the appropriate value in assessing its demand for spatial interaction. We know that a place's wealth has a bearing on its demand for spatial interaction, so a place's income may be a more appropriate measure of complementarity than is its population. In addition, the basic gravity model ignores the effect of intervening opportunities on spatial interaction. In the example, city B with its huge population has no effect on the expected volume of spatial interaction between cities A and C. That volume is expected to be the same as that between cities A and D, even though there is no intervening city on that route. Finally, as you will see shortly, transferability may not be adequately measured by the physical distance between places.

In many cases, distance is only an indirect measure of the declining demand for spatial interaction between places. The cost of spatial interaction has a more direct bearing on its volume, and although it is often closely related to distance, they are not always the same thing. In general, the cost of spatial interaction increases with increasing distance, but the effect of its cost varies in two ways. First, as long as the cost of spatial interaction is relatively low compared to the price of a good or service entering into exchange, then the volume of spatial interaction is not necessarily affected by long distances. On the other hand, even short distances can limit the demand for spatial interaction if the cost of movement is high relative to the price of the good or service entering into exchange. Second, the impact of cost on frequency and volume of spatial interaction can vary with ability to pay. In the United States, for example, people with higher incomes enjoy higher mobility simply because they are better able to afford it (Figure 6.5). This brings us back to another chicken and egg proposition;

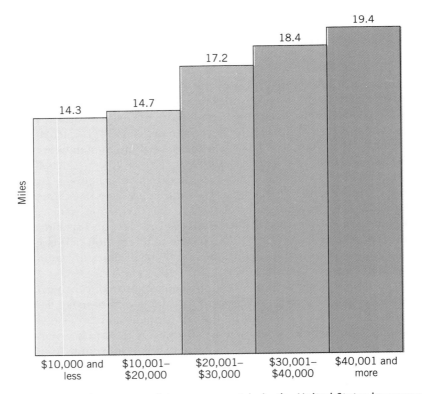

Figure 6.5 The average distance per car trip in the United States increases with annual income. SOURCE: Federal Highway Administration, U.S. Department of Transportation, 1991. *Highway Statistics 1991.*

spatial interaction leads to increases in wealth, and wealth leads to increases in spatial interaction.

➤ INSIGHTS 6.3
Transport Routes, Accessibility, and Spatial Structure

Transport arteries define connections between places that reveal the spatial structure of a geographical system. Spatial structure can be illustrated in two ways: by a map and by a matrix indicating the connections between places in a system in a binary format; 1 indicates that places are connected, 0 indicates that they are not. The map shows Air New Zealand's jet routes around 1980. As you can see, and might expect, the highest density of Air New Zealand's routes are focused on New Zealand's three largest cities: Auckland, Wellington, and Christchurch. Connections on the network are most frequent between the cities in New Zealand and the three Australian cities in the system. Non-Australian cities only connected directly with Auckland and, for several of the cities, that was their only connection in the system.

The connectivity matrix in the table also describes Air New Zealand's spatial structure. The places in the network are listed as both row and column headings in the matrix. If two places have a direct connection, such as Singapore and Auckland, then the corresponding element in the matrix is 1; if two places are not connected directly, such as Hong Kong and Sydney, then the corresponding element in the matrix is 0. The matrix is symmetrical because a connection between any two places on the network runs both ways. For example, Samoa is connected to Auckland so Auckland must also be connected to Samoa. Connec-

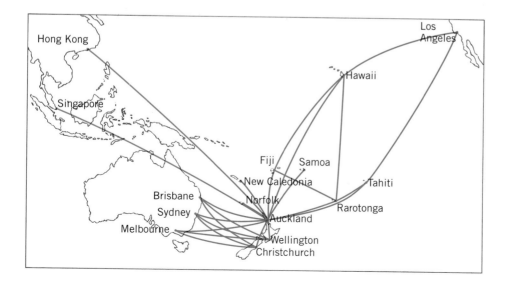

Air New Zealand's Spatial Structure circa 1981

Place/Node	1	2	3	4	5	6	7	8	9	10	11	12	13	14	15	16	Total
1. Hong Kong	-	0	0	0	0	0	0	1	0	0	0	0	0	0	0	0	1
2. Singapore	0	-	0	0	0	0	0	1	0	0	0	0	0	0	0	0	1
3. New Caledonia	0	0	-	0	0	0	0	1	0	0	0	0	0	0	0	0	1
4. Brisbane	0	0	0	-	0	0	0	1	1	1	0	0	0	0	0	0	3
5. Sydney	0	0	0	0	-	0	0	1	1	1	0	0	0	0	0	0	3
6. Melbourne	0	0	0	0	0	-	0	1	1	1	0	0	0	0	0	0	3
7. Norfolk Is.	0	0	0	0	0	0	-	1	0	0	0	0	0	0	0	0	1
8. Auckland	1	1	1	1	1	1	1	-	1	1	1	1	1	1	1	0	14
9. Wellington	0	0	0	1	1	1	0	1	-	0	0	0	0	0	0	0	4
10. Christchurch	0	0	0	1	1	1	0	1	0	-	0	0	0	0	0	0	4
11. Fiji	0	0	0	0	0	0	0	1	0	0	-	0	1	0	1	0	3
12. Samoa	0	0	0	0	0	0	0	1	0	0	0	-	0	0	0	0	1
13. Raratonga	0	0	0	0	0	0	0	1	0	0	1	0	-	0	1	0	3
14. Tahiti	0	0	0	0	0	0	0	1	0	0	0	0	0	-	0	1	2
15. Hawaii	0	0	0	0	0	0	0	1	0	0	1	0	1	0	-	1	4
16. Los Angeles	0	0	0	0	0	0	0	0	0	0	0	0	0	1	1	-	2
Total	1	1	1	3	3	3	1	14	4	4	3	1	3	2	4	2	50

An entry of "0" indicates that the two places are not linked by a direct connection. Places with direct connections have a corresponding entry of "1."

tions are only counted between places, so the principal diagonal of the matrix, where places are matched with themselves, is marked by a dash (-).

Describing a transport system in terms of connections only, and ignoring frequency of service, route capacities, and so on, reduces the system to its simple topology. This simple topology, however, defines the basic spatial structure of the system in the same way maps describe it graphically. If you wanted to, you could duplicate the map of Air New Zealand's routes by piecing together the connections contained in the matrix. Row or column sums on the matrix indicate the degree of accessibility, with respect to number of connections, of any place on the network. Samoa, for example, is tied with some other places with the lowest level of accessibility on the network as indicated by its row and column sums of 1. At the other extreme, Auckland is the most accessible place on the network as indicated by its row and column sums of 14. The relative sparseness of the entire system is indicated by the number of actual connections between places compared to the number of possible connections. The number of actual connections in the Air New Zealand system is 50, which is a relatively small proportion of the possible total of 120 $((16 \times 15)/2)$ connections between places that could exist.

➤ INSIGHTS 6.4
The Doubly Constrained Spatial Interaction Model

The gravity model of spatial interaction (Equation 6.2) is best used to accurately describe the flows between two places over fairly long distances. At shorter distances and for flows among a number of places, a different type of spatial interaction model is often used. This model takes the general form

$$T_{ij} = \frac{A_i B_j O_i D_j}{e^{\gamma C_{ij}}} \tag{6.3}$$

In this model, T_{ij} is the number of trips between origins, i, and destinations, j. The number of trips starting at the origins, O_i, and ending at destinations, D_j, are known, and flows in the model are constrained to equal both ends, hence the name "doubly constrained." The origin constraint is defined as

$$A_i = \frac{1}{\sum\limits_{j=1}^{n} B_j D_j / e^{\gamma C_{ij}}} \tag{6.4}$$

and the destination constraint is defined as

$$B_j = \frac{1}{\sum\limits_{j=1}^{n} A_i O_i / e^{\gamma C_{ij}}}. \tag{6.5}$$

Because A_i and B_j are just scaling coefficients and O_i and D_j are known values, the interesting part of the doubly constrained model is in the denominator of Equation 6.3. The value of e is the base of the natural logs, which turns out to be a fairly accurate value with respect to calibrating distance decay, which is defined with respect to cost, C_{ij}, in this model. The remaining value in the denominator, γ, is a calibration coefficient that describes the importance of travel cost for the flow in question. For example, transport cost may have a different effect on business travel than on travel for recreation.

This model has a foundation in probability as opposed to the physical analogy that underlies the unconstrained gravity model. It can also be derived from some behavioral theory that is useful in applying it and related models to situations where locational choices can be made. Finally, note that travel cost, rather than distance, is the interaction's limiting factor in this spatial interaction model. Related models use travel time, rather than distance or cost, to account for "distance" decay in spatial interaction.   ◄

TRANSPORTATION COSTS

Transportation is a service provided by various modes under a variety of pricing systems. The most basic form of transport pricing is called a *postage stamp rate* because a single price is charged for an item's transport throughout the service territory of the company selling the transport service. The name is taken from the type of service offered by most postal authorities. The U.S. Postal Service, for example, charges a fixed price for delivery of an item weighing one ounce or less, and of a certain dimension, anywhere within the United States. The price of having a letter delivered across the street is the same as that of having it delivered across the country. The costs of delivering the letter vary by distance, of course, but the high volume of such mail has led the Post Office to charge by its average (and subsidized) cost rather than its marginal cost with respect to distance.

Blanket transport rates are similar to postage stamp pricing because they also are based on the average costs of providing a transportation service. Unlike postage stamp rates, however, blanket rates vary from place to place within a company's service area on a regional basis. UPS, for example, has divided the United States into several districts for pricing purposes. Whether one is sending a package from Chicago to Boston or Chicago to New York, the price is the same under this blanket rate system because Boston and New York are in the same shipping district. Sending a package from Denver to New York or Boston has a different charge because Chicago and Denver are not in the same district.

Perhaps the most common form of transportation pricing is simply based on the distance a product is shipped or a person is moved. The costs of providing transportation generally increase with distance, but transport costs are affected by economies of scale. *Economies of long distance,* a class of economies of scale, are very important in the provision of transportation services. Because of economies of long distance, the total cost of transportation increases with distance at a decreasing rate (Figure 6.6). The costs of transport can be divided into two components: *terminal costs* and *line-haul costs.* Terminal costs are fixed expenses associated with providing a transport service such as maintenance of a warehouse, insurance costs, property taxes, and finance charges on a fleet of vehicles. They may also include some variable costs associated with loading and unloading shipments, documentation, and so on. As illustrated in Figure 6.6, transport costs are above zero because of terminal costs even before any distance has been covered.

If total terminal costs can be allocated over many miles, average cost per mile decreases, total costs increase more slowly, and a *tapering freight rate* is the result. For example, if it costs you $150 to load a truck and you drive the truck 1 kilometer, you have paid $150/km to load the truck. If you drive the truck 10 kilometers, the distance-based average loading charge decreases to $15/km, and if you drive it 1000 kilometers the average goes down to 15¢/km. All terminal costs can be allocated over distance in the same way. Most of the line-haul costs increase fairly uniformly with distance. For example, truck fuel and wear and tear on tires are likely to increase the line-haul costs of truck transport with distance traveled on an almost one-to-one basis. However, labor costs can decrease with distance, especially if an hourly rate is in force. A truck driver is probably going to be paid the same amount for traveling 120 kilometers in an hour as for traveling 100 kilometers in an hour, so average labor costs decrease with

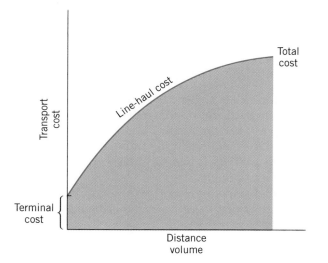

Figure 6.6 Transportation is marked by economies of scale as revealed in the tapering freight rate. Total costs of transportation increase at a decreasing rate with distance and with volume of shipment because average costs decrease with length and size of shipments.

distance the faster the truck is driven. This decrease in average line-haul costs contributes to the tapering total cost of transport with distance.

Economies of scale with respect to volume of shipment also affect transportation (Figure 6.6). The ability to spread costs of transport across a large number of individual items in a shipment lowers average costs in the same way that spreading costs over many miles lowers average costs. For example, if sending a rail freight car from Chicago to Denver costs $500, then sending one package on the car yields an average cost per package of $500. If 100 packages are sent in the single freight car, the average cost per package decreases to $5, and so on. The greatest source of *economies of large volume* in transportation is the reduction in handling and associated charges that occurs when larger consignments are shipped. If a freight car cannot be filled, for example, then the requirements for handling its contents can easily double or more. On- and off-loading increases, multiple stops may be required, and more paperwork accumulates in addition to the logistical complications. Sellers of transport services charge premiums on an average price basis for smaller consignments because of their associated loss of scale economies.

SYSTEMS OF FREIGHT CONSOLIDATION

A transportation service called *freight-forwarding* provides a type of wholesale link between sellers and purchasers of transport services that takes advantage of economies of large volume. Rather than purchase transport services directly, small volumes of freight (LTL or less-than-truck load, LCL or less-than-car [rail] load, LPL or less-than-plane load, as opposed to TL, CL, and PL, respectively) are consigned to freight-forwarders that consolidate a number of small shipments into larger ones. For example, let's say a railroad charges $100 per unit of shipment between Denver and Los Angeles for LCL lots but only $60 per unit of shipment for CL lots. A freight-forwarder might charge $80 per unit of shipment for LCL shipments, consolidate them, and purchase CL service from the railroad at $60 per unit. Small shippers pay the freight forwarder a lower price than they would pay the railroad, so they are happy; the railroads achieve their economies of large volume, so they are happy; and the freight-forwarders are happy as long as their businesses are profitable.

A similar type of freight consolidation was developed in the trucking industry, with companies specializing in LTL shipments as carriers rather than as freight-forwarders. Their method of using *hub-and-spoke transport systems* relies on feeding a central point of consolidation, the hub, by a series of smaller routes, the spokes. Hub-and-spoke systems achieve *economies of flow*, which are a special form of economies of large volume. The small feeder routes ensure maximum capacities and full economies of volume on major routes of interaction between the hub and other hubs or other major centers. Airlines in the United States use hub-

and-spoke networks to move people in the same way. Smaller flights originating in smaller centers are consolidated at hub airports into larger, fuller flights that then go on to other major airports. Centralized baggage handling and other airline facilities further enhance possibilities to achieve economies of scale at hub airports.

Economies of large volume also serve as the foundation for one of the most important developments in transportation since the invention of the wheel. *Freight containerization*, developed by shipping magnate Malcolm McLean in the 1950s, lowers handling costs significantly by prepacking freight consignments into large boxes or trailers. Containerization has lowered transport costs in three ways. First, handling costs are decreased significantly when freight is containerized. Containers can be packed by producers and sent directly to customers, so that third parties are not required to handle cargo at all. Before containerization, a *break-in-bulk freight system* of loading and reloading cargoes required relatively labor-intensive shifts of freight from truck to pier and from pier to ship. Furthermore, the more people who handled the freight, the greater the loss due to damage and theft. Containerized cargoes can be sealed before transit, so the shipper has much less liability than under the break-in-bulk system.

The second way that containerization has lowered transport costs has been by increasing economies of large volume. Container ships have holds that can be packed tightly, in conformance with the shape of the containers, so that there is no unused space below decks. More important, containers can be stacked on decks of ships and on flatbed truck trailers, so that more cargo can be moved by individual carriers than before.

The third major savings afforded by containerization comes from increased flexibility. Containerized freight is highly suitable to shifts from one transport mode to another; containers can be lifted directly from ships to rail cars or from rail cars to flatbed truck trailers. Some containers have removable wheels so that they can be pulled by trucks or on the railroads. This increased flexibility improves the ability of shipments to be sent directly from their point of origin to their point of destination. Transport speed is increased while handling costs go down.

OTHER INFLUENCES ON TRANSPORT COSTS

The costs of providing transport services, and the prices paid to buy them, are based to a large degree on volume and distance of shipment. Other factors, however, are important, too. The type of cargo being shipped affects the cost of transportation because of differences in care that different cargoes require. Coal, for example, is very cheap to ship in bulk because it requires very little care. It can get wet, and it can be exposed to subfreezing temperatures without any loss of its value. Glass panes, on the other hand, require special care because breakage in transit eliminates their value altogether. Fresh foodstuffs and some other items require temperature and moisture controls that raise the cost of their shipment relative to goods that do not require refrigerated transit.

The availability of competing modes of transport also affects the price paid to purchase transport services, and indirectly the costs of providing the service as well. To some degree, however, competition between the various modes of transport is limited by some of their particular cost characteristics. Transport services have a tendency to be selected by distance of shipment. In the United States, for example, coastal shipping freight runs have the longest average distance, followed by air freight, rail, inland rivers and canals, and finally truck (Figure 6.7). The availability of coastal shipping is limited by nature, as is shipping on rivers and canals, but the water-borne transport is often preferred by long-distance shippers of bulk cargoes. Its line-haul costs are low because a small crew

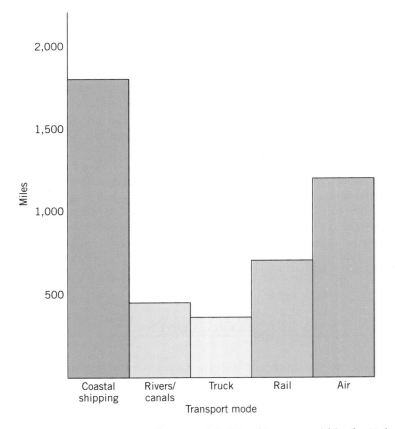

Figure 6.7 The average distance of freight shipments within the United States varies with transport mode.   Source: U.S. Department of Transportation, 1990. *National Transportation Strategic Planning Study* (Washington, D.C.: U.S. Government Printing Office), pp. 5–28.

on a single ship can move thousands of tons of cargo. The average distance of air-freight shipments is also fairly long. In the case of air freight, speed of shipment seems to be the most important factor. In Europe, time savings of air shipments, as compared to shipments by truck, appear to become important around distances of 550 kilometers and dominate the choice between the two for comparable shipments around 700 kilometers. The time factor is similar with respect to trains, with air freight gaining preference over rail freight at about 600 kilometers. Otherwise, equally suited shipments almost always are sent by air freight rather than by road or rail, when distances of more than 1,000 kilometers are involved.

Perhaps the two most potentially competitive modes of freight transport are trucks and trains. For similar European cargoes, rail transport tends to be preferred over truck transport at distances over 400 kilometers. The average length of shipment by train in the United States is about double the distance of the average truck shipment. The choice of trucks for shorter distances and trains for longer distances can be attributed to their differences in terminal costs and line-haul costs (Figure 6.8). Average terminal costs are lower in the trucking industry than in the rail industry, so short-distance shipments by train are relatively expensive. The average line-haul costs are less for a rail shipment than for a comparable truck shipment, however, and rail's lower line-haul costs make it more competitive than trucking at longer distances.

Distance and choice of transport mode are linked in personal travel as well as in shipping freight. In the United States, for example, walking is used only

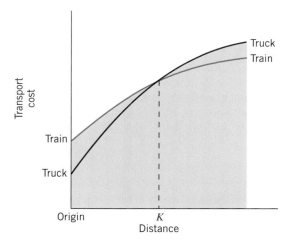

Figure 6.8 On average, trucking has lower terminal costs but higher line-haul costs than rail freight. The difference in the two modes' cost structures tends to make trucking more efficient for transport over shorter distances and trains more efficient over longer distances. In this illustration, freight would be sent by truck between the origin and point *K*, but by rail for longer distances.

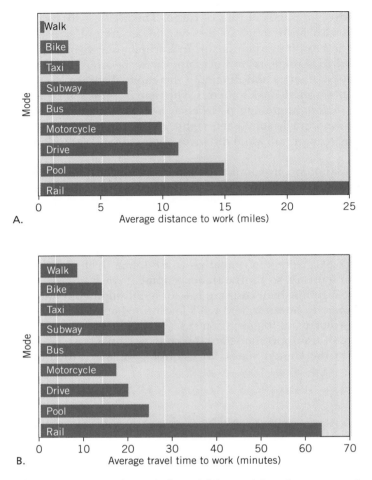

A.

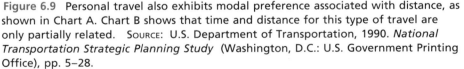

B.

Figure 6.9 Personal travel also exhibits modal preference associated with distance, as shown in Chart A. Chart B shows that time and distance for this type of travel are only partially related.   Source: U.S. Department of Transportation, 1990. *National Transportation Strategic Planning Study* (Washington, D.C.: U.S. Government Printing Office), pp. 5–28.

for getting to work over very short distances. Bicycles are used for longer distances, but most transport of this kind takes place by automotive modes or by rail (Figure 6.9). The distribution of modes by distance is representative only of richer countries. More expensive transport modes, especially personal automobiles but also motorcycles, are unaffordable in many poorer countries where walking is a much more common mode of transport for commercial as well as personal reasons. In the United States and other wealthy countries, the selection of transport mode for personal purposes results from a number of considerations, including time, cost, convenience, and simple personal preference.

TRANSPORT REGULATION AND DEREGULATION IN THE UNITED STATES

Even though the basic operating economics of the various modes of transport helps determine which of them is chosen for moving a particular shipment or for personal travel, there is still room for competition at most distances no matter what the cargo. Changes in technology, in market perceptions among companies that sell transport services, and in government policies have all worked together in recent years to promote competition among transportation modes. Competition between airlines and bus companies, for example, is new, as is the potential for competition between trucking and railroads implied in Case 6.1. Not too long ago, the travel time differential between airplane and bus was considered to be sufficient on its own to separate the two systems from direct competition over routes that covered much distance. Furthermore, price differences segregated their markets significantly, with air travel reserved for fairly well-off individuals and business travelers, while bus service focused on connections between rural areas and urban centers that had little business traffic and on less well-heeled individuals traveling for personal reasons. In freight markets, trucks didn't often compete against trains for economic reasons, but not all of the differences between the two markets were results of fundamental differences in their operating costs. Much of their market segregation was the result of their regulation by the federal government. As the nature of such regulation has changed, so has the potential for competition between the two modes of transport.

Regulation of transportation began in the United States in 1887 with the establishment of the Interstate Commerce Commission under the Act to Regulate Commerce. The purpose of regulation was to eliminate the railroads' practice of charging excessive rates and other discriminatory practices against their *captive markets*, those unserved by alternative modes of transport. The practice at the time was to charge very high rates for shipments where waterway alternatives did not exist, as in the Great Plains, and to undercharge customers near coasts and other waterways. Regulation was also established to limit collusion among railroad companies that reinforced their dominance over captive markets.

Regulation held benefits for the railroads that were designed to offset the costs it presented. The thinking at the time, encouraged by the railroads, was that they held *natural monopolies* that developed from the high start-up and fixed costs of their operation. Because of these high costs, it was especially important that they maintain high volumes that lowered their average costs and, therefore, the prices they charged their customers. Competition, by reducing economies of scale, meant higher prices to customers of the railroads, and so it was inefficient; that's why the monopoly was termed "natural." Under regulation, the monopolies were protected by the government. Companies wishing to start railroad service and to expand existing services into other markets required government permission, but that permission was very hard to get.

Over time, federal regulation of transportation in the United States was extended to almost all forms of interstate movement of goods and passengers.

Pipeline transport, inland and ocean water carriers, trucking, airlines, and bus systems were all subject to regulation. In the case of pipelines and to a lesser degree, water-borne shipping, the "natural monopoly" argument was used as the basis for regulation. Where it could not be used, as in trucking and later the airline industry, regulation was imposed in the interest of achieving a comprehensive and integrated national transportation system. It was argued that the integration of the nation's transport was weakened if half of it was regulated and the other half was not. Since no one thought deregulating the railroads was a good idea, other carriers were regulated in the interest of uniformity in policy.

Eventually, most interstate transportation in the United States consisted of a series of geographical monopolies or near-monopolies operated by a series of carriers in each mode of transport. Direct competition within modes only existed on routes where demand for spatial interaction was considered to be great enough to maintain economies of scale for all the competitors. Service areas were guaranteed as monopolies, with prices based on cost-plus principles rather than on competitive processes. *Cost-plus pricing*, in which transport prices were effectively set by government boards to cover transport service costs plus a "reasonable" profit, reinforced the effect of distance on choice of transport mode described in the preceding section. In return for price guarantees, transport providers guaranteed service on routes within their service areas that would be unprofitable under competitive conditions. Losses on these routes could be compensated by extra earnings on routes that were more heavily in demand within the monopolized area.

By the mid-1970s, it became widely recognized that transportation service in America was not all it could or should be. The railroad industry in particular was under stress, with the rail freight carriers in the Northeast, most notably the Penn Central Railroad, facing bankruptcy. Revenues and service quality suffered under regulation and poor management, and deregulation was held to be the answer to the country's transportation problems. The purpose of economic deregulation of transportation was to allow more service to be provided at lower prices. More-for-less is not a common occurrence, but theoretically the shift from a regulated monopoly to a competitive market has that result. In Figure 6.10, the regulated supply S_R is represented as a vertical line that is typical of monopolistic supply curves. Supply Q_R of transport services is brought to the market at regulated price P_R. That quantity of transport services falls short of that supplied by market equilibrium, as identified by the intersection of the demand curve, D and the competitive supply curve, S_C. The equilibrium price is P_C, which is lower than the regulated price, and under competition the quantity of transport services supplied is Q_C, which is more than the supply under regulation.

Economic deregulation of American transportation began with the Railroad Revitalization and Regulatory Reform Act of 1976 and continued legislation that further deregulated rail transport and other modes of transport. By 1986, most systems were deregulated to their current (and likely maximum) extent. Significant regulation persists, however. Captive markets are still protected; that's why the Canadian Pacific rail line in Maine discussed in Case 6.1 had to have its closure permitted by the ICC. Furthermore, environmental and safety regulations remain in place and are occasionally strengthened.

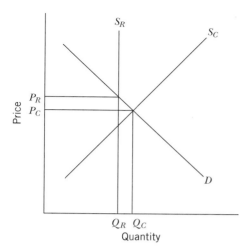

Figure 6.10 A regulated price of P_R yields a quantity of service Q_R when supply is offered on monopolistic terms as indicated by S_R. Under competitive conditions, the intersection of the supply curve S_C and the demand curve D yields a quantity of service Q_C at price P_C defined by market equilibrium.

Although the general effect of deregulation of transportation in the United States has been positive and as intended in the aggregate, its effects are mixed when taken on more specific bases. Competition has led to cost-cutting in an effort to reduce prices. Established carriers that had been operating under cost-plus rules found themselves hard pressed to compete on the basis of price because their costs remained high after deregulation took effect. That's why Greyhound was hovering on the edge of bankruptcy in the early 1990s. Deregulation forced several major carriers in all modes of transportation to shut down and caused hardship for many of their stakeholders, including employees and shareholders. In addition, although aggregate service levels did increase because of regulation, service to specific areas was eliminated, and many places have become effectively isolated from the mainstream American economy. Under regulation, unprofitable routes were served, but losses were compensated by earnings from more profitable ones. Now that profit margins have been cut, surplus earnings can no longer support service on money-losing runs. If regulation no longer requires them, unprofitable routes are rapidly dropped by transportation companies.

PRODUCER PRICING

We have mentioned several times that the costs of spatial interaction can be treated as transaction costs. Transport costs, as costs of spatial interaction, are transaction costs that play an important role in determining the market areas of companies that either produce goods or distribute services. Other things being equal, the volume and frequency of exchange diminish as transportation costs increase. Because this distance decay obviously affects the boundaries of a company's market, the pricing policy a company adopts with respect to delivering its products to its customers is an important factor in determining its revenues. As you read Case 6.2, for example, you will see that transport prices can vary significantly for an otherwise uniform product and that delivery prices can either be set to accommodate an existing market or be used as part of a company's competitive strategy.

The three basic types of pricing policies are FOB/CIF pricing, uniform delivered pricing, and base-point pricing. The extent of a company's geographical market is most heavily affected by an *FOB (free-on-board) / CIF (cost, insurance, and freight) pricing* policy. This type of pricing combines a fixed price for a product at its point of production or central point of distribution and a delivery charge based on distance and handling. The difference between the designations FOB and CIF is that the FOB price is the price quoted at the point of production and the CIF price is the quoted price on the delivered product. For example, say a product is sold for $1,000 at the factory gate and carries a $1/kilometer delivery charge. Its FOB price is $1,000, and its CIF price is $1,100 at 100 kilometers from the factory, $1,400 at 400 kilometers from the factory, and so on.

FOB/CIF pricing defines the market area of a company in terms of a spatial gradient (Figure 6.11). The spatial gradient begins at the point of production, marked M in Diagram A of Figure 6.11, and from there the delivered price of a product increases with distance. At the factory site, M, the product is offered at its lowest price, FOB without any additional delivery charges. As the delivery

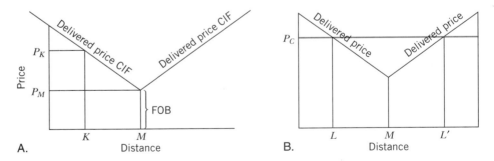

Figure 6.11 Diagram A shows the partition of a product's price under an FOB/CIF pricing system. The point of production is M, and the vertical line from that point represents the FOB price of the product. That price, P_M, is the price that would be paid for the product if it were purchased at the factory. The other part of the product's price is derived from its cost of delivery. The gradients on the diagram represent the product's CIF price as it increases with distance. While price P_M would be paid at the factory, a higher CIF price, P_K, would be paid at distance K. Diagram B illustrates the determination of a company's market boundary by the intersection of its delivered price gradients and a line, P_C, that represents the ceiling price that buyers are willing to pay for the company's product.

charges add to the delivered price of the product, demand for the product is likely to decrease. In Diagram B of Figure 6.11, market limits for a product are shown as the segment L to L'. Those limits correspond to the intersection of the delivered price gradients with a line, P_C, that represents the ceiling, or maximum, price that consumers are willing to pay for the product. Within the segment L to L', the delivered price is lower than the ceiling. Outside the segment the delivered price is more than consumers will pay, so L to L' defines the extent of the company's market area.

As an alternative to FOB/CIF pricing, a company can follow a *uniform delivered pricing* policy. This policy seems straightforward because a product simply has the same price wherever it is sold. As indicated at the top of Figure 6.12, the price of the product doesn't change with distance from its point of production,

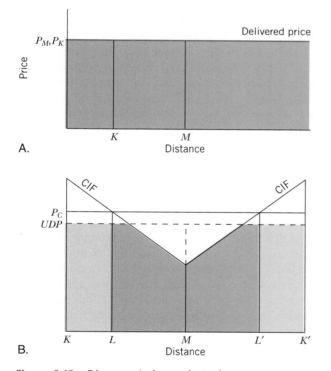

Figure 6.12 Diagram A shows that when a company uses uniform delivered pricing, the price of its product is the same everywhere in its market. In Diagram B, the geographically discriminatory nature of uniform delivered pricing is illustrated by its comparison to an FOB/CIF system in the same region. The difference between the dashed line marked UDP for uniform delivered pricing, and the CIF gradients shows that nearby customers are overcharged under uniform delivered pricing and more distant customers are undercharged. By using uniform delivered pricing, the company can price its product everywhere in the region below P_C, the ceiling price buyers are willing to pay for the product. Therefore, uniform delivered pricing extends the company's market from *LL'* to *KK'*.

so distance decay in demand is not a factor in determining a company's market area because there are no spatial price gradients. Uniform delivered pricing is often opposed as a pricing policy for two reasons. First, it is a geographically discriminatory form of pricing. As illustrated in the bottom half of Figure 6.12, in comparison to FOB/CIF pricing, uniform delivered pricing overcharges nearby customers and undercharges more distant customers. Nearby customers effectively subsidize more distant customers, and the company's market area is expanded by uniform delivered pricing as compared to a pricing system based on cost.

The second reason why uniform delivered pricing is often opposed is that it can easily be used to hide the true costs of production and distribution and so can be manipulated in a way that limits competition in markets. Price collusion among companies is often a problem in markets with relatively few producers. Rather than compete, they are often tempted to share a market by entering illegal agreements as to product prices, delivery volumes, or other aspects of market service. Uniform delivered pricing allows these companies to hide cost variations that would lead to price differences among them. They then argue that their pricing similarities arise by astounding coincidence. As mentioned in Case 6.2, regulators prefer to "unbundle" transport charges from product prices so that cost differences among companies are more difficult to hide. The problems described in that case arise largely from a mandated shift from a type of uniform delivered pricing to FOB/CIF pricing—a good move in general, but one that backfired in this instance.

The third type of pricing policy, *base-point pricing*, also has been used to fix prices and limit competition within markets. Base-point pricing is a form of FOB/CIF pricing that uses an arbitrary or otherwise artificial origin for a product instead of its actual point of production. This policy is most often followed as a matter of convenience. In pricing agricultural commodities, for example, it would be very impractical to quote delivered prices from individual fields. A shipment of tons of grain may have its price quoted as if it were all being delivered from a single point such as Minneapolis, even though it was not grown there or at any other single place. Most base-point pricing is limited to commodity shipments now, but until the 1940s it was used for manufactured products as well.

The best known case of base-point pricing, and one found to be illegal, was the "Pittsburgh Plus" system which was used under collusion by the biggest steel corporations in the United States in the early 1900s. Under that system, steel was priced as if it were produced in Pittsburgh whether or not it was actually produced there (Figure 6.13). The Pittsburgh Plus system was advantageous to the steel producers in two ways. First, by making its customers indifferent as to their source of steel, the producers could maintain their economies of scale in the mills in and around Pittsburgh, their major place of investment. Second, if steel from a nearby mill was priced as if it were coming from Pittsburgh, that price yielded a high profit because customers were paying charges for transport services that were never supplied. The Pittsburgh Plus system was declared illegal in 1924, and base-point pricing for manufactured goods was effectively banned in the United States in 1948 because of its potential for abuse.

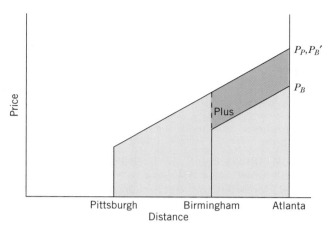

Figure 6.13 In the Pittsburgh Plus base-point pricing system, the price of steel was quoted FOB Pittsburgh, even if it was produced somewhere else. In the illustration here, both Birmingham and Pittsburgh are locations of steel production, and Atlanta is the location of steel consumption. Under conventional FOB/CIF pricing, consumers in Atlanta would prefer to buy their steel from Birmingham with its delivered price P_B instead of from Pittsburgh with its delivered price P_P. Under the Pittsburgh Plus system, however, all steel was priced as if it was coming from Pittsburgh, so the price of steel produced in Birmingham was raised to $P_{B'}$ in Atlanta.

☑ *CASE 6.2*
Effects of Unbundling

When federal regulators separated the cost of pipeline transportation from natural gas sales, the "unbundling" was supposed to foster competition and reduce bills—even for customers at the end of the pipelines in the Northeast.

The change gave large commercial or industrial customers the chance to save some money by negotiating their own deals on gas purchases and delivery, and by paying the local gas company to move the gas from the pipeline to the customer's door.

But some Connecticut industries are complaining that their opportunities to save have evaporated in the past two years because the local gas companies have boosted their charges for transportation services.

The industrial customers argue that the transportation charges of Connecticut's gas utilities—Connecticut Natural Gas Co., Yankee Gas Services Co. and Southern Connecticut Gas Co.—are so high that they discourage customers from bypassing the utility to make their own gas purchases from producers or brokers.

They also say the transportation charges in Connecticut far exceed what gas utilities are charging in neighboring Rhode Island and Massachusetts.

The result is that out-of-state competitors have an advantage because they have more opportunities to reduce their energy costs. And that advantage is costing Connecticut companies business and jobs, said Frank J. Johnson, director of governmental affairs for the Manufacturing Alliance of Connecticut, Inc.

"The greatest complaints that I hear are about costs in Connecticut that are beyond the control of the manufacturer. Energy costs certainly rank high as a topic of complaint in Connecticut, and among the most frequently mentioned outrages is the cost of transporting gas from [the local gas company's] city gate to a manufacturing customer."

The city gate is where gas supplies enter the local gas company's distribution system from the interstate pipelines.

The industrial customers are arguing about the transportation rate to so-called interruptible customers—commercial or industrial users equipped to burn either natural gas or another fuel, depending on which is cheaper. The alternate fuels are generally oil or propane.

—Until a few years ago, the gas companies based their transportation charges to interruptible customers on what it cost them to provide the service. But in response to competition in the industry—and with the approval of state regulators—the companies now base the charge on the value of the transportation service.

That value is determined primarily by looking at the cost of the alternative sources of fuel or supply available to interruptible customers. The charge can vary considerably among customers.

Ansonia Copper & Brass, Inc. has not been able to competitively buy its natural gas since April of 1993, said Craig Schatzlein, operations service manager for the copper-alloy rod and wire manufacturer, one of the few heavy metal producers left in Connecticut.

"Our problems started in April 1993, when our transportation rates started to climb," Schatzlein said. "Prior to that, we were transporting gas through a third party. Since then, we havn't transported on the interruptible rate."

In 1991–92, Schatzlein said, his company's average transportation price from Yankee gas was roughly 50 cents per thousand cubic feet. In 1995, the price is about $1.30. "I don't know many things that have gone up that much," he said.

The company now uses gas supplied by Yankee Gas when it is available and competitively priced with its alternate fuel, No. 6 fuel oil, Schatzlein said. But the company has lost an opportunity to cut energy costs by $5,000 to $8,000 a month because it cannot negotiate its own gas purchases, he said.

In Bridgeport, Peter Kappel sees out-of-state competitors taking trailor truckloads of work out of Connecticut, work that could otherwise be done by his company, Connecticut Metallurgical Processes, or any of the state's 25 other commercial heat-treating companies.

Kappel's company, in business since 1915, employs 23 people. About 20 percent of its costs are energy-related. Kappel uses natural gas and propane as an alternate fuel.

"Our competitors in surrounding states can buy gas from many sources, including the wellhead in Texas, at the best price they can find, and their local distribution company must deliver it from the city gate to them at a regulated price. In Connecticut, the maximum amount a {local gas company} can charge to transport gas is not regulated," Kappel said.

For example, Kappel said, he was able to buy gas in March from the Texas-Mexico border and have it delivered 1,800 miles to the city gate of Southern Connecticut Gas for $2.22 per thousand cubic feet of gas. But the gas utility wanted to charge him $3.02 to move the gas from the city gate to his plant.

"They want to make it so expensive that you won't do it," Kappel said.

SOURCE: "Burning Issue," by Susan E. Kinsman, *Courant* Staff Writer, in *The Hartford Courant Business Weekly*, May 1, 1995, pp. 1, 12–13. By permission of the *Hartford Courant.*

FOR DISCUSSION

Describe some arguments for regulation and some arguments against regulation of the transportation sector.

POINTS IN SUMMARY

1. Transport arterials are one component of economic infrastructure, the basic physical framework of the economy.

2. Government operation or subsidy of transport systems may be necessary because of the market's failure to value the complete set of benefits a system may provide.

3. Transport infrastructure can lead to an increase in wealth, but wealth is required to develop transport infrastructure.

4. The density of transport services within a region is a function of population and economic specialization.

5. Economic specialization generates demand for high densities of certain types of transportation services, and a supply of transportation services allows certain types of economic specializations to develop.

6. When transport systems change, so does accessibility, and when accessibility changes, so does the pattern of land use.

7. Because of locational inertia, contemporary surface routes often follow routeways established for other modes of transportation in earlier times.

8. While the demand for transport services is driven by population and economic specialization, the supply of transport services responds to an additional factor: competition.

9. The geographical pattern of transport links among places identifies their demand for spatial interaction.

10. As advances in transport technology take place, the volume of spatial interaction increases.

11. The supply and demand for spatial interaction is often assessed by means of a gravity model that relies on the principle that demand for spatial interaction between two places increases with their populations but decreases with their distance.

12. The actual cost of spatial interaction has a more direct effect on the volume of spatial interaction than does simple distance.

13. Spatial interaction leads to increases in wealth, and wealth leads to increases in spatial interaction.

14. The most common form of transportation pricing is based on the distance a product is shipped or a person is moved.

15. Economies of scale are powerful in transportation.

16. Freight containerization is one of the most important developments in transportation since the invention of the wheel.

17. Competition between the various modes of transport is limited by some of their particular cost characteristics.

18. Regulation of transportation began in the United States in 1887 with the establishment of the Interstate Commerce Commission under the Act to Regulate Commerce.

19. The purpose of economic deregulation of transportation, beginning with the Railroad Revitalization and Regulatory Reform Act of 1976, was to allow more service to be provided at lower prices.

20. Environmental regulations and safety regulations remain in place and are occasionally strengthened.

21. Transport costs are transaction costs that play an important role in determining the market areas of companies that either produce goods or distribute services.

TERMS TO REMEMBER

base-point pricing	economic infrastructure	freight-forwarding	postage stamp rate
blanket transport rates	economies of flow	gravity model	spatial structure
break-in-bulk freight system	economies of large volume	hub-and-spoke transport system	tapering freight rate
captive markets	economies of long distance	intervening opportunity	terminal costs
CIF pricing		line-haul costs	transferability
complementarity	FOB pricing	locational inertia	uniform delivered pricing
cost-plus pricing	freight containerization	natural monopolies	

SUGGESTED READING

Bianco, Lucio, Domenico Campisi, and Massimo Gastaldi. 1995: "Which Regions Really Benefit from Rail-Truck Substitution? Empirical Evidence for Italy." *Papers in Regional Science*, Vol. 74, pp. 41–62.

The authors find that Italy's freight transport favors truck over rail in most sectors and regions. Rail's primary competitive problems are price and inflexibility. A new north-south rail line may improve rail's ability to compete with trucks by reducing the latter problem.

Brunn, Stanley D., and Thomas R. Leinbach, eds. 1991: *Collapsing Space and Time: Geographic Aspects of Communications and Information*. London: HarperCollins Academic.

Spatial interaction is affected by connections that transport ideas as well as goods and people. This is a collection of 18 papers that focus on the role of telecommunications advances in making the world smaller and interaction easier.

Dempsey, Paul Stephen. 1989: *The Social and Economic Consequences of Deregulation: The Transportation Industry in Transition*. New York: Quorum Books.

Dempsey argues for regulation of transportation because, by his reckoning, the social costs of lost services outweigh the gains in economic efficiency that freer transport markets provide.

Goddard, Stephen B. 1994: *Getting There: The Epic Struggle Between Road and Rail in the American Century*. New York: Basic Books.

This book describes the political economy of the switch from rails to highways in the United States during the first half of the twentieth century. Goddard describes the coalition of auto, steel, concrete, and other producers that overthrew the railroads' political machine and became the "driving" force in American transport policy.

Haynes, Kingsley E., and A. Stewart Fotheringham. 1984: *Gravity and Spatial Interaction Models*. Vol. 2 in Sage Scientific Geography Series. Beverly Hills, Calif.: Sage).

This is an excellent primer on gravity models in concept and in application to both economic and political problems.

Horvath, Ronald J. 1974: "Machine Space." *Geographical Review*, Vol. 64, pp. 167–188.

Horvath considers the automobile to be the "sacred cow" of the Western world, especially the United States. This article describes the geographical impact that the automobile, a machine, has at the local scale in territorial terms.

O'Sullivan, Patrick. 1980: *Transport Policy: Geographic, Economic and Planning Aspects*. Totowa, N.J.: Barnes & Noble.

O'Sullivan describes both the economic and social foundations for the design and provision of transportation systems. Transport issues are examined at three scales: local/urban, interregional, and international.

U.S. Department of Transportation. 1990: *National Transportation Strategic Planning Study*. Washington, D.C.: U.S. Government Printing Office.

This volume contains the general plan for American transport to the year 2015. It provides a multimodal overview of the state of transport in the United States in the late 1980s and contains projections of future demands for transport and how they might be met by appropriate investment in infrastructure.

Vonderohe, A. P., L. Travis, R. L. Smith, and V. Tsai. 1993: *Adaptation of Geographic Information Systems for Transportation*. Washington, D.C.: National Academy Press.

This is a "how to" guide for GIS in planning, design, building, and operating transport systems.

Werner, Christian. 1985: *Spatial Transportation Models*. Vol. 5 in Sage Scientific Geography Series. Beverly Hills, Calif.: Sage.

Werner provides a solid introduction to some of the more technical approaches to the geographical analysis of transport networks and flows, including the linear programming of the transportation problem.

Chapter 7

The Location of Manufacturing

This chapter

- describes some current large-scale patterns in the geography of manufacturing.

- presents a series of selected location factors in manufacturing.

- describes the relationship between changes in manufacturing processes and changing locational requirements in manufacturing.

- provides an overview of basic location models for manufacturing in the context of market structure and competition.

- use the product life-cycle model to illustrate the dynamic nature of locational requirements in manufacturing.

- analyzes the location of foreign direct investment in manufacturing.

Courtesy of Ford

Manufacturing is a little more complicated in its locational patterns than any economic activity we have looked at so far. In general, both agriculture and the natural resource industries are best located in places where two general locational requirements can be met. One is on the production side; coal mining requires the presence of coal, and wheat farming can't proceed unless certain environmental characteristics are in sufficient local supply. The second requirement is market access; if transport services aren't available at the place of production, then production won't take place in more than subsistence amounts. Manufacturing is more complicated in its location because it has a little more locational freedom. For example, as long as transport services are available so that interaction can take place, a factory can be located where the raw materials it uses are in abundance, or it can be located right in the market where most of its production is sold (or anywhere in between). You don't have that kind of locational choice in agriculture or in the natural resource industries. Over time, the mobility of manufacturing has been increasing as more and more locations have been made accessible by the spread of transport networks. In addition, other advances in materials and process technology have reduced the costs of spatial interaction in manufacturing.

THE SHIFTING GEOGRAPHY OF MANUFACTURING

As an economic activity, manufacturing can be measured in two basic ways. One is by its inputs, such as the volume of raw materials and energy it consumes. Labor input, or employment, is often used to measure manufacturing, and changes in manufacturing employment are used to gauge its health. Manufacturing jobs are considered especially valuable by both politicians and workers, and policies that promote the growth or retention of manufacturing employment therefore become the focus of regional and local economic policies. The alternative approach to measuring manufacturing is by its output. Output measures include volume of production, as in numbers of automobiles produced, and weight of production, as in tons of steel.

Perhaps the most frequently used measure of manufacturing combines inputs and outputs in terms of their prices to derive the *value added in manufacturing*. Value added is simply calculated as the price of a product going out the factory door minus the cost of its inputs, including labor, energy, raw materials, semifinished components, taxes, and insurance. Although labor is only one of many costs, it is often the single largest one.

When measured by value added, the geography of manufacturing around the world is quite concentrated. On a proportional basis, the great majority of manufacturing is found in the world's richest countries (Figure 7.1). In fact,

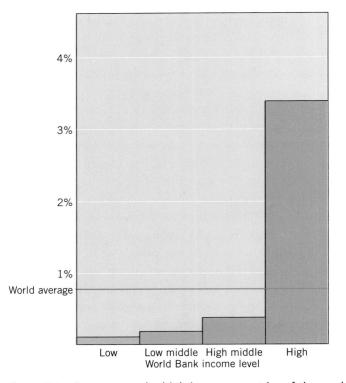

Figure 7.1 On average, the high-income countries of the world have a much larger proportion of the world's value added in manufacturing than do the world's poorer countries. Source: World Bank, 1994: *World Development Report 1994* (New York: Oxford University Press).

more than half of the world's value added in manufacturing in 1992 was located in just five countries: Italy, France, Germany, the United States, and Japan. The last three countries accounted for over 40% of the world's value added in manufacturing. The five countries with the largest manufacturing sectors outside of the high-income group—Brazil, China, South Korea, Mexico, and Russia— contributed only about 10% of the world's value added in manufacturing in the early 1990s. The lesson seems fairly easy: manufacturing and high incomes go together, and that is another reason why governments so often stress manufacturing in their economic policies.

The lesson, however, is not as straightforward as it seems. Historically, manufacturing in many of the world's wealthier countries, in terms of its proportion of a country's employment and of national income, initially tends to grow with a country's economy but then declines as part of the pattern of sectoral shifts (see Chapter 5). While at present the world's richest countries do have the greatest share of the world's value added in manufacturing, the service sector provides the majority of their jobs and is the single largest sectoral source of their national incomes. From 1980 to 1992, average rates of growth in manufacturing

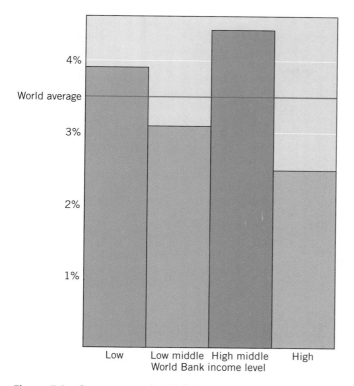

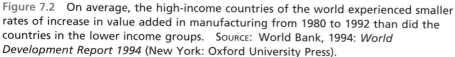

Figure 7.2 On average, the high-income countries of the world experienced smaller rates of increase in value added in manufacturing from 1980 to 1992 than did the countries in the lower income groups. SOURCE: World Bank, 1994: *World Development Report 1994* (New York: Oxford University Press).

among the World Bank's income groups were lowest in the high-income countries (Figure 7.2). This recent trend can be expected to continue as manufacturing becomes relatively less important in already wealthy countries and more important in developing countries around the world.

Manufacturing is geographically concentrated at the global scale but is undergoing dispersion at a fairly steady rate. The same kind of dispersion has taken place over time within the United States. U.S. manufacturing was born in the river valleys of southern New England and soon spread into the Middle Atlantic states of New Jersey, New York, and Pennsylvania. By the beginning of World War II, a manufacturing region that just about encompassed the northeastern quadrant of the United States seemed to be firmly established. While manufacturing was certainly established in other parts of the country, particularly in the Southern Piedmont, Texas, and California, it did not approach the levels of geographical concentration found in America's leading manufacturing region. In 1967, over 60% of U.S. manufacturing employment was located in the Midwest and Northeast Census regions of the United States (Figure 7.3 A and B). By 1989, however, a shift had occurred that saw a marked decline in the Northeast

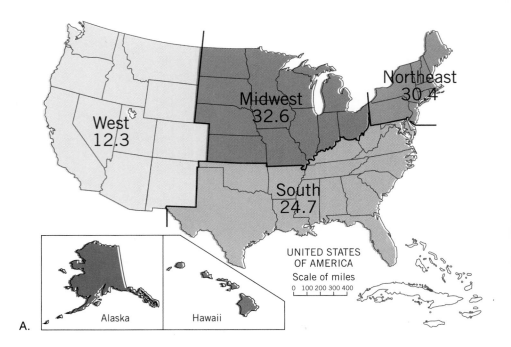

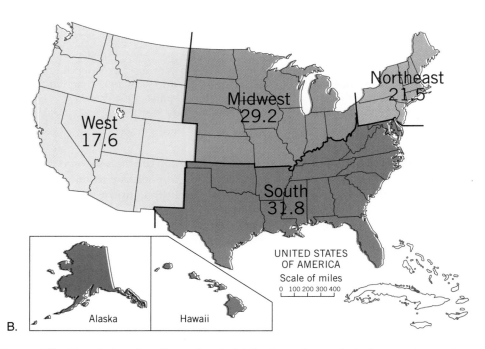

Figure 7.3   Map A describes the regional distribution of manufacturing employment in the United States in 1967, and Map B shows its distribution in 1989.   SOURCE: Robert W. Crandall, 1993: *Manufacturing on the Move* (Washington: The Brookings Institution).

region's share of manufacturing employment, a smaller decline in the Midwest's share, and large increases in the South and West. Of the four large U.S. Census regions, the South had the single largest share of manufacturing employment by 1989.

The same geographical trend occurred in manufacturing output, but the shift was not as extreme as that experienced by employment. In 1969, the Midwest and the Northeast combined accounted for about 63% of the country's share of manufacturing output but that share dropped to about 53% by 1989 (Figure 7.4 A and B). Although the Midwest had dropped to second place (behind the South) in manufacturing employment by 1989, it did retain its leading position in terms of output. The gap was relatively narrow, however, and the South had surpassed the Northeast's output by a large margin. Interestingly, the Northeast declined in both employment and output during the period while the South gained in both, even though by 1989 the Northeast was the most productive of the four regions and the South was the least productive (when productivity is measured as the region's share of output divided by its share of employment). One explanation for this disparity is that production costs in the Northeast are too high to be competitive with those in the South, even when the Northeast's productivity advantage is considered.

LOCATION FACTORS AND TRENDS

Why is there a trend toward geographical dispersion of manufacturing around the world? The answer is more easily stated in general than in specific terms because manufacturing is a very diverse sector of the economy. The general answer is that, over time, the relative profitability of manufacturing locations has changed.

Manufacturing, like any other sector of the economy, can enjoy location rent, and as location rents change, manufacturing's locations shift. These changes in location rents can occur in four ways, the first of which involves the characteristics of a location that make it yield rent to a manufacturing enterprise. For example, a raw material source that once served a factory well may finally run out. Second, transaction costs, especially the costs of spatial interaction, may change, so that once economically remote places become feasible locations for manufacturing. In the United States, lower transport costs that were achieved by establishing the Interstate Highway System have helped spread manufacturing along its routes. Third, manufacturing processes may change so that characteristics of a place that formed the basis of manufacturing rents under older manufacturing methods no longer generate rent when new methods are applied. For example, unlike the situation in the nineteenth century, few factories today need to be located on rivers so that running water can fulfill their energy requirements. Finally, the market structure, or type of competition, faced by the manufacturing enterprise can change, and with it the quality of its location(s). In many cases,

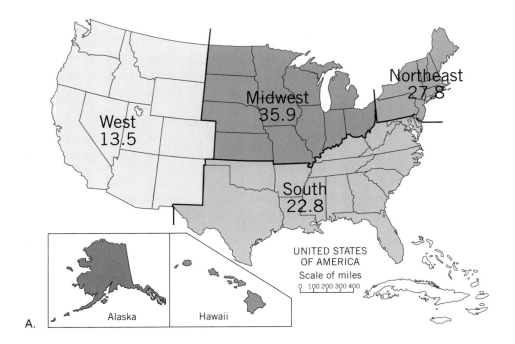

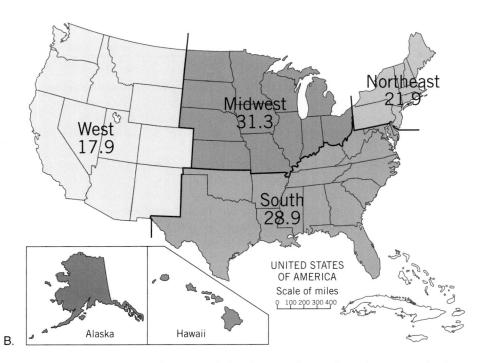

Figure 7.4 Map A describes the regional distribution of manufacturing output in the United States in 1969, and Map B shows its distribution in 1989. Source: Robert W. Crandall, 1993: *Manufacturing on the Move* (Washington: The Brookings Institution).

manufacturers establish branch plants in foreign countries in order to match their competitors' actions.

The specific answer as to why manufacturing shifts occur can be found in the specific locational requirements of manufacturers. All economic enterprises have production functions that are determined by what they produce and how they produce it. (Recall the discussion of production functions in Chapter 3.) A general production function is often written

$$Q = (K, L) \tag{7.1}$$

where Q stands for quantity of output, K for quantity of capital inputs, and L for quantity of labor used in production. Manufacturing and other enterprises also have *location of production functions*, which are simple extensions of the basic production function to include locational considerations, such as

$$Q_P = (K_P, L_P, M_P) \tag{7.2}$$

where Q_P is production at a particular place, P, and all the factors of production are made place-specific, too. The factors K and L are still capital and labor, respectively, but production at a place depends on their accessibility, defined in terms of cost. Another factor that must be accessible to a place of production is the market, M, a factor that is not usually included in general production functions but is of vital consideration when the location of production is considered.

Just as labor and capital in the general production functions can be employed in different combinations by different producers, the location factors in the location of production function can be used in different "combinations" as well. Some manufacturing enterprises can maximize their location rents by utilizing large amounts of cheap labor; others may require a location that is in their primary marketplace in order to stay in tune with current consumer tastes; and so on. Often, the best location factor combinations change over time, so that locations change, too. Again, changes in location factors, in their relative accessibility, in production processes, and in market structure can effectively alter the location of production function and thereby alter the quality of a particular location for manufacturing a particular product.

The location of production function is given in a general and limited form in Equation 7.2, but in reality location factors are more specific and can vary by geographical scale. Some location factors are relevant on a national or even international scale; others are more critical at the regional level; and still others concern the quality of specific plant sites. A comprehensive list of location factors of interest to manufacturers would probably contain dozens of items, but a recent survey of people involved in plant location decisions resulted in a list of six that are considered "essential": adequacy of services, labor availability, market access, business climate, access to raw materials and components, and quality of life and the environment.

ADEQUACY OF SERVICES

Two types of services of interest to manufacturers are infrastructure, including transportation routes and facilities, telecommunication links, and public utility hookups; and more specific services such as specialized financial or engineering consultants, for example. If such consultants are available locally, their cost should be lower and the quality of their service should be higher owing to their greater familiarity with their clients. Since many larger manufacturing companies provide the bulk of their specialized service needs in house, those services are not an important factor in determining their location. A recent trend, however, even in the largest corporations, has been the spinning off of in-house service operations as a cost-cutting measure. As a result, the proximity of independent service enterprises is becoming a more important location factor.

LABOR AVAILABILITY

The phrase "labor availability" has different connotations for different types of manufacturing. In labor-intensive manufacturing, proximity to large pools of inexpensive labor helps to keep labor costs low and to ensure continuity of production. Critical factors for other types of manufacturing may be the availability of labor with a certain set of skills and the cost of that labor in terms of wages and benefits. The tradeoff between labor cost and labor productivity must always be considered. Labor at $5 per hour that produces $50 of output per hour is no bargain compared to labor at $15 per hour that produces $200 of output per hour.

MARKET ACCESS

A market's relative accessibility varies with geographical scale. Some American manufacturers are interested in having a presence within the European Union countries in general, but may select the specific country in which they locate for nonmarket reasons. In turn, many foreign manufacturers want to locate some production within the United States in order to be in the American market, but whether they wind up in South Carolina or Illinois is determined by other factors. In some circumstances, access to a regional market is the primary factor. A manufacturing enterprise may find it necessary to have a presence in the U.S. South, for example, but whether it starts production near Atlanta or near Jacksonville will be determined by other factors. For some producers who supply parts or services to other manufacturers, market access may require that they locate on the site of their most important customers in the interest of a *just-in-time manufacturing* (JIT) system. This system requires close coordination between supplier and manufacturer in altering production runs to suit short-term changes in markets (Insights 7.1).

> ➤ **INSIGHTS 7.1**
JIT and Flexibility

Firms practicing JIT reduce inventories at all stages by purchasing just in time to produce and producing just in time to sell. These practices represent a drastic departure from traditional purchasing and production practices in the United States. Accordingly, firms adopting JIT must confront the problems the traditional practices were designed to accommodate.

To reduce inventories of materials and supplies, firms are changing their purchasing practices under JIT. Traditional practices called for infrequent orders of large lots of materials and supplies, well in advance of when needed for production. Such practices were intended to minimize ordering and transportation costs and to allow time for late deliveries and inspection of goods upon arrival.

In contrast, just-in-time purchasing calls for frequent orders of small lots of material and supplies, just in time to produce. Upon delivery, materials and supplies are whisked directly onto the assembly line. For example, Hewlett-Packard orders materials and supplies in lots of just a few hours worth of production, several times a day.

Just-in-time purchasing requires rapid delivery by suppliers. To speed delivery, suppliers are encouraged to locate near the buyer. For example, suppliers of General Motors' Buick division are all located within one shift (eight hours) of the manufacturing plant. In addition, many suppliers are switching from trains to trucks as their primary delivery mode. Trucks are more economical than are trains when delivering small lots. Trucks are also more flexible, permitting delivery directly to the assembly line to eliminate unnecessary handling.

To reduce inventories of finished goods, manufacturing firms are also changing their production practices under JIT. Traditional manufacturing practices called for production of large batches of goods, which were then stored as inventories until inspected and sold. These practices were intended to minimize the costs of setting up for a production run and to ensure an adequate supply of the finished goods in case of defects, strikes, or a surge in demand.

JIT entails frequent production runs of small batches. Ideally, manufacturers should produce goods continuously at roughly the same rate the goods are sold. That way, if sales decline, production declines in step to prevent inventories from accumulating. To provide for an increase in sales, on the other hand, manufacturers must maintain excess production capacity to avoid missing sales.

JIT also requires firms to reduce the time needed to set up for production of a particular good, in order to respond quickly to new orders. Setup times are being reduced in several ways. Manufacturers are installing more flexible machinery that can be quickly switched between production of different goods. For example, automobile makers are installing computer-aided machinery that is quickly reprogrammed to produce a variety of different components. And instead of bolting machines to the floor, manufacturers are using quick-release clamps so machines can be moved quickly between stations where different goods are produced.

Just-in-time purchasing and production both require improved quality control since firms hold smaller inventories against defects. To improve quality, manufacturers and their suppliers are using computer programs to control quality. These programs monitor the dimensions of goods produced and automatically halt production if the dimensions exceed the desired specification. In addition, the technique of ordering and producing in small lots improves quality because defects are detected sooner.

SOURCE: "Will Just-In-Time Inventory Techniques Dampen Recessions?", by Donald P. Morgan, *Economic Review*, Federal Reserve Bank of Kansas City, March–April 1991, pp. 24–25.

BUSINESS CLIMATE

Places with good business climates often develop as a result of governments that are "pro" business, as evidenced by relatively low tax rates and limited regulatory requirements. A good business climate in a state is frequently indicated by a *right-to-work law* (Insights 7.2). These laws, though fairly insipid on paper, send a signal that organized labor is not a strong political force and that business has the upper hand. Governments often try to foster "good" business climates, subsidizing manufacturing and other enterprises, by offering financial incentives designed either to lure a company to a location or to keep it there. These subsidies may take the form of low-interest loans or outright grants, as described in Case 7.1. Other subsidies include lower property tax rates, income tax holidays, and the absorption of labor training and other operating costs.

> ➤ INSIGHTS 7.2
Right-to-Work in Louisiana

RIGHT TO WORK

S. 981. Declaration of public policy

It is hereby declared to be the public policy of Louisiana that all persons shall have, and shall be protected in the exercise of the right, freely and without fear of penalty or reprisal, to form, join and assist labor organizations or to refrain from any such activities.

S. 982. Labor organization

The term "labor organization" means any organization of any kind, or agency or employee representation committee, which exists for the purpose, in whole or in part, of dealing with employers concerning wages, rates of pay, hours of work or other conditions of employment.

S. 983. Freedom of choice

No person shall be required, as a condition of employment, to become or remain a member of any labor organization, or to pay any dues, fees, assessments, or other charges of any kind to a labor organization.

S. 984. Certain agreements declared illegal

Any agreement, understanding, or practice, written or oral, implied or expressed, between any employer and any labor organization in violation of the provisions of this Act is hereby declared to be unlawful, null and void, and of no legal effect.

S. 985. Penalties

Any person who directly or indirectly places upon any other person any requirement or compulsion prohibited by this Act shall be guilty of a misdemeanor, and upon conviction thereof shall be subject to a fine not exceeding one thousand dollars and/or imprisonment for a period of not more than ninety days.

S. 986. Injunctive relief

Any employee injured as a result of any violation or threatened violation of the provisions of this Part shall be entitled to injunctive relief against any and all violators or persons threatening violation, and may also recover any and all damages of any character resulting from such violation or threatened violation. Such remedies shall be independent of and in addition to the penalties and remedies described in other provisions of this Part.

SOURCE: Legislature of Louisiana, 1976, House Bill No. 637, Act 97.

◁

◪ *CASE 7.1*
Manufacturing Location Subsidies Gone Bad

BEFORE

Lured by a state incentive package, a New Jersey company is doubling the size of its South Windsor manufacturing operation and creating about 350 new jobs.

Nytronics, Inc., which considered moving to other states before deciding to consolidate operations in Connecticut, will receive a $3.5 million incentive package that includes a $2.15 million grant and a $1.35 million loan.

"We had looked at eight different states and were ready to move operations to South Carolina when the state of Connecticut presented a very unique opportunity that allowed us to stay in the area," Charles K. Rivard, Nytronics' president and chief executive officer, said in a statement.

The corporation's Hi-G Co. Inc. subsidiary already is in South Windsor. Under the deal with the state, Nytronics will move its corporate headquarters and another subsidiary from New Jersey to Connecticut.

The two subsidiaries make electro-mechanical switching devices for the military and the areospace industry.

The move will double the size of the company's operations in South Windsor. It is building a 50,000-square-foot addition, and is planning to hire new workers to staff the facility rather than transfer employees from New Jersey.

"We are hiring new people in Connecticut," said Howard McCormick, plant manager at Hi-G. "We're trying to hire local people as much as possible."

"It's all-around a good deal for everyone," said Joseph Cohen, a spokesman for the state Department of Economic Development.

Hi-G officials said two of the key factors in their decision were the state aid package and the existence of a skilled work force.

"What caught our attention was the quality of the work force here in Connecticut and the fact that the state was able to provide us with this assistance," Rivard said in his statement. "If we had moved to the Sun Belt like we had planned, we would have had to train a whole new work force."

AFTER

Five months after giving a New Jersey company millions to expand its South Windsor operations, the state has taken over the property, the company is facing tax delinquencies and employees are facing uncertainty.

The state has bought the Hi-G Co. Inc. property and equipment for $1 from Nytronics, Inc., its New Jersey parent company, according to documents filed in the town clerk's office.

In June, the state gave Nytronics a $3.5 million incentive package to move its corporate headquarters to Connecticut and expand the South Windsor operations. That package included a $2.15 million grant and a $1.35 million loan.

But, more recently, the state feared Hi-G, which makes switching devices, was in danger of failing.

"The state, in an effort to secure its financial assistance to Hi-G/Nytronics, took collateral in the form of Hi-G's buildings and other assets, said Joseph Cohen, spokesman for the state Department of Economic development.

Under the deal with the state, Nytronics Inc. agreed to move its corporate headquarters and another subsidiary from New Jersey to South Windsor. A 50,000-square-foot addition to the South Windsor plant was being built and 350 new jobs were supposed to be created.

"Nobody is any longer talking about consolidation or expansion," Cohen said. "This has boiled down to survival."

Cohen said he was not sure what ultimately would happen to the company or the more than 300 people who now work there.

"The state is trying to preserve the company and the employees' jobs in what is a very difficult situation," Cohen said. "We're still making the jobs our first priority, but this is a pretty difficult situation and it's hard to be optimistic."

SOURCES: "Firm Decides to Consolidate in Connecticut," by Andrew Julien, in *The Hartford Courant*, June 23, 1994, p. B1, and "State Takes Over Hi-G Co. Property," by Cindy Murphy, in *The Hartford Courant*, November 19, 1994, pp. F1, F2. By permission of the *Hartford Courant*.

FOR DISCUSSION

Should governments subsidize companies in the way this case describes?

ACCESS TO RAW MATERIALS AND COMPONENTS

Easy access to raw materials and components lowers production cost by reducing the costs of spatial interaction on the input side. The importance of this access, however, has decreased over time, for two reasons. First, transportation costs have decreased, so that even geographically remote sites can be mined and their ore brought to points of production at fairly low costs. As those costs have decreased, other location factors have become more important in the location of manufacturing. At one time steel production, for example, was strongly tied to raw material sites, but because of declining transportation costs, steel now is produced in closer proximity to its markets. Second, manufactured goods are produced more efficiently and require fewer raw materials than they once did.

In contrast, the relative importance of access to component suppliers has been increasing. Manufacturing processes are being modified in many industries, largely in response to rapidly changing consumer markets. Many producers are now using *flexible manufacturing* processes that use smaller production runs of a larger variety of goods than in traditional manufacturing. Flexible, sometimes called agile, manufacturing is based on the achievement of *economies of scope*, which are a special form of economies of scale. With economies of scope, several similar products are produced in the same factory using the same flexible machinery and labor. This approach yields economies because average production costs decrease as the production volume of similar goods increases. For the economies to be achieved, the goods must be fairly similar, or "within scope." A flexible auto manufacturer, for example, would build several makes or related models on the same production line and be able to vary individual levels of output in reaction to demand in the market. It would not make automobiles in the morning, televisions in the afternoon, and switch to brewing beer on the night shift because those activities are not within scope of each other. To a great degree, flexibility requires significant purchasing of components from suppliers rather than in-house production (Insights 7.1). Thus, proximity to the suppliers of the components is a very important location factor to flexible manufacturers.

QUALITY OF LIFE AND THE ENVIRONMENT

As traditional location factors become less important in response to changing production processes and decreasing relative costs of transportation, a place's social, educational, and recreational characteristics, as well as its cost of living, are taking on more importance in location decisions. So-called *footloose manufacturing* has few or no ties to conventional location factors, and quality of life could be a determining factor in the location of that type of enterprise. For most manufacturers, however, quality of life is not a leading consideration in plant location decisions but instead is used as a tie breaker in selecting among a number of otherwise equally attractive places.

In the future, environmental considerations will play an increasingly important role in manufacturing location. For most of the history of industrialization, manufacturers externalized the costs of environmental degradation, but increasing environmental regulation is now forcing them to internalize those costs. When environmental regulations, and therefore internal costs of compliance, vary from one jurisdiction to another, then their cost differences will influence the location decision. For example, many environmentalists opposed the establishment of the North American Free Trade Agreement (NAFTA) between Canada, Mexico, and the United States on the grounds of Mexico's weak environmental record. Because of free trade, they argued, environmentally irresponsible producers from Canada and the United States could simply relocate to Mexico and still serve their home market without incurring the costs of environmental responsibility. As long as environmental regulation and enforcement varies among the countries, the possibility that manufacturers will take advantage of the differences continues to exist. The same possibility exists within countries as long as they contain geographical variations in environmental costs.

INDUSTRIAL AGGLOMERATION

Every enterprise has a specific location of production function in which location factors are implicitly weighted to form a particular combination. Manufacturers that produce similar products tend to have equivalent functions, and as a result they are often found in geographical concentrations. In the United States, for example, about 70% of all household furniture is produced in the Piedmont of North Carolina and southern Virginia. Historically, as noted in Chapter 1, automobiles, steel, and, more recently, the computer industry have developed in agglomerations of a number of similar producers. Such agglomerations tend to be self-reinforcing. They are based on a suitable supply of initial factors of production at a place, which serves as a seedbed for the industry. Once an industry's growth begins, however, the place's characteristics tend to change in further support of the agglomeration. For example, local labor markets become specialized toward the needs of the agglomeration, and local services are especially developed to supply the markets provided by the agglomeration. Agglomeration economies develop as a result of the development of specialized local labor and services, and costs of spatial interaction within the industry decrease. In combination with the high transaction costs associated with physically shifting production sites from one place to another, agglomeration economies tend to lead to *industrial inertia*—the maintenance of industrial regions even after the location factors that originally led to their development are no longer relevant to the industry.

For example, furniture manufacturing in the Piedmont developed as part of the region's forest industry, and it relied on large local supplies of wood as a raw material. The wood used in manufacturing furniture in the region now comes from all over the world, and large local supplies of specialized labor and services for the furniture industry have become the most significant location factors in the region. The specialized labor and services developed in tandem with the industry as part of the process of its agglomeration, and now are vital to the health of furniture manufacturing in the region.

LOCATION MODELS

The theory of industrial location, or the location of any type of economic enterprise for that matter, is profit maximization. The best location is the one where location rent, and therefore profits, are maximized. Profits are the difference between revenues on one hand and costs of production on the other. Profits can be maximized by maximizing sales and minimizing costs. Although the strategy is simple to state, it's much harder to put into practice in a locational context because the places where the highest revenues might be earned are infrequently the same as the places where the costs of production are going to be at their lowest. Finding the best location most often involves tradeoffs between revenue and cost considerations, and in practice costs are never minimized nor are revenues ever maximized in the extreme sense. Profits are much more easily maximized in theory than in the real world, where *satisficing search behavior* leads to the selection of economic locations that provide satisfactory, or reasonable, levels of relevant cost and revenue characteristics. True profit maximization requires that people making a plant location decision have perfect and complete information concerning costs and revenues at all possible sites and, just as unrealistically, be able to use that information perfectly. Satisficing requires a simpler short list of possible locations that are expected to provide acceptable levels of profit, and the selection of the best site on the basis of particular production circumstances.

Whether we think of the theoretical approach to industrial location of profit maximization or the more realistic satisficing approach, the same problem remains: low-cost sites are not often the sites from which higher revenues can be earned. Which side of the coin should be given the most weight, cost reduction or revenue growth? The answer is often determined by the *market structure* of the industry. The three basic types of market structure, or types of competition, are monopoly, oligopoly, and perfectly competitive markets.

Monopolies exist when a single company so thoroughly controls either the production or distribution (or both) of a product that it can control the product's price. Because large-scale monopolies don't face true competition, governments often regulate their prices and other parts of their operation. Monopolies are always geographical and have boundaries, with some of them covering entire countries, but most existing on a regional basis, like electrical utilities in the United States, or on a local level, like many retail franchises.

Oligopolies are industries in which production and distribution are controlled by just a few enterprises and contain more true competition than do monopolies. Members of an oligopoly have some price control in the market, but their pricing power is limited by other members of the oligopoly. Any unilateral price increase in an oligopoly can result in a loss of market share. Members of this type of competition tend to raise prices, and sometimes lower them, in unison so that a competitive balance is maintained in their industry. For example, the breakfast cereals sold by the leading producers—an effective oligopoly in the United States—have very similar prices.

Finally, perfectly competitive markets contain a sufficient number of producers/distributors so that no individual member of the industry can exercise any control over prices (recall from Chapter 2). The difference between the profit that would be earned in a competitive market and the profit earned under monopolistic conditions is called *monopoly rent,* which, like location rent, is a return that exceeds "normal" levels.

Why does market structure make a difference in industrial location? The key difference in market structure is between the monopolists and oligopolists on one side and producers facing more perfect competition on the other. Because monopolists and to a lesser degree oligopolists have some control over prices, their locational choices are weighted more toward revenue considerations than toward cost considerations. Within limits, these companies can pass along higher costs to customers by way of higher prices, so that revenue considerations come first in their location decisions. Companies in more competitive markets can't pass along higher costs so easily. Price increases simply lower a company's sales because customers can buy the product from many other producers or distributors. For companies in competitive markets, cost reduction is the path to higher profitability, so the best locations are those with the lowest associated costs. In summary, different market structures lead to different locational strategies, and different locational strategies lead to different emphases on locational characteristics, and different "optimum" locations (Insights 7.3).

➤ INSIGHTS 7.3
The Market Potential Model and the Aggregate Travel Model

The "best" location for a manufacturer or any other business depends upon the company's approach to profit maximization, which in turn depends upon the market structure of its industry. Revenue maximization, as an approach to profit maximization, is most often associated with companies operating under monopolistic or oligopolistic conditions. In order to determine the best location under these circumstances, a company should use a *market potential model* to assess locational quality. The market potential model takes the general form

$$M_i = \sum_{j=1}^{n} \frac{P_j}{D_{ij}} \tag{7.3}$$

where M_i is the market potential of the *i*th place, P_j is the population (or other gross measure of demand) at the *j*th place, and D_{ij} is the distance between the place of production and the place of consumption. If $i = j$, meaning production and consumption occur at the same place, then $D_{ij} = 1$. This model is similar to the gravity model described in Chapter 6 because it indicates, as does the gravity model, that demand for a product at a place increases with that place's population, but decreases with distance from the product's place of production. The optimum location with respect to revenue maximization is that place where market potential is maximized.

If a manufacturer, or other business, is operating under more competitive conditions, it would best follow a cost-minimizing strategy in order to maximize its profits. Instead of evaluating its possible location using the market potential model, it should use the *aggregate travel model*:

$$A_i = \sum_{j=1}^{n} P_j D_{ij} \tag{7.4}$$

where A_i is the aggregate travel associated with supplying customers from the *i*th place. In this model, population is multiplied by distance, rather than divided as in the market potential model. The optimum location with respect to cost minimization is that place where aggregate travel is minimized.

A brief hypothetical example can easily illustrate the differences in the approaches on which the two models are based on. Let's say that there is a road 110 miles long with four villages scattered along it in the following way:

population   100   250   100   400

Village   A____B_____C_____D

distance   10   30   70

The market potentials of each of the places are as follows:

$$M_A = \frac{100}{1} + \frac{250}{10} + \frac{100}{40} + \frac{400}{110} = 131.14$$

$$M_B = \frac{100}{10} + \frac{250}{1} + \frac{100}{30} + \frac{400}{100} = 267.33$$

$$M_C = \frac{100}{40} + \frac{250}{30} + \frac{100}{1} + \frac{400}{70} = 116.54$$

$$M_D = \frac{100}{110} + \frac{250}{100} + \frac{100}{70} + \frac{400}{1} = 404.84$$

Place D, where market potential is maximized, is the optimal location with respect to revenue maximization. Of course, the calculated values don't have much specific meaning, but their relative magnitudes indicate market potential proportions that can be specified by indexing them to the highest value, at place D in this example. Dividing all the values by 404.84, the indexed market potential values are $M_A = 0.32$, $M_B = 0.66$, $M_C = 0.29$ and, of course, $M_D = 1$. These values indicate that a company locating at place A can expect 32% of the revenue it would earn if it located at D, the place where revenues are maximized in the region. It could earn 66% of the maximum revenues at place B, and only 29% at place C, the region's poorest location with respect to revenue maximization.

The aggregate travel values for the places are calculated as follows:

$$A_A = (100 \times 1) + (250 \times 10) + (100 \times 40) + (400 \times 110) = 50,600$$

$$A_B = (100 \times 10) + (250 \times 1) + (100 \times 30) + (400 \times 100) = 44,250$$

$$A_C = (100 \times 40) + (250 \times 30) + (100 \times 1) + (400 \times 70) = 39,600$$

$$A_D = (100 \times 110) + (250 \times 100) + (100 \times 70) + (400 \times 1) = 43,400$$

Place C, where aggregate travel is minimized, is the optimal location with respect to cost minimization. Again, the calculated values don't have much specific meaning, but their relative magnitudes indicate aggregate travel proportions that can be specified by indexing them to the lowest value, at place C in this example. Dividing all the values by 39,600, the indexed aggregate travel values are: $A_A = 1.28$, $A_B = 1.12$, $A_D = 1.10$, and, of course, $A_C = 1$. These values indicate that a company locating at place A can expect to pay 28% higher locational costs than if it located at C, the lowest cost location. Locational costs are 12% higher at place B than necessary, and 10% higher at place D, the region's optimum location with respect to revenue maximization, but just second best when it comes to cost minimization.

THE LÖSCH MODEL

If monopolistic firms can pass along higher costs to consumers by increasing prices, why should they worry about revenues in their location decisions? In addition to any government regulation of prices that may affect a monopoly's revenues, a monopoly's prices are also limited by price elastic demand, which leads to a decrease in sales of a product with an increase in its price. Distance decay is the geographical manifestation of price elastic demand. As prices increase because of spatial interaction costs, the demand for spatial interaction—in this case a sale by a producer to a customer—declines. The locational effects of distance decay in defining the market areas of geographical monopolies are the focus of a location model developed by the economist August Lösch, based on some earlier work by the geographer Walter Christaller. (We discuss Christaller's work in more detail in Chapter 8.)

Lösch's initial model used brewing as its example. The location of the first brewery in a hypothetical region is marked as *B* in Figure 7.5. For purposes of simplification, let's assume that the region is a homogeneous plain, unmarked by any variations in topography, transport costs, or population density. Demand for beer is greatest right at the brewery because that's where the product is cheapest. The price of beer increases with distance from the brewery because an additional cost is associated with spatial interaction, either a transport charge for the beer or a travel cost of getting to the brewery. At distance *K* (or *K'*) from the brewery, the additional costs of spatial interaction make the beer too expensive, and it is not in demand in any quantity. The distance over which a good is sold is the *range of the good*, and the maximum distance over which it can be sold is called the ideal limit of the good's *outer range*. The outer range of beer, in this example, is the distance from *B* to *K*.

In order for the brewery to stay in business, it must maintain a minimum operating scale, or *market threshold*. The geographical extent of that threshold market is the *threshold range*, which defines the area that contains just enough consumers to keep the producer operating. In Figure 7.5 A and B, the brewery's threshold range is defined by the so-called 0,1 demand function, illustrated by the rectangular box associated with distance segment *D* to *D'*. As long as the brewery has that large a market, it can stay in business. Accordingly, any sales it makes beyond its threshold range generate excess profits. These excess profits are monopoly rents because they are earned in the absence of competition. The

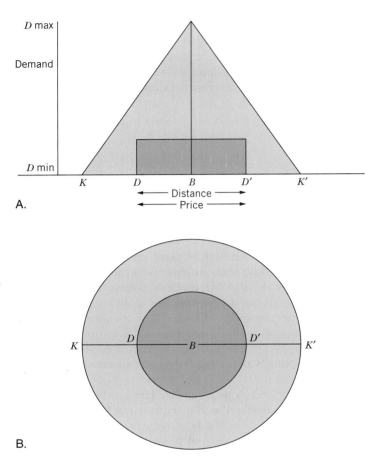

Figure 7.5 The location of the first brewery in a region is marked B. Diagram A represents the region in horizontal cross-section, and Diagram B represents a mapped, or bird's eye view. The maximum extent of its market is defined by segment *K* to *K'*, which is derived from distance decay in the regional demand for beer. That segment is the diameter of the circular market area shown in the map view of the market. The segment *D* to *D'* represents the minimum market required by the brewery to stay in business.

area over which monopoly rents can be earned, however, is limited by the distance decay in the demand for beer that results from spatial interaction costs. If the brewery raises the price of beer too high, it can put itself out of business by reducing demand below its threshold necessary to survive. The need to maintain market threshold demand limits the ability of the brewery in Figure 7.5 and that of most other monopolies from exercising too much price power or otherwise being too insensitive to the market.

The entry of additional breweries will erode the monopolistic edge enjoyed by the initial brewery, as illustrated in Figure 7.6 A and B. Diagram A indicates the boundary between the market of the first brewery at *B* and that of the second brewery at B_2 at distance *M*, where their prices are equal. Customers at *M* have a choice of beers, which are assumed to have identical taste (as do the customers). All other customers in the region, however, simply buy their beer at the lowest price, which in this case means they buy it from the nearest brewer. In Diagram B, a consumer at distance *M* is contributing to the monopoly rent of one brewery or the other. In the lower diagram of Figure 7.6, however, the breweries are close enough together so that only threshold market levels are maintained in the center of the region. Additional breweries could be located in the region until all the breweries have market areas defined by their threshold ranges. The result would be what seems a contradiction in terms—monopolistic competition,

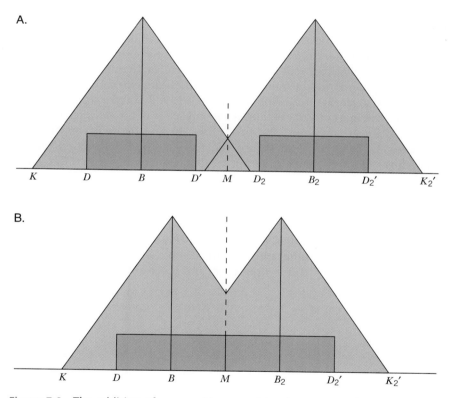

Figure 7.6   The addition of a second brewery introduces competition to the region's market for beer. In Diagram A, the regional beer market is divided at *M*, the distance from each brewery where their prices are equal. Some monopoly rents are maintained in the region's center if the breweries are located as they are in the upper diagram. In Diagram B, the monopoly rents are lost in the center because breweries are close enough together so that only threshold market levels are maintained.

in which many producers compete at one geographical scale, the region in this case, but maintain monopolies at smaller geographical scales.

THE HOTELLING MODEL

Even in the presence of monopolistic competition, a monopoly has, by definition, effective control of a market. The first locational lesson to draw from the spatial monopoly model is that profits are higher if you're the first entrant in a market, especially if the market is a large one. The second lesson is that monopolistic advantage is difficult to maintain in a locational context, and that even one competitor can have a significant effect on the size of a single enterprise's market. A model developed by Harold Hotelling (recall the name from Chapter 5) illustrates the role of location in determining the market share of an enterprise that is a member of a duopoly, a two-member version of an oligopoly.

Let's assume that there is a market that can be represented as in Figure 7.7 A and B by a straight line, and along the line the market holds a uniform distribution of demand, with customers a constant distance from each other. An initial seller could locate at one end of the market and still exercise a geographical monopoly over the market's full extent. A second seller of an identical product, however, could locate anywhere else in the market and detract from the first entrant's sales. In Diagram B of Figure 7.7, for example, the second seller's location reduces the first seller's market to the segment between *M* and the endpoint of the market where the first seller is located. As you can imagine, the second seller's location wouldn't sit well with the first seller, who could move to the left of the second seller in order to increase market share at the second seller's expense. That move, in turn, would cause the second seller to move and so on and so on until a locational pattern could be found from which neither seller could move without losing, rather than gaining, market share.

As it turns out, such a location does exist, and it is right at the center of the

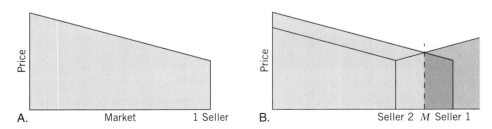

Figure 7.7   Diagram A shows that the first seller in a geographical market enjoys a monopoly even with a "bad" location. Diagram B illustrates the competitive effect of location in the same market with two sellers.

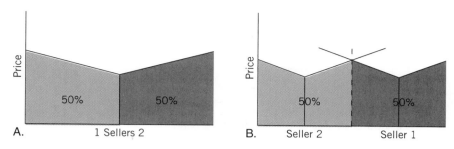

Figure 7.8 Diagram A illustrates a spatial market equilibrium developed by two competitors locating together at the center of the market. Diagram B illustrates a social equilibrium that is unlikely to be maintained because the locations of the two sellers are not economically stable.

market (Figure 7.8 A and B). If the two sellers are located back-to-back at the center, one serving the eastern half of the market and the other the western half, a *spatial equilibrium* is achieved. The central locations are stable because a unilateral shift in location can only hurt the seller that moves. If either of the sellers moves to either the east or to the west of the center, that seller will lose market share. The proximity of their locations is a result of the *principle of minimum differentiation*, which holds in all oligopolies and not just duopolies. This principle is that sellers of the same sort of product try to make their own brands as similar to each other's as possible. Prices, other qualities, and locations are all similar in the oligopoly's geogaphical context.

While an independent move can only hurt one of the sellers, they can move in tandem to positions that would maintain their market shares and lower prices to consumers on the borders of the market. If the sellers locate at quartile positions (each halfway between one endpoint and the center), each will also have one-half of the market (Figure 7.8). Quartile locations yield a social equilibrium because any shift in location by one or both producers would cause prices for their product to rise somewhere in the market. This social equilibrium is not an economic one, however, because locational shifts toward the center can increase a mover's market share. Unless the sellers fully trust each other, the duopolists should locate at the center of the market in order to ensure market stability.

The location models for either monopolies or the oligopolistic market have nothing to say about cost. Again, because monopolies and companies that belong to oligopolies can determine the prices they charge for their products, they can pass along a lot of their costs without reducing profits. Their location rents, therefore, are derived more from their location's market effects than from their location's factor costs. In more competitive markets, however, the focus is on cost reduction because prices are determined by the customers in the market so that location rents are highest where costs of production and distribution are lowest. As described in Case 7.2, the costs of production can vary significantly from place to place. Obviously, if the same jet engine can be built in Georgia as in Connecticut, Pratt & Whitney makes more money on the one built in Georgia because its costs there are so much lower.

◪ *CASE 7.2*
Comparative Costs in Jet Engine Manufacturing

A production worker in Connecticut makes, on average, $40,160 a year.

A similar worker in Georgia makes, on average, $26,980, nearly one third less.

And in those statistics from DRI/McGraw Hill, an economic forecasting firm, lies one of the major problems confronting manufacturers in Connecticut.

The costs of labor, as well as the costs of land, taxes, energy and workers' compensation, have become so steep that numerous manufacturers have moved or expanded operations elsewhere, in places where such costs are substantially less.

The scourge of high costs never has seemed more dramatic than on Wednesday, when Pratt & Whitney announced plans to close plants in East Hartford and Southington, and move some of the production to Georgia and Maine.

Karl Krapek, Pratt's president, emphasized that costs were central to the decision, saying, "our fiercely competitive industry doesn't allow the less-competitive costs structure we face in Connecticut."

Krapek said in a statement that Pratt determined that "plants in Maine and Georgia offer substantial savings, caused by a more favorable business environment, plus benefit and wage differences," in comparison with plants in Connecticut.

Indeed, in their recent discussions with Connecticut lawmakers and union officials, Pratt officials cited figures that roughly peg wages, fringe benefits, taxes, and other operating costs at $31.05 per worker per hour in Connecticut. The comparative costs in Maine are $25.85 per worker per hour, and $24.20 per worker per hour in Georgia, say sources familiar with the discussions.

Connecticut's comparatively high costs are largely a legacy of the mid- and late-1980s, boom years that also were a time of severe labor shortages. The labor shortages helped boost wages sharply. Per-capita income nearly doubled in Connecticut during the 1980s.

The boom of the 1980s concealed the start of what has become an unbroken trend—the steady decline of manufacturing jobs in Connecticut. Those losses began in 1985, and accelerated with the exodus of several prominent manufacturing operations.

Since 1990, Bic Corp., The Stanley Works, First Brands, Inc., and Hamilton Standard have moved important parts of their businesses to the South or West, where labor, land and energy cost less than in Connecticut. In addition, United Parcel Service and Saab Cars USA Inc. have moved their headquarters from Connecticut to Georgia.

Ronald F. Van Winkle, a West Hartford economist, said the news from Pratt that it may shift operations to Georgia and Maine represents "the most dramatic example of a company telling the state it's not a good place to do business. To have the premier manufacturer in the state say, 'We can't afford to be here,' is a very serious statement . . . about the adverse business climate in Connecticut. It's the kind of high-tech, high value-added firm we cannot afford to lose."

Kenneth O. Decko, president of the Connecticut Business and Industry Association, also spoke ominously about Pratt's decision. "If we want manufacturing jobs in Connecticut," Decko said in a statement, "we must act now to reduce costs and improve the business climate."

In particular, Decko urged the General Assembly to enact "workers' compensation reforms that truly reduce costs, health-care reforms to make health care more affordable while . . . making it more accessible, and a budget that controls spending so that business won't feel the sting of more taxes."

Comparing Pratt's Manufacturing Costs

	Connecticut	Maine	Georgia
Hourly Wage	$15.00	$12.50	$12.75
Benefits	7.50	6.00	5.40
Workers' Compensation	0.50	0.25	0.05
Energy	3.80	3.50	2.50
State and Local Taxes	4.25	3.60	3.50
Total (worker/hour)	$31.05	$25.85	$24.20

SOURCE: "State's Labor Costs Scaring off Manufacturers," by W. Joseph Campbell, in *The Hartford Courant*, April 15, 1993, p. A15. By permission of the *Hartford Courant.*

FOR DISCUSSION

Do you expect the cost differential between Georgia and Connecticut to continue, or do you think that the production costs will eventually become about the same in the two states?

THE WEBER MODEL

The most influential industrial location model emphasizing cost minimization was developed early in the twentieth century by Alfred Weber. His model focused on minimizing transport costs associated with both procuring raw materials for

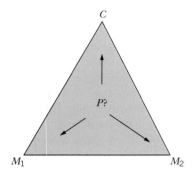

Figure 7.9   The Weber triangle, named for the developer of an early least-cost location model, is formed by the locational pulls of the market at *C*, one type of raw material at *M*$_1$, and another type of raw material at *M*$_2$ on a plant's location, *P*.

production and delivering of finished products to the market. In the model, sites where necessary raw materials are found and the place where the product is sold exert locational pulls on the factory (Figure 7.9). Any manufacturing that requires large amounts of a particular localized raw material, such as copper, is drawn toward places where that raw material is found so that its cost of transportation is lowered. Manufacturing that uses large volumes of ubiquitous raw materials such as water found in most places should locate closer to its markets so that the cost of transporting finished products is lowered. Weber calculated a *material index, M_I*, to make generalizations about the raw material/market orientation of a particular manufacturing process:

$$M_I = \frac{\text{localized material transport cost}}{\text{finished product transport cost}} \qquad (7.5)$$

If $M_I > 1$, then the process has a raw material orientation and is likely to have lower transport costs if located in proximity to its necessary raw materials. If, on the other hand, $M_I > 1$, then the process has a market orientation and should be located in proximity to its market. A manufacturing process can be market oriented, according to this index, only if it uses a ubiquitous raw material, which is not included in the index's numerator.

Weber considered location factors other than material and product transport costs in his model, but in a secondary way. Cheap labor could draw a plant's location away from the site with the lowest transport cost, and so could opportunities to achieve agglomeration economies, but only if the additional savings outweighed any increase in transport costs of materials and finished products that would be associated with the move to a location where they would be available. Case 7.3, concerning Mexico's relatively low labor costs but higher costs in some other areas of production, illustrates Weber's point in a current context. The case implicitly illustrates another point—that while the costs of individual location factors must be considered in current comparison to one another, the basis for their comparison can change over time. The issue of the attractiveness of low-cost Mexican labor became a big one because the cost of Mexican access to the American market decreased after NAFTA was established (also see Chapter 10). Without a decrease in tariffs, the lower cost of Mexican labor, regardless of any other production costs, was largely offset by high tariff payments.

For a more general illustration, let's consider a factory located at place *P* in Figure 7.10. Under the old production system in which the plant was established, the costs increase uniformly, as marked by isocost lines, at a fairly steep rate. Three low-cost alternative factory sites are also labeled on the figure. Let's say the factory can save $20 in labor costs per unit of output if it locates at L_1, $15 if it locates at L_2, and $10 if it locates at L_3. (It's not necessary that the savings come from cheap labor. They could be derived from lower priced electrical service, or lower taxes, or any other location factor.) Under the old system of production, none of these cheap labor sites would be attractive as the plant's location because other costs of operation would increase by a larger amount than the lower cost labor would save. Under the new production system, however, operating costs increase less rapidly with distance from the initial lowest cost site, and each of the places with low-cost labor would now be an overall lower cost site of production than the initial one. The plant should be moved if the costs of closing the old plant and establishing a new one and the resulting

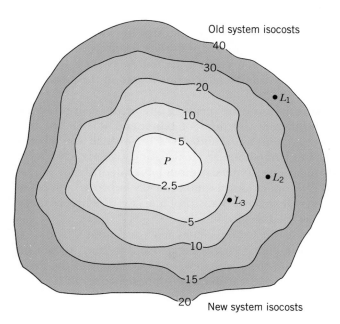

Figure 7.10 Isocost lines define uniform areas of cost increases with distance from a factory's lowest initial cost location at *P*. Places marked L_1, L_2, and L_3 are alternative low-cost sites for the factory that may be preferable if the current location's costs change, or if transport costs, production technology, or government policies change.

operational cost savings add up to a higher discounted present value than that of the current plant and its operation.

◢ CASE 7.3
Manufacturing Costs in Mexico

MEXICO CITY—As Mexico's low wages emerge as a major issue in the debate over the North American Free Trade Agreement, U.S. business executives and Mexican officials are arguing that problems of infrastructure and a range of other economic factors make Mexican labor far less of a bargain than first appears.

Mexico's highway system is falling apart, its railroads are dangerously decrepit, bureaucratic hassles and corruption abound, the phone system doesn't work and Mexican labor can be unreliable, U.S. executives here say. When the scores of risks and drawbacks are included in the equation, they say, many companies will realize they are better off staying in the United States.

Some large and mid-sized U.S. companies, including General Motors, already are finding that Mexico is not the cost-effective manufacturing venue it used to be.

For example, GM decided this summer to shift production of the 1995 Chevrolet Cavalier from a plant in northern Mexico to Lansing, Mich., because, said spokeswoman Nicole Solomon, "It's not just wages, but the entire calculation."

Mustafa Mohatarem, chief economist for GM, said that the lower wages paid to Mexican auto workers were not enough to offset other relatively higher costs of doing business here. "Transportation costs, potential delays at the border and . . . higher inventory storage costs in Mexico" contributed to the move back to Lansing, Mohatarem said.

In large part, business executives who are speaking out on Mexico's problems hope to counter the well-publicized assertions of billionaire Ross Perot that American jobs would hemorrhage southward under NAFTA—which would break down trade barriers among the United States, Mexico, and Canada, creating a free-trade area of some 360 million consumers. Although President Carlos Salinas de Gortaru has engineered economic reforms and radically improved the country's business climate, they say, Mexico has many problems to solve before it can live up to the image Perot has tried to give it.

"It's astounding to me that the United States fears us," said Claudio X. Gonzalez, director general of Kimberly Clark of Mexico and Salinas' advisor on foreign investment. "We're the smallest, least-developed economy of the three [NAFTA signatories]. We're the weaker partner in this whole equation. How are we a threat?"

Mexico's infrastructure problems continue to be a major deterrent for American manufacturing comapnies that use modern "just in time" production schedules to reduce inventories and keep storage costs down.

Unanticipated delays, a daily aspect of life in Mexico, can scramble delivery schedules, said Steve Knaebel, president of Cummins Engine of Mexico. "It's the unpredictability of the place," he said. "You never know when or where the problems will arise."

Knaebel estimated that each time he uses the telephone for a simple business call, for example, it takes three or four attempts before the call is completed. "This is the main tool I use for managing my business," he said, "and I can't even be sure if I'm going to get a line out."

He said Mexico's highway system is so dilapidated that truck transportation can take 30 to 40 percent longer here than in the United States, and fuel costs are 60 percent higher. A new system of better-quality toll roads has improved some routes, but the cost is widely regarded as prohibitive for commercial traffic.

"Labor costs look cheap up front, but the total cost can be very high," said a financial analyst at a major Mexican bank. "You're not saving money if it takes two or three times before you can get a job done right."

Bringing Mexicans up to American levels of quality and productivity carries a high price, and there is no guarantee that a trained employee will stay with a company once it has given him a marketable skill, said Ron E. Shaver, an operations manager of Hughes Aircraft Co.

SOURCE: "NAFTA Issue Is Muddied by Hidden Costs," by Todd Roberson of the *Washington Post*, October 2, 1993. (c) 1993 *The Washington Post*. Reprinted with permission.

FOR DISCUSSION

Describe this case in the context of the Weber model.

THE EVANS MODEL

Alan Evans, an economist, has suggested an alternative least-cost industrial location model that is based on the associations between the cost of certain location factors and the city population size. The cost of real estate, whether purchased or rented, tends to increase with city size and so do wages (Figure 7.11). The costs of necessary business services, however, tend to decrease because of agglomeration economies. If the three factors are weighted equally, the best location for a producer is in a small to medium-sized city. Most producers, however, would have location requirements weighted toward one or two factors. Manufacturers that require large amounts of floor space and relatively little labor and external services have their lowest cost locations in small towns, as do manufacturers requiring large amounts of labor. Producers with small labor and floor space requirements, but high frequencies of spatial interaction with both suppliers and consumer markets, would find their lowest cost sites in larger cities.

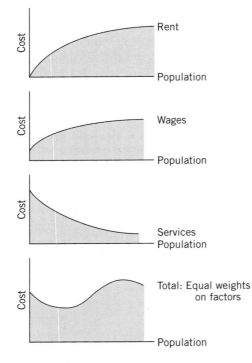

Figure 7.11 Costs of renting floor space, wages, and services all vary systematically with city population. Source: After Alan W. Evans, 1972. "The Pure Theory of City Size in an Industrial Economy." *Urban Studies*, Vol. 9, pp. 49–77.

THE PRODUCT LIFE CYCLE AND LOCATIONAL SHIFTS

Market structure has a strong bearing on the locational requirements of a manufacturing enterprise. As we have seen, monopolies and members of oligopolies focus more on the revenue side of the profit equation, whereas more competitive market structures lead companies to focus on lowering their operating costs. Over time, however, market structures can change and locational requirements change along with them.

The *product life-cycle model* illustrated in Figure 7.12 was originally developed to describe a product's projected level of sales over its life in the market place. As you can see, a product's life cycle can be divided into four sales stages. The first stage is marked by rapid growth in sales, and growth continues at a slower pace in the second stage. Sales level off during the third stage as the market for the product becomes saturated, and demand for the product actually decreases in the fourth stage as it is replaced by a new product beginning its own life cycle. Product life cycles exist; they are drawn from market histories. Examples include black and white television and its replacement by color TVs and and the relative decline in aspirin use with the advent of other over-the-counter pain relievers.

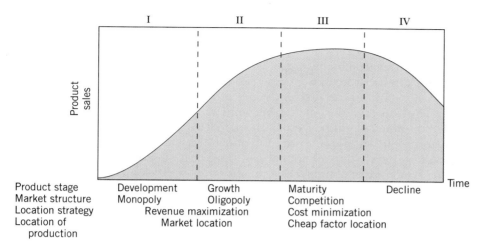

Figure 7.12 The product life-cycle model has implications for the location of production that are associated with changing market structure.

Market structures and locational strategies can be expected to change as a product proceeds through its life cycle. During the first stage, a product is just being developed. It is unlikely that its development will occur simultaneously in several places and by several companies; rather, it will probably occur at one place and under a single company's control. The product's market structure in the first stage of its life cycle is monopolistic, therefore, and the company controlling the product would follow a strategy of revenue maximization. The location of the product's production would be within the market, not only as part of the company's overall revenue maximization strategy, but also because new products are more likely to be developed in places where their characteristics are in great demand.

During the growth stage of the product life cycle, the monopolistic advantages held by the product's developer are eroded as additional companies begin to produce the product. The market structure of the product becomes oligopolistic as a limited number of producers, often in countries different from the product's country of origin, are established. The original producer as well as the new ones also modify the original product in response to the tastes of certain geographical or other segments of the product's growing market. Revenue maximization remains the locational strategy in manufacturing the product, and the modification of the product to suit particular markets requires a market location for production to ensure an accurate response to customer preferences.

The market matures over the third stage of the product life cycle, with sales flattening out. By the third stage, methods of manufacturing the product are fairly well known, and a more competitive market is developed as a result of a relatively large number of producers. Because of competition, cost minimization becomes the appropriate strategy for companies manufacturing the product, and production begins to shift to locations where cheap production factors are available. The trend of locational shifts continues into the fourth stage, when sales of the product are actually shrinking and only the lowest cost producers can operate profitably.

In reality, few companies manufacture a product over its entire life cycle. Most companies that actively pursue product development prefer to operate almost entirely within the first two stages of the life cycle. Once product sales start to level off and the market becomes more competitive, they shed the product's production entirely, establish specialized subsidiaries, or even subcontract it to producers who are used to competitive manufacturing. In any case, they focus on developing additional new products. The low-cost producers, on the other hand, are seldom involved in new product development, so they don't have to shift their production from low- cost sites to locations that are better situated with respect to new markets. In many cases, then, any shifts in the location of manufacturing associated with the product life cycle are more apparent than real because production isn't being relocated within a company. Instead, certain companies only produce products at certain stages of the product life cycle and never relocate any production at all.

The product life cycle is a generalization that applies to many but not all products. The same thing is true of the effect of changing market structure on the locational requirements and locational strategies of manufacturing (and other) enterprises. Companies in competitive markets do emphasize low-cost production, but they can't ignore revenue-increasing strategies, and although monopolies and members of oligopolies do emphasize revenues, their production costs have to be kept within reasonable limits. Review Case 7.2 on Pratt & Whitney and its analysis of comparative costs. Jet engines do go through product life cycles but not in precisely the way described in the product life-cycle model. The jet engine life cycle involves the development of one generation of engine and replacement by a newer generation, but at no stage of the cycle has production ever been marked by many producers and competitive markets. Jet engine production takes place in an oligopolistic market with just a few producers, most notably Pratt & Whitney, General Electric, and the British producer Rolls Royce (long split off from the luxury auto producer).

Pratt & Whitney's concerns over production costs are fairly new. After all, the big differences in costs between Pratt & Whitney's production sites didn't develop overnight; they've always been there, and it's not as if no one noticed them before. Instead, the cost differential between Pratt's Connecticut and other sites, particularly the site in Georgia, has recently become bothersome because of Pratt's loss of much of its military market as the defense budget of the U.S. government has shrunk. When Pratt's defense sales were larger, most of its product development and other costs of production were simply passed along to the government. Because the same basic engines were sold to Pratt & Whitney's customers in the airlines, the government purchases effectively subsidized the civilian purchases. At the time, Pratt & Whitney didn't really care if costs were 30% higher in Connecticut than in Georgia because the difference was borne by the government and didn't affect sales.

The decline in military orders of Pratt & Whitney's jet engines means that the government subsidy of civilian sales, which now form the majority of the market, no longer exists to any great extent. As a result, Pratt's costs became too high relative to those of General Electric and Rolls Royce, and it lost money in its efforts to maintain market share within the limited price range prevailing in the oligopoly. Just as distance from the center of the market in a spatial oligopoly causes a company's market share to decrease, so can distance from the figurative price "center" of the oligopoly (another example of the principle of minimum differentiation at work).

FOREIGN DIRECT INVESTMENT IN MANUFACTURING

Investments can be classified as portfolio and direct. *Portfolio investments* usually include shares of stock in individual corporations, mutual fund shares, corporate bonds, and bonds issued by all levels of government. The common characteristic of all portfolio investments is, by definition, that they carry no control over the operations of the entity in which the investment is made. If you buy a U.S. Savings Bond, you have no more influence over the American government's fiscal policy than does anyone else. If you buy a corporate bond, or some shares of stock, any suggestions you have concerning the corporation's operations and policies are just as likely to be ignored by the board of directors and other management as the suggestions of anyone else. The other category of investments, direct investment, does carry some element of control. On a superficial basis, any investment that holds 50% or more of an entity's assets can be considered direct investment, but practically speaking, direct investment levels can be much less. If, for example, you owned 10% of the stock in any corporation, the board of directors and other management would pay attention to your suggestions. Most of the time, however, we think of portfolio investment as pertaining to individuals and direct investment as a financial flow directed by a business enterprise of some type, usually a corporation.

Foreign direct investment (*FDI*) is direct investment whose origin is in one country and its destination in another. (It's not just the geography of the flow that's important, however, but also the geography of the control over the investment; see Chapter 11 for more of this issue.) FDI is carried on by enterprises over the entire spectrum of the economy; natural resource corporations (especially oil companies), service-sector operations (including everything from financial services to fast food outlets), as well as manufacturing enterprises use FDI as part of their business strategies. Most of the world's larger corporations today are multinational corporations, and if they are manufacturers, they likely control the production of goods in more than one country.

Flows of FDI around the world form a complex web of investment among countries. Although virtually all countries are both origins and destinations of FDI, however, there are only three major sources of FDI in the global economy. Called the triad by the UN, the three are the European Union (or Community), Japan, and the United States, and while FDI occurs in all economic sectors it's no coincidence that the triad comprises the world's major manufacturing centers.

Two basic patterns of FDI originate in the triad. First, a distance decay effect can be seen in FDI from the triad to places outside. A significant share of FDI originating in the United States has destinations in Latin America, whereas the EC's FDI emphasizes East Europe and Japan's FDI is concentrated in East Asia (Figure 7.13). The second basic pattern is the significant FDI among the triad members themselves (Figure 7.14).

At the level of the individual manufacturing enterprise, places are selected for FDI for the same reasons that domestic locations are selected as places for

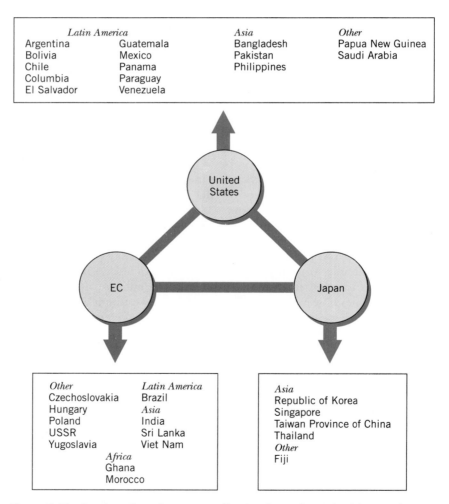

Figure 7.13 Foreign direct investment flowing from the United States, the E.C., and Japan has a regional orientation. Source: Transnational Corporations and Management Division, Department of Economic and Social Development, 1992, *World Investment Report: Transnational Corporations as Engines of Growth* (New York: United Nations), p. 33.

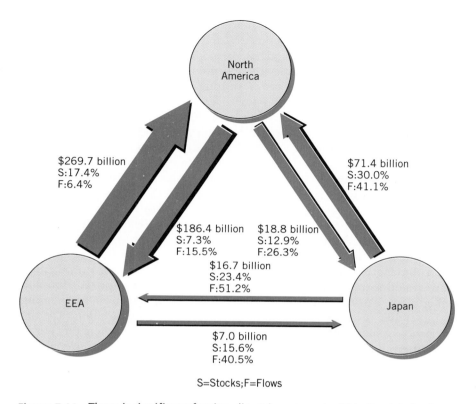

$269.7 billion
S:17.4%
F:6.4%

$71.4 billion
S:30.0%
F:41.1%

$186.4 billion
S:7.3%
F:15.5%

$18.8 billion
S:12.9%
F:26.3%

$16.7 billion
S:23.4%
F:51.2%

$7.0 billion
S:15.6%
F:40.5%

North America

EEA

Japan

S=Stocks;F=Flows

Figure 7.14 There is significant foreign direct investment within the triad. SOURCE: Transnational Corporations and Management Division, Department of Economic and Social Development, 1992, *World Investment Report*: *Transnational Corporations as Engines of Growth* (New York: United Nations), p. 33.

production. Some FDI has a market orientation, and some FDI is undertaken in order to take advantage of lower production costs than are available in the domestic economy. Because the basic locational motives hold whether a domestic or foreign direct investment is undertaken, the industrial location models that have already been described are applicable to FDI as well as domestic location decisions (as described in Cases 7.3 and 7.4, for example). The product life-cycle model, in particular, has been used to describe international shifts in the location of production that could guide FDI. The first stage of the product's life cycle begins in the manufacturer's home country, and production is established in other countries, with important markets in the second stage. By the third stage, new manufacturing facilities are established in low-cost production sites, and perhaps production is shifted to even lower cost sites by the fourth stage of the product life cycle.

Initially, the product life-cycle model was used to describe the spread of production from richer industrial countries to poorer developing countries.

Now, however, the geographical shifts that might occur aren't so simple. New products are often developed in industrializing countries, and over their life cycle production may never shift at all. In addition, the flexibility of many multinational manufacturers permits the selection of a single site for production that eliminates the transaction costs of shifting manufacturing sites, thereby minimizing the average cost of production over the entire life cycle.

Although the question of "where" to locate FDI in manufacturing is not so different from the question of "where" in domestic location decisions, the question of "when" to proceed with FDI is another matter. For a long time, manufacturing enterprises have recognized cost advantages and market opportunities that they were unable to take advantage of because long distances, managerial inexperience, and government restrictions limited the geographical spread of FDI. The geographer Peter Dicken, in his book *Global Shift*, has written of *enabling technologies* that facilitate control of production in one country by an enterprise in another. Two of these technologies are of the conventional sort: telecommunications and transportation. These technologies are sufficiently developed as linking mechanisms at the global scale to allow foreign production to be integrated within a manufacturing corporation's overall production and marketing plans. A third technology is not a function of advanced engineering ability, but rather is based on developments in business organization: it is the *multinational corporation (MNC)*. MNCs provide an institutional context for coordinating an international production and marketing system. To the three enabling technologies proposed by Dicken, we can add the liberalization of government restrictions on international investment as a major factor enabling the spread of FDI (see also Chapter 11).

The enabling technologies affect timing in a generic way, but the timing of a particular enterprise's FDI may depend on the size of a particular foreign market. There are three basic ways to gain access to a foreign market. One is to export: simply produce a product at "home" for sale in the foreign market. Another is to arrange a licensing agreement under which the product is manufactured by a licensee producer within the foreign market that pays a royalty on sales to the licenser. The third method of access is FDI. Of the three methods, exporting has the lowest fixed cost and the highest variable costs of market service. It doesn't require significant up-front investment in new plant and equipment, but the costs of long-distance market service are high. In some circumstances, foreign governments establish strict quotas on imports or require the payment of very high import tariffs so that the costs of serving a market through exporting become prohibitive (see Chapter 10). The fixed costs of licensing are higher than that for exporting, but the variable costs are lower. With licensing, the foreign producer's production facilities have to be modified, which can be expensive. However, some of the market service costs can be shared with the foreign producer, so those costs are lower. FDI requires the most substantial up-front investment of the three methods of market access, but once a physical presence in the market is established, distribution, marketing, and other costs of serving the market are relatively low.

The relationships between the cost of the three methods of foreign market access and market size are portrayed in Figure 7.15. The graph can be interpreted

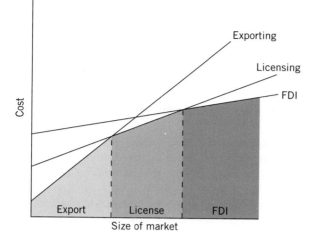

Figure 7.15 In the market model of FDI, the size of the market determines whether exporting, licensing, or foreign direct investment is the most efficient form of access to a foreign market. SOURCE: After Peter J. Buckley and Mark Casson, 1981: "The Optimal Timing of a Foreign Direct Investment," *The Economic Journal*, Vol. 91, pp. 75–87, Figure 4.

in two ways. First, in a static context the *market model of FDI* indicates that exporting is the most efficient method of foreign market access to small markets, licensing is the most efficient form of access to intermediate markets, and FDI is the best method of access to the largest markets. Second, the market model suggests a strategy for foreign market penetration that is similar to the conservative one followed by the Stanley Works, as described in Case 7.4. Access to the market is initially gained by exporting. As the market for the company's products grows, licensing agreements are established in order to get more of the products to the market, often with local modifications not included in the earlier exports. Finally, when demand has reached sufficient size, manufacturing facilities are established in the foreign market. This slow-going approach to foreign market access is not unusual, even among long-established MNCs.

Once the decision to proceed by FDI is made, whether for reasons of improving market access or taking advantage of low production costs, the investment can take three forms. The establishment of a completely new manufacturing facility, perhaps under the control of a new corporate subsidiary, is called *greenfield FDI*. This facility is fairly risky, especially in locations that are not familiar to the investing corporation. In addition, greenfield FDI projects carry high start-up costs but do not generate any operating income until they are fully on-line. FDI projects are able to generate positive cash flows almost immediately if they are carried out by *foreign acquisition* or through a takeover of a producer already operating in the location. In addition, foreign acquisitions bring with them foreign expertise, allowing new entrants to a country to rapidly obtain knowledge of relevant business customs and operating procedures. Often a local partner is found necessary or is even required by some governments so that *international joint ventures*, partnerships between domestic and foreign enterprises, are common forms of FDI.

■ CASE 7.4
Stanley, Hardware, and International Manufacturing

Throughout the Stanley Works' eleven manufacturing units, the push is on to increase sales and, in many cases, operations outside North America. "This is our new frontier," said Gil Julian, plant manager for the hardware division in New Britain.

Taming the offshore "frontier" is a highly complex venture at Stanley, as no two units have the same expansion needs; some are in consumer goods, some industrial; some have major overseas facilities, some don't.

One division—Stanley Tools, which makes hand tools—decades ago began forging a worldwide network of sales, distribution, and manufacturing. For it and other Stanley units, international markets are hardly a frontier, although many populous markets remain barely trodden.

Other divisions, including Stanley Hardware, have lagged overseas until recently, despite their market prowess at home in America. Hardware gained a foothold in Southeast Asia last year and won a contract to supply hinges for the twin Petronas towers in Kuala Lumpur, Malaysia, which will open next year as the world's tallest building.

Still others are strong in some global pockets. Access is established and growing in Western Europe, and only recently began eyeing Asia. Stanley Fastening Systems, maker of fasteners and pnuematic nailers, and staplers, planted its flag in Poland, China, Indonesia and Malaysia in the past four years.

Seen as a whole, the effort is a natural progression for Stanley, company officials and outside experts say, and it sheds light on how an old-line U.S. maufacturer with major sales and operations overseas becomes a truly global company across all divisions.

"It's becoming more planned," said Richard H. Ayers, chairman and chief executive since 1989. "We're now at the stage where we're beginning to recognize those international opportunities on a larger scale."

For the past few years, international sales have hovered around 30 percent of total revenues, which reached $2.5 billion last year. Stanley's goal: to boost non-North America sales to 40 percent as total revenues grow by 10 percent a year. Manufacturing operations would follow a similar pattern.

To that end, key executives from headquarters and the various divisions are coordinating efforts through a newly formed "world markets group." Stanley has already moved toward more aggressive—but never hostile—takeovers. And it will seek more joint ventures in difficult markets such as Japan, China and Eastern Europe, where Stanley Tool opened a pincers and pliers plant with a Polish firm in 1991.

In parts of Asia and Latin America, economies are growing at double-digit rates, with strong construction sectors that bode well for Stanley products.

Ayers and other Stanley executives cite two chief reasons why the company has stepped-up its offshore moves.

First, the company faces growing competitors in every region as markets open and tariffs decline. Second, customers such as Wal-Mart, Home Depot and Makro in Europe are becoming more international themselves.

In a reorganization that finished in 1993, Stanley merged 23 divisions into 11, consolidating regional units such as Stanley Tools Europe. Now, each unit has a global reach for its products.

''We're trying to find the best of all worlds . . . to find an affordable solution to get Stanley products marketed all over the world.'' Ayers said.

ACCESS TECHNOLOGIES

One side of the 100,000-square-foot Stanley Access Technologies plant—formerly Stanley Magic-Door—is dominated by the electronics section, where circuits that form the heart of the automatic doors come together.

Four computerized machines use tiny light beams and rapid movements to show employees where to place components on a board. A room with the latest equipment spits out test results after simulating long use, and thick ovens put the electronics through radical changes in temperature.

This section of automatic door manufacturing, which employs about 60 people, will not be duplicated overseas as Access expands in Europe and Asia, said Claude ''Robbie'' Robertson, vice president of manufacturing for the division.

''We want to maintain close control of the electronics,'' Robertson said.

While keeping its core high-tech operation close to home, Access is looking to expand small plants in France, the Netherlands and Italy. It already has a larger plant in England and a sales office in Germany.

Access is also laying groundwork to move into Asia, where the automated door market is four or five times larger than in the U.S. In the past year, sales representatives for the division have set up shop in Thailand, where Stanley has several divisions operating in a single complex.

''During the next five years, most of our growth will be in Europe. And beyond five years, our growth will be in the Far East, said Henning N. Kornbrekke, the division president and general manager.

INTERNATIONAL MARKETING

The Petronas towers deal in Kuala Lumpur, Malaysia, expected to total 50,000 heavy-guage, stainless steel hinges made in New Britain, is a case study in Stanley's new international marketing push.

Stanley Hardware—maker of more than 12,000 varieties of door hinges, hasps, hooks and wire goods—assembled an 11-person East Asia sales and marketing team early last year.

The director, Bill Remy, set up in Bangkok, Thailand.

His job? "To know everything about every major building project in in the Far East," said Scott A. Bannell, vice president of international operations for Stanley Hardware.

Back in New Britain—where Stanley Hardware employs more than 700 people—Gil Julian, the plant manager, kept a close eye on the first shipment of 15,000 hinges for Petronas, the state oil company. "We baby-sat that one," he said.

"Scott doesn't necessarily get the kind of lead time we'd like," Julian said. "That's the nature of the international business. . . . You can't accept every order."

For another project in Malaysia, an Exxon building, Bannell contacted the chairman of the Dallas-based energy giant. "Literally a week later our sales rep gets a call from the Exxon-Malaysia office," he said. "We're working on it as we speak."

For now, Stanley Hardware sells less than 10 percent overseas.

Bannell doesn't know why the division never expanded much outside North America. Ironically, he said, Hardware had one of Stanley's first overseas acquisitions, in Germany in 1923.

CONSERVATIVE EXPANSION

Traditionally, where Stanley has expanded overseas it has followed a familiar, conservative progression.

It starts with exporting order-by-order, expands to a relationship with a distributor, then Stanley dispatches its own sales representatives to the region, Bannell said.

The company would then progress to opening its own warehouse and distribution network, followed by alliances and investment in a plant.

"The first thing is to learn as much as you can about the market," Bannell said. "We have people make many trips to the Far East, spend weeks at a time, not sell anything, talk to architects."

Ayers said Stanley will continue the steady, conservative approach.

Stanley's push to open new world markets and establish global facilities for the nontool divisions began around six years ago, when Ayers succeeded Donald W. Davis.

But Ayers is adamant that his legacy will not be as the architect of international expansion.

"Businesses today aren't single-person entities. They're the collection of the minds and thoughts and skills of an awful lot of people."

His legacy, he said, will be "creating a situation where more people are involved in the decision-making."

He has started by instituting a policy of informal dress, where appropriate.

He and Stanley President R. Alan Hunter are pictured in the latest annual report in casual attire.

But, perhaps satisfying overseas expectations, they are shown in dark suits and ties in the Stanley world brochure.

Ultimately, Stanley's Connecticut employees want to know whether the company's overseas expansion means a loss of jobs here. Stanley executives point to indications showing the opposite.

Employment in New Britain has remained steady at about 2,000 even as Stanley has targeted worldwide growth.

And the local tape rule plant, which was automated in 1982, is the lowest-cost site for tape rules, which are made in France, England, Mexico, Brazil, Thailand, and Taiwan, said Stewart Gentsch, the Stanley Tools president.

"I don't think we're going to lose jobs," Gentsch said.

SOURCE: "Stanley's World," by Dan Haar, *Courant* Staff Writer, in *The Hartford Courant Business Weekly*, June 19, 1995, pp. 1, 8–9. By permission of the *Hartford Courant.*

FOR DISCUSSION

Does the material in this case support or contradict the product life-cycle model?

POINTS IN SUMMARY

1. The experience of many of the world's wealthier countries is that manufacturing, in terms of its proportion of a country's employment and in terms of its proportion of national income, tends to grow initially with a country's economy but then declines as part of the pattern of sectoral shifts.

2. Manufacturing can earn location rent like any other sector of the economy, and as location rents change, manufacturing shifts in its locations.

3. Governments often try to develop good business climates by offering financial incentives designed either to lure a company to a location or to keep it there.

4. The relative importance of access to raw materials has decreased over time.

5. Flexible manufacturing is based on achievement of economies of scope, which are a special form of economies of scale.

6. Traditionally, manufacturers internalized the costs of environmental degradation, but increasing environmental regulation is now forcing manufacturers to internalize those costs.

7. Agglomerations tend to be self-reinforcing.

8. The best location is the one where location rent, and therefore profits, are maximized.

9. Distance decay is the geographical manifestation of price elastic demand.

10. The location rents of monopolies and oligopolies are derived more from their location's market effects than from their location's factor costs. In more competitive markets, however, location

rents are highest where costs of production and distribution are lowest.

11. The costs of individual location factors must be considered as relative in current comparison to one another; the basis for their comparison can change over time.

12. A factory should be moved if the discounted present value of closing it, establishing a new one, and the operational cost savings sum to a higher discounted present value than that of the current plant and its production.

13. Market structures and locational strategies can be expected to change in the manufacture of a product as it proceeds through its life cycle.

14. Locational shifts in production are expected over a product's life cycle because market structure changes, but that does not mean that individual manufacturers are expected to keep shifting their production locations over time.

15. Investments can be classified in two categories: portfolio and direct.

16. FDI is carried on by enterprises in all sectors of the economy.

17. There are three major regional sources of FDI in the global economy: the EC, Japan, and the United States.

18. The question of "where" to locate FDI in manufacturing is not so different as the question of "where" in domestic location decisions, but the question of "when" to proceed with FDI is another matter.

TERMS TO REMEMBER

aggregate travel model
economies of scope
enabling technologies
flexible manufacturing
footloose manufacturing
foreign acquisition
foreign direct investment (FDI)
greenfield FDI
industrial inertia

international joint venture
just-in-time manufacturing
location of production functions
market model of FDI
market potential model
market structure
market threshold
material index

monopoly
monopoly rent
multinational corporation (MNC)
oligopoly
outer range of a good
portfolio investment
principle of minimum differentiation
product life-cycle model
range of a good

right-to-work law
satisficing search behavior
spatial equilibrium
threshold range of a good
value added in manufacturing

SUGGESTED READING

Alonso, William. 1967: "A Reformulation of Classical Location Theory and Its Relation to Rent Theory." *Papers of the Regional Science Association*, Vol. 19, pp. 23–44.

You should recall the authors' name in association with land-use theory described in Chapter 2. Here, he shows the equivalence of land rent theory and industrial location theory that exists under certain assumptions concerning production costs.

Crandall, Robert W. 1993: *Manufacturing on the Move.* Washington, D.C.: The Brookings Institution.

This book focuses on the problems associated with the regional shifts in manufacturing that occurred during the 1960s, 1970s, and early part of the 1980s. Brookings is a Washington "think tank" that develops public policy positions, and this book has solid suggestions for state and local policies in support of manufacturing.

Dicken, Peter. 1992: *Global Shift: The Internationalization of Economic Activity*, 2nd ed. New York: Guilford.

Dicken provides an excellent volume on the international economy especially with respect to case-by-case analyses of FDI in manufacturing and multinational corporations in general. This is the second best book ever written by a geographer on the international economy.

Graham, Edward M., and Paul R. Krugman. 1989: *Foreign Direct Investment in the United States*. Washington, D.C.: Institute for International Economics.

This book provides a good introduction to the topic of FDI and then focuses on the sectoral distribution of investment by foreign interests in the United States. Its general tone is that FDI in the U.S. economy is a good thing and that restrictive policies are not appropriate reactions to growing foreign investment.

Hamilton, F. E. I., ed. 1978: *Contemporary Industrialization: Spatial Analysis and Regional Development*. New York: Longman.

Ian Hamilton led the development of geographical interests in industrial systems in the 1970s and early 1980s. These interests concern manufacturing in its regional economic, social, and political contexts more than the location of production in its more narrow sense. This volume of 14 papers by various authors provides an introduction to the industrial systems school of economic geography.

Hanink, D. M., and R. G. Cromley. 1987: "A Risk-Return Model for Multiregion and Multiproduct Diversification of the Firm." *Environment and Planning A*, Vol. 19, pp. 81–92.

This paper applies a financial portfolio model to the complex location problems faced by companies that produce a number of products in different factories in different places.

Hekman, John S. 1980: "The Product Cycle and New England Textiles." *The Quarterly Journal of Economics*, Vol. 94, pp. 697–717.

Hekman examines the historical record of the decline of textile production in New England at the same time the industry was growing in the U.S. South. The evidence he cites in this article strongly supports the locational effects of the product life cycle in this manufacturing sector.

Perrucci, Carolyn C., Robert Perucci, Dena B. Targ, and Harry Targ. 1988: *Plant Closings: International Context and Social Costs*. Sawmill, N.Y.: Aldine de Gruyter.

The authors are sociologists and psychologists, and so provide a special perspective on the disruptive effects of plant closings on local communities and on affected individuals.

Smith, David M. 1981: *Industrial Location: An Economic Geographical Analysis*, 2nd ed. New York: John Wiley & Sons.

This book covers almost all of basic location theory and then some, especially the least-cost models. In addition to theory and related models, the book provides case studies and an introduction to applied industrial location analysis.

Webber, Michael J. 1984. *Industrial Location*. Vol. 3 in Sage Scientific Geography Series. Beverly Hills, Calif.: Sage.

If you would prefer more of a summary of basic industrial location theory to the more comprehensive presentation by David Smith, then this short volume (94 pages) is for you. Despite its brevity, it covers all the bases and even contains some short case studies.

Chapter 8

The Location of Services

This chapter

- describes the global distribution of services and their relative concentration in high-income countries.
- divides services into two major sectors: tertiary and quaternary.
- introduces central place theory and related models in describing the importance of market proximity as a location factor in the tertiary sector.
- describes the various location factors affecting the quaternary sector.
- emphasizes the growing importance of the service MNC in the global economy.

Arthur James M.P.A./The Canadian Architect

The primary sector, including agriculture and other direct uses of natural resources, has locational requirements that are fairly confining. As we have already seen, wheat can't be grown commercially unless certain environmental conditions are locally present, and copper isn't mined unless copper ore is in sufficient quantity and of sufficient quality to provide an economic resource. The primary sector has a supply-side locational orientation that cannot be avoided. However, as described in the preceding chapter, the manufacturing, or secondary, sector of the economy is split between general location preferences. Some manufacturing, especially its more competitive industries, is best located where factor costs are low, and some of manufacturing is best located with market factors in mind.

Traditionally, the service sector has been thought to be locationally confined to markets in the same way that the primary sector is confined by supply considerations. Services can't be stored, at least in the conventional sense, so they must be provided where they are consumed. Because of technological change, however, the necessity for many enterprises selling or otherwise providing a service to be physically located in a market is declining. Improvements in transport facilities and increasing mobility in consumer populations allow more locational flexibility in the service sector than existed just a few years ago. Telecommunications advances permit many services to be provided over long distances, even internationally. Rather than being locationally confined like the primary sector, it seems that the service sector is now more like manufacturing, with different types having different locational priorities and different emphases on cost and revenue as location factors.

THE GROWTH OF SERVICES

The tendency of national and regional economies to undergo sectoral shifts as they grow was described in Chapters 5 and 7. Recall that over the course of economic growth, the natural resource extraction industries and agriculture are displaced by the secondary sector, or manufacturing, as an economy's major provider of both jobs and income. As growth continues, the secondary sector is in turn overtaken by the service sector as the most important contributor to an economy. Richer economies are often referred to as postindustrial because they are dominated by their service sectors.

Although the sectoral shifts don't always take place smoothly, there is a strong association between an economy's wealth and the size of its service sector. As illustrated in Diagram A of Figure 8.1, the average proportion of national income derived from services progresses in a uniform way with national income

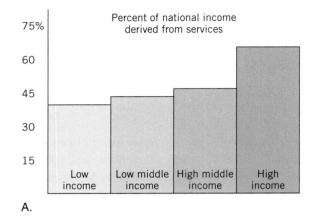

A.

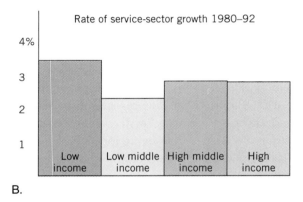

B.

Figure 8.1   The percentage of national income derived from services increases with national income in a predictable way. From 1980 through 1992, however, low income countries had faster service-sector growth than any other World Bank income group.

level. Low-income countries earn, on average, about 40% of their national income from services, and high-income countries earn an average of nearly 65% of their national income from services. Diagram B in Figure 8.1 shows that the low-income countries have been catching up to the others with respect to service-sector growth, but the higher income countries are continuing to experience healthy service-sector growth.

What accounts for the growth of the service sector? A simple, and correct, answer is its breadth. What we popularly refer to as a single-service sector encompasses a wide variety of activities, ranging from fast food restaurants to investment banking and employing a large number of people in various occupations from hair cutters to U.S. government cabinet secretaries (and also the U.S. president). The U.S. government's classification of industries in Table 8.1 indicates the breadth of activities that can be considered to be types of services. The major divisions include transportation, wholesale trade, retail trade, *FIRE* (finance,

Table 8.1 Major Divisions of the Service Sector in the U.S. Standard Industrial Classification

Division E. Transportation, Communications, Electric, Gas, and Sanitary Services
Major Group 40. Railroad transportation
Major Group 41. Local and suburban transit and interurban highway passenger transportation
Major Group 42. Motor freight transportation and warehousing
Major Group 43. U.S. Postal Service
Major Group 44. Water transportation
Major Group 45. Transportation by air
Major Group 46. Pipelines, except natural gas
Major Group 47. Transportation services
Major Group 48. Communication
Major Group 49. Electric, gas, and sanitary services
Division F. Wholesale Trade
Major Group 50. Wholesale trade—durable goods
Major Group 51. Wholesale trade—nondurable goods
Division G. Retail Trade
Major Group 52. Building materials, hardware, garden supply, and mobile home dealers
Major Group 53. General merchandise stores
Major Group 54. Food stores
Major Group 55. Automotive dealers and gasoline service stations
Major Group 56. Apparel and accessory stores
Major Group 57. Furniture, home furnishings, and equipment stores
Major Group 58. Eating and drinking places
Major Group 59. Miscellaneous retail
Division H. Finance, Insurance, and Real Estate
Major Group 60. Banking
Major Group 61. Credit agencies other than banks
Major Group 62. Security and commodity brokers, dealers, exchanges, and services
Major Group 63. Insurance
Major Group 64. Insurance agents, brokers, and service
Major Group 65. Real estate Major Group 66. Combinations of real estate, insurance, loans, law offices
Major Group 67. Holding and other investment offices
Division I. Services
Major Group 70. Hotels, rooming houses, camps, and other lodging places
Major Group 72. Personal services
Major Group 73. Business services
Major Group 75. Automotive repair, services, and garages
Major Group 76. Miscellaneous repair services
Major Group 78. Motion pictures
Major Group 79. Amusement and recreation services, except motion picture
Major Group 80. Health services
Major Group 81. Legal services
Major Group 82. Educational services
Major Group 83. Social services
Major Group 84. Museums, art galleries, botanical and zoological gardens
Major Group 86. Membership organizations
Major Group 88. Private households
Major Group 89. Miscellaneous services
Division J. Public Administration
Major Group 91. Executive, legislative, and general government, except finance
Major Group 92. Justice, public order, and safety
Major Group 93. Public finance, taxation, and monetary policy
Major Group 94. Administration of human resources programs
Major Group 95. Administration of environmental quality and housing programs
Major Group 96. Administration of economic programs
Major Group 97. National security and international affairs

SOURCE: Executive Office of the President, Office of Management and Budget, 1972: *Standard Industrial Classification Manual* (Washington, D.C. U.S. Government Printing Office), pp. 6–7.

insurance, and real estate), and public administration, in addition to those activities specifically referred to as services (Division I in Table 8.1). Given that services encompass so many functions, it's not surprising that they contribute so much to most economies.

In analyzing the growth of the service sector and its locational patterns, it can usefully be divided into different components. Frequently, it is considered to be two related, but distinct, economic sectors. The *tertiary sector* consists of those activities such as transport, government, wholesale and retail trade, and the general business and personal services that make up most of the listings in Table 8.1. The *quaternary sector* includes FIRE and management services, and is sometimes called the information sector because providing and managing information is its fundamental business. Another important distinction between services is defined not by what they provide, but by their market. Whether they issue from the tertiary or the quaternary sector, services sold to households are called *consumer services*. Those services sold or otherwise provided to business are called *producer services*. As you should expect, businesses that sell consumer services and businesses that sell producer services usually have different locational patterns.

The tertiary sector contains those services that are expected to increase their contribution to a national or regional economy as it grows. Producer services in the tertiary sector have to expand as growth takes place in either the primary or secondary sector. For example, any good manufactured or any crop grown for commercial purposes has to be distributed to its consumers. Distribution is therefore, a service, that must be provided along with the manufacture of a good or any other type of production in the economy.

As production grows, its distribution requirements increase as well. Distribution and other producer services can be expected to grow at least at the same pace as goods production in an economy simply because the growth of goods production creates demand for producer services. (This type of integrated growth is discussed in detail in Chapter 9.)

The conventional wisdom has been that manufacturing growth leads growth in services because real wealth can only be embodied in tangible things and material accumulation. Many people, politicians among them, are often concerned about the "decline" of manufacturing and its replacement by services as a source of employment and income. However, as shown in Case 8.1, which describes the growth of narrowly defined service employment in Chicago, the relationship between manufacturing and services is not as straightforward as it once appeared.

Growth in consumer services is generated by increasing personal incomes. According to *Engel's law,* as incomes increase, decreasing proportions of incomes are required to purchase the necessities of life. People with higher incomes have more money available for discretionary spending, and money they don't save is often spent on consumer services. Wealthier people, for example, are able to spend more money on entertainment than can be afforded by poor people. In addition, the wealthy can spend more money on insurance, education, travel, and many other consumer services. The geographical disparity in the contribution of services to national income illustrated in Figure 8.1 is easily explained when the income-based demand for most of the consumer services of the tertiary sector is added to the production-generated demand for producer services.

The impact of the quaternary sector also must be taken into account. The quaternary sector consists of consumer and producer services that respond to growth in income and production in the same way that they do in the tertiary sector, and therefore are more likely to be found in richer than in poorer places. In addition, the quaternary sector also includes most of the new service products associated with the digital electronic revolution that is currently affecting all parts of society in almost all parts of the world, particularly the wealthier countries. Much of the quaternary sector's growth in recent years is associated with increased demand for new information and knowledge products, such as software, which are really services that generate demand for manufactured goods (computers, discs, etc.) rather than the other way around.

◪ CASE 8.1
The Recent Growth of Services in Chicago

Economic regions, such as Chicago, compete with each other in order to maintain or enhance their share of national output of goods and services. Regions that outperform others expand their market, while regions that lag behind lose market share. Any evaluation of a region's economic performance requires a comparison of that region with the nation as a whole.

Nationally, service employment surpassed manufacturing employment in 1982. In Chicago, this watershed was reached in 1980. In both the nation and Chicago, service employment approximately doubled between 1970 and 1987. (Services here are limited to include hotels, personal services, business services, auto repair, amusement, health and legal services. They do not include retail and wholesale trade, finance, insurance, real estate, and transportation services.) Over the same period, manufacturing employment, while somewhat constant in the nation, declined in Chicago. The fall in Chicago's manufacturing employment was steady in the 1970s and sharper in the 1980s (see Figures 1 A and B).

In the last two decades, Chicago's manufacturing employment experienced a gradual decline relative to manufacturing employment in the nation. Chicago's share of national manufacturing employment decreased from 4.9 percent in 1970 to 3.4 percent in 1987. Over the entire period, this constitutes a 31 percent decline in Chicago's manufacturing employment base relative to the nation (see Figure 1 C).

Prior to the 1970s, growth in Chicago's manufacturing sector was aided by a number of factors. The availability of natural resources, easy access to waterways and railroads, and close proximity to major consumers located in the Midwest and East made Chicago an attractive place to site manufacturing activity. As these advantages declined over time, so did Chicago's ability to draw manufacturing.

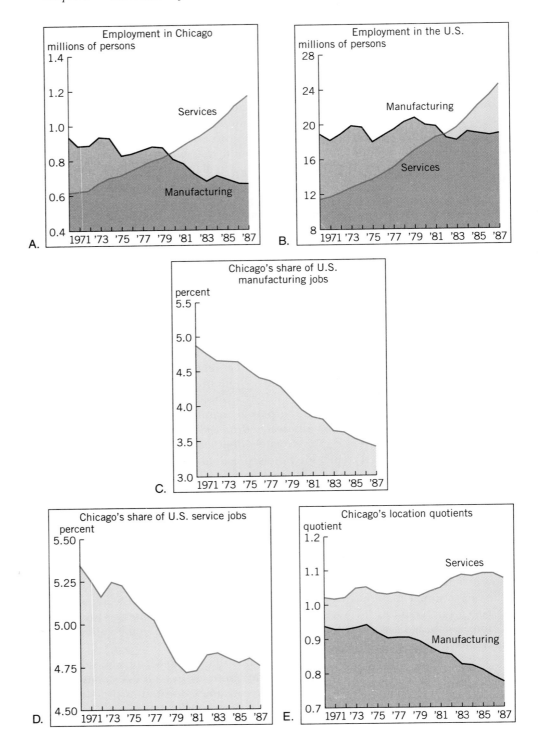

In addition, relatively expensive labor and electricity further eroded the manufacturing base.

Other structural factors, such as a higher than average proportion of mature industries, played a prominent role in the restructuring of Chicago. Such mature industries as steel and automobiles which were highly energy intensive were also inefficient users of energy. This drawback hardly mattered, given the abundant availability of cheap oil in the 1950s and 1960s. But the oil price increases of 1973 and 1979 rendered part of the capital stock in such industries obsolescent. Meanwhile, the stricter environmental regulations of the early 1970s raised costs by requiring considerable capital investment in pollution control devices. The net effect on the Chicago region was to raise manufacturing costs and lower productivity in the short run.

Chicago's service industry, on the other hand, showed substantial growth in employment from 1970 to 1987. However, employment growth in Chicago's service industry was slightly lower than that of the nation between 1970 and 1979. As a result, Chicago's share of national service employment declined from 5.3 percent in 1970 to 4.8 percent by 1979. From 1979 onwards, Chicago's service employment growth has kept pace with national service employment growth, and remained at a constant 4.8 percent of national service employment (see Figure 1 D).

The steady growth in Chicago's service employment in the face of declining manufacturing employment runs counter to conventional wisdom, which considers manufacturing the prime mover behind all employment growth. A decline in manufacturing employment should be accompanied by a decline in service and other nonmanufacturing employment. This line of thinking can be wrong, at least in Chicago, where the service sector grew even as manufacturing employment declined. But such counterintuitive growth does not necessarily diminish the importance of the manufacturing sector. Indeed, manufacturing-service linkages grew stronger in Chicago in the post-1979 period.

To study the structural relationship between Chicago and the nation, we use location quotients. Location quotients measure the importance of a sector in the local economy relative to the importance of the same sector in the national economy. A location quotient value less than one implies that the given sector has a smaller role to play in the local economy than in the nation as a whole. Similarly, a location quotient greater than one implies that (in terms of the variable being measured), the given sector has a larger role to play locally then in the nation as a whole.

Specifically, location quotients are ratios of ratios and are of the form (A/B)/(C/D). For example, A would be Chicago employment in manufacturing, while B would be total Chicago employment.

Thus A/B tells us what proportion of Chicago's total employment is accounted for by the manufacturing sector. C would then be national manufacturing employment, while D would be total national employment. Thus C/D would tell us what proportion of the nation's total employment is accounted for by the manufacturing sector. The ratio of these two ratios would then enable us to gauge whether a particular industry is more important to Chicago than it is to the nation. Furthermore, one is not restricted to using employment values alone. One can also obtain income and output location quotients.

Manufacturing and service sectors location quotients are graphed in Figure 1 E. The service sector employment location quotient was greater than one over the last two decades, rising from 1.02 in 1970 to 1.09 by 1987. Thus a larger proportion of Chicago's overall employment came from the service industry than was the case with the nation. Manufacturing location quotients were, however, lower than those for the service sector, and differed both in levels as well as trends. The location quotient for manufacturing fell from 0.93 in 1971 to 0.79 in 1987.

These numbers clearly indicate that, over the last two decades, manufacturing employment has had an increasingly smaller role in Chicago's overall employment, not only in absolute terms but also relative to manufacturing at the national level.

SOURCE: "Chicago's Economy: Twenty Years of Structural Change," by Philip Israilevich and Rama-mohan Mahidhara, in *Economic Perspectives*, Federal Reserve Bank of Chicago, Vol. 14, 1990, pp. 15–17, 18, and 22.

FOR DISCUSSION

This case describes the replacement of manufacturing by services in Chicago's economy. Explain this replacement in the context of the sectoral shifts described in Chapters 5 and 7.

LOCATION IN THE TERTIARY SECTOR

Service establishments in the tertiary sector are almost always found at their market. Their location results mainly from the fact that most services can't be stored, at least in the usual meaning of the word. Because their production and consumption take place simultaneously, the "best" locations for most retailers and other consumer service providers are in places with a high market density. The guide to retail site selection in Insights 8.1 outlines the importance of such items as traffic flows and population densities in selecting a site for a new retail store. The same list of location criteria applies to most consumer service businesses in the tertiary sector. Recall from Chapter 2 that businesses requiring highly frequent interaction with their customers earn their highest location rents at centers of regional accessibility where transport costs are low. Tertiary-sector consumer services are just those sorts of businesses, and so they tend to be found in clusters at road intersections and at other easily accessible points.

Providers of producer services have a little more locational leeway than do businesses selling consumer services. Producer services typically require less frequent interaction between seller and buyer than is found in the consumer service market. Businesses selling producer services can therefore earn higher location rents at less accessible places than those required by sellers of consumer services. Wholesalers, for example, aren't often found in downtown commercial areas or in the same neighborhoods as suburban shopping centers because those locations earn higher rents for businesses selling consumer services. But while accessibility is less important to sellers of producer services than it is to sellers of consumer services in the tertiary sector, market proximity remains an important location factor because of distance decay that occurs in producer service transactions. Even retail bank services sold to producers are marked by distance decay (Table 8.2), although the actual costs of distance in conducting this type of business are so low as to be negligible. Often, however, proximity breeds a comfortable familiarity between seller and buyer in the tertiary sector, even in

Table 8.2 Percent of Bank Services Acquired by Business Within Various Distances

Service/Business Type	Percent of Services						
	70	75	80	85	90	95	
Deposit Accounts							
Total Sample	3	4	5	5	8	15	m
Suburban	3	4	5	8	12	20	i
Manufacturer	4	5	6	8	12	20	l
Suburban Manufacturer	5	8	10	12	15	22	e
Large	5	5	·5	7	10	20	s
Loans							
Total Sample	3	5	6	9	12	25	m
Surburban	4	5	8	13	25	35	i
Manufacturer	5	7	9	15	19	25	l
Suburban Manufacturer	8	10	13	20	25	35	e
Large	6	7	10	20	30	65	s
Other Services							
Total Sample	3	3	5	6	9	20	m
Suburban	3	3	5	6	12	22	i
Manufacturer	5	5	6	9	12	22	l
Suburban Manufacturer	8	10	12	15	22	35	e
Large	4	5	6	6	10	25	s
Total Services							
Total Sample	3	4	5	6	10	20	m
Suburban	3	4	5	8	12	22	i
Manufacturer	5	5	7	10	13	22	l
Suburban Manufacturer	8	10	12	13	20	25	e
Large	5	5	6	8	15	35	s

SOURCE: "Geographic Banking Markets," by Paul R. Quatro, in *Economic Commentary* (Federal Reserve Bank of Cleveland, September 12, 1983), p. 2.

the producer service end of things. Accessibility, therefore, remains an important location factor because it helps ensure a share of the market for reasons other than minimizing the transaction costs of spatial interaction.

Retail Site Selection

IMPORTANCE OF A GOOD LOCATION

Often an owner-manager, for whatever reason, is faced with renewing the lease or choosing a new or perhaps an additional site for the business. At this crucial time the owner should consider the value of a traffic count to be sure the new location can draw customers into the store.

In the central business district, land values and rents are often based on traffic counts. The site in the central business district that produces the highest traffic count with regard to the type of traffic desired by a particular store is considered its 100 percent location. However, a 100 percent location for one type of store may not be 100 percent for other types. For example, a site which rates 100 percent for a drugstore may be only 80 percent for a men's clothing shop or 60 percent for an appliance store.

FACTORS TO BE CONSIDERED

Three factors confront you as an owner-manager in choosing a location: selection of a city; choice of an area or type of location within a city; and identification of a specific site.

If you are going to relocate in another city, naturally you consider the following factors:

- Size of the city's trading area.
- Population and population trends in the trading area.
- Total purchasing power and the distribution of the purchasing power.
- Total retail trade potential for different lines of trade.
- Number, size, and quality of competition.
- Progressiveness of competition.

In choosing an area or type of location within a city, you evaluate factors such as:

- Customer attraction power of the particular store and the shopping district.

- Quantitative and qualitative nature of competitive stores.
- Availability of access routes to the stores.
- Nature of zoning regulations.
- Direction of the area's expansion.
- General appearance of the area.

Pinpointing the specific site is particularly important. In central and secondary business districts, small stores depend upon the traffic created by large stores. Large stores in turn depend on attracting customers from the existing flow of traffic. Obviously, you want to know about the following factors when choosing a specific site:

- Adequacy and potential of traffic passing the site.
- Ability of the site to intercept traffic en route from one place to another.
- Complementary nature of the adjacent stores.
- Adequacy of parking.
- Vulnerability of the site to unfriendly competition.
- Cost of the site.

SOURCE: *Using a Traffic Study to Select a Retail Site*, by James R. Lowry (Washington, D.C.: U.S. Small Business Administration), p. 2.

CENTRAL PLACE THEORY

For the most part, businesses and other service providers in the tertiary sector have a market orientation to their location strategies. Because of their market orientation, the appropriate location model for assessing locational patterns in the tertiary sector is based on *central place theory*, a theory of the location of market centers first developed by the German geographer Walter Christaller in the early 1930s and expanded upon by the economist August Lösch. You should remember that Lösch's model was used in the last chapter to describe the theoretical location preferences of firms that hold geographical monopolies, and much of the same model holds for a large part of the tertiary sector because of the impact of distance decay on sales areas. Many retailers, for example, expect most of their customers to travel relatively short distances to make purchases. Travel expenses, again, are a form of transaction cost that reduces exchange.

Briefly, recall that each business requires a market threshold to maintain its existence, and its threshold population is contained within a particular range of the business if its sales are subject to distance decay. (It might be a good idea to review Figures 7.5 and 7.6 and the related text in Chapter 7 on these points.) Businesses have different thresholds and ranges, depending on the *order of the service or good* (the "product"). The order of a product is determined by four characteristics: price, typical frequency of purchase, threshold, and range. High-order products have high prices and are therefore purchased infrequently. As a result, their sellers usually require high population thresholds. High-order products also have long ranges. Their high-selling prices mean that distance-based transaction costs are proportionately low, so people will travel long distances to purchase a high-order product. As you might expect, low-order products have the opposite characteristics. They are inexpensive, and so they can be purchased frequently. Because they are purchased frequently, low-market thresholds can support sellers of low-order goods because even a limited number of consumers make many purchases. Finally, low-order products have short ranges because their low prices make any cost of travel required to obtain them proportionately high.

In short, high-order products require larger markets than do low-order goods and are less subject to distance decay in their sales. As examples, let's compare the retailing of two similar products: newspapers and books. Newspapers are low-order products; they have low prices and are purchased fairly frequently by most people who read them. The range of a newspaper is very short. Few people would travel any significant distance to buy one because any cost incurred in travel would rapidly rise to a level that is higher than the price of the paper itself. In addition, the threshold population for selling newspapers is apparently low because they can even be sold in vending machines with very limited capacities. Books, on the other hand, have the characteristics of a higher order product. They are higher priced and are purchased less frequently. Their ranges are longer because travel costs to purchase them are relatively less than the travel costs to purchase a newspaper. Threshold populations required by book sellers are higher than those required by those selling newspapers, and book-vending machines are unusual.

According to central place theory, the order of a product indicates two critical characteristics of the locations from which it is sold: locational frequency and spacing between sellers. Because low-order products are purchased frequently and have short ranges, such products are sold in many locations, and the sellers are located fairly close to each other. Because high-order products are purchased infrequently, there are relatively few locations where such products are sold, and the sellers should be found relatively far apart from each other. This market geography, however, is based on some strong assumptions that don't often apply to real-world businesses.

The most important assumption is that businesses sell undifferentiated products, but the reality is that there is most often some competition within the same product lines in the tertiary sector. How often do you drive through an intersection that has more than one gas station or find more than one fast food restaurant in adjoining locations? The two (or three or four) gas stations at the same intersection don't sell the same brand of gas, and the two (or more) fast food restaurants aren't owned by the same company, so spatial monopolies are maintained. Thus, "monopolies" exist, but only if judged from a restricted viewpoint. Unless a consumer has unusual brand loyalty, such markets are competitive ones that seem to favor the locational model of oligopolistic competition described in Chapter 7 rather than the monopolistic central place model.

HIGH- AND LOW-ORDER PLACES

Although principles of central place theory are applicable in many cases to the location of individual businesses, Christaller developed it in the analysis of the size and relative spacing of places: villages, towns, and cities. In central place theory, the *order of a place* is derived from the orders of the products that are available in it. A low-order place can provide only a limited number of low-order products, whereas a higher order place, by definition, offers a wider variety of goods and services, including those of a higher order than are available in a low-order place. Higher order places effectively serve two geographical markets. They are sources of low-order products over a relatively small adjoining market area, and they are sources of higher order goods over larger, but still adjacent, market areas. A higher order place is also a lower order place because basic central place theory assumes a *nested hierarchy of functions*. Any higher order place has everything to offer that a lower order place does, in addition to its offering of higher order products. This means that while consumers from low-order places may have to buy things from higher order places, a consumer in a higher order place would have no reason to buy anything from a lower order place.

Higher order places must have larger populations than lower order places because the higher order products they provide require higher threshold populations. In turn, a high-order place's high-threshold population means that it automatically includes the smaller threshold populations required to offer low-order products. From the other side of the scale, low-order places are of low order simply because their populations are insufficient to support a market for higher orders of products. Their residents, as well as residents of the surrounding area, must travel to higher order places for higher order products, and they can do so because higher order places have relatively long ranges to their market areas as a result of the higher order products they offer.

A theoretical layout of a central place system along a line is illustrated in Figure 8.2. Each of the places A-L is a low-order central place that serves itself and a surrounding area that just encompasses its threshold. Each place's threshold range defines its local geographical market, and there are no unserved areas in this system of monopolistic competition among places. Place A's low-order market directly borders place B's low-order market, place B's market borders place C's, and so on. Only six of the twelve places in the illustration are higher order places (B, D, F, H, J, and L). Note that their spacing is uniform; they are every second place. Their relative location on the line gives each of them a total of two lower order markets over which they sell their higher order products

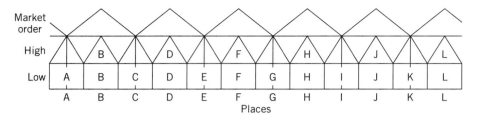

Figure 8.2 In a central place system, low-order places such as A-L each have their own market areas. Some of the low-order places (B, D, F, H, J, L), by virtue of their relative locations, also function as higher order places that contain themselves and parts of other lower order places in their market areas.

(assume that the line continues indefinitely to both its right and left). Place D, for example, sells its higher order products to itself, as a lower order market, and to half of the lower order markets of places C and E ($1 + 1/2 + 1/2 = 2$ markets).

A central place system on a plane develops hexagonal market areas as illustrated in Figure 8.3. The hexagonal shape avoids any market overlaps, which

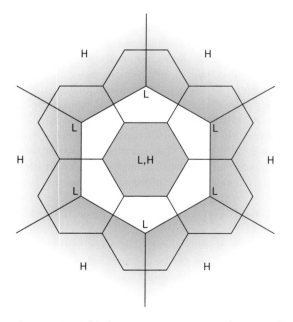

Figure 8.3 A bird's eye, or map, view of a central place system illustrates the hexagonal shape of its ideal market areas, which eliminates both direct competition between centers and unserved market areas. The market areas of low-order places (L) are divided among higher order places (H), except when a lower order place is also a higher order place.

would violate the principle of spatial monopoly and therefore a place's ability to ensure its threshold. Furthermore, the hexagonal market areas work to limit the distance costs of traveling to, or distribution from, a market center across its market area. In the particular central place system shown in Figure 8.3, a higher order place serves its own and one-third of six surrounding lower order market areas for a total number of three low-order markets for every higher order one. There are additional geometries of central place systems, and several variations in the relationships between orders have been developed. But the basic principles of threshold and range are the critical features of any version of central place theory.

IS CENTRAL PLACE THEORY REALISTIC?

Central place theory has been criticized for being too unrealistic to be of much use in analyzing actual geographical patterns of either businesses or settlements. Some people have argued that central place theory is incorrect because the size and spacing of places that it describes with some geometrical rigor simply don't exist in the real world. This is a silly argument when you think about it, because topographical variation alone—the fact that there are rivers and mountains and coastlines and so on—is enough to break up most of the regularity in the distribution of places that the theory predicts over a homogeneous plain.

A more interesting criticism concerns the balance of payments in a central place system. How can such a system last if low-order places are always buying things from high-order places and never the other way around? Sooner or later, the low-order places would run out of money. One answer to this problem actually lies outside the central place trade system. If we assume that the lowest order places provide products from the primary sector, especially food, to the higher order places, then the balance of payments can adjust itself. Primary-sector production is based on the location and supply of natural resources, and not market density. Therefore, low-order places can provide these products without violating the general principles of central place theory concerning threshold and product orders.

One example of the applicability of the principles of central place theory is revealed in grocery store prices in many rural areas of the United States and Canada. Many settlements in northern Michigan, for example, are small towns or villages with insufficient thresholds to support more than one or two grocery stores. Because groceries are low-order goods, consumers don't travel too far to purchase them, and the lack of local competition allows some of the grocery stores to earn excessive location rents. Under such circumstances, grocery prices can be raised to levels that are just under the price of groceries plus the costs in time and money of traveling to more distant stores. Central place theory tells us about the same thing that the gravity model of spatial interaction tells us. The attractiveness of a place because of its particular characteristics is countered by our distance from that place. This fundamental geographical proposition is used to analyze the retail market areas of both cities and individual shopping centers, as described in Insights 8.2 and 8.3.

Location in the tertiary sector has a strong market orientation, but government policy almost always plays a strong role in selecting a specific site. Local zoning regulations, in particular, often lead to the development of small-scale retail agglomerations that reinforce what market processes can be expected to bring about—concentrated shopping districts. In larger metropolitan areas, larger retail malls are surrounded by stand-alone establishments, including restaurants and automotive service centers. In addition, clusters of unattached, large-scale specialized discounters and movie theaters have been agglomerating in *power centers* in areas adjacent to established suburban shopping areas. Traditionally, the congestion of transport arterials has been the chief local regulatory concern of businesses in the tertiary sector. As transport arterials are improved, land that becomes more accessible is zoned for retail, and related uses and less accessible land are reserved for other purposes.

Recently, additional concerns over location practices in the tertiary sector have been raised. One concern is that large projects have disproportionate impacts not only on transportation in an area, but also on an area's existing retail sector and even its quality of life. Wal-Mart is frequently criticized for being a "bull in a china shop" when it opens a new store, as described in Case 8.2. Another concern is one of decline rather than growth. Increasingly, businesses in the tertiary sector abandon inner-city neighborhoods as suburbanization continues. Even grocery stores are not easily found in many central city neighborhoods. Poor people are especially affected by the local loss of service establishments because the cost of obtaining services increases as a result of their relatively distant location. Since the government cannot force a business to stay open, location subsidies rather than regulations are being used to maintain service provision in some places.

➤ INSIGHTS 8.2
Reilly's Law of Retail Gravitation

The geographical extent of a place's market area can be assessed by invoking *Reilly's law of retail gravitation*. This law states that a place will attract retail trade from its surrounding area in direct proportion to the population of the place and in inverse proportion to the square of the distance from the place. The law boils down to

$$R_i = \frac{P_i}{D_i^2} \tag{8.1}$$

where R_i is the retail attractiveness of the ith place, P_i is its population, and D is distance. You can see that Reilly's law is close in its specification to the gravity model of spatial interaction described in Chapter 6. The difference between the two is that Reilly's law considers only a one-way attraction, while the gravity model addresses the mutual attraction that two places may have.

For a quick example of Reilly's law in action, let's consider the following set of places:

population	25,000	10,000	30,000
place	A	B	C
distance (km)	20	15	

Place B is a lower order place, based on population differences, than the other two. If a resident of place B wants to purchase a higher order good, say a refrigerator, she must travel to either place A or place C. Reilly's law tells us which trip she is most likely to make in the following way. First, calculate the retail attractiveness of places A and C for a resident of place B.

$$R_A = \frac{25,000}{20^2} = 62.5 \text{ and } R_C = \frac{30,000}{15^2} = 133.3$$

Now, the numbers 62.5 and 133.3 don't tell us anything in themselves, but they are used to allocate shopping trips from place B to places A and C by proportion (P):

$$P_A = \frac{62.5}{62.5 + 133.3} = 0.319 \text{ and } P_C = \frac{133.3}{62.5 + 133.3} = 0.681$$

The proportions add up to one because of the way they are calculated, which assumes that someone from B will travel to either A or C but not anywhere else. The proportions can be interpreted in two ways. At the level of the individual, they indicate that on any given day, an individual in B that requires a higher order good has about a 32% chance of buying that good in place A and about a 68% chance of buying it at C. (Note that C has the higher probability for two reasons: it's closer to B than is A, and it's larger than place A.) The other interpretation of the proportions is more aggregate in that, over a cetain time period such as a month or year, we can expect that about 32% of all the refrigerators purchased by residents of place B came from a store in place A and about 68% came from a store in place C.

If we evaluated Reilly's law for places A and C over the entire distance between them, the proportions of the market that they attract would be as illustrated in Figure 8.4. This figure reveals an important characteristic of Reilly's law and of real-world spatial interaction. No place can count on capturing an entire geographical market. Even though it is very small, there is some probability that the residents of place A will travel to place C to purchase items, and there is also a small probability that residents of place C will travel to place A for their shopping. Market areas are more regions of influence than regions that can be counted on for sales. Although places are likely to exert a dominant influence nearby, it decays over distance. The *market breakpoint* occurs where the influences

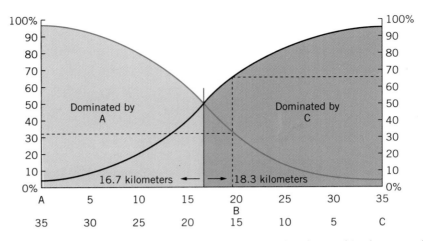

Figure 8.4 This figure illustrates the numerical results obtained in the example of an application of Reilly's law of retail gravitation and the calculation of the market breakpoint.

of two competing regions are equal ($R_A = R_C$). The breakpoint, in distance from a competing center, can be calculated as

$$B_A = \frac{D_{AC}}{1 + \sqrt{P_C/P_A}} \qquad (8.2A)$$

where B_A is the market breakpoint distance from A, and D and P are distance and population. The equation is subtly modified to determine the breakpoint distance from place C:

$$B_C = \frac{D_{AC}}{1 + \sqrt{P_A/P_C}} \qquad (8.2B)$$

Plugging in our numbers:

$$B_A = \frac{35}{1 + \sqrt{30,000/25,000}} = 16.7 \text{ miles}$$

and

$$B_C = \frac{35}{1 + \sqrt{25,000/30,000}} = 18.3 \text{ miles}$$

The mileages correspond to the 0.5/0.5 proportion intersection in Figure 8.4.

Recommended reading: W. Reilly, 1931: *The Law of Retail Gravitation* (New York: Pilsbury).

➤ INSIGHTS 8.3
Competing Destinations

Recall that the gravity model of spatial interaction considers only two of the three bases for spatial interaction. It incorporates complementarity and transferability, but does not include any consideration of intervening or alternative opportunities. A model developed by the geographer David Huff to assess the market areas of retailers and similar enterprises does directly incorporate intervening opportunities for shopping in addition to characteristics representing complementarity and transferability. Like Reilly's law, this *competing destinations model* is used to calculate probabilities that consumers will shop at a particular place. The specification of the competing destinations model makes it look more complex than it really is:

$$P(C_{ij}) = \frac{\dfrac{S_j}{T_{ij}^{\,k}}}{\displaystyle\sum_{j=1}^{n} \dfrac{S_j}{T_{ij}^{\,k}}} \tag{8.3}$$

where $P(C_{ij})$ is the probability that a consumer from the ith origin will shop at the jth shopping center, S_j is the selling floor space of the shopping center, and T_{ij} is the travel time between an origin and a shopping center. The value of the superscript k on travel time is used in calibrating the model for specific regions. (We'll assume $k = 1$ in the example below.)

In the competing destinations model, complementarity is measured as retail selling floor space, a variable that is designed to capture both the variety and quantity of goods and services available at a shopping center. Transferability is captured in travel time, not distance, because the model is applied in retail analyses of individual metropolitan regions. Within these areas, travel time usually is more meaningful in assessing distance decay in markets than is actual distance. Traffic conditions and different grades of transport routes, from superhighway to back street, mean that travel times can vary considerably over similar distances. Using distances would hide time variations and oversimplify the market's geography. The origins in the model are most often residential zones, such as census tracts. The numerator in the competing destinations model accounts for the attractiveness of a single shopping center, and the denominator accounts for the attractiveness of all shopping centers in the region or intervening/alternative opportunities.

For a quick hypothetical application of the competing destinations model, let's say we are interested in a region's probable shopping patterns with respect to three malls: Mall 1, with 1 million square feet of selling floor space, Mall 2 with 1.5 million square feet, and Mall 3 with 1 million square feet. Let's also say that there are four residential zones in the region—A, B, C, and D—with travel times to each of the malls identified in the following matrix.

DESTINATIONS

O		1	2	3	
R	A	10	10	20	minutes
I	B	15	17	25	minutes
G	C	20	20	15	minutes
N	D	25	15	10	minutes
S					

Plugging in our numbers, we have

$$P(C_{A1}) = (1/10)/((1/10) + (1.5/10) + (1/20)) = 0.333$$
$$P(C_{A2}) = (1.5/10)/((1/10) + (1.5/10) + (1/20)) = 0.500$$
$$P(C_{A3}) = (1/20)/((1/10) + (1.5/10) + (1/20)) = 0.167$$
$$P(C_{B1}) = (1/15)/((1/15) + (1.5/17) + (1/25)) = 0.342$$
$$P(C_{B2}) = (1.5/17)/((1/15) + (1.5/17) + (1/25)) = 0.453$$
$$P(C_{B3}) = (1/25)/((1/15) + (1.5/17) + (1/25)) = 0.205$$
$$P(C_{C1}) = (1/20)/((1/20) + (1.5/20) + (1/15)) = 0.261$$
$$P(C_{C2}) = (1.5/20)/((1/20) + (1.5/20) + (1/15)) = 0.391$$
$$P(C_{C2}) = (1/15)/((1/20) + (1.5/20) + (1/15)) = 0.348$$
$$P(C_{D1}) = (1/25)/((1/25) + (1.5/15) + (1/10)) = 0.166$$
$$P(C_{D2}) = (1.5/15)/((1/25) + (1.5/15) + (1/10)) = 0.417$$
$$P(C_{D3}) = (1/10)/((1/25) + (1.5/15) + (1/10)) = 0.417$$

The probabilities are usually put in a matrix for easy comparison:

DESTINATIONS

O		1	2	3
R	A	.333	.500	.167
I	B	.342	.453	.205
G	C	.261	.391	.348
N	D	.166	.417	.417
S				

Note that the probabilites sum to one because we are assuming that the consumers in the region are going to choose one of the three shopping centers and not go outside the area.

Further market analysis using competing destinations models takes into account the incomes and spending habits of the populations within each of the origins so that forecasts of actual retail sales at individual shopping centers can be derived. The forecast of retail sales can be used to supply the revenue values that are used in cost-benefit analyses of competing projects. In most applications, the cost-benefit analyses would compare the costs and revenues of competing projects on the basis of net income per square foot of selling floor space.

Recommended reading: D. L. Huff, 1963: "A Probabilistic Analysis of Shopping Center Trade Areas," *Land Economics*, Vol. 39, pp. 81–90.

◪ CASE 8.2
Is Bigger (and Cheaper) Better?

STURBRIDGE, MASS.—Before it opened its first store in New England in 1991, Wal-Mart Stores, Inc. had used its base in the Midwest and South to become the nation's largest retailer. Since then, however, Wal-Mart has made up for lost time, opening a total of 39 stores in the region, with others in the planning stage.

But this growth has not always come easy.

Wal-Mart was rebuffed by the citizenry of Greenfield last year and withdrew a proposal in Westford because of strong local opposition.

And tonight, opponents of a 330,000-square foot shopping center will turn out in Sturbridge to say they don't want Wal-Mart, either. More than 1,000 residents of the community of 8,500 signed petitions to call the special town meeting.

Opponents in the various communities have expressed concerns that the huge Wal-Mart stores—typically 100,000 square feet or larger—would cause excessive traffic, environmental damage and competition that would threaten other stores.

But there is another element to the opposition.

There is "a kind of mystique with them being the largest in the country and being an unknown quantity," said John Hurst, president of the Retailers Association of Massachusetts.

And there is concern about the effects of the Arkansas-based company's aggressiveness, especially in the rural areas where it typically places its stores. "They undercut prices until they're the only store in town. Then they'll have free rein," said Carol Goodwin, leader of the opposition group Save our Sturbridge, which petitioned for tonight's town meeting, at which a non-binding vote will be taken.

A spokeswoman for the company, which had 1993 sales of $67.4 billion and operates more than 2,000 stores in every state except Vermont, said the opposition in New England has been surprising. But she defended company practices.

"It's competition," said Betsy Reithemeyer. "We offer quality products at low prices. We don't apologize for that."

She said Wal-Mart is "a good corporate neighbor," supports local causes and provides competitive wages.

"Once they get to know a Wal-Mart they'll like us," Reithemeyer said.

During this period of slow economic growth, many communities have welcomed Wal-Mart stores.

But Wal-Mart has yet to open a single store in Vermont, largely because of a state law requiring extensive statewide review of any project large enough to affect a single community.

Residents of Williston, Vt., have opposed a store in that community—one of three proposed in the state—because they fear it would draw shoppers away from the downtown area.

Wal-Mart has been highly successful elsewhere, opening 11 stores in New Hampshire, 14 in Maine, two in Rhode Island and 10 in Massachusetts since 1991 (See Map).

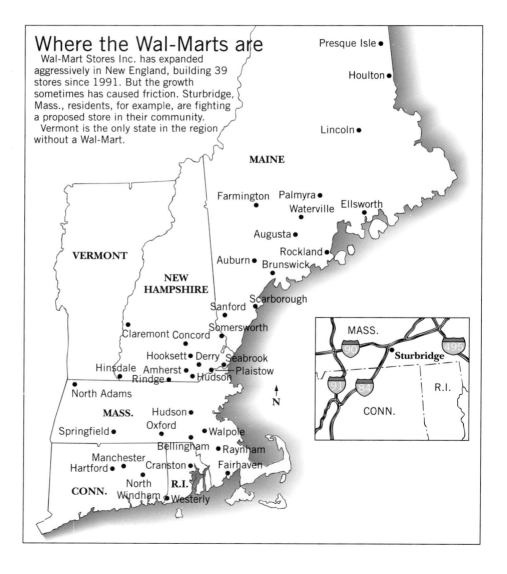

Where the Wal-Marts are

Wal-Mart Stores Inc. has expanded aggressively in New England, building 39 stores since 1991. But the growth sometimes has caused friction. Sturbridge, Mass., residents, for example, are fighting a proposed store in their community.
 Vermont is the only state in the region without a Wal-Mart.

Presque Isle •

Houlton •

Lincoln •

MAINE

Farmington • Palmyra •
Waterville • Ellsworth

Augusta •

VERMONT

Rockland •
Auburn • Brunswick

NEW HAMPSHIRE

Scarborough

Sanford •

Claremont Concord • Somersworth

Hooksett • Derry Seabrook
Hinsdale Amherst • — Plaistow
Rindge • Hudson

North Adams

MASS. Hudson •
Oxford
Springfield • • Walpole

Bellingham • Raynham
Manchester
Hartford • • Cranston • Fairhaven
CONN. North
Windham • Westerly
R.I.

MASS.
90 495
Sturbridge
91 84
CONN.   R.I.

N

And while there is opposition in Sturbridge, residents are far from unanimous.

"I think the town needs someting like that," said Jeanne Hopfe, who owns an antique store near the site proposed for the Wal-Mart shopping center, which would also include two smaller clothing stores, other retail space, a bank, a restaurant and an 8-screen movie theater.

Wal-Mart's plans to improve traffic flow through the area would stop speeding on Route 20 in front of the store, Hopfe said. Trucks routinely drive past at 50 mph now.

The retail company proposes to widen the road from four to six lanes and to install several traffic lights at nearby intersections.

But Goodwin said traffic elsewhere in the largely residential community would increase greatly because of a Wal-mart store, changing the character of the town.

"Sturbridge always had an elegant simplicity about it," she said. "I think the traffic's going to change all that." She fears the town would become a "shopping mecca" if the Wal-Mart store wins final approval of the town's planning commission next month.

SOURCE: "Something There Is That Doesn't Love a Wal-Mart," by Robert S. Capers, in *The Hartford Courant*, August 18, 1994, pp. A1, A12. By permission of the *Hartford Courant*.

FOR DISCUSSION

Explain the impact of a new Wal-Mart in an area in the context of the competing destinations model described in Insights 8.3.

LOCATION IN THE QUATERNARY SECTOR

All the services in the quaternary sector revolve around the management of information and knowledge, but locational criteria in the sector are far from homogeneous because the sector is quite diverse. One characteristic that varies widely across the services of the quaternary sector is their frequency of purchase. Some services, specialized management consulting, for example, are purchased fairly infrequently. Other services, such as retail banking, are classified as quaternary activities but are difficult to distinguish from any consumer service in the tertiary sector. In general, the producer services of the quaternary sector are purchased relatively infrequently in comparison to the consumer services in the sector. Because of their relatively infrequent transactions, quaternary producer services are much less uniformly distributed with respect to population than are the sector's consumer services, which require more frequent market interaction.

In a sense, producer services are the sector's high-order products, so they are available in fewer locations than the sector's low-order consumer services.

Because consumer services in the quaternary sector are so much like tertiary services, their overriding location factor is market accessibility. In contrast, a wider variety of location factors affect the producer service segment of the quaternary sector. The question of market access for much of the producer service segment is a large-scale one, because many markets are national, if not international, in size. The quality and frequency of available airline service is often taken as the measure of a place's accessibility in this context. Agglomeration economies are also important to producer service location because local supplies of experienced labor and a specialized supporting infrastructure help to lower costs in all economic sectors. Because the locations of many producer service businesses are not confined by specific market requirements, local quality of life can often be an important location factor.

Recent technological developments and changes in public policy have gone a long way in changing the locational pattern of the quaternary sector within countries and also internationally (see the next section). The most important technological advances are the development of electronic digital processing and advanced telecommunications, including the transmission of information via satellite and optical fiber cables. The development of digital technology has proven important in providing productivity gains in a sector where such gains were once thought to be nearly impossible. Productivity, or output per worker, has increased dramatically, so that the sector's businesses can now compete in their markets through cost reductions in a way that was not possible before. Additional cost competition has been made possible by the ability to send information, the sector's major product, over long distances. Basic information processing and other *back-office tasks* that don't require immediate contact between service buyer and seller can be carried out in low-cost locations at great distances from a service's actual market. In many cases, locational criteria have diverged within many service businesses: their front-office work has more of a market orientation, and their back-office tasks are located on the basis of cost minimization. Chicago, for example, is cited by *Best's Review* (November 1994) as the best location for an insurance company's headquarters, whereas Des Moines is considered the best location for the back-office tasks of the insurance industry.

The most important changes in public policy concerning the quaternary sector have to do with deregulation, especially of financial services. The bulk of financial service deregulation has focused on market access. In the American banking industry, for example, interstate banking was a difficult prospect because of a variety of state and federal regulations that only began to give way in the late 1980s. Because most banks were limited to specific geographical markets in selling many of their services, growth was difficult, and economies of scale were not easily achieved. As interstate banking began to open up, interstate bank mergers were accomplished that have had significant impacts on the location of the banks' back-office and management functions, even though locational change at the retail level is largely unaffected. Mergers have also led to reductions in back-office and managerial employment as the result of the ''operating efficiencies,'' or economies of scale, that they bring about. Staff reductions in both areas have been politically controversial because they tend to be geographically concentrated. Two headquarters are often reduced to one, and two or more data processing centers are reduced in number so that one city's employment gains come at the expense of another city's losses.

As described in Case 8.3, the decline of Wall Street as a financial center has resulted from the combination of technological advances, deregulation, and advancing obsolesence of the district's office buildings. The stock brokerage business was largely deregulated in the United States in the mid-1970s. This deregulation led to competition among brokers based on price rather than on service quality, and the new digital computing technologies and more recent telecommunications technologies allowed many broker functions to be relocated in places with lower operating costs than found in downtown Manhattan. The New York Stock Exchange, the anchor of the Wall Street financial district, has also experienced strong competition from the *North American Securities Dealers Automated Quotations* (*NASDAQ*), a stock exchange that has no actual location at all. The NASDAQ exchange has no trading floor like the New York and American Stock Exchanges, but exists in the form of a computer network linking brokers all over the United States.

Wall Street has also suffered from the ongoing suburbanization of office work that began in the late 1970s. Central cities and their downtowns have expensive land, and as their office buildings grow old, it's less costly to build new ones in suburban areas. Not only is land less expensive in suburbs than in most central city locations, but suburban accessibility is now markedly better than in the earlier era, before the construction of expressways, when the down-town office districts were established. In the case of Wall Street, some of the district's businesses may only have moved to midtown Manhattan, but many have moved across the river to Bergen County, New Jersey, and to Fairfield County, Connecticut. Both of these counties are within greater New York, but generally offer lower cost suburban sites for activities that were once much more limited in their locational opportunities.

◤ *CASE 8.3*
The Decline of Wall Street

NEW YORK—The windows of the proud, prewar skyscrapers are black, their lobbies dead as tombs, their "FOR SALE" and "WILL DIVIDE" signs yellow and cracked with age. When another bank or brokerage moves out, it takes the landlord three or four years to find a new tenant.

This is Wall Street today. Quietly, almost while we weren't looking, it became more adjective than noun, more of a state of mind than a place.

There are still "Wall Street analysts" and "Wall Street profits," but no Wall Street, at least not as we knew it.

Wall Street, the industry, has fled its birthplace, like Hollywood did. Now Wall Street is in midtown Manhattan and New Jersey and Los Angeles, in suburban office parks and home offices.

But Wall Street, the neighborhood—the street itself and its immediate environs, an area covering a quarter-square-mile in the core of lower Manhattan—is going one way: down.

It has fallen victim to the age and obsolesence of its buildings, to decentralization and downsizing in the financial services industry, to the lure of other business districts with newer buildings, easier commutes, better food.

A third of the district's office space is vacant. A tower at 55 Broad St. has been empty since its chief tenant, Drexel Burnham Lambert, went ignominiously out of business. "ENTIRE BUILDING FOR LEASE" is stenciled on the glass facade. A doorman stands morosely in the dim lobby, the Maytag repairman of Manhattan real estate.

Since the 1987 stock market crash lower Manhattan has lost a fifth of its workforce—100,000 jobs. Most probably aren't coming back.

"In '92, people still thought it was a cyclical downturn," says Elliot Schlar of Columbia University, a planning expert. "It's becoming clear it's more than that."

The computer, the fax and their ilk have reduced the need for a dense, high-rise office district. At the same time, the financial services industry has become more competitive; even as profits increase, firms employ fewer workers and use less space.

The industry has also spread out. Less than a third of the firms in the Securities Industry Association are even in Manhattan. Big mutual funds like Fidelity and Vanguard are in Massachusetts and Pennsylvania. And many clerical jobs once done on Wall Street can now be done elsewhere.

"The trend is toward an ever broader definition of Wall Street," says Charles Shapiro of the real estate firm Austrian Roth, "one that might be found on the information highway."

Even if they stay in New York, businesses want big, open, rectangular floors so they can rearrange their offices as needed. They want high ceilings, so they can raise floors to accommodate computers and wiring. They want extra electrical capacity, efficient air conditioning and fast elevators.

But most Wall Street buildings went up before 1940, and were designed with smaller floors so workers would be closer to the best source of light and air—the window. Many have irregularly shaped floors (a legacy of the district's curving old streets), lots of columns, antiquated wiring and slow elevators.

Ten years ago, businesses settled for anything with four walls. But now Manhattan is awash in vacant office space—50 million square feet, roughly as much as built in the 1980s. These new towers, says Schlar, "sucked the life out of Wall Street."

Merrill Lynch and Shearson Lehman moved to the World Financial Center, over on downtown's booming waterfront. Kidder Peabody, Paine Webber and Bear Stearns decamped to midtown.

Midtown is downtown's real competition—Pennsylvania Station and Grand Central Terminal offer access to the suburbs. Downtown has lots of subway lines to Brooklyn and Queens, but straphanging secretaries and clerks don't sign long-term leases.

The real estate firm Jones Lang Wooten says Wall Street's next big need could be "demolition and site clearance." "For the first time in 400 years," predicts Columbia's Schlar, "we're gonna take buildings away downtown instead of putting them up."

More probable is a gradual cycle of decline, in which the city lowers tax assessments and landlords lower rents, opening the area to fledgling businesses, nonprofit institutions and government. It won't be the old Wall Street, but at least it won't be a parking lot.

SOURCE: "Once Mighty Wall Street Crumbling as Center of Finance," by Rick Hampson, Associated Press, August 5, 1994. By permission of the Associated Press. ◪

FOR DISCUSSION

Should city governments intervene in real estate markets to preserve special urban districts such as Wall Street?

THE SERVICE MNC

An interesting advertisement appeared in one of the July issues of *The Economist* in 1995. It was placed by the Jardine Matheson Group, a multinational holding company based in Hong Kong, in the interest of soliciting business for its operations in Vietnam. The operations it listed included trading and distribution, engineering and construction, aviation and shipping, security and environmental services, financial and property management services, insurance, automobile sales and rentals, and restaurants. Each of the operations involves the sale of a service. Some of them are in the tertiary sector, for example, restaurants, and some of them are in the quaternary sector, such as its financial and property management services. Jardine Matheson's slogan is "the multinational at the heart of Asia," and it could easily be expanded to "the service multinational at the heart of Asia."

Most of the early MNCs were involved in the primary sector, from mining and petroleum to agriculture. Currently, when most people think of MNCs, they probably think of big international manufacturers in industries such as electronics and automobile production. Although MNCs do operate extensively in both the primary and secondary sectors, those in service business, like Jardine Matheson, and the service holdings of diversified MNCs that operate in all economic sectors are growing rapidly. In 1990, for example, services led all sectors in FDI by American interests (Figure 8.5A), and it also led all sectors of FDI coming into the United States (Figure 8.5B). The growth of FDI in services

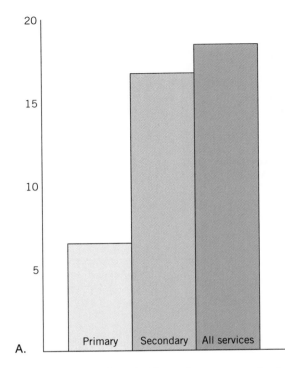

A.

Figure 8.5   American FDI in services was greater in 1990 than its FDI in either the primary or secondary sectors (Figure 8.5A). FDI in the United States followed the same relative proportions, but with an even larger share in services (Figure 8.5B). SOURCE: United States Department of Commerce, 1991: *Survey of Current Business*, Vol. 71, No. 8 (Washington, D.C.: U.S. Government Printing Office).

and the increasing spread of service-based MNCs is not surprising on two counts. First, the size of the tertiary and quaternary sectors alone means that services should play a major role in global business. Second, the nature of many services, especially their inability to be stored, means that they can't be exported, at least in the same way as goods produced in the primary and secondary sectors.

The services that are exported in the conventional way are the *factor services* of capital and labor. Labor is a service in and of itself, and when people cross international boundaries to work and send their earnings back to their home countries they are exporting a service. Capital services are exported when investment in one country results in payments of interest, dividends, or royalties in another. The services that make up the bulk of the tertiary and quaternary sectors, however, are different from the factor services of labor and capital, and it is often impossible from a practical standpoint to export them. Grocery stores, for example, or fast food restaurants, don't often deliver across town, much less internationally. Most businesses selling services have a market orientation that requires their physical presence within a country's borders if they want to serve that country's market. Even those services that are ''exported'' within a country

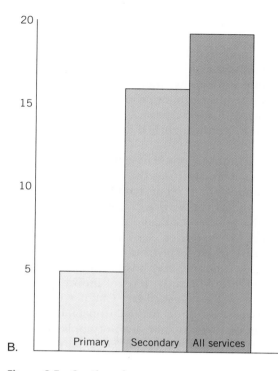

B.

Figure 8.5　Continued.

are not often exported across international boundaries. For example, the international insurance industry, described in Case 8.4, relies on market proximity, rather than sales from a limited number of centers, and insurance MNCs are marked by a physical front office presence within the national markets they serve.

Service businesses often have different characteristics than manufacturing or primary sector companies, including their locational criteria, and many FDI models are too narrowly focused on manufacturing to be easily applicable to tertiary or quaternary enterprises. The product life-cycle model, for example, was developed for manufacturing, and although some of the locational shifts it describes are applicable to back-office operations, international locational shifts in the interest of minimizing costs still do not play a large role in determining the geography of a service MNC. Case 8.4 does suggest, however, that service MNCs are increasingly faced by locational splits in the global economy.

The economist John Dunning has developed an *eclectic model of FDI* that is general enough to be applicable to the tertiary and quaternary sectors as well as to manufacturing and FDI in the primary sector (Insights 8.4). Parts 1 and 2 of the model are especially relevant to FDI in services, although part 3 applies because the market is a location factor. Intangible assets of expertise and "know-how" have proven to be of critical competitive importance in the international expansion of service MNCs. For example, Case 8.5 indicates that the international management consultant business is marked by service MNCs that sell their expertise as a product. In most instances, however, the expertise is the basis for market expansion and is not sold as product because of imperfect markets for knowledge. As described in part 2 of the eclectic model, MNCs find it advantageous to use their intangible assets in foreign countries themselves rather than to sell or lease them. Because the assets are intangible and because they are rarely bought and sold, companies have a hard time determining an appropriate price for their use. Instead, MNCs maintain a practice of *market internalization* that transfers the use of the asset across national boundaries through FDI at the same time the asset remains within the corporation.

The geographical spread of service MNCs would not have been possible without advances in communications technology, but the role of government policy has perhaps been even more important. It seems paradoxical at first, but both restrictive and liberal policies toward the service sector have led to the growth of service MNCs. The restrictive policies facilitated the growth of service MNCs within the set of the world's richer countries. Services are often heavily regulated, and governments have taken an especially active interest in the the FIRE services. In the United States, for example, both insurance and banking are regulated not only at the national level but at the level of individual states as well. Before the European Union was well established (see Chapter 10), many MNCs had to have separate operations in each country of the European Economic Community because of service-sector regulations that did not apply to other sectors of the economy. In effect, service imports were limited by service trade policies; therefore, MNCs were required to establish a foreign subsidiary in each country that had an attractive market. Because service trade restrictions have been eased with the development of the European Union, and in other wealthy countries, it would not be surprising if some foreign subsidiaries are merged within MNCs in order to achieve economies of scale.

Although service trade restrictions led to FDI in richer countries, service investment restrictions limited the role of MNCs in many of the world's developing economies. Since the mid-1980s, however, the trend in the developing countries has been toward more openness to foreign investment, including FDI by service MNCs. As the developing markets open, especially the more rapidly growing ones, service MNCs have been establishing both front-office and back-office operations in them, with the result being continued expansion of the global service economy.

> ➤ INSIGHTS 8.4
The Eclectic Model of FDI

1. It possesses net ownership-specific advantages vis-à-vis firms of other nationalities in serving particular markets. These ownership advantages largely take the form of the possession of intangible assets, and/or of coordinating or risk-reducing advantages which are, at least for a period of time, exclusive or specific to the firm possessing them.

2. Assuming condition one is satisfied, it must be more beneficial to the enterprise possessing these advantages to use them (or their output) itself rather than to sell or lease them to foreign firms; this it does through existing value-added chains or the involvement of new ones. These advantages are called internalization advantages.

3. Assuming conditions one and two are satisfied, it must be in the global interests of the enterprise to utilize these advantages in conjunction with at least some factor inputs (including natural resources) outside its home country; otherwise foreign markets would be served entirely by exports and domestic markets by domestic production. These advantages are termed the locational advantages of countries.

SOURCE: John Dunning, 1988: "The Theory of International Production." *The International Trade Journal*, Vol. 3, pp. 45–46.

◄

◤ *CASE 8.4*
The International Insurance Industry

THE FRONT OFFICE

The significance of FDI in the insurance industry is reflected in the transnationalization of the largest insurance firms. Twenty-seven of the world's thirty largest insurance companies in 1986 were transnational in structure. Two of them had more than one hundred foreign affiliates; six had more than fifty affiliates; and eight, more than ten affiliates.

Approximately 30 percent of the foreign affiliates of the top insurance firms and 15 percent of the foreign affiliates of the reinsurance firms were located in developing countries. However, both the absolute and relative number of foreign affiliates in insurance decreased in all host regions of the world. Even with this decline, foreign firms comprise 10 to 40 percent of all firms in the host regions that include developing countries.

In addition to the establishment of affiliates, many different forms of market intermediation have become very important in international insurance delivery. At one extreme there are the small-scale brokers who concentrate on personal and small-business insurances. They are often able to differentiate their products very successfully with consumers and carry profitable premium rates. In most countries, they are closely tied to particular insurers through long standing goodwill, credit arrangements and links with company representatives. Competing with these brokers would involve the establishment of a large local sales force, able to cultivate business and provide the technical support and encouragement that such small scale operators require. Such a process takes time and money. An alternative solution is to purchase companies, which enables the retention of the acquired firm's reputation and links and, often, management.

However, this is a costly alternative and it also implies a lack of direct control. Direct intervention in retail insurance markets is, therefore, not a preferred option for foreign insurers, unless they are prepared to contemplate a long-term commitment, involving heavy management costs.

Larger brokers and agents often operate across regional or national markets, often specializing in large-scale risks, which they place with local or foreign insurers (when the latter's presence is not prevented by regulation). Large-scale risks constitute a more congenial market for entry by foreign insurers, for price is a more important consideration. They can often attract business on that basis, sometimes collaborating with local companies through co-insurance agreements.

Intermediation takes place on an international scale through large insurance brokers. The operations of these brokers are at least as important as the overseas activities of the large insurance companies, with some generating revenues of over one or two billion dollars. Brokers provide one of the main points of access into the international insurance market. They place large individual risks, seeking competitive rates, negotiating reinsurance arrangements for local companies and providing a range of technical and business services otherwise unavailable to local markets, especially in developing countries.

International transactions in insurance thus take place within a complex institutional framework. They involve a wide variety of products within many different market and technical environments. While insurers nearly always prefer proximity to consumers, often for competitive reasons, the technical necessity for proximity varies considerably between products. Life insurance may provide an example where technical and marketing considerations combine to make proximity very important. On the other hand, marine insurance, and the reinsurance of most forms of insurance, appear to require very little proximity and have successfully substituted alternative institutional arrangements that make proximity unnecessary.

These different requirements for product delivery are complemented by a similar variety of different types of international delivery and organization. Foreign direct investment through wholly-owned local branch offices or subsidiaries is preferred for those types of insurance where proximity is essential. When circumstances make this impossible or difficult, insurers appear to operate satisfactorily, though less willingly, through the market access or presence provided through joint ventures, locally managed associates, reinsurance or through local intermediaries.

THE BACK OFFICE

Advancements in information technology permit many insurance tasks to be performed thousands of miles away from where the work is needed, and are now reshaping the mode of cross-border delivery in the insurance industry.

Currently, three United States insurance companies, CIGNA, Massachusetts Mutual Life Insurance and New York Life Insurance, have set up claims-processing centers in Ireland, and Travelers Corporation operates an office there to write computer software for its own use. In Ireland, the English-speaking population is well-educated, the unemployment rate has been persistently high (15.5 percent in 1991) and the Government of Ireland provides attractive financial incentives to TNCs locating affiliates in Ireland.

The Ireland offices of the United States insurance companies are typically connected to computer centers in the United States, with Irish subsidiaries performing on-line data entry. CIGNA, for example, has an office of 115 staff in Loughrea where 4,000 group insurance claims are processed each day. Claims are flown daily from New York to Shannon International Airport and are delivered to Loughrea by ground transportation. After manual review and approval, data are keyed and transmitted over two trans-Atlantic leased lines to CIGNA's IBM mainframe center in the United States at Windsor, Connecticut. Massachusetts Mutual Life Insurance has established one of its ten claims-processing centers in Tipperary. According to the company, 25 to 30 percent in processing costs are saved.

New York Life Insurance Company, a pioneer in establishing a claims-processing center in Ireland, is now processing 30,000 claims monthly, about 10 percent of the company's total claims, in the Castleisland office that employs 55 people. Despite high telecommunications charges in Ireland and an additional bill for shipping the insurance-claims forms, the company's claims-processing costs in Ireland are 25 percent less than those of a similar job in the United States.

These examples illustrate the impact of new information technology on the strategy of an insurance company and the conduct of international insurance business. They, however, highlight the importance of the use of information technology in terms of efficiency within the existing structure of the business, which involves presence through foreign direct investment. All the companies acknowledge that they have set up the affiliates in Ireland because of the availability of a highly educated, relatively inexpensive English-speaking labor force and the near zero staff turnover rate—a rate that is between 10 to 30 percent in the United States.

SOURCE: The Transnational Corporations and Management Division, UN Department of Economic and Social Development, *International Tradability in Insurance Services: Implications for Foreign Direct Investment in Insurance Services*, ST/CTC/SER.A/25 (New York: UN, 1993), pp. 12–14 and 23.

FOR DISCUSSION

Interpret Case 8.4 in the context of the product life-cycle model that was described in Chapter 7.

◪ CASE 8.5
International Management Consulting

United States-based transnational corporations dominate the consulting industry in most countries. Only five of the top 40 consulting companies in the world are not headquartered in the United States and the only country in which local firms have a significant market share is the United Kingdom. In Germany, four of the top management consultants are United States firms—McKinsey (the largest in the country), Boston Consulting Group, Arthur D. Little and Booz Allen. Roland Berger & Partners GmbH, a subsidiary of the Deutsche Bank AG (but with the majority of voting shares held by Roland Berger, the original founder), is the second largest firm. In Belgium the largest domestic firm, Buck Consultants, employs only 170 professionals. In the Netherlands, Coopers and Lybrand employs a staff of 2,800, while the domestic firm Van de Bunt (founded in 1933) employs only sixteen.

There are several possible explanations for the dominance of United States companies. Consulting was first developed in the United States and United States consultants had a head start in the theory and practice of consulting, including the development of tacit firm-specific methods of managing. The experience curve is of great significance in consulting as in other fields. Furthermore, these firms followed their large United States clients to foreign markets, in particular to Western Europe. When large domestic companies were ready to employ consultants, these companies were already on hand. Second, most countries outside the Anglo-Saxon world did not have large stock exchanges. The large firms did not publish financial figures; many of them were owned by their founders or by financial institutions and were not professionally managed. The convention of greater corporate secrecey was coupled with a strong suspicion of outsiders. industries are generally underdeveloped, and advice to business companies is given, if it is given, by consulting divisions of large domestic banks. For many years, employing a consultant was interpreted by management outside of the United States as a sign of weakness, pointing to an ailing situation. Thus, only the unfortunate were perceived as needing help—not those who could learn better ways to enhance performance.

By the end of the 1980s, a major debate among management-consulting experts was on the future of the so-called "mega firm" (or the service conglomerate). One view of the future of the industry is that of polarization, where the majority of consultants will work for large, global, diversified "mega firms," offering a full line of services and achieving economies of scope. These firms will take advantage of the client contact each consultant has developed and increase repeat business by offering a wide variety of services. A minority will specialize, carving a niche for themselves. Mid-sized firms will disappear.

The scenario makes some strong assumptions on the preferences of clients as well as on the means of achieving a global competitive advantage. On the demand side, it assumes that clients prefer to buy their services from the same firm. Yet clients are becoming increasingly sophisticated and may prefer to shop among a wide range of different suppliers. Clients often want to meet the actual team who will carry out the assignment rather than rely solely on name. Sophisticated clients may buy not only the experience embedded in individuals, but also the accumulated experience of the whole firm, and may choose different firms for different assignments.

On the supply side, the ability to serve a client in different markets is of crucial importance to large management-consulting firms. To serve profitable transnational markets, small firms had to rely on international alliances to create networking. Thus, Prommer Consultants in Munich established Technical Investment Partners, an association of small consulting firms in Germany, France and the United Kingdom. M.A.C. Group tapped the services of 400 business school professors on a part-time basis. However, these alliances are extremely difficult to coordinate.

To reiterate, successful large transnational management-consulting firms must develop a set of intangible assets that enables them to achieve higher performance. These intangible assets enable large transnational corporations to retain the loyalty of their other major assets—the consultants themselves—and to gain reputations and recognition among clients. This includes the accumulated stock of knowledge and competence, links with clients, formal and informal (on-the-job) training and other investments in human resources, investment in marketing and information management, data-bases of accumulated experience and other information, and organization and information structure. Transnational corporations are drawing on accumulated past experiences for solutions or ideas in carrying out current tasks, further gaining advantages over small firms.

SOURCE: The Transnational Corporations and Management Division, UN Department of Economic and Social Development, *Management Consulting: A Survey of the Industry and its Largest Firms,* ST/CTC/SER.A/25 (New York: UN, 1993), pp. 17–19.

FOR DISCUSSION

Interpret Case 8.5 in the context of the eclectic model of FDI described in Insights 8.4.

POINTS IN SUMMARY

1. Richer economies are often referred to as postindustrial because they are dominated by their service sectors.

2. Services are divided into two related, but distinct, economic sectors: the tertiary sector and the quaternary sector.

3. Services are also divided by their markets into two groups: consumer services and producer services.

4. Consumer service growth is generated by increasing personal incomes.

5. Much of the quarternary sector's growth in recent years is associated with increased demand for its new information and knowledge products, such as software, that are really services that generate demand for manufactured goods (computers, discs, etc.) rather than the other way around.

6. Tertiary-sector consumer services earn their highest location rents at centers of regional accessibility, so they tend to be found in clusters at road intersections and other points of high accessibility in an area.

7. Producer services typically require less frequent interaction between seller and buyer than is found in the consumer service market, so businesses selling producer services can earn relatively high location rents at less accessible places

than those required by sellers of consumer services.

8. The order of a product is distinguished by four characteristics: price, typical frequency of purchase, threshold, and range.

9. According to central place theory, the order of a product indicates two critical characteristics of the locations from which it is sold: locational frequency and spacing between sellers.

10. Central place theory has been criticized as being too unrealistic to be of much use in analyzing actual geographical patterns of either businesses or settlements, but not by people that understand it well.

11. Producer services are the service sectors' high-order products, and so are available in fewer

locations than the sector's low-order consumer services.

12. Productivity has increased dramatically in the service sectors because of technological advances.

13. Locational criteria have diverged within many service businesses; their front-office work has more of a market orientation, and their back-office tasks are located in the interest of cost minimization.

14. Even those services that are exported within a country are not often exported across international boundaries.

15. Intangible assets of expertise and "know-how" have proven to be of critical competitive advantage in the international expansion of service MNCs.

TERMS TO REMEMBER

back-office tasks	factor services	Securities Dealers	producer services
central place theory	FIRE	Automated	quaternary sector
competing destinations	market breakpoint	Quotations	Reilly's law of retail
model	market internalization	(NASDAQ)	gravitation
consumer services	nested hierarchy of	order of a place	tertiary sector
eclectic model of FDI	functions	order of a service/good	
Engel's law	North American	power centers	

SUGGESTED READING

Berry, Brian J.L. 1967: *Geography of Market Centers and Retail Distribution.* Englewood Cliffs, N.J.: Prentice-Hall.

   This volume considers the geographical distribution of retail and other service businesses in the context of central place theory. In doing so, it provides a series of case studies and an excellent summary of central place theory and related principles.

England, Kim V.L. 1993: "Suburban Pink Collar Ghettos: The Spatial Entrapment of Women?'' *An-*

nals of the Association of American Geographers, Vol. 83, pp. 225–242.

   This paper explores the implications for women of the recent suburbanization of a large part of the American service sector.

Goss, Jon. 1993: "The 'Magic of the Mall': An Analysis of Form, Function, and Meaning in the Contemporary Retail Built Environment.'' *Annals of the Association of American Geographers* Vol. 83, pp. 18–47.

Goss provides a noneconomic view of shopping centers and describes the architectural design implications of shopping as entertainment.

Harrington, James W., Jr. 1995: "Empirical Research on Producer Service Growth and Regional Development: International Comparisons." *The Professional Geographer*, Vol. 47, pp. 66–69.

This is an introduction to a series of short papers concerning producer services in Europe and North America. The papers are not just literature reviews, but also contain good summaries of current locational and structural trends in producer services. The other papers, all in the same volume, are: Antoine S. Bailly, "Producer Services Research in Europe," pp. 70–74; William J. Coffey, "Producer Services Research in Canada," pp. 74–81; Peter W. Daniels, "Producer Services Research in the United Kingdom," pp. 82–87; and James W. Harrington, "Producer Services Research in U.S. Regional Studies," pp. 87–96.

Hughes, J., K. Miller, and R. Lang. 1992: *The New Geography of Office Buildings*. New Brunswick, N.J.: Center for Urban Policy Research, Rutgers University.

This study contains information on the suburbanization of the real estate market for office space that took place in the 1980s, with special emphasis on metropolitan New York.

King, Leslie. 1984: *Central Place Theory*. Vol. 1 in Sage Scientific Geography Series. Beverly Hills, Calif.: Sage.

King provides both the descriptive and analytical background to central place theory, as well as the theory itself, in a reader-friendly way. The emphasis of this brief volume is placed appropriately on Christaller's original approach to central place systems.

Lanvin, Bruno, ed, 1993: *Trading in a New World Order: The Impact of Telecommunications and Data Services on International Trade in Services*. Boulder, Colo.: Westview Press.

A series of papers commissioned by the Atwater Institute on the impact of technological advance in communications on services in the global economy are collected in this volume. The services considered are finance, insurance, software services, and travel.

Laulajainen, Risto. 1987: *Spatial Strategies in Retailing*. Dordrecht: D. Reidel.

This book provides over 50 cases of retail chain expansion drawn from restaurant, food chain, department store, specialty store, and discounting businesses. The author finds that the expansion of retail chains often conforms to spatial diffusion models, especially if a corporation's operating space is well defined.

O'hUallachain, Breandan, and Neil Reid. 1991: "The Location and Growth of Business and Professional Services in American Metropolitan Areas, 1976–1986." *Annals of the Association of American Geographers*, Vol. 81, pp. 254–270.

This paper describes the uneven geographical growth of the service sector in the United States over a recent 10 year period. The authors show that service-sector employment tends to be concentrated in America's largest metropolitan centers in a way that suggests that the sector benefits from agglomeration economies.

The Transnational Corporations and Management Division, UN Department of Economic and Social Development, publishes the series *TCMD Current Studies*, which includes several titles that concern services in the global economy. In addition to those studies that provide Cases 8.4 and 8.5 in this chapter, you should read:

Key Concepts in International Investment Arrangements and Their Relevance to Negotiations on International Transactions in Services, ST/CTC/SER.A/13 (New York: UN, 1990), and *International Property Rights and Foreign Direct Investment* ST/CTC/SER.A/24 (New York: UN, 1993).

Chapter 9

Urban and Regional Economic Growth

This chapter

- describes recent geographical trends in urbanization

- emphasizes the role of agglomeration economies in city growth

- examines the role of exports in regional growth

- introduces shift-share analysis and input-output analysis as techniques for assessing regional growth patterns

- summarizes a variety of government policies designed to encourage local and regional economic growth

Corning Photography

Economic growth is unevenly distributed. Economic agglomerations are everywhere apparent to even the most casual observer. Perhaps the most evident of all geographical differences is that between city and countryside. Cities exist for many reasons, but the stronger ones most likely are associated with the economic efficiencies they provide for many industries. All cities are not alike, however, and they vary considerably in size from villages to metropolitan areas with many millions in population. Why aren't all cities the same size? We have already considered at least two reasons: factor costs can vary as a function of city size so that producers prefer different-sized centers (Chapter 7), and central place theory tells us that as long as everybody doesn't live in only one place, settlements will vary in size depending on their relative locations (Chapter 8).

In addition to city-country differences and differences in city sizes, geographical concentrations in the economy are also apparent at regional and local scales. Most countries, for example, have regional variations in their economies that mean that some of their population is better off than the rest simply because of where they live, and the same geographical effect can be found within individual metropolitan areas. Markets, and market failures, tend to build up geographical differences in economies, and government often develops policies designed to smooth out the differences.

URBANIZATION AND BIG CITIES

Cities exist for several reasons. Some settlements have been established at or near sacred sites as centers for religious practices, and many others owe their original existence to collective needs for defense. Even without specific purposes, it is likely that cities would exist because people are social animals who seem both to want and to need the company of others. Aside from social factors, however, the most compelling basis for the existence of cities is economic. In the previous chapter, we discussed the role of cities as distribution centers—as central places; cities also play important economic roles as places of production. Although their function as centers of distribution underlies the relative spacing and size of cities, their role as production centers tells us a lot about why cities grow.

Why are cities important as centers of production? First of all, their importance to production is rather new in historical terms. After all, even in those European countries where the Industrial Revolution first took hold, as well as in the United States, agriculture was the dominant economic sector until well into the late 1800s. Cities, of course, are not centers of agricultural production; during the early years of our nation, cities were not important to manufacturing either. Early factory sites were decidedly rural; most often factories were built at raw material sites and at places where the energy needed to power early machinery was cheap. Rural New England and the countryside of the Southern Piedmont in the United States are sprinkled with the ruins of old factories wherever streams provided sufficient flows to literally keep the wheels of production turning.

By the mid-1800s, however, the ties between cities and manufacturing were quite apparent, and urban locations for manufacturing were developing in two ways. One was the growth of cities around manufacturing sites, as in Manchester in the United Kingdom and Pittsburgh in the United States. The other was the growth of manufacturing in cities that already existed, such as London and New York. Since the mid-1800s, the growth of manufacturing, national wealth, and urbanization have been strongly tied together around the world. Currently, the world's richest countries, which also have the world's largest share of manufacturing (recall from Chapter 7), have the most urbanized populations. At the other end, the low-income countries, which have the smallest share of the world's manufacturing, have the smallest proportion of their populations living in cities (Figure 9.1).

The link between national wealth and urbanization rates is not a coincidence. Cities tend to be good places not only for manufacturing, but also for tertiary and

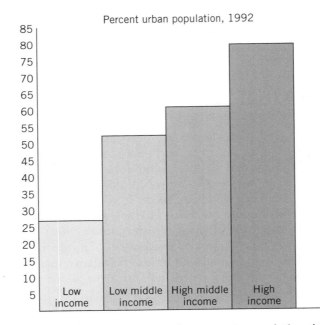

Figure 9.1 The proportion of a country's population that is urbanized varies, on average, with national income. The average low-income country has less than 30% of its population living in cities, while the average high-income country has about 80% of its population classified as urban.   Source: *World Development Report 1994* (New York: Oxford University Press).

quaternary sector activities. Chapter 1 introduced the concept of agglomeration economies of scale, or decreases in the average cost of production that often occur when that production takes place in geographical concentrations of economic activity. All producers have need of spatial interaction in their activities. If production occurs in an agglomeration, the costs of spatial interaction can be reduced so that average costs of business operations can be reduced.

LOCALIZATION AND URBANIZATION ECONOMIES OF SCALE

There are two basic types of agglomeration economies of scale *localization economies* and *urbanization economies* (Figure 9.2). Localization economies come into play when there is a concentration of linked businesses within a region. The automotive industry around Detroit and the movie industry around Hollywood are examples. Producers within such an agglomeration benefit from low costs of supplier-customer interaction, especially under just-in-time systems. They also can take advantage of specialized services that develop around industrial concentrations. Legal, financial, and distribution services in a region often become specialized, and therefore more efficient, around a major regional industrial concentration. Labor markets also become specialized, and labor training costs

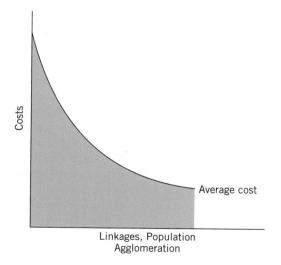

Figure 9.2 Agglomeration economies can be divided into two types. Localization economies occur when a geographical concentration of linked enterprises leads to a decrease in their average cost curves. Urbanization economies are defined as a decrease in the average cost curve because of a geographical concentration of population.

are often borne by specialized local educational institutions that have been established in response to the specialized nature of the region's labor market. In addition, regional production centers are often centers of industrial innovation as well. The agglomeration of computer companies in California's Silicon Valley is an example. Businesses outside of such agglomerations may be subject to higher product development costs because they are not able to share in information as readily as those companies in the agglomeration.

Localization economies can be achieved outside of individual big cities. The North Carolina Piedmont, for example, is a regional center for household furniture production in the United States, but the industry is dispersed over a number of intermediate-sized cities such as High Point and Hickory that are well-linked by transport infrastructure. Although localization economies can have a wider regional extent, urbanization economies are more dependent on a concentration of population in one place. Urbanization economies are more general in nature than are localization economies, but they occur for the same reasons. Spatial interaction costs are reduced in large cities because transactions between producers and a large number of consumers can take place over fairly short distances. Furthermore, large cities are centers of infrastructure, the publicly provided capital that is so important in reducing costs of interaction in an economy. The existence of urbanization economies indicates that cities are efficient places to do business, and their efficiency is an important basis for the higher incomes enjoyed in the world's more urbanized countries.

URBAN GROWTH TRENDS

Although richer countries are more urbanized than poorer ones, the poorer countries are urbanizing at a faster rate (Figure 9.3). One reason for the poor countries' more rapid urbanization is that the richer countries are approaching a type of cap on the proportion of their population that can live in cities. Except for city-states like Singapore, in every country some of the population lives in rural places simply because of the demands of its primary economic sector. Another reason for the poorer countries' faster urbanization rates is that their population growth rates in general are higher than in richer ones (see Chapter 5), so their cities can be expected to grow at a faster rate, too.

The differences in production functions between rich and poor countries provide an additional explanation for the differences in urbanization rates. Growth in manufacturing output is occurring in both rich and poor countries, but its growth in poor countries is taking place under more labor-intensive production while capital-intensive production is more typical of the richer countries. Labor-intensive methods simply require more people, and as manufacturing grows in cities in poorer countries, those cities are going to experience a rapid increase in their populations. Most of the increase results from rural to urban migration of the labor force. Manufacturing jobs often pay more than primary-sector employment, and people are drawn from the country to the city in the

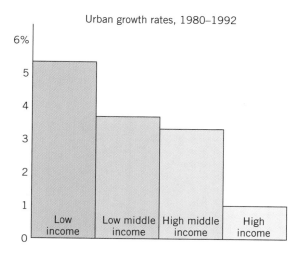

Urban growth rates, 1980–1992

Figure 9.3 Low-income countries are rapidly urbanizing, with average urban growth rates that are much greater than those found in countries at higher income levels. SOURCE: *World Development Report 1994* (New York: Oxford University Press).

hope of increasing their standard of living. Manufacturing centers like Detroit and Manchester grew rapidly in the same way, but at a time when their manufacturing industries were a lot more labor intensive than they are today. Now output can easily grow in the richer countries even as employment declines. Thus, growth in production is no longer associated with population growth as it was (and is in poorer countries) under more labor-intensive production processes.

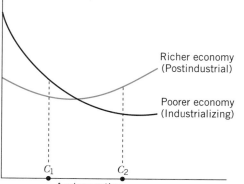

Figure 9.4 Agglomeration economies may be differentiated between industrializing and postindustrial economies. Although decreases in average costs occur in both economies at lower levels of agglomeration such as C_1, there is a difference at larger levels of agglomeration. For example, agglomeration economies still obtain at C_2 in industrializing countries as average costs continue to decline. In postindustrial countries, however, agglomeration diseconomies occur at C_2, with average costs on the increase.

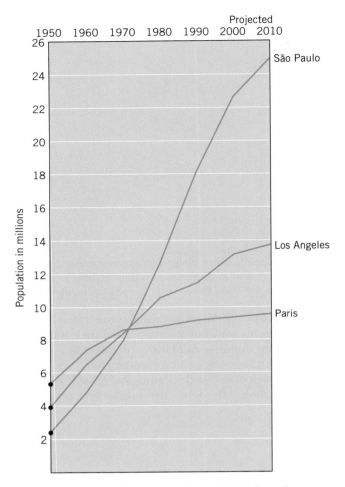

Figure 9.5   São Paulo, Los Angeles, and Paris have been among the world's largest agglomerations since 1950, but their individual growth paths since that year, and projected to 2010, are quite different.   SOURCE: *World Urbanization Prospects: The 1992 Revision,* UN Department of Economic and Social Information and Policy Analysis (New York: United Nations, 1993), pp. 126–127.

Yet another reason why poor countries have higher urbanization rates lies in the differences in agglomeration economies. As we have seen, many of the operating efficiencies that lower average costs of production in large cities exist because the costs of spatial interaction are lower in large cities than elsewhere. In richer countries, however, the spread of infrastructure has led to a lowering of spatial interaction costs throughout their national economies, so an urban location is less beneficial. Agglomeration economies may exist in smaller centers in richer countries, as illustrated by point C_1 in Figure 9.4, but tend to diminish in cities with larger populations. Place C_2, for example, would provide *agglomeration diseconomies,* or increasing average costs, in a richer economy, whereas the same-sized center would still be beneficial to a producer in a poorer economy. In richer countries, producers can take advantage of cheaper property, cheaper labor, and lower taxes that exist in smaller centers but still be able to interact with suppliers and customers at a fairly low cost because of geographically widespread infrastructure. In poorer countries, the centralization of infrastructure is a result of its high cost, and that centralization in turn ensures a leading role for agglomeration economies in the centralization of the economy.

The demographic and economic processes that affect urban growth differently between richer and poorer countries lead to the type of differential growth paths illustrated in Figure 9.5. All three cities—Paris, Los Angeles, and São Paulo—are manufacturing centers. Paris is the oldest as both a major city and as a manufacturing center, with Los Angeles in an intermediate position and São Paulo a relative latecomer as a world-class industrial center.

Table 9.1   The World's Largest Agglomerations: 1950, 1970, 1990, 2010

1950 Agglomeration	Population*	1970 Agglomeration	Population*
1. New York	12.3	1. Tokyo	16.5
2. London	8.7	2. New York	16.2
3. Tokyo	6.9	3. Shanghai	11.2
4. Paris	5.4	4. Osaka	9.4
5. Moscow	5.4	5. Mexico City	9.1
6. Shanghai	5.3	6. London	8.6
7. Essen	5.3	7. Paris	8.5
8. Buenos Aires	5.0	8. Buenos Aires	8.4
9. Chicago	4.9	9. Los Angeles	8.4
10. Calcutta	4.4	10. Beijing	8.1
11. Osaka	4.1	11. São Paulo	8.1
12. Los Angeles	4.0	12. Moscow	7.1

1990 Agglomeration	Population*	2010 Agglomeration	Population*
1. Tokyo	25.0	1. Tokyo	28.9
2. São Paulo	18.1	2. São Paulo	25.0
3. New York	16.1	3. Bombay	24.4
4. Mexico City	15.1	4. Shanghai	21.7
5. Shanghai	13.4	5. Lagos	21.1
6. Bombay	12.2	6. Mexico City	18.0
7. Los Angeles	11.5	7. Beijing	18.0
8. Buenos Aires	11.4	8. Dacca	17.6
9. Seoul	11.0	9. New York	17.2
10. Rio de Janeiro	10.9	10. Jakarta	17.2
11. Beijing	10.9	11. Karachi	17.0
12. Calcutta	10.7	12. Manila	16.1

* in millions

SOURCE: *World Urbanization Prospects: The 1992 Revision,* UN Department of Economic and Social Information and Policy Analysis (New York: United Nations, 1993), pp. 126–127.

In 1950, Paris was the largest of the three, and São Paulo was the smallest. In the mid-1970s, the three cities were about the same size, but after that period São Paulo experienced explosive growth whereas Paris's metropolitan population effectively stabilized. Los Angeles also experienced population growth from the mid-1970s on, but not on the same order as São Paulo. São Paulo is a center of manufacturing growth in an economy with relatively labor-intensive production and geographically concentrated infrastructure. In addition, Brazil has a relatively high rate of population growth. Manufacturing growth still takes place in Paris and Los Angeles, but it is not so labor intensive and the populations of France and the United States are not growing very rapidly.

In 1950, many of the world's largest agglomerations were in Europe and North America, and their large size was a result of the manufacturing that occurred there (Table 9.1). By 1990, only New York and Los Angeles remained on the list of largest agglomerations, with all the European centers gone. According to current projections for 2010, Tokyo, at the top, and New York, in ninth place, are the only agglomerations among the world's 12 largest that are located in currently richer economies. The geographical shifts that occur between 1950 and the projections for 2010 underline the relationship between cities and their economic contexts.

REGIONAL EXPORTS AND GROWTH

Although some cities, and the surrounding areas that comprise their metropolitan agglomeration, can get very large indeed, most settlements remain relatively small. In addition, some regions are prosperous, and some have reputations as economic backwaters where incomes and employment always seem to lag (more about this in Chapter 11). Why do some places grow into world-class metropolitan agglomerations while others remain villages? Why are some regions rich and other regions poor? If we could answer these questions easily, we would be a long way down the road to solving many of the world's most pressing problems.

Unfortunately, the answers aren't easy because they aren't consistent from case to case. In some instances, apparently regional economic growth can be traced only to luck. The fact that Henry Ford lived there at the right time has a lot to do with Detroit's growth into a major industrial agglomeration. Detroit was a big city in the late 1800s, but it was about the same size as Milwaukee and Cleveland, two other major ports on the Great Lakes. By the 1920s, however, Detroit was a much larger center than any other on the Great Lakes with the exception of Chicago, and its size was due to its development as the center of the American automotive industry. Although automobile production would likely have developed around Detroit even if Henry Ford had never been born, it is unlikely that the scale of the industry in the region would have been the same. Furthermore, if Ford had lived in Buffalo, or Cleveland, or maybe even Passaic, then that city would probably have become the center of the American car industry.

Of course, having the right person in town at the right time isn't the only reason why certain places grow. Some places grow because they have an advantage with respect to raw materials. Manchester, England, for example, and Pittsburgh in the United States, as mentioned above, owe most of their size to abundant local mineral resources. But while local natural resources have proved important in some places, perhaps the most important historical advantages for growth are tied to a place's suitability as a distribution center. In the United States, for example, the first city to achieve a population of over 100,000 was New York, just after 1800. No other cities reached that size (within their political limits) until the mid-1830s, when both Baltimore and New Orleans passed the 100,000 mark. Boston, Philadelphia, and Cincinnati passed the mark in the mid-1840s, and St. Louis and Chicago by 1860. All these cities are ports and serve as distribution centers on coasts or on interior waterways. Although each is now a manufacturing center, they achieved significant size before manufacturing was an important factor in metropolitan growth.

The cities grew as distribution centers because their market areas were growing. Notice the geographical progression of cities just listed. New York served the northern part of the United States in its European trade and gained considerable advantage in its region with the opening of the Erie Canal in 1825. Baltimore served the southern part of the United States in its Atlantic trade, a region smaller than that served by New York, and New Orleans served the smaller Gulf Coast region and the area up the Mississippi River. As regional populations grew, so did market areas, and more cities reached 100,000 in population as their role as distribution centers expanded.

Remember from the presentation of central place theory in Chapter 8 that low-order central places are small, and have small markets and small market areas. High-order central places, on the other hand, have large markets and large market areas. It follows that central places can grow if their market areas grow, and that's just what happened with the cities listed above because they served as central places for growing markets.

THE CENTRAL PLACE MULTIPLIER

We can think of the relationship between a central place's size and the size of its market using the following identity:

$$C_P = k(C_P + M_P) \tag{9.1}$$

where C_P is the population of a central place, M_P is the population of its external market, and k is the proportion of the central place's population that is required to serve itself and also the external market $(0 < k < 1)$. If we use multiplier notation, the identity can be written as

$$C_P = \left(\frac{1}{(1 - k)} \right) k M_P \qquad (9.2)$$

where $1/(1 - k)$ is the *central place multiplier*. In this format, you can readily see that any increase in a central place's external market leads to an increase in the size of the central place, too.

So, central place theory tells us not only about the relative size and spacing of cities, but something about city growth as well. Although the specific relationship between central place and market size can vary, the important point remains that cities (and their surrounding areas) grow because they are linked to external markets. In the central place model, those markets should be contiguous to the central place. However, while that sort of contiguity was important at one time, it no longer seems to be a necessary condition for city and regional growth.

THE ECONOMIC BASE MULTIPLIER

The contiguity condition no longer holds, in part because transportation technology has developed to such a degree that there is significant market overlap among distribution centers. Another reason is that the growth of manufacturing has led to the establishment of many cities as centers of production and not as centers of distribution that would conform to central place principles. The city of Pittsburgh, for example, reached 100,000 in population in the mid-1870s because the demand for steel was growing throughout the country, and not just in western Pennsylvania; similarly, Detroit did not achieve its size because so many people in southeastern Michigan bought automobiles. According to the central place multiplier in Equation 9.2, the growth of a central place, as a central place, is determined as a multiple of growth in its surrounding market area. However, a more contemporary multiplier is often derived by splitting the economy of a city or region into two market sectors. The *basic sector* consists of all goods and services that are purchased by enterprises and consumers from outside the local market. The *non-basic sector* consists of all goods and services that are purchased by enterprises and consumers inside the local market.

It's not always easy to determine what is part of the basic sector. Sometimes *location quotients*, which measure activities in local economies against expectations based on national conditions (recall Case 8.1), are calculated. Greater than expected concentrations $(LQ > 1)$ are taken as evidence of basic activity (Case 9.1). Traditionally, manufacturing was almost synonymous with basic activity, but services can be basic as well because both tertiary and quaternary services can be sold outside a region in which they are produced. In fact, a good or service doesn't have to be sold outside of the local area to qualify for inclusion in the region's basic sector, it only needs to be sold to an enterprise or consumer from outside the region. Tourism, for example, is part of the basic sector, with consumers from outside the region consuming a host of locally provided recreational and educational services.

A city's, or region's, employment can be divided among the two sectors:

$$E = B + N \tag{9.3}$$

where E stands for all employment and B and N are basic employment and nonbasic employment, respectively. We can think of nonbasic employment as a proportion of total employment, or

$$N = kE, \qquad (0 < k < 1) \tag{9.4}$$

so by substitution,

$$E = B + kE \tag{9.5}$$

Again using multiplier notation, we have an employment identity:

$$E = \left(\frac{1}{(1 - k)} \right) B \tag{9.6}$$

Note the similarity to the central place multiplier given in Equation 9.2 above, but in this case we have what's called an *economic base multiplier*. This multiplier is drawn out from *economic base theory*, which holds that all local growth is ultimately derived from growth in the basic sector, or expansion of external markets (contiguous or not). Growth in sales to external markets leads directly to growth in income and employment in the local area. Additional indirect growth effects are realized because increases in income and employment in the basic sector lead to increased local demand for goods and services. If a factory expands its employment, for example, the new employees will buy groceries, go to movies, use local government services, and consume other local goods and services in a way that causes employment and income in the region's nonbasic sector to increase. That additional employment will generate still more, and so on, through several rounds of economic expansion.

Economic base theory correctly identifies the importance of ties to external markets as a basis for economic growth in a region, but it also tends to overlook the importance of local factors as contributors to a region's growth. Infrastructure, for example, provides services to a local economy that are vital to any region's economic success. It may be, in fact, that a region's economic growth ultimately rests on the quality of the nonbasic services that are required for the basic sector to function.

◪ CASE *9.1*

The Service Exports of Four Texas Cities

Based on location quotients (LQ), a list of service-sector imports and exports was developed using the assumption that exports occur if the LQ is greater than 1.2 and imports occur if the LQ is less than 0.8 (see list). Interpretation of location quotients requires great care, especially when applied to cases as specific as the cities I have chosen. Still, the broad pattern of service-sector strengths described here conforms to images held by knowledgeable observers of the cities. These results probably contain some new insights as well.

HOUSTON

Houston is an oil and natural gas center for the world, and the location quotients for oil and gas mining (16.75) and pipeline transportation (9.11) vividly illustrate this point. Of the top fifteen publicly held firms headquartered in Houston (ranked by annual revenues in 1988), nine are related to oil and gas: Tenneco, The Coastal Corporation, Enron, Lyondell Petrochemical, Panhandle Eastern, Transco, Baker-Hughes, Permian Partners, and Pennzoil.

Much of Houston's apparent strength in services stems from oil and gas as well. Trucking, transportation services, and water transportation are almost certainly linked to the Port of Houston. Based on tonnage, it is the largest U.S. port, and petrochemicals and refined energy products (along with agricultural products) are the top exports from the port.

The strength of the miscellaneous services category results at least in part from the large construction engineering firms in Houston such as Fluor Daniel, Brown and Root, and M.W. Kellogg. Houston is a national and global center for the design and construction of large petrochemical and refining plants. Houston's large number of engineering jobs, and the apparent strength of construction in these data (LQ=1.33), can be attributed to the petrochemical construction boom along the Texas Gulf Coast that began in 1987. Even Houston's apparent exports of real estate, holding and investment companies, and legal services are probably tied to the volume of oil and gas projects financed through the city.

DALLAS

Dallas, in contrast to Houston's dependence on petroleum, is a more widely diversified city with a major role in national and regional distribution. As in Houston, oil and gas is an important business in Dallas, as the LQ of 6.14 for oil and gas mining indicates. Unlike Houston, the most striking aspects of the Dallas service sector are its strengths in wholesale trade and in a range of retail services that are normally purely local activities.

Dallas is a center for regional and national headquarters, and Texas Instruments, LTV, J.C. Penney, Dresser Industries, Southland Corporation, Kimberly Clark, Electronic Data Systems (EDS), and Frito-Lay illustrate the diversity that exists among the types of industries with headquarters in the city. Dallas is physically located to serve as a distribution hub for the Southwest and for parts of the Midwest as well. The huge World Trade Center is the most conspicuous sign of the city's broad role in national distribution.

The location quotients for Dallas show exports in sales in industries such as food stores, eating and drinking establishments, department stores, automobile dealerships, and miscellaneous retail stores. Dallas' strength in eating and drinking places, hotels, and personal services ties in to its large number of convention visitors and other business travellers to the city. The large Dallas-Fort Worth Airport and American Airlines headquarters in the city stand out very strongly (LQ = 2.60). Dallas shows a much stronger financial sector than Houston, with exports of banking, real estate, and insurance.

SAN ANTONIO AND FORT WORTH

These smaller metropolitan areas, in contrast to Dallas and Houston, have fewer service-sector exports and far more imports. In San Antonio, the large location quotients for the federal government reflect the city's dependence on the payrolls of Ft. Sam Houston and four major Air Force facilities. Exports of personal services, hotels, and eating and drinking places are related to tourism. Service-sector exports from Fort Worth are confined to retail furniture, personal services, museums, and a strong transportation sector (railroads and air transportation). Both cities import a wide range of services, especially financial and business services.

Wilbur Thompson (*A Preface to Urban Economics*, 1965, Baltimore: The Johns Hopkins Press) proposed four stages of urban growth: (1) the expansion of an export-based economy led by one export; (2) the rise of an export complex, as other competing exports develop; (3) the achievement of economic maturity as regional manufacturing displaces imports; and (4) the development of a regional metropolis with service-sector exports.

Any stage theory of this kind is an oversimplification, but this description seems useful in light of findings for these four cities. Dallas and Houston have achieved the final stage—status as a regional metropolis, providing services to other cities throughout the Southwest and United States. San Antonio and Fort Worth, on the other hand, remain at an earlier stage of development. They are probably mature in the sense of stage 3, but as yet they show only limited service-sector exports.

List of Service Exports and Imports of Four Major Texas Cities, 1987

- Houston's Exports: trucking; water transportation; transportation services; wholesale trade; pipelines; retail apparel; electric, gas, and sanitary services; real estate, legal services, holding and investment companies, miscellaneous services

- Houston's Imports: security and commodity brokerage; insurance carriers; federal civilian government; federal military government
- Dallas' Exports: air transportation; communications; general retail merchandise; wholesale trade; food stores; eating and drinking establishments; auto dealers; miscellaneous retail; banking and credit agencies; insurance carriers; insurance agents; holding and investment companies; real estate; hotels; personal services; business services
- Dallas' Imports: railroad transportation; security and commodity brokerage; amusements; social services; private education services; museums; federal civilian government; federal military government
- Fort Worth's Exports: railroad transportation; air transportation; retail furniture; personal services; museums
- Fort Worth's Imports: transportation services; communications; electric, gas, and sanitary services; security and commodity brokers; banking and credit agencies; insurance carriers; real estate; retail apparel; miscellaneous repair; holding and investment companies; hotels; business services; private educational services; membership organizations; miscellaneous services; federal civilian government; state and local government
- San Antonio's Exports: building materials; eating and drinking establishments; food stores; auto dealers; personal services; insurance carriers; hotels; federal military government; federal civilian government
- San Antonio's Imports: air transportation; transportation services; electric, gas, and sanitary services; miscellaneous retail trade; wholesale trade; insurance agents; security and commodity brokerage; holding and investment companies; business services; legal services; amusements; membership organizations; miscellaneous services

SOURCE: "Identifying Service-Sector Exports from Major Texas Cities," by Robert W. Gilmer, in *Economic Review*, Federal Reserve Bank of Dallas, July, 1990, pp. 7, 9, 11–13.

For Discussion

Higher education can be classified as a quaternary activity. Can it also be classified as a basic activity in the context of economic base theory?

INPUT-OUTPUT ANALYSIS

Growth in any economic activity, basic or nonbasic, is likely to have direct or indirect multiplier effects throughout a regional economy. The multiplier effects result from the integrated supply and demand relationships across economic sectors that can be assessed through *input-output analysis* (Appendix 9.1). The inputs of many economic activities can also be viewed as the outputs of other economic activities. For example, a tire produced by one corporation is placed on an automobile produced by another. Another example is the service produced by a public accounting firm that is purchased by a mining corporation. Input-output analysis tracks the flows of outputs-as-inputs through an economy and can be used to determine the multiplier effects of growth in individual industries. For example, input-output analysis can be used to determine the full impact that a certain amount of agricultural growth will have on manufacturing, both in its direct effect as more farm machinery is required and in its indirect effect as more machine tools are needed to build farm equipment. The Swedish economist Gunnar Myrdal called the concept of growth breeding growth in a region *circular and cumulative causation*. An initial boost in a region can cause its economy to experience an upward spiral as input-output relationships come into play.

Unfortunately, what goes up can also come down, and multiplier effects can also result in economic contraction, and downward spirals in regional economies. A decline in agricultural output, for example, would also lead to direct and indirect declines in manufacturing. The state-by-state employment effects of expected cuts in American defense spending, as assessed through input-output analysis, are described in Case 9.2. The effects of the defense spending cuts are diluted because the economies of the individual states are diversified enough in aggregate to adjust to the employment impacts within short time periods. On a more local scale, however, such declines can lead to a *ghost-town syndrome*, where the loss of a critical local industry results in widespread economic decline and a place's eventual abandonment.

◪ CASE 9.2
Impacts of Cuts in Defense Spending on States

NEAR TERM EFFECTS ON STATES

The regional impact of defense purchasing cuts depends on the distribution of affected industries. States with high concentrations of ordnance or aircraft manufacturing would experience much greater employment losses than states without such concentrations.

Data on gross state products (GSP) identify each state's industrial composition. I use these data to translate near-term industry effects into state effects by assigning each state a share of industry employment according to its share of industry output. By assumption, if Alabama produces 10 percent of the country's shoes, 10 percent of the country's shoe manufacturing jobs are in Alabama.

In the near term, defense purchasing cuts would cause relatively large percentage-rate employment declines in Connecticut and Alaska (Map A). The rate of employment losses in Connecticut would be almost twice the national average.

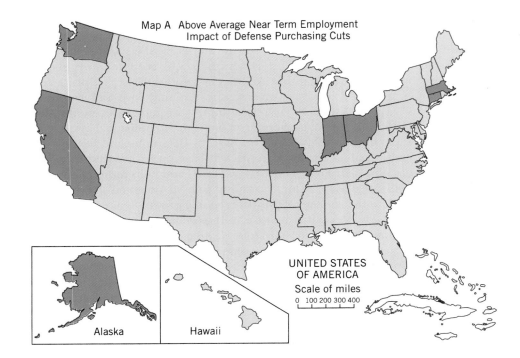

Map A Above Average Near Term Employment Impact of Defense Purchasing Cuts

UNITED STATES OF AMERICA
Scale of miles
0 100 200 300 400

Alaska   Hawaii

Connecticut would lose 0.44 percent of its employment, or almost 7,500 jobs, if Congress cut real defense purchasing by 10 percent. In contrast, states in the Upper Great Plains and the Mid-Atlantic region have relatively small shares of affected industries and should lose few jobs from purchasing cuts.

Connecticut would have the greatest percentage of job losses because firms that manufacture military transportation equipment and electronics play dominant roles in the state's economy. On the other hand, South Dakota would have the smallest percentage of job losses from purchasing cuts because it produces few defense-related products and supplies few defense contractors. South Dakota would lose only .12 percent of its employment, or less than 400 jobs, if Congress cut real defense purchasing by 10 percent.

In all but two of the states with above-average employment losses, the transportation equipment industries would lose the most jobs from defense purchasing cuts. In Alaska, the mining industry would lose the most jobs, while in Massachusetts the electronics industry would lose the most jobs.

Multiplier effects push Ohio, Indiana, and Alaska into the category of states with above average employment losses. In Ohio, for example, total job losses in primary metals manufacturing should exceed losses in electronics or communications equipment. In Indiana, total losses in primary metals manufacturing should exceed losses in ordnance manufacturing.

Although average job losses would be negligible in many states, specific communities within those states might still experience significant job losses. Analysis at the state level blurs significant employment changes at the local level.

Some communities would experience job losses significantly greater than their state's average. Other communities may lose no jobs at all. The state employment effects are better estimates of local employment effects when all parts of the state are integrated into a single economy. In states with many regional economies, such as California or Texas, local economic effects may differ dramatically from the state average.

LONG TERM EFFECTS ON STATES

Labor is a very versatile input. Over time, the economy will find new uses for the labor displaced by defense cuts, and the national economy will return to full employment. In the process, the distribution of industries will change slightly. Defense-dependent industries, such as ordnance and aircraft manufacturing, will play smaller roles in the national economy. Industries that absorb significant quantities of displaced labor will play somewhat larger roles.

Two factors will minimize the redistributional effects of defense purchasing cuts on industries. First, the labor displaced by defense purchasing cuts represents only a small fraction of the national labor supply. Second, many industries will reabsorb labor in the long term, diffusing the impact of any cuts. Because a relatively small quantity of labor will be distributed over a wide variety of industries in the long term, no industry's employment would increase by more than 0.33 percent of its initial employment following a uniform 10-percent cut in defense purchases.

The long term effects of defense cuts on states equal the reabsorbed labor minus the near-term employment losses. Some states should absorb more labor in the long term than they lose in the near term. Other states will absorb too little labor to compensate for near-term losses. Each state's absorption of labor depends on its pattern of job creation.

If the geographic distribution of characteristics that significantly influence state employment growth remains stable, then the states that have created the most jobs in the past are the most likely to create jobs in the future. Thus, states with the highest historical growth rates for employment appear to be the states most likely to reabsorb the labor displaced by defense purchasing cuts.

Historically, Nevada, Alaska, Arizona, and Florida created jobs faster than other states. Over the past thirty years, employment in each of these states grew at a rate more than double the national average of 2.4 percent annually. These states should absorb relatively more labor than other states in the long run.

On the other hand, employment growth rates have been lowest in New York, Pennsylvania, and Illinois. Employment in these states grew at a rate less than one-half the national average during the same period. Consequently, they should absorb a smaller share of the labor displaced by cuts in defense purchasing (Map B).

Although several states would lose jobs even after reabsorption, losses would be negligible in every state except Connecticut. Connecticut's industry mix leads to the greatest proportional job losses in the near term, and the state's employment growth historically has been low. Connecticut would lose 0.24 percent of

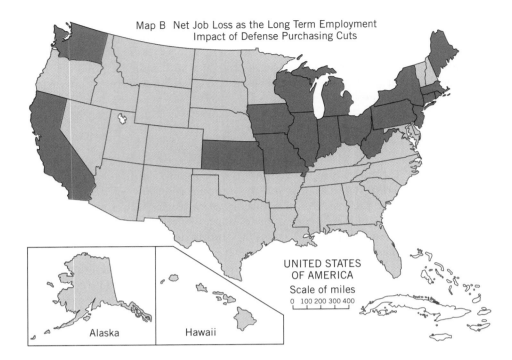

Map B   Net Job Loss as the Long Term Employment Impact of Defense Purchasing Cuts

UNITED STATES OF AMERICA

Scale of miles

0   100 200 300 400

Alaska   Hawaii

its employment, or roughly 4,000 jobs, in the long term if defense purchasing were cut by 10 percent.

Three states—Nevada, Arizona, and Florida—should gain significantly more jobs than all other states in the long term. Nevada should gain the most jobs, proportionally. Nevada's employment should increase by 0.35 percent, or roughly 2,000 jobs, after reabsorption. Employment should increase in Arizona by 0.29 percent and in Florida by 0.28 percent. These states should gain jobs in the long term because they have demonstrated above-average historical growth.

SOURCE: "Reduced Defense Purchasing: Anticipating the Impact on State and Industry Employment," by Lori L. Taylor, in *Economic Review*, Federal Reserve Bank of Dallas, November 1990, pp. 19–23.

FOR DISCUSSION

Should the federal government consider employment effects in formulating its defense budget?

LOCAL AND REGIONAL GROWTH POLICIES

The importance of government policy in influencing locational choices in the economy has been considered in every chapter of this book so far. Some of the locational effects of government policy are unintended, as with most of U.S. agricultural policy. Many government policies, however, are designed to have locational effects, and just as national governments have a host of economic policies designed to promote their country's economic interests, subnational governments like those at the state and municipal levels in the United States have policies designed to promote their economic interests, too. In general, state and local economic growth policies can be placed in one of two categories. The first category is general in its geographical scope and entails efforts to reduce the costs of doing business within a political jurisdiction. The second category consists of policies that are more specifically targeted at recruiting, or retaining, selected industries and even selected individual businesses.

Business costs in an area can be reduced in a number of ways, but development and maintenance of infrastructure has been found to be about the most effective general policy for facilitating economic expansion. As described in Chapter 6, high-quality transport and communications infrastructure lowers business costs by reducing the costs of spatial interaction within an area. In addition, such infrastructure provides low-cost links to places outside a region and is therefore especially important in supporting activities in the basic sector. In addition to providing good physical infrastructure, education systems and related services comprise a type of institutional infrastructure that also can serve to lower business costs and encourage local economic growth. A well-educated population provides a productive labor force and one that is fairly flexible. Ultimately, continued attention to both physical and institutional infrastructure is effective as a policy both to promote economic growth and to improve an area's quality of life for its residents.

As described above, the benefits of infrastructure are a major source of agglomeration economies. In the 1960s and 1970s dozens of countries around the world practiced *growth center policy*. This policy was based on a variant of economic base theory that concerned the establishment of a leading industry in a depressed region that would, through a multiplier effect, generate regional economic growth and eventual industrial diversification. The leading industry, or *growth pole*, was given an initial advantage in the targeted growth center by the establishment of productive infrastructure and other government-sponsored inducements of agglomeration economies. Hydroelectric plants have been used in this way in some countries. For the most part, growth center strategies were not fully implemented because of cost or other political considerations.

GROWTH CENTERS AND ENTERPRISE ZONES

A more current variation of growth center policy is the *enterprise zone*, a concept that was first widely promoted by Jack Kemp, then a Republican member of Congress from Buffalo, New York. Enterprise zones are local areas targeted by government for special economic incentives. They are similar to growth centers because they are designed to invigorate, or reinvigorate, economies of particular places. The zones differ in scale from the areas targeted by growth center strategies in that they are much smaller, most often consisting of a limited number of blocks in an urban area. Because of their typical location within metropolitan areas, especially central cities, and their small scale, infrastructural projects are not emphasized in establishing enterprise zones. Instead, a variety of direct cost-cutting benefits are offered, including tax abatements or tax holidays, special employment credits, and labor training assistance. The enterprise zone described in Case 9.3 is typical in the array of locational inducements it provides. The primary purpose of enterprise zone policies is to generate local employment. A secondary purpose is to encourage local entrepreneurship by lowering the costs of starting a business in neighborhoods where capital costs are often higher than the average for the region or where credit is often unavailable through conventional sources because of lending practices that effectively discriminate against poor neighborhoods.

The tax breaks in enterprise zones are probably their most attractive feature, and reduced business taxes are likely the most commonly used method of decreasing the costs of doing business in an enterprise zone. Tax decreases are achieved in three different ways: (1) tax rate reductions that reduce the proportion of a company's earnings that are due the government; (2) tax credits that lower the cost of new capital equipment or job additions; and (3) narrowing the tax base through such means as excluding some sales taxes, for example, or excluding capital equipment from property taxes. Tax reduction policies must always be balanced by the need for sufficient expenditures to maintain the quality of a place's physical and institutional infrastructure, however, or its goal of encouraging economic growth is likely to go unrealized.

In addition to cost-cutting measures, economic growth is often encouraged by directly marketing and advertising a place's qualities as a business location. This is accomplished through normal outlets such as business magazines and television commercials. Trade shows and other exhibitions are also used as promotional venues. In addition, most American states, and some municipalities, even have promotional offices in foreign countries designed to attract foreign investment and other economic links between outside economies and their own. Most state and local promotion of economic development in the United States is handled either by the office of a jurisdiction's chief executive, a governor or mayor, for example, or more often by a special bureau or commission directly charged with promoting economic growth.

◪ CASE 9.3

An Enterprise Zone in East Hartford, Connecticut

The downtrodden south end of Main street received a ray of hope Wednesday from the state Department of Economic Developmnet.

Arthur H. Diedrick, the department's commissioner, handed Mayor Robert M. DeCrescenzo a certificate designating the huge chunk of town where Pratt & Whitney sits as an enterprise zone. That means certain businesses in the area, or planned for the area, may apply for everything from tax breaks to utility cost discounts.

"Certainly, it would behoove you to get into the zone if it's available," Councilwoman Marylee A. Hickey said after Diedrick's announcement. Hickey was among a half dozen smiling local and state officials who attended the commissioner's press conference at Pratt's new customer training center.

DeCrescenzo said he chose the state-of-the-art building as the site because he views it as a symbol of what's to come.

"We've really taken it on the chin over the years," he said of the town. "But let me tell you, we are fighting back."

Defense cuts at Pratt are the main reason the area was picked for the designation. Former state Rep. Gary LeBeau, D-East Hartford, said he proposed changing the law on enterprise zones in a way that would benefit the town a few years ago. Eventually, with help from state Sen. Kevin Rennie, R-South Windsor, and state Rep. Melody Curry, D-East Hartford, the law was changed.

The new law reserves two enterprise designations for areas that lost at least 2,000 jobs through base or plant closings or cutbacks. East Hartford is one of those; Southington may be the other.

Once the law was changed, the town and state worked together on the application, which DeCrescenzo described as "voluminous."

East Hartford's targeted 1,600 acres is roughly bounded by the Connecticut River and Route 2, Brewer Street, the Pratt property line and the Hockanum River.

For manufacturing and service businesses, the benefits of an enterprise zone include:

- A five-year, 80 percent abatement of local property taxes on real estate improvements and personal property purchases.

- A 10-year, 50 percent corporate business tax credit, and a grant of up to $1,500 per position, when at least 30 percent of new employees are either residents of the zone or eligible for federal job training subsidies.

- Exemption from state real estate conveyance taxes and sales taxes on manufacturing replacement parts.

- Job training and placement assistance.

Commercial and residential building owners may be eligible for tax deferrals and abatements, among other things.

SOURCE: "Good News for a Needy Town Zone," by Christine Dempsey, in *The Hartford Courant*, July 20, 1995, p. B2. By permission of the *Hartford Courant*.

FOR DISCUSSION

Determine the government agency responsible for local development efforts where you live and assess some of the promotional efforts it makes.

BUSINESS RECRUITMENT AND RETENTION

The second category of local and regional economic growth policies, those that target specific industries, is currently being relied upon more heavily in most places in the United States than general policies designed to lower costs or otherwise improve business conditions. *Industrial recruitment* is the common practice of attempting to pursuade a company to relocate, or at least expand, its operations in a different jurisdiction than where it is currently located. Targeting industries or individual companies for recruitment to a place is not always an easy thing to do, and it's not always a risk-free proposition either (recall Case 7.1). Typically, those industries or particular companies that pay higher than average wages and salaries are preferred targets, as are those that appear to have larger multiplier effects. Issues in regional industrial recruitment include whether large or small companies will have greater employment impacts over time, and whether service businesses or manufacturers are better targets. One method of identifying promising prospects is through *shift-share analysis*, which is a method of analyzing the components of a region's growth and of the growth of specific industries (Appendix 9.2). Shift-share analysis is particularly useful in identifying targets for special efforts toward industrial retention, which is easily as important a basis for local economic growth as the recruitment of new industries or companies.

Emphasis on *industrial retention*, or keeping existing local businesses in place, has been increasing as a response to increased efforts at industrial recruitment. Jurisdictions often find themselves competing with each other in offering packages of benefits, and in making counteroffers, in ways that are reminiscent of the free agent markets of American major league professional sports. Although the economic gains from such activity are uncertain, it appears to be politically important for local governments to at least appear to be making an effort to compete with other jurisdictions in the interest of promoting economic growth.

POINTS IN SUMMARY

1. Cities exist for social as well as economic reasons.

2. Currently, the world's richest countries, which also have the world's largest share of manufacturing, have the most urbanized populations.

3. Spatial interaction costs are reduced in large cities because transactions between producers and a large number of consumers can take place over fairly short distances.

4. Labor-intensive production requires people, and as manufacturing grows in cities in poorer countries, those cities are going to experience a rapid increase in their populations. Most of the increase results from rural to urban migration.

5. In poorer countries, the centralization of infrastructure results from its high cost, and its centralization in turn ensures a leading role for agglomeration economies.

6. In some cases it seems that regional economic growth can be traced to luck.

7. Central place theory tells us not only about the relative size and spacing of cities, but about city growth as well.

8. A good or service doesn't have to be sold outside of the local area to qualify for inclusion in the region's basic sector; it only needs to be sold to an enterprise or consumer from outside the region.

9. Indirect growth effects are realized as increases in income and employment in the basic sector lead to increased local demand for goods and services.

10. Economic base theory correctly identifies the importance of ties to external markets as a basis for economic growth in a region, but it also tends to overlook the importance of local factors as contributors to a region's growth.

11. State and local economic growth policies can be placed in one of two categories. The first category of such policies is general in its geographical scope, and entails efforts at reducing the costs of doing business within a political jurisdiction. The second category consists of policies that are more specifically targeted at recruiting, or retaining, selected industries and even selected individual businesses.

12. The primary purpose of enterprise zone policies is to generate local employment.

13. Local economic growth is often encouraged by directly marketing and advertising a place's qualities as a business location.

14. Industries that pay higher than average wages and salaries, and those that appear to have larger multiplier effects, are preferred targets of industrial recruiting.

TERMS TO REMEMBER

agglomeration diseconomies	economic base multiplier	growth center policy	localization economies
basic sector		growth pole	location quotient
central place multiplier	economic base theory	industrial recruitment	nonbasic sector
circular and cumulative causation	enterprise zone	industrial retention	shift-share analysis
	ghost-town syndrome	input-output analysis	urbanization economies

SUGGESTED READING

Castells, Manuel, and Peter Hall. 1994: *Technopoles of the World: The Making of Twenty-First-Century Industrial Complexes.* Routledge: London.

This book describes the emergence of planned high-tech developments from the regional scale down to the level of the new industrial park. It emphasizes the policies and practices that bring technopoles into being and includes a chapter of policy recommendations drawn from their examination of high-tech winners and losers around the world.

Clark, Gordon L., Meric S. Gertler, and John Whiteman. 1986: *Regional Dynamics: Studies in Adjustment Theory.* Boston: Allen & Unwin.

Although the "dynamics" in this book are not the sort of most economic-geographical analyses, it does cover a lot of interesting topics, including labor and capital markets, and wages and prices.

Ge, Wei. 1995: "The Urban Enterprise Zone." *Journal of Regional Science,* Vol. 35, pp. 217–231.

This article examines the use of enterprise zones as a policy of local/regional development. While analysis indicates that urban enterprise zones are beneficial to urban renewal and regional economic growth, the author notes that their draw-down effects on neighboring regional economies may be a problem.

Hansen, Niles, Benjamin Higgins, and Donald J. Savoie. 1990: *Regional Policy in a Changing World.* New York: Plenum Press.

This book covers regional policy in general, but consists mainly of its development in seven countries. Canada, France, Great Britain, the United States, and Australia are considered as representation of the industrial countries, and Malaysia and Brazil are used in representing the developing countries with their different set of regional issues.

Isard, Walter. 1975: *Introduction to Regional Science.* (Englewood Cliffs, N.J.: Prentice-Hall and 1985; Ithaca, N.Y.: Cornell University Department of City and Regional Planning.

Isard is the founder of the discipline of regional science that combines regional economics, spatial economics, and analytical economic geography. Regional science has a strong methodological bent, but Isard provides a palatable introduction to the discipline in this interesting overview.

Jones, Emrys. 1990: *Metropolis.* Oxford: Oxford University Press.

Jones writes about important cities in this book, with their importance measured in qualitative terms as well as with respect to their population. Its approach is historical; Jones considers different eras of the past and speculates on the future of great cities in the world.

Pred, Allan. 1965: "Industrialization, Initial Advantage, and American Metropolitan Growth." *Geographical Review,* Vol. 55, pp. 158–185.

In this essay on the growth of the American system of cities, Pred draws together a number of historical, economic, and geographical concepts and principles, including central place theory, external economies of scale, and circular and cumulative causation.

Rogers, Andrei. 1985: *Regional Population Projection Models,* Vol. 4 in Sage Scientific Geography Series. Beverly Hills, Calif.: Sage.

Population change is a vital component of regional economic growth (or decline). This short volume by Rogers is mathematically challenging in its treatment of regional population forecasting, but its succinct nature makes it an excellent introductory reference on the topic.

Scott, Allen J. 1993: *Technopolis*: *High-Technology Industry and Regional Development in Southern California.* Berkeley: University of California Press.

Scott has studied the region of Southern California long and hard, and the results of his efforts are contained in this book. The volume begins with the historical and geographical background of the high-tech agglomeration in the region and proceeds with sector-by-sector presentations.

The three special papers on urbanization listed here, along with brief commentaries on their contents, have been published in *Proceedings of the World Bank Annual Conference on Development Economics, 1991.* Each paper deals with the special concerns of rapidly growing cities during the process of economic growth.

Mabogunje, Akin L. "A New Paradigm for Urban Development," pp. 191–208.

Mills, Edwin S. "Urban Efficiency, Productivity, and Economic Development," pp. 221–235.

Williamson, Jeffrey G. "The Macroeconomic Dimensions of City Growth in Developing Countries: Past, Present, and Future," pp. 241–261.

Appendix 9.1

Input-Output Analysis

Input-output analysis is a useful method of tracing the relationships among the various sectors of the economy. It was developed largely by the economist, Wassily

Leontief, who was later awarded the Nobel Prize in economics for this important contribution. Basically, input-output analysis consists of a set of linear equations that describe the linkages of production and consumption in an economy. Input-output analysis is fairly sophisticated and requires some knowledge of linear algebra, so hang on to your hat.

For starters, let's define a simplified economy that contains the four economic sectors: primary, secondary, tertiary, and quaternary. Each of the sectors consumes some of its own output, as well as output from the other sectors. In addition, households consume some output in final demand. For now, we will assume a closed economy so that none of the output is exported and there are no imports. In tabular form, our hypothetical economy looks like this:

Hypothetical Sectoral Production and Consumption

Units of Production Sectors	Units of Consumption					
	Sectors				Final Demand	Total Output
	P	S	T	Q		
Primary	20	70	10	10	10	120
Secondary	40	100	50	50	50	290
Tertiary	30	50	100	100	120	400
Quaternary	20	70	100	100	100	390

Note that the entries in the table are in some sort of "standard" units, such as money. The first part of the analysis is the calculation of technical input-output coefficients. These coefficients only concern the flows between the sectors, and not final demand or total output, so an interindustry transactions matrix, **R**, is extracted as follows:

Interindustry transactions matrix

	P	S	T	Q
P	20	70	10	10
S	40	100	50	50
T	30	50	100	100
Q	20	70	100	100

The technical coefficients are a matrix, **A**, that is calculated as follows:

$$\mathbf{A} = \mathbf{R} \times \hat{\mathbf{X}}^{-1} \qquad (9.7)$$

where $\hat{\mathbf{X}}^{-1}$ is the inverse of the diagonalized total output vector. In this case, we have:

Diagonalized total output vector

P	120	0	0	0
S	0	290	0	0
T	0	0	400	0
Q	0	0	0	390

and

The inverse of the diagonalized total output vector

P	0.0083	0	0	0
S	0	0.0034	0	0
T	0	0	0.0025	0
Q	0	0	0	0.0025

Resulting in the following:

The technical coefficients

	P	S	T	Q
P	0.167	0.241	0.025	0.026
S	0.333	0.345	0.125	0.128
T	0.250	0.172	0.250	0.256
Q	0.167	0.241	0.250	0.256

The technical coefficients tell us the amount of input from each sector that is required directly by a sector to produce one unit of its output. For example, the quaternary sector needs 0.026 unit of primary inputs, 0.128 unit of secondary inputs, and 0.256 unit of inputs from the tertiary sector and from itself to produce one unit of output. If we square the technical coefficients matrix ($\mathbf{A} \times \mathbf{A}$), we can find indirect input requirements that arise from multiplier effects. For example, when a unit of quaternary output is produced, it directly requires certain amounts of inputs from all sectors including itself, and these inputs in turn are outputs that require inputs, and so on and so on in so-called rounds of expansion. In this case, the second round coefficients are as follows.

The technical coefficients at the second round

	P	S	T	Q
P	1.119	0.134	0.047	0.048
S	0.223	1.252	0.115	0.118
T	0.204	0.225	1.154	0.158
Q	0.213	0.228	0.151	1.165

The full intersectoral impact of producing one unit of output is found by calculating a matrix called the Leontief inverse, $\mathbf{L}$, where

$$\mathbf{L} = (\mathbf{I} - \mathbf{A})^{-A}$$

$$(9.8)$$

where **I** is an identity matrix. In this case we have:

Leontief inverse

	P	S	T	Q
P	1.663	0.796	0.286	0.293
S	1.333	2.460	0.690	0.708
T	1.283	1.316	1.905	0.928
Q	1.237	1.419	0.929	1.952
Total	5.516	5.991	3.810	3.881

Each entry in the Leontief inverse matrix is an input-output multiplier on a sector-by-sector basis, and the sum of a column in the Leontief inverse is the aggregate multiplier for an individual sector. For example, after all the multiplicative effects are considered, an initial increase in demand of one unit of quaternary services would lead to an increase of 0.293 unit of primary-sector output, 0.708 unit of secondary output, 0.928 unit of tertiary services, and a total of 1.952 units of quaternary services. Altogether, an increase in demand for one unit of quaternary services leads to an aggregate output increase in the economy of 3.881 standard units.

Interregional input-output analysis is conducted in a similar way, except the input-output tables must have sectoral labels that also contain geographical information. In the following table, P1 and P2 stand for primary sectors in regions 1 and 2, respectively, and S1 and S2 concern the secondary sector in those regions.

	P1	P2	S1	S2
P1	20	0	50	20
P2	0	30	30	70
S1	50	50	100	70
S2	30	50	100	150

This example table shows a high level of interregional integration, except in the primary sector where the zero entries indicate that primary products are produced and consumed without any intrasectoral exchange. Again, technical coefficients can be calculated, as above:

Technical coefficients

	P1	P2	S1	S2
P1	0.222	0.000	0.185	0.061
P2	0.000	0.231	0.111	0.212
S1	0.555	0.385	0.370	0.212
S2	0.333	0.385	0.370	0.455

and, of course, they also show the lack of geographical integration within the primary sector. When the second-round impacts are calculated, however, the primary sector does reveal an indirect integration, with nonzero entries in all cells of the second-round matrix.

Technical coefficients at the second round

	P1	P2	S1	S2
P1	1.172	0.095	0.132	0.080
P2	0.132	1.178	0.145	0.169
P3	0.400	0.313	0.361	0.290
P4	0.431	0.406	0.410	1.387

SOURCE: Geoffrey J.D. Hewings, 1985: *Regional Input-Output Analysis*, Vol. 6 in Sage Scientific Geography Series (Beverly Hills, Calif.: Sage).

Appendix 9.2

Shift-Share Analysis

Shift-share analysis provides a decomposition of a region's economic change against the background of economic changes in the entire country. Usually, shift-share analysis concerns employment, but it can also be used to analyze revenues or other measures of economic activity. For an illustration of the shift-share method, let's use the following hypothetical data.

	Regional Employment*		National Employment*	
	Time		Time	
Sector	1	2	1	2
Primary	2	2	30	20
Secondary	5	7	100	90
Tertiary	8	10	100	150
Quaternary	3	5	75	90

*In thousands.

Look at some of the differences between the region and the country as a whole. For example, although primary-sector employment declined sharply across the whole country, it remained stable in the region. Secondary-sector employment increased in the region, but it declined at the national level.

Shift-share analysis considers that the changes in a region's employment can be divided into three components: a national share (NS), a regional share (RS), and an industry mix share (IM). The national share component is simply the region's portion of the national pattern of employment change. The regional share is that part of employment change that is due to special economic conditions in the region, and the industrial mix share takes into account the specific industrial structure of the region. The following equations are used to calculate the three shares:

$$NS = \sum_{i=1}^{n} e_i^0 \frac{E^t}{E^0} - \sum_{i=1}^{n} e_i^0 \qquad (9.9)$$

$$RS = \sum_{i=1}^{n} \left(e_i^t - e_i^0 \frac{E_i^t}{E_i^0} \right) \qquad (9.10)$$

$$IM = \sum_{i=1}^{n} \left(e_i^0 \frac{E_i^t}{E_i^0} - e_i^0 \frac{E^t}{E^0} \right) \qquad (9.11)$$

where E refers to national employment, e refers to regional employment, superscripts 0 and t indicate, respectively, the beginning and end of a time period, and the subscript i indicates an individual sector or industry. As a check, we have the condition that total change in regional employment equals the sum of the components, or $\Delta e = NS + IM + RS$. An additional measure is called total shift, TS, which expresses the difference between the actual change in regional employment and the change that would have occurred if the region's sectors grew at the national rates:

$$TS = IM + RS \qquad (9.12)$$

Plugging in the numbers from above:

$$NS = (2.30 + 5.75 + 9.20 + 3.45) - 18 = 2.70$$
$$RS = 0.67 + 2.50 + -2.00 + 1.4 = 2.57$$
$$IM = -0.970 + -1.25 + 2.80 + 0.15 = 0.73$$

and, finally,

$$TS = 0.73 + 2.57 = 3.30$$

So, during the time period the region gained 2.7 thousand jobs as its share of national employment change. Because of its particular characteristics, as measured in its regional share, almost 2.6 thousand jobs were added. In this case, its poor performance in the tertiary sector was overcome by strong growth in the other sectors. Its industrial mix was just barely positive as a source of regional job gains over the period, contributing only 730. By national standards, it has too much primary- and secondary-sector employment. However, it also has a large portion of fast-growing tertiary-sector employment. Finally, the region's total shift is the difference between its national share of employment change and its total change in employment of 6,000 jobs.

SOURCE: Hannu Tervo and Paavo Okko, 1983: "A Note on Shift-Share Analysis as a Method of Estimating the Employment Effects of Regional Economic Policy," *Journal of Regional Science*, Vol. 23, pp. 115–121.

Chapter 10

International Trade: Patterns and Management

This chapter

- describes the contemporary global pattern of trade

- outlines the geography and product composition of recent American trade

- provides a summary of various theories of international trade and their locational implications

- contains an outline of trade management within MNCs

- summarizes the various policies used by national governments to manage their country's international trade

- presents an outline of the current version of the General Agreement on Tariffs and Trade (GATT)

- covers environmentalists' concerns with international trade treaties

- raises the theoretical and practical issues of regional trade agreements among countries

Courtesy of New York Convention & Visitors Bureau Inc.

Trade and location can be taken as the two sides of a coin. International trade is the spatial interaction between two countries that arises from their complementarity with respect to supply and demand for goods and services. When you think about it, the complementarity that drives trade between two countries arises from differences in their locational characteristics. One of the countries, the country of demand, must be a relatively poor location for producing the traded product. Its relative costs of producing the product may be too high to satisfy domestic demand in terms of quality or quantity, or both. On the other hand, the country of supply must be a good location for producing the product, with relative costs that are low enough to promote production in excess of any domestic demand.

The statement that complementarity is the basis for trade is a truism that applies to trade between villages in the same local district as much it applies to international trade. What, then, makes international trade different from local trade? For one thing, the average distances involved are greater, so the transaction costs of spatial interaction can often be of critical concern to trade at the international scale. More importantly, there is a different, additional, set of transaction costs in international trade that does not affect local trade within countries. Trade between countries means trade between places with different governments and often very different political interests. Theoretically, free trade unhindered by governmental restriction should yield spatial interactions in the global economy that increase the economic efficiency of each trading country. While increasing its country's economic efficiency is usually an interest of any national government, that interest is often tempered by its interest in social equity for its country's population and often by interest in preserving its political power. Ultimately, patterns of international trade are based as much on political-economic foundations as they are on the economic complementarities among countries.

GLOBAL TRADE PATTERNS

International trade may be the dominant form of spatial interaction in the global economy, but its relative importance to the economies of individual countries varies on a number of counts. When we hold per capita national incomes constant, for example, we see that trade tends to be inversely proportional to the physical area of a country. Again holding per capita national incomes constant, we see a tendency for trade to be inversely proportional to the size of a country's economy as measured by its GNP. Both tendencies follow simple rules of spatial interaction. If the area of a country is large, the goods and services produced near its center may have relatively low levels of transferability compared to the goods and services produced near the border. Long internal distances don't detract much from the international transferability of products produced in a country with a small area. In addition, if a country's domestic economy is large, it provides a relatively large number of intervening opportunities for domestic trade as compared to the market potential of countries with smaller economies.

We don't really want to hold per capita national income constant for very long when we study international trade, however, because the importance of international trade to a country's economy is, in fact, related to its variation. Countries with low per capita national incomes export the least, on both an aggregate and a proportional basis, and rich countries export the most (Figure 10.1). This relationship between exports and income is one that is expected

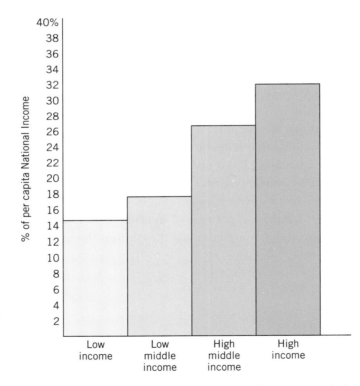

Figure 10.1 The value of per capita exports increases consistently with national wealth as a proportion of per capita national income. About 15% of per capita national income can be attributed to exports in the world's low-income countries, while 32% of per capita national income is earned from exports in the average high-income country. SOURCE: *World Development Report 1994* (New York: Oxford University Press).

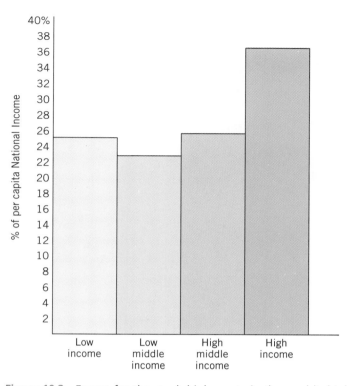

Figure 10.2 Except for the much higher rate in the world's high-income countries, the average country has per capita imports that are equivalent in value to about 25% of per capita national income. Source: *World Development Report 1994* (New York: Oxford University Press).

when international trade is viewed as a form of spatial interaction. Richer economies, simply by virtue of their wealth, are likely to form more complementary relationships with other countries than can poorer economies. Much of the wealth of rich countries comes from their ability to produce a wide variety, and large quantity, of goods and services. These goods and services that rich countries supply, in turn, are in demand in poor countries that do not produce such wide varieties and large quantities of goods and services, and they are in demand in other rich countries, too (Figure 10.2).

The composition of a county's exports also varies with its per capita national income (Figure 10.3). High proportions of the poorer countries' exports originate in their primary sectors (also see Chapter 11). They export commodities such as agricultural products and industrial raw materials, but relatively few manufactured goods. The proportion of manufactured exports increases consistently with a country's per capita national income, with nearly three-quarters of the average rich country's exports consisting of manufactured products. The high proportion of manufactured goods in rich countries' exports doesn't mean

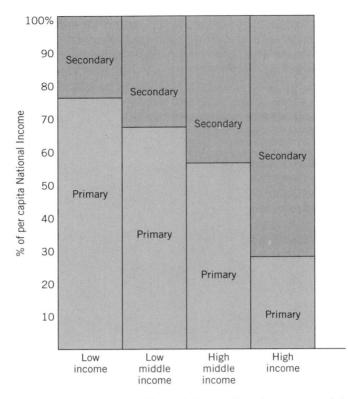

Figure 10.3 The composition of the merchandise exports of the world's low-income countries is heavily weighted toward commodities from the primary sector. The importance of primary exports decreases as incomes rise, and the world's richest countries have most of their merchandise exports originating in their secondary sectors. Source: *World Development Report 1994* (New York: Oxford University Press).

that they don't have significant primary-sector exports. Indeed, rich countries such as the United States, Canada, and Australia have significant exports of agricultural products and industrial raw materials. The proportion of manufactured goods in the composition of rich country exports doesn't indicate a shortage of primary products; instead, it points to the relative breadth of goods that rich countries have to offer in international markets as compared to the more limited exports of poorer countries.

Rich countries can also export a larger variety of services than poor countries can normally offer. You will recall from Chapter 8 that services are traded internationally and that their trade is increasing over time. In 1990, the global value of nonfactor services (excluding, for example, worker remittances) was ''only'' about one-sixth the value of merchandise trade at $3.2 trillion—but a half trillion dollars ($500,000,000,000) worth of trade is nothing to sneeze at. Many traded services, especially those involving tourism and even transportation can readily be supplied to international markets from a large number of countries regardless of their per capita national incomes. There are, however, many traded services such as business consulting and insurance that we would only expect to enter the global market from sources among the world's high-income economies.

The geographical pattern of international trade, at the global scale of analysis, is related to variations in per capita national incomes among countries as well, simply because those incomes go such a long way in determining the composition of trade between countries. The largest share of international trade is among the world's high-income countries; there is a smaller share of trade between rich countries and poor countries; and the smallest share of world trade at this scale is among the world's poorer countries. Rich countries are strongly complementary to each either because they are places with high levels of demand as well as places of large supply. There is less complementarity between rich and poor countries because poor countries sustain less demand in international markets than rich ones can, and the degree of complementarity between two poor countries is usually low because they are limited in both supply and demand.

This gross pattern of trade is expected from a gravity model of spatial interaction (see Chapter 6) that uses per capita national income as its measure of complementarity. Following the gravity model, we expect the greatest per capita trade flows around the world to occur between rich countries that are neighbors

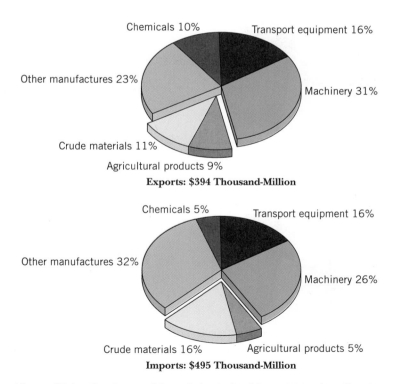

Figure 10.4 The Composition of the United States' Merchandise Exports and Imports in 1990. Source: Bureau of the Census, Economics and Statistics Administration, US Department of Commerce.

and the leanest flows in trade to take place between poor countries that are far apart. Although there are some exceptions, the expectations of trade patterns derived from the gravity model are usually fulfilled in the real world of the international economy.

Case 10.1, which focuses on the world's *big emerging markets* (*BEMs*), illustrates two common patterns of international trade. The BEMs are countries with large, growing economies. None of them, however, has a per capita national income that would place it among the world's high-income group. Currently, the BEMs' imports are led by capital equipment and other manufactured goods that are not readily available in their domestic economies. For the most part, the composition of their imports requires that they trade heavily with rich countries, and of the ten BEMs described in the case, the United States, Japan, or Germany is the leading source of imports for eight.

Where does the United States fit into the general pattern of world trade? Measured by per capita national income, the United States is one of the world's high-income countries and the composition of its exports is typical of the group (Figure 10.4). Four-fifths of its commodity exports came from its secondary

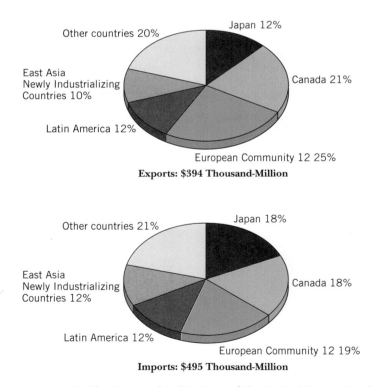

Exports: $394 Thousand-Million

Imports: $495 Thousand-Million

Figure 10.5 The Geographical Pattern of the United States' Merchandise Trade in 1990. Source: Bureau of the Census, Economics and Statistics Administration, US Department of Commerce.

Figure 10.6 Export Regions of the United States. SOURCE: "The International Flows of Industrial Exports from U.S. Regions," by Rodney A. Erickson and David J. Hayward, in *Annals of the Association of American Geographers*, Vol. 81, 1991, pp. 371–390.

Table 10.1 Leading Destinations of Foreign Industrial Exports from the United States and its Regions in 1987.*

Exports from:	Order of Trade Partners		
	First	Second	Third
United States	Europe	North America	Asia
Rocky Mountains	Asia	Europe	North America
Southwest	Asia	Central America	Europe
Plains	North America	Europe	Asia
Great Lakes	North America	Europe	Asia
South Central	Europe	North America	Asia
New England	Europe	Asia	North America
Mid Atlantic	Europe	North America	Asia
South Atlantic	Europe	Asia	North America

* See Figure 10.6.

SOURCE: "The International Flows of Industrial Exports from U.S. Regions," by Rodney A. Erickson and David J. Hayward, in *Annals of the Association of American Geographers*, Vol. 81, 1991, pp. 371–390.

sector, with machinery holding the largest share of six broad trade categories. Most of the United States' imports in 1990 came from the secondary sector, too, with transport equipment comprising the same share of American imports as American exports. Primary-sector commodities contributed 21% of imports and 20% of exports. In general, the United States appeared to have exported about the same kinds of goods that it imported in 1990 (a trade flow we consider again in the next section).

The geographical pattern of the United States' trade flows in 1990 was also typical of the trade geography of the world's other high-income countries (Figure 10.5). The bulk of American imports came from other high-income countries: Canada, Japan, and members of the European Community (now the European Union). Its exports followed the same basic tracks, with some adjustment in proportion. Regional analysis has revealed a geographical bias in American exports, which is likely due to distance decay effects in spatial interaction (Figure 10.6 and Table 10.1). The western parts of the country trade most heavily with Asia, especially Japan, and the eastern parts of the country have a greater proportion of their exports going to Europe. The central regions of the Great Lakes and Plains have their leading export destinations in other countries of North America, especially Canada.

◪ CASE 10.1
Big Emerging Markets in International Trade

The U.S. Department of Commerce is actively involved in promoting exports. In 1993, President Clinton announced a National Export Strategy for the United States, described as "a comprehensive plan that upgrades and cordinates the government's export promotion and export finance programs to help American firms compete in the global marketplace." In particular, the National Export Strategy identifies past problems with with U.S. trade promotion efforts and recommends improvements to current ones. This includes enhancing existing trade finance ones such as the Exim Bank and the Overseas Private Investment Corporation and creating a Tied Aid Fund to help U.S. firms compete on a level playing field. As an outcrop of this initiative, Commerce identified ten foreign nations as big emerging markets (BEMs) of the upcoming century, markets where the potential for trade growth is the largest.

It has long been recognized that exports play an important role in the U.S. economy because they support jobs and they represent a significant component of gross domestic product (GDP). Over the last few years, U.S. exports have contributed significantly to overall GDP growth. But targeting emerging markets is a new concept for the U.S. In the past, the nation could expect trade to expand steadily with its traditional trading partners—mainly Europe, Canada, and more recently, Japan. As the National Export Strategy was being developed, however, it became clear that the U.S. could not rely on these partners as a source of continued growth. In fact, trade with our traditional trading partners has been, and is projected to continue to be, flat. The next logical step was to determine where growth was likely to occur. Thus was born the BEM initiative.

In addition to growth potential, the ten BEMs have other traits in common. They are all physically large with large populations, have recently undergone some program of economic reform, are politically important to their region of the world, and are likely to spur growth within their regions. Where are these markets? Geographically they represent several parts of the world. In Asia they are China, Indonesia, India, and South Korea; in Latin America they are Mexico, Argentina, and Brazil; in Central and Southern Europe they are Poland and Turkey; in Africa it is South Africa.

Commerce estimates that the BEMs and other less developed countries will be the fastest growing import markets through the year 2010. By then, the BEMs are expected to account for 27 percent of total world imports, three times their 1992 share. U.S. firms will want to capture as much of that market as possible.

The Growing BEM Market

The BEM's share of world imports grew from 7.7 percent in 1988 to 9.3 percent in 1992. In the latter year, the BEMs imported $357 billion in commodities. The U.S. captured the largest share with nearly 22 percent, up from 20 percent in 1988. Japan held second place with approximately 14 percent, down from 17 percent in 1988. Germany captured nearly 9 percent, as it did throughout the period. South Korea and China are by far the largest of the BEMs in terms of total imports. In 1992, each of those two countries imported around $81 billion in goods. Mexico was the next largest with nearly $48 billion.

Two things stand out about the types of goods that the BEMs imported in 1992. First, the single largest import commodity was petroleum and petroleum products (mostly crude petroleum and fuel). Second, the next four largest import commodities were all in machinery and transportation equipment—electrical machinery (such as household appliances and switchgears), machines for special industries (such as textile and leather machinery), road vehicles, and general industrial equipment (such as heating and cooling equipment). Combined, these five commodity categories accounted for $124 billion, or about 35 percent of total BEM imports.

This collective import profile of the BEMs shows an emphasis on production rather than consumer goods, reflecting a desire to develop the capacity to produce their own goods for consumption or export. Given this desire, the BEMs need machinery imports to build an industrial structure or upgrade an existing one. Thus, several of the Asian BEMs' machinery imports are in the textile and apparel industries. Road vehicles, telecommunications, and electronics and electrical machinery are in demand in the Latin American BEMs, and machinery for special industries is in demand in several others, for example, industrial food processing machinery in Poland. To fuel these industries (literally), petroleum and petroleum products are needed—for the factories, equipment, workers' homes, workers' transportation, and so on.

Total import growth for the BEMs over the 1988–92 period was nearly 59 percent. By comparison, total world imports grew by 21 percent, U.S. imports grew by 21 percent, Japan's by 25 percent, and Germany's by 63 percent. Germany's spectacular increase can be attributed to the country's reunification and the increased demand resulting from the effort to bring the former East Germany up to par with the rest of the country (East Germany was not included in the 1988 data). In addition, the BEMs as a whole registered a higher average annual import growth rate than did either the U.S. or Japan, both of which have experienced recent periods of economic slowdown. However, Germany still outperformed the BEMs (on average) for the reason noted above.

Individually, BEM import growth ranged from a high of 179 percent for Argentina to a low of 7 percent for South Africa. In addition to Argentina, Mexico and Indonesia also had above-average import growth, rising 145 percent and 106 percent, respectively. South Africa's weaker gains were likely due to its overall stagnant economic growth that persisted through the early 1990s.

To summarize, the import profile of the BEMs over the last few years indicates that they are indeed growth markets. Import growth in seven of the ten BEMS exceeded world import growth, the types of goods the BEMs import are those most needed to support growing economies, and the major industrialized countries of the world have recognized the importance of serving these markets.

SOURCE: ''Big Emerging Markets and U.S. Trade,'' by Linda M. Aguilar and Mike A. Singer, in *Economic Perspectives*, Federal Reserve Bank of Chicago, Vol. 19, Issue 4, pp. pp. 2–6.

FOR DISCUSSION

Do the trade patterns described in this case conform more to factor endowment theory or to overlapping market theory?

THEORIES OF INTERNATIONAL TRADE

You will recall from earlier chapters that the locational requirements of producers can vary depending on whether their markets are competitive, oligopolistic, or monopolistic. Market structure plays an important role in determining optimal patterns of trade, too, which is not surprising because trade and location are the two sides of the same coin. Trade theories, like location theories, have been developed over time to deal with different market structures as well as changing technologies and even changing forms of business organization. However, the dominant theory of international trade, *comparative advantage theory*, applies to competitive markets. Like the location theory for competitive markets, comparative advantage theory focuses on differences in production costs between locations, which are most often taken as entire countries in the analysis of international trade.

COMPARATIVE ADVANTAGE

The theory of comparative advantage in international trade can be traced to the classical economist, Adam Smith. In 1776, he described the advantages of economic specialization in his book *The Wealth of Nations*. He wrote of the benefits that were achieved by the tailor sticking to sewing clothes and the cobbler sticking to the shoe business. Because they specialized in their efforts, more shoes and more clothes were available to the local villagers than if the tailor and cobbler each tried to make some shoes and some clothes. Smith's suggestion was that specialization led to greater efficiency in production, that each of the tradespeoples' skills were made greater as their experience in production grew. (Of course, in today's economy we would expect the tailor and cobbler to merge, forming an integrated apparel corporation that would subcontract most of its production to manufacturers in East Asia and Central America.)

Smith argued that what was good for the village's economy was good for the world economy as well. If individual countries specialized in their production, each would become more efficient and produce surpluses that could be traded for the surpluses produced in countries specializing in the production of other goods. The question that remained, however, was, which country should specialize in what product? That question was answered by David Ricardo, whose contribution to land-use analysis was described in Chapter 2. Ricardo demonstrated that national specializations in production could be selected on the basis of comparative costs, with the comparisons taking place both within and across national economies (Insights 10.1). Because some countries could produce certain products at comparatively lower costs than others, they were more efficient *locations* for production of those products. Efficiency leads to surplus, and the surplus is entered into international trade for the surpluses of the other products produced in other least-cost, specializing locations. With production based on specialization determined by comparative advantage, production costs are minimized, with the savings passed on to the world's consumers.

The comparative cost assessment indicates a competitive market in which consumer surplus is maximized and producer surplus, or location rent at the national scale, is eliminated. The increase in consumer surplus brought about by trade based on comparative advantage forms the foundation of most arguments for the benefits of free trade. If trade is restricted by government intervention, as free trade proponents argue, the gains to consumers from production patterns based on comparative advantage can't be realized. Free trade is required for countries to be able to specialize in production but still have the full variety of goods available for their citizens to consume. If trade is restricted, countries must produce goods and services in which they are relatively inefficient; in the absence of trade, costs go up, as does the potential for rents to producers, but consumer surpluses are lost.

➤ INSIGHTS 10.1
Comparative Advantage in Televisions and Tractors

The law of comparative advantage provides gains to participants in free trade as long as their costs of production are not perfectly identical. We'll use a hypothetical example of trade between Freedonia and Ruritania (two countries on the planet Xenon) in televisions (TVs) and tractors. The accompanying table lists initial conditions for developing trade based on comparative advantage and also provides a quantitative example of how the gains from trade might be realized.

The production costs of TVs and tractors are different in the two countries (see part A of the table). Reducing costs to hypothetical "factor units," we see that tractors are less expensive to produce in Ruritania than in Freedonia, and the same goes for TVs. (Except for cost of production, we'll assume that there is no difference between either the TVs or tractors produced in the two countries.) At the prevailing production costs in both countries, let's say they produce TVs and tractors in the amounts shown in part B of the table. Initially, they consume exactly what they produce, and no more, because trade between the two countries does not exist.

Even though Ruritania enjoys an absolute advantage in the production of both TVs and tractors, the law of comparative advantage guarantees it can gain from trade with Freedonia. As you might guess, it wouldn't do any harm for Freedonia to trade with Ruritania either. The benefits of trade have their source in the comparative costs of production of the two items, as described in part C of the table. Based on its domestic costs, every time a television is produced in Ruritania, that country gives up one-third of a tractor; and every time one tractor is produced, Ruritania gives up three TVs. In Freedonia, every time one TV is produced, one-half of a tractor is given up, and two TVs are given up for every tractor that comes off the production line.

Part C of the table allows us to compare costs between the two countries. The opportunity costs of tractor production are higher in terms of the number of foregone TVs in Ruritania (3) than in Freedonia (2), and the opportunity costs of TV production are higher in terms of the number of tractors foregone in Freedonia (0.500) than in Ruritania (0.333). These comparative opportunity costs lead us to the geographical pattern of trade. If all exchange is by barter, then we would have to pay three TVs for each tractor in Ruritania but only two TVs for each tractor originating in Freedonia. On the other hand, the cost of TVs in Ruritania is one-third of a tractor, but the price is higher, at one-half a tractor, in Freedonia. If you have TVs and want to buy tractors, buy them in Freedonia; if you have tractors and want to buy TVs, buy them in Ruritania.

TVs are comparatively cheaper in Ruritania, and tractors are relatively cheaper in Freedonia.

Based on their comparative costs, both Freedonia and Ruritania would be better off if they could specialize in producing what they produce more cheaply on a comparative basis. Such specialization can yield more output for any given level of cost, and the cost advantages should be passed along so that consumer surplus is raised in both trading countries. One possible result of trade between Ruritania and Freedonia in TVs and tractors is shown in part D of the table. Freedonia has given up TV production altogether to concentrate on producing tractors while Ruritania produces a lot more TVs than it did before trade. In this example, the gains from specialization in production and trade are taken in the form of tractors, with their consumption increasing in both countries without an addition to aggregate production costs.

TVs, Tractors, and Comparative Advantage

A. Production Costs

	Factor Units	
	TVs	Tractors
Ruritania	10	30
Freedonia	20	40

B. Production and Consumption without Trade

	Production		Consumption	
	TVs	Tractors	TVs	Tractors
Ruritania	600	200	600	200
Freedonia	300	150	300	150

C. Domestic Comparative Costs and Barter Terms of Trade

	Comparative Costs		Barter Terms of Trade	
	TVs/Tractors	Tractors/TVs	TVs/Tractors	Tractors/TVs
Ruritania	10/30 (0.333)	30/10 (3.000)	3/1	1/3
Freedonia	20/40 (0.500)	40/20 (2.000)	2/1	1/2

D. Possible Production and Consumption with Trade

	Production		Consumption	
	TVs	Tractors	TVs	Tractors
Ruritania	900	100	600	225
Freedonia	0	300	300	175

FACTOR ENDOWMENT THEORY

Although Ricardo answered the question of how a country's specialization in production could be determined by analysis of comparative costs, his explanation in turn raised the question of why costs should vary from country to country in the first place. This question was answered by the economist Bertil Ohlin in his extension of comparative advantage theory called *factor endowment theory*. According to this theory, the source of any cost advantage in a country, or any region for that matter, is its factor endowments. Some countries are relatively well endowed with capital as a factor of production, for example, whereas other countries may be relatively well endowed with labor or with certain kinds of raw materials. The relative abundance of those factors means that they have relatively low costs that lead to comparative advantage in a certain type of production. Now, recall that different industries have different factor intensities (Chapter 3); that is, some use relatively more of one factor of production than other factors. Locational efficiency arises when matches are made between regions that are well endowed with a particular factor and industries that use that factor intensively in their production. As in Ricardo's version of comparative advantage theory, least-cost production generates surpluses that can be traded for the surpluses of different products produced in different countries with different factor endowments.

As you can see, factor endowment theory is as much a least-cost theory of location as it is a theory of international (or interregional) trade. Trade in the factor endowment model can be viewed, in some respects, as secondary in importance to the optimization of production locations, both in terms of minimizing costs and maximizing consumer surplus through the elimination of location rents. Trade is not even a perpetual activity if we follow factor endowment theory to its logical conclusion. If industries with the appropriate factor intensities are located in those countries with the appropriate factor endowments, then the efficient use of the cheap factors in producing surpluses will eventually drive the price of the factors up. The consumption of the factors diminishes their endowment and therefore undermines the region as a least-cost location. This is most apparent in the case of natural resource industries, especially those using nonrenewable resources. The best, or cheapest, resource is consumed initially, but then more costly lower quality resources will have to be used in order to maintain production (see Chapter 5).

Eventually, the cost of production would rise to a point that would be equal to its cost in other regions, even though those regions had smaller initial endowments. Such *factor price equalization* leads to the elimination of trade based on comparative factor costs, because factor costs no longer vary from region to region. Factor costs can equalize across regions even if they are not physically consumed by intensive use. The cost of labor, for example, should increase as more and more labor-intensive industry is established, and the cost of capital should rise in the same way. In addition, factor mobility can lead to factor price equalization across countries. If labor is paid less in one country because of its large endowment, then workers can migrate to regions where they can earn more. If relatively low interest rates indicate that capital is in effective surplus, than investment can flow across borders to countries where it is paid more for its services. Labor migration from poorer countries to richer countries is a common enough form of spatial interaction, and has been for centuries. International capital flows are also becoming increasingly common in the global economy (recall the discussion of FDI in Chapter 7).

Factor price equalization is a corollary of the *law of one price*, which states that the price of any mobile good or service will eventually be the same in every place where it is sold. This "law" results from the tendency of mobile goods and services to flow from places where their price is low, where they are in surplus, to places where their price is higher, where they are in short supply. As in the case of factor price equalization, the flow away from places of surplus causes the surplus to shrink, while the flow into places with shortages causes supplies to rise. Eventually, surpluses are reduced and shortages are filled so that supplies, and therefore prices, are equal everywhere.

The law of one price is violated as often as laws prohibiting teenagers smoking cigarettes. Because it is so easily violated, factor price equalization is only approached, but never achieved, and so we can expect international trade to continue well into the future. There are several reasons why factor price equalization is difficult to realize in the real world and why the law of one price is so easily broken. One reason is that many goods are subject to *factor intensity reversals*; that is, at one point, their production is intensive in one factor, and at another point, either in time or geographically, their production is intensive in another factor. Textile production, for example, is capital intensive in Western Europe, Japan, and the United States, but labor intensive in China, Southeast Asia, and Central America. The product life-cycle model considered in Chapter 7 describes a locational shift in a product's production over time which is effectively based on a change in its factor intensity. As its factor intensity changes, its best location for production switches to places with the appropriate factor endowment. Because of the ability to relocate production, the flows that would ordinarily equalize factor prices don't get a chance to do so.

Even beyond the possibility of factor intensity reversals, institutional, social, and cultural factors serve to maintain relative factor prices in the face of trade or to change factor prices in a way that cannot be accomplished by flows across markets. The use of child labor and the violation of labor laws in order to keep costs low are described in Case 10.2. In some countries, the use of child labor is acceptable, but in others it is not. In some countries, labor organizations bargain with management for their rates of pay, and in other countries they do not. The use of child labor can be viewed as a method of ensuring that wages do not rise to the higher levels enjoyed in countries where child labor is prohibited, and labor organizations try to ensure that their members' wages don't decrease to levels that prevail where organized labor is less successful. Both child labor and unions repress a market tendency toward wage equalization.

In addition to potential factor intensity reversals and important differences in culture and institutions, real-world economies, as opposed to theoretical ones, have to contend with the costs of spatial interaction. The cost of spatial interaction in trade and the way it reduces its consumer benefits from theoretical levels are illustrated in Figure 10.7. The cost of transportation draws down consumer surplus and raises potential economic rents to domestic producers. In effect, transport costs are an additional cost of production that domestic producers don't have to pay. Domestic producers are like the farmers near the center of the market in the von Thünen land-use model discussed in Chapter 2. Rents are greater where transport costs are lower in that context, and they are in this one, too. Higher rents mean lower consumer surplus, and transport costs affect domestic consumers and domestic producers in the same way; benefits are reduced. (Tariffs in international trade act the same way as do transport costs, as you will see later in this chapter.)

Transport costs are additions to costs of production in one place that are actually imposed in another place. This strange-sounding situation keeps the law of one price from ever being perfectly enforced either in international or interregional markets. There are other conditions that limit "free" trade, which

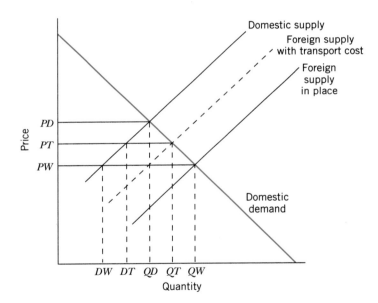

Figure 10.7 In the absence of transportation costs, trade allows consumers to take advantage of a supply shift to the right, from domestic levels to world levels. At equilibrium, domestic demand would pay price *PW* for quantity *QW* with trade, as opposed to the higher domestic price of *PD* for the smaller quantity *QD* if trade did not exist. The impact of transportation costs, however, is the effective shift to the left of the foreign supply schedule, raising prices at equilibrium to *PT* and shrinking quantity consumed to *QT* from the larger supply *QW* that could be consumed if transport costs did not exist. Producer surplus is reduced with trade as prices decrease and domestic production is cut from *QD* to *DW*. With transport costs, however, some of the domestic producer surplus is restored with production levels raised to *DT*.

only affect interaction in international markets. Some of these conditions arise from corporate and government efforts to manage trade flows between countries for their own particular purposes. Currency exchange rates are a particularly important consideration in international trade flows. The particular value of a country's currency as measured in the currency of another country can result from several conditions (Insights 10.2). If exchange rates are determined in financial markets instead of goods markets, they can have an effect on prices that is unrelated to production costs in the way that comparative advantage theory describes.

➤ INSIGHTS 10.2
How Currency Exchange Rates Are Determined

Exchange rates can be determined in three basic ways. One way is by comparing prices across countries. For example, if a loaf of bread in Canada costs C$2.00 and the exact same kind of loaf costs US$1.50 in the United States (and the same relative prices hold across a wide variety of products), the American dollar will be worth worth 1.33 Canadian dollars (2.00/1.50), or the Canadian dollar will be worth 75 U.S. cents (1.50/2.00). In other words, relative prices give each American dollar the purchasing power of 1.33 Canadian dollars, or each Canadian dollar has the purchasing power of 75 cents in the United States.

Second, money supply comparisons can be used to determine the exchange rate. Continuing with our hypothetical comparison of the United States and Canada, let's say that the American economy is exactly 10 times the size of the Canadian economy, but the United States only has 7.5 times the amount of its dollars in circulation as there are Canadian dollars in circulation. Based on their relative money supplies, the American dollar would be worth C$1.33 simply because of the disparity in their money supplies as compared to the difference in the size of their economies. For all practical purposes, the relative money supplies tell us the relative purchasing powers of the two currencies.

The third basic way of determining exchange rates is through comparison of capital markets. For example, let's say that after all taxes and other transaction costs are accounted for, the real rate of interest in Canada on a 30-day loan is 5%, and it's only 3.75% in the United States. The interest rate difference simply means that you can earn more money investing in Canada than investing in the United States. Under this condition, each American dollar is worth 75 Canadian cents and each Canadian dollar is worth U.S. $1.33. This exchange rate is, of course, just the opposite of what was derived under the hypothetical conditions given earlier, and, indeed, it's not unusual for goods markets to tell foreign exchange traders one thing and investment markets to tell them another. Because of disparities between short-term financial conditions and longer term conditions in economies, exchange rates tend to fluctuate as they are determined in one way for a short term and in another, perhaps conflicting, way for longer term purposes.

Governments frequently try to change market-based currency valuations by actively participating in currency markets. If a government thinks its currency is undervalued, for example, it can buy it from foreign sources at higher than the going market rate using other currencies it has on hand. This kind of intervention tends to have more of a symbolic than a real effect, however, because currency markets are so large that government purchases represent only a tiny proportion of their volume.   ◄

■ *CASE 10.2*
Comparative Advantage in Labor-Intensive Production

News Item 1: In a widening investigation of the apparel industry, the U.S. Labor Department notifies more than a dozen of the nation's largest retailers that goods made by 70 illegal Thai immigrants working in virtual slavery in El Monte, Calif., may have ended up in their stores. The goods are seized under a federal law known as the "hot goods" provision.

News Item 2: The National Labor Committee, a New York organization that lobbies for worker's rights in the U.S. and abroad, accuses the Gap of contracting with an El Salvador firm that has sweatshop conditions.

News Item 3: U.S. Sen. Tom Harkins, D-Iowa, introduces a bill that would ban imported goods made by children under age 15.

Sweatshops? Child labor? Hot-goods raids? The clothing industry is certainly no stranger to these ills, but most consumers probably think sweatshops went out with bloomers.

Well they haven't.

Americans want lower prices and better deals. In an effort to supply such merchandise, retailers are sometimes less than stringent in checking on working conditions of their suppliers.

"The momentum is for the contractor to bid as low as possible so he gets the work," Maria Echaveste, head of the wage and hour division of the U.S. Labor Department said on "60 Minutes" last week. "In turn, the contractor wants to get some kind of profit, but where does that profit come from? By not paying attention to the labor laws, by denying people their minimum wage and overtime."

This can cause headaches for shoppers who want to have a clear conscience when clothes shopping.

What do you do then? Ask the Clerk at The Gap where the shirt was made?

"No, that's not really effective," says the Rev. David Schilling of the Interfaith Center on Corporate Responsibility in New York. "What you need to do is let the corporate offices of the clothing companies know this is an issue you care about."

The Gap has a set of sourcing principles and guidelines stating that the company doesn't tolerate discrimination, forced labor or child labor and that it encourages safe working conditions and legal wages and hours.

"The tough part is enforcing these codes of conduct," Schilling says. "We hear that Levi Strauss is a company with a good track record in that area."

"We make our products all over the world and do have subcontractors," says company spokesman Sean Fitzgerald. "But we have teams of auditors who check the factories to make sure the vendors are following our codes of conduct. If they don't, we often give them some time to fix the problems. But if that fails, we cancel the contract."

Levi's is a manufacturer as well as a merchant.

Filene's, for the most part, is a merchant, although May Department Stores, its parent company, does contract for private-label clothing.

"We have our code of conduct printed right on our purchase orders," says Jim Abrams, vice president of corporate communications for the May Co. "We expect our vendors to meet the Fair Labor Standards Act."

Abrams said the company "is still looking into" whether any of the merchandise seized by the Labor Department during the Aug. 14 raid at the El Monte factory was headed for May stores.

READ THE LABELS

Labelling can offer some clues for a shopper who wants to do the right thing.

Merchandise carrying labels with either the ILGWU (International Ladies Garment Working Union) or the ACTWU (Amalgamated Clothing and Textile Workers Union) assures that the workers received a fair wage. The two unions recently merged into UNITE, with a combined membership of 401,000, and a new label is being designed for future use.

Garments that say either "Made in the USA" or "Crafted with Pride in the USA" means the items are from fabric made and assembled in this country.

"Does that absolutely, positively mean that everyone got a fair wage? I can't guarantee that 100 percent, but we do everything we can to make sure that's true," says Robert Swift, executive director of Crafted with Pride. "I wasn't surprised about the El Monte raid. It just shows that they are bringing sweatshop conditions that are prevalent in Southeast Asia into this country."

CHILD-LABOR ABUSES

Recently, the U.S. Department of Labor issued a report, "By the Sweat of Children: The Use of Child Labor in American Imports." The National Consumers League, a fraud information center, condensed the report in its March issue of *Child Labor Monitor.*

Among the countries cited for child-labor abuses in the garment industry were Bangladesh, Brazil, China, Guatemala, India, Indonesia, Lesotho, Mexico, Morocco, the Philippines, Portugal and Thailand.

On May 20, the Child Labor Coalition, run by the National Consumers League, called for a boycott of clothing from Bangladesh to protest the rejection by that country's garment makers of a plan to end child labor in their industry. The league advised shoppers to "check the label and refuse to buy garments made in Bangladesh."

The United States buys about 60 percent of the garments made there. In 1994, the U.S. imported nearly $900 million in Bangladesh apparel. On July 4, a Memorandum of Understanding was signed to set up a survey of factories and to establish appropriate school programs for the children put out of work.

"We hope that if consumers voice enough concern about this, then something will get done," Schilling says. "It's a complicated world-wide issue, and not easily fixed."

Source: "The Sweatshop Dilemma: How Can we Buy with a Clear Conscience?" by Donna Larcen, in *The Hartford Courant*, August 23, 1995, pp. E1, E3. By permission of the *Hartford Courant*.

FOR DISCUSSION

Should human rights issues be treated separately from trade issues in international treaties?

TRADE IN OLIGOPOLISTIC AND MONOPOLISTIC MARKETS

Comparative advantage theory and its extension in factor endowment theory concern trade in competitive markets, so they have to be modified for use in analyzing trade in oligopolistic or monopolistic markets. For example, although factor costs are critical to factor endowment theory's determination of the optimal location of production, other production cost variations should be considered when assessing trade flows in many industries. If an industry can enjoy economies of scale in its production process, then its cost of production will decrease as its output increases regardless of its factor costs. This means that certain industries are more efficiently located in large markets, even if labor costs, or the costs of other factors of production, are high. Think of the big auto producers around the world, such as General Motors, Volkswagen, and Toyota. Although they all have production sites in a number of places, the bulk of their production takes place not where production costs are low, but where markets are large. The economies of scale that they achieve in large markets overcome the typically higher costs of factors in those places.

Many industries are like the automobile industry—oligopolistic and subject to economies of scale in production. Sometimes trade in the goods produced in these industries is called *noncompetitive trade* because the market sizes necessary to generate their economies of scale don't exist in many countries around the world. Small markets can't support production of such goods, so they certainly aren't going to be exporting them. When you think about it, noncompetitive trade is not too different from the kind of regional trade described in central place theory. Countries with large markets providing economies of scale are the high-order places of the international economy, and those countries with small markets and lacking economies of scale are the lower order places.

MARKET THEORIES OF INTERNATIONAL TRADE

If we think of economies of scale as a factor of production in their own right, then factor endowment theory can help explain a lot of trade that takes place in the world today: trade between rich and poor countries. Rich countries export capital-intensive and economies-of-scale intensive goods and services to poor countries for labor-intensive goods and services. Factor endowment theory doesn't do such a good job, however, of explaining the dominant pattern of trade: trade between rich countries, and exports and imports of the same types of goods. These flows contradict factor endowment theory because: (a) trade is taking place between countries with the same factor endowments (heavy on the capital side), and (b) trade in the same type of goods, or *intraindustry trade,* means that the specialization required for trade isn't based on differences in production cost.

The economist Staffan Burnestam-Linder developed an *overlapping market theory of international trade* that accounts for just the type of trade that can't be explained by factor endowment theory. In this theory, trade between countries results from their overlapping markets: similarities in their demand and preferences for particular types of goods and services. If the similarities are strong, then trade between the two countries can be expected to be heavy; if the similarities are weak, then trade between the two countries can be expected to be light. Any good, and many services, produced in a country can be considered a potential export (or a potential import). If consumers in another country like its style or durability or any other quality, they will want to import it. If a country produces a product that is unwanted in other countries' markets, on the other hand, then the product's export potential will be low. Because this theory focuses on demand, and not production costs, it is especially applicable to those markets with oligopolistic or monopolistic structures.

Burnestam-Linder suggested that the degree of similarity between two markets could be approximated by the closeness of two countries' per capita national incomes. People with about the same income like the same things and will trade heavily with each other. If incomes are far apart, then there is little overlap and the potential for trade is low, unless the trade is based on comparative advantage. Although this theory implies that trade between two poor countries is likely because of income similarities, such trade is limited because low incomes make demand weak. The potential for trade between two wealthy countries is very

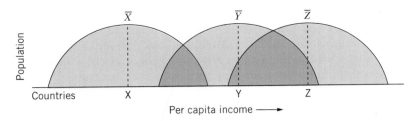

Figure 10.8   The means of the income distributions of countries X, Y, and Z are labeled $\bar{X}$, $\bar{Y}$, and $\bar{Z}$, and show the center points of the three markets. Shaded areas indicate overlaps in the income distributions that are equivalent to the potential for trade among the three countries that would be expected under overlapping market theory.

high because their wealth makes their markets strong and wealthy countries generally produce a wide variety of goods and services that can be traded. The geographer Andreas Grotewold extended the overlapping markets theory to include industry as well as individual consumers. If industrial patterns are similar, as they often are among rich countries, then the demands of the industrial sector will be similar as well and contribute to the potential for trade.

The trade effect of overlapping markets is illustrated in Figure 10.8. Trade between countries Y and Z would be the greatest of any pair of countries in the figure, because their income distributions have the greatest overlap. The poorer people in country Z have about the same incomes as the richer people in country Y, and a similarity in their preferences and demand for goods and services is expected. With less overlap in the incomes of people in countries Y and X, the potential for trade is less. The richest people in X do not have the incomes of the poorest people in Z, so trade between countries X and Z is not expected.

According to *differentiated market theory*, people with different incomes will demand not only a different variety of goods and services, but also a different variety of a single good or service. The effect of this relationship on international trade between overlapping markets can be illustrated in the context of some automotive exports to the American market. In Figure 10.9, the American market

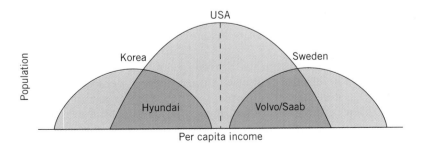

Figure 10.9   American imports of automobiles from Sweden and from Korea can be considered an example of trade based on overlapping markets.

is represented in the central income distribution; it's not the richest of the three economies based on per capita income, but it does have the largest market. Sweden has a higher per capita income, and its market overlaps with the high end of the market in the United States. The Republic of (South) Korea has a lower per capita income with a distribution that overlaps with the lower end of the income distribution of the United States. Based on these overlapping market characteristics, it's not surprising that Korea exports inexpensive Hyundais to the United States, whereas Sweden sells Americans the more expensive Volvos and Saabs.

Many variations exist, but two general trade theories seem to be applicable to today's global economy. First, factor endowment theory (an extension of the theory of comparative advantage) serves pretty well in telling us about the spatial interaction across competitive markets in the world economy. It provides an explanation for trade between rich and poor countries (and all trade in raw materials) based on principles of cost minimization that are also relevant to locational analysis for businesses in competitive markets. Second, the overlapping market theory accounts for trade between countries with the same factor endowments and in the same products. It has the same focus on markets in international trade that applies to the location models for businesses that operate in oligopolistic and monopolistic markets.

Both factor endowment theory and overlapping market theory concern the attributes of countries, or regions, as the bases for their trade patterns, but they omit the important consideration of the effects of distance on trade. Distance is important, of course, because it has a bearing on prices. In addition, distance between places also acts to limit the market knowledge of both producers and consumers. Producers, even when they are geared especially toward export markets, are more likely to produce for known tastes and preferences than unknown or uncertain ones. Consumers, on the other hand, develop their tastes and preferences from their experience with goods and services that they know, and their knowledge of foreign products can be expected to decrease with distance from their source. Trade has expanded around the world so rapidly over the last few years in part because people are becoming more familiar, through both personal experience and mass media channels, with goods and services produced in more distant places. Spatial interaction has an effective positive feedback loop in many circumstances, including international trade, so that once it begins it tends to increase in frequency and scope.

THE MNC AND MANAGED TRADE

The trade theories we've just reviewed were developed to explain trade that occurs under conditions free from the interferences that alter international flows. However, many companies pursue *trade management* policies that are designed to alter trade flows and trade volumes in ways that they they expect to be advantageous to their particular interests. In some circumstances, special corporations have been established to handle the international trade of other corporations that actually manufacture goods or provide services. The corporations are linked, even though they are legally distinct entities. Their separation allows them to specialize in a way that would have made Adam Smith happy, and their specialization allows them to be better at what they do. The most famous of the trading corporations are the *sogo shoshas* of Japan. When many Japanese products are purchased in the United States, for example, they are not purchased directly from their producer in Japan, but from the sogo shosha which acts as a type of international wholesaler.

Another form of managed trade takes place within multinational coporations (MNCs), which operate their own systems of international spatial interaction. Because most units of an MNC are potential producers and potential consumers, most MNCs participate in *intracorporate trade*, in which buying and selling takes place across national boundaries but within the corporation. This process is illustrated in Case 10.3 on Asea Brown Boveri, a European MNC. It has been estimated that intracorporate trade may amount to 40% of all American trade, and because the United States has been running a chronic trade deficit, American-headquartered MNCs are often targeted as strong contributors to the shortfall. Often MNCs are called *transnational corporations* in recognition not only of their global extent but also of their apparent indifference to the interests of individual countries. Recent estimates reveal that if trade balances were calculated using transactions involving American interests rather than transactions crossing national boundaries, the United States would have a positive trade balance.

Intracorporate trade has two basic motives. One motive is simple economic efficiency in production and results in trade that conforms to international trade theory, even though it occurs within a single corporation. For example, the geographical extent of an MNC may allow it to produce the individual components that make up a finished product in different parts of the world based on their factor intensities. If one component of a good is capital intensive in its production, it can be produced where capital is relatively inexpensive. If another part required in the finished good is labor intensive in its production, then it can be manufactured where there is a large relative endowment of labor. When the finished good is finally assembled, it will have been built with parts from other countries, but not necessarily parts from other companies. Some governments encourage intracorporate trade by implementing special low tariff rates on goods assembled outside of their own borders using parts produced within their national territory. The United States' *Caribbean Initiative*, for example, is a policy designed to spur economic growth in that region by encouraging American companies to assemble products there for import back into the United States. Many European countries have the same sort of trade provisions with many of the poorer countries that they used to hold as colonies.

Another motive for intracorporate trade is tax avoidance, which is legal, and sometimes even tax evasion, which is not. Most countries collect income taxes on corporate earnings, but there are many differences from country to country concerning which earnings qualify for taxation, investment tax credits, and so on. MNCs can use *transfer pricing*, a special system of preferential pricing between entities within the corporation, to manipulate their tax bills. This system is most often used to make costs of operation look high, and therefore profits look low, in countries with high income tax rates. Companies can produce in a high-tax country, sell their output to another corporate division in a low-tax country at a loss, and not have to pay any income taxes. In turn, the corporate division in the low-tax country sells the product at market prices and appears to make all the profits, but at the lower tax rate.

Some countries are *tax havens*, with little or no real tax liabilities placed on producers. Tax haven countries use their low-tax rates to recruit foreign producers, with the payoff of improving their citizens' employment prospects and generating domestic multiplier effects (see Chapter 9). Ireland, for example, has operated as a tax haven for manufacturers, and many have arranged for the bulk of their profits to show up on the books of their Irish operations by using transfer pricing methods.

◪ CASE 10.3
International Production and Trade in an MNC

There are probably only a few MNCs in the world today which could be called truly global firms, and that own, organize and manage an international production network. Among those few firms is Asea Brown Boveri (ABB), which was formed in a 1987 merger of the Swedish firm Asea with the Swiss firm Brown Boveri.

The structure and management practices of ABB place it among the few truly global corporations operating in the world economy: it comprises 1,300 companies located throughout the world, 130 of them in developing countries; its eight corporate board members are from five different countries; it has adopted an official language (English) for major transactions; and its 5,000 profit centers report all financial information in United States dollars to a single location, to allow for cross-border analysis. The firm is organized into a matrix structure, in which businesses are responsible to both a global leader as well as a national president. Leaders of the 50 business areas of ABB are based throughout the world and manage their operations on a global basis, devising overall strategies as regards exports, capacity and employee development; the leader of the power transmission business, for instance, is a Swede based in Germany, managing 25 factories in 16 countries. At the same time, the 1,300 individual companies that make up the 50 Business Areas each belong to a national company, and must prove themselves competitive on a national basis. This structure, which the company's president and CEO characterizes as "multidomestic," allows ABB to compete as if it were a national company in industries where local presence is important (such as locomotives), while at the same time drawing on the corporation's global resources in such areas as core technologies, design, component manufacturing, managerial expertise and finance. The management strategy of combining the advantages of globalization (economies of scale in both production and purchasing), along with the responsiveness of a national firm (ABB has companies in 140 countries), has led to the emergence of a globally integrated production and distribution system which involves extensive cross-border flows of goods and services, people, technology and know-how.

The operations of ABB reflect many of the trends of the new world economy, in which MNCs account for an increasing share of the world's trade, technology, financial and knowledge flows; in which economic distances are being shortened by new communication and information technologies; and in which regional integration is leading to the emergence of regional MNC-controlled production networks. From very low levels in 1989, the exports of ABB have grown to $1 billion and are expected to double in the next few years, particularly as North American and Eastern European operations achieve targeted export levels; its 1991 R&D budget totalled $2.3 billion; it has created its own private satellite networks to communicate with affiliates in countries with poor communications infrastructure; it manages its own Business Information Center; its World Treasury Center mobilizes financial resources for its global operations; and it makes large investments in management training for its newly-acquired personnel. Developing countries, where ABB employs some 34,000 employees and which account for $6 billion in revenues, currently serve mainly as markets for ABB exports from North America and Europe as well as sites for local-market production. ABB has targeted the Asian region, which currently accounts for about 15 percent of revenues, for major growth in the next few years. Selected developing countries, such as Brazil, are also emerging as important export bases for the global distribution network of ABB.

In addition to cross-border flows of goods, capital equipment and training, technology and know-how are important resource flows within the ABB network. Business areas regularly rotate personnel to share expertise. Moreover, a corporate R&D organization regularly combines resources from several parts of the organization, to centralize efforts that promise to yield company-wide benefits. At a less formal level, ABB consolidates research data, knowledge and experiences from various affiliates to be utilized in product development throughout the firm.

Finally, flows of goods, technology, information and management are complemented by movements of capital and services within ABB. The firm's Financial Services business, offering a full range of services including finance, treasury operations and insurance, is managed as a separate profit center which competes with outside financial service providers for the financing of ABB operations. As such, its relations with ABB's industrial operations are carried out on an arm's-length basis, with the goal of maximizing synergies within the organization.

The structure of ABB and the geographical scope of its activities are at the forefront of a relatively small number of companies whose operations may be characterized as ''global.'' To the extent to which other companies adopt similar strategies, they lay the foundation for a global production system, integrating both industrial as well as service activities. Under such a system, countries are integrated into the international economy through the activities of MNCs, involving not only investment but also cross-border flows of goods and services, information, technology, personnel and finance.

SOURCE: "Asea Brown Boveri: An International Production Network," Box X.2 in *World Investment Report 1992: Transnational Corporations as Engines of Growth* (New York: United Nations).

FOR DISCUSSION

Consider the balance of FDI and trade within ABB
in the context of the eclectic model of FDI described
in Chapter 8.

GOVERNMENT AND MANAGED TRADE

Governments manage trade as part of their overall economic policy and as a means of providing benefits to particular interest groups. The most common instrument of trade management is the *import tariff*, which is a tax collected on goods or services as they enter one country from another. *Specific tariffs* are fixed taxes collected by the weight or volume of a shipment, and *ad valorem tariffs* are taxes determined as a proportion of the price of the foreign product. In either form, tariffs are like most taxes on producers because they wind up being paid by consumers (Insights 10.3). Their general results are to limit imports, raise domestic prices, provide government revenue, and lower consumer surplus by increasing the potential rents of domestic producers. In most countries, tariff collections are not major contributors to government revenue; their primary purpose is therefore *trade protectionism*, the protection of selected domestic producers from foreign competition.

Two types of industries traditionally have been chosen for trade protection: *infant industries*, those that are just getting established in a domestic economy, and *sunset industries*, those that have seen better days in domestic markets and appear to be heading toward decline. Infant industry protection is usually designed to give start-up industries time to develop without competition from foreign producers that may have advantages in competition due to their economies of scale. As the protected producers grow, they achieve their own economies of scale, and the tariffs can be reduced to less protective levels. For example, the early textile industry and the early auto industry in the United States were both protected as infant industries. Some governments have attempted to induce domestic industrial growth by enacting very high tariffs over most products in a policy of *import substitution*. These policies have not been effective; many of them have backfired and caused domestic economies to stagnate rather than grow (see Chapter 11).

The protection of sunset industries, such as current textile or steel production in Western Europe and the United States, is most often based on the political economy of entrenched interests pursuading their government to provide them with what amounts to a fixed share of the domestic market. It is not unusual for trade protection of sunset industries to result from a rare coordination of efforts by both management and labor toward their common purpose of keeping their jobs. The most common argument for protection of sunset industries is that the foreign competition faced by domestic producers has unfair advantages, or that their own government provides them with undue burdens, that keep the sunset industry from maintaining its traditional large share of the domestic market.

➤ INSIGHTS 10.3
Domestic Gains and Losses Associated with Tariffs

A domestic economy has three interests that may be affected by the imposition of a tariff (or any instrument of trade management): its producers, its consumers, and the government itself. In general, any tariff will raise producer incomes, lower consumer welfare, and provide the government with some revenue. The gains to the producers and the government are paid for by the consumers who pay higher prices than when trade is unrestricted.

The specific gains and losses associated with the imposition of a tariff are illustrated in Figure 10.10. Let's say that there is some initial world price, *PW*, being paid in a country for a particular product, semiconductors, for example. Only a few suppliers in the country represented in Figure 10.10 can serve the domestic market at the world price, and domestic production only provides *SW* quantity of semiconductors, with the rest of domestic demand satisfied by imports. Let's also say that the government, after due deliberation and consultation with members of the domestic semiconductor industry, imposes a tariff that raises the price of semiconductors from *PW* to *PT*. The higher price allows the domestic industry to supply quantity *ST* of semiconductors to domestic demand, and shrinks imports by the difference between quantities *SW* and *ST*.

As you know, when prices rise without any increase in associated production costs, producers enjoy increasing economic rents. The imposition of a tariff, by raising prices, causes producer rents to increase in this example by the amount represented in area 1 of Figure 10.10. Producer rent comes at the consumers' expense. In this case, the tariff causes consumers to pay an additional amount for semiconductors that is equal to the sum of areas 1, 2, 3, and 4 in the diagram. The government collects an amount equal to area 3, so the final tally of the tariff's effect is producers and government win, and consumers lose.

Note that we have a little discrepancy between the amounts of gain to producers and government on one hand and the loss to consumers on the other. The two triangles labeled areas 3 and 4 in Figure 10.10 represent amounts that don't wind up in either producer or government pockets. They combine as a so-called deadweight loss to the domestic economy, an amount over and above the extra consumer spending on semiconductors that is not just a transfer from consumers to producers or the government. Some trade analysts would add two more amounts to the economy's deadweight loss incurred through trade

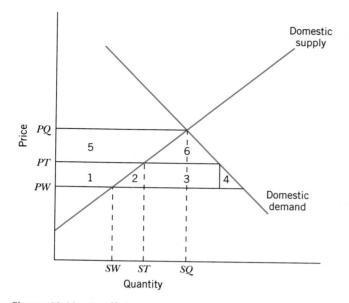

Figure 10.10 Tariffs have an impact on domestic prices and production.

restrictions. One amount is the cost that the government imposes on itself of administering the trade restriction. In this example, the collection of the tariff would require some government expenditure. The other amount is the semiconductor industry's costs of lobbying and otherwise influencing the government to first impose and then maintain the tariff.

Under some circumstances, governments impose prohibitive tariffs that raise prices to such a level that importing stops. Price PQ in Figure 10.10 represents the imposition of a prohibitive tariff because that is the equilibrium price for the domestic semiconductor market. At that price, the sum of all the numbered areas (1–6) is the additional cost to the consumer over and above the world price, with the sum of areas 1 and 5 providing tariff-induced rents to domestic producers. There are no government revenues derived from the imposition of a prohibitive tariff because there are no imports to tax.

DUMPING

Sometimes foreign producers are accused of *dumping*, or predatory pricing, in the domestic market. Dumping can take two forms: selling products in a foreign market for less than the price commonly charged in the home market, or selling products in a foreign market at prices that are lower than their cost of production. For example, some European producers have been accused of dumping bearings in the American market.

The first, milder, form of dumping may not be true predatory pricing at all, but may rather be a business policy called *pricing-to-market*. This policy takes into account that many products are income-elastic in their demand. That is, people with low incomes buy less of them than people with high ones. This pattern of demand can be offset by charging lower income consumers lower prices, while higher income consumers are charged higher prices. The higher revenues earned in wealthier markets compensate for the lower revenues earned in poorer markets. American pharmaceutical companies have been accused of pricing-to-market, with Americans paying much higher prices for drugs than consumers in, for example, Latin America. The drug companies argue that the higher prices paid by Americans support the very high costs of research and development incurred in their business, and if they didn't pay the higher prices there would be fewer drugs on the market, especially those that have been developed to treat rare illnesses. They believe this pricing-to-market is a fair policy, with a payment system that charges people fairly when their incomes are taken into account.

The second type of dumping, selling products at prices below their cost of production, is much more likely to result from an actual policy of predatory pricing. Predatory pricing tactics begin with entry into a market at prices below existing levels; if those prices are less than production costs, then the product is sold at a loss. The losses are expected to last only a short time, however, because predatory pricing is designed to drive competitors out of a market by forcing them out of business. Once the competition is bankrupted, the predatory pricer raises prices to levels high enough to make up for earlier losses, and the higher prices have to be paid by consumers because no other source of the product is left in the market. In some cases, governments impose *countervailing duties*, tariffs that raise the price of the product in the domestic market to what is considered fair by domestic interests. Countervailing duties are levied at rates that should eliminate any big differences in prices between the foreign producer's home market and the market where the producer is accused of dumping.

STRATEGIC INDUSTRIES

In addition to infant industries and sunset industries, another class of businesses called *strategic industries* is now considered worthy of protection from international competition. The word "strategic" is most often associated with military purposes, and the first so-called strategic industries were those associated with military production. The steel industry, for example, and also shipbuilding were traditionally considered as strategic industries because their products were required to maintain supplies of arms to a country's military forces. These industries have often received special government subsidies and special types of trade protection, so that they remain in business even if they are inefficient by international standards. Countries don't want to be put in the position of having to import products they need for their own defense.

Newer strategic industries include the semiconductor industry and other electronics producers and producers in biotechnology. These industries are strategic in a military sense in today's high-tech military systems, but they are also strategic in an economic sense. A country's future economic growth may depend on the quality of its domestic high-tech producers. If they are lost to foreign competition, proponents of strategic industry protection argue that a country's entire economy is put in peril.

NONTARIFF BARRIERS

Tariffs aren't the only instrument of government trade management. Several *nontariff barriers to trade (NTBs)* can also be used to intentionally alter trade flows, and some NTBs arise unintentionally as a result of other government policies. NTBs fall into three different classes: (1) NTBs, such as import quotas, that intentionally and primarily alter a country's geographical pattern of trade; (2) NTBs, such as product safety or other product standard requirements, that have a secondary purpose of altering a country's geographical pattern of trade; and (3) NTBs that arise unintentionally from the implementation of other government polices, such as tax credits that reduce production costs for certain domestic businesses, therefore allowing them to lower their products' prices below those of foreign competitors.

The most common form of NTB is the *import quota*, which is a quantitative restriction on imports by weight, volume, or value. Quotas have the same effect on domestic markets as do tariffs (Insights 10.3), except that they don't contribute to government revenue. Quotas are established in two ways. First, government may simply declare that only a limited amount of a certain product will be be allowed to enter a country from foreign sources over a particular period of time. Sometimes governments even put geographical limitations on quotas by allocating proportions of the product's quota to producers in particular countries. Textiles and apparel, for example, enter the United States under such a quota. Another method of imposing quotas is through what are called voluntary export restraints—quotas that are negotiated with foreign producers and are effectively enforced by the foreign producers as well. Exports of Japanese cars to the United States were under voluntary export restraints during the 1980s and early 1990s.

Trade protection measures, whether in the form of tariffs or NTBs, have uneven impacts on a national economy. Unless trade protectionism is enacted across the board, the industries singled out for special treatment will likely prosper, at least in the short term, at the expense of industries that don't receive this special protection. Targeted industries will employ labor and capital that they couldn't afford unless they were protected, and they will be drawing these factors away from more efficient uses. There is also a geographical imbalance in the effects of trade protection because industries tend to be found in agglomerations. Such geographical imbalance is especially evident in large countries like the United States, as described in Case 10.4. The unevenness is compounded by the general loss of consumer surplus that results from trade protection and by the more geographically and sectorally specific increases in potential producer rents that are generated in the selected industries and their more specific labor force impacts.

☑ CASE 10.4
State Employment Effects of American Trade Protection

THE MODEL

Trade restraints increase employment in the protected industry by raising the price or limiting the supply of competing imported goods. Industries that supply to the protected sector also gain employment. Industries that purchase the protected product as an input face higher costs. These higher costs are then passed on to the consumer and reduce sales. Thus, employment declines in these related industries.

Because trade restraints cause both positive and negative employment effects on the economy, the net effect of protection on aggregate labor demand is unclear. Trade protection may lead to either an excess demand for or an excess supply of labor. In an economy with flexible wages and a functioning labor market, wages will adjust to ensure that the economy remains fully employed. In the long run, trade protection simply alters the composition of employment.

I estimate the gains and losses in employment for different industries using an input-output model of the United States. A study by Hufbauer, Berliner, and Elliot (*Trade Protection in the United States: 31 Case Studies*, Washington: Institute for International Economics, 1986) provides estimates of the initial increase in domestic production and price of the protected commodity caused by trade restraints in place in 1984 (on textiles and apparel, steel, and automobiles). I apply the increase in domestic production estimates to the input-output model to examine the gains in employment in industries supplying to the protected sector. I also apply the increase in domestic price estimates to the input-output model, in a different manner, to estimate the losses in employment in industries using the protected product.

Because I assume the national labor supply is fixed, aggregate employment is not affected by trade restraints. To ensure that aggregate employment remains constant, any net gains (losses) generated by the input-output model are subtracted from (added to) the individual industries in proportion to their shares of total employment. This procedure is intended to approximate the employment effects of equilibriating wage adjustments, assuming that industries respond in a similar manner to changing wages.

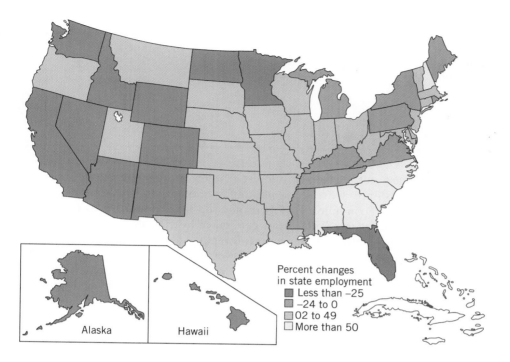

Percent changes
in state employment
■ Less than −25
■ −24 to 0
□ 02 to 49
□ More than 50

Alaska   Hawaii

REGIONAL EFFECTS OF PROTECTION

Even if national employment remains constant, trade protection can cause significant shifts in employment. Trade protection leads to increases and decreases in the production of goods and, therefore, labor shortages and surpluses in affected industries. Because labor is relatively mobile across states, workers will move from where there is an excess supply of labor to where there is an excess demand for labor.

I estimate the changes in state employment caused by U.S. trade protection by allocating the total net changes in an industry's employment among the states in accordance with their shares of national production in the industry in 1984. The accompanying map shows which states are the winners and losers from U.S. trade barriers in terms of percentage changes in their employment.

As the map displays, the gains from trade protection are concentrated among a few states, while the losses are spread across many states. Furthermore, the gains and losses are separated geographically by region. The eastern portion of the United States tends to gain employment, while the western portion of the country tends to lose employment from the trade restraints.

SOURCE: "U.S. Trade Protection: Effects on the Industrial and Regional Composition of Employment," by Linda C. Hunter, in *Economic Review*, Federal Reserve Bank of Dallas, January 1990, pp. 1–2, 10–11.

FOR DISCUSSION

Does economic base theory, as described in Chapter 9, apply to international trade?

EXPORT MANAGEMENT

Governments are not, of course, interested solely in managing their country's imports; they also are active in promoting the exports of goods and services produced in their economies. Export promotion takes a number of forms and does not really differ too much from general industrial promotion policies. A major form of export promotion occurs indirectly—for example, through different forms of production subsidies that lower costs and make products more competitively priced in foreign markets. More direct efforts at export promotion are made through government-directed banks that finance export sales by providing loans to foreign purchasers of their country's products. Lately, it seems that U.S. export promotion policy has been largely one of threatening foreign countries with curbs on American imports of their products if sales of U.S.-made products don't increase in their home markets.

Many countries have established *free trade zones (FTZs)* to encourage exports in general as well as to lure exporting companies to particular locations. FTZs are fairly small regions, sometimes as small as enterprise zones or even single buildings, in which goods can be imported without any tariffs. The ideal import in an FTZ is an intermediate product that is then used in the final assembly of a finished good headed for international markets. Because the intermediate product can be imported duty-free, production costs of the export good are lower in FTZs than they would be in other parts of the country. Forms of FTZs have been used at least since the Middle Ages, when the Hanseatic League was comprised of a series of free ports on the Baltic Sea. The earliest and best known of the modern FTZs is located at Shannon International Airport in Ireland. Established in the early 1950s, the Shannon FTZ was successful in luring manufacturing; similar FTZs were established in Southhampton, England, and Hamburg, Germany, among other places.

Although government economic policy encourages exports, sometimes political and social policy takes priority and exports are limited or entirely cut off to particular countries by embargo or other *trade sanctions*. The U.S. government has used trade sanctions frequently, sometimes on its own and sometimes in coalitions with other countries, to achieve its political objectives. In the past, most of the trade sanctions were targeted at countries in the former Soviet bloc, including the Soviet Union itself. Cuba was a special object of such sanctions because of its proximity to the United States, and the political-economic clout of Cuban refugees and other emigrés living in the United States. Sanctions have been imposed against Iraq and Iran, on both the import and export side, and apparently played a role in dismantling the system of racial apartheid in South Africa and the establishment of real democracy in that country.

Perhaps the best known case of export sanctions, and those with the greatest impact at least in the short term, occurred during the 1970s. In October 1973, an embargo was placed on Arabian oil shipments to the Netherlands and the United States because those countries had supported Israel in the "October War" against Egypt, Syria, and others in the Middle East. Following the embargo, the Organization of Oil Exporting Countries (OPEC) raised prices consistently over the next seven years. OPEC is an oil cartel, an association of producers that attempts to control both the price and production of oil in world markets to its own advantage. In 1970, the price of Saudi Arabian oil was $1.80 a barrel; in 1973, after the formation of the cartel, the price rose to $5.04, and it reached $11.25 in 1974. Oil prices peaked in 1983 at $34 per barrel and then began to decline as more and more sources of oil not controlled by OPEC became productive (just as we would expect having read Chapter 5). By 1987, the price had dropped to about $17.50 per barrel, and OPEC was in disarray. Later disagreements on pricing policy within OPEC, especially between Iraq and Kuwait, led to the Gulf War in 1990.

Politics aside, governments undertake both export and import management in order to provide benefits to certain interests in their domestic economies that those interests would not enjoy if trade followed so-called market forces. Governments also use trade management policies to generate broad macroeconomic changes that are especially geared to keeping trade balances positive. Import and export management policies are not effective in controlling trade balances, however, because trade balances are tied more to the general spending and saving habits of a country's citizens. For the most part, trade management by governments is more effective in steering a country's trade flows than it is in controlling a country's balance of trade.

MULTILATERAL TRADE AGREEMENTS

Trade policies tend to be cyclical. When domestic economies are strong, national governments generally argue for the benefits of free trade, but when a country experiences high rates of unemployment or other symptoms of economic distress, its government often blames domestic problems on "unfair" foreign competition. Protectionism, however, has come to be considered a major contributing factor to the depth and duration of the Great Depression of the 1930s, so since the end of World War II the general trend in government management of trade has been toward more open domestic markets. As you can imagine, opening an economy to international trade is not easily accomplished on a unilateral basis. Any government would find it politically difficult to make concessions to foreign economic interests without being able to show gains in the way of easier entry to foreign markets for its own industries. In addition, because international trade can get geographically complex, with many countries tied into the production of even a single good, significant trade liberalization has been accomplished only through multilateral agreements involving many countries.

The most comprehensive multilateral trade treaty is the *General Agreement on Tariffs and Trade (GATT)*. The GATT began small, with only eight countries signing the original treaty in 1948: Australia, Belgium, Canada, France, Luxembourg, the Netherlands, the United Kingdom, and the United States. The GATT's purpose is to eliminate discrimination in trade policy between countries and provide the "level playing field" in international trade that politicians are always talking about. The treaty is complex and has undergone eight major revisions since its beginning. Its current version, called the Uruguay Round because its negotiations were begun in Punta del Esta, was signed by representatives of 109 different countries in early 1994.

Over time, and in its different versions, the GATT has always incorporated three different principles of free and fair trade. One is *transparency* of trade regulations, meaning that all trade regulations should be visible—open and above-board—to all countries. A second is that each country be granted *most-favored-nation* status, meaning that individual countries should not be singled out for better or worse treatment in international trade. There are exceptions to the most-favored-nation principle for poorer countries, as in the special treatment of Caribbean countries by the United States, and for regional trading partners, as in the European Union. The third general principle of the GATT is *reciprocity*, meaning that any easing of trade regulations offered by one country should be met by eased trade regulations in other countries. (Negative reciprocity is prohibited.)

The current version of the GATT was negotiated in order to improve trade relations in several vital areas. One of its aims is to open markets by reducing the use of voluntary quotas, relaxing rules against dumping, phasing out subsidies to domestic industries that affect trade, simplifying customs procedures and entry rules, and opening up government purchasing policies that currently restrict the use of imports in fulfilling government contracts in many countries. Important advances in specific trade relationships among countries contained in the new GATT concern intellectual property, textiles and apparel, agricultural products, and services.

Intellectual property includes items covered by copyrights, patents, trademarks, and simple reputation in some circumstances. There has been a growing problem of infringement of intellectual property rights due to counterfeiting and forgery. Many Rock 'n Roll stars, for example, lose income because of counterfeited CDs sold in international markets. Similar losses occur in a number of industries, from cosmetics to software. The new GATT makes international enforcement of copyright and similar laws easier to accomplish.

Trade in textiles and clothing has been accomplished for a number of years under a series of coordinated but bilateral quotas called the *Multifiber Arrangement*. This arrangement is a side-agreement of the GATT, not part of the main treaty, which has been used to allocate shares of rich country markets to producers in poorer countries (also see Chapter 11). Its primary purpose was to maintain relatively high-cost textile and apparel production in the richer countries in the face of competition from much cheaper merchandise originating in poorer countries. It has succeeded in its primary purpose of limiting import penetration, but its success has led to higher prices for textile and apparel products in richer countries and a drag on the economic growth of the poorer countries, where textile and apparel production has been limited by the constraints in the world market. Under the new GATT, the Multifiber Arrangement will be phased out over 10 years, and trade in textiles and apparel will come under the GATT proper and be subject to the provisions of the more general trade treaty.

New agreements concerning trade in agricultural products center on the reduction of subsidies, including support prices, and the removal of quotas as barriers to international agricultural trade. Some subsidies are still permitted, especially those like crop insurance programs which are not directly intended to provide advantages in international markets. In addition, any environmental or conservation programs remain allowable under the new GATT. Tariffs are expected to be reduced 36% from their 1986 levels by the year 2000.

For now, trade in services will be conducted under its own special treaty called the *General Agreement on Trade in Services (GATS)*, another side-agreement of the GATT. International trade in services, as you recall from Chapter 8, is new and growing rapidly. The GATS is a response to a widely perceived need for some international coordination of service trade and its rules, but it is really only a framework on which to base future discussions. For the most part, most service trade will remain regulated by bilateral agreements rather than multilateral ones until the GATT undergoes another revision.

One of the more controversial outcomes of the new GATT was the establishment of the *World Trade Organization (WTO)*. Until the WTO, the GATT was more or less enforced by mutual agreements by the countries that were in conflict over trade. The WTO, on the other hand, means that a third party will judge trade conflicts, and the judgment will be enforced through the potential for retaliatory trade sanctions by all members of the WTO—that is, all the countries signing the new GATT. Some observers viewed the establishment of the WTO with alarm because it means that part of a country's sovereignty is given up to a multilateral organization. Governments traditionally have held certain powers as their own: notably, the power to tax, the power to raise military forces, and the power to control flows across the country's borders. With the WTO, the power to control flows across borders is lost, to some degree, because what actions constitute fair and unfair trade practices are now to be determined by an international body, and not by the national government.

The new GATT was received with mixed feelings on other counts in addition to the controversy raised by the establishment of the WTO. In the United States, for example, organized labor's response to the new GATT was strongly negative, while the response on the side of capital was rather positive (Insights 10.4). The same positions were held by those interests in other countries, too. An additional issue raised by the new GATT concerns the effect of more open international trade on the Earth's environment, particularly in the developing countries. Under the GATT, free trade means that one country can't place restrictions on another country's style of production because such restrictions can easily be used as a smokescreen designed to limit trade. Apart from requiring basic sanitation standards to be met in exported products, the new GATT contains nothing in the way of environmental production standards that must be met before a good can be legitimately entered into international commerce. Many opponents of the GATT based their opposition on its lack of environmental coverage, while many of its proponents argued that the environment should be considered separately and in different forums.

Some special multilateral trade treaties expressly concern environmental issues. The purpose of the Convention on International Trade in Endangered Species of Wild Fauna and Flora (CITES) is to promote biodiversity and reduce species extinctions by limiting international trade in some species and banning trade in certain plants and animals and their products, such as carved ivory, that are endangered species. Another treaty, the Basel Convention on Control of Transboundary Movements of Hazardous Wastes and Their Disposal, has been signed by nearly 60 countries since 1989. It concerns the identification, reduction, and control of hazardous waste shipments across international boundaries. A related agreement, the Bamako Convention on the Ban of Imports into Africa and the Control of Transboundary Movement of Hazardous Wastes within Africa, has the same purpose as the Basel Convention, but is specifically targeted at Africa so that its poorer countries don't become international dumping grounds. The reduction of hazardous waste production and transport is an important environmental goal around the world, especially in its poorer countries (Insights 10.5).

➤ **INSIGHTS 10.4**

Conflicting Views of Labor and Capital on the Uruguay Round of the GATT

CAPITAL'S VIEW

The Investment Policy Advisory Committee ("INPAC") was created pursuant to the Trade Act of 1974 to provide advice from the private sector to the President, the Congress, and the United States Trade Representative on investment policy issues related to international economic activity. Part of INPAC's statutory mandate is to assess the "implementation, operation, and effectiveness of recently concluded multilateral and bilateral trade agreements." In fulfillment of this responsibility, INPAC has prepared this report on the investment-related provisions of the Uruguay Round of the General Agreement on Tariffs and Trade ("GATT"). The investment-related provisions are embodied primarily in the Agreement on Trade-Related Investment Measures ("TRIMS Agreement").

The report begins with a review of the effect of transnational investment on U.S. and global economic growth, concluding that fostering more open transnational investment promotes the economic interests of the United States. The report then compares the TRIMS Agreement with the relevant negotiating objectives set by Congress in the Omnibus Trade and Competitiveness Act of 1988 (''1988 Trade Act''), as well as the goals set by GATT members at the outset of the Uruguay Round negotiations in the 1986 Punta del Este Declaration and the negotiating objectives of the U.S. private sector.

The report concludes that the TRIMS Agreement will bring some improvement in the treatment of international investment, while the Uruguay Round as a whole will advance U.S. economic interests. INPAC is disappointed that the TRIMS negotiations were not a major success, but this disappointment does not justify opposition to the Uruguay Round. The TRIMS negotiations were an area where the United States attempted to take bold strides toward a more open world investment system, and the rest of the world unfortunately failed to follow. Given this difficult environment, U.S. negotiators are to be commended for their diligence in taking the negotiations as far as they could.

The progress achieved will leave U.S. investors better off than they would be without an agreement. INPAC supports approval and implementation by Congress of the overall Uruguay Round Agreement.

SOURCE: *Report of the Investment Policy Advisory Committee (INPAC) on the Invesment-Related Provisions of the Uruguay Round of the General Agreement on Tariffs and Trade,* January 15, 1994 (Washington, D.C.: U.S. Government Printing Office), pp. 1–4.

LABOR'S VIEW

The Labor Advisory Committee for Trade Negotiations and Trade Policy (LAC) was established by the Trade Act of 1974, as amended, to provide advice and information to the United States Trade Representative and the Secretary of Labor with respect to, among other items, the negotiating objectives and bargaining positions of the United States in international trade negotiations.

The LAC has been an active participant in this negotiation, beginning with the 1986 Ministerial meeting that launched the Uruguay Round. The Committee has met countless times with government officials over the last seven years to consult and make proposals to eliminate the inequities present in the international trading system, and hopefully address America's serious trade problems.

The public discussion of what policies are needed to redress the economic impact of international trade and investment all too frequently degenerate into a sterile debate over labels—so-called free trade and so-called protection. For the LAC, the overriding issue in discussions of trade and development is not free trade versus protection, more trade versus less trade, open markets versus closed markets, more investment versus less. Rather, it is how economic ties among nations, each with its own set of rules and practices governing production and trade, affect the lives of working people.

We learned long ago that unfettered markets are not nearly as wonderful as many people tell us they are. We know very well that when market forces are left to their own devices we cannot expect them to bring sustained, equitable economic growth and social progress. Most of the historic achievements of the labor movement, and indeed of the United States as a whole—the establishment of the minimum wage, the abolition of child labor, the development of workplace health and safety laws and of environmental protection, collective bargaining itself—are intended to temper and restrain some of the most brutal effects of the "free" market. Markets need to be restrained and channeled in certain directions if economic activity is to serve the interests of the majority of America's people.

Regrettably, this view of the world is not reflected in the Uruguay Round Agreements. While it is no doubt true that international trade can increase competition, and that competition can reduce costs, costs can be reduced by either increasing productivity or by lowering wages and/or workplace or social standards. The failure of the Uruguay Round to address the social side of the production equation—worker rights and standards and environmental protection—is a major shortcoming. Absent progress in these areas, pressure to harmonize standards downward in order to remain "competitive" will continue to grow.

When the Uruguay Round of Trade Negotiations formally began in 1986, the U.S. trade deficit had reached the previously unimaginable level of $138 billion. While shrinking somewhat over the last few years, the deficit is again growing rapidly and will exceed $115 billion for 1993, a 40 percent increase from the 1992 level. Over the past decade, this country's trade shortfall has totalled more than a trillion dollars and has made the U.S. the world's largest debtor nation.

It is widely acknowledged that the magnitude and persistence of the U.S. imbalance is both harmful and ultimately unsustainable. Unchecked, the deficit portends even more painful reductions in the living standards of working Americans. The external debt of the United States, which continues to grow, must be serviced and, ultimately, repaid.

Central to America's trade problem is the imbalance in manufactured goods trade. Eleven years ago, the U.S. enjoyed a trade *surplus* in this vital sector. 1993 will see this deficit grow to more than $113 billion. This rapid and massive shift in trade has severely weakened America's industrial base, and has had a major negative impact on employment. While total employment has grown over the last ten years, that growth has taken place solely in the service sector. Employment in manufacturing has declined substantially. From 1979 to 1992, 2.8 million manufacturing jobs have been lost in America.

To address these problems, the LAC made recommendations to U.S. negotiators in all subjects addressed by these talks.

- The inclusion in GATT rules of provisions that would address trade advantages gained by the denial of internationally recognized worker rights or the maintenance of repressive working conditions;

- Reform of the GATT to directly address the continuing problem of large external imbalances;

- The strengthening of U.S. trade remedy laws;

- The elimination of gross inequities in market access among contracting parties, as well as the removal of "special and differential" treatment that has been provided for even the most advanced "developing" countries.

SOURCE: *Statement of the Labor Advisory Committee for Trade Negotiations and Trade Policy (LAC) on the Uruguay Round of Multilateral Trade Negotiations,* January 11, 1994 (Washington, D.C.: U.S. Government Printing Office), pp. 1–3.

➤ INSIGHTS 10.5
Agenda 21 on International Flows of Hazardous Wastes

ENVIRONMENTALLY SOUND MANAGEMENT OF HAZARDOUS WASTES, INCLUDING PREVENTION OF ILLEGAL INTERNATIONAL TRAFFIC IN HAZARDOUS WASTES

Introduction

Effective control of the generation, storage, treatment, recycling and reuse, transport, recovery and disposal of hazardous wastes is of paramount importance for proper health, environmental protection and natural resource management, and sustainable development. This will require the active cooperation and participation of the international community, Governments and industry.

Prevention of the generation of hazardous wastes and the rehabilitation of contaminated sites are the key elements, and both require knowledge, experienced people, facilities, financial resources and technical and scientific capacities.

There is international concern that part of the international movement of hazardous wastes is being carried out in contravention of existing national legislation and international instruments to the detriment of the environment and public health of all countries, particularly developing copuntries.

In section I of resolution 44/226 of 22 December 1989, the General Assembly requested each regional commission, within existing resources, to contribute to the prevention of the illegal traffic in toxic and dangerous products and wastes by monitoring and making regional assessments of that illegal traffic and its environmental and health implications. The Assembly also requested the regional commissions to interact among themselves and cooperate with the United Nations Environment Programme (UNEP), with a view to maintaining an efficient and coordinated monitoring and assessment of the illegal traffic in toxic and dangerous products and wastes.

OVERALL TARGETS

The overall targets are:

a. Preventing or minimizing the generation of hazardous wastes as part of an overall integrated cleaner production approach; eliminating or reducing to a minimum transboundary movements of hazardous wastes, consistent with the environmentally sound and efficient management of those wastes; and ensuring that environmentally sound hazardous waste management options are pursued to the maximum extent possible within the country of origin (the self-sufficiency principle). The transboundary movements that take place should be on environmental and economic grounds and based upon agreements between the states concerned;

b. Ratification of the Basel Convention on the Control of Transboundary Movements of Hazardous Wastes and their Disposal and the expeditious elaboration of related protocols, such as the protocol on liability and compensation;

c. Ratification and full implementation by the countries concerned of the Bamako Convention on the Ban of Import into Africa and the Control of Transboundary Movement of Hazardous Wastes within Africa and the expeditious elaboration of a protocol on liability and compensation;

d. Elimination of the export of hazardous wastes to countries that, individually or through international agreements, prohibits the import of such wastes, such as, the contracting parties to the Bamako Convention, the fourth Lomé Convention or other relevant conventions, where such prohibition is provided for.

SOURCE: *Report of the United Nations Conference on Environment and Development*, Volume I, *Resolutions Adopted by the Conference* (New York: United Nations, 1993), pp. 335–336.

REGIONAL TRADE AGREEMENTS

The Multifiber Arrangement, the GATS, CITES, and the Basel Convention are multilateral treaties concerning trade in specific sectors. The Bamako Convention concerns a specific sector and a specific region of concern: Africa. Regional trade agreements, which are more comprehensive than the Bamako Convention, are often considered a complement to the GATT in promoting a region's special trade interests. Sometimes they are viewed as superior to the GATT because the individual interests of countries in a regional trade agreement carry more weight than they can in the set of 100-plus countries in the new GATT.

There are four basic types of regional trade agreements. One is the *free trade union*, in which countries in a region remove the barriers to trade among themselves, but maintain their own individual policies concerning trade with countries outside of the union. Another is the *customs union*, which has the free internal trade of the free trade union plus a uniform set of policies among its members toward trade with nonmember countries. A third type is the *common market*, which has the characteristics of a customs union and also allows the free movement of factors of production within its member countries. Common markets, for example, allow the citizens of one of its member countries to work in another member country without requiring any special permits or visas. The fourth type of regional trade agreement is *economic union*. An economic union is the effective integration of the economies of its members. Not only would the countries in an economic union have the same internal and external trade policies, but they would also have the same tax and monetary policies, and use the same currency.

Regional trade agreements have three different effects. *Trade creation* results when the barriers to trade among a group of countries in a region are lowered, and the lowering of transaction costs increases the volume and frequency of their spatial interaction through trade. The other side of trade creation, however, can be *trade diversion*, which is a loss of trade by countries outside of a regional agreement that occurs not because their costs are rising, but because their trade barriers to the member countries' markets remain in place. If trade diversion occurs, the trade gains within the customs union are achieved in part at the expense of trade lost by countries outside the union. Finally, the free trade union form of regional trade agreements can lead to *trade deflection*. Deflection occurs when one country in a free trade union imports goods from nonmember countries only to re-export them—without tariffs—to countries that are members of the free trade union. To limit trade deflection, free trade unions can use *domestic content rules* that limit free trade within the union's set of countries to only those goods that have been produced within the union's boundaries.

Since the mid-1950s, dozens of regional trade agreements have been attempted in various forms, but few of them have been successful to any meaningful degree. What are the ingredients of a successful trade agreement? So far, it seems that regional trade agreements are most successful when their membership is fairly large, trade accounts for a relatively small proportion of the members' individual economies, their members already have a high proportion of their trade with other members even before the agreement is reached, and there are large differences in production costs among member countries so that comparative advantage can be realized as a basis for some of the region's internal trade.

THE EUROPEAN UNION

The most successful regional trade agreement is the *European Union (EU)*. The EU had its beginnings in the European Coal and Steel Community (ECSC) that was established in 1951. The ECSC was a remarkable achievement so soon after World War II because its members included both West Germany and Italy, former Axis members, along with Belgium, France, Luxembourg, and the Netherlands, all countries that had been invaded, devastated, and occupied by the Axis countries during the war. The purpose of this limited regional agreement was to promote the efficiency of the related coal and steel industries in the reconstruction of Western Europe in the war's aftermath. Evidence of the ECSC's success was its extension to the much more comprehensive European Economic Community (EEC) in 1957, made up of the same members as the ECSC. The EEC expanded, with the United Kingdom, Ireland, and Denmark joining in 1973; Greece in 1981; and Portugal and Spain in 1986. Austria, Finland, and Sweden joined the EU, the current expanded version of the EEC, in 1995. In the future, almost all of the European countries, including Turkey and Russia which extend into Asia, are likely to become EU members.

In its current format, the EU is a comprehensive common market that involves common policies among its members not only with respect to trade and factor movements, but also to the areas of agricultural programs, regional development policies, and efforts toward economic development in other parts of the world, especially in those countries that are former colonies of European powers. In its recent revision and expansion that began with the Single European Act of 1986, the stage was set for full economic union, including the use of a common currency. The steps toward full union, however, are on hold for now. The requirements of full union and the use of a common currency are hard to meet, even among the EU's more similar members, because each country in the EU still has its own domestic economic problems. As long as inflation rates and unemployment rates, for example, vary between the members of the EU, it is difficult for the individual countries to agree on a common set of specific domestic policies.

NAFTA

One goal of the EEC and now EU is to create a single, unified market as large as that in the United States. Even the United States, however, which is the world's single largest market, has found it worthwhile to enter a free trade union called the *North American Free Trade Agreement (NAFTA)* with Canada and Mexico. Originally, NAFTA included only Canada and the United States, two countries with a long history of heavy mutual trade and an earlier free trade agreement covering the automotive industry. About two-thirds of the trade between Canada and the United States was not subject to tariffs even before the first NAFTA was signed in 1988. The inclusion of Mexico in the NAFTA was accomplished in 1994.

The current NAFTA covers a wide variety of trade issues among the three countries over and above its general intention of tariff reductions and the elimination of other barriers to trade. It specifically targets trade in autos, for example, with its elimination of performance standards on foreign producers in Mexico who were once required to export a certain proportion of their Mexican output. NAFTA also concerns investment patterns, with the elimination of any restriction on the establishment of U.S. and Canadian financial service subsidiaries by the year 2000. This action effectively deregulates Canadian and U.S. banking, securities brokering, and insurance operations in Mexico. Truck transport is another service affected by NAFTA, with full access to the Mexican market opened to Canadian and American trucking companies by the end of 1999.

The NAFTA covering the United States and Canada was controversial in Canada because many Canadians feared that their national economy would simply become an extension of the U.S. economy once the agreement was signed. Their fear was based on the relative size of the two economies, with the U.S. economy more than ten times the size of the Canadian economy. Many Canadians were, and remain, concerned about the erosion of Canada's national identity with the increased blending of the Canadian and U.S. economies.

The NAFTA covering the United States and Canada went almost unnoticed in the United States, but extension to Mexico was especially controversial there and in Mexico, too. The Mexicans' concerns mirrored those of the Canadians. Many arguments against NAFTA were based on the disparity in the sizes of the Mexican and U.S. economy, a difference much larger than that between the U.S. and Canadian economies. The strongest proponents of NAFTA in the United States were the political and business interests located in the Southwest that already had strong ties with the Mexican economy (Case 10.5). Because of their proximity to the Mexican market, they knew they would benefit most, especially in the short run, from freer trade with Mexico because thay already had their feet in the water. Any decrease in trade restrictions would only lower their costs of existing flows in spatial interaction and cause their existing levels of trade to expand.

The opposition to NAFTA in the United States came from an unlikely coalition of members of organized labor, environmentalists, and followers of the Texan billionaire H. Ross Perot. Both the labor unions and Perot were concerned that once trade barriers were removed, the lower costs of production in Mexico would attract U.S. investment at such a rate that a "giant sucking sound" would be heard as American factories closed up shop in the United States and moved to Mexican locations. With NAFTA, companies could produce in Mexico but have free access to the lucrative American market. This opposition was probably unfounded. The U.S. tariff barrier to imports from Mexico averaged only 5% before NAFTA went into effect, so NAFTA did not materially raise the incentive to invest in Mexico. Furthermore, a free trade zone called the *maquiladora zone* had been in operation along almost the whole Mexico–U.S. border for some time. This zone was established for companies from the United States to use as low-cost locations for production that would be exported to the United States. In effect, NAFTA has simply extended this maquiladora zone to all of Mexico.

Although the maquiladora zone was effective as a free trade zone, it was also cited frequently by environmentalists opposed to NAFTA's extension to Mexico. Much of the maquiladora zone is like an open sewer with an added dose of toxic waste dump. A major city in the maquiladora zone, Ciudad Juarez, located across the border from El Paso, Texas, has over a half-million people but no sewer system. Infrastructure such as sewers is expensive, and Mexico is still a fairly poor country. Where environmental and sanitation infrastructure is available, standards are enforced on an irregular basis. Many unscrupulous companies owned and operated by U.S. interests have used the maquiladora zone as locations for their production that is especially harmful to the environment. They know that their plants' discharges of polluted water and polluted air will go unfined and often unchallenged by most local interests. Environmentalists are concerned that the extension of the maquiladora zone effected by NAFTA will also mean an extension of its environmental problems to the rest of Mexico. They are also worried that relatively weak Mexican environmental standards and, therefore, low costs of compliance, will attract "dirty" companies from the United States and Canada that will find it cheaper to move their production facilities than to find ways to produce at their present location with lower levels of pollution and waste.

NAFTA, like the GATT, has little concern for environmental issues written explicitly into the treaty. The main text only indicates that the members of NAFTA don't have to violate their own environmental laws in enforcing the new NAFTA regulations on trade. Environmental concerns were addressed in a separate agreement called the North American Agreement on Environmental Cooperation and by the establishment of an Agreement on the Border Environment Cooperation Commission, which is more or less a study group. The separation of the environmental and trade issues has led environmentalists to conclude that the environment is a back-seat issue when it comes to trade, and that commercial interests are of much more importance to the governments forming the new NAFTA than are the environmental issues faced by North America.

◪ *CASE 10.5*

Texas' Merchandise Exports to Mexico and the State's Employment

THE LINK BETWEEN TRADE AND EMPLOYMENT

Nationally, import and export changes have few lasting effects on the level of employment. Over time, workers displaced by increased import competition find jobs in other industries. Similarly, workers hired by growing export firms generally surrender existing jobs. While the composition of employment can change dramatically, the level remains essentially unchanged.

Regionally, however, the situation is very different. As employment patterns shift in response to trade, workers can move geographically, as well as occupationally. After all, the cultural and legal barriers that make it difficult to move across national borders in response to labor market conditions seldom inhibit movement across state lines. Thus, when an increase in exports attracts workers to the petrochemical industry, it also attracts them to states like Texas that are home to petrochemical firms. Furthermore, because proximity to Mexico can reduce transportation costs, increases in exports to Mexico also encourage firms in those export-oriented industries to locate in Texas rather than in other states.

Unfortunately, data on Texas' trade in services and merchandise imports from Mexico are not available. Therefore, we focus our analysis on the role that Texas' merchandise exports to Mexico play in the state's economy. Given this narrow focus, our analysis reveals only part of the influence that increasing trade with Mexico has had on the Texas economy. However, because merchandise exports to Mexico represent nearly 5 percent of Texas gross state product (GSP), our analysis describes an important part of the total trade picture.

EMPLOYMENT CONSEQUENCES OF INCREASING MERCHANDISE EXPORTS TO MEXICO

Although Texas' merchandise exports to Mexico have nearly tripled since 1987, they still represent less than 5 percent of GSP. Therefore, it would be surprising if merchandise export growth could explain a large percentage of Texas employment growth. Our analysis indicates that 6.1 percent of Texas employment growth between first-quarter 1987 and fourth-quarter 1994 can be attributed to increasing merchandise exports to Mexico. On average, 3 percent of Texas employment growth can be attributed to the direct effects of increases in merchandise exports to Mexico, while another 3.1 percent of Texas employment growth can be attributed to corresponding multiplier effects.

While merchandise export growth cannot explain much of total employment growth, it has had a considerable influence on the composition of the Texas economy. As Figure A indicates, increasing merchandise exports to Mexico encouraged workers to shift towards industries that manufacture durable goods like electronics and other electrical equipment and transportation equipment. (Figure A indicates the difference in employment share between first-quarter 1987 and the predicted employment for each industry in fourth-quarter 1994. The predicted employment for each industry is the sum of the actual employment in first-quarter 1987 and the total change in employment attributable to increasing merchandise exports to Mexico between first-quarter 1987 and fourth-quarter 1994.) The electronics and other electrical equipment industry gains the most employment share because exports to Mexico represent a disproportionately large percentage of that industry's production. Especially rapid export growth produced gains in employment share for the transportation equipment industry.

When some industries gain employment share, others must necessarily lose it. Not surprisingly, our analysis indicates that increases in merchandise exports cause employment to shift away from industries that do not produce merchandise exports. Multiplier effects determine the extent of the losses for these industries. Industries that are closely linked to merchandise exporters—such as the transportation services industry—lose less employment share than industries that are not closely linked.

A. Changes in Employment Composition Due to Changes in Real Texas Merchandise Exports to Mexico, 1987–94

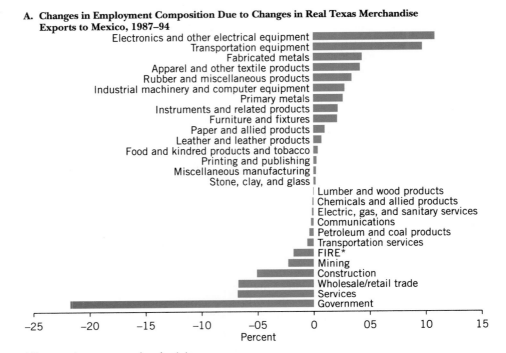

*Finance, insurance, and real estate

B. Ratio of Employment Share to Predicted Employment Share Absent Growth In Merchandise Exports to Mexico, 1994

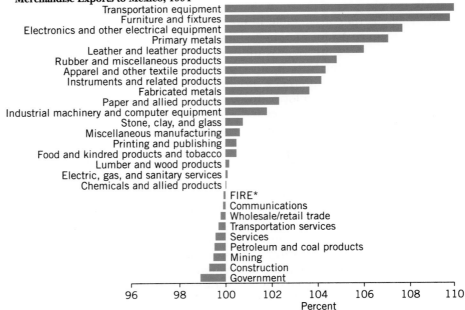

*Finance, insurance, and real estate

In Figure B, we compare the actual employment composition in 1994 with the employment composition we predict would have occurred if merchandise exports to Mexico had not changed. This analysis allows us to isolate those industries in which increasing merchandise exports to Mexico have had a significant influence on employment shares. We find that four industries—transportation equipment, furniture and fixtures, electronics and other electrical equipment, and primary metals—would have had much smaller shares of Texas employment had merchandise exports to Mexico remained unchanged. We estimate that since 1987, all the gains in employment in the electronics and other electrical equipment and furniture and fixtures industries, and more than half of the gains in the primary metals industry, can be attributed to increasing merchandise exports to Mexico. Furthermore, we calculate that employment in transportation equipment manufacturing would have fallen much more rapidly over the past few years if increases in merchandise exports to Mexico had not partially offset declines in defense spending by the U.S. government.

A common denominator among three of the four industries that have gained considerable employment share through increasing merchandise exports is that major components of these industries are classified as high-technology manufacturers by the Bureau of the Census. To be classified as a high-technology manufacturing industry, spending on research and development must be more than 50 percent above the U.S. average. We estimate that increasing merchandise exports to Mexico can explain all of Texas' employment growth in high-tech manufacturing since 1987. However, the relationship need not be causal because our analysis does not discriminate between increases in Texas merchandise exports that reflect increasing Mexican demand and increases in Texas merchandise exports that reflect export firms relocating to Texas from other states.

SOURCE: "The Role of Merchandise Exports to Mexico in the Pattern of Texas Employment," by Lindy A. George and Lori L. Taylor, in *Economic Review*, Federal Reserve Bank of Dallas, First Quarter 1995, pp. 22–23, 24, 26–27, 29.

FOR DISCUSSION

Which regions of the United States do you think are most significantly affected by the U.S.–Canada link in NAFTA?

POINTS IN SUMMARY

1. Countries with low per capita national incomes export the least, and rich countries export the most.

2. The proportion of manufactured exports increases consistently with a country's per capita national income.

3. There are many traded services, such as business consulting and insurance, that we only would expect to enter the global market from sources among the world's high-income economies.

4. Following the gravity model, we expect the greatest per capita trade flows around the world to occur between rich countries that are neighbors and the leanest flows in trade to take place between poor countries that are far apart.

5. Trade theories, like location theories, have been developed over time to deal with different market structures as well as changing technologies and changing forms of business organization.

6. Adam Smith wrote that if individual countries specialized in their production, each would become more efficient and produce surpluses that could be traded for the surpluses produced in countries specializing in the production of other goods.

7. The increase in consumer surplus that trade based on comparative advantage brings about forms the foundation of most arguments for the benefits of free trade.

8. Locational efficiency arises when matches are made between regions that are well endowed with a particular factor and industries that use that factor intensively in their production.

9. Both trade and factor mobility can lead to factor price equalization across countries or regions.

10. There are institutional, social, and cultural factors that serve to maintain relative factor prices in the face of trade or to change factor prices in a way that would not be accomplished by flows across markets.

11. International transport costs are an additional cost of production that domestic producers don't have to pay.

12. Countries with large markets providing economies of scale are the high-order places of the international economy, and those countries with small markets and lacking economies of scale are the world's lower order places.

13. Factor endowment theory tells us about the spatial interaction across competitive markets in the world economy.

14. Overlapping market theory accounts for trade between countries with the same factor endowments and in the same products.

15. One reason that trade has expanded around the world so rapidly over the last few years is that people are becoming more familiar, through both personal experience and mass communications media, with goods and services produced in different parts of the world.

16. The geographical extent of an MNC allows it to produce the individual components that make up a finished product in different parts of the world based on their factor intensities.

17. Governments manage trade as part of their overall economic policy and also as a way of providing benefits to particular interest groups.

18. Traditionally, two types of industries have been chosen for trade protection: infant industries and sunset industries. In addition, strategic industries are now often considered worthy of protection from international competition.

19. Governments aren't interested only in managing their country's imports; they also are active in promoting the exports of goods and services produced in their economies.

20. Import and export management policies are not effective in controlling aggregate trade balances, which are the result of the general spending and saving habits of a country's citizens.

21. Trade policies tend to be cyclical; they are more restrictive during hard times and more liberal during periods of economic growth.

22. The GATT's original and continuing purpose is to eliminate discrimination in trade between countries.

23. Important advances in sectoral trade relationships among countries contained in the new GATT concern intellectual property, textiles and apparel, agricultural products, and services.

24. Many opponents of the GATT based their opposition on its lack of environmental coverage, whereas many GATT proponents argued that the environment should be considered separately and in different forums.

25. Since the mid-1950s, dozens of regional trade agreements have been attempted in various forms, but few of them have been successful to any meaningful degree.

26. The EU is a comprehensive common market that involves common policies among its members not only with respect to trade and factor movements, but also to the areas of agricultural programs, regional development policies, and efforts toward economic development in other parts of the world.

27. The NAFTA covering the United States and Canada was controversial in Canada because many Canadians feared that their national economy would simply become an extension of the U.S. economy once the agreement was signed.

28. The extension of NAFTA to Mexico concerned many Americans who felt that investment and jobs would be rapidly drawn to Mexico because of its low costs of production.

29. NAFTA is like the GATT, with very little concern for environmental issues written explicitly into the treaty.

TERMS TO REMEMBER

ad valorem tariff
big emerging markets (BEMs)
Caribbean Initiative
common market
comparative advantage theory
countervailing duties
customs union
differentiated market theory
domestic content rules
dumping
economic union
European Union (EU)
factor endowment theory

factor intensity reversal
factor price equalization
free trade union
free trade zone
General Agreement on Tariffs and Trade (GATT)
General Agreement on Trade in Services (GATS)
import quota
import substitution
import tariff
infant industries
intracorporate trade
intraindustry trade

law of one price
maquiladora zone
most-favored-nation
Multifiber Arrangement
noncompetitive trade
nontariff barriers to trade (NTBs)
North American Free Trade Agreement (NAFTA)
overlapping market theory of international trade
pricing-to-market
reciprocity
sogo shoshas
specific tariff

strategic industries
sunset industries
tax havens
trade creation
trade deflection
trade diversion
trade management
trade protectionism
trade sanctions
transfer pricing
transnational corporations
transparancy
World Trade Organization (WTO)

SUGGESTED READING

Bergstrand, Jeffrey H. 1985: "The Gravity Equation in International Trade: Some Microeconomic Foundations and Empirical Evidence." *Review of Economics and Statistics*, Vol. 67, pp. 474–481.

Bergstrand derives the gravity model from economic theory and tests it on international trade flows. An interesting finding in this article is that a gravity model of spatial interaction without any economic content (i.e., price information) works just as well in accounting for trade flows as a gravity model with economic content.

Bhagwati, Jagdish N. 1988: *Protectionism.* Cambridge, Mass.: MIT Press.

Bhagwati is a leading expert on trade and its management through commercial policy. This short volume elegantly and eloquently summarizes the economic distortions raised by trade protection and the special problems of protectionism for developing economies.

Erickson, Rodney A., and David J. Hayward. 1991: "The International Flows of Industrial Exports from U.S. Regions." *Annals of the Association of American Geographers* Vol. 81, pp. 371–390.

Based on a comprehensive set of data developed for the U.S. Census Bureau, the authors describe the foreign trade of the major American census regions. Regional trade with other countries, with some exception, is shown to conform to patterns expected under an extended gravity model of spatial interaction.

Grotewold, Andreas. 1992: *Patterns of World Trade.* Grove City, PA: American Book Distributors.

This slim (71 pages) book describes global trade patterns from the perspective of Grotewold's "regional theory of world trade." That theory concerns trade based on differences and similarities in production systems among various regions of the world.

Hanink, Dean M. 1994: *The International Economy: A Geographical Perspective.* New York: John Wiley & Sons.

Don't wait for the movie! Buy several copies (it makes a great gift).

Hoare, A. G. 1993: "Domestic Regions, Overseas Nations, and Their Interactions Through Trade: The Case of the United Kingdom." *Environment and Planning A*, Vol. 25, pp. 701–722.

This article is a good comparison piece for the Erickson and Hayward article cited above. Hoare uses a different analytical method in assessing the United Kingdom's regional trade with other countries than the one used by Erickson and Hayward, but both works are pioneering efforts at assessing regional-international trade patterns.

Ohlin, Bertil. 1967 (original 1933): *International and Interregional Trade,* revised edition. Harvard Economic Studies, Vol. 39. Cambridge, Mass.: Harvard University Press.

This may be the most influential volume ever written on international trade. It contains the detailed development of factor endowment theory of trade and its less well-known application to location analysis. Ohlin also addresses the importance of studying economic geography as the basis for understanding how the world works.

Tyson, Laura D'Andrea. 1992: *Who's Bashing Whom: Trade Conflict in High-Technology Industries.* Washington, D.C.: Institute for International Economics.

Dr. Tyson wrote this book just before assuming her post as President Clinton's chairperson of the Council of Economic Advisors. She argues for strategic trade protection in its contemporary sense of advancing the national interest by protecting high-tech industries from international competition.

UNCTAD Secretariat. Annual: *Trade and Development Report.* Geneva: United Nations Conference on Trade and Development.

This volume provides annual updates and general coverage of world trade trends, especially with respect to policy. In addition to a consistent annual coverage of trade, each volume focuses on a special topic. In 1994, for example, it contained an initial assessment of the Uruguay Round of the GATT.

Two Journals: *Economic Geography* (Vol. 65, No. 1) and *Environment and Planning A* (Vol. 24, No. 1), have published special issues containing papers on the geography of foreign trade. The set of papers in *Economic Geography* is eclectic in covering a variety of topics, whereas the set in *Environment and Planning A* focuses on the regional trade blocs in Europe and North America.

Chapter 11

Economic Growth and Development: National Patterns and Processes

This chapter

- contains a description of the global distribution of rich and poor countries

- emphasizes the importance of human capital as the basis of economic growth

- suggests the differences between economic development and economic growth

- details some of the regional effects of economic development

- outlines models of economic development that focus on a country's internal conditions

- considers the effects of trade on a country's economic development

- reviews the debt problems of the developing countries

- describes the potential benefits of FDI for economic development and the role of MNCs in fostering economic growth

Courtesy of The World Bank.

We have already considered some issues in regional economic growth in Chapter 9. This chapter raises some additional issues, but now our attention will be focused on national rather than local and regional concerns. Another difference between this chapter and Chapter 9 is in locational emphasis. The discussion of regional growth largely concerned disparities in economic conditions across regions in wealthy countries. Now we'll consider the economic problems of entire countries, especially the poorer ones. Beyond the change in geographical scale and location, our concern in this chapter goes beyond economic expansion in poorer countries to their full economic development at a time when opening international markets require these countries to balance domestic priorities with the practical realities of global competition.

Keep in mind as you read this chapter that the geography of economic development has experienced significant historical changes. Right now, the highest living standards around the world, on average, are in a limited number of countries in West Europe, North America, and East Asia. It wasn't so long ago however, by historical standards, that many of these places were crude and undeveloped as compared to the world's most developed regions in China, India, and even earlier in Egypt and other parts of the Middle East. It could easily be, in the not too distant future, that an entirely different set of places will be considered "most developed."

NATIONAL INCOME

National wealth can be measured in a variety of ways. The extent of a country's territory could be used, for example, as a measure of its resource base, and in the past it was certainly a strong indicator of its prestige and political and military strength. Not too long ago, the amount of gold that a country held in its national treasury was the standard measure of wealth. Gold was (and is) valued across cultural and political boundaries around the world and was easily used to make purchases before contemporary monetary systems were established. The current international standard for measuring a country's wealth, however, doesn't have to do with how much gold it has or its command over natural resources. Instead, the current standard focuses on the amount of production that occurs in a country as measured by either its gross national product (GNP) or gross domestic product (GDP).

Values of GNP and GDP are taken from a system of *national accounts* which attempt to measure the activity or output of an economy. The details of the measure of GDP and GNP, which are closely related amounts, are described in Insights 11.1, but in simple terms they are the sum in money terms of the value of output of goods and services produced in a country's economy over the period of a year. (Many countries measure their output over shorter terms, especially for calendar quarters of three months. For our purposes, however, GNP and GDP values are annual ones.) It's important to keep in mind that using output as a standard of national wealth is drawn from a system of Western values that include the idea that economic growth is a virtue in and of itself. The contemporary measures of national wealth, therefore, are drawn from a particular cultural context.

The world's largest economy is that of the United States, and this has been the case for some time (Table 11.1). In the mid-1990s, the U.S. economy was followed by Japan's, Germany's, France's, and Italy's. If you add the United Kingdom's economy to the list, you have the six national economies that had output valued in U.S. currency at over one trillion dollars ($1,000,000,000,000). In the mid-1990s the combined output of those six economies was greater than the combined output of all the other countries of the world.

Table 11.1   The World's 20 Largest Economies in 1993

Country	GNP (×1,000,000)	Per Capita GNP	Population (×1,000,000)
United States	$5,935,496	$23,240	255.4
Japan	3,509,655	28,190	124.5
Germany	1,856,218	23,030	80.6
France	1,277,724	22,260	57.4
Italy	1,182,588	20,460	57.8
United Kingdom	1,028,262	17,790	57.8
Canada	567,454	20,710	27.4
China	546,234	470	1,162.2
Spain	546,227	13,970	39.1
Brazil	426,303	2,770	153.9
Russia	373,990	2,510	149.0
Netherlands	311,296	20,480	15.2
Australia	302,050	17,260	17.5
South Korea	296,723	6,790	43.7
Mexico	294,950	3,470	85.0
India	273,916	310	883.6
Switzerland	248,952	36,080	6.9
Sweden	234,987	27,010	8.7
Belgium	208,800	20,880	10.0
Argentina	200,255	6,050	33.1

SOURCE: World Bank, *World Development Report 1994* (New York: Oxford University Press).

➤ INSIGHTS 11.1
How GNP and GDP Are Calculated

Gross national product (GNP) and gross domestic product (GDP) are measures of national income that are rooted in the national product identity developed by the influential economist John Maynard Keynes. That identity is

$$\text{National Product} = \text{Consumption} + \text{Investment} + \text{Government Spending}$$

The terms "national product" and "national income" are virtually synonomous. National product is measured as the sum in money of the flow of final goods and services in an economy. (Final goods and services are consumed as products in themselves, and not as parts of other products.) National income is taken as the sum of earnings in the economy, including both wages and other factor costs of production as well as profits. This brings us to another accounting identity:

$$\text{Price} = \text{Cost} + \text{Profit}$$

with price taken from the product account and cost and profit calculated as income because they are the payments to either factors of production or producers. That's why product and income amounts are equal, and the terms national "product" and national "income" are synonymous.

The accompanying table summarizes the components of GNP and GDP in a general way. Consumption refers, again, to final goods and does not include used, second-hand, merchandise. It also doesn't include the large part of any country's economy that is "off the books," including illegal purchases and transactions in what is called the *informal sector.* The informal sector includes cash and barter transactions that are part of everyday life in most places, but go unrecorded by government agencies. In poorer countries, the informal sector is often quite large and actually accounts for a large share of national employment. The informal sector exists at a smaller scale in wealthier countries where transactions are more easily monitored by third parties because the same technology that facilitates the transactions also facilitates recording them.

Gross capital formation, or investment, comprises new structures and machinery that help the economy advance its production. The word "gross" is important here. Remember, we're talking about gross national and domestic products, not "net" products, so depreciation is not a consideration in this type of accounting system. This limitation has led to recent criticism of standard national accounting procedures for not subtracting the value of natural resources lost in production from the measure of national wealth. In fact, because gross measures are used, the faster resources are consumed, the wealthier a country appears to be. This type of accounting is not useful at all when a measure of sustainability of a country's economy is needed. (Sustainable development is taken up in the next chapter.)

An economy's international activity is taken into account by netting out its trade: exports less imports, and adding that value to consumption of domestic production and investment to arrive at GDP. When the net value of factor income derived from foreign sources is added to GDP, the result is GNP. The basic difference between the two measures is that GNP is the income of a country's citizens, wherever they might live, and GDP is the income of the country's resident population. Most countries around the world now use GDP as the basic measure of their economies, and calculate it on a quarterly and calendar-year basis. The calendar GDP or GNP, when divided by the country's population, yields per capita GDP or GNP, respectively.

The United Nations' National Accounting System

+ Consumption
+ Gross capital formation (investment)
+ Exports
− Imports

= Gross domestic product
+ Net factor income from abroad

= Gross national product

MEASURING LIVING STANDARDS

Gross output measures such as GDP and GNP tell us about the wealth of a national economy on an aggregate basis, but they often mask variations in standards of living that exist across countries. For example, three countries, Canada, China, and Spain, had about the same GNP in 1993, but the standards of living for the "average" person in each country was different. The most commonly used measure used in assessing a country's average standard of living is *per capita GNP* (or *GDP*), which is simply a country's GNP divided by its population, or GNP per "head." In 1993, Canada's per capita GNP was $20,710, about 50% larger than Spain's $13,970 and more than 40 times larger than China's $470. The three countries had about the same GNP despite the differences in their per capita GNP because of the differences in the size of their populations. China is the world's most populous country, by a long shot, so even though its per capita GNP is small, its aggregate output is huge. Spain's population is about 50% larger than Canada's, and that compensates for its smaller per capita GNP in roughly equating its aggregate output with that of Canada, the country with the smallest population of the three.

The use of per capita GNP as a measure of a country's standard of living has been criticized on a number of counts. One problem with using this measure is that it is almost always expressed in U.S. dollars when international comparisons are made. Changes in exchange rates between the U.S. dollar and a country's own currency can cause changes in GNP figures when no real changes have occurred in a country's economy. Furthermore, prices of goods and services that can't be traded, such as housing, can be very different among countries. Such price differences can't be accounted for in per capita GNP, but they can have quite an impact on standards of living.

Recently, efforts have been made to comprehensively measure *purchasing power parity* across countries. This parity indicates the buying power of the average person in a country in an "international dollar" (which is very closely related to the U.S. dollar but is not so subject to exchange rate changes). In general, when purchasing power parities are used rather than values of per capita GNP, the disparities in living standards between richer and poorer countries are lessened. As indicated in Figure 11.1, the purchasing power of the average person

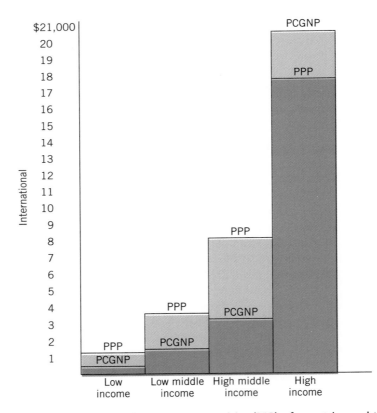

Figure 11.1 The purchasing power parities (PPP) of countries and their per capita GNPs (PCGNP) are similar on average, but lower income countries tend to have their purchasing power underestimated by their per capita GNP and the world's highest income countries tend to have their relative purchasing power overestimated by their per capita GNPs. SOURCE: World Bank, 1994: *World Development Report 1994* (New York: Oxford University Press).

in poorer countries is higher than would be indicated by the country's per capita GNP. The reverse holds for the richer countries, with their purchasing power parities falling below their average per capita GNPs. Even though these parities lessen the measurable discrepancy in living standards between rich and poor countries, as compared to the discrepancies indicated by per capita GNP, the differences are still great. The average purchasing power in the world's poorest countries is just over $1,100 per person per year, but it is nearly $18,000 per year (international dollars) in the world's richest countries.

Using purchasing power parities as a measure of national living standards has also been criticized because it considers, as does per capita GNP, that an individual's consumption of goods and services is all that matters in their quality of life. Alternative measures of living standards often consider other factors, in addition to consumption, as contributing to living standards. For example, literacy rates, access to health care and employment, infant mortality, and other related measures have been used in various comparisons of international living standards. In one of these types of assessments, the United Nations puts a limit of $5,000 on per capita GNP's contribution to an index of human development that it compiles. The limit is designed to suppress the overstatement of living standards, on a comparative basis, that can occur in the case of countries with higher per capita GNPs.

RICH AND POOR COUNTRIES

Throughout this book, we have used per capita GNP to classify the world's countries into four groups: low income, low middle income, high middle income, and high income. In most circumstances where this distinction is drawn, it reveals important differences among the world's countries: differences in population, agricultural practices, trade, and so on, and in purchasing power parities as well. You probably are also aware that locational differences exist among the world's countries when they are classified by their per capita GNP. Most of the world's richest countries are found around the North Atlantic, especially in West Europe, and some are in East Asia and in the Southwest Pacific (Figure 11.2). The world's poorest countries, called the *least developed countries (LDCs)* by the United Nations, are mostly in Africa. They are also found in the South Pacific and in South Central and Southeast Asia (Figure 11.3). Haiti is the only LDC in the Western Hemisphere. The general geography portrayed in the maps of rich and poor countries has led to the almost literal geography of a *North-South division* of the world based on national wealth and development. Aside from such obvious exceptions as Australia and New Zealand, the world's richest countries are found in a northern tier, while its poorer countries are located to their south. Although the geography of North and South is far from perfect, many people consider the term useful because it emphasizes a clear-cut distinction between the world's poor and rich countries.

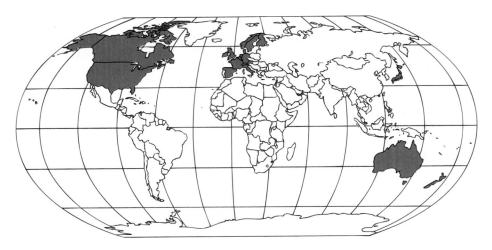

Figure 11.2 The world's richest economies, as measured by per capita GNP, are geographically clustered in West Europe, North America, and the West Pacific Rim. SOURCE: World Bank, 1994: *World Development Report 1994* (New York: Oxford University Press).

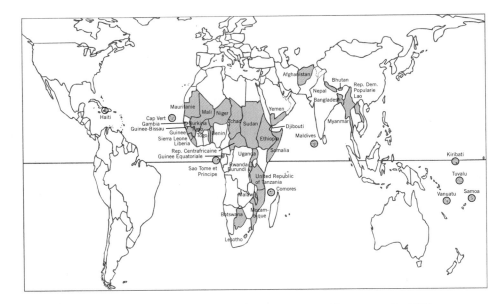

Figure 11.3 The world's poorest economies, as measured by per capita GNP, are found in what the United Nations calls the least developed countries (LDCs). Most of the LDCs are in Africa, with secondary clusters in the Pacific and in Southeast Asia. SOURCE: United Nations Conference on Trade and Development, 1992: *Paris Declaration and Program of Action for the Least Developed Countries for the 1990s* (New York: United Nations), p. viii.

In the context of Western values, big is beautiful and growth is good. Large GNPs are better than small ones, high per capita GNPs suggest individual well-being, and economic growth is an appropriate objective of every government of every country. *Economic growth*, meaning an increase in an economy's output, is necessary under currently dominant production systems and values to ensure both the maintenance and improvement of living standards. If a country's economy grows faster than does its population, then per capita GNP will increase over time. If GNP grows at the same rate as population, the average rate of consumption won't grow, but at least it will be maintained. Unfortunately, in recent years the very countries that are most in need of economic growth have been experiencing declines in the size of their economies while their populations continue to grow (Figure 11.4). From 1980 through 1992, the average low-income and low-middle-income countries experienced absolute declines in their economies once inflation was taken into account. Ironically, the only countries that experienced real economic growth during the period, on average, were those that already had high values of per capita GNP. It seems that the adage "it takes money to make money" holds for countries as much as it does for individual people.

Actually, the 1980–1992 period was a particularly bad one for many economies around the world, but the general relationship of stronger growth in the world's richer countries than in the world's poorer countries is a consistent one in other time periods, too. Why is there a consistent difference in growth rates,

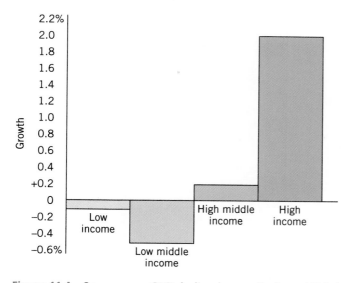

Figure 11.4 On average, GNP declined annually from 1980 through 1992 in the world's poorest countries. Although GNP experienced slight annual increases in the high-middle-income countries during that period, its annual growth rate in the world's richest countries was a relatively high 2%. Source: World Bank, 1994: *World Development Report 1994* (New York: Oxford University Press).

with higher rates typical of rich countries and lower ones typical of poorer ones? This is a big question, with no certain answer. However, a number of characteristics distinguish rich countries from poor ones, beyond their different incomes, which may provide the foundation for the gap between rich and poor in rates of economic growth. One important difference between the two is that the rich countries are more likely to benefit from economies of scale. Internal economies of scale require larger levels of output that, in turn, are dependent on having larger markets. Rich countries, almost by definition, are larger markets than poorer ones and so are more likely to achieve economies of scale in their production. Apparently, the higher rates of economic growth in richer countries are due in large part to the benefits of economies of scale. And these benefits allow the rich to get richer.

Rough measures of economic efficiency, or productivity, across the national

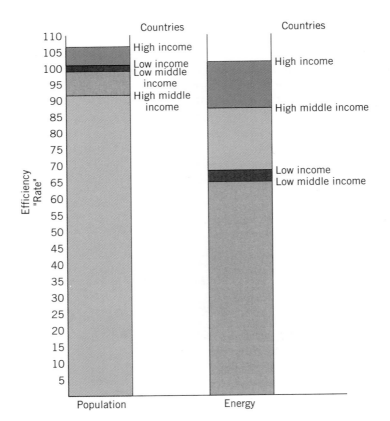

Figure 11.5 Productivity with respect to population was roughly consistent regardless of national income in 1990. Productivity with respect to energy was not consistent, however, but varied with average national income. Source: D. M. Hanink, 1994: *The International Economy: A Geographical Approach* (New York: John Wiley & Sons).

income groups are illustrated in Figure 11.5. An efficiency rating of 100 in the figure would lead to constant income with respect to the factor in question: population (labor) or energy (capital). A rating less than 100 points to declining income and a rating greater than 100 points to rising income; keep in mind, however, that the values are rough and small differences aren't important. On average, efficiency with respect to population increases—a very rough approximation of labor productivity—is about the same across the four national income groups, with the high-income countries in the lead. On the other hand, the differences in efficiency with respect to energy, an approximation of capital efficiency, are quite large. Furthermore, only the high-income countries have an efficiency rating that is higher than 100, with the lower income countries having ratings below 70.

The clustering of population (labor) efficiency ratings together with the big difference in energy (capital) efficiency ratings seems to point to differences in technology between the income groups. Rich countries are much more often the sources of inventions and innovations that improve technology than are poor countries, and new and improved technology is more efficient than old technology. The use of new technology, therefore, generates more wealth, and the increases in wealth can be used to purchase more technology, and so on. Technological differences between countries, like economies of scale, account for the rich getting richer and are also a probable cause for the gap in economic growth rates between rich and poor countries. But, if we accept technology as an answer to our question concerning differences in growth rates, then we have another question to answer; why are rich countries more likely to be sources of technological advance than are poor countries?

The answer to this question is probably found in the differences in *human capital* that occur between richer and poorer countries. Human capital assets include education and health, and just as physical capital improves the productive capacity of an economy, human capital does, too. Better educated people are better able to contribute to a country's society and economy than people who are poorly educated, and healthier, well-nourished people are also more productive than ill-fed people with chronic health problems. Technological development is most likely to result from high investments in human capital than from anything else. Although brilliant inventions are possible anywhere, concerted effort at education—basic, general advanced, and technical—appears to result in many rewards, including widespread technological advances. Like physical capital, however, human capital is expensive to develop and maintain, and average levels of education in countries vary with their national income (Figure 11.6). Health quality, too, is often associated with national income because health care is expensive. Infectious diseases lead to hardship and suffering for people, but their economic consequences are felt most strongly in the world's poorest countries. The devastating impact of AIDS on economic growth in many of the LDCs is described in Insights 11.2. Although AIDS is a major health problem that inhibits economic activity in poorer countries, it is only one of a number of health problems, including those associated with poor nutrition, that limit the potential of human capital contributions to economic growth.

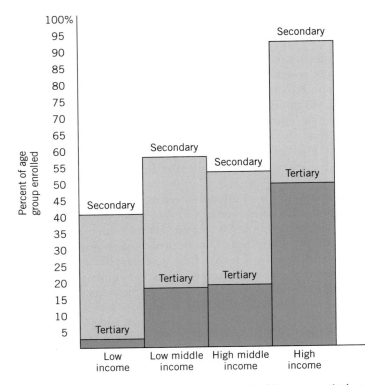

Figure 11.6 Education, an important aspect of human capital, varied with average national income in 1991. SOURCE: World Bank, 1994: *World Development Report 1994* (New York: Oxford University Press).

> ➤ INSIGHTS 11.2
AIDS and Economic Development

Apart from its devastating impact on health performance, AIDS is threatening the social fabric and economic life in many countries suffering from the pandemic.

Since numerous members of the same family and community may be infected, and since many of the victims are the mainstay of their households, surviving family members are forced to alter their patterns of consumption as well as those of savings and investment. The contraction of AIDS may dramatically reduce a person's life expectancy, possibly inducing dissaving (depending on what arrangements the infected person makes for his or her dependents); it can also have a "disruptive effect" on the productivity of survivors, parents and friends of the victim, weakening the capacity of households to purchase food and other necessities and the ability to participate in the labor force.

Another consequence is that the capacity of affected households to finance their children's schooling diminishes, so enrollment rates are likely to fall. Young women may be disproportionately affected as they are traditionally expected to care for the sick. Enrollment rates will also be reduced as children are forced to leave school to replace female labor. Moreover, child mortality rates, which had substantially improved in the last decade, are again rising to their pre-1980s level. Such trends will inevitably erode the productive capacity of the labor force even more.

The AIDS epidemic affects all levels of economic activity. Although the impact on investment is hard to measure, it may well be as important as the direct effect on the labor supply. The impact on agricultural production is already evident in countries where farmers are switching from cash to subsistence crops. At the level of the firm, AIDS will not only lower the productivity of workers and increase absenteeism but also reduce the number of skilled workers and increase health care costs. Since AIDS seems to hit the more productive and educated elements of the population, the urban community, which is most affected by the disease, is experiencing a reduction of its productive labor force. In rural communities, AIDS is affecting the availability of peak seasonal labor. Consequently, as food supplies decline as a result of lower agricultural production, nutritional levels are likely to fall.

AIDS is an unusual epidemic, both because of the very high levels of fatality among the infected and because its transmission is controllable by human behavior. The best "cure" for aids is thus prevention. However, a recent study by the World Health Organization (WHO) Global Program on Aids indicates that prevention costs for all developing countries would amount to $1.5–2.9 billion a year (10 to 15 times current spending), adding to the already overstretched budget allocated to AIDS.

A report by WHO issued in 1989 concluded that the epidemic would be most serious in countries already experiencing slow or negative rates of per capita GDP growth. After studying 10 African countries most affected by the disease, the World Bank found that AIDS had a negative impact on average growth of GDP per capita, as it was positively related to the number of infected skilled workers and the share of AIDS treatment costs financed from savings. Another World Bank study on the productive segment of the population shows that, on the assumption that 50 percent of the treatment costs are financed from savings and each education class has double the risk of the benefit beneath it, AIDS will reduce growth in GDP per capita by about one-third. While the negative impact on GDP growth seems small, the World Bank argues that reduction of up to 0.3 percentage points would mean a reduction of 30 percent in the growth rate of per capita income.

SOURCE: United Nations Conference on Trade and Development, 1994: Box 18: "Least Developed Countries and the Economic and Social Implications of AIDS," in *The Least Developed Countries, 1993–1994 Report* (New York: United Nations), p. 119.

ECONOMIC DEVELOPMENT

The formation of human capital and economic growth are intertwined processes; one increases the potential for the other. The same sort of intermingled association holds for economic growth and the process of economic development. Most of the time we think of the terms "economic growth" and "economic development" as the same thing, but it's useful to think of development as something more than just the increases in production that define economic growth. As opposed to simple growth, *economic development* is the integration of an economy's productive resources and markets. Integration in an economy permits smooth flows of goods, services, payments, and investment with low transaction costs. Integration effectively makes a number of smaller markets a single larger one, therefore allowing for economies of scale and economies of scope to yield efficiencies in production that boost consumer surpluses. Integration of productive resources leads to flexibility in investment, production, and marketing so that an economy's production system can be more responsive to consumer needs. (Defined in this way, economic development can be observed at a number of geographical scales, from local to international. This chapter, however, focuses on national economic development.)

Economic development is associated with economic growth, of course, and the more developed national economies are the world's wealthier ones, too, for the most part. Their development improves economic efficiency and generates wealth that can be invested in further development efforts such as infrastructural improvements that improve the physical integration of a country's economy or the establishment of institutions that may facilitate the integration of financial markets. On the other hand, poorer economies are less developed, and the poorest ones least developed, with their poverty and lack of development reinforcing each other. The lack of development, or lack of integration in poor country production and marketing systems makes their economies fairly inefficient. Because they are undeveloped, or underdeveloped, it is difficult for poor country economies to generate the surpluses that are required for investment in projects that promote economic development.

The relationship between economic growth and economic development can be illustrated by the bell-shaped curve in Figure 11.7. The economist William Alonso (whom we met in Chapter 2) has suggested that five characteristics of a society follow a predictable path as economic development progresses: its population growth rate, its economic growth rate, its geographic concentration, its regional inequality, and its social inequality. We've already considered the bell-shaped curve of population growth rates, using different terminology, in the context of the demographic transition model (see Chapter 5).

A developing economy starts out by growing slowly. The pace of growth increases, and then slows down again as development progresses. Simple initial advances in economic integration should be expected to yield significant gains in production because they lower costs so much. The establishment of infrastructure that ties together the regions of a country, for example, decreases the costs

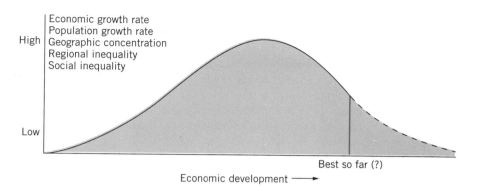

Figure 11.7   Five characteristics of a society tend to follow a bell-shaped track during the process of economic growth. Together, the change in these characteristics may be considered the process of economic development. This process is not fully complete in any country.   Source William Alonso, 1980: "Five Bell Shapes in Development," *Papers of the Regional Science Association*, Vol. 45, pp. 5–16.

of spatial interaction among the regions dramatically, and the savings are readily translated into production increases. Additional growth is facilitated by infrastructural improvement, but the rate of increase in production shouldn't be expected to equal the rate of increase accomplished by the initial establishment of infrastructure. For example, a new rail line linking together two regions of a country will do much more to advance their connection and improve economic growth than will later improvements to the rail line. The improvements may be important, but they are unlikely to have the dramatic effect of the rail line's initial construction. Growth slows down as development advances because the cost reductions from later development efforts tend to be less than those achieved by earlier ones. In effect, the returns to increased integration are always positive, but they do diminish as development progresses.

Do growth rates follow a bell-shaped curve with economic development? That was, in fact, the general experience from about the end of World War II to 1980. Since that time, however, the richest countries (and presumably the most developed) have enjoyed higher rates of growth than countries in any other income group (review Figure 11.4). A reasonable explanation for the change in relative growth rates is given later in this chapter.

REGIONAL INEQUALITY

The tracks of geographical concentration, regional inequality, and social inequality tell us the most about economic development in a country. You'll remember from our discussion in Chapter 9 of the world's largest cities that agglomeration economies of scale are most beneficial in industrializing economies and that rates of urbanization are higher in poorer than in richer countries. In poorer countries economic growth tends to be geographically concentrated in larger cities because both private and public investment is more efficient in a geographical concentration when investment levels are low. Geographical concentration in poorer countries is often revealed by a condition called primacy in their urban systems. A *primate city* is one that is many times larger than any other city in a country. There are primate cities in richer countries, too (London is an example), but primacy is more often associated with poorer countries. As development progresses, the importance of agglomeration economies decreases and geographical concentrations begin to disperse.

Regional income inequality is usually associated with geographic concentration in an economy. Incomes in the region containing or surrounding a primate city, for example, can be expected to be higher than in other regions in a country. The geographical concentration of investment and employment opportunities means that standards of living in the primate city region will be higher than in other regions. In Mexico, for example, living standards around Mexico City, a primate city, and two other large centers, Tijuana and Monterrey, are much higher than in other regions of the country. Frequently, regional differences can be boiled down to an urban-rural dichotomy. People living in urban places have higher living standards than people living in rural places simply because

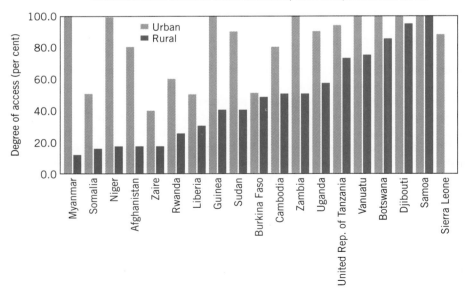

Figure 11.8 Differences in access to health care between urban and rural residents is one of many inequalities facing a developing country's population. Source: *The Least Developed Countries, 1993–1994 Report* (New York: United Nations).

of the concentration of opportunities in cities and the lack of opportunities in the countryside. This disparity affects not only employment access and income, but access to basic human services as well (Figure 11.8). As the degree of geographic concentraion in an economy declines, its degree of regional inequality can be expected to decline, too.

Not all regional inequality, however, is a function of geographic concentration. In some countries, regional inequality results from settlement patterns of racial or cultural minorities that have resulted in geographical segmentation. Regions with high proportions of a country's minority population are often subject to economic discrimination. Regional inequality due to economic imbalances caused by geographical concentrations in a national economy can be reduced by infrastructural investment. Regional inequality that results from social inequality is less easily dealt with. Social integration, however, is easily as important a part of a country's economic development as regional integration. Aside from its immorality, the involuntary segregation of ethnic, racial, or cultural groups from a society's majority is wrong because it is economically inefficient. Gender biases in employment and educational opportunities also generate inefficencies that retard growth in an economy (Insights 11.3). Groups of people, like regions, must be integrated in an economy before the economy can be said to be developed. Although economic development is farther along, in general, in the world's richer economies than in its poorer ones, it is an ongoing process in every country.

➤ INSIGHTS 11.3
Educating Women and Economic Development

Most women in the least developed countries (LDCs) have been left out of the development process. While many governments provide for women in their official plans, there is little evidence that the political rhetoric has been matched by an improvement in the status of women. Education is one crucial area in which women have suffered.

A review of the adult literacy rates for males and females in 1990 in LDCs is revealing. With few exceptions, the female adult literacy rate was about half that of males. In most of the countries for which data were available, it was below 30 percent and in 10 countries it was under 20 percent.

WHY DO WOMEN FARE SO POORLY?

There has been much research suggesting the existence of gender bias in education, for a number of reasons. In many LDCs, the parents' decision to educate their daughters is related to their beliefs about the economic returns in terms of earning potential, and about the costs associated with their education. They often believe, with good reason, that the economic returns are low, and hence they enter into a "vicious circle" of not educating their daughters and thereby ensuring that their potential earnings are low. Early marriage reduces parents' incentive to invest in female education, especially when education is costly and they will be unlikely to reap the benefits.

In most LDCs, parents view the costs as being too high relative to the returns. Some of these costs are direct (e.g. school fees, books, and associated expenses). There are also opportunity costs that enter into the decision-making process. Girls fill an important household role in developing countries and they often free their mothers by helping with household chores and tending to their siblings, thus allowing their mothers to work outside the home. They may also be sent to work themselves, or may work in the family business, be it farming or in the informal sector. Any time spent at school would detract from these duties.

Cultural traditions and concerns about the safety and honor of girls also enter into the education decision. For example, if schools are far from the home or not equipped with separate toilets for girls, parents are hesitant to send their daughters there. The shortage of female teachers, and the inappropriateness of the school curriculum and textbooks are also cited as reasons for not sending girls to school.

WHY IS THE EDUCATION OF WOMEN SO IMPORTANT?

Equal access for women to education can ensure both a private and social gain. The private return to education is increased earnings potential which, despite discrimination in the labor market in both wages and access to jobs, gives women greater control over their lives. Education brings with it the awareness of rights; along with some degree of economic independence gained from earning their own income, this empowers women, giving them the ability to cope with, and even address, the discrimination and marginalization from which they suffer.

The social gains to be made from female education are numerous and have implications for health, population growth and labor productivity. Women become much more aware of basic standards of hygienic and nutritional requirements. In addition, the health of children is often left in the hands of the mothers in LDCs, with the result that maternal education has been found to be an important determinant of child survival and health. Indeed, studies have revealed that an additional year of schooling reduces under-5 mortality by up to 10 percent, possibly because education increases a mother's ability to recognize the signs of illness and thus shortens her response time. Her ability to follow medical instructions is also enhanced. Women's education may increase the economic status of their families through additional income, which in turn improves child survival status. In addition, research has shown that mothers are more likely to spend their income on food and on the children than are fathers.

In terms of population and fertility, a recent study found that secondary female education lowers fertility rates and that its effect increases when combined with family planning programs. Knowledge about the availability of and desire to use contraceptives and family planning services, comprehension of family planning messages and the empowerment of women through the understanding and control of their bodies are explanations for the effect of education on fertility. There are many economic links between the two as well. For example, education increases women's economic opportunities and earnings potential, thereby raising the opportunity costs of childbearing and rearing, and studies have shown that the economic benefits of female education reduce the desired family size. Education also raises the age of marriage, which has the effect of reducing the fertility rates.

HOW CAN ACCESS TO EDUCATION IMPROVE FOR GIRLS?

A number of suggestions have been made in this respect. In many LDCs, where the provision of education is limited, schools tend to reserve places for boys rather than girls although reserving places for girls would increase enrollment. Malawi and the United Republic of Tanzania have both pursued such policies. Another option is to reduce the distance to schools by providing classes closer to home, in, for example, a house or a free room in the community. In Bhutan, for example, the Government has created extended classrooms, which provide the early primary grades at locations around the local primary school. Parents who are unwilling to let their daughters attend the primary school due to the distance are thus encouraged to enroll them in complementary schools closer by.

Increasing the number of female teachers provides girls with role models and also reassures the parents about sending their daughters to school. Improving the school facilities, making the curriculum more relevant and providing separate toilets are other ways of attracting female students. Scholarships reduce the direct costs of education; if they were provided for girls, parents might have less excuse to choose between educating their sons and their daughters.

These are just a few ways of increasing female enrollment in schools and dispelling some of the fears and anxieties that beset parents in LDCs when confronted with the education decision. As the benefits of female education are so widespread, influencing many facets of the development process, it is essential that Governments explore all available options in ensuring that girls have access to quality education.

SOURCE: United Nations Conference on Trade and Development, 1994: Box 21: "Women and Education", in *The Least Developed Countries, 1993–1994 Report* (New York: United Nations), pp. 128–129.

INTERNAL PROCESSES OF ECONOMIC GROWTH AND DEVELOPMENT

Economic growth and economic development are complex processes that have been described in simplistic ways. From the late 1800s to the mid-1900s, *environ-*

mental determinism was a widely held theory of economic growth. According to this theory, the differences in productive capability between countries, or regions, were based largely on the differences in their physical environments, especially the differences in their climates. Why were the West European countries, Canada, and the United States the most productive countries? Because they had the most invigorating climates. Some climates are too cold, according to environmental determinism, and some climates are too hot for industrial growth to proceed. The mid-latitude climates, however, are like baby bear's porridge; they are just right for economic progress.

Environmental determinism was appealing because it served easily to explain the North-South geography of the world's economic development. Its explanatory power was superficial, however. If, for example, you compared the fifteenth-century economies of West Europe and those of the Middle Atlantic region of North America at that time, you would certainly see important differences. Shipbuilding technology, for example, was quite different. Other technological differences allowed different living styles and production systems to be maintained within similar environmental conditions then, and they continue to do so today. There are, of course, environmental constraints to different types of production, with practical limits to various forms of agriculture coming to mind immediately. Environmental conditions affect what's possible in economic practices, but to call on them as determinants of economic outcomes in places is to fall prey to a single factor fallacy.

In the mid-1950s, the single factor fallacy of environmental determinism gave way to another single factor fallacy: *cultural determinism.* The concept holds that variations in cultural characteristics determine variations in productivity levels around the world and, therefore, variations in the geography of economic development. Different religious traditions, for example, are thought to promote "industriousness," while others are viewed as pushing their adherents away from material concerns, thereby making them less inclined to save and invest. It's true that Western styles of production and the growth orientation of Western economies have come to dominate other production systems around the world. The spread of the growth psychology away from European centers to other parts of the world is as much an indicator of cross-cultural flexibility, however, as it is of cultural domination. Culture, as a shared, comprehensive set of ways of doing things among people, has important effects on geographical patterns in the international economy, but it's not their sole determinant.

THE NEOCLASSICAL MODEL

Environmental determinism and cultural determinism are not really concerned with the economics of growth and development; instead, they attempt to establish a foundation for economic progress. The dominant model of growth economics, the *neoclassical economic growth model,* is concerned with economic growth as a process. The neoclassical model indicates that output grows in response to additions to production of the two basic factors of labor and capital (Figure 11.9). The model suggests relative balance in factor use; the law of diminishing returns makes it inefficient to use too much labor or too much capital; that's why the isoquants (curves tracing the same amounts of production over a series of input combinations) are curved the way that they are in Figure 11.9. As illustrated in the figure, initial inputs of L_1 amount of labor and C_1 amount of capital yield output level 1. When the factors are doubled to L_2 and C_2, then output is doubled, too.

The model is quite simple, though not simplistic, and it has large implications. It implies, for example, that labor and capital must work in an interdependent fashion in order for production to expand efficiently. Such interdependence can be achieved only if factor markets are integrated in such a way that labor and capital can serve as partial substitutes for each other. This type of integration

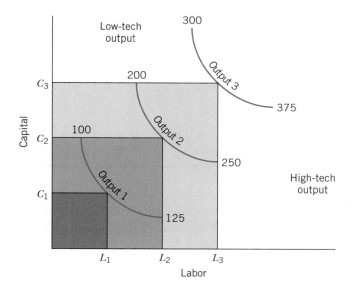

Figure 11.9 Basic economic growth theory tells us that relatively balanced additions of capital and labor lead to increases in production, or economic growth. High technology and/or high rates of human capital allow richer economies to be more efficient in production than are poorer countries that typically suffer from technology and human capital shortfalls. In this diagram, for example, the same input levels (L_2 and C_2) yield 200 units of output under low-tech conditions, but 250 units of output under high-tech conditions.

is a characteristic of economic development. It also implies, however, a constraint to production that we don't really observe in the real world because it suggests that similar labor and capital combinations should yield similar levels of output across all economies and that differential growth rates across economies are possible only when production factors are added at differential rates. We don't observe the constraint because of the effects of technology that are not incorporated in the neoclassical model.

This brings us back to the question of differential growth rates between rich and poor countries that was raised earlier in this chapter. From the immediate post–World War II period to about 1980, the developing economies did indeed have faster rates of growth than the richer, more developed economies, and that's why growth rates were described as following a bell-shaped curve as development progresses. The reason for their relatively fast rates of growth was that both labor and capital were being organized and put to use in many of these countries in efficient ways that had not occurred in earlier periods, so their output increased dramatically. Since about 1980, however, strong growth has been harder to achieve because contemporary production methods had been widely established, so that additional rapid gains were harder to achieve from simply adding factors of production. Instead, the average economy among the developing countries either stagnated or even experienced relative decline owing to a series of problems—environmental, political, and economic—which effectively halted their development and associated economic growth. The more rapid growth experienced by the richer economies since 1980 has resulted from their generally higher levels of development, as well as their better technology and higher levels of human capital. Technology and human capital, along with economies of scale, effectively make factor productivity unequal, as illustrated in Figure 11.9. They continually work in favor of the world's richer economies.

MODERNIZATION THEORY

One of the leading theories of economic development, as something more than economic growth, is *modernization theory*. We have already considered two models drawn from modernization theory: one was the model of the demographic transition, and the other was the model of sectoral shifts—primary to secondary to tertiary—that take place with economic growth. The basic premise of modernization theory is that historical processes are predictable and hold into the future. The past experience of some countries can be used to predict the future experiences of other countries. With respect to the demographic transition, some countries can expect a decline in their population growth rate in the future because other countries have experienced such declines in the past. Sectoral shifts can be expected in some countries because they have already happened in others.

The most comprehensive version of modernization theory is presented by

W. W. Rostow in his description of the five stages of economic development. The first stage is "traditional society." This stage is characterized by limited technology, an economy consisting almost completely of primary-sector activities, and low levels of capital investment. The second stage establishes the "preconditions for takeoff." These preconditions come about because of increased agricultural productivity. The productivity improvements in agriculture ultimately provide output surpluses that can be sold. Those earnings become the capital surpluses needed for infrastructural development, which, in turn, improves productivity in the economy because it serves to integrate the regions of the developing country.

The third stage of development is called the "takeoff," and as the name implies it is a period of rapid economic growth (recall the supposed bell-shaped curve of growth rates during economic development). During this stage, rapid economic growth is brought about in response to the demands of a single-growth industry for labor and capital. The single-growth industry has a multiplier effect on the whole economy (recall from Chapter 9). The fourth stage is the "drive

Table 11.2 Initial Years of Entry to Economic Development Stages: Selected Countries

Country	Takeoff	Drive to Maturity	High Mass Consumption
United States	1815	1870	1910
Canada	1896	1915	1919
United Kingdom	1783	1830	1920
France	1830	1870	1920
Germany	1840	1870	1925
Sweden	1868	1890	1925
Australia	1901	1920	1925
Italy	1895	1920	1950
Japan	1885	1905	1955
Russia-USSR	1890	1905	1956
Argentina	1933	1950	ne
Brazil	1933	1950	ne
Mexico	1940	1960	ne
Taiwan	1953	1960	ne
Turkey	1933	1961	ne
India	1952	1963	ne
Iran	1955	1965	ne
China	1952	1968	ne
Republic of Korea	1961	1968	ne
Thailand	1960	ne	ne

Note: "ne" indicates not entered as of 1978.

Source: Walt W. Rostow, 1978: *The World Economy: History and Prospect* (Austin: University of Texas Press).

to maturity." At this point, the economy is broadened as the production processes that were once employed only in the dominant growth industry are now used in other industries. Rapid rates of growth give way to slower but stable rates as a country's resource use approaches its maximum level of efficiency given prevailing technological limits (again recall the bell-shaped curve). The final stage of development is that of "high mass consumption" in which manufacturing becomes oriented toward the production of consumer goods and the service sector becomes the dominant one in the economy.

As an historical account, Rostow's version of modernization theory is a very interesting one. It provides particular years when different countries entered the various stages of development (Table 11.2), and describes particular events that were pivotal in the progress of national economic conditions. Its general applicability as a theory of development with respect to currently developing economies is questionable, however, if only because the relevance of eighteenth- and nineteenth-century European history appears to be rapidly declining in the contemporary global economy. In addition, the decade of the 1980s has shown us that the path of economic growth and progress is not as smooth and predictable as modernization theory implies.

COEVOLUTIONARY DEVELOPMENT

Like modernization, most theories of economic growth and economic development assume that all countries will develop along Western lines. In addition, they imply that all countries *should* develop along Western lines, and they adopt the principles that (1) "big is beautiful," and (2) "growth is good." For some, however, growing concerns for the environmental degradation and rapid cultural change associated with efforts at rapid economic growth and development have called into question the appropriateness of the Western "model" in many regions around the world (even the West!). An alternative approach that sees smaller scale processes of *coevolutionary development* taking place around the world has been suggested as a remedy to many of the problems that are now often associated with development practices, especially in the LDCs.

Coevolutionary development occurs through the interaction of local culture and the local environment in producing technologies that are beneficial with respect to production but have very small environmental impacts. Historically, regional economic growth and development have proceeded in a preindustrial fashion in many places. Local groups, over time, have experienced a coevolution of their culture and economy given the possibilities presented by their local environment. Production methods that are particularly suited to local circumstances, sometimes called appropriate technology (Chapter 3), arise from cultural-environmental requirements that facilitate regional growth and development in a sustainable form (see Chapter 12). When you think about it, the idea of coevolutionary development contradicts both environmental determinism and cultural determinism because it considers that environment and culture are interwoven, each influencing the other.

A good example of the success of coevolutionary development before the spread of modernization is in the Iroquois Nation of Native Americans as it existed before significant contact with Europeans. This nation consisted of a confederation of several bands of people living mostly in what is now New York State and part of Ontario. The Iroquois were politically sophisticated and had a well-developed agricultural economy, with established interregional trade patterns among themselves and with other groups. Their economy was developed, but not rich by European technological and material standards. The effects of European technology and modernization on the Iroquoian group were disastrous because European and Iroquois economic practices were mutually exclusive. The introduction of Western technology and modernization caused the Iroquois Nation's economy to go into rapid decline, and it regressed from its level of development.

In another context, Tanzania devised a series of development policies in the late 1960s and in the 1970s that were designed to promote growth and development using indigenus practices instead of simply adopting Western-style production policies. The general approach was called *ujamaa* and focused on African-proved methods of economic growth in agriculture rather than European-proved methods of growth in manufacturing. Small-scale operations were emphasized as local village economies were used as building blocks in the development process. Emphasis was also placed on providing the basic forms of human capital with respect to health and education. The policy of *ujamaa* has not been successful, however, for several reasons. One is that it was implemented under a strict regime that sometimes forced people to leave their own village for a new *ujamaa* village, causing many to balk at the whole system. It was also instituted under a concurrent system of agricultural price controls that inhibited production. Finally, Tanzania faced the same problems that limited economic growth in other LDCs during the 1980s, no matter what types of policies they had implemented to spur economic development.

BARRIERS TO ECONOMIC DEVELOPMENT

What happened in the 1980s to slow down, and sometimes halt or even reverse, the average economic progress of those countries in the South? To be sure, there were some "success" stories in the 1980s, but most of them began much earlier and involved economies such as those of the Republic of (South) Korea, Taiwan (called Taiwan Province of China by the United Nations), Mexico, Brazil, and Argentina that already had strong economies by international standards. The economic development story in the LDCs during the 1980s was almost uniformly bleak, with the earlier economic gains of the 1960s and early 1970s stalled by a number of barriers to continued progress. The special problems of the LDCs in the 1980s (and they still apply in the mid-1990s) are described in Insights 11.4. The major problems affecting the LDCs are low agricultural productivity, rapid population growth, environmental degradation, instability in macroeconomic policies, government-imposed market rigidities that create barriers to development, and problems in external relationships.

Links among the first three issues take us right back to Ricardo's land-use model (Chapter 2). Low rates of agricultural productivity cause poorer and poorer quality land to be put into food cultivation as population grows. The low-quality land used to increase production is not substandard simply because of its poor soil quality or lack of moisture for farming, but also because it is easily degraded by cultivation. Soil erosion, for example, and desertification are environmental problems that are created by the spread of agricultural practices into physically marginal lands in many LDCs. (We'll return to this subject in more detail in Chapter 12.)

Macroeconomic policies concern fiscal practices, such as taxation, and monetary issues, including interest rates and currency exchange rates. Macroeconomic instability, or fluctuations in such government policies, hinders investment in an economy because it creates uncertainty. Most investments, for example, are made in the context of taxation policy. If tax policies change, the expectations concerning investment returns change, too. Most investors are uneasy about putting their money to work in countries (even their own) where tax and interest rate policies are unpredictable.

Governments can impose market rigidities in several ways. They can require, for example, that corporations maintain certain levels of investment or employment in order to remain in business. Governments can also impose "official" prices that either suppress investment in some activities because the official prices are too low, or subsidize investment in other activities where official prices are artificially high (remember the problem of price suppression in agricultural markets described in Chapter 3). Governments can also overregulate and overadminister their economy in such a way that high transaction costs bog down the interactions that are required for more efficient production. Market rigidities are a major barrier to the economic diversification and economic growth of the LDCs.

The problems of market rigidity are the problems of a less developed economy. The "rigidities" basically are barriers among markets and sectors in an economy that impede their integration and limit economic progress. In an effort to remove such barriers to development, the governments of many LDCs recently have undertaken policies of *structural adjustment* that are designed to integrate their domestic economies and so promote more efficient use of their factors of production. In general, structural adjustment programs involve limiting the government's role in the economy and stabilizing macroeconomic policy. The way to reduce the government's role in the economy most quickly is to reduce its spending; this approach also permits tax reductions and fiscal and monetary stabilization. Government-owned enterprises are also sold to the private sector, and private enterprise and entrepreneurship are encouraged. Another way that governments induce structural adjustment is to loosen or eliminate wage and price controls that affect interactions in domestic markets.

Structural adjustment and the decline of government activity in the economy have often led to increased unemployment as government workers are let go. State-owned enterprises have a greater political than profit motive, and their employment levels usually drop dramatically when they are taken into the private sector. In addition, general decreases in government spending and increases in interest rates are often aspects of structural adjustment that help to stabilize macroeconomic policy but initially lead to economic contraction and job losses in the private sector as well. In addition, the relaxation of wage and price controls usually means that wages go down while prices for many necessities increase.

Adjustment programs are expensive to institute because they create economic shocks, and most of these programs have required significant financial backing from institutions such as the International Monetary Fund and the World Bank (discussed later in this chapter). But even though such programs are wrenching to a country's economy, the hope is that the negative impacts are short-term and that long-term benefits will be the result. Less government intervention in the economy should lead to a rationalization of wages and prices based on markets rather than politics, and a country's factors of production should be used more efficiently when rigidities, which create barriers to interaction, are removed from the economy.

Although many governments are withdrawing from more heavy-handed intervention in their economy, they can and do play an important role in facilitating economic development. For example, macroeconomic policy is by definition in the hands of a country's government, and it can be designed in ways that promote economic growth. Human capital investment, at least at basic levels, is also an area of government concern. Furthermore, as illustrated in Case 11.1, some governments have been successful in guiding private investment in effective ways. In developing economies, for example, governments can be particularly useful in making certain types of private investment more attractive by providing income insurance or some other type of guarantee that is not otherwise available. Finally, government plays an important role in its country's external relationships. Government controls trade and investment flows across its country's borders, and it can facilitate such flows in its policy efforts.

➤ INSIGHTS 11.4
Internal Issues in Economic Development

National Policies and Measures

Fundamental to the problems faced by the LDCs in achieving sustained long-term growth and sustainable development in the 1980s were rigidities in their economies, fiscal imbalances, monetary (and in some cases political) instability and pricing policies. While much weight was put on the role of the State in development, insufficient attention was paid to individual initiative and enterprise. The experience gained in implementing development plans to transform the social and productive basis for development confirmed the need to improve macro-economic policies, implementation mechanisms and institutions, and to put in place policy measures which would enable LDCs to adjust better to external shocks. In some countries, internal disturbances and instability, sometimes aggravated by destabilization originating from outside, also had an adverse effect, particularly where scarce resources otherwise available for economic and social development were diverted for other purposes.

For many of the LDCs only one or two sectors contributed to economic growth, domestic revenue and foreign-exchange earnings, so rendering their economies heavily dependent on, and vulnerable to adverse changes in, the international economy. To achieve broad-based growth, LDCs therefore need to diversify their productive bases—a process which required structural change, and corresponding capital inputs, which were not available domestically, nor in many cases forthcoming from foreign private investment.

Many LDCs introduced structural adjustment programs particularly in the latter half of the decade. They were usually supported by the International Monetary Fund (IMF) and/or the World Bank, in order to achieve short-term economic stabilization and to promote long-term development. However, the success rate in the 1980s was mixed. A number of these programs could not be implemented fully or in a timely fashion, for a number of reasons. These include weakness in the design or implementation of early programs, inadequate attention to the specific development characteristics of individual LDCs, inadequate external support and too much emphasis on measures to restore economic and financial stability, with too little on the need to maintain an essential minimum of investment in key areas. More recent structural adjustment programs, profiting from this experience, are showing more promise, although the benefits of these programs have yet to be fully realized and evaluated.

Agriculture, the most important sector of the economies of the LDCs, played a key role in providing food, employment, raw materials for industry and export revenues. While some progress was noted, agricultural performance during the 1980s was generally disappointing, since food production lagged behind population growth in many cases. The reasons for this included marketing price and land-reform policies, inadequate and unsuccessful investment, damage done to the environment, natural disasters (flood, drought, locusts); bottle-necks in transport, seeds and fertilizers; and shortage of credit. External trade restraints were also a serious deterrent to agricultural production and diversification. These factors also affected rural development plans adversely.

In most LDCs, the high rate of population growth was a fundamental problem adversely affecting efforts to alleviate poverty, the efficient allocation of resources, the adequacy of social services, food security and the quality of the natural environment. During the 1980s, limited investment led to cuts in expenditure on health and education which often weighed hardest on the most vulnerable groups, such as children, the aged and the rural and urban poor. The experience of this period also underscored the importance of adequate participation in the decision-making process at all levels, thus further promoting the economic, social, cultural, civil and political rights of all people and thereby allowing their natural talents to flourish.

Despite the efforts undertaken by various national and international bodies, women continued to face the following obstacles which prevented them from being full agents and beneficiaries of development, such as: attitudes which tended to perpetuate the inferior status of women; the unequal access of women to education, training, employment, earnings and to the means of production; the inadequate participation of women in decision-making; and inadequacies in government policies and structures with regard to the integration of women in development.

Sound environmental management in the LDCs during the 1980s also suffered, largley on account of lack of resources devoted to this purpose. In the majority of LDCs, most of the pressing environment problems resulted directly from endemic poverty and population pressure. These have often compelled the poor to adopt unsound farming, grazing and fishing methods, or to settle on ecologically fragile marginal lands. To these may be added a general low level of awareness among the people in LDCs of the issues relating to environment, particularly in rural areas.

Eighty percent of the population of the LDCs lives in rural areas. The diminishing capacity of the agricultural sector to sustain a growing population triggered a rapid urbanization process, placing an unbearable burden on the urban infrastructure.

During the 1980s, private sector development began to play an increasing role despite the lack in many cases of an appropriate legal and institutional framework for the conduct of private entrepreneurship. There was greater recognition that the operation of public enterprises in the LDCs and the role of private initiative and competition should be approached in a more balanced and pragmatic manner. Measures have been taken to improve the efficiency of the parastatal sector including by reducing subsidies, but given the weakness of many institutions, further sustained efforts will be required. In some cases, programs of divestiture have been implemented, but have encountered constraints owing to the small size of the investing public and the undeveloped nature of capital markets, associated with the low level of domestic savings and the lack of foreign investment.

SOURCE: United Nations Conference on Trade and Development, 1992: *Paris Declaration and Program of Action for the Least Developed Countries for the 1990s* (New York: United Nations), pp. 9–13.

◣ CASE *11.1*
Government-Induced Rents in East Asia

The centerpiece of industrial policy in East Asia has been the provision of incentives to induce firms to increase production capacity and productivity and to compete aggressively for increased market share. The incentives have been provided through a mix of selective protection, competition and "subsidies."

Industrial deepening proceeded furthest in those countries where the international competitiveness of national firms was steadily built up, i.e. Japan, Republic of Korea and Taiwan province of China.

"Subsidies" to support industrial development were applied selectively and used particularly in the initial phases of establishing new industries. Fiscal support was provided by a range of special tax measures which reduced government revenue but promoted the accumulation of earnings by firms and their stability in the face of cyclical fluctuations or (as in the case of special depreciation allowances) reduced investment risks by shortening the period of investment recovery. But perhaps the most important "subsidies" came from keeping down interest rates and allowing domestic prices to deviate from international ones.

A critical feature of "getting the prices right" in order to encourage industrialization involved getting them "wrong" in the sense of not letting them reflect existing scarcities of factors of production. This has been demonstrated by the World Bank in its recent major report on the "East Asian Miracle." In respect to conformity of national prices with international prices, the report shows that Taiwan province of China, the Republic of Korea and Japan fall within the fifth and sixth deciles of developing countries, with greater levels of price distortion than Brazil, India, Mexico, Pakistan and Venezuela.

It has recently been argued that "state-created rents" were an important mechanism through which industrial policy provided incentives to set up new industries. This view is based on the observation that the risks of establishing new industries in late industrializing countries are very high and that, as with any innovative activity, high entrepreneurial profits are consequently required. For innovators at the frontier of technology, entry barriers associated with innovation result in rents which provide incentives for doing "new things." In late industrializing countries, however, the market mechanism alone cannot provide such rents. Even though a new activity may be highly risky, firms borrowing and adapting foreign technology face established competitors who have much greater experience. Consequently, if the development of industry relies on the private sector, it is the State that has to create rents for the early entrants, particularly through the application of protectionist measures and by repressing interest rates and credit provision. It has been argued that industrial policy in the Republic of Korea worked through these rents, and that the most lucrative "subsidies" provided by the Government took the form of profits from sales on domestic markets made possible by protection which was conditional on export performance.

The incentives provided by rents were most effective when the latter were distributed on a competitive basis. Private firms competed vigorously to win monopolistic positions, e.g. when government technology screening and the sequencing of acquisition of technology by different firms interacted to improve the process of technology importation.

The notion that the creation of rents was central to the establishment of new industries contradicts the political economy of rent-seeking of the 1970s and 1980s under inward-oriented trade regimes. Four critical differences would seem to lie behind the success of rent creation in promoting industrialization in the newly industrialized economies. Firstly, it was achievable through directly productive activities which served national interests. Secondly, rent-seeking costs, a form of transaction costs incurred in seeking rents (through activities like information collection, influence-peddling and bargaining) were kept low. Thirdly, governments acted to close off other nonproductive channels of wealth accumulation, such as agricultural landlordism, urban real estate speculation and the exploitation of military and bureaucratic office for private gain. Fourthly, the realization of rents (and also other subsidies) was related to performance standards, including a requirement to export. This was of critical importance in the Republic of Korea and Taiwan province of China, where domestic markets could not support the cutthroat oligopolistic competition which prevailed in Japan during its high-growth period.

SOURCE: "Rents as Incentives," in UNCTAD, 1994: *Trade and Development Report, 1992* (New York: United Nations), pp. 68–69.

FOR DISCUSSION

Discuss this case in the context of the modernization theory of economic development.

EXTERNAL LINKS AND ECONOMIC GROWTH AND DEVELOPMENT

Terms such as rich and poor are not necessarily absolute; rather, they are often used for comparison. The same holds for the descriptive terms and classifications used in describing the geography of economic development. The term "least developed countries (LDCs)" used by the United Nations, for example, requires that there also be at least one other group of countries that are "most" (more?) developed. Another term used to collectively describe the world's poorer countries is *third world*, which implies that there are at least two more "worlds" on the planet as far as economic development is concerned. In fact, the term "third world" was initially a reference to a political category. The first world consisted of the industrial democracies, such as the United States, Japan, and Germany, which have dominated much of the global economy since the mid-1950s. The economic systems in these countries rely mainly on markets to allocate goods and services. The second world is now gone, but it consisted of the countries, such as the Soviet Union, that had industrial economies with centrally planned allocations of goods and services and decidedly nondemocratic governments. The third world consisted of a group of countries with a mixture of political and economic systems, but unified by the fact that their economies were not industrialized.

Over time the industrial-nonindustrial split, with the first two "worlds" on the one hand and the third world on the other, simply boiled down to the rich versus poor categorization that is now most often described in North-South terms. The North-South categorization also conforms to the *core-periphery model* of economic development. A core economy contains an agglomeration of vertically integrated manufacturing and service industries. In a vertically integrated industry, producers sell products to other producers in a chain that begins with raw material production and ends with output for final demand. The geographical concentrations of vertically integrated industries that define core regions also make them virtually self-sufficient in supply and demand relationships, except in their need for raw materials that are not always domestically available. In addition, core producers usually are interested in serving external markets because of their potential for increasing economic rents.

Peripheral economies are marked by specialization rather than the economic diversification that exists in the core. They tend to obtain most of their earnings either from raw material sources or other primary-sector products, or from their ability to employ labor cheaply. The domestic markets of peripheral economies are limited because incomes are low; thus external markets are of critical importance to their growth.

The differences between core (North) and periphery (South) economies have led to a call for a *New International Economic Order (NIEO)* in the United Nations. In the NIEO resolution passed by the General Assembly in 1974, the United Nations called for economic redistribution between rich and poor countries that would close the gap in living standards between the average citizen of the world's wealthier countries and the average citizen of the world's poorer economies. Nothing much has come from the NIEO, but it does underscore the importance of interaction between the North and South in boosting the South's prospects for economic growth and development.

The process of modernization outside of its Western European origin can be considered the result of spatial interaction between core and periphery. In Chapter 3 spatial diffusion was described as a form of interaction in which certain agricultural technologies were spread from rich countries to poorer ones. Spatial diffusion can also spread more general technologies and technologies applicable to manufacturing processes from rich countries to poor ones. The Meiji Restoration and the growth of the Japanese economy in the late nineteenth century and again after World War II are often considered as illustrative of modernization resulting from spatial diffusion. The Japanese, alone among the nations of East Asia, adopted and adapted Western technology and economic practices to a degree that they were able to withstand the military and economic domination by Western powers that reached its height in the nineteenth and early twentieth centuries.

An optimistic view is that technological diffusion from core to periphery can go a long way toward raising peripheral incomes because technology is so important in improving productivity. Many times, however, while the spread of technology does occur from core to peripheral locations, it is often in second-best form. In the early 1990s, for example, an entire General Motors plant was dismantled in Pontiac, Michigan, and shipped in pieces to China. In China it was reassembled and is now operated as a light truck factory. Machine tools that are obsolete by American standards are shipped to Brazil and installed for use in factories. Telephone switching equipment that only has scrap value where the best telecommunications systems are in use is installed in South Asia, where telephone systems are of poor quality and inhibit the integration of regions within countries. In all these cases, the physical diffusion of capital equipment and the technology that it contains are beneficial to its new user in the periphery, but it is no longer considered productive at its origin in the core.

Even though the technology is often second-best, technological diffusion from core to periphery is an important link between the rich and poor countries, and it does carry the potential for improving the economic prospects of the South in a meaningful way. Two other major forms of interaction between North and South are trade and investment. Unfortunately, the 1980s and 1990s were years of difficulties in these areas, especially for the LDCs (Insights 11.5). Leading problems in trade between the South and North concern weak prices for primary products and generally declining terms of trade. Many core economies retain barriers to the import of products from the periphery, especially its manufactured products. Conditions for financial assistance have become more restrictive, and lending has declined in favor of direct investment as a source of financing for projects in peripheral economies. Official aid, too, has declined in some instances, but debt burdens remain severe. We'll take up the role of trade in economic development first, and then we will turn to the issue of international finance.

> INSIGHTS 11.5
External Issues in Economic Development

EXTERNAL ENVIRONMENT

In the field of trade, the international economic environment of the 1980s has been difficult, especially for the LDCs, given the heavy dependence of most LDC economies on the export of a handful of commodities. With their very weak manufacturing base, exports were almost exclusively of unprocessed primary commodities. The prevailing trend over the 1980s of a decline in world prices for raw materials of interest to the LDCs weakened the LDCs' export earnings and their imports and debt-servicing capacity. Since prices of goods imported by the LDCs continued to rise, the terms of trade of the LDCs worsened significantly, causing a significant trade loss. The two main international compensatory financing schemes, the IMF Compensatory and Contingency Financing Facility (CCFF) and the EEC STABEX arrangement, helped to reduce the adverse impact on many LDC economies, but coverage of such schemes was limited.

Special tariff preferences have been granted to LDCs and extended during the 1980s. However, trade barriers have affected actual and potential exports and discouraged diversification. Thus, certain LDC exports (especially textiles, vegetable oils, tobacco and sugar) faced tariff and nontariff barriers in various parts of the world. In addition, some LDCs were excluded by certain importing countries from the full benefits of the generalized system of preferences (GSP) and the "Special measures in favor of LDCs" adopted at the Tokyo Round. Moreover, consumer prices for tropical products have been kept relatively high in GSP donor countries through the application of high internal taxes. And in a large number of GSP schemes, semiprocessed forms of products tend to be subject to considerably higher tariffs than the primary form, with ensuing disincentives for LDCs to process primary products for exports. Furthermore, more than 15 percent of LDC exports, especially clothing, were subject to various nontariff measures. Many LDCs lacked the expertise to derive full benefit from the various GSP schemes. Others, while aware that their products could find additional markets, lacked the resources to improve the quality and appearance of such products to the required standard.

The 1980s have been marked by a slow-down in the rate of increase of official development assistance (ODA) and the drastic fall in private flows such as export credits and direct investment, with the virtual stoppage of commercial lending. As LDCs resource needs grew substantially during that period, in particular in connection with additional financial requirements to support rehabilitation and adjustment programs and growing debt-service obligations, the volume of ODA has been generally insufficient, taking into account the virtual disappearance of private flows. Although a number of donor countries met or exceeded the 0.15 percent aid target, or increased very substantially their aid to LDCs, donors' ODC/GNP ratio remained at the average of 0.09 percent throughout the 1980s.

Among the problems identified by donors and/or recipients were cumbersome procedures, protracted negotiations, failure to identify or agree on priorities, too much tied aid, difficulty of meeting local costs and insufficient use of local products or skills. The adverse external environment also affected the ability of the LDCs to generate resource flows internally. The 1980s witnessed a significant depletion in the savings capacity of the LDCs in the face of rising population, declining economic growth and foreign-exchange constraints.

External debt servicing emerged as a major problem for most LDCs during the 1980s. By the end of 1986, total accumulated external debt of the LDCs represented over 60 percent of their combined GDP; and service payments alone absorbed about 30 percent, and in many cases as much as 50 percent, of their exports of goods and services. Over one-third of ODA to the LDCs (mainly from international financial institutions) was provided in the form of loans, albeit on highly concessional terms, with consequent debt implications for the LDCs. Increasing debt-service obligations to multilateral institutions and the weight of debt to private (commercial) creditors constituted a considerable burden on LDCs.

SOURCE: United Nations Conference on Trade and Development, 1992: *Paris Declaration and Program of Action for the Least Developed Countries for the 1990s* (New York: United Nations), pp. 13–15.

THE ROLE OF TRADE

Is trade between North and South beneficial to peripheral economic growth and development? There are, as you might expect, different opinions. On the negative side, it has been argued that the different natures of core and perpheral economies leads to trade imbalances between them that limit peripheral growth. The core can offer the periphery a wide variety of products because of its diversified economy. Peripheral countries, however, can only export a limited number of products because of their specialization in either the primary sector or in producing manufactured goods that require large amounts of cheap labor in their production. Trade will always be unbalanced between core and periphery, it is argued, simply because their economies are at different levels of development. Flows between economies at different levels of development only serve to maintain their differences, at best, or even cause the gap between the two types of economies to get larger.

In addition to the economies of scale available to producers in the core, their efficiency is also increased by their higher level of technology. Because of their high technology, producers in rich countries have a type of monopoly power that keeps producers from poorer countries, with their lower technology, from entering the market. High technology producers are able to earn economic rents in poor country markets, and maintain those rents because of their competitive edge (see Case 11.1). Finally, producers in poor countries are often at a disadvantage simply because they operate in an undeveloped economy. The structural adjustment programs described above were often undertaken not only with domestic considerations in mind, but also to make exports more competitive in world markets.

Because of their differences, trade between core countries, with their economies of scale and associated production efficiencies, and poorer countries, with relatively small markets and production inefficiencies, could actually undermine the development of domestic economic diversification in the periphery. The goods flowing from the core would be more attractive because of higher quality and lower prices than could be achieved in domestic markets, so trade would cut off the growth of domestic industries in the periphery. The answer to this potential problem is protection of the domestic market in poorer countries, so that their economies can grow without facing the unfair advantages held by producers from the core economies. Following this general line of thinking, many poorer countries around the world developed policies of import substitution (see Chapter 10) in the 1950s and 1960s that used trade protection to encourage the establishment and growth of their domestic producers. The intention of this type of policy is to encourage local production to replace goods normally purchased as imports from the core economies.

Although imports from the core are to be avoided, according to the arguments made for import-substitution policies, exports are always expected to have positive impacts on the growth and development of a country's economy. Most of the benefits of exporting in international markets are the same as those described for regions in Chapter 9. In addition, the benefits of free trade, especially on the export side, are those that were described in Chapter 10, and include the increase of production efficiency as markets increase in size. Exporting, however, is not the only side of the trade equation that can have a positive impact on a country's domestic economy. Proponents of free trade argue, for example, that imports often contain technology that is unavailable in the domestic market and may be critical to increasing production efficiency in a poor country's domestic production. Remember Case 10.1, which described the world's big emerging markets. Those countries, you will recall, are industrializing most rapidly, and they are all importing capital equipment from core economies to accomplish their rapid growth. The same point is illustrated in Case 11.2, which describes the importance of opening domestic economies to imports in order to fuel increases in export sectors.

Trade is often called the "engine of growth," and the countries in Case 11.2 are good examples of countries that have achieved significant economic progress over the last 30 years or so by developing coordinated programs of exporting and importing. None of the countries described in the case are from the group of LDCs, and each of the countries in the group has a large manufacturing sector. Among the LDCs, however, manufacturing is less important, and the primary sector is the dominant one. Primary products, with some exceptions, are not often considered to have the same potential for export-induced economic growth that is often associated with manufactured goods.

Countries that export primary products are often affected by poor *terms of trade* in international markets. Terms of trade are usually defined as unit export values divided by unit import values, with the result multiplied by 100 so that they are expressed in index form (Figure 11.10). If a country's terms of trade are equal to 100, then the average value of its exports is equal to the average value of its imports. If its terms of trade are less than 100, then it is importing products with a higher average value than its exports carry. Usually, manufactured goods have a higher average value than do primary goods, so countries that export mostly primary goods often have poor terms of trade. Poor terms of trade, in and of themselves, do not mean that a country will necessarily run trade deficits. They do carry that potential, however, and export volumes must grow rapidly if a country expects to accumulate foreign exchange if its terms of trade are poor. Unfortunately for the LDCs, primary product markets don't grow very rapidly because technological advances usually cause demand for natural resources to grow slowly, if at all.

Exporting primary products has led to national economic development, but only in unusual circumstances. According to the *staple theory of development*, Canada achieved its status as a rich industrial country utilizing earnings gained from exports from its primary sector. It did not specialize in a single primary product, however, but was able to substitute one primary product for another as international markets changed. Initially, fish from the Grand Banks were exported, then fur from the interior, followed by lumber, wheat, and then energy resources. Currently, countries such as Nigeria, Indonesia, Iraq, and Iran are trying to use proceeds from their oil exports to finance internal development projects, but

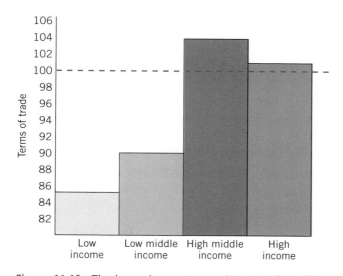

Figure 11.10 The lower income countries typically suffer from poor terms of trade. Their export values are less than their import values, a relationship indicated by a number less than 100 in this illustration. On the other hand, richer countries have average terms of trade that indicate that the value of their exports is greater than the value of their imports.

earnings from those exports fluctuate with international market prices and so their development efforts fluctuate as well.

Export earnings are more consistent when exports are diversified across economic sectors. A major challenge for the LDCs has been to expand their export bases from the primary sector to the secondary one. Bangladesh has been successful in its efforts to diversify its exports in this way (see Case 11.3), but international markets are not easy to penetrate because of their maze of trade restrictions. For example, the Multifiber Arrangement (see Chapter 10) has been used to restrict access by peripheral textile and apparel producers to the markets of core economies. While it is scheduled to end by 2000 with textiles and apparel coming under GATT rules, its use in the past illustrates the sort of trade barriers faced by LDCs and other developing countries that need to be significantly lowered for trade to provide them with an "engine of growth."

Sir W. Arthur Lewis, the Nobel Prize-winning development economist, summarized the problems of the developing countries in today's global economy (from *The Evolution of the International Economic Order*, p. 76):

1. The principal cause of the problem of the developing countries, and of their poor factoral terms of trade, is that half of their labor force (more or less) produces food at very low productivity levels. This limits the domestic market for manufactures and services, keeps the propensity to import too high, reduces taxable capacity and savings, and provides goods and services for export on unfavorable terms. To alter this is the fundamental way to change less-developed country/more-developed country relations. But this takes time.

2. Meanwhile less-developed countries need a more rapid rate of growth of exports, to pay for needed imports and to meet their debt obligations. More-developed countries should make more space for the less-developed countries in world trade, by reducing their barriers to less-developed country exports of manufactures and agricultural products. This is the best and most effective way of helping the less-developed countries.

◪ *CASE 11.2*

Exports and Economic Growth in Some Developing Countries

An examination of successful export experiences illustrates the fact that developing countries have used very different strategies to build export success and have been able to combine protection for the domestic market with export promotion in many different ways. However, aside from liberalization of imported inputs used by export sectors, other forms of import liberalization have not necessarily been an ingredient of successful trade policies.

The Republic of Korea is the best known example among developing countries of active industrial policies and targeting. The availability of directly allocated long-term credit to target industries was an important element of this strategy. The country also used export subsidies for a large part of its long export boom. Rapid growth took off after the launching of a comprehensive export promotion program in 1964–1965, which included the active use of export and credit subsidies and export targeting. A moderate liberalization of quantitative restrictions (QRs) on imports took place in 1967, but tariffs remained high and direct import controls extensive until as late as 1978, when a gradual preannounced program of import liberalization was initiated. In 1973, however, the Government launched an ambitious heavy and chemical industries promotion plan, which included the granting of fiscal and credit incentives and increased protection for some of the targeted industries. After important problems associated with the world recession of the early 1980s, this plan became the basis for the export industries of the second half of the decade.

Despite the general characterization of the economies of Latin America as inward-oriented, most countries in the region abandoned active import-substituting industrial policies in the mid-1970s. Brazil and Mexico were among the few countries in the region which continued to follow active policies of this nature until the debt crisis. They used a mixture of policy measures and actions, including high tariffs (more so in Brazil than in Mexico), high non-tariff barriers, special industrial programs, domestic content requirements and direct investment by public enterprises. For almost two decades, starting in the late 1960s, Brazil succeeded in combining high protection with rapid export growth and an improvement in the composition of its manufacturing exports. It did so by using a combination of export incentives and gradual devaluation, adopting an import liberalization program only in 1991. The interruption of its export boom in the mid-1980s was a consequence of the major problems created by the macroeconomic imbalances in the country, rather than of deficiencies in trade policies.

China is one of the most notable examples of a country with rapid growth in the 1980s, based on a program of measures adopted in the late 1970s. These included a significant devaluation of the currency; the decentralization of the managment of foreign trade; an export contract system, by which the foreign trade corporations entered into contracts for the implementation of the plan (in terms of foreign exchange earnings, production costs for exports and total size of the trade deficit); the active use of Hong Kong's commercial agents and facilities; and the establishment of several Special Economic Zones (which did not make an important contribution to export expansion until the second half of the decade). Although foreign trade continued to be highly regulated and protected, real exports tripled in the decade following these reforms.

Malaysia is an example of a country which underwent rapid export growth in the 1980s through the establishment of export processing zones. Together with other countries of Southeast Asia, it has also enjoyed significant external economies resulting from the relocation of industrial operations from Japan and the leading newly industrialized countries of the region. This relocation has been brought about by the latter countries' loss of competitiveness in the most labor-intensive activities and by the imposition of nontariff restrictions against them by developed countries. Although Malaysia has low nontariff barriers and relatively low tariffs, domestic trade policies are not neutral. Effective tariff protection rose, particularly in the machine and capital goods sector, as a result of a heavy industrialization program launched in the early 1980s. On the export side, taxes on many of the agricultural and mineral raw materials in which the country has a strong comparative advantage have been used to generate incentives to the processing of such materials; some of these were abolished only in 1991.

These country experiences indicate that export success has involved at least three different strategies, or a combination of them: very active industrial policies and targeting; active management of the exchange rate and use of export subsidies (such as direct cash payments, preferential and subsidized export credits and income tax allowances) in the early stages of export growth; and the establishment of export processing zones. More generally, successful export growth has also involved maintaining competitive exchange rates and enabling exporters to acquire raw materials, intermediate goods and, in some cases, capital goods duty-free.

Except for the imported inputs used by export sectors, import liberalization has been introduced only after the upturn of exports, sometimes well after the upturn. This suggests that trade reform should not only be implemented gradually but should also follow a sequence in which protection is reduced substantially only after rapid export growth is already in place, i.e. after export supply capabilities have been built up. Whereas exchange rate policies are crucial, the role of import liberalization in export success is less clear.

Finally, it should be noted that rapid export growth has been accompanied in some of the countries examined by sharp, even dramatic, reductions in real wages. However, there is no clear pattern of the effects of trade policy reform on income distribution. The evidence from Colombia, the Republic of Korea and Malaysia shows that increasing real wages can accompany sustained export growth in the long run; the effects of real devaluation on this trend were marginal in the latter two countries. In contrast, in Mexico, Turkey and Chile real wages fell considerably in the early stages of the export boom. However, even in these countries the relative contribution of trade policies to this outcome is unclear because they were accompanied by other, equally far-reaching, economic and political events.

SOURCE: "Some Country Experiences," in UNCTAD, 1992: *Trade and Development Report, 1992* (New York: United Nations), pp. 109–111.   ◩

FOR DISCUSSION

Based on the experiences of the countries described in this case, design a basic set of policies that would promote economic growth in a hypothetical developing country.

◩ *CASE 11.3*
Export Diversification in Bangladesh

The diversification of the economy of Bangladesh during its brief history has been considerable. Agriculture remains the dominant sector, but its share of GDP has declined from 57.8 percent in the year of independence (1971) to 37.8 percent in 1990. The growth of the economy has been mainly in public administration (including defense), trade and professional services and the transport, storage and communications sectors. Industry, which expanded during the first five-year plan (1973–1978), did not increase its share in GDP thereafter.

The pattern of merchandise exports changed dramatically during the 1980s. The locus in dynamism in export performance lay in the continued expansion of the "nontraditional" items. At the beginning of the decade raw jute and jute products accounted for approximately two-thirds of total export earnings. Although these items continue to be important, their export earnings declined sharply and the ready-made garment industry became the main export earner: in 1989/90 exports amounted to $609 million and in 1990/91 to an estimated $724 million, or 42.5 percent of total exports. A closer look at the "new" export products reveals the high degree of specialization in the garment industry. On the basis of disaggregated data at the four-digit level, there are three products for which export earnings in 1988/89 exceeded $50 million, namely men's and boy's shirts, jackets and overcoats. This performance was achieved in spite of rising barriers to exports such as the anti-dumping action brought by the United States against shop towels from Bangladesh in 1991.

Explanations of this "success" have focused on the positive impact of the country's textile quota under the Multifiber Arrangement; export opportunities of competing countries were limited, while importers (in the first instance from the Republic of Korea and India) were drawn to the Bangladesh market. However, at the present stage of development of the garment industry the quotas are no longer a major requirement for its further expansion.

Industrial expansion faces many critical constraints: the industrial base is narrow, contributing less than 15 percent to GDP, of which manufacturing, with a high import content, comprises about half; hence industrialization is likely to remain import-intensive. Unemployment and underemployment are widespread and the bulk of the labor force is unskilled. Labor productivity is low and income and wage policies are not linked to efficiency. Furthermore, the manufacturing sector is beset with a number of other problems, including limited purchasing power in the domestic market and inefficiencies and sustained losses in the oversized public sector. This is exacerbated by the lack of accountability by management and labor, as well as the prevalence of many loss-making enterprises in the private sector, reflecting poor choices by the nationalized industrial financing institutions.

Import liberalization has been the hallmark of trade policies in recent years and has taken the form of significant tariff reductions and rationalization of the tariff system, progressive removal of items from the list of restricted imports (from 186 items in 1985 to 113 in 1991), simplification of procedures, enlarging the number of freely importable items, etc. Schemes have been introduced for bonded warehouses, duty drawback for export production, foreign investment incentives and export processing zones.

The current export strategy includes "rationalization" of the value of the taka (Banglaedesh's currency); promotional measures for individual export categories such as leather, prawns, electronics, computers and engineering services, agricultural products, and backward-linking manufacturing activities; development and expansion of supporting infrastructure; export market expansion through continuous market surveys; greater participation in trade fairs abroad and the organization of trade missions. However, to generate additional export opportunities further tariff reductions and selective import liberalization will be needed to realize the full potential of the textile, garment, leather and assembly industries.

SOURCE: Box 19: "Successful Diversification in Bangladesh," in UN Conference on Trade and Development, 1991: *The Least Developed Countries* (New York: United Nations), p. 90.

FOR DISCUSSION

Describe the industrial diversification of Bangladesh in the context of the product life-cycle model described in Chapter 7.

FINANCING ECONOMIC GROWTH AND DEVELOPMENT

A major international economic crisis of the 1980s resulted from the inability of many peripheral countries to pay the interest on the mountains of foreign debt that they had accumulated during that decade and in the 1970s. A combination of international economic recession, high oil prices, and miscalculation on the parts of both lenders and borrowers led to the debt crisis. Although the crisis eased in the early 1990s, debt remains a serious problem for many of the world's poorer countries, especially those classed among the LDCs. In 1992, the average debt of the LDCs equaled over 200% of their annual export earnings and almost two-thirds of their GNPs. Even the middle-income economies retained high debt levels after the crisis ended, with both low-middle income and high-middle income countries running debt amounting to about 150% of their exports, and 40% and 30% of their respective GNPs.

Because of the debt crisis, most private bank lending to developing economies has declined considerably. The bulk of financial flows to the periphery, aside from export earnings, come either from multilateral sources, foreign aid, or foreign direct investment (see the next section). The two leading multilateral financial institutions are the *International Monetary Fund (IMF)* and the umbrella organization now called the *World Bank*. Both the IMF and the World Bank were established at an international conference held at Bretton Woods, New Hampshire in 1944, which dealt with the reorganization of the world economy after World War II. Both are UN organizations, but their ties to the United Nations are quite weak. Their headquarters, for example, are in Washington, D.C., not New York.

The IMF is not a bank, but a different type of financial organization that was designed to provide an institution to guide the expansion of international trade and finance. It uses a quota system of governance which allocates voting rights to its members based on the size of their economies. The United States and other core-economy countries dominate policy formation in the IMF, therefore, and also provide most of its financial base. Since its beginning, the IMF has been concerned primarily with its members' balance-of-payments problems (financial shortages caused by excesses of imports over exports) and has not focused on the international problems of developing countries alone. Over the last few years, however, the IMF has become more involved with the internal economic conditions of the LDCs in addition to their trade-financing problems.

The World Bank has always been concerned with economic development. The two largest banks in this organization are the International Bank for Reconstruction and Development (IBRD) and the International Development Association (IDA). The IBRD had its greatest successes in the reconstruction of Western Europe after World War II. It specializes in lending money for development projects in the same way that private banks do. It requires cost-benefit analyses of the projects on which it is asked to lend, and its government borrowers must show that they are good credit risks. The IDA lends money to countries that can't meet the stricter credit requirements of the IBRD. Its geographical focus, therefore, is the LDCs, and its loans are financed through gifts rather than the commercial borrowings used by the World Bank to finance IBRD loans.

Recently, the World Bank has come under heavy criticism for ignoring environmental concerns in its lending policies during most of its existence. Transport, hydraulic, and forestry projects, in particular, were often judged on limited financial merits without any concern for their larger environmental costs. Recently, environmental concerns have begun to play a major role in World Bank lending (see Chapter 12). Another recent change in World Bank practice has been to coordinate its efforts on specific projects with those of *nongovernmental organizations (NGOs)*. NGOs are social assistance and medical assistance agencies, such as HABITAT and CARE, that work especially well in the LDCs. They have local expertise and are often highly trusted by the populations with whom they work, and can often provide a positive link between the World Bank and the community in which a development project is located.

Both the IMF and World Bank became involved in implementing structural adjustment policies in developing countries in the mid-1980s. Both provided financial resources to governments that could support export incentives and cover lost revenues as tax systems were changed. They financed deregulation of agriculture and manufacturing and helped pay for the higher energy prices that resulted from their decontrol. These supports have not been forthcoming, however, without cost to the developing countries. The IMF, in particular, but also the World Bank have imposed various controls on the domestic economic policies of the countries to which they offer structural adjustment assistance. Many of the countries using IMF and World Bank financing have complained that many of the conditions imposed by these multilateral financial agencies have eroded their sovereignty. Financial and monetary policies, including those affecting exchange rates, are taken out of government hands, at least to some degree, and are determined by the IMF and World Bank. The relationship between lenders and borrowers has grown antagonistic in many cases, mainly because the benefits of structural adjustment in the LDCs are yet to be realized on any large scale. The influence of the IMF and World Bank remains strong, however, because other financial sources, especially private ones, are so limited.

FOREIGN DIRECT INVESTMENT, MULTINATIONAL CORPORATIONS, AND ECONOMIC DEVELOPMENT

Foreign direct investment (FDI) (see Chapter 7) has picked up some of the slack in financing in poorer countries resulting from the decline in bank lending. However, it remains a relatively small proportion of all investment in the world's poorer economies. In the mid-1990s, FDI accounted for only about 5% of investment in the LDCs and about 7% of investment in the middle-income countries. The rest came from the multilateral agencies, individual governments, some lending, and the majority from domestic sources. Though small in proportion of total investment, FDI and other activities of multinational corporations (MNCs) provide an important link between core and periphery in the international economy. (Keep in mind that most, but not all, MNCs are headquartered in core economies. There are several huge MNCs based in industrializing countries such as the Republic of Korea and Brazil. The focus here, however, is on links between core and periphery).

In addition to capital investment, MNCs have the potential to aid economic development in other ways. For example, MNCs may facilitate exports and improve a country's balance of payments. They may also speed structural adjustment because of their more sophisticated use of a developing country's factors of production. They may raise employment levels in a country and may also pay higher than prevailing wage rates because of their high productivity. In addition, it has been suggested that MNCs are particularly effective in promoting the diffusion of technology from richer to poorer countries, and that, by establishing subsidiaries in poorer countries, MNCs provide the propulsive industry that may be the key to a developing country's modernization.

Each argument for the benefits of MNCs in developing countries can be countered by an argument that MNCs cause poorer economies more harm than good, or at best they have a neutral effect on economic development. For example, in some cases MNCs actually cause a country's balance of payments to decline because of their high rate of imports and their use of transfer pricing policies, as described in Chapter 10. Even the economies of rich countries, such as the United States, may be negatively affected in this way. In addition, many MNCs may crowd out domestic employers in an economy by taking their workers, making their employment contributions an illusion, and they are unikely to pay higher than prevailing wage rates if their production in the developing economy is based on its large supply of cheap labor. MNCs may impose costs on their poorer country hosts by setting up manufactures in these countries that are especially harmful to the environment because of their polluting byproducts. Also, MNCs may be so functionally removed from the rest of a poorer country's economy that they don't make any contribution to necessary structural adjustment.

The question of technological diffusion through the activities of MNCs is also open to debate. Although they may facilitate the diffusion of technology, this diffusion may be limited in its geography to subsidiaries operated within the core economies. Even when technology does diffuse from core to periphery within an MNC, there is some question as to whether it is actually spread beyond the corporation into any of the domestic economy. It has been suggested that technological spread within an economy requires both high-quality infrastructure and existing technological expertise. Both of these conditions are anything but typical of poorer economies, particularly those of the LDCs. Again, it appears that much of the technology that does diffuse from richer to poorer countries is second-best, and this diffusion results from transactions between rich-country sellers and poor-country buyers rather than from transfers within MNCs.

In spite of the arguments that MNCs have negative effects on the develop-

ment prospects of poorer countries, the current trend among peripheral governments is to relax restrictions on FDI within their countries and even encourage
it (Insights 11.6). Tax rates on foreign investment and sectoral restrictions have
been eased not only in the LDCs but in the middle-income countries of Latin
America as well. Much of this encouragement of FDI is due to the scarcity of
loans, but some of it is also due to the realization that more spatial interaction
in the international economy, rather than less, has led to economic growth in
a number of peripheral economies. In the 1950s and 1960s, many governments
of developing countries simply took control of, or nationalized, the interests of
foreign corporations operating within their boundaries. They feared that the
presence of MNCs was simply another form of colonialism. The relationship
between MNCs and many governments of poorer countries is now geared toward
partnership rather than confrontation. Governments often promote partnerships
between domestic and foreign companies as guarantees of positive impacts on
their economies from FDI and the presence of MNCs.

➤ INSIGHTS 11.6
FDI in the LDCs

The "program of Action for the Least Developed Countries for the 1990s stipu-
lates that "Private enterprises . . . can play a greater role in transforming LDC
economies and achieving national development objectives. Investment by foreign
enterprises can provide a significant range of new skills which can over time
facilitate the progressive integration of areas of economic activity of the LDCs
into the international economy" (paragraph 70). To date, however, foreign
investors have been in general very reluctant to invest in LDCs, and the flow of
foreign direct investment (FDI) to these countries has remained negligible.

Given the potential contribution of FDI to the modernization of the productive and technological base in LDCs and the fact that it does not create any
additional debt, FDI should indeed play a greater role in these economies. The
fundamental problem faced by policy makers in LDCs in this respect can be
succinctly described as follows: What should be done by the LDCs to stimulate
private investment and, in particular, to attract substantially greater foreign
participation in their development process.

A greater involvement of private investors in the modernization of the technological and productive base of the LDCs presupposes a stronger commitment
by Governments of LDCs to private sector development. Accordingly, they should
make greater efforts to provide an appropriate environment for FDI, e.g. by
pursuing macroeconomic policies (trade, exchange rate, interest rate and tax
policies) that would encourage private investment, providing appropriate infrastructural facilities (in particular public utilities, transport and communications)
and setting up a legal framework which is reliable and enables potential investors
to perceive clearly the benefits of investing in the country. In addition, regulations
restricting the activities of potential investors, such as limitations regarding access

to certain sectors, the number of expatriates that can be employed or the the extent of ownership by residents of foreign countries, should be reduced, if not completely eliminated, or replaced by incentive measures. Moreover, Governments of LDCs should actively support promotional activities abroad, including participation in trade fairs, the establishment of trade promotion centers and the dispatch of trade missions.

Changes recently introduced in regulations and legislation concerning FDI in some LDCs, including Burkina Faso, Central African Republic, Djibouti, Guinea-Bissau, Haiti, Lesotho, Malawi, Maldives, Niger, Sudan, Togo, Vanuatu and Samoa, have reflected a liberal approach in certain aspects, but were somewhat more selective in others. Thus, several countries accord differential incentives to foreign investors depending upon the importance of the investment to the economy. Preferential treatment is given under what is called a "privileged regime", and is generally limited to agriculture and forestry, agroindustry, mining, tourism and handicrafts. Other requirements for benefits under the privileged regime affect regulations concerning the employment of local and expatriate labor. In Djibouti, for example, where the scope of the privileged regime has been further widened, stipulations concerning the creation of permanent employment for locals have been made more explicit. While the eligibility of investors for tax concessions has been broadened in Sudan, other concessions, such as discounted prices for land and transportation costs, have been abolished under the new code regulating foreign investment. In Togo, benefits to enterprises operating under the privileged regime have been increased. However, at the same time, foreign ownership in small- and medium-sized ventures has been limited to a maximum of 49 percent.

The FDI laws promulgated recently in some LDCs which used to pursue a more restrictive attitude also reflect the trend toward greater liberalization. Bangladesh, the Lao People's Democratic Republic, Nepal, Rwanda, Somalia, Sierra Leone, Yemen, among other LDCs, have recently adopted legislation promoting FDI. In particular, provisions relating to such questions as the authorization of investment, ownership, fiscal incentives and the use of local materials and labor aim to stimulate the interest of potential investors.

SOURCE: Insight 13: "Promotion of Foreign Direct Investment in LDCs," in UN Conference on Trade and Development, 1991: *The Least Developed Countries* (New York: United Nations), p. 65.

POINTS IN SUMMARY

1. The current standard for assessing national wealth is the production that occurs in a country as measured by either its gross national product (GNP) or gross domestic product (GDP).

2. Using output as a standard of national wealth is

drawn from a system of Western values that include the idea that economic growth is a virtue in and of itself.

3. In general, when purchasing power parities are used rather than values of per capita GNP, the

disparities in living standards between richer and poorer countries are lessened.

4. The world's richest countries generally are found in a northern tier, while its poorer countries are located to their south.

5. Rich countries, almost by definition, are larger markets than poorer countries and so are more likely to achieve economies of scale in their production.

6. Rich countries are much more often the sources of inventions and innovations that improve technology than are poor countries.

7. Human capital is expensive to develop and maintain, and average levels of education in countries vary with their national income.

8. Integration in an economy, as opposed to segmentation, allows for smooth flows of goods, services, payments, and investment with low transaction costs.

9. Poorer economies are less developed, and the poorest ones least developed, with their poverty and lack of development reinforcing each other.

10. Additional growth is facilitated by infrastructural improvement, but the rate of increase in production shouldn't be expected to equal the rate of increase accomplished by the initial establishment of infrastructure.

11. Regional income inequality is usually associated with geographic concentration in an economy.

12. Regions with high proportions of a country's minority population are often subject to economic discrimination.

13. Groups of people, like regions, must be integrated in an economy before the economy can be said to be developed.

14. Environmental conditions affect what's possible in economic practices, but to call on them as determinants of economic outcomes in places is to fall prey to a single factor fallacy.

15. Culture, as a shared comprehensive set of ways of doing things among people, is surely important in effecting geographical patterns in the international economy, but it's not their sole determinant.

16. The neoclassical economic growth model indicates that labor and capital must work jointly and interdependently in order for production to expand efficiently.

17. The general applicability of modernization theory to currently developing economies is questionable because the relevance of eighteenth- and nineteenth-century European history appears to be rapidly declining in the contemporary global economy.

18. Growing concerns for the environmental degradation and rapid cultural change associated with efforts at rapid economic growth and development have called into question the appropriateness of the Western ''model'' in many regions around the world.

19. The major problems affecting the LDCs are low agricultural productivity, rapid population growth, environmental degradation, macroeconomic instability, government-imposed market rigidities, and problems in external relationships.

20. Although many governments are withdrawing from more heavy-handed intervention in their economy, they can and do play an important role in facilitating economic development.

21. In a vertically integrated economy, producers sell products to other producers in a chain that begins with raw material production and ends with output for final demand.

22. Many core economies retain barriers to the import of products from the periphery, especially its manufactured products.

23. An optimistic view is that technological diffusion from core to periphery can go a long way in raising peripheral incomes because technology is so important in improving productivity.

24. It has been argued that the different nature of core and peripheral economies leads to trade imbalances between them that limit peripheral growth.

25. Because of their high technology, producers in rich countries have a type of monopoly power that keeps producers from poorer countries, with their lower technology, from entering the market.

26. Free trade proponents argue that imports often contain technology that is unavailable in the domestic market, and the very technology that's imported may be critical to increasing production efficiency in a poor country's domestic production.

27. Trade is often called the "engine of growth."

28. Export earnings are more consistent when exports are diversified across economic sectors.

29. Debt is a serious problem for many of the world's poorer countries, especially those classed among the LDCs.

30. Many of the countries using IMF and World Bank financing have complained that the conditions imposed by the multilateral financial agencies have eroded their sovereignty.

31. FDI and the other activities of multinational corporations (MNCs) provide an important link between core and periphery in the international economy.

32. Each argument for the benefits of MNCs in developing countries can be countered by an argument that MNCs cause poorer economies more harm than good.

33. Partnerships between domestic and foreign companies are often promoted by governments as guarantees of positive impacts on their economies from FDI and the presence of MNCs.

TERMS TO REMEMBER

coevolutionary development
core-periphery model
cultural determinism
economic development
economic growth
environmental determinism
human capital

informal sector
International Monetary Fund (IMF)
least developed countries (LDCs)
modernization theory
national accounts
neoclassical economic growth model

New International Economic Order (NIEO)
nongovernmental organizations (NGOs)
North-South division
per capita GNP
primate city

purchasing power parity
staple theory of development
structural adjustment
terms of trade
third world
ujamaa
World Bank

SUGGESTED READING

Alonso, William. 1980: "Five Bell Shapes in Development." *Papers of the Regional Science Association,* Vol. 45, pp. 5–16.

This article was Alonso's presidential address to the Regional Science Association. It contains a good summary and synthesis of some of the observed (and anticipated) geographical effects of modernization.

Amin, S. 1977: *Imperialism and Unequal Development.* New York: Monthly Review Press.

This volume sums up the "development of underdevelopment" school of thought that is not covered in this text. This work is thought provoking to be sure, but is divorced from consistent reality. Remember the United States was once a series of colonies, too.

Bunge, W. W., and R. Bordessa. 1975: *The Canadian Alternative: Survival, Expeditions and Urban Change,* Geographical Monographs, No. 2, Department of Geography, Atkinson College. Toronto: York Univesity.

Bunge and Bordessa describe the problems of "modernization" at a variety of scales and use the same scales to prescribe more humanistic ways of living. If you can't find this volume, try to find some other work by Bunge. All of it is interesting.

Holloway, Steven R., and Kavita Pandit. 1992: "The Disparity Between the Level of Economic Development and Human Welfare." *The Professional Geographer*, Vol. 44, pp. 57–71.

This article describes the problem of equating per capita output with individual well-being in describing economic development. It contains a mapped comparison of output and quality of life measures, and describes some sources of their different geographies.

Lewis, W. A. 1977: *The Evolution of the International Economic Order*. Princeton, N.J.: Princeton University Press.

The Jamaican-born economist W. Arthur Lewis was knighted by Queen Elizabeth and was awarded the Nobel Prize in Economic Science for his work on economic development. If you read this book, you'll understand both why he was so recognized and much of the problems and promise of the developing world.

Myrdal, G. 1957: *Economic Theory and the Under-developed Regions*. London: Duckworth.

Myrdal's work, like Lewis's, was awarded the Nobel Prize for its insights on economic development. It describes the effects of "circular and cumulative causation" on both upward and downward development paths.

Norgaard, Richard B. 1994: *Development Betrayed: The End of Progress and a Coevolutionary Revisioning of the Future*. London: Routledge.

Norgaard is an environmental economist who often challenges the applicability of conventional neoclassical economics in assessing natural resource and environmental issues. In this book, he describes coevolutionary economic development as the antidote to the global problems brought about by efforts at modernization.

Rostow, Walter W. 1978: *The World Economy: History and Prospect*. Austin: University of Texas Press.

This is not Rostow's original work on modernization, but it contains material on this subject and a much more comprehensive description of the steps toward "modernization" that most of the world's countries had taken by the mid-1970s.

UN Conference on Trade and Development. Annual: *The Least Developed Countries*. New York: United Nations.

This annual publication describes general concerns of the world's poorest countries, with a special topic addressed in each volume. It also contains a statistical section which presents data on the set of countries.

The World Bank publishes two annual volumes of special interest to students of economic development: *World Development Report* (New York: Oxford University Press) and *Global Economic Prospects and the Developing Countries* (Washington, D.C.: World Bank). Each volume covers a different special topic. *World Development Report* is an especially useful source of data on most of the world's countries.

Chapter 12

Geographic Perspectives on Sustainable Economic Growth and Development

This chapter

- provides a definition of sustainability in the context of cost-benefit analysis
- uses the principles of the Rio Declaration to develop an overview of global environmental-economic issues
- presents a discussion of the potential for sustainable development in the world's poorer countries
- takes up problems of waste in the industrial economies
- describes problems of transboundary environmental degradation

Courtesy of U.S. Department of Energy.

W e'll wrap up our work in economic geography by focusing on the relationship between the Earth's physical environment and its human population's constant attempts at economic growth and development. Emphasizing environmental concerns helps underline the "geo" in geography, and also stresses the importance of our planet's role in any type of economic endeavor. The relationships between the environment and economy are many, and each is complex. In this chapter, therefore, the environmental issues are limited in their selection and simplified in order to draw out some of their basic economic geography. One part of that economic geography arises because regional differences in income seem to lead to regional differences in dominant environmental issues. Poorer countries are faced with demands for rapid economic growth while maintaining their stock of environmental resources, and richer countries are faced with problems of reducing their industrial and household wastes while maintaining high standards of material consumption. These differences, of course, are in addition to a host of environmental issues that are common to people all over the world, regardless of their income.

A second part of the basic economic geography of the environment is, in fact, concerned with the interaction between regions. Flows in the atmosphere and oceans don't pay any attention to political boundaries, and many environmental problems also arise because the impact of political boundaries on economic flows is decreasing as well. Again, scenarios are simplified in this chapter to make them easier to consider. In the real world where economic geography and environmental issues are interacting all the time, life becomes much more complicated. It wouldn't be an easy road, but an interesting one to travel is one that takes you into further study and understanding of how the world works in its geographical contexts of economy and environment. Ask your geography instructor for more details, or write me at Hanink@UConnvm.UConn.edu.

SUSTAINABLE ECONOMIC GROWTH AND DEVELOPMENT

The phrase *sustainable development* is commonly used, but it has several definitions. To some, sustainability is an economic concept, and sustainable development means that standards of living, including material consumption levels, will be maintained into the future. To others, sustainability refers to environmental maintenance, with necessary reductions in conventional economic activity being part of the price of ecological preservation. For most people, however, the concept of sustainability in economic development and growth is one of balance between economic and environmental concerns. The environment at large and in its particulars is viewed as a resource that must be used, but used conservatively, in providing the basis for economic well-being.

Sustainable development was first raised widely as an issue in the *Brundtland Report*, named for the chairperson of the body that issued it, the World Commission on Environment and Development, in 1987. (It was published in New York as *Our Common Future* by Oxford University Press, 1987.) It defined sustainable development as "meeting the needs of the present generation without compromising the needs of future generations." The definition is a good one in general, but it's a vague one, too.

Can an economy meet the needs of its present generation without compromising the needs of future generations? It can be argued that the economies of the richer countries, the North, have been practicing sustainable economics for some time. Longer term trends show that living standards have been increasing in Western Europe, Japan, Canada, and the United States for several generations. In retrospect, their earlier economic growth and development did not detract from their current relative prosperity, and so their past practices were sustainable under the definition given above. In the same sense, the economic practices in the world's poorer countries, the South, have also been sustainable. Despite their recent rapid growth in population, their living standards have not really declined over the last two generations and some of their number have experienced significant increases in per capita income.

To suggest that sustainable economic practices have been in use on any large scale anywhere, North or South, is a hard thing to do. Most of the income gains that have been experienced in the North and the success of the South in not collapsing into deeper poverty have been achieved by borrowing against a future that is coming ever closer. The sustainabilty of their economic practices is an illusion when measured by income gains or maintenance, in the same way that spending money that you've borrowed can provide the illusion that you have a steady source of income. True sustainability requires conservation of resources and preservation of the environment in a way that can continue to be effective in supporting reasonable levels of output forever—a goal that seems impossible to achieve. Difficult yes, impossible no. In a sense, sustainable economies are those that can violate the law of diminishing returns by effectively broadening their environmental resources.

We have already considered two ways in which sustainability can be accomplished when we studied the use of natural resources way back in Chapter 5. One approach is by technological enhancement. Methods continue to be developed that facilitate the conservation of environmental resources. Raw materials can be used more efficiently because of technological advances, and technological advances also help us reduce atmospheric, water, and land pollution. The second approach is by substitution. Shortages in one natural resource are made up by use of another natural resource. Substituting renewable resources for nonrenewable ones is the most effective method of promoting sustainable production, and recycling and reuse of resources also contribute to sustainability.

The principles of sustainable growth are in place, but the practice of sustainable economics is still on the horizon.

How can we tell if we are practicing sustainable economics? One way to approach the question is through cost-benefit analysis. In Chapter 1 we calculated the net present value of a project, NPV_P, as

$$NPV_P = \sum_{t=0}^{t} \frac{(B - C_t)}{(1 + r)^t} \tag{12.1}$$

where benefits, B, and costs, C, are considered over several time periods, t. Some discount rate, r, is assigned, depending on our preference for consuming things now rather than in the future. (You may want to review some of the related material in Chapter 1.) Cost-benefit analysis is often regarded as the enemy of sustainable economic growth and development because its use of discounting indicates that current consumption is preferable to consumption in the future. The higher the discount rate, the less the value placed on the future. However, the discount rate employed in cost-benefit analyses can also be used to promote sustainability.

The sustainability of an economic project can be determined by using the rate of population growth as a *social discount factor* that requires net per capita benefits in the future to be the same as they are in the present. This would lead to sustainability in a narrow economic sense, but it would not necessarily promote environmental conservation. Broader sustainability would be promoted by setting the discount rate to zero, and therefore make the future benefits of a project equal in importance to its current benefits. Overconsumption today, with its high costs, would not be subsidized by future consumption costs that are made lower by a positive discount factor. It has even been suggested that true sustainability requires that negative discount rates be used. Think about it; if positive discount rates promote current consumption, then negative discount rates would accomplish the opposite. Future benefits would carry a premium and current benefits would have less value, so future generations would have priority in economic appraisal and current preservation of environmental resources would carry a high value.

SUSTAINABLE DEVELOPMENT IN THE SOUTH

Sustainabilty and economic growth are often taken as contradictory goals, and many people fear that efforts at environmental conservation are likely to limit current economic expansion. In some circumstances, however, environmental conservation is easy to accomplish because it can make immediate financial sense. Many governments subsidize resource use in order to promote high rates of economic growth. In related circumstances, the costs of environmental pollution and other forms of degradation are borne by society in general rather than charged to any individual producer. The costs of production are lowered artificially in both ways, but total production may actually be reduced because of waste, as illustrated in Figure 12.1. In that diagram, resource waste actually reduces gross output to point *A* on curve *QG*, below its potential peak at point *B*. The loss of government subsidy of resource costs can cause a shift from lower to higher levels of output in the same way that other forms of structural adjustment (see Chapter 11) can raise output by improving efficiency. When producers have to pay their full costs, they are more careful to avoid waste in their economic actions.

Governments and producers should quickly recognize the benefits of reducing resource use from the levels associated with output at point *A* to the levels associated with output at point *B* because gross yields increase with less resource consumption. This reduction, labeled shift 1 in Figure 12.1, would be much easier to accomplish than shift 2, which also reduces resource use but at the cost of reducing total output. This shift is associated with a move from output levels associated with point *B* on curve *QG* to output level *C* on curve *QN*. The net output is actually at its peak at point *C*, because this volume incorporates environmental costs in production. Point *B* has higher gross output, but does not consider environmental costs as portrayed by curve *EC* in the diagram. Shift 2 requires external environmental costs to be internalized by producers, so production declines. The decrease in production makes shift 2 hard to accomplish, and

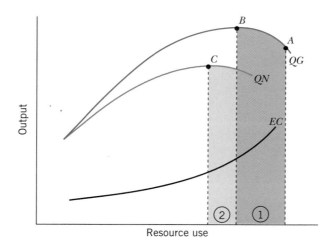

Figure 12.1 Gross output, *QG*, is traced as a function of resource use. It peaks at point *B*, but lower output at *A* may result from wasting resources because their use is subsidized. Net output, *QN*, takes environmental costs into account. It peaks at point *C*, which is less than peak gross output at *B*, but is a more efficient and sustainable level of production because it generates lower environmental costs. The reduction in resource use marked shift 1 is more easily accomplished than the further reduction marked shift 2. Source: Mohan Munasinghe, 1990: *Energy Analyisis and Policy* (London: Butterworths Press).

often unpopular among producers and consumers alike (and, therefore, not favored by government). Shift 2 does not allow environmental costs to be passed on to others, either in the future or in a different place.

Figure 12.1 illustrates the basic problem of achieving sustainable economic growth and development that exists for all economies. It also underscores the special problem of the countries of the South, which are not faced with maintaining high living standards and environmental quality at the same time, but with dramatically improving current living standards without ruining their prospects for future economic well-being. Because of their requirements for rapid growth, the problem of sustainability is considered especially acute in the world's poorer countries. In response to calls for solutions to the problems of sustainability in the South, the United Nations sponsored the Conference on Environment and Development, popularly referred to as the *environmental summit*, in Rio de Janeiro in June 1992. The environmental summit resulted in two major publications. One is the detailed *Agenda 21*, so-called because it lists what must be done in the twenty-first century to ensure sustainable economic development. The other is known as the *Rio Declaration*, and contains 27 principles for sustainable development that were agreed upon at the conference (Insights 12.1).

Environmentalists consider many of the Rio Declaration's principles unsatisfactory because they are too general. Other principles have been criticized for being too lenient and providing loopholes that seem to place economic above environmental interests. To some degree, however, the loopholes make the principles useful for practical plans of action because they do recognize that even though sustainable economic growth and development is of global concern, that concern can be expressed in different priorities in different countries. Furthermore, the principles are correct in their recognition that countries, whether in the North or South, cannot treat sustainable development as a national issue alone. It can only be achieved in an international context.

Many of the most important and pressing environmental issues in the poorer economies concern rapid resource exhaustion. Depletion of soil quality through waterlogging and salinization associated with irrigation is typical in areas where agricultural output is increasing rapidly. Overgrazing and stripping vegetation for fuel leads to *desertification* in some cases, with once productive land turned to desert as its moisture-holding capacity is severely reduced. Deforestation results from agricultural expansion and, to a lesser degree, the export of timber to international markets. These problems are briefly described for a small selection of countries in Case 12.1. In each country, rapid depletion of soil resources carries the potential of limiting the future economic well-being of its population.

The world's least developed countries (LDCs) have particularly severe problems of achieving sustainable economic development because their economies are so weak and their environments are often deeply degraded owing to attempts at rapid economic growth. The situation in Sierra Leone is described in Case 12.2. The country suffers from extensive poverty, high international debt, and extreme degradation of its resource base. Two of its principal economic activities, mining and commercial fishing, suffer from resource exhaustion because of attempts to use their stocks at faster rates to raise incomes. Mining also leads to environmental pollution, especially of fresh water, but clean-up costs are prohibitive in such a poor country. Water pollution is a special problem not only because of mining, but also because of the lack of household sanitation and sewerage facilities. In Sierra Leone, as in most LDCs, environmental problems often pose immediate health problems, and the health care system is almost always inadequate to their solution. Sierra Leone has developed a broad plan of action to promote sustainable development but is not in any financial position to begin its implementation. It also lacks the contemporary technology that would greatly assist its efforts toward more efficient resource use and pollution abatement.

Both the financial and technical problems associated with policies of sustainable development in poorer countries are being addressed by the *Global Environmental Facility (GEF)* sponsored principally by the World Bank. The GEF assists in the diffusion of technology and also its local development. It finances projects that should lead to more efficient energy use, and also the development of renewable energy sources. Furthermore, it provides money for treating both household and mining wastes and for developing sustainable forestry practices. In addition to the GEF, both the IMF and World Bank now encourage sustainable economic practices in their other programs, and work closely with NGOs in emphasizing environmental protection in undertaking economic projects in the South.

➤ INSIGHTS 12.1
Principles of the Rio Declaration on Environment and Development

PRINCIPLE 1

Human beings are at the center of concerns for sustainable development. They are entitled to a healthy and productive life in harmony with nature.

PRINCIPLE 2

States have, in accordance with the Charter of the United Nations and the principles of international law, the sovereign right to exploit their own resources pursuant to their own environmental and developmental policies, and the responsibility to ensure that activities within their jurisdiction or control do not cause damage to the environment of other States or of areas beyond the limits of national jurisdiction.

PRINCIPLE 3

The right to development must be fulfilled so as to equitably meet developmental and environmental needs of present and future generations.

PRINCIPLE 4

In order to achieve sustainable developement, environmental protection shall constitute an integral part of the development process and cannot be considered in isolation from it.

PRINCIPLE 5

All States and all people shall cooperate in the essential task of eradicating poverty as an indispensable requirement for sustainable development, in order to decrease the disparities in standards of living and better meet the needs of the majority of the people of the world.

PRINCIPLE 6

The special situation and needs of developing countries, particularly the least developed and those most environmentally vulnerable, shall be given special priority. International actions in the field of environment and development should also address the interests and needs of all countries.

PRINCIPLE 7

States shall cooperate in a spirit of global partnership to conserve, protect and restore the health and integrity of the Earth's ecosystem. In view of the different contributions to global environmental degradation, States have common but differentiated responsibilities. The developed countries acknowledge the responsibility that they bear in the international pursuit of sustainable development in view of the pressures their societies place on the global environment and of the technologies and financial resources they command.

PRINCIPLE 8

To achieve sustainable development and a higher quality of life for all people, States should reduce and eliminate unsustainable patterns of production and consumption and promote appropriate demographic policies.

PRINCIPLE 9

States should cooperate to strengthen endogenous capacity-building for sustainable development by improving scientific understanding through exchanges of scientific and technological knowledge, and by enhancing the development, adaptation, diffusion and transfer of technologies, including new and innovative technologies.

PRINCIPLE 10

Environmental issues are best handled with the participation of all concerned citizens, at the relevant level. At the national level, each individual shall have appropriate access to information concerning the environment that is held by the public authorities, including information on hazardous materials and activities in their communities, and the opportunity to participate in decision-making processes. States shall facilitate and encourage public awareness and participation by making information widely available. Effective access to judicial and administrative proceedings, including redress and remedy, shall be provided.

PRINCIPLE 11

States shall enact effective environmental legislation. Environmental standards, management objectives and priorities should reflect the environmental and developmental context to which they apply. Standards applied by some countries may be inappropriate and of unwarranted economic and social cost to other countries, in particular developing countries.

PRINCIPLE 12

States should cooperate to promote a supportive and open international economic system that would lead to economic growth and sustainable development in all countries, to better address the problems of environmental degradation. Trade policy measures for environmental purposes should not constitute a means of arbitrary or unjustifiable discrimination or a disguised restriction on international trade. Unilateral actions to deal with environmental challenges outside the jurisdiction of the importing country should be avoided. Environmental measures addressing transboundary or global environmental problems should, as far as possible, be based on an international consensus.

PRINCIPLE 13

States shall develop national law regarding liability and compensation for the victims of pollution and other environmental damage. States shall also cooperate in an expeditious and more determined manner to develop further international law regarding liability and compensation for adverse effects of environmental damage caused by activities within their jurisdiction or control to areas beyond their jurisdiction.

PRINCIPLE 14

States should effectively cooperate to discourage or prevent the relocation and transfer to other States of any activities and substances that cause severe environmental degradation or are found to be harmful to human health.

PRINCIPLE 15

In order to protect the environment, the precautionary approach shall be widely applied by States according to their capabilities. Where there are threats of serious or irreversible damage, lack of full scientific certainty shall not be used as a reason for postponing cost-effective measures to prevent environmental degradation.

PRINCIPLE 16

National authorities should endeavor to promote the internalization of environmental costs and the use of economic instruments, taking into account the approach that the polluter should, in principle, bear the cost of pollution, with due regard to the public interest and without distorting international trade and investment.

PRINCIPLE 17

Environmental impact assessment, as a national instrument, shall be undertaken for proposed activities that are likely to have a significant adverse impact on the environment and are subject to decision of a competent national authority.

PRINCIPLE 18

States shall immediately notify other States of any natural disasters or other emergencies that are likely to produce sudden harmful effects on the environment of those States. Every effort shall be made by the international community to help States so afflicted.

PRINCIPLE 19

States shall provide prior and timely notification and relevant information to potentially affected States on activities that may have a significant adverse transboundary environmental effect and shall consult with those States at an early stage and in good faith.

PRINCIPLE 20

Women have a vital role in environmental management and development. Their full participation is therefore essential to achieve sustainable development.

PRINCIPLE 21

The creativity, ideals and courage of the youth of the world should be mobilized to forge a global partnership in order to achieve sustainable development and ensure a better future for all.

PRINCIPLE 22

Indigenous people and their communities and other local communities have a vital role in environmental management and development because of their knowledge and traditional practices. States should recognize and duly support their identity, culture and interests and enable their effective participation in the achievement of sustainable development.

PRINCIPLE 23

The environmental and natural resources of people under oppression, domination and occupation shall be protected.

PRINCIPLE 24

Warfare is inherently destructive of sustainable development. States shall therefore respect international law providing protection for the environment in times of armed conflict and cooperate in its further development, as necessary.

PRINCIPLE 25

Peace, development and environmental protection are interdependent and indivisible.

PRINCIPLE 26

States shall resolve all their environmental disputes peacefully and by appropriate means in accordance with the Charter of the United Nations.

PRINCIPLE 27

States and people shall cooperate in good faith and in a spirit of partnership in the fulfillment of the principles embodied in this Declaration and in the further development of international law in the field of sustainable development.

SOURCE: UN Conference on Environment and Development, 1993: *Report of the United Nations Confer- ence on Environment and Development, Volume I, Resolutions Adopted by the Conference* (New York: United Nations), pp. 3–8.

◪ CASE 12.1
Issues of Sustainability in Four Countries

MEXICO

The rise in environmental concern in Mexico was illustrated by then President Salinas's major address on World Environment day in June, 1990 and the nation- wide planting of five million trees, but the continuing problems are daunting. Mexico City, home to nearly a quarter of the country's population, is the largest city in the world and one of the most environmentally damaged. It suffers from horrific air and water pollution, thanks to a heavy concentration of industry and a motor vehicle fleet that has grown six times as fast as the population over the past 40 years. Throughout the country, nearly a million acres of forest are lost each year and desertification proceeds apace. Forty percent of rural Mexicans are malnourished, and basic food grains must be imported. Real wages fell at least 20 percent in the 1980s as oil prices dropped and debt payments consumed half of export earnings. Restless and rebellious, the voters of Mexico in 1988 seriously challenged the ruling party for the first time in 60 years.

EGYPT

Egypt may be poor in natural resources—only 4 percent of its land is arable, its water supplies are uncertain, and its known oil reserve could be exhausted in 15 years—but it is rich in human resources. Its chief asset is a resilient, industrious, and educated people, three million of whom work overseas and send part of their wages home, thereby fueling an informal economy that belies official statistics. Population doubled between 1952 and 1980, but economic growth kept pace and the progressive social policies that Egypt adopted allowed it to avoid the extremes of wealth and poverty found in many developing countries.

But in the 1980s, oil prices collapsed and debt payments rose, putting Egypt in a financial bind at the same time that the balance between population and resources began to shift. Soil and water degradation plague both rural and urban areas. Damming the Nile at Aswan allowed regulated irrigation that greatly increased food production in the short term, but also led to the waterlogging and salinization that affect perhaps one-third of Egypt's arable land. Some irrigated land, once lush and green, is now salt-encrusted, and food production is off by an estimated 10 percent.

The cities, where nearly half the population lives, don't have adequate water or sanitation systems, and urban air is dirty. At current growth rates, Egypt's population of 50 milion will double by 2012. Will the country's limited and already severely strained resource base be able to support so many people? No development scenario yet proposed can keep up with such rapidly growing population pressure on land and water resources. Environmental degradation and population rarely surface in discussions of Egypt's security, but their uncontrolled growth threatens economic prospects and political stability.

KENYA

Kenya is in many ways the most promising state in sub-Saharan Africa. It has met various economic, political, and ethnic challenges and has survived the 1980s' drought without loss of life. But Kenya's economy is hostage to many factors beyond its control: the vagaries of the world coffee and tea markets, the fads and fears of European tourists, the price of imported oil, and the weather. With one of the world's highest fertility rates—eight children per woman during the early 1980s—Kenya doubled its population from 8 million to 16 million between 1960 and 1980. And if present increases continue, the population is expected to reach 40 million by the end of the century and 80 million by 2020 or so.

Meanwhile, Kenya's arable land—20 percent of the total land area—is losing productivity at an alarming rate. Thanks to soil erosion caused by deforestation and other land-use changes, crop yields in some areas are expected to fall 50 to 75 percent by 2000. Although only 3 percent of Kenya is forested, fuelwood provides 74 percent of the country's energy. The government is pushing tree planting, but this burgeoning fuelwood crisis demands much more agroforestry training and higher energy-efficiency gains than are presently in the pipeline. Water is also a problem, both for urban areas straining to absorb rural migrants and urban babies and for subsistence farmers in the country's vast semiarid regions. Since Kenya is East Africa's leading market economy, its management of these natural-resource problems will have repercussions far beyond its borders.

PHILIPPINES

"If we have a revolution in this country," a Philippine official once said, "it will start in the uplands." His logic is impeccable, for the uplands—where up to one-quarter of the population now lives—bear the brunt of the country's environmental problems. The Philippine population more than tripled between 1948 and 1988, from 19 million to 63 million.

A small group of wealthy families owns most of the good cropland, so throngs of impoverished, landless migrants push into the uplands, where they clear steep, forested slopes to raise food for their families. Heavy rains of the twice-yearly monsoons rush down the denuded slopes and carry off topsoil that silts streams, damages hydroelectric plants, and spoils fish-spawning grounds—a particular disaster for a people whose main protein source is fish. Commercial logging, much of it illegal, also contributes to deforestation. Logging so wasteful and corrupt that it can only be described as rapacious was a hallmark of the Marcos government. But destruction of mangrove forests, dynamiting of coral reefs, and overfishing are still commonplace in spite of environmental laws.

SOURCE: "Developing Nations: Four Environmental Profiles," by Janet Welsh Brown in *EPA Journal*, Vol. 16, No. 4, 1990, pp. 42–43.

FOR DISCUSSION

Why is the agricultural sector a consistent source of environmental degradation in the countries described in this case, as well as in most other countries?

◢ CASE 12.2
Toward Sustainable Development in Sierra Leone

Problem Areas

- Widespread poverty;
- Negative balance of trade and massive external debt. Debt servicing takes up about 67% of annual exports;
- Population growth stands at 2.76% per annum. The pattern of rural-urban population is unbalanced and 41% of the total population are under 15 years of age;
- Decline in agricultural production;
- Deforestation, soil erosion and soil degradation;
- Over-exploitation of natural resources, especially minerals and fisheries;
- Degradation of the environment due to mining activities. On the other hand, gold and diamond mining has been suffering from illicit trade and smuggling;
- Waste management;
- Water pollution from mining activities and household wastes. River-borne diseases, such as river blindness, are prevalent;

- Sierra Leone is concerned about toxic and hazardous wastes that may be dumped within her territorial boundaries;
- Poor housing and unsanitary environmental conditions both in urban and rural areas. In Freetown itself, almost all urban services have either totally failed or operate at a very poor level;
- Inadequate health system. Only 38% of the population have access to health services. Peripheral health units are unevenly distributed and most often ill-equipped and poorly maintained;
- The overall literacy rate is 28% and for women the figure drops to 22%. Illiteracy is therefore one of the obstacles to the implementation of policies and thus public awareness is very low;
- The educational system is characterized by inadequate infrastructure and learning materials as well as low morale for teachers due to irregularity of payment and a drop in real wages;
- High rate of inflation arising from a series of exchange rate adjustments;
- Rising urban unemployment and increasing employment in low productivity activities in the informal and traditional sectors;
- A lot of programs and projects are never carried out due to inadequate institutional arrangements, lack of funds and logistical support as well as lack of political will to implement decisions;
- Lack of effective implementation of policies and legislation.

Past and Present Capacity Building Initiatives

- Successive governments have instituted measures to revive economic growth and to improve environmental and national resource management through:
  - the formulation and implementation of macro and sectoral policies;
  - the setting up of institutions;
  - the enactment of laws on natural resources;
  - the formulation and implementation of development programs and projects
  - collaborating with international and national NGOs in dealing with economic and environmental issues.
- Sierra Leone has recently developed a policy for women in response to the Lagos Plan of Action which called for the mobilization of all resources including those of women to facilitate the acceleration of a self sustaining and self reliant form of development. The policy measures aim at promoting women's role in development.
- The National Population Policy, formulated in 1988, is designed to reinforce and enrich national development, especially human resources development, improve the quality of life and enhance human welfare and dignity. Special emphasis is laid on regulating population size, enhancing

population quality and improving the health and welfare of women and children;

- The National Population Commission, with the assistance of task forces, is undertaking sector action planning as a pre-implementation activity of the Population Policy.

- A National Environmental Policy (NEP) has recently been adopted by the government (May 1990).

- As part of the institutional reforms carried out with effect from 1985, the Ministry of Lands, Housing and Environment was created as a focal point to ensure inter-ministerial and inter-sectoral coordination at the national level;

- Although not fully implemented, the Agricultural Sector Support Project (ASSP), supported by the World Bank, focused on the major constraints limiting agricultural development as a whole, and instituted measures for tackling them.

- A number of forestry projects have been proposed for donor support;

Recommendations and Priorities on Environment & Development

- Promotion of food self sufficiency and food security through revitalizing successful traditional farming methods and involving local communities in the design and implementation of policies for using agricultural lands, forest and water resources;

- Alleviation of poverty by encouraging self-employment through the provision of middle level manpower training;

- Management of demographic change by guaranteeing access to maternal and child health and family planning services for all Sierra Leoneans;

- Reorientation of policy and planning approaches by applying environmental impact assessment to sectoral decision-making and by coordinating inter-sectoral policy;

- Enactment of new national environmental legislation;

- Improving housing;

- Creation of a population and environmental data bank;

- Encouragement of NGOs;

- Recognition of the role of women in improving the environment and population planning;

- Promotion of environmental education;

- Strengthening existing health facilities;

- Protection and conservation of the forest and its resources;

- At the international level, Sierra Leone recommends the following:

- Opening the markets of the industrialized countries to Sierra Leone's primary commodities and the payment of fair prices for her exports;
- The World Bank's and the International Moneatry Fund's lending policies should incorporate both economic and environmental criteria with respect to the conditionalities attached to loans;
- Ease the debt burden to allow Sierra Leone to devote more of her foreign exchange earnings to development rather than to debt servicing;

Financial Arrangements and Funding Requirements

- Sierra Leone suffers from a lack of financial resources to enable her to effectively implement her programs and projects;
- Out of the numerous forestry projects proposed for donor support, one project, the "Community participatory forestry for fuelwood production in the Western area," has been implemented with support from UNDP and other donors;
- In the fisheries sector, two projects are being implemented with external donor support;
- Foreign-owned fishing companies that operate in Sierra Leone's territorial waters mainly pay licensing and royalty fees and are required to sell part of their catch in the Sierra Leone market. But these arrangements have not been very beneficial to the government in terms of receipts and the fishery resources have been over-exploited;

International Cooperation

- Various programs and projects have been formulated and implemented by the government with technical and financial assistance from UN agencies and multilateral and bilateral agencies. In this context, the posts and telecommunications systems, which were in a seriously dilapidated state, were improved with assistance from UNDP and the EEC;
- Sierra Leone expects increased international cooperation in the global economic and environmental crisis including the willingness of the developed countries to assist small developing countries like Sierra Leone, with enormous natural resource potential, to pursue the path of sustainable development;
- To contribute to reducing the global environmental crisis, Sierra Leone will adhere to and implement those international treaties and conventions to which she can meaningfully contribute.

SOURCE: "Sierra Leone," in UN Conference on Environment and Development, 1993: *Nations of the Earth Report, National Reports Summaries, Volumes II* (New York: UN), pp. 283–287.

FOR DISCUSSION

Sierra Leone is addressing both domestic and international factors in its concerns for sustainable development. Should either the domestic or international factors be given priority in Sierra Leone's policies?

SUSTAINABLE DEVELOPMENT IN THE NORTH

As we have noted at several points, differences among countries' environmental concerns are often related to differences in national income. In 1992, the World Bank's *World Development Report* noted that the low-income economies tend to have low levels of sanitation and high levels of aeresol particles polluting their air. The air in middle-income countries is marked by high concentrations of sulfur dioxide, and their land is particularly susceptible to deforestation. The world's high-income countries have high levels of industrial and household waste, and are the leading sources of emissions of carbon dioxide into the atmosphere. The most distinctive feature of the richer countries' environmental problems, as compared to those of the poorer ones, is that they often result from the wastefulness that accompanies their affluence. In the North, sustainable growth and development requires that waste be reduced while fairly high living standards are maintained.

Historically, waste has been a byproduct of economic growth in every country. Raw material use is hardly ever fully efficient in the sense that an entire pound of a raw material is used completely in production. Refining, by definition, means that some portion of a raw material is unfit for use in certain types of production. Even when materials are used in final consumption, they are rarely used completely. The gasoline you use in your car is a good example. A lot of it burns up and is true fuel, but a significant portion of it does not burn and goes out the exhaust pipe and contributes to atmospheric pollution. Even the technological advance that marks growing economies leads to waste. Today's machines will soon be obsolete because of technological improvements, and although some of their components will be recycled, most of them will simply be tossed out as worthless. There is a growing industry involved in the sales and distribution of second-hand computers and peripheral equipment, but most of this type of equipment is consigned to the trash heap as obsolete.

Conventional economics, using the concept of diminishing returns, tells us that there is an acceptable level of pollution. The marginal cost of pollution abatement is constantly increasing, meaning that a lot of pollution is inexpensive to get rid of, but eliminating 100% of any pollution, or waste for that matter, is very expensive (Figure 12.2). Fortunately, the cheapest part of the pollution to abate is also the most costly with respect to the damage it causes. For example, a water body that is completely polluted can impose huge health costs as well as the costs associated with its use for recreation. Initial clean-up efforts may only require shutting down a source of pollution, but this action brings large

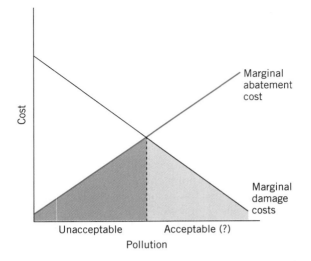

Figure 12.2 Marginal abatement costs increase as the marginal damage costs of pollution decrease. In an economic context, the relationship yields unacceptable pollution, to the left of the hatched line, and acceptable pollution, to the right of the hatched line.

benefits. Once the source of pollution is eliminated, the water body may renew itself fairly quickly. Most potential health problems will be eliminated, and the water will become fit for recreational use in a short time. However, the sediments at the bottom of the water body may still contain toxic material even after the source of pollution is shut off. As long as these pollutants remain undisturbed, they have no immediate health or recreational effect, so their current damage cost is nothing. The costs of eliminating the toxic pollutants from sediments is enormous, however, and economic analysis indicates that any money spent in this way is wasted. When the marginal costs of reducing pollution or waste are greater than the marginal costs of the damage they cause, then the pollution or waste is economically acceptable. In the context of cost-benefit analysis, the present value of a pollution- or waste-reduction program under these conditions would be negative, and therefore not worth the effort.

Beyond the fact that some amounts of pollution and waste are "acceptable", another reason why they are widespread consequences of economic growth is that their costs are often realized as externalities. As you recall from Chapter 4, negative externalities are costs imposed on one by the actions of another. Water pollution, land pollution, and in particular, air pollution, are often the source of negative externalities. Corporations and individuals can use air, land, and water to dispose of wastes at little cost to themselves but at significant costs to society at large. If the costs of pollution are imposed on the polluters, rather than imposed on others as externalites, then pollution and other forms of waste would be reduced.

Figure 12.3 illustrates the results of following the *polluter-pays principle*. The private supply line holds when the costs of pollution associated with a certain type of production are externally imposed. The market price, defined by the intersection of the demand line and the private supply line, yields a relatively large level of production and consumption. When the polluter pays, however, through the imposition of an environmental tax on production, then the social supply line is relevant with its higher costs of production.

The intersection of the social supply line with the demand line results in a relatively lower level of production and consumption, and their lower level means that pollution is reduced, too. The reduction in consumption associated with the polluter-pays principle makes this practice unpopular. A proposal by the Clinton administration to impose a BTU tax in order to reduce energy consumption in the United States—the same type of tax illustrated in Figure 12.3 and designed to have the same effect—was about as popular as a case of hives. Apparently, environmental costs are preferred in their indirect form as externalities rather than in their direct form; this observed preference is another argument for the "acceptability" of some levels of pollution and waste.

Externalites are more common than directly imposed environmental costs in part because of the difficulty in determining the full extent of environmental damage associated with many types of production and consumption practices. As described in Insights 12.2, *life-cycle analysis*, tracing the full environmental impact of a project from its inception to completion, is difficult to accomplish. Many of the costs are imposed on future generations and at great distances from

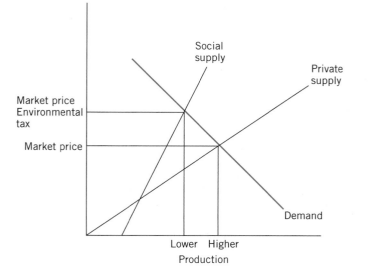

Figure 12.3 The imposition of a tax that would compensate for its environmental costs would lower production in comparison to the volume of output when environmental costs are left unpaid.

the locations where the benefits are achieved. Ontario Hydro, for example, maintains that it is limited in assessing all the environmental costs of generating electricity because some of the costs are imposed in other provinces and even in another country, the United States. In many circumstances, the fact that environmental costs are often removed either temporally or geographically from the area where the benefits of a project are received provides the illusion that the costs are quite low. It has been suggested that *environmental distancing*, or the geographical separation of environmental costs from the benefits of economic actions, is the primary reason why such costs are often virtually ignored at or near their source.

Some people who actively enjoy the benefits of production and consumption also actively oppose paying some of their costs by blocking the establishment of local facilities designed to reduce pollution and waste. The well-known *not-in-my-backyard (NIMBY)* syndrome illustrates the political problems often incurred in siting environmental facilities. The NIMBY syndrome also arises, and often justifiably, on the receiving end of environmental distancing. For example, when wastes produced in one place are targeted for storage or incineration in another, the population of the second place often feels it has been selected unjustly to pay the environmental costs of benefits enjoyed elsewhere.

In some circumstances, distancing has raised questions of environmental justice. In the United States, for example, many hazardous waste sites are located in low-income areas far from where the wastes were generated. Their location often breeds suspicion of *environmental racism* because the waste sites, along with particular environmental health problems such as lead poisoning, are often found in areas with large African-American and Hispanic populations. Native groups also are subjected to environmental distancing, with energy projects in Quebec and Alaska, for example, designed to provide economic benefits to nonresidents while their costs are borne in native tribal areas.

➤ INSIGHTS 12.2
Environmental Projects and Geographical and Temporal Equity

Ontario Hydro's Demand and Supply Plan (DSP) states the importance of considering the entire life cycle of a project or program, and the broad temporal scope. Programs are considered in the light of the effects of their facilities in all stages of development, construction, operation, and retirement. The DSP also accounts for the impact of fuel and its life cycle. This approach facilitates consideration of environmental impact over time, and the problems that may be faced by future generations. It will assist decision makers in determining long-term costs and effects, which may not be apparent in the immediate future.

However, Hydro has determined that some of these life-cycle effects are beyond its range of analysis. It has pointed out that some of the activities associated with its proposals will be beyond its direct control and, in some cases, will be beyond the geographical and jurisdictional boundaries of the Province (e.g.

uranium and coal mining which will take place in other Provinces or in the United States).

This situation raises questions about how to deal with consequences that may be significant but beyond the jurisdiction of the proponent. Indeed, the proponent is not responsible for the fact that environmental regulations and standards differ between Provinces, let alone between countries. Since the impact may be significant and far-reaching—and it is no less real for its disqualification from analysis because of jurisdictional boundaries—legislative authorities should develop a policy for dealing with it. Perhaps the impact should be assessed by an independent agency rather than by the proponent.

The DSP could potentially affect all parts of Ontario and have some impact outside the Province. Given that Hydro is responsible for providing energy to Ontarians, its geographical scope includes the entire Province. The scope of inquiry should include all regions, providing an opportunity to evaluate the cumulative and aggregate impacts of all proposed activities.

The Ontario Ministry of Environment is critical, however, in reviewing this aspect of the DSP. Ministry officials point out that Hydro has estimated the impact of pollutants on regions primarily by estimating the amounts of effluents, air emissions, and solid waste that would be produced. The Ministry argues that there was no attempt to estimate the current impact of Hydro's transmission and generating facilities; and no attempt to estimate the cumulative impact of upgrading or adding new facilities. Reviewers also criticized the lack of baseline environmental data, which would assess current levels of environmental impact, both from Hydro facilities and other sources.

The issue of equity is explicitly stated as being within Ontario Hydro's scope of analysis. This is clear recognition that the provision of energy is not only responsible for a certain social impact, but that this impact may be positive or negative. An additional issue is whether there should be an effort to ensure that the risks and benefits are distributed so as to avoid large inequities. The Ontario Hydro study addresses in a general manner situations in which communities may be compensated.

SOURCE: Economic Commission for Europe, 1992: "Ontario Hydro 25-Year Energy Plan (Derived from a Review of Several Federal and Provincial Plans)" in *Application of Environmental Impact Assessment Principles to Policies, Plans, and Programs* (New York: United Nations), pp. 11–12.

SUSTAINABLE ECONOMIC GROWTH AND DEVELOPMENT: INTERNATIONAL ISSUES

The existence of environmental distancing points to the importance of a geographical context for sustainable growth and development. Remember, the Brundtland Report's definition of sustainability is that the needs of the present generation are achieved without compromising the needs of future generations. In a geographical context, sustainability might also require that the needs of one place not compromise the needs of another. Such geographical sustainability implies the necessity of both environmental and economic justice. It also requires that the sustainable practices be designed in such a way that the geographical interactions in the economy and in the environment are always taken into account.

The different environmental problems of countries with varying levels of wealth were emphasized in the preceding sections of this chapter. But the differences in environmental issues faced by countries, whether based on income or something else, are more than balanced by the environmental problems held in common by all countries. A list of some of the more pressing global economic-environmental issues is provided in Table 12.1. Some issues, such as global climate change and the different pollution problems, result from unintentional environmental distancing. The atomic radiation from the disaster at Chernobyl spread into much of the rest of Europe and beyond; sulfur dioxide emissions in the United States may lead to acid precipitation in Canada; and oil spills spread rapidly in oceanic currents from one country's territory to another. None of these occurrences was or is intentional, but each is an example of the transnational split of costs from benefits. Some of the problems listed in the table, including maintaining biological diversity, trade-related environmental issues, and international waste shipments are direct results of the increasing level of spatial interaction that is occurring in today's global economy. Whether the problems are directly or indirectly international, their solution goes beyond the ability of any single country.

International solutions to international environmental problems can be achieved through international institutions, both private and public. For better or worse, the MNC is the leading form of private institution with an international

Table 12.1 Selected International Issue of Environmental Quality

1. Global climate change
2. Stratospheric ozone depletion
3. Biological diversity maintenance
4. Forest protection/tropical deforestation
5. Preservation of the Antarctic environment
6. Marine pollution
7. Transboundary water pollution
8. Transboundary air pollution
9. International waste shipment
10. Trade and the environment

SOURCE: Congressional Research Service, 1991: *Selected Major International Environmental Issues: A Briefing Book* (Washington, D.C.: U.S. Government Printing Office).

presence. For the most part, MNCs are associated with the process of environmental distancing. They have been accused, for example, of using poorer countries as pollution havens. Because of their international production and marketing networks, they are able to site more polluting production in poor countries with less developed environmental laws or lax enforcement, but sell the products in richer countries. They earn economic rent by effectively exporting the higher environmental costs in their richer markets to poorer countries. Even when trade is not an issue, many MNCs are accused of utilizing lower environmental standards and taking more environmental risks in poorer countries than in the richer countries where the MNCs are most often headquartered.

Perhaps the most telling environmental disaster in this respect occurred at Bhopal, India in 1984. A joint venture between Union Carbide, a U.S.-based MNC, and some minority-partner Indian financial institutions in Bhopal resulted in over 4,000 deaths when a toxic gas leaked from a chemical plant. After the *Bhopal disaster*, Union Carbide was severely criticized both for the way the plant was operated and for its weak response to the resulting deaths. The Indian government issued a warrant for the arrest of Union Carbide's chairman on murder charges, but efforts at extradition failed. (More recently, Union Carbide has been widely recognized for its later efforts in compensating the Bhopal survivors.)

Partly in response to the negative public opinion resulting from Bhopal, partly in response to legal requirements, and partly in response to basic business demands, several MNCs have developed policies on the environment in the last few years. Case 12.3 describes some of these policies with respect to atmospheric pollution. As the last part of the case shows, MNCs still seem to have different policies and more concern for the environment in their home countries than for the environment in the developing countries where they operate.

Because of their commercial purpose, MNCs are unlikely to take the lead in providing solutions to international economic-environmental problems. Instead, international agencies such as the United Nations and other multilateral efforts by governments are likely to continue as the primary mechanisms for tackling these issues. The most successful multilateral initiative on the global economy-environment so far is probably the Montreal Protocol on Substances That Deplete the Ozone Layer. The *Montreal Protocol* was signed by more than 65 countries in 1987 and was later expanded to over 90. It committed the countries to a phased reduction of chlorofluorocarbons (CFCs) in production because they have been found to deplete atmospheric ozone to a degree that is harmful to the Earth's inhabitants. The Protocol is divided in its requirements; the industrial countries are supposed to eliminate use of CFCs by 2000, and the developing countries, by 2010. A fund has been established to support the shift away from CFCs in the poorer countries and to facilitate the diffusion of the relevant industrial technology, using CFC-free processes, from rich to poor countries.

The Montreal Protocol's fund underscores cost as one of the most important issues limiting international agreements on environmental preservation. Poorer countries are hard pressed to fund such programs in their own countries, especially if there are additional short-term opportunity costs of foregone production or consumption. Financial contributions from the North to the South are needed, and some innovative methods of environmental finance have been designed.

The problem of maintaining biodiversity in tropical and semitropical areas is a case in point. Preservation of forest ecosystems in many countries is associated with a loss in income that the forest sector provides. This is true in the United States and other rich countries as well as in poorer ones. In addition, many poorer countries have requirements for agricultural land expansion that spills over onto forests, and if forests are preserved some agricultural output must be foregone. A method of compensating poorer countries for their forest preservation and related maintenance of biodiversity is through a *debt-for-nature swap*. These swaps allow the foreign debt of a country to be traded, or swapped, for expenditures related to the county's environmental preservation actions. Effectively, the swaps mean that foreign debt is forgiven if governments use most, if not all, the money for domestic environmental programs.

Foreign financing, even if necessary and useful, often brings along elements of foreign control. Debt-for-nature swaps aren't very controversial, but some people in the developing countries feel that too much domestic control is given up to international agencies and their standards in the name of international environmental preservation. Many observers in industrial countries feel the same way (see Insights 12.3). The conflicts between national and international interests in the environment are often the same sorts of conflicts that arise concerning national versus international interests in the global economy. As in international trade and finance, however, the future trend in environmental issues is likely to be increasing recognition that national and international interests often are one and the same.

➤ INSIGHTS 12.3
Are There Conflicts Between National Interests and International Controls of Environmental Degradation?

YES

Concerns about the greenhouse effect, the ozone layer, the loss of biodiversity, and the tropical rain forests have led to calls for "globalizing" environmental policy. Just as the U.S. EPA was created to assume control of state and local environmental affairs, we now need a global environmental protection agency to protect Mother Earth, so the argument goes. Only centralization, it appears, can eliminate the conflict of interest that forces nation-states to choose between environmental quality and economic growth.

However, before rushing to turn in our citizenship papers, we should consider what was sacrificed in federalizing U.S. environmental policy and whether global institutions are likely to advance global environmental goals. First, consider the U.S. experience under federalized environmental policy.

Prior to federalization, the states, like nations today, varied widely in their interests in environmental issues and their economic ability to resolve them. More environmental quality (a "good thing") had to be traded off against more economic wealth (a "good thing"). States that emphasized environmental quality to the detriment of economic growth could lose their tax base. The impact of their choices was felt clearly and directly.

Once EPA was formed, however, the pressure to make tradeoffs disappeared. People cannot simply move away from their country the way they can move from state to state. Federalization made it easier to spend more money, to mandate costly private expenditures on pollution controls, and to impose uniform standards across a very diverse nation. Whether this was something the American people wanted is unclear. Indeed, whether federal policy has even advanced environmental goals is unclear. Urban air remains polluted; most of our waters are not much cleaner.

Federalization separated people from power by creating an additional layer of bureaucracy and making it harder to enlist people in the fight for a quality ecology. In principle, environmental policy is made only after "public participation." In reality, most people lack the time and interest to affect public policy, to become expert on such issues as whether efficient refrigerants should be banned or what the future of the Amazon basin should be. Those devoting the time to such pursuits are highly motivated, either because of economic interests or ideological committment. Such groups are unlikely to represent the views of the public at large; yet, in a politicized setting their voices are the ones most likely to prevail.

Federalization weakened the principle that polluters should bear all environmental damage costs. Politically well-connected polluters—older firms and city governments, for example—are treated far more leniently than oil, chemical, or other "pariah" polluters. Political status, rather than damage to the environment, becomes the metric for apportioning responsibility. Of course, this tendency makes a mockery of the major goal of centralization, uniform treatment of all polluters.

This politicization has caused EPA's resources to be diverted to low-priority environmental goals such as eliminating asbestos in school buildings, even in the face of research suggesting it would be safer to leave the asbestos in place, or cleaning up abandoned waste sites posing minimal risk. Politics has too often used new environmental arguments to justify old pork-barrel programs. EPA's 1987 publication, *Unfinished Business,* documents the resulting misprioritization.

Globalization is all too likely to follow the path we have seen with federalization. Narrow, vocal interests will hold sway, and the concerns of the organized environmental groups will probably prevail over those of Third Worlders. We are likely to emphasize the eradication of trace pesticide levels rather than the improvement of basic diets and to be concerned with disposing of "hazardous" wastes rather than treating disease-carrying contaminated water. Globalization, like federalization, is likely to mean that environmental priorities will be set by the shrill rather than the serious.

Too, the lack of world government means that enforcement of global environmental policies will not be easy. International environmental agreements take the form of treaties, official promises by one government to another. History does not encourage us to expect such promises always to be honored. Indeed the OPEC experience suggests that nations find it hard to enforce agreements even when they share common goals. A global warming treaty—given that warming will create widely varying costs and benefits among nations—would be far more complex to enforce. Moreover, America's disastrous record of negotiating international agreements in such areas as trade and telephone service does not indicate that the United States will fare well under a global environmental regime. (Written by Fred Lee Smith, Jr.)

NO

That individual American states were "best served by a *laissez-faire* posture in environmental regulations" is a flawed premise. States that welcomed polluting industries did indeed accrue short-term benefits in the shape of jobs and tax revenues. Over the longer term, however, these benefits were far outweighed by the costs of health care, productivity losses due to environmentally caused illness, and the cost of cleaning up polluted water and land. The tradeoff turned out to be a Faustian bargain.

One of the notable developments of the past decade or two has been the growing recognition that the same pattern holds true on an international scale. Countries differ widely in their commitment to environmental protection and in their readiness—and capacity—to spend governmental dollars on it. But in sharp contrast to the situation only a short while ago, no country now sees it as being in its national interest to attract international business or investment by becoming a so-called pollution haven.

While many countries lack the bureaucratic capacity, the political will, or the fiscal ability to strengthen weak environmental regulations, few see weakness in this area as a national asset. The tragic lessons of Bhopal and Cubato, Brazil's "Valley of Death," have been well learned.

Bhopal has become a household world for industrial disaster, but Cubatao, a slow-motion industrial disaster brought on by extreme concentration of industries with lax or nonexistent pollution controls, is less well known. Cubatao was so polluted during the 1970s and early 1980s that hundreds died and emergency evacuations became commonplace. Even without an accident or extreme concentration of industry in one place, the chronic and worsening environmental crisis in Eastern Europe stands as a stark warning of the long-term costs of industrializing without paying adequate attention to environmental protection.

Global environmental trends—loss of species, ozone depletion, deforestation on a scale that affects world climate, and accelerating buildup of greenhouse gases—all pose potentially serious losses to national economies, defy solution by one or a few countries, and render geographic borders irrelevant. By definition, then, they pose a major challenge to national sovereignty.

In this the environmental trends are not alone. Many policies and practices once considered purely domestic matters now spill over into the international arena. The integration of the global economy—with its internationalization of markets, sources of supply, and capital—makes industry increasingly mobile, thereby undercutting governments' rights to tax and regulate.

The notion of what constitutes national security is also changing. As the concept of national security broadened in the 1970s to include economic strength, the element of common security gained ground, as exemplified, for instance, by efforts to manage monetary policy cooperatively and to achieve free trade.

Environmental concerns shift the center of gravity still further toward common security. Global environmental degradation threatens nations' economic potential and thereby their internal political stability. But the potential fallout goes far beyond economics. Ozone depletion may put their citizens' health at risk because of increased ultraviolet radiation. The worst-case scenarios associated with global warming call into question some nations' very existence—the biggest national security threat of all.

Thus for both economic and environmental reasons, the notion of collective global security is slowly replacing that of individually defined national security. Nation states are not going to disappear, nor is world government in the offing. But nations are seeing irrefutable evidence that their future well-being rests increasingly on actions taken far from their shores, an insight that is putting an unprecedented premium on international cooperation.

The idea that nations might gain from competing in the environmental realm, either by becoming pollution havens or by hoping to emerge as a "winner" from global climate change, has little support. Instead, nations are acting as though they believe that they have a strong mutual interest in cooperation, as demonstrated most spectacularly by the tightened chlorofluorocarbon and financing agreements under the Montreal treaty reached by 93 nations meeting in London in June 1990.

Turning this mutual interest into effective international environmental management remains a distant goal. The answer does not lie in a vain attempt to apply uniform environmental standards to a community of nations whose members differ by one hundredfold in per capita income and have vastly different cultures, climates, religions, resources, and attitudes towards nature.

Instead, answers will be found only through institutional innovations as sweeping as those that inaugurated the postwar period we're now emerging from. The present international system was set up to preserve the status quo and to manage and contain conflict. The new system that will allow us to deal with the problems ahead must be designed to catalyze cooperation. Instead of the glacial pace required to negotiate treaties that set particular performance standards, we need fluid international processes that can respond quickly to changes in scientific understanding and that set all nations moving in the same direction at whatever pace is realistic for each nation's particular circumstances. (Written by Jessica Tuchman Mathews.)

SOURCE: "National Sovereignty and Environmental Imperatives: Two Views," by Fred Lee Smith, Jr. and Jessica Tuchman Mathews, in *EPA Journal*, Vol. 16, No. 4 (1990), pp. 25–28.

◢ CASE *12.3*
Air Pollution and Multinational Corporations

Atmospheric issues are of pivotal importance to the responding corporations. Reasons why corporations appear more concerned about atmospheric protection than any other United Nations Conference on Environment and Development (UNCED) issue are: (a) Air quality and atmospheric protection are areas highly regulated by most governments. The United States Clean Air Act is one of the most comprehensive and costly environmental regulations in the world, and international discussions on ozone depletion and climate change have signaled to the corporate community that the future will see further initiatives in that field; (b) The quality of the air is a tangible issue for most people, and public awareness is high in that area; (c) Historically, air-pollution legislation has been given priority attention by governments; and (d) Ozone protection ranks high on the international agenda.

By sheer volume, carbon dioxide, produced principally by the combustion of fossil fuels, is the most important of greenhouse gases. It is responsible for about 50 percent of the global warming problem. CFCs, however, also contribute to at least 15 percent of the global warming. This is because the greenhouse effect of these compounds per molecule, relative to carbon dioxide, equals several hundred to 20,000, depending on the compound. That effect is compounded by the fact that their lifetime is 100 years or more. Moreover, CFCs and halons deplete the Earth's ozone layer. Other greenhouse gases such as nitrous oxides, sulphur dioxides, methane, and tropospheric ozone, the cause of acid rain and of smog in cities, also result from the production and use of fossil fuels.

Approximately 50 percent of all greenhouse gas emissions can be traced directly or indirectly to transnational corporations (TNCs). That amount includes about half of the oil-production business, virtually all the production of road vehicles in the industrialized world, most CFC production, and significant portions of electricity generation and use.

In addition to the impact on the global climate, a number of chemical substances such as asbestos, dioxins, polychlorinated biphenyls (PCBs) and volatile organic compounds (VOCs) produced and used by TNCs, when emitted into the atmosphere, can pose serious health problems because of their toxicity. Those substances can also contaminate land or water.

STATISTICAL FINDINGS

Ozone-depleting Activities

As seen in Figure A, a large number of respondents to the Benchmark Survey participated in activities which involve products or processes generating greenhouse gases, ozone-depleting gases and high-hazard pollutants, principally in the automotive, chemical, metal, oil and gas, and paper industries.

Three-quarters of the firms in the finished-goods sector, which includes the

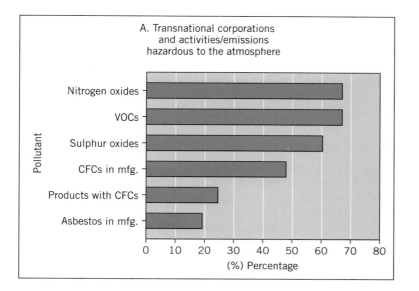

A. Transnational corporations
and activities/emissions
hazardous to the atmosphere

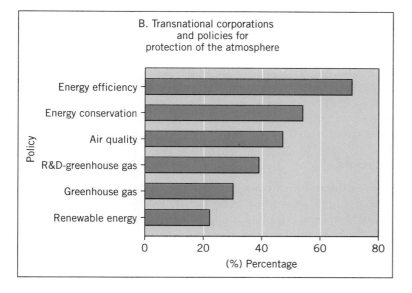

B. Transnational corporations
and policies for
protection of the atmosphere

automotive, electrical, electronics, machinery and metal products industries, used CFCs and related compounds in their manufacturing processes. Forty percent stated that they manufacture products containing CFCs. A similar trend appeared among all respondents. Twice as many firms reported using CFCs in manufacturing processes as those firms selling products containing such chemicals. That may imply that perhaps it is easier to substitute the CFCs used in certain products, but not in the manufacturing process. It should be pointed out that the electronics sector, particularly, had made impressive progress in eliminating CFC use in the cleaning of components.

The extent of CFCs usage nonetheless raises the following question: will the production and use of CFCs be phased out internationally by the year 2000, the target date of the Montreal Protocol? CFCs remain for a long time in the stratosphere, so that even after the chemical is phased out, ozone damage will occur for most of the next century.

Transboundary Pollution

Sulphur dioxide and nitrogen oxide emissions from industrial and mining activities cause acid rain. The combustion of fossil fuel in urban areas, mainly from transportation and industrial activities, is also responsible for the formation of those and other pollutants such as ground-level ozone. The environmental damage caused by transboundary air pollution is abundantly documented in Europe and North America. The European and North American regions are the only areas for which reliable time-series data and computer calculations on the transfrontier dispersion of air pollutants exist.

Sixty percent of the respondents to the Benchmark Survey stated that they emitted sulphur dioxide and 67 percent stated that they emitted nitrous oxides. Those numbers are quite high considering the level of awareness about the damage already suffered due to acid rain and urban smog in the regions where the corporate headquarters of the respondents are located. Alternatively, the results may indicate the degree to which those gases are endemic to modern manufacturing processes. Volatile organic compunds (VOC) were also found to be emitted by 67 percent of the respondents. The Asia-based (Japan) respondents were more likely to emit sulphur dioxide and nitrous oxides than the Europe- and North America-based firms.

High Hazard Pollutants

Asbestos has been considered a carcinogen since the early 1970s. It becomes a health hazard when its fibers become airborne and are inhaled. Inhaling asbestos fibers can result in asbestosis, a crippling lung disease, as well as in various forms of cancer. Asbestos has been used extensively for insulation, noise reduction and fire retardation.

Despite the common knowledge of asbestos' carcinogenic nature, 19 percent of the respondents to the Benchmark Survey indicated that they used asbestos in manufacturing. The regional breakdown showed the Europe-based respondents as less likely to use asbestos than their North American and Japanese counterparts. A likely explanation for the smaller number of European firms using asbestos could be the existence of European Community directives laying down provisions on asbestos removal and worker protection in industrial plants. In the United States on the other hand, the 1986 Asbestos Hazard Emergency Response Act mandated asbestos removal or management only in public schools. Among industrial sectors, as expected, the finished-goods and extractive-based sectors were the most likely to use asbestos, and firms in the top third were twice as likely as those in the bottom third to use asbestos in manufacturing.

Policies and Programs

Atmospheric protection was cited more frequently as a top corporate concern than any other environmental issue. That concern was demonstrated, in varying degrees, by having in place policies and programs on air pollution, on reduction of generating greenhouse gases and energy efficiency.

Forty-seven percent of the respondents stated that they had corporate-wide policies on air quality or pollution beyond those required by national legislation. The Asia-based firms were more likely to have such policies, 66 percent, compared to 47 percent and 29 percent, respectively, for the North America- and Europe-based firms. The extractive-based and finished-goods sectors led the other sectors with 60 and 56 percent of positive responses, respectively. Concern with air quality policies was associated with the emissions resulting from industrial operations in those sectors.

Policies reducing greenhouse-gas generation which go beyond national legislation, however, do not appear to have received the same corporate attention. This may be due to the fact that greenhouse-gas generation reduction policies were more specific and had not been as formalized as those for air quality. In general, 30 percent of the respondents had greenhouse-gas reduction policies, another quarter found them to be inapplicable to the firm's operations.

It is encouraging, however, that a larger number of respondents, 39 percent, undertook environmentally-oriented research and development programs for the reduction of greenhouse-gas generation. The Europe-based firms led (43 percent) in such programs implying that action in this area was ahead of policy formulation.

Programs for the conservation of energy supplies were given importance by the majority of respondents (Figure B); 54 percent of the respondents stated that they had such programs. Economic considerations may be the driving force for having such programs. The regional distribution of having such programs, however, appeared quite uneven. Over three-quarters of the North America-based firms had such programs compared to slightly more than half of the Asia- (Japan) and Europe-based firms.

Sustainable Development Programs

Renewable energy sources such as solar, photovoltaic and wind energy were being utilized by over one-fifth of the respondents. That usage demonstrated that some firms were already taking a long-term view with regard to energy use. The finished-goods and extractive-based sectors, possibly because of their usually high energy requirements, led in the use of such renewable resources. Firms in the top third by sales were more likely to use renewable energy resources.

Almost three-quarters of the respondents had undertaken research and development for energy effficiency production methods. All three regions appeared to be attentive to the matter, with the Europe-based firms slightly behind the Japan-based and North America-based respondents. As with the programs for renewable energy sources, research and development for energy efficiency were undertaken mainly by the extractive-based and finished-goods sectors. Again, firms in the top third by sales were more likely to undertake such research and development.

The picture with regard to practices in developing countries was rather mixed. Twenty percent of the respondents reported using CFCs or related products in developing countries. As with previous questions regarding the use of CFCs, the finished-goods sector was ahead of the other sectors in such use. When it came to monitoring air emissions in developing countries, however, only about a third of the respondents reported that they monitored, and an equal number did not. More disconcerting was the fact that a quarter of the respondents indicated that they did not have sufficient data at headquarters to answer the question, and another 13 percent did not know whether CFCs are used in their developing-country operations. This lack of information could be related to the decentralized nature of the respondents' operations. Given the heightened sensitivity with regard to ozone depletion or accidents in developing-country affiliates, those answers give cause for concern.

SOURCE: United Nations Conference on Trade and Development, Program on Transnational Corporations, 1993: *Environmental Management in Transnational Corporations: Report on the Benchmark Corporate Environmental Survey*, Environment Series No. 4 (New York: United Nations). The quoted material is from pp. 101–106.

FOR DISCUSSION

Should there be an international agency, like the United Nations, with the sole responsibility of solving international environmental problems and maintaining globally consistent environmental standards?

POINTS IN SUMMARY

1. The environment at large and in its particulars is a resource that must be used, but used conservatively, in providing the basis for economic well-being.

2. In a sense, sustainable economies are those that can violate the law of diminishing returns by effectively broadening their environmental resources.

3. Cost-benefit analysis is often regarded as the enemy of sustainable economic growth and development because its use of discounting indicates that current consumption is preferable to consumption in the future.

4. Many governments subsidize resource use in order to promote high rates of economic growth.

5. Because of their requirements for rapid growth, the problem of sustainability is considered especially acute in the world's poorer countries.

6. Many of the most important and pressing environmental issues in the poorer economies concern rapid resource exhaustion.

7. Historically, waste has been a byproduct of economic growth in every country.

8. When the marginal costs of reducing pollution or waste are greater than the marginal costs of damage they cause, then the pollution or waste is economically acceptable.

9. In a geographical context, sustainability requires that the needs of one place not compromise the needs of another.

10. International solutions to international environmental problems can be achieved through the use of both private and public international institutions.

11. Recently, many MNCs have developed policies on the environment.

TERMS TO REMEMBER

Agenda 21

Bhopal disaster

Brundtland Report

debt-for-nature swap

desertification

environmental distancing

environmental summit

environmental racism

Global Environmental Facility (GEF)

life-cycle analysis

Montreal Protocol

not-in-my-backyard (NIMBY)

polluter-pays principle

Rio Declaration

social discount factor

sustainable development

SUGGESTED READING

Adams, W. M. 1995: "Sustainable Development?" in *Geographies of Global Change: Remapping the World in the Late Twentieth Century,* edited by R. J. Johnston, Peter J. Taylor, and Michael J. Watts. Oxford: Blackwell, pp. 354–373.

This piece by Adams focuses on the history and politics of defining "sustainability," and describes some of the term's geographical implications.

Ashworth, William. 1995: *The Economy of Nature: Rethinking the Connections Between Ecology and Economics.* Boston: Houghton Mifflin.

This book is especially interesting in its genre because it concentrates on land-use issues. It's not so radical as it is conservative in the environmental sense.

Buchholz, Rogene A. 1993: *Principles of Environmental Management: The Greening of Business.* Englewood Cliffs, N.J.: Prentice Hall.

Buchholz both describes recent efforts by business in America to become "green" and encourages them to do more. He lays out selected environmental problems in a very accessible way.

Cline, William R. 1992: *The Economics of Global Warming.* Washington, D.C.: Institute for International Economics.

Cline is a relatively conservative environmental economist, but this book suggests that global warming is a serious and costly economic issue. It is also a good example of very long-term cost-benefit analysis.

Commission for Racial Justice, United Church of Christ. 1987: *Toxic Wastes and Race in the United States: A National Report on the Racial and Socio-economic Characteristics of Communities with Hazardous Waste Sites.* New York: Public Data Access.

This report, written under the direction of Ben Chavis, was the catalyst of the environmental justice movement in the United States. It contains both descriptive and statistical arguments that geographical inequity compounds environmental problems.

Manes, Christopher. 1990: *Green Rage: Radical Environmentalism and the Unmaking of Civilization.* Boston: Little, Brown.

Manes describes the radical environmental movement in the United States (Earth First!) and around the world (Greenpeace). He's part of the movement, too, and describes its vision of radical economic change as the only hope for the planet's future.

Turner B. L., II, William C. Clark, Robert W. Kates, John F. Richards, Jessica T. Mathews, and William B. Meyers, eds, 1990: *The Earth as Transformed by Human Action.* Cambridge, Mass.: Cambridge University Press with Clark University.

This comprehensive volume contains more than 40 papers on the historical geography of interaction between people and their environment. Some of the papers are topical, and others are regional in providing global coverage of environmental impacts of human actions.

UN Conference on Environment and Development. 1992–1993: *Nations of the Earth Report, National Reports Summaries,* Vol. I-III. New York: United Nations).

The summaries of the much lengthier national reports on economic growth, development, and environment made by the members of the United Nations in association with the Rio environmental summit are contained in these volumes.

UN Conference on Environment and Development. 1993: *Report of the United Nations Conference on Environment and Development,* Vol. I, *Resolutions Adopted by the Conference.* New York: United Nations.

This is the main publication of the United Nations' Conference on Environment and Development that took place in Rio de Janeiro in June 1992. It contains the famous ''Agenda 21,'' which describes the current problems facing developing countries with respect to environmental-economic interactions, and some paths toward their solution.

World Bank. 1992: *World Development Report 1992.* New York: Oxford University Press.

Subtitled *Development and the Environment,* this volume contains a systematic description of the environmental problems that arise from economic growth and development.

The British journal *Progress in Human Geography* published three articles in 1995 (Volume 19) that consider environmental issues in the context of economic geography: Cutter, Susan L., ''Race, Class and Environmental Justice,'' pp. 111–122; Hanink, Dean M., ''The Economic Geography in Environmental Issues: A Spatial Analytic Approach,'' pp. 372–387; and Robinson, Kelly, ''Industrial Location and Air Pollution Controls: A Review of Evidence from the USA,'' pp. 222–244.

Glossary

A

absolute location A geometric construct; designated by at least two directional coordinates.

ad valorem **tariff** Tax determined as a proportion of the price of an imported product.

ad valorem **tax** Property tax determined as a proportion of the property's value in its highest and best use.

Agenda 21 A document published by the United Nations describing the necessary actions for sustainable development that should be taken in the twenty-first century.

agglomeration A geographical concentration of people or industries.

agglomeration economies of scale Decreasing average costs that occur because of the lower costs of spatial interaction within a geographical concentration.

agglomeration diseconomies Increasing average costs associated with a geographical concentration.

aggregate travel model Model used to determine the optimal location of an enterprise with a uniform delivered pricing system.

agricultural systems Crops and the environmental, social, economic, and technological contexts in which they are grown.

agricultural zoning Government designation of certain areas of land as limited to agricultural production.

agro-ecosystems The interaction across natural and social contexts of crop production.

appropriate technology Technology that improves productivity without raising social and environmental costs in its application.

appropriative water rights The principle of "first come, first served", with use of water based on a temporal priority.

arable land Land that can be used for agriculture.

B

back-office tasks Tasks that don't require immediate contact between service buyer and seller.

base-point pricing A form of FOB/CIF pricing that uses an arbitrary or otherwise artificial origin for a product instead of its actual point of production.

basic sector All goods and services that are purchased by enterprises and consumers from outside the local market.

Bhopal disaster The deaths of over 4,000 people when toxic gas leaked from a chemical plant owned jointly by Union Carbide, a U.S.-based MNC, and some minority-partner Indian financial institutions in Bhopal, India.

bid-rent curve A diagramatical representation of the maximum bid anyone should make for using a location.

big emerging markets (BEMs) Developing countries with large and growing economies.

biotechnology Productive methods or techniques that incorporate living things into their design.

blanket transport rates Transport rates that are uniform within a region.

break-in-bulk freight system The unloading of freight from one mode of carriage and loading on another mode of carriage.

Brundtland Report The popular name of the report issued by the World Commission on Environment and Development in 1987.

C

capital-intensive production Production that uses relatively more capital than labor.

captive markets Markets served by only one mode of transport.

Caribbean Initiative   American policy designed to spur economic growth in the region by encouraging American companies to assemble products there for export to the United States

catch and release fishing   The practice of releasing fish caught for sport with as little harm as possible.

central place multiplier   A value describing the local growth-inducing effect of the expansion of a place's external market area.

central place theory   A theory of the location of market centers.

CIF pricing   FOB pricing from the customer's point of view.

circular and cumulative causation   An initial trigger to growth, or decline, in a region that will lead to continued growth, or decline.

clear-cutting   The forestry practice of simply cutting every tree in a wood holding.

coevolutionary development   The interaction of local culture and the local environment in producing technologies that are beneficial with respect to production but have small environmental impacts.

Common Agricultural Policy (CAP)   The set of agricultural subsidies, price supports, and restraints to international trade in agricultural products used in the European Union.

common market   Market that has the characteristics of a customs union and also allows the free movement of factors of production across its member countries.

comparative advantage theory   Trade theory that focuses on differences in production costs between locations.

competing destinations model   A location model that considers alternative shopping opportunities in calculating probabilities of spatial interaction between consumer origins and retail destinations.

complementarity   Supply and demand across locations.

congestible good   A good that is nonrival at lower levels of aggregate demand but rival at higher levels.

consumer services   Services sold to households.

consumer surplus   The difference between the most that people would be willing to pay for a product and what they do pay for it.

contagious diffusion   Spatial diffusion marked by distance decay.

contract rent   Price paid for an asset's use over a limited period.

core-periphery model   Economic development model based on geographical interaction.

cost-plus pricing   The practice of setting transport and other prices to cover costs plus a "reasonable" profit.

countervailing duties   Tariffs that raise the price of the product in the domestic market to what is considered fair by domestic producers.

county supremacy movement   The belief that the federal lands in the United States are held unconstitutionally and any federal or state policy that affects land is unconstitutional as well.

cultural determinism   Theory that variations in cultural characteristics determine variations in productivity levels around the world and variations in the geography of economic development.

cumulative zoning   Hierarchical zoning in which "better" land uses are allowed in addition to specified land use(s).

customs union   Union that removes the barriers to trade among its members and has common trade policies toward countries outside the agreement.

D

debt-for-nature swap   Exchange of a country's foreign debt for expenditures related to its domestic environmental programs.

deforestation   The process of forest reduction.

demographic gap   The difference between the crude birth rate and the crude death rate.

demographic transition   The expectation that human populations will move from a high-level to a low-level equilibrium of birth rates and death rates.

desertification   A form of soil degradation.

differentiated market theory   The proposition that people with different incomes will demand not only different types of goods and services, but also different varieties of a single good or service.

discount rate   A value used to account for inflation and the time value of money in evaluating economic projects.

diseconomies of scale   An increase in average cost with an increase in production.

distance decay   The decline in interaction that occurs with distance between locations.

domestic content rules   Trade barriers that concern a product's place of production.

dumping   Selling products in a foreign market for less than the price commonly charged in the home market, or selling products in a foreign market at prices lower than their cost of production.

E

eclectic model of FDI   A general model of FDI that takes both corporate and location factors into account.

economic base multiplier   A value describing the local growth-inducing effect of the expansion of a place's basic sector.

economic base theory   The theory that all local growth is ultimately derived from growth in the basic sector, or expansion of external markets.

economic development   The integration of an economy's productive resources and markets.

economic geography   (The study of) the spatial distribution and interactions of locations of production and consumption in the economy.

economic growth   An increase in an economy's output.

economic rent   The difference between the price paid for a good or service and the cost of providing the good or service.

economic resources   Resources that could be employed at current prices.

economic union   The effective integration of the economies of otherwise independent countries.

economies of flow   A special form of economies of large volume derived from hub-and-spoke transport systems.

economies of large volume   Decreases in transport costs per mile with increasing size of load.

economies of long distance   Decreases in transport costs per mile with increasing distance of haul.

economies of scale   Decreases in average cost with an increase in production.

economies of scope   Decreases in average costs that occur when several similar products are produced in the same factory using the same flexible machinery and labor.

enabling technologies   Those that facilitate control of production in one country by an enterprise in another.

Engel's law   As income increases, decreasing proportions of it are required to purchase the necessities of life.

enterprise zone   Usually a small district within an urban area that is targeted for growth by the provision of subsidies to business.

environmental determinism   Theory that the differences in productive capability between countries, or regions, is based largely on the differences in their physical environments.

environmental distancing   The geographical separation of environmental costs from the benefits of economic actions.

environmental racism   Bias that results in waste sites, along with particular environmental health problems such as lead poisening, often found in areas with large African-American and Hispanic populations.

environmental summit   UN-sponsored Conference on Environment and Development held in Rio de Janeiro in June 1992.

European Union (EU)   The collection of European countries that have relatively integrated national product and factor markets.

exactment   A form of in-kind payment that governments may require in exchange for a permit to develop land.

exhaustible resources   Those resources that can be consumed in their entire useful amount without any hope of replenishing their geological supply.

F

factor endowment theory   Modern version of comparative advantage theory that identifies the source of any cost advantage in a country in its factor endowments.

factor intensity reversal   Theory that at one point production is intensive in one factor, and at another point, in time or geographically, production is intensive in another factor.

factor price equalization   The tendency for realtive factor prices to become the same across countries engaged in free trade.

factor services   The services of capital and labor.

factors of production   Inputs required for production.

FIRE   Finance, insurance, and real estate.

flexible manufacturing   Manufacturing that can respond rapidly to market changes and changing production costs.

FOB pricing   The combination of a fixed price for a product at its point of origin plus a delivery charge.

footloose manufacturing   Manufacturing with little or no ties to conventional location factors.

foreign acquisition   The takeover of an enterprise already operating in a foreign country.

foreign direct investment (FDI)   Direct investment that has its origin in one country and its destination in another.

free trade union   A set of countries with little or no barriers to trade among themselves.

free trade zone   Region in which goods can be imported without any tariffs.

freight containerization   The packing of freight consignments into large boxes or trailers.

freight-forwarding   A type of wholesale link between sellers and purchasers of transport services that takes advantage of economies of large volume.

fundamental economic activities   Production, distribution, and consumption.

G

game species   Animals prohibited from commercial harvest; may only be killed by people in the interest of recreation or by accident.

General Agreement on Tariffs and Trade (GATT)   The most comprehensive multilateral trade treaty.

General Agreement on Trade in Services (GATS)   A side-agreement of the GATT concerning international service trade.

geographic information system (GIS)   Software that comprises spatial databases, and the ability to integrate geographical information, and provides analysis as well as display of geographical relationships.

ghost-town syndrome   The loss of a critical local industry leading to widespread economic decline and a place's eventual abandonment.

Global Environmental Facility (GEF)   Organization sponsored principally by the World Bank, to financially assist the diffusion of technology from core to periphery as well as its local development in the periphery.

gravity model   A model of spatial interaction adapted from Newton's equation for the gravitational force between two objects.

greenfield FDI   The establishment of a completely new facility in a foreign country.

green revolution   The development of certain high-yielding varieties of cereals by hybridization.

gross national product (GNP)   The value of final goods and services produced and provided in a country's economy during one year.

growth center policy   The establishment of a leading industry in a depressed region that should, through a multiplier effect, generate regional economic growth and eventual industrial diversification.

growth pole   The lead industry used in a growth center policy.

H

hierarchical diffusion   Spatial diffusion marked by point-to-point interaction.

highest and best use   Use of the land that would earn the highest economic rent.

Hotelling Rule   Principle that states the value of a mine's output is related to the discount rate.

hub-and-spoke   A transport system—A system that feeds a central point of consolidation, the hub, from a series of smaller routes, the spokes.

human capital   Resources including education, health, and other characteristics that improve the productive capacity of people.

I

import quota   Quantitative restriction on imports by weight, volume, or value.

import substitution   Attempt to induce domestic industrial growth by enacting very high import tariffs.

import tariff   Tax collected on goods or services as they enter one country from another.

induced greenhouse effect   Result of additional greenhouse gases put into the atmosphere through human activities, such as the release of carbon dioxide when fossil fuels are burned.

industrial inertia   Maintenance of industrial regions even after the location factors that originally led to their development are no longer relevant.

industrial recruitment   Common practice of attempting to pursuade a company to relocate, or at least expand, its operations in a different jurisdiction from where it is currently located.

industrial retention   Keeping existing local businesses in place.

Industrial Revolution   Beginning in the mid-1970s, the replacement of animate energy by inanimate energy in production processes.

infant industries   Industries that are just getting established in a domestic economy.

informal sector   Sector that includes cash and barter transactions that are part of everyday life in most places but go unrecorded by government agencies.

input-output analysis   A method of assessing supply and demand relationships across economic sectors.

international joint venture   A partnership between enterprises with headquarters in different countries.

International Monetary Fund (IMF)   Monetary organization designed to provide an institutional framework for the expansion of international trade and finance.

intervening opportunity   An alternative origin or destination in spatial interaction.

intracorporate trade   Buying and selling across national boundaries but within a corporation.

intraindustry trade   International exchange of similar products.

isocost line   A diagramatic representation of the factor combinations that could be used in production at a particular constant cost.

isoquant   A diagramatic representation of equal quantities of output.

J

just-in-time manufacturing   Production that requires coordination between manufacturers and their suppliers.

L

labor-intensive production   Production that uses relatively more labor than capital.

labor productivity   The value of output per worker.

land rent   Economic rent earned by land.

land-tenure system   The legal context in which land is held and used.

latifundia   An estate system of agriculture most often associated with Latin America.

law of diminishing returns   Production increases at a diminishing rate as either the labor-to-capital ratio or capital-to-labor ratio increases.

law of one price   The principle stating that the price of any mobile good or service will eventually be the same in every place where it is sold.

least developed countries (LDCs)   The UN designation of the world's poorest countries.

life-cycle analysis   Analysis that traces the full environmental impact of a project from its inception to completion.

line-haul costs   Variable expenses associated with carrying freight or passengers between an origin and a destination.

localization economies   Decreases in average costs associated with a geographical concentration of an industry.

location equilibrium   A balance in the supply and demand for locations.

location of production function   A simple extension of the basic production function to include locational considerations.

location quotient   A measure of local economic activities against expectations based on national conditions.

location rent   Economic rent earned from a location.

locational inertia   A stable geographical pattern of production and consumption.

M

made land Land that results from engineering rather than as a natural endowment.

Malthusian model Vision of the world's future as one of "overpopulation."

Malthusian scarcities Absolute quantitative resource scarcities.

Malthusian trap The point at which population growth exceeds the carrying capacity of an economy's natural resources.

maquiladora zone A Mexican free trade zone along its border with the United States.

marginal cost Cost of producing, or purchasing, an additional unit of output.

marginal product The last unit produced.

market The supply and demand for a good or service.

market breakpoint A boundary splitting an area between two market centers.

market capitalization The price of an asset as determined by its earnings over its useful life.

market-clearing price The price at which market equilibrium is achieved.

market equilibrium Matching of the quantity in demand and the quantity in supply.

market failure The inadequate determination of costs and prices owing to incomplete information or the inability to use information completely.

market internalization The transfer of an asset across national boundaries but within an MNC.

market model of FDI Model indicating that exporting is the most efficient method of foreign market access to small markets, licensing is the most efficient form of access to intermediate markets, and FDI is the best method of access to the largest markets.

market potential model Model used to determine the optimal location of an enterprise with an fob pricing system.

market structure The type of competition faced in a market.

market threshold Demand for a good or service that yields its minimum operating scale.

material index Ratio of the weight of localized raw materials to the weight of the finished product.

mineral endowment The amount of a resource in the Earth's crust that occurs in mineral ore.

minifundia The agricultural smallholdings of Latin America.

modernization theory The theory stating that current patterns of economic development are predictable from historical conditions.

monopoly A single company's control of either production or distribution (or both) of a product to such an extent that it can control the product's price.

monopoly rent Producer surplus available to monopolies because of lack of competition.

Montreal Protocol Treaty that committed countries to a phased reduction of chlorofluorocabons (CFCs) in production.

most-favored-nation Country with best trade treatment.

Multifiber Arrangement A side-agreement of the GATT concerning trade in textiles and apparel; currently being phased out of existence.

multinational corporation (MNC) A corporation with operations in more than one country.

multiple use The management policy of allowing competing uses to share stakes in public land.

multiple-use zoning Government-imposed restriction that limits land to selected uses.

N

national accounts Measures of the activity or output of an economy.

natural greenhouse effect An effect that results from gases such as carbon dioxide and water vapor forming an atmospheric thermal blanket around the Earth, trapping the warmth of sunlight and making the Earth habitable.

natural monopolies Those monopolies that develop from the high start-up and fixed costs of their operation.

negative externalities Cost imposed on people from actions taken by others.

neoclassical economic growth model Growth of output in response to the addition of the two basic production factors of labor and capital.

nested hierarchy of functions The notion that any higher order place has everything to offer that a lower order place does, plus its additional offerings of higher order goods.

net present value The value in today's money that is obtained by adding the actual current and forecasted future net costs and benefits of a project over its anticipated useful life.

New International Economic Order (NIEO) Economic redistribution between North and South that would close the gap in living standards between the average citizen of the world's wealthier countries and the average citizen of the world's poorer economies.

nonbasic sector Sector that comprises all goods and services that are purchased by enterprises and consumers inside the local market.

noncompetitive trade Trade in products that cannot be produced in more than a few places.

noncumulative zoning Exclusive zoning that prohibits any nonspecified land use.

nongovernmental organizations (NGOs) Social assistance and medical assistance agencies that work especially well in the LDCs.

nonpoint source pollution Pollution that does not come from a single source.

nontariff barriers to trade Methods other than taxation that are used in governement management of trade.

North American Free Trade Agreement (NAFTA) The treaty that established a free trade area including Canada, Mexico, and the United States.

North American Securities Dealers Automated Quotations (NASDAQ) A leading stock exchange that exists in the form of a computer network linking brokers in many locations.

North-South division Figurative geography of the world based on national wealth and development; North is the rich core and South is the poorer periphery.

not-in-my-backyard (NIMBY) Phrase that illustrates the common aversion to the nearby location of environmental facilities.

O

oligopoly An industry in which production and distribution are controlled by just a few enterprises.

opportunity costs Result from taking one action, or picking one location, when another action or location would yield greater economic rent.

order of a place Concept derived from the orders of goods and services that are available in it.

order of a service/good A collection of characteristics that determine the locational pattern in which a product will be sold.

Organization of Petroleum Exporting Countries (OPEC) A multinational oil-producing cartel that attempts to control output and prices in the world market.

outer range of a good The maximum distance over which a good (or service) is sold.

overlapping market theory of international trade Theory that trade between countries results from their overlapping markets: similarities in their demand and preferences for particular types of goods and services.

P

per capita GNP (or GDP) A country's gross national product (or gross domestic product) divided by its population.

perfectly competitive market A market that has so many buyers and sellers that neither group can ordinarily fix the price of a product.

physical infrastructure Capital that serves the economy in general, such as transport and other communications systems.

point source pollution Pollution that comes from a single source.

political economy The process of groups using government to effect favorable allocations of goods and services.

polluter-pays principle The idea that the costs of pollution should be borne by the polluter rather than imposed as an externality on society.

portfolio investment An investment that doesn't carry any control over the operations of the entity in which the investment is made.

positive externalities Free benefits to people from actions taken by others.

postage stamp rate A single price charged for an item's transport throughout the service territory of the company selling the transport service.

potential (resource) supply That part of the resource base that can be used given current exploration efforts.

power centers Retail clusters of unattached, large-scale specialized discounters and movie theaters.

price elastic demand Demand for a good or service inversely related to changes in its price.

pricing-to-market Business policy that takes into account that many products are income-elastic in their demand.

primate city A city that is many times larger than any other city in a country.

principle of minimum differentiation Sellers of the same sort of product try to make their brands as similar to each other's as possible.

private goods Goods that are exclusive and rival in their consumption.

producer services Services sold to businesses.

producer surplus The difference between the actual price at which something is sold and the minimum price at which it would be sold.

production function The relationship between the quantity of inputs to the production process and the quantity of output.

productivity Output per unit of productive input.

product life-cycle model A model that describes the projected level of sales of a product over its life in the marketplace: has locational and trade implications.

public goods Goods that are nonexclusive and nonrival in their consumption.

purchase of development rights Land-use preservation policy in which government purchases the development rights to a piece of property so that its current use must be maintained.

purchasing power parity The buying power of the average person in a country in an "international dollar."

pure economic rent Rent derived from an increase in demand without any increase in supply.

Q

quaternary sector Sector that includes FIRE and management services, and is sometimes referred to as the information sector because it mainly provides and manages information.

R

range of a good Distance over which a good (or service) is sold.

reciprocity The notion that any easing of trade regulations offered by one country should be met by eased trade regulations in other countries.

reforestation Process of forest recovery.

Reilly's law of retail gravitation The idea that a place will attract retail trade from its surrounding area in direct proportion to the population of the place and in inverse proportion to the square of the distance from the place.

relative location Location in relationship to other relevant places.

renewable resources Resources that can be replenished in supply even as they are consumed.

reserves Particular deposits of a mineral resource.

residual land use A use that occupies land that is left over after commercial interests are satisfied.

resource base Entire amount of a mineral resource available in the Earth's crust.

resource pyramid Diagram often used to illustrate the relative quantities of a particular mineral resource.

Ricardian rent A term named for the economist David Ricardo: rent gained from land as a result of an increase in the demand for food.

Ricardian scarcities Named for the economist David Ricardo, scarcities that occur as better supplies of a resource diminish and poorer quality resources come on stream.

right-to-work law A law stating that membership or nonmembership in a labor organization cannot be a condition of employment.

Rio Declaration Published by the United Nations, the principles for sustainable development that were agreed upon at the environmental summit in 1992.

riparian water rights Rights granted to those who occupy the riparian zone (shore, river bank, etc.), allowing reasonable use of the water supply.

rule of 72 The doubling time of any growing population: 72 divided by its rate of growth.

S

satisficing search behavior Behavior that leads to the selection of economic locations that provide satisfactory, or reasonable, levels of relevant cost and revenue characteristics.

sectoral shifts Movements of labor and income from the primary sector's activities directly associated with natural resources, such as farming and mining; to the secondary sector, mainly manufacturing; to the tertiary sector, which includes both producer and consumer services, government, and everything else not included in the primary and secondary sectors.

shift-share analysis A method of analyzing the components of a region's growth and of the growth of specific industries.

single-use zoning Government-imposed restriction that limits land to a single use.

social discount factor Factor used to consider the rate of population growth in cost-benefit analysis.

sogo shoshas Japanese trading corporations.

space–time convergence The effective decrease in distance brought about by technological advances that accelerate spatial interaction.

spatial diffusion A form of spatial interaction; the geographical spread of a thing or idea from its origin to other places.

spatial equilibrium A market regionalization or other spatial pattern that is stable under current market conditions.

spatial interaction The flows between locations.

spatial structure Geographical pattern.

specific tariff Fixed tax collected by the weight or volume of a shipment.

staple theory of development Canada's industrialization was made possible by investing its earnings gained from exports from its primary sector.

strategic industries Industries that provide a product vital to a country's well-being.

strategic resource A resource that is necessary for the survival of a country's economy.

structural adjustment Government policies designed to integrate the domestic economies and so to promote more efficient use of factors of production.

sunset industries Industries that are declining in a domestic economy.

sustainable development Defined in the Brundtland Report as "meeting the needs of the present generation without compromising the needs of future generations."

T

taking The lack of compensation for land value that is illegally diminished by government regulation.

tapering freight rate Diagramatic representation of economies of scale in transportation.

tax havens Countries with little or no tax liabilities for producers.

technology Productive methods and techniques.

terminal costs Fixed expenses associated with providing a transport service.

terms of trade Unit export values divided by unit import values, with the result multiplied by 100 so that they are expressed as an index.

tertiary sector Activities such as transport, government, wholesale and retail trade, and general business and personal services.

third world The world's poorer, less developed countries.

threshold range of a good A distance that defines a market area for a good (or service) that just contains its market threshold.

total fertility rate The average number of children each adult woman will bear over her lifetime.

trade creation A condition that results when the barriers to trade among a group of countries in a region are lowered, and the lowering of transaction costs increases their trade volume and frequency.

trade deflection A condition that occurs when one country in a free trade union imports goods from nonmember countries only to reexport them to countries that are members of the free trade union.

trade diversion   Loss of trade by countries outside of a regional agreement that occurs not because their costs are rising, but because their trade barriers to the member countries' markets remain in place.

trade management   The use of policies that are designed to alter trade flows and trade volumes in ways that they they expect to be advantageous to their particular interests.

trade protectionism   Protection of selected domestic producers from foreign competition.

trade sanctions   Trade restrictions designed to augment political policies.

tragedy of the commons   A parable written by Garret Hardin that describes the problem of commonly held resources.

transaction cost   The cost of making a sale or purchase.

transfer pricing   A special system of preferential pricing between individual interests within a corporation designed to manipulate taxes.

transferability   The relative ease of spatial interaction.

transnational corporations   A name for MNCs that recognizes not only their global extent but also their apparent indifference to the interests of individual countries.

transparency   Policy that all trade regulations be visible to all countries.

U

ujamaa   Rural-oriented development policy implemented in Tanzania under Julius Nyrere.

uniform delivered pricing   A policy of charging a single delivered price for a product wherever it is sold.

urban sprawl   The spread of the built-up area of a metropolitan region.

urbanization economies   Decreases in average costs associated with a geographical concentration of population.

use-based taxation   Property taxes determined as a proportion of the property's value in its current use.

V

value added in manufacturing   The price of a finished product minus its cost of production.

W

World Bank   A group of development financing agencies, with its two largest operations being the International Bank for Reconstruction and Development (IBRD) and the International Development Association (IDA).

World Trade Organization (WTO)   Recently established body that handles trade disputes between

Index